QUALITATIVE AND QUANTITATIVE METHODS IN LIBRARIES

THEORY AND APPLICATIONS

Proceedings of the International Conference on QQML2009

QUALITATIVE AND QUANTITATIVE METHODS IN LIBRARIES

THEORY AND APPLICATIONS

Proceedings of the International Conference on QQML2009

Chania, Crete, Greece 26 – 29 May 2009

Editors

Anthi Katsirikou
University of Piraeus Library, Greece

Christos H. Skiadas
Technical University of Crete, Greece

World Scientific

NEW JERSEY • LONDON • SINGAPORE • BEIJING • SHANGHAI • HONG KONG • TAIPEI • CHENNAI

Published by

World Scientific Publishing Co. Pte. Ltd.

5 Toh Tuck Link, Singapore 596224

USA office: 27 Warren Street, Suite 401-402, Hackensack, NJ 07601

UK office: 57 Shelton Street, Covent Garden, London WC2H 9HE

British Library Cataloguing-in-Publication Data
A catalogue record for this book is available from the British Library.

QUALITATIVE AND QUANTITATIVE METHODS IN LIBRARIES
Theory and Applications
Proceedings of the International Conference on QQML2009

ISBN-13 978-981-4299-69-5
ISBN-10 981-4299-69-3

Printed in Singapore by World Scientific Printers

Preface

The present volume includes most of the keynote and contributed papers that were presented at the Qualitative and Quantitative Methods in Libraries International Conference (QQML2009) held in Chania, Crete, Greece, May 26-29, 2009, which was organized under the umbrella of ASMDA International Society.

The conference aims to serve as the intermediate between theory and applications, in this case between Quantitative and Qualitative Methodologists and Library and Information Scientists. As expected, the conference, consequently its proceedings, is addressed to the library professionals in a more general sense: professors, researchers, students, administrators, librarians, technologists, museum scientists, archivists, decision makers and managers.

Qualitative and Quantitative Methods (QQM) have proven to be popular tools for Library scientists, because of their usefulness to the everyday professional life. QQM are involved in the improvement of the services, the measurement of functional effectiveness and efficiency, decision-making and fund allocation.

The book covers a wide variety of themes in both theoretical and applied such as the modern methodological approaches, the library's management and marketing, the change of libraries, the digital resources and the new library models, the focus on users and user groups, the information literacy, the qualitative options, the application of the QQM in digital library education and research, the evaluation and the impact assessment, the information and communication technology services, the support to research and the application of QQM to the catalogues and manuscripts. The papers come from all over the world and referred to every kind of libraries, so the book helps the reader to have a holistic view on the subject.

Some of the subjects that are discussed in the enclosed papers are: teaching methodologies to LIS students mixed methods, leadership, the quality of information, e-resource management, semantic Web, personalised virtual digital libraries, user evaluation of library services, information behavior, information ecology, user profiles, quality management, quality metrics, digital library education, knowledge management, open access, performance based software, self-efficacy, infopragmatics, web dynamics etc.

We acknowledge the support of MAICh in Chania, Greece. Sincere thanks must be recorded to colleagues, friends and partners who worked hard for the success of the conference and especially the conference committees, speakers and keynote speakers, authors and reviewers. Finally, we would like to heartily thank Aggeliki Oikonomou, Mary Karadima, Iro Tzorbatzaki, Aris Meletiou, Ioannis Dimotikallis and George Matalliotakis for their valuable support.

Athens, November 1, 2009

Anthi Katsirikou, University of Piraeus Library, Greece

Christos H. Skiadas, Technical University of Crete, Greece

Honorary Committee

International Scientific Committee

Keynote Talks

Carla Basili
Consiglio Nazionale delle Ricerche - (Italian National Research Council), Rome, Italy, Lumsa University - Rome
Measuring Information Literacy Policies

Norbert Fuhr
Department of Computational and Cognitive Sciences, University of Duisburg-Essen, Germany
Evaluation Approaches for Digital Libraries

Henk Harmsen
Head of the Development & Acquisition Department, The Netherlands Institute of Scientific Information (NIWI-KNAW)
Guidelines for Repositories Assessment and Review of the Quality of Operations for Data Repositories

Peter Hernon
Graduate School of Library and Information Science, Simmons College, Boston, MA, USA, Co-editor, Library and Information Science Research
The Next Managerial Leadership: Continuation of a Research Agenda

Niels Ole Pors
Department of Library and Information Management, The Royal School of Library and Information Science, Copenhagen, Denmark (www.db.dk/nop)
Measuring the Quality of Leadership and Service Provision in Libraries

Contents

Chapter 7. Quality

Chapter 8. Using Qualitative and Quantitative Methods in Digital Library Education and Research

Chapter 9. Evaluation

1. Methods

Teaching Information Science Students for the Use of Different Methodologies

Fernanda Martins[1]

[1]Faculdade de Letras, Universidade do Porto, Portugal

Abstract: The Information Science course of the University of Porto in Portugal has a learning unit designed Research Methodology. As a teacher of this discipline I encourage students to develop research studies using either qualitative or quantitative methods applied to possible future professional scenarios, namely when analyzing librarians' users satisfaction. The aim of this communication is to present some examples of those research essays and to discuss future ways for teaching and learning those issues as well as different professional frames where those methods are needed to solve problems.

Keywords: Librarian students; Information Science Students; Teaching quantitative methods; Teaching qualitative methods; Librarians' users satisfaction.

1. Introduction

Since 2001 the University of Porto in Portugal has an Information Science course that resulted from a partnership between Faculty of Arts and Faculty of Engineering. It is based on a large and integrated perspective considering subjects of different interdisciplinary areas and is organized according to the spirit of Bologna Declaration in what concerns professional profiles and competences (Ribeiro, 2005).

The curriculum design supposes that technical procedures of information's representation (such as description or classification) are a part of any information system, namely archives or libraries. This unitary perspective also aims to synthesize the so called Information Systems (technological systems devoted to the storage and retrieval of information) that are increasingly implemented inside organizations in general. Thus, learning contents include: (1) theory and research methods, (2) systems analysis, (3) technical procedures for organizing and representing information related to storage and retrieval, and (4) informational seeking and behavior. Complementary subjects include applied components of Information Science related to the different kind of information systems (archives, libraries or technological information systems). This Information Science course has a strong technological component and is oriented to information management problems in any organizational context (Ribeiro & de Pinto, 2009).

The main goal of the Bologna Process is to be capable of creating until 2010 a European Higher Education Area making it possible for students to choose from multiple high quality courses and have easier recognition procedures with comparable degrees across Europe. It supposes the idea of an educational system based on the development of competences rather than on the transmission of knowledge and is planned for a lifelong learning and development. It meant a total reorganization of curricula and teaching methods in every cycle of study in order to development of a reformed and modernized system.

In order to fit these new educational ideas, either the general curricula of courses or the particular learning activities proposed in each discipline had to be modified. If the system is supposed to develop competences it has to tell what a graduate of an education must be able to do in order to graduate. This also means students must show in action that they are competent, that is, that they are able to interpret the situation and have a repertoire of possible actions to choose which have been trained and were previously found to succeed. Regardless of training, competence grows through experience and the extent of an individual to learn and adapt.

In the same sense, the fast development of working life and technology requires an equally fast development of competences and knowledge which implies a lifelong learning carried out in close cooperation with the education system, and society.

The new educational challenges are, in some way, related with some classic pedagogical issues: (1) the importance of learning by doing, (2) the need for learners to take the responsibility of their learning and (3) learner-centered model. In reference to the first aspect, Jerome Bruner following the ideas of Dewey and Piaget proposed the so called discovery learning a constructivist approach to education and states that discovering for oneself teaches how to acquire information making it more ready in problem solving (Bruner, 1961). However Mayer (2004) points out that more important than being behaviorally active is to be cognitively active. The discovery learning is also a method of instruction through which students interact with their environment by exploring and manipulating objects, wrestling with questions and controversies, or performing experiments.

Finally according to the learner-centered model (McCombs & Whisler, 1997) learners bring to the learning process diverse references as a consequence of their previous experiences. To learn is seen as a constructive process that is facilitated when learning issues are relevant to learners and when they are actively involved creating their own knowledge and comprehension putting together their previous knowledge and experiences. Teaching methods must attend students' goals and promote the self regulation learning through experiences of self regulated teaching and learning.

2. The discipline of Research Methodology

As already said the Bologna Declaration obliged curricula to include aspects of some similarity all over European countries and to implement the development of professional competencies which was also the case of this Portuguese Information Science course. This course has a learning unit designed Research Methodology that has as fundamental objective to prepare students in order (1) to adopt a critical attitude toward professional problems (2) to question the logic of the social processes of scientific production, (3) to characterize and to apply different methodologies in the scientific production of Social Sciences (4) to critically apply and analyze different data collection instruments (5) to know and to apply formal norms for research presentation. Students must also (1) know scientific research fundamentals, (2) develop a critical and creative spirit when confronting problems related with their future profession (3) present skills for team work, (4) develop skills for organizing and presenting individual work and (5) organize and plan research work based on acquired knowledge.

One of the main objectives of the discipline of Research Methodology is to develop research competencies on students through the planning of short research studies where typical methods of data collection and treatment used in Social Sciences are applied. To be capable of doing research planning, data collection and treatment and to know how to write and present research results means students have learned by doing.

As seen before authors point out the importance of developing competences by doing and this way students measure their difficulties and can update their theoretical knowledge in order to accomplish their work. This application component of the discipline is based on: (1) theoretical aspects of research planning steps, namely documental research, (2) data collection methods (observation, interviews and surveys) and (3) data treatment methods (content analysis and statistical methods using statistical analysis software). All these aspects are usually present in Social Sciences some in qualitative and some others in quantitative research. Special importance is given to the construction of surveys and to the use of interviews in data collection as well as to the application of statistical methods with the use of the SPSS software. Among qualitative methods the one proposed by De Bruyne (1974) in which evaluation is based on four poles or elliptical stages (epistemological, theoretical, technical and morphological) is presented as an alternative that fits the needs of a qualitative research. Some colleagues of the teacher team (Silva & Ribeiro, 2009) have already used this method to study information evaluation seen as a methodological operation, and applied to information in any context of production and use, in the scope of Information Science. In that study authors proposed criteria and parameters in order to apply evaluation taking into account the information's life cycle, the renewal and obsolescent of knowledge and the importance of memory for the long time preservation of informational products.

In this learning unity students, as already said, develop some research studies applying the methodology proper of Social Sciences. This means that most works focus on the opinion of information users either it is related with libraries or any other context of information use. Once one of the possible Science Information professional careers is related with libraries, the objective of this paper is to present some examples of students' work related with libraries' context.

In the great majority of the works students choose to use a survey as it is an easier and more rapid way of obtaining data than it is interview, for instance, and it allows applying statistical methods. Both issues are felt as important needing some training in order to be able to use them in the future.

Some of their studies are presented below and some methodological aspects are referred namely the main objective, the participants, the data collection method and the main results and conclusions.

Study 1 (1)

This study aimed to understand the degree of knowledge showed by the users of the library of the Faculty of Arts and Humanities of Porto, namely, the familiarity with the electronic resources available and their regular use. It also analyzed if those resources are public and used by them.
The information collected during this research work corresponds to a sample of 127 Library users of the Faculty of Arts and Humanities of Porto (FLUP). An inquiry comprising 15 questions was given to this sample of the library users. Its aim was to understand to what extent the academic community is familiar with the use of electronic resources.
The inquiry is composed of four major points: (1) characterization of the interviewees regarding gender, age and academic qualifications, (2) the interviewees' general information technology knowledge, (3) direct and objective answers about their concrete knowledge of what electronic resources are (this question was later object to a content analysis). The library users were also asked if they were aware of which electronic resources were available, they were asked to express if they felt the need of attending training courses to fully use the available resources, and how they learned about them and (4) different electronic resources available in the library were listed and interviewees must answer about their knowledge and importance given to these resources, as well as about the frequency of their use.
Results showed that age, gender and academic qualifications are important to determine the interviewees' degree of knowledge and how they use the electronic resources available also affecting the importance users give to the presence of those resources.
Although the library made a considerable investment in new technologies in order to provide different electronic resources the potential of these tools is still far from being fully explored. However there is a continuous development and promotion of the library's electronic resources.

Study 2

The aim of the study was to know the degree in which students of both Faculties (Engineering and Arts and Humanities from the University of Porto) were opened to the existence of e-books and other digital documents and to point out the possible differences between Faculties.
A survey was presented to 40 students, 20 from each School. Responses were given to sentences in a 5 point scale from totally agree to totally disagree.
Results showed that students didn't know much about e-books, especially about the free availability of them on the Web. However a great percentage read books (60%) although not digital ones (only 20%) but in the Library (60%) and know few digital Libraries (only 20%). There were no differences statistically significant between Faculties.

Study 3

This study analyzed the differences between a random sample of 50 students from the Faculty of Arts and Humanities in their use of Libraries. Some differences between courses were found but the main differences were between sexes. Female students go to the Faculty Library more frequently than males.

Study 4 (2)
The aim of the work was to know which methods of information research, first year university students from some Faculties of the University of Porto use in the first place when they have to make a research, namely the Internet versus the Library.
A questionnaire was constructed for the aim of the study and was presented to a sample of 20 students from each of five faculties (Arts Faculty, Engineering Faculty, Law Faculty, Science Faculty, and Medicine Faculty) in a total of 100 surveys.
Generally students prefer the Internet to search the information needed for their studies although the vast majority of respondents know that the information from that environment is not always reliable or valid. University students of the first year prefer to make research on-line saying that it has the capacity to catch more information and to accede to an enormous number of contents in a fast form. However, students prefer Libraries to study because they think they have a more reflective and calm environment.
Universities must inform students about information sources at their disposal and the best way of using them.

3. Conclusions

The possibility students have to plan and carry out research work is a way to developing different capacities. They have the opportunity of applying the acquired knowledge but also of confronting themselves with their difficulties. Normally the themes of their research work are freely chosen by them making it possible to serve their interests providing that they are related with Information Science questions and analyzed by scientific methods of research. Those are also moments of creativity and team work implying task division and, most of the times, direct contact with situations of the real world and with people (the respondents) either they are other students or professionals particularly those working in the area of Information Science in libraries or other kind of Institutions or even in a company.
Students are encouraged to do rigorous work in order to present it in international Science encounters. This is a way of challenging them and of making them follow the norms of doing research and writing scientific reports but it is also a moment of learning and confronting themselves with their strong and weak abilities.
In their future professional settings many will be the times where assessing users preferences, needs or satisfaction will be necessary to better plan manage and evaluate their performance or, for instance, the impact of new technologies in people´s lives. Being capable of organizing a research to answer some of these questions is an important outcome of their professional education.
These kinds of teaching and learning activities are important tools in any area of knowledge particularly in disciplines that have a practical component that can be applied in the future.

References

Bonwell, C. & Eison, J. (1991). *Active Learning: Creating Excitement in the Classroom AEHE-ERIC Higher Education Report No.1*. Washington, D.C.: Jossey-Bass.

Bruner, J. S. (1961). The act of discovery. *Harvard Educational Review* 31 (1): 21–32.

De Bruyne, P., Herman, J., & De Schoutheete, M. (1974). *Dynamique de la recherche en sciences sociales. Les pôles de la pratique méthodologique*. Paris: PUF.

Mayer, R. (2004). Should there be a three-strikes rule against pure discovery learning? The case for guided methods of instruction. *American Psychologist* 59 (1): 14–19.

Ribeiro, F. (2005). Formação em mercado de trabalho em informação e documentação em Portugal. Salamanca: *VI Coloquio Internacional de Ciencias de la Documentción.*

Ribeiro, F., & de Pinto, M. M. G. (2009). *IFLA SET Bulletin: IFLA Section on Education & Training*, IFLA, Volume 10, Issue 1, 6-11.

Silva, A. M., & Ribeiro, F. (2009). Perspectivar a avaliação como operação metodológica no âmbito da Ciência da Informação. Valencia: *IX CONGRESO ISKO-ESPAÑA - Nuevas perspectivas para la difusión y organización del conocimiento* , Universitat Politècnica de Valencia, Volume 1, 246-261.

Silva, A., Selas, M., Peixoto, J., Graça, R., & Martins, F. (2009). *The use and implementation of electronic resources in the FLUP Library, Porto:* BOBCATSSS. http://www.bobcatsss2009.org/programme/abstracts.html#posters1

Miranda, A., Capitão, G., Moreira, F., Vaz, F., Freitas, H., Correia, J., & Martins, F.(2009). *Preferred information sources: first year university students.* Porto: BOBCATSSS. http://www.bobcatsss2009.org/programme/abstracts.html#posters1

(1) This study resulted in a poster that was presented at the BOBCATSSS Conference – Porto, Portugal, 28-30 January 2009.

(2) This study resulted in a poster that was presented at the BOBCATSSS Conference – Porto, Portugal, 28-30 January 2009.

A Glance at the Characteristics of Mixed Methods and Importance of its Applications in LIS Researches

Hossein Pashaeizad

Department of Library and Information Science, University of Tehran and Payame Noor University, Iran, E-mail: Pashaeizad@pnu.ac.ir; Pashaeizad@gmail.com

Abstract: Mixed methods research is becoming increasingly articulated, attached to research practice, and recognized as the third major research approach or research paradigm, along with qualitative research and quantitative research. Inquiry and investigation about problems of an interdisciplinary and multidisciplinary domain, such as library and information science studies require decision to be taken about an appropriate research design. In making such a decision, the researcher must tacitly assume a philosophical point of view or a research paradigm. There are four research paradigms which construct the basis of the selection of research methodology and research methods designs. These paradigms include: a) positivism, b) interpretivism, c) critical theory, and d) post-structuralism (Bazargan, 2007). Positivism is the basis of quantitative research method, and of the qualitative research methods are the three paradigms mentioned above (namely; interpretivism, critical theory, and post-structuralism). Because of the nature and complexity of problems in library and information science settings and also the newly matters evolved in this multidisciplinary field, such as information technologies, digital libraries and so on, neither of the quantitative nor qualitative research methods, alone, are able to investigate problems pertaining to them thoroughly. Therefore, researchers of this domain require have a shift toward applying a combination of quantitative and qualitative research methods designs that is named mixed methods research. In this article, first of all we concisely review the philosophical point of views (paradigms) which construct the basis of research methods. Thereafter history and the characteristics of mixed methods research will be reviewed. Finally, applications of mixed methods research in the library and information science (LIS) are discussed.

Keywords: Mixed methods; Mixed methods research; Paradigms; Qualitative research; Quantitative research; Library science; Library and information science.

1. Introduction

Research by library and information science (LIS) practitioners is needed to create new knowledge and thereby contribute to the growth of LIS as a profession or discipline. It is needed to improve problem solving and decision making in the workplace, to make professional practitioners critical consumers of the research literature, and to better equip librarians to provide optimal information services to researchers in other fields. Reading and conducting research can contribute to career advancement for librarians. It can also improve an individual's ability to think critically and analytically, improve staff morale, and enhance the library's status within its community (Powell, 1997). There are so many definitions of research that is not easy to choose one. Basically, research is an inquiry process that includes the components for collective inquiry, research design, methodology, data collection and analysis, concluding with the communication of the findings. It later appears in a published form. The research process is not the same in all scientific fields. In the social sciences, research is more problem-oriented and may not be aimed at developing cumulative theory. It might fulfill other functions, such as description or evaluation. Library and information science (LIS) has emerged, not only as a profession and the educational program that supports it, but also as a research discipline. Research is needed to create new knowledge and thereby contribute to the growth of LIS as a profession or discipline. If research is absent, non-existent or even scarce, there is no profession, but only an occupation grounded in techniques, routine and common sense. This is, of course, the important reason why research is conducted into LIS (Juznic and Urbanija,2003).
LIS is known as a multidisciplinary and interdisciplinary scientific field. According to Holland (2008), Information science has incorporated a number of distinct disciplines, including library science, information technology, sociology, communications, computer science, AI into its mainstream and peripheral research. Collaboration is being promoted within many disciplines as a source of innovation and theory progression, including information science (Borgman, 2004; cited in Holland, 2008). Interdisciplinary studies may be defined as a process of answering a question, solving a problem, or addressing a topic that is too broad or complex to be dealt with adequately by a single discipline or profession. The key defining feature of interdisciplinarity is integration of disciplinary methods and

arguments, as captured in the following definition:
"Interdisciplinary research requires integration of knowledge and/or methods from the various disciplines brought together to address an issue or problem"
Multidisciplinary work refers to the simple juxtaposition of two or more disciplines, focused on the proximity of the disciplines rather than the transformative effort to produce new forms of knowledge (Moran, 2002; cited in Holland, 2008). Possible collaborative efforts between LIS and a variety of disciplines would prove useful to explore. For example, philosophy can provide numerous relevant arguments concerned with the nature of knowledge that could deeply integrate into LIS. Likewise sociology presents theories of considerable interest to LIS research that delves into group dynamics and cultural trends for information use. Cognitive science is another discipline that has much to offer based on its strong collaborative nature. LIS has involved cognitive science in research and theories in varying degrees for a significant period of its history. Birger Hjørland provides an account of the history of cognitive science in LIS and finds strong evidence of collaboration at least from 1977 onwards (Hjørland, 2002). Given that information science has relationships with multiple disciplines at work, it's research problems may be complex and multifaceted. LIS researchers need a large toolkit of methods and designs to address complex, multidisciplinary and interdisciplinary research problems. This researchers may be part of a team of researchers with individuals bringing to the table different research skills and training-most likely skills in both quantitative and qualitative research (Creswell & Plano Clark, 2007). These skills are needed to study the increasingly complex problems facing LIS scientists.

2. Research paradigms

A paradigm is a perspective based on a set of assumptions, concepts, and values that are held and practiced by a community of researchers (Johnson and Christensen, 2008). From the 1960s the word paradigm has referred to thought pattern in any scientific discipline or other epistemological context. The Merriam-Webster Online dictionary defines this usage as "a philosophical and theoretical framework of a scientific school or discipline within which theories, laws, and generalizations and the experiments performed in support of them are formulated; broadly : a philosophical or theoretical framework of any kind" (Wikipedia, 2008). Bryman defines paradigm as a 'cluster of beliefs and dictates which for scientists in a particular discipline influence what should be studied, how research should be done, how results should be interpreted, and so on' (Bryman, 1988; cited in Barron, 2006). Thomas Kuhn gave the word paradigm its contemporary meaning when he adopted it to refer to the set of practices that define a scientific discipline during a particular period of time. As Kuhn (1970) declares, "there is no such thing as research in the absence of a paradigm" (p. 79). Kuhn himself came to prefer the terms exemplar and normal science, which have more exact philosophical meanings. However, in his book **The Structure of Scientific Revolutions** Kuhn (1970) defines a scientific paradigm as:

- what is to be observed and scrutinized
- the kind of questions that are supposed to be asked and probed for

answers in relation to this subject
- how these questions are to be structured
- how the results of scientific investigations should be interpreted

Kuhn's elaboration of the function of paradigms helps us to understand how normal research can take place with the confidence that results will be cogent and not a random gathering of facts. A paradigm is:

> Like an accepted judicial decision in common law, it is an object for further articulation and specification under new or more stringent conditions. To see how this can be so, we must recognize how very limited in both scope and precision a paradigm can be at the time of its first appearance. Paradigms gain their status because they are more successful than their competitors in solving a few problems that the group of practitioners has come to recognize as acute. (Kuhn, 1970, p. 23)

Kuhn's argument is that researchers who share a commitment to a particular paradigm are committed to the same rules and standards for scientific practice. His approach has been influential within the social sciences within which two broad research paradigms are often identified – the quantitative and the qualitative. Each paradigm rests upon distinctive foundations and applies a specific approach to researching the social world. For instance, quantitative research is a research strategy that emphasizes measurement in the collection and analysis of data. The quantitative approach is underpinned by a distinctive epistemological and ontological nature.

For the most of the 20th century the quantitative paradigm was dominant (Johnson and Christensen (2008). The epistemological basis for quantitative research is typically, but not exclusively, characterized as positivist. Positivism advocates the application of the methods of the natural sciences to the study of social reality. The general principles of the positivist paradigm are that only phenomena, and therefore knowledge, confirmed by the senses can genuinely be warranted as knowledge; that the function of theory models is to generate hypotheses that can be tested and that will allow explanations of law to be considered. Ultimately, according to the positivist school, the scientific study of society must be undertaken in a manner that is value free that is predicated upon an objective study of the social world. The positivist approach rests upon an epistemological foundation, which emphasizes the principles of measurement, causality, generalization and replication. These theoretical underpinnings therefore presume a certain category of research methods, which are conducive to an objective, positivistic approach such as surveys, questionnaires, structured interviews, experiments, quasi-experiments and official statistics, and content analysis of documents.

The second dominant research paradigm is qualitative research. During the 1980s, the qualitative paradigm came of age as an alternative to the quantitative paradigm, and it was often conceptualized as the polar opposite of quantitative research (Johnson and Christensen (2008).The qualitative research strategy differs markedly from the quantitative approach and is underpinned by very different epistemological and ontological foundations. This approach emphasize the need to understand society as social actors perceive and interpret it, and interpretations of social phenomena can vary markedly according to the standpoint of the social actor. In light of such an epistemological grounding, qualitative researchers do not typically seek objective appraisal of social phenomena, therefore the arsenal of research methods utilized differs from the quantitative tradition and includes participant observation, unstructured/ semi-structured interviews, focus groups, case studies, ethnographic research and discourse analysis (Barron, 2006).

The difference between quantitative and qualitative research is often seen as quite fundamental, leading people to talk about 'paradigm wars' in which quantitative and qualitative research are seen as quarrelsome and incompatible factions. Many researchers define themselves as either quantitative or qualitative. This idea is linked to what are seen as the different underlying philosophies and worldviews of researchers in the two 'paradigms' (also called 'epistemologies'). According to this view, two fundamentally different worldviews underlie quantitative and qualitative research. The quantitative view is described as being 'realist' or sometimes 'positivist', while the worldview underlying qualitative research is viewed as being 'subjectivist'. Realists take the view that what research does is uncover an existing reality. 'The truth is out there' and it is the job of the researcher to use objective research methods to uncover that truth. This means that the researcher needs to be as detached from the research as possible, and use methods that maximize objectivity and minimize the involvement of the researcher in the research. This is best done using methods taken largely from the natural sciences (e.g. biology, physics, etc.), which are then transposed to social research settings. Positivism is the most extreme form of this worldview. According to positivism, the world works according to fixed laws of cause and effect. Scientific thinking is used to test theories about these laws, and either reject or provisionally accept them. In this way, we will finally get to understand the truth about how the world works (Muijs,2004).

A lot of researchers, both quantitative and qualitative, take a pragmatist approach to research, using different methods depending on the research question they are trying to answer. In some cases this will lead them to quantitative research, for example when they need to give a quantitative answer to a question or generalize findings to a population, or are looking to test a theory mathematically; in other cases they will employ qualitative methods. Sometimes a mixed methods approach combining quantitative and qualitative methods will be the most appropriate. Although the modern roots of mixed research go back to the late 1950s (and its historical roots go much further back in time), some researchers think that mixed research truly became the legitimate third paradigm with the publication of the **Handbook of Mixed Methods in Social and Behavioral Research** (2003) by Tashakkori and Teddlie. At the same time, mixed research has been conducted by practicing researchers throughout the history of research (Johnson and Christensen, 2008). Different schools of thought have presented in figure1.

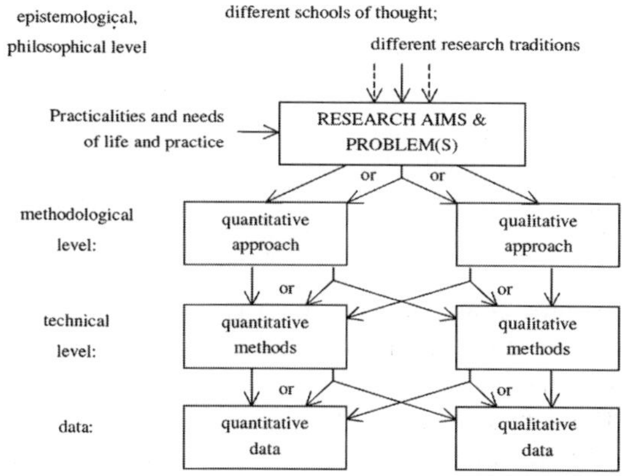

Figure1. The levels of research in practice (adapted from Niglas 1999)

3. Mixed methods research

Since the 1960s, an increasing number of researchers in various fields of social and behavioral sciences have been advocating the combining of quantitative and qualitative approaches to the study of various social phenomena (Creswell & Plano Clark, 2007; Tashakkori & Teddlie, 2003). The combining of qualitative and quantitative approaches is most commonly known as mixed methods research. As noted by Johnson and Onwuegbuzie (cited in Collins, Onwuegbuzie & Jiao, 2007) mixed methods research is formally defined as the class of research where the researcher mixes or combines quantitative and qualitative research techniques into a single study. Mixed methods research is the processes and procedures for collecting, analyzing and inferring both quantitative and qualitative data in a single study or in sequential studies, based on priority and sequence of information (Tashakkori & Teddlie, 1998; Creswell & Plano Clark, 2007). Mixed methods is an approach to inquiry in which the researcher links, in some way (e.g. merges, integrates, connects), both quantitative and qualitative data to provide a unified understanding of a research problem (Creswell & Plano Clark, 2007).Teddlie & Tashakkori (2003) define truly mixed approach methodology as a methodology that incorporates multiple approaches in all stages of research from problem identification to research questions, data collection, data analysis, and final inference; and includes a transformation of the data and their analyses through the other approach (i.e. quantification and qualitization of data).

Creswell and Garrett (2008) point out that mixed methods research has come into its own as a research approach in the last 20 years. To understand the beginnings of mixed methods, we need to return to the 1980s. Prior to this decade, authors wrote about the importance of gathering both quantitative and qualitative data and debated the merits of combining qualitative and quantitative data. These early writers had not conceptualized mixed methods as a distinct approach to inquiry. Several writers working independently in different parts of the world conceptualized mixed methods as we know it today. Tashakkori and Teddlie (2003) argue that mixed methods designs evolved from the notion of 'triangulating' the information from different data sources. However, mixed methodology evolved as a "third methodological movement" originated from the "paradigm wars," in which each camp was criticizing the other's methods of study, rigor of its procedures and the validity of its outcomes. There are some essential theoretical assumptions that should be taken into consideration and adhered to when conducting a mixed methods study. These are the pragmatist philosophy, compatibility thesis and fundamental principle of mixed methods research (Teddlie & Tashakkori, 2003; Creswell & Plano Clark, 2007). The pragmatist philosophy keeps the researchers away from pointless philosophical arguments and enables them to mix the research components in the way they believe to work for the given research problem and context. This is also consistent with the fundamental principle of mixed methods research, since this principle expresses that the "methods should be mixed in a way that has complementary strengths and nonoverlapping weaknesses" (Johnson & Turner, 2003; Creswell & Plano Clark, 2007). Lastly, as for the compatibility thesis which refers to the assumption that quantitative and qualitative methods are compatible and can be mixed (Teddlie & Tashakkori, 2003; Creswell & Plano Clark, 2007). It would be impossible for any researcher to even propose such a study, if this thesis were not assumed. In addition to the above mentioned fundamental assumptions, Creswell, et al. (2003) state four additional assumptions or criteria implicit in the design of the studies:

1. Implementation of data collection referring to the sequence in which the researcher collects qualitative and quantitative data, which also affects data analysis and written report. Both qualitative and quantitative data collection might occur either concurrently or sequentially. This implementation approach also raises an issue of iterative cycles, where researcher may go back and forth between qualitative and quantitative data collection. In addition to the sequencing, researchers can also mix different qualitative and quantitative data collection techniques by utilizing intra- or inter-method mixing. Intra-method mixing is defined as concurrent or sequential use of a single method, e.g. using both open- and close-ended items in a questionnaire, whereas inter-method mixing utilizes two or more methods concurrently or sequentially, e.g. using questionnaires and interviewing. These two different kinds of method mixing are also called "data triangulation" and "method triangulation" respectively.
2. Priority refers to which method, either quantitative or qualitative or both, is given more priority, weight and attention in the study.
3. Stage of integration, which stands for the phase in the research process where the mixing or connecting of the quantitative and qualitative data occurs. It might occur in different phases of the study, e.g. problem description, research questions, research methods, data collection and analysis, and inference processes.
4. Theoretical perspectives refer to researchers' personal stances toward the topics they are studying based on their personal history, gender, experience, culture and class.

Based on these criteria Creswell et al (2003) specify six different types of major mixed methods research: sequential explanatory, sequential exploratory, sequential transformative, concurrent triangulation, concurrent nested, and concurrent transformative.

Philosophically, mixed methods research is the "third wave" or a third research movement, a movement that moves past the recent paradigm wars by offering a logical and practical alternative. Philosophically, mixed research makes use of the pragmatic method and system of philosophy. Its logic of inquiry includes the use of induction (or discovery of patterns), deduction (testing of theories and hypotheses), and abduction (uncovering and relying on the best of a set of explanations for understanding one's results). The past decade has seen a proliferation in the number of mixed methods studies undertaken. The popularization of mixed methods research has led to an increase in the number of publications devoted to methodological issues in this field-the most comprehensive of which, to date, has been the Handbook of Mixed Methods in Social & Behavioral Research (Tashakkori & Teddlie, 2003), which has provided researchers with some theoretical and practical tools for conducting mixed methods research. Nevertheless, as noted by Teddlie and Tashakkori (2003), six unresolved issues and controversies in the use of mixed methods in the social and behavioral sciences still prevail, namely, (a) the nomenclature and basic definitions used in mixed methods research, (b) the utility of mixed methods research, (c) the paradigmatic underpinning for mixed methods research, (d) design issues in mixed methods research, (e) issues in making inferences in mixed methods research, and (f) the logistics of conducting mixed methods research. Moreover, Onwuegbuzie (2007) has identified the following four crises or challenges that researchers face when undertaking mixed methods research: representation, legitimation, integration, and politics.

In addition to triangulation, the third methodological movement has been given many names such as blended research, integrative research, multimethod research multiple methods, triangulated studies, ethnographic residual analysis, and mixed research. An advantage of the broader term mixed research, is that it does not suggest a limitation of mixing to methods only. Mixed methods research has become the most popular term used to describe this movement. It is important to keep in one's mind, however, that the word methods should be viewed broadly. Some researchers believe that a broad interpretation and use of the word methods (in mixed methods) allows inclusion of issues and strategies surrounding methods of data collection (e.g., questionnaires, interviews, observations), methods of research (e.g., experiments, ethnography), and related philosophical issues (e.g., ontology, epistemology, axiology). Others believe each of the three major approaches to research include assumptions, principles, and values about these kinds of methodology and practice-related issues as parts of the research paradigm(Johnson, Onwuegbuzie & Turner, L.A.(2007).

Mixed methods can be used to enhance our understanding of a topic typically studied from just a qualitative or quantitative perspective. Alongside social scientists' increasing shift toward thinking that qualitative and quantitative orientations are complementary rather than competing perspectives, there has been interest in developing strategies to combine qualitative and quantitative data collection and analytical approaches. Researchers can consider both causal (quantitative) and interpretive (qualitative) questions when designing their research projects (Kalof, Dan and Dietz, 2008).

A number of factors have contributed to the evolution of mixed methods research.

The complexity of our research problems calls for answers beyond simple numbers in a quantitative sense or words in a qualitative sense. A combination of both forms of data can provide the most complete analysis of problems. Researchers can situate numbers in the contexts and words of participants, and they can frame the words of participants with numbers, trends, and statistical results. Both forms of data are necessary today. In addition, qualitative research has evolved to a point where writers consider it a legitimate form of inquiry in the social and human sciences. Quantitative researchers, we believe, recognize that qualitative data can play an important role in quantitative research. Qualitative researchers, in turn, realize that reporting only qualitative participant views of a few individuals may not permit generalizing the findings to many individuals. Audiences such as policy makers, practitioners, and others in applied areas need multiple forms of evidence to document and inform the research problems. A call for increased sophistication of evidence leads to a collection of both quantitative and qualitative data. In recent years, many authors have begun to advocate for mixed methods research as a separate methodology or design. Tashakkori and Teddlie (2003) called mixed methods research the "third methodological movement". This means that in the evolution of research methodologies, mixed methods now follows quantitative approaches and then qualitative approaches as the third movement. Unquestionably, many scholars are interested in mixed methods research as it has evolved during the last few decades (Creswell, 2008).

4. Challenges in mixed methods research

Some researchers (for example; Collins, K.; Onwuegbuzie, A. J. and Jiao, Q. G. ,2007) have mentioned four challenge including challenge of representation, challenge of legitimation or validity, challenge of integration, and challenge of politics for mixed methods research. The challenge of representation refers to the fact that sampling problems characterize both quantitative and qualitative research. With respect to quantitative research, the majority of studies utilize sample sizes that are too small to detect statistically significant differences or relationships and utilize nonrandom samples that prevent effect-size estimates from being generalized to the underlying population. In qualitative research, the challenge of representation refers to the difficulties researchers encounter in capturing lived experiences via their social texts. In mixed methods research, the challenge of representation often is intensified because both the qualitative and quantitative components of studies bring to the study their own unique challenges. In mixed methods studies, the challenge of representation refers to the difficulty in capturing (i.e., representing) the lived experience using text in general and words and numbers in particular.

The second challenge in mixed methods research pertains to legitimation or validity. With respect to quantitative research, the importance of legitimation, or what is more commonly referred to as ''validity,'' has been long acknowledged and is well documented in the literature, including measurement-related validity (e.g., construct-related validity, criterion-related validity, content-related validity) and design-related validity (e.g., internal validity, external validity). With respect to the qualitative research paradigm, the issue of legitimation has been more controversial. As is the case for the challenge of representation, the challenge of legitimation is greater in mixed methods studies than in monomethod studies (i.e., quantitative research or qualitative alone). The challenge of legitimation refers to the difficulty in obtaining findings and/or making inferences that are credible, trustworthy, dependable, transferable, and/or confirmable.

The third challenge in mixed methods research pertains to integration. This challenge compels mixed methods researchers to ask questions such as the following: Is it appropriate to triangulate, expand, compare, or consolidate quantitative data originating from a large, random sample with qualitative data arising from a small, purposive sample? How much weight should researchers and/or consumers place on qualitative data compared to quantitative data?

The fourth challenge in mixed methods research is the challenge of politics. This challenge refers to the tensions that come to the fore as a result of combining qualitative and quantitative approaches. These tensions include any conflicts that occur when different investigators are used for the qualitative and quantitative components of an investigation, as well as the contradictions and paradoxes that come to the fore when qualitative and quantitative data are compared and contrasted. The challenge of politics also pertains to the difficulty in persuading the consumers of mixed methods research, including stakeholders and policy makers, to value the findings stemming from both the qualitative and quantitative phases of a study.

5. Applications of mixed methods research in LIS

As mentioned in production section of this article, LIS as an multidisciplinary field have interaction with many disciplines such as psychology, linguistics, information technology, computer science, communications, sociology and so on…, therefore need to use proper research methods, especially mixed method, for facing with and studying of the problems evolving from those disciplines. For a long time, the quantitative and qualitative research paradigms were dominant and prevalent in social science researches (Bowler & Large, 2008). With the research issues and problems being more complex in social science, none of those research methods are not able to solve the newfangled multifaceted research problems in a multidisciplinary areas such as LIS anymore, so needs to use the new research methods designs and approaches for study of the those problems came out. Although mixed methods research has been used in various disciplines (for example sociology, education, nursing, anthropology, management, social policy, healthcare, and psychology), there are not sufficient evidences about using that in library and information science to date. The status of mixed methods research in LIS can be revealed through examining books and articles about research methods in LIS and by analyzing published research reports. For finding how did this approach shape research in LIS, Fidel (2008) conducted an analysis of 465 articles published in four major LIS research journals. Findings of study revealed that 22 articles (5%) employed mixed methods research. However the recognition of mixed method research by name or as a research method was absent from these articles and from the methodological literature in LIS. Therefore he concluded that mixed methods research is not common in library and information science (LIS) and has not been discussed in its literature. He adds the various strengths of mixed methods research suggest that being cognizant of its possible use in LIS would benefit researchers in the field. Findings of Fidel's study revealed that the term mixed methods is missing from most methodological Books.

To LIS researchers, the most familiar form of mixed methods research use is triangulation, one of the methods to test the validity and accuracy of a study. Triangulation is employed primarily in qualitative research. However, not all triangulations require the use of mixed methods research. For example, Patton (2002, cited in Fidel, 2008) identified four types of triangulation:

1. Methods triangulation: Checking the consistency of findings generated by different data collection methods
2. Triangulation of sources: Checking the consistency of different data sources within the same method
3. Analyst triangulation: Using multiple analysts to review findings
4. Theory/perspective triangulation: Using multiple perspectives or theories to interpret the data

LIS researchers can use mixed methods research when no single approach can fully investigate the phenomenon, particularly when the phenomenon is complex and multifaceted. Another case is when qualitative, exploratory investigation generates hypotheses to be tested. Hypotheses generated this way add depth to the evidence available for testing them. Eventually, using mixed methods research allows LIS researchers to address issues more widely and more completely than one method could, which in turn amplifies the richness and complexity of the research findings. For example, you can suppose a researcher is interested in understanding the Web searching behavior of under graduate students. For that purpose he can develop and test a few hypotheses about the association between variables describing the student population (independent variables) and those illustrating web searching behavior (dependent variables). He can collect data through a multiple-choice questionnaire that he administers to students. To make sure that the sample is representative of all students, he needs to know how to stratify the population before administering the questionnaire. To answer this question, he observes class and Web searching sessions, and conduct open-ended interviews with several students to explore their perception of the differences among students. This qualitative investigation provided additional useful information. At its conclusion, researcher may re-considers his study design after than he discovered that teachers were important players in shaping students' searching behavior. He may decide to include them in the investigation. Researcher can use this qualitative analysis to enhance data collection as well. Through his interactions with the participating students he will create rapport with the potential respondents to the questionnaire; this will help him achieve a satisfying response rate.

An example of mixed methods research use in study is Web searching behavior of elementary school students. Researcher, however, prefers to explore it to provide a thick description of the process. For that purpose, she collects data through observation and open-ended interviews. To support her study design and data collection, she initially administers a simple questionnaire to the student population from which she would draw her qualitative sample. The data collected from the questionnaires will help her to improve the study in several ways. Through them she creates a profile of the population which guides her sampling. This was particularly important because she has planned to employ purposeful sampling. To select the participants, she needs information about individuals that will be collect only from the students themselves—such as their searching experience or whether they have Internet connection at home. In addition, the questionnaires provide background information about each participant that she takes into consideration when she conducts the observation and interviews with individual students—such as the student's first language or favorite topic. Analyzing the qualitative data, she may discover some prominent themes in the students' searching behavior. She thinks these are important findings but she can not generalize them because she draws the participants from a relatively small sample of students in only one school. To generalize the findings, she administers questionnaire to a diverse population. The data collected this way also may verify her interpretation of the qualitative results.

6. Conclusion

Today's research world is becoming increasingly interdisciplinary, complex, and dynamic; therefore, many researchers need to complement one method with another, and all researchers need a solid understanding of multiple methods used by other scholars to facilitate communication, to promote collaboration and to provide superior research. Taking a non-purist or compatibilist or mixed position allows researchers to mix and match design components that offer the best chance of answering their specific research questions. Because no single research method can tap all dimensions of a complex research problem, it is often valuable to combine two or more methods, drawing conclusions from a synthesis of the results. Multiple method use, also called triangulation, unquestionably results in a broader perspective on the problem and often more persuasive findings for policymakers. Similar results from two or more methods could increase the credibility of the findings, whereas dissimilar results might raise new questions about alternative interpretations. Awareness of mixed methods research among LIS researchers can be increased through various channels. When authors who employ the approach explain their motivation for its use- along with its advantages and challenges and the mixing procedures they followed-readers enrich their understanding of these issues and may be exposed to new ways of thinking about the approach and its implementation.

Mixed methods research also is an attempt to legitimate the use of multiple approaches in answering research questions, rather than restricting or constraining researchers' choices (i.e., it rejects dogmatism). It is an expansive and creative form of research, not a limiting form of research. It is inclusive, pluralistic, and complementary, and it suggests that researchers take an eclectic approach to method selection and the thinking about and conduct of research. What is most fundamental is the research question- research methods should follow research questions in a way that offers the best chance to obtain useful answers. Many research questions and combinations of questions are best and most fully answered through mixed research solutions.

Mixed methods designs hold a great deal of promise for the researcher who wants to tackle complex issues that reside at multiple levels- the individual as well as the social. It can enhance the type of information gathered and can serve to increase the validity of both qualitative and quantitative projects. There is the idea that by using both approaches can bring out the best in both methods (increasing the validity of a given study through triangulation, for example), while offsetting the weaknesses of the other. The idea, as we have noted earlier, is that "The Whole is greater than the sum of its parts". However, having said this, there are a range of caveats from the conceptual to the practical that one must consider when using mixed methods designs. Mixed methods blur the line between research paradigms, and it is unclear how concerned researchers should be about this. There are those " pragmatists" who advocate for whatever methods work, sometimes with little regard for issues of epistemology and methodology, while others, known as "purists", see such boundary crossings as violating the very foundations of scientific thought. Many others take positions between these views on what we see as a continuum of opinions on matter. Mixed methods is not a panacea; a magic elixir that one pours onto a research project to make it work. Mixed methods are techniques for getting as knowledge building. More is not necessarily better; the sum may not be greater than its parts.

References

Bazargan,A. (2007). "Mixed methods design: A preferable approach in educational inquires", Journal of Psychology and Education, Vol. 37, No.3, 101-119.

Barron, L. (2006). " Paradigm" in The Sage Dictionary of Social Research Methods, Compiled and edited by Victor Jupp, London: Sage, 212-213.

Borgman, C. (2004), E-Science, Digital Libraries and Knowledge Communities, Oxford Internet Institute, Oxford.

Bowler, L. and Large, A. (2008). Design-based research for LIS, Library & Information Science Research Vol. 30, No. 1, 39-46.

Collins, K.; Onwuegbuzie, A. J. & Jiao, Q. G. (2007). A Mixed Methods Investigation of Mixed Methods Sampling Designs in Social and Health Science Research, Journal of Mixed Methods Research, Vol.1, No.3, 267-294.

Creswell, J.W. (2008). "Mixed methods research" in The Sage Encyclopedia of Qualitative Research Methods, LISA M. GIVEN (Ed.) , London:Sage, 526-529.

Creswell, J.W. (ed.)(2008). Research Design: Qualitative, Quantitative, and Mixed Methods Approaches, Thousand Oaks, CA: Sage.

Creswell, J.W. & Garrett, A. L. (2008). The "movement" of mixed methods research and the role of educators, South African Journal of Education, Vol. 28,321-333

Creswell, J.W & Plano Clark, V.L. (2007) . Designing and conducting mixed methods research. Thousand Oaks, CA: Sage.

Fidel, R.(2008) . Are we there yet? : Mixed methods research in library and information science, Library & Information Science Research 30, 265–272.

Hjørland, B. (2002), "Epistemology and the socio-cognitive perspective in information science", Journal of the American Society for Information Science and Technology, Vol. 53 No.4, 257-70.

Holland. G. A. (2008). Information science: an interdisciplinary effort? Journal of Documentation, Vol.64, no.1, 7-23.

Johnson, B. & Christensen, L. (2008). Educational Research: Quantitative, Qualitative, and Mixed Approaches, Thousands Oakes, CA. : Sage.

Johnson, B.; Onwuegbuzie, A.J. & Turner, L.A.(2007). Toward a Definition of Mixed Methods Research, Journal of Mixed Methods Research, 1, 112-133.
Juznic, P. & Urbanija, J.(2003). Developing research skills in library and information science studies, Library Management, Vol. 24, No. 6/7, 324-331.
Kalof, L.; Dan, A. & Dietz, T. (2008). Essentials of Social Research, London: McGraw-Hill.
Kuhn, T. S. (1970). The structure of scientific revolutions (2d ed.). Chicago: University of Chicago Press.
Kwon,N.(2008). A Mixed-Methods Investigation of the Relationship between Critical Thinking and Library Anxiety among Undergraduate Students in their Information Search rocess, College & Research Libraries, March- Vol. 69, No.2, 117-131.
Moran, J. (2002), Interdisciplinarity, Routledge, London.
Talja, S., Tuominen, K., Savolainen, R. (2005), "'Isms' in information science: constructivism, collectivism and constructionism", Journal of Documentation, Vol. 61 No.1, pp.79.
Muijs,D. (2004) Doing Quantitative Research in Education with SPSS,London: Sage.
Niglas, K. (1999). Quantitative and Qualitative Inquiry in Educational Research: is there a paradigmatic difference between them? Paper given at ECER99, Lahti, 22–25. September 1999; Education Line http://www.leeds.ac.uk/educol/documents/00001487.htm
Onwuegbuzie, A. J. (2007). Mixed methods research in sociology and beyond. In G. Ritzer (Ed.), The Blackwell encyclopedia of sociology, Oxford, UK: Blackwell.
Powell, R.R. (1996). Recent Trends in Research: A Methodological Essay, Library Research Seminar I, Florida State University, Tallahassee, November l-2
Powell,R.R.; Baker, L.M. & Mika, J.J.(2002). Library and information science practitioners and research, Library & Information Science Research, 24, 49–72.
Tashakkori, A. & Teddlie, C. (Eds.). (2003). Handbook of Mixed Methods in the Social and Behavioral Science. Thousand Oaks, CA: Sage.
Tashakkori, A. & Creswell, J.W. (2007). The new era of mixed methods, Journal of Mixed Methods Research, 1, 3-7.
Tashakkori A. & Teddlie, C. (1998). Mixed methodology: Combining qualitative and quantitative approaches. Thousand Oaks, CA: Sage.
Todd, Z. et. al. (eds.) (2004). Mixing Methods in Psychology : The integration of qualitative and quantitative methods in theory and practice, East Sussex: Psychology Press.
Wikipedia (2008). "Paradim", http://en.wikipedia.org/wiki/Paradigm

Bibliometric Analyses on Repository Contents for the Evaluation of Research at Wageningen UR

Marco G. P. van Veller, Wouter Gerritsma, Peter L. van der Togt, Charles D. Leon and Corrie M. van Zeist

Wageningen UR Library, PO Box 9100, 6700 HA Wageningen, The Netherlands

Abstract: Since the last two decades, Wageningen UR Library has been involved in bibliometric analyses for the evaluation of scientific output of staff, chair groups and research institutes of Wageningen UR. In these advanced bibliometric analyses several indicator scores, such as the number of publications, number of citations and citation impacts, are calculated. For a fair comparison of scientific output from staff, chair groups or research institutes (that each work in a different scientific discipline with specific publication and citation habits) scores of the measured bibliometric indicators are normalized against average trend (or baseline) scores per research field. For the collection of scientific output that is subjected to the bibliometric analyses the repository Wageningen Yield (WaY) is used. This repository is filled from the research registration system Metis in which meta data for scientific output is registered by the secretaries of the research groups of Wageningen UR. By the application of a connection between the meta data of publications in WaY and citation scores in Thomson Reuters' Web of Science, custom-made analyses on the scientific output and citation impact of specific entities from Wageningen UR can be performed fast and efficiently. Moreover, a timely registration of new scientific output is stimulated (to ensure their inclusion in future bibliometric analyses) and the quality of meta data in WaY is checked by the library staff and research staff from the research entities under investigation, thus promoting communication between the library and customers.

Keywords: Bibliometric analysis; Citation impact; Repository; Research evaluation; Library.

1. Introduction

One of the main activities of doing scientific research involves the publication on this research in scientific literature. It is for this reason that measurement of scientific output and impact of scientific publications may be used to estimate the productiveness and importance of the underlying research activities. Both productiveness and importance of research are essential criteria for making decisions regarding further development of research at institutes or universities. Therefore, policy makers and boards of these research organizations are interested in quantitative measurements on the output and impact of scientific publications for monitoring and evaluation purposes.

Since the last two decennia, the library of Wageningen University and Research (or Wageningen UR) has been involved in various quantitative analyses on scientific publications produced by staff of the university and institutes. These advanced bibliometric analyses were performed for various periods of time on scientific output of staff, chair groups and research institutes (or entities) of Wageningen UR.

Originally, the scientific output, on which the bibliometric analyses were performed, was selected by doing a retrospective search in citation enhanced bibliographical databases for the Wageningen UR entities under consideration. Thereby it was very important to be as complete as possible in the retrospective search in order to select all scientific output on which the analyses should be based. For this reason, the results from the retrospective search were checked by the Wageningen UR entities for which the bibliometric analysis was performed. Missing publications were added and corrections were made before the scientific output was subjected to the bibliometric analyses.

The additions and corrections on scientific output, however, were not registered and needed to be made for each subsequent bibliometric analysis. It is for this reason that since 2009 the library of Wageningen UR uses the repository Wageningen Yield (WaY) for bibliometric analyses for Wageningen UR entities. This repository contains the meta data of all publications (as well as a link to the full-text of the publication if available) that have been published by the staff and employees from Wageningen UR. For this reason WaY is a very comprehensive source for the scientific output that is subjected to the bibliometric analyses. This paper discusses the application of the repository in the bibliometric analyses performed by Wageningen UR Library as well as the mutual advantages to both the bibliometric analyses and the repository that results from this combination.

2. Choice of bibliographic databases for bibliometric analyses

The aim of a bibliometric analysis is to obtain a quantitative overview of the scientific output and the impact of citations to this scientific output published by a researcher, research group or research organization. At Wageningen UR bibliometric analyses are made at regular intervals as part of the continuous research evaluation of staff, research groups or institutes. The advanced bibliometric analyses performed by Wageningen UR Library are based upon scientific articles that are published in scholarly journals or serials that are covered by the bibliographic database Web of Science (WoS) from Thomson Reuter Scientific.

In WoS almost 8000 current peer reviewed journals in different scientific disciplines are covered. This selection of journals is considered to include the most important peer reviewed journals for science. In addition to standard bibliographical data, WoS contains for each of the articles (in the covered journals) the number of citations to each article. The latter is updated on a regular basis.

Besides WoS, Thomson Reuters Scientific also produces the database Essential Science Indicators (ESI) which provides the world average number of citations of articles for 22 different research fields. The world averages are updated five times per year and a series of world averages over a certain number of years is called a baseline. Besides world averages, ESI also provides the average number of citations per year for the top 0.01%, 0.1%, 1%, 10%, 20% and 50% most cited articles per research field. In an advanced bibliometric analysis combination of WoS and ESI is essential for the calculation of the impact of citations because citation counts for an article should be obtained from WoS, the baselines follow from ESI and the journals are classified in the research fields in ESI.

3. Normalization of citation impacts

The impact of citations to an article is normalized for one of the 22 different research fields to which the article belongs. Thereby, the research field for an article is determined on basis of the journal in which it has been published and can be found in the ESI. For each article, the citation impact is normalized by benchmarking the number of citations against the world average citation value, obtained for the same year in which the article has been published via the baseline for the research field to which the article belongs. The reason to normalize citation impacts lies in the different publication and citation cultures that apply to different research fields (e.g. the world average number of citations for publications in Molecular biology & Genetics are approximately eight times larger than in Mathematics). It is for this reason that only by normalizing citation impacts, monitoring and evaluation of these impacts over different research fields can be performed.

Normalization of citation impacts of a series of articles (e.g. published by a particular research group that is subject to a bibliometric analysis) can be done in two alternative ways. Both ways of normalization result in a measure that shows the relation of the impact of the analyzed set of articles to the world average of 1. One normalized measure for the citation impact is obtained by dividing the sum of citations to all considered articles by the sum of the world average citation rates for these articles. This ratio leads to the Citation Impact (CI or Crown Indicator sensu van Raan, 2004) for the series of articles. Alternatively, normalization of citation impacts of a series of articles can also be carried out at the level of individual articles. In this case, a citation impact is calculated for each article separately and normalization is accomplished by calculation of the mean of these impacts. This approach on the level of individual articles leads to a measurement for the citation impact known as the Relative Impact (RI sensu Gerritsma, 2006).

4. Advanced indicators for bibliometric analyses

Besides normalized citation impacts also other indicators result from a bibliometric analysis. In bibliometric analyses at Wageningen UR Library for a series of articles (e.g. for a particular Wageningen UR entity) the following indicators are measured:

- N = Total number of articles in series that is examined $= \sum_{t=1}^{T} n_t$
- C = Total number of citations to the N articles $= \sum_{t=1}^{T} \sum_{i=1}^{n_t} C_{t,i}$
- CPP = Average number of citations per article $= \dfrac{\sum_{t=1}^{T} \sum_{i=1}^{n_t} C_{t,i}}{N}$
- CI = Citation Impact $= \dfrac{\sum_{t=1}^{T} \sum_{i=1}^{n_t} C_{t,i}}{\sum_{t=1}^{T} \sum_{i=1}^{n_t} Wavg_{t,i}}$
- RI = Relative Impact $= \dfrac{\sum_{t=1}^{T} \sum_{i=1}^{n_t} \dfrac{C_{t,i}}{Wavg_{t,i}}}{N}$
- %T10 = Percentage of the 10% most cited articles compared to the total number of articles in the series $= \dfrac{N(C_{t,i} \geq C_{10\%,t,i})}{N} * 100\%$
- %T1 = Percentage of the 1% most cited articles compared to the total number of articles in the series $= \dfrac{N(C_{t,i} \geq C_{1\%,t,i})}{N} * 100\%$
- %NC = Percentage of non-cited articles compared to the total number of

$$\text{articles in the series} = \frac{N(C_{t,i} = 0)}{N} * 100\%$$

With
n_t = Number of articles published in year t
$C_{t,i}$ = Number of citations to article i, published in year t
$Wavg_{t,i}$ = World average number of citations for articles in same research field as for article i for the year t in which article i has been published
$C_{10\%,t,i}$ = Average number of citations for 10% best cited articles in same research field as for article i for the year t in which article i has been published
$C_{1\%,t,i}$ = Average number of citations for 1% best cited articles in same research field as for article i for the year t in which article i has been published

Via these eight indicators Wageningen UR Library tries to give an impression of both the scientific productivity (by counting the number of articles published by the Wageningen UR entities) as well as the impact of this output in the form of citations (by calculation of Citation or Relative Impacts of articles published by the Wageningen UR entities).
For the eight advanced bibliometric indicators both the CI and RI are preferred for the measurement of citation impact because they have been normalized to the research field in which the Wageningen UR entity is working. Because of the different way of normalizing citation impacts of articles differences can be found between these two indicators. Hereby, the RI measures citation impact on an individual basis and may be susceptible to outliers due to articles with high citation scores related to their corresponding world averages. The CI, to the contrary, applies normalization to the complete set of articles as a whole and thereby gives a relative larger weight to the number of citations for older articles and articles in highly cited research fields.
Although the CPP is not normalized to a particular research field, it gives (in relation to the CI) an impression on the world average number of citations per article for the most dominant research field in which the Wageningen UR entity has published. In general, the CPP shows an increasing trend with the age of the articles for which the CPP has been calculated. Both the %T10 and %T1 give indications for excellent cited Wageningen UR entities. Finally, high values of %NC weigh down the values of CPP, RI and CI in bibliometric analyses.

5. Repository contents as a source for bibliometric analyses

In order to perform a bibliometric analysis on the scientific output of a particular Wageningen UR entity, first the series of articles for which the eight different indicators will be calculated need to be selected. As indicated above, these articles need to be published in scientific journals or serials that are covered by WoS. By examining these articles only, one is able to obtain the number of citations for each article from WoS and relate it to values of the applicable baseline for normalization.
Besides selection of articles from journals covered by WoS it is important that the series of articles that has been selected is identified as the set of articles published by the Wageningen UR entity that is evaluated over a certain period of time.

Hereby it is important that a complete set of articles is obtained and that no mistakes are made by selection of articles from other persons, groups or institutes than the one(s) that is evaluated. Selection of the right series of articles for a particular Wageningen UR entity is based upon the meta data (such as affiliation information of the authors) of the articles.

Meta data of the scientific output of whole Wageningen UR are collected in a research registration system (called Metis) and made accessible to users via the repository WaY. Registration of new publications in the research registration system is done by the secretaries of the research groups and both the research registration system Metis and the repository WaY are (further) developed and maintained by Wageningen UR Library.

The repository WaY contains besides the meta data also links to scientific output of the Wageningen UR entities. Further, also affiliation data and all work relations of the staff of Wageningen UR with various Wageningen UR entities (and others outside Wageningen UR) and the research theme or graduate school in which the staff member participates is recorded in great detail. The in-house registration and dissemination of meta data of scientific output from Wageningen UR staff enables a more reliable selection of a series of articles for a bibliometric analysis (for a particular Wageningen UR entity) than selection of these articles on the basis of affiliations mentioned in the articles. Also, if the registration of meta data for new scientific output in the repository WaY is complete and timely, the chances of missing articles in a bibliometric analysis are minimized.

6. Connection between the repository and bibliographical database for bibliometric analyses

For a bibliometric analysis of a series of articles (published by a particular Wageningen UR entity) selected from the repository WaY a connection needs to be made between the meta data for the selected articles in the research registration system Metis and the bibliographical information for the same articles in WoS.

By searching in WoS on affiliation Wageningen UR and its various institutes a list of articles from authors that work (or have worked) at Wageningen UR is obtained. The bibliographical records for these articles are matched with records for the articles that are registered in Metis by using information from the Digital Object Identifier, ISSN in combination with volume and page number or title. As a result of this matching for each article in Metis (which can be identified in Metis by a unique article number), it's ISI-number is obtained from WoS. The ISI-number is entered in the record for the article in WaY and can be used for identification of the article in WoS. Since the ISI-number of each article is stored in WaY the matching between bibliographical data from Metis with WoS needs to be done for each (added) article only once.

With the meta data in WaY on affiliation and work relations different selections can be made for series of articles published by one (or more) Wageningen UR entity (or entities) that will be subjected to a bibliometric analysis. For a particular selected series of articles ISI-numbers are collected from WaY and used to obtain the number of citations ($C_{t,i}$ in formulas above) per article from WoS. Because this number of citations changes over time it needs to be collected from WoS on a frequent basis. Besides the number of citations also the world average number of citations ($Wavg_{t,i}$ in formulas above) and the average number of citations for 10% and 1% most cited articles (respectively $C_{10\%,t,i}$ and $C_{1\%,t,i}$ in formulas above) are updated for each research field from ESI frequently.

The values of the bibliometric data $C_{t,i}$, $Wavg_{t,i}$, $C_{10\%,t,i}$ and $C_{1\%,t,i}$ are used to calculate the different indicators that are mentioned in the formulas above. Hereby the research field of an article is obtained by making a connection (on basis of ISSN; obtained from WaY) between the journal in which the article has been published and information obtained from ESI on the classification of journals in the different research fields.

7. Example of a bibliometric analysis for a research group of Wageningen UR

An example of the results from a bibliometric analysis that has been performed for the scientific output of a research group of Wageningen UR is given in the two tables below. Table 1 gives yearly results for the different indicators whereby publications from different research field may have been combined per year. Table 2 is based on the same series of articles from this research group but lists the different indicators per research field whereby publications from different years may have been combined in a research field. From the two tables trends in the scientific output and impact over years can be derived as well as information on the most prominent research fields in which this research group published.

Table 1: Indicators calculated from a bibliometric analysis on 139 articles published by a research group from Wageningen UR in the years 2002-2007.

Year	N	C	CPP	CI	RI	%T10	%T1	%NC
2002	10	527	52.7	3.46	4.92	50%	30%	0%
2003	21	545	26.0	1.54	1.89	33%	5%	0%
2004	25	509	20.4	1.71	2.53	28%	8%	0%
2005	25	323	12.9	1.35	1.83	28%	4%	0%
2006	26	319	12.3	2.52	3.22	38%	15%	8%
2007	32	285	8.9	3.73	4.69	38%	19%	13%
All years	139	2508	18.0	2.01	3.10	35%	12%	4%

Table 2: Indicators calculated from a bibliometric analysis on 139 articles published by a research group from Wageningen UR in five different research fields.

Research Field	N	C	CPP	CI	RI	%T10	%T1	% NC
Plant & Animal Science	73	1427	19.6	4.08	4.29	49	19	4
Molecular Biology & Genetics	38	686	18.1	1.03	1.17	18	0	0
Biology & Biochemistry	21	365	17.4	1.85	2.69	19	10	14
Environment/Ecology	6	16	2.7	0.54	0.78	0	0	0
Agricultural Sciences	1	14	14.0	12.96	12.96	100	100	0
All research fields	139	2508	18.0	2.01	3.10	35	12	4

8. Mutual advantages to the use of repository contents in bibliometric analyses for Wageningen UR entities

The application of the Wageningen UR repository WaY for the selection of articles for the evaluation of scientific output and citation impact of Wageningen UR entities gives advantages to the efficiency and quality of both the repository and the bibliometric analyses.

For the repository, complete coverage and timely registration of new publications is stimulated because by registration of these publications in WaY, the Wageningen UR entities ensure that also their new scientific output will be included in future bibliometric analyses. The meta data in WaY is entered by the secretaries and checked by the research staff of Wageningen UR at the registration of new publications in Metis as well as double checked on a regular basis by staff from Wageningen UR Library. Besides these checks, errors in the meta data and coverage of the scientific output from Wageningen UR in WaY is checked when bibliographical records in Metis and WaY are matched with the corresponding ones in WoS. Additions as well as corrections that are made on the bibliographic records for Wageningen UR scientific output are registered in Metis and WaY and thereby are ensured for inclusion in future analyses and uses of meta data such as generation of publication lists, etc.

For the advanced bibliometric analyses that Wageningen UR Library performs on Wageningen UR entities, quality is improved by a more precise selection of the right articles for the entities under evaluation due to reliable and updated registration of affiliation data and work relations. Moreover, by using the repository for selection of scientific output, custom-made bibliometric analyses can be performed almost "on the fly" and comparative research evaluations can be performed in a fast and efficient way.

By the establishment of a connection between meta data on affiliation and work relations in the repository WaY and bibliometric data from WoS and ESI a system has been developed in which bibliographical information on new publications is entered when they are registered in the research registration system Metis. For this system updates on the bibliometric data can be performed efficiently and on a regular basis. Finally, the bibliometric analyses performed by Wageningen UR Library in this way has improved awareness of library services considerably. Wageningen UR Library is consulted for questions with regard to steps that can be taken to improve publication strategies for staff members, research groups or institutes.

References

Gerritsma, W., (2006). Een systeem voor citatieanalyses in de praktijk. *InformatieProfessional*, 10, 12-17.

Van Raan, A.F.J., (2004). Measuring Science. Capita Selecta of Current Main Issues, in *Handbook of Quantitative Science and Technology Research : The use of Publication and Patent Statistics in Studies of S&T Systems*, Moed, H.F., Glänzel, W., and Schmoch, U. (eds). (Kluwer Academic Publishers, Dordrecht), pp. 19-50.

2. Management and Marketing

The Next Managerial Leadership: Continuation of a Research Agenda

Peter Hernon

Professor, Graduate School of Library and Information Science, Simmons College, USA
Co-editor, Library & Information Science Research

Leadership and management are two terms that are often used interchangeably. In fact, they describe entirely different concepts, as leadership is more than a component of the functions of management. Management is the process of administering and coordinating resources to ensure than an organization accomplishes its mission and goals. Library and information science (LIS) has a managerial focus; librarians manage the infrastructure of a library: its collections, staff, technology, and facilities. For this reason, the interconnection between management and leadership is the domain of LIS theory and practice. The purpose of leadership is to challenge the status quo as libraries undergo a transition in organizational culture, the services they offer, and workforce restructuring as they try to better fulfill the organizational and broader institutional mission. Management, on the other hand, prepares the infrastructure for that transition.

As early as 1950s, the term *managerial leadership* was coined, but its definition was imprecise. "No definition of the phrase 'managerial leadership' has gained general acceptance. In fact, it is often referred to but left undefined" or merely equated to particular leadership theories and styles. [1] The term recognizes (or at least should) that leadership is not exclusively a top-down process between the *boss* as a leader and subordinates.

This paper, which aligns with the program in managerial leadership in the information professions at Simmons College, [2] views managerial leadership as encompassing an examination of leaders, followers, the interaction between the two groups, and, in this context, leadership becomes a process whereby people influence others to develop, accept, and carry out a shared vision that guides future actions of the organization. As a result, that process is longitudinal and involves events (actions, impacts, and accomplishments). Because leadership is not always effective or positive, [3] it should not automatically be assumed that goals and events are always successfully met or that staff members are sufficiently motivated or inspired to challenge themselves and others. The purpose of this paper is to build on the international research agenda that Candy Schwartz and I presented in 2008 and that illustrates that LIS research needs to go beyond a preoccupation with understanding the style, personality, traits, and other characteristics of the boss and that person's influence on organizational dynamics and performance. [4]

1. LEADERSHIP

In addition to focusing on a shared vision, leadership is about giving people confidence to meet organizational expectations and to serve as change agents. It also encourages them to seek, be given, and benefit from team coaching and mentoring aimed at enhancing their knowledge, skills, abilities, effectiveness, and commitment to the transformation process. A library's staff might consist of both followers and leaders who are willing to collaborate with other institutional partners. As well, the director, if that person is truly a leader, might be more so within the organization than in representing the library to other stakeholders (or vice-versa).

With so many libraries organized into teams or small groups and involved in managing change; with new staff members expected to work together to plan, implement, administer, and evaluate services; and with libraries forging new partnerships at the institutional, local, and other levels, more librarians are becoming increasingly interested in knowing about and applying leadership theories, styles, traits, and roles. They are also trying to develop their leadership potential. Within this context, there is much interest in transformational leadership and emotional intelligence, which

> helps leaders move beyond basic "people skills" to understanding how one's own reactions and feelings impact how one is perceived by others. Leaders and managers need to understand their own emotions and recognize and understand the feelings of those around them. Leaders are more successful when they pay attention to their social interactions with others in the workplace and the impact they as leaders have on those around them. It is also important for leaders to understand the impact that others' emotions have on them. When leaders are aware of the emotional side of the workplace, they are better able to create a working environment that encourages excellence. [5]

As librarians gain an understanding of such theories, it is important to remember that, as Peter Northouse points out, leadership has "many different meanings;" this is evident when people "finish the sentence 'Leadership is ....'" [6] Their responses might ignore social influence, add new elements, or confuse leadership with someone holding a managerial position. They might also fail to recognize that there are also spiritual, legacy, moral, ethical, charismatic, and other types of leadership. Each of these areas actually produces separate leadership theories that have been long investigated but rarely connected to LIS.

2. CONTEXT

Even though this paper focuses on topical areas for future research and selected methodologies, it is important to remember that methodologies do not frame a research study. Research, which engages in problem-solving, is shaped by a reflective inquiry (problem statement, literature review and theoretical framework, logical structure, objectives, research questions, and hypotheses). These components, as well as the study procedures and data quality, comprise a framework in which each component should be bonded to the others through, what David R. Krathwohl calls, a "chain-of-reasoning." That "chain," he points out, "is only as strong as its weakest link" and "all links ... should be built to about the same strength." He further explains that, "as the work load is picked up by the first link [the problem statement] and passed to successive links, the work load—and therefore the nature of each link—is determined by the previous links."

Furthermore, "where several links together join those above and below them, there may be trade-offs to compensate for weaknesses. [7]

It is beyond the scope of this paper, however, to present and relate the entire chain-of-reasoning. Still, I would be remiss if I did not underscore the importance of the theoretical framework. Vincent A. Anfara, Jr. and Norma T. Mertz provide an excellent overview of theatrical frameworks and the impact of "good and useful" theory on the chain-of-reasoning. [8] In the case of managerial leadership, like other areas within LIS, there are numerous theories, some of which fit a given problem statement and set of objectives better than others. One such theory might be constructive-development theory, which relates directly to leadership and which offers a way to view the complex problems that organizations face from multiple perspectives. This theory describes "how adults develop more complex and comprehensive ways of making sense of themselves and their experience." [9] Another concept relates to trust, which is an essential component in motivating or inspiring others and which is more than a trait. [10]

3. RESEARCH DESIGNS

As a prelude to methodologies, research designs for leadership research might call for a longitudinal study and a comparison of several (comparable) organizations. Widely used research designs center on either a case study or the application of grounded theory. A case study is a means "for learning about a complex instance, based on a comprehensive understanding of that instance obtained by extensive description and analysis of that instance taken as a whole and in its context." [11] Grounded theory, on the other hand, "is a method for discovering theories, concepts, hypotheses, and propositions directly from data, rather than from a priori assumptions, other research, or existing theoretical frameworks." [12] Theory emerges from, and is grounded in, the data themselves.

DATA-GATHERING TECHNIQUES

This section focuses on some of the most prevalent methodologies used in leadership research, especially within LIS. As such, it builds from Karin Klenke's work on leadership research. [13] It is increasingly common for researchers to apply qualitative methods. The accompanying table offers examples of some methodologies applicable to the study of leadership in LIS that will not be discussed in the body of this paper. The sources in that table came from an extensive review of the vast literature on leadership produced outside LIS.

The largest number of research studies related to leadership involves the distribution of a self-report survey or questionnaire. Such surveys are often in paper-and-pencil format, although more recently Web-based surveys have appeared with increasing frequency. The survey might involve the use of a pre-developed, behavior-based leadership assessment tool (e.g., the Mayer-Salovey-Caruso Emotional Intelligence Test (MSCEIT), which is an ability-based test; see http://www.eiconsortium.org/measures/msceit.html) that is distributed to those heading the organization or to subordinates who are asked to evaluate the director or boss as a leader or their immediate supervisor. As an alternative, surveys might probe respondent preference for a particular leadership theory or style and ask them to rate themselves or identify the most important attributes for individuals in their position.

Complementary to a questionnaire that is mailed (e-mail or other) or otherwise distributed, investigators might use personal or focus groups interviews. Responses to open-ended questions might be subjected to content analysis, which "is a set of procedures for transforming nonstructured information into a format that allows analysis." [14] On occasion, biographies of people identified as leaders have been developed and their content subjected to analysis for discussions of leadership. Available historical records, however, might focus more on their accomplishments than the story behind those accomplishments: how did the individual co-opt and navigate different stakeholders and the staff to bring about that change? If a shared vision emerged, how was it developed?

Some other means of data collection include an analysis of citation patterns of a body of works on leadership and a characterization of the most cited works (e.g., names of journals and publishers) and authors, as well as the age of the cited material. Additional insights might be gained from a consideration of the journal's impact factor and the number of copies of a work that libraries hold (as reflected in *WorldCat*).

Assuming the availability of a body of independent studies focused on the same aspect of leadership and that describes the research design, the methodologies and data-collection instruments used, information about the population and sample, and so on, meta-analysis might be appropriate. Such analysis refers to a set of statistical procedures used to summarize and integrate those studies. [15] It reveals sources of bias and is helpful for posing research questions for future study. Among other things, it cannot exceed the limits of what the researchers report.

Another method, known as the Delphi study or technique, is a procedure relies on the use of sequential questionnaires in which experts share their perspectives on issues. [16] The Delphi technique is not necessarily designed to generate consensus, but it does involve a systematic refinement of prior responses. It has been applied to seeing which leadership attributes are most critical for future managerial leaders.

Concept Mapping

Concept mapping is both a process for representing data in the form of pictures or maps and a structured methodology for organizing the ideas of a group or organization. The goal is to bring together groups of multiple "stakeholders … and help them rapidly form a common framework that can be used for planning, evaluation, or both." [17]

The maps represent the groups' thinking about a topic, show how their ideas are related to each other, and, in general, indicate "which ideas are more relevant, important, or appropriate." [18]

Interviews and other techniques might produce datasets that might be examined by the use of concept maps. These maps provide a graphic illustration of patterns among the findings. Jan Schilling, for instance, takes interview data about negative leadership and produced maps that show the antecedents of such leadership, negative leadership behaviors, and the consequences of negative leadership. [19]

Simulation and Scenarios

A simulation study, as G. Yukl explains, involves a realistic task that continues for several periods of time and asks participants (e.g., team members) to assume the role of top executives in an organization and to engage in team and organizational learning. Simulation "is also relevant for understanding how collective learning occurs among people whose decisions and actions affect organizational processes and performance." [20]

Instead of doing a simulation exercise, researchers might develop scenarios that make projections for the next fifteen years; forecaster Joseph P. Martino indicates that the accuracy in predicting what will likely occur declines dramatically with a longer time frame. [21] According to Dana Mietzner and Guido Reger,

> scenarios, as a prime technique of future studies, have long been used by government planners, corporate managers and military analysts as powerful tools to aid in decision making in the face of uncertainty. The idea behind them is to establish thinking about possible futures which can minimi[z]e surprises and broaden the span of managers' thinking about different possibilities. [22]

They recommend that the number of scenarios not exceed four and that any scenario should meet criteria such as *plausibility* (each is capable of happening), *differentiation* (each differs from the others and together they offer multiple futures), *decision-making utility* (each offers insights into the future that help in planning and decision-making), and *challenging* (each challenges conventional wisdom about the future). [23]

4. RESEARCH AGENDA

The accompanying figure, which updates the depiction that Schwartz and I created, centers on three broad areas that relate to planning:

1. Accomplishments (translating vision into effective organizational performance);
2. People (creating an organizational climate that values staff and inspires them); and
3. Transformation abilities (focusing on the change process that brings people together to accomplish the organization's mission and goals—preparing the organization of the future).

These areas match those that guide the doctoral program in managerial leadership in the information professions (Simmons), which the Institute of Museum and Library Services has funded since 2005 with two multi-year grants. Those areas, originally modeled by the National Center for Healthcare Leadership, cover twenty-five distinct leadership competencies.

Under each of the broad areas, numerous topic areas emerge. At the same time, relationships among the areas might be probed. As directors or other members of the senior management team retire or depart, their replacement might be someone who serves on an interim basis. Are such people leaders or care-takers? The answer might take into account the library but also engagement beyond the library, transformation abilities, mentoring, and talent management. Focusing solely on talent management, many businesses engage in succession management or planning, but do libraries? Succession planning and management are not synonymous with mentoring. In some countries, if there is leadership, it might be characterized as autocratic. Such leadership merits analysis. Finally, various aspects of the figure might be probed in the present recession (2008-2009) as libraries make significant decisions about collections and staff that will likely have a long-term impact.

Turning to other topics, James G. Neal discusses "feral library professionals," which refers to the hiring of more people into traditional and non-traditional library positions who do not have the credentialed degree from an accredited library school program." [24] Comparative case studies might analyze the emergence of leadership in organizations that employ both feral and non-feral professionals and that include staff who represent different generations. How cohesive are staff within and across departments? Do they share a common vision—do they need to share one?

Studies might probe LIS educational programs and see whether (or how) they incorporate leadership as a student learning outcome, one that reflects what students have learned throughout their program of study and demonstrates what they can apply upon graduation. Some other possible topics include the role of power in effective leadership, the major trends in making leadership effective, the communication networks of leaders, transformational leadership and its relationship, for instance, to

- Emotional intelligence, which deals with one's ability to manage emotions and relationships and to use this ability to advance the organization's mission and goals. Emotional intelligence presumably requires *sense-giving* or shaping how people understand themselves, their work, and others engaged in that work.
- Resonant leadership, which focuses on self-awareness and self-renewal, and which enables individuals to recognize and cope with work stress.
- Distributed or shared leadership, which views leadership as more than a top-down approach. Leadership moves up the organization as well and is distributed among a number of people working in teams and groups.
- Servant leadership, which recognizes that leadership is not confined to those in formal managerial positions and who lead as a way to extend service to others. The servant leader focuses on the needs and the development of followers.

Recognizing that libraries serve multicultural communities, employ a diverse staff, and deal with myriad stakeholders, it is critical to assess different leadership theories, recognizing the strengths and weaknesses of each. Many of the prevailing theorists have not considered how multiculturalism influences what they propose. Perhaps the best illustration of this comes from Linda Sue Warner and Keith Grint, who adopt a historical perspective and compare American Indian and western approaches and perspectives on leadership. There are differences between the practice of leadership in a tribal setting (including tribal colleges) and in other organizational settings. [25]

5. EXAMPLE

Although library directors cannot be equated with the president of the United States and other heads of government, political commentators have identified areas in which the leadership of those aspiring to be president might be probed. Prompted by the lack of penetrating questions raised in presidential debate and the quality of the responses, David Gergen and Andy Zelleke identify a series of important questions that deal with leadership and that require answers of more than a number or brief response. [26] Their categories and questions have been reorganized and combined with the categories that Jack and Suzy Welch would like considered. [27]

The revamped questionnaire was pre-tested with one university library director and one library consultant. Based on their comments the questionnaire was revised (see Appendix). As of this time, the author of this paper is conducting a study to fine-tune the instrument and to gauge the responses of some library leaders. Instead of presenting preliminary data, this section probes relevant methodologies that might be used to address the open-ended questions and determine the relative rating of the categories.

The methodology section of a hypothetical study might be based on a survey that is most likely administered in the form of an interview, either in-person or by telephone. Directors might be unwilling to devote the time necessary to complete a paper-and-pencil survey or be unwilling to write detailed responses to each question (e-mail or Web-based survey). It might be difficult to find a time when five to ten directors could meet and participate in a focus group interview. For additional data collection, the investigator might ask for historical documentation or visit the institutional repositories of selected institutions to gather data for event history analysis, assuming such information has been gathered and is publicly available.

Interview results might be analyzed in terms of grounded theory and content analysis. The rating of the categories on a se4ven-point scale might be visualized in terms of concept mapping, and such mapping might also apply to the responses to the various questions within a category, especially if responses can be gathered from the same scale.

A follow-up study might concentrate on selected categories and probe responses more deeply. For instance, under "Coalition Building/Advocacy," participants might meet and be asked for an example of when they became a catalyst who brought groups with polarized opinions together so that all voices were at the table. The examples generated might be cast in terms of a concept map, or the investigator could make the topics recurring most frequently and pursue them more with the Delphi technique.

A different study might recast question responses to the initial study or one focusing on selected categories as scenarios (for projecting what study participants believe likely for the next fifteen years) or as simulation exercises. It is also possible to take selected responses from the first study and select particular sites for in-depth case study analysis.

In summary, the instrument portrayed in the appendix does not promote or study any particular leadership theory or style. That instrument, however, is framed in such a way that the research focuses on leadership as events and assorted methodologies are applicable. Leadership, after all, "is a process, a series of activities and exchanges engaged in over time and under varied circumstances." [28] As such, accomplishments might be viewed as events in that leadership is an ongoing, never-ending process.

6. CONCLUSION

To gain a more complete understanding of the phenomena under investigation, it is common for studies on leadership, like other topical areas, to incorporate more than one method of data collection. Mixed methods, which are most prevalent with case studies, integrate quantitative and qualitative methods into one study and therefore strengthen the chain-of-reasoning presented in study findings. [29] While it is important to expand the methodological tool-chest that researchers within LIS use, it is also important to shift from studying leaders to investigating leadership events. Many aspects of leadership presented in the figure have not been addressed, and a need emerges for a fuller body of evidence-based research relevant to change management within libraries and similar complex organizations on a global basis. It is also important that those within LIS contribute to the broader literature on leadership and that their works be recognized by those in other disciplines.

NOTES

1. See Peter Hernon, "Leadership in Academic Libraries Is No Fad," in *Making a Difference: Leadership and Academic Libraries*, edited by Peter Hernon and Nancy Rossiter (Westport, CT: Libraries Unlimited, 2007), p. 253.
2. Simmons College, Graduate School of Library and Information Science, "Managerial Leadership in the Information Professions" (Boston, MA). See http://www.simmons.edu/gslis/academics/programs/doctoral/phdmlip/
3. There is an emerging literature on ineffective, bad, negative, and destructive leadership. See, for instance, Barbara Kellerman, *Bad Leadership: What Is It, How Does It Happen, and Why It Matters* (Boston: Harvard Business School Press, 2004); "Special Issue on Destructive Leadership," *The Leadership Quarterly* 18, no. 3 (2007): 171-280; Jan Schilling, "From Ineffectiveness to Destruction: A Qualitative Study on the Meaning of Negative Leadership," *Leadership* 5, no. 1 (2009): 102-128. Also relevant is Juan M. Madera and D. Brent Smith, "The Effects of Leader Negative Emotions on Evaluations of Leadership in a Crisis Situation: The Role of Anger and Sadness," *The Leadership Quarterly* 20, no. 2 (April 2009): 103-114.
4. Peter Hernon and Candy Schwartz, "Leadership: Developing a Research Agenda for Academic Libraries," *Library & Information Science Research*

30, no. 4 (December 2008): 243-249.

5. Peter Hernon, Joan Giesecke, and Camila A. Alire, *Academic Librarians as Emotionally Intelligent Leaders* (Westport, CT: Libraries Unlimited, 2008), pp. 8-9.

6. Peter G. Northouse, *Leadership: Theory and Practice*, 4th ed. (Thousand Oaks, CA: Sage Publications, 2007), p. 2.

7. David R. Krathwohl, *Social and Behavioral Science Research: A New Framework for Conceptualizing, Implementing, and Evaluating Research Studies* (San Francisco: Jossey-Bass, 1985), p. 52. For an extended discussion of problem statements, see Peter Hernon, *Statistics: A Component of the Research Process* (Norwood, NJ: Ablex, 1994), pp. 8-13; Peter Hernon and Candy Schwartz, "What Is a Problem Statement?," *Library & Information Science Research*, 29 (2007): 307-309; Peter Hernon and Cheryl Metoyer-Duran, "Problem Statements: An Exploratory Study of Their Function, Significance, and Form," *Library & Information Science Research* 15, no. 1 (Winter 1993): 71-92; Cheryl Metoyer-Duran and Peter Hernon, "Problem Statements in Research Proposals and Published Research: A Case Study of Researchers' Viewpoints," *Library & Information Science Research* 16, no. 2 (1994): 105-118.

8. Vincent A. Anfara, Jr., and Norman T. Mertz, *Theoretical Frameworks in Qualitative Research* (Thousand Oaks, CA: Sage Publications, 2006), p. xvii.

9. Cynthia D. McCauley, Wilfred H. Drath, Charles J. Palus, Patricia M. G. O'Connor, and Becca A. Baker, "The Use of Constructive-development Theory to Advance the Understanding of Leadership," *The Leadership Quarterly* 17, no. 6 (2006): 634.

10. C. Shawn Burke, Dana E. Sims. Elizabeth H. Lazzara, and Eduardo Salas, "Trust in Leadership: A Multi-level Review and Integration," *The Leadership Quarterly* 18, no. 6 (2007): 606-632.

11. U.S. General Accounting Office [now the Government Accountability Office], Program Evaluation and Methodology Division, *Case Study Evaluations*, Transfer Paper 10.1.9 (Washington, DC: General Accounting Office, 1990), p. 14.

12. Steven Taylor and Robert Bogdan, *Introduction to Qualitative Research Methods*, 2nd ed. (New York: Wiley and Sons, 1984), p. 126. See also Ken W. Perry, "Grounded Theory and Social Process: A New Direction for Leadership Research," *The Leadership Quarterly* 9, no. 1 (1998): 85-105.

13. Karin Klenke, *Qualitative Research in the Study of Leadership* (Bingley, United Kingdom: Emerald Group Publishing Ltd., 2008).

14. U.S. General Accounting Office [now the Government Accountability Office], *Content Analysis: A Methodology for Structuring and Analyzing Written Material*, Transfer Paper 10.1.3 (Washington, DC: General Accounting Office, 1989), p. 1. See also Tamara L. Friedrich, Christina L. Byrne, and Michael D. Mumford, "Methodological and Theoretical Considerations in Survey Research," *The Leadership Quarterly* 20, no. 2 (April 2009): 57-60.

15. See Eric Trahan, "Applying Meta-Analysis to Library and Information Science Research," *The Library Quarterly* 63, no. 1 (1993): 73-91. See also C. Shawn Burke, Kevin C. Stagl, Cameron Klein, Gerald F. Goodwin, Eduardo Salas, and Stanley M. Halpin, "What Types of Leadership Behaviors Are Functional in Teams? A Meta-analysis," *The Leadership Quarterly* 17, no. 3 (2006): 288-307.

16. Robert M. Hayes, *Use of the Delphi Technique in Policy Formulation: A Case Study of the Public Sector/Private Sector Task Force* (Los Angeles: University of California, Graduate School of Library and Information Science, 1982), p. 1. See also John B. Harer, *Performance Measures of Quality for Academic Libraries Implementing Continuous Quality Improvement Programs: A Delphi Study* (Ph. D. diss., Texas A&M University, 2001). Available from *Dissertations & Theses: Full Text* (AAT 3011718).
17. Mary Kane and William M. K. Trochim, *Concept Mapping for Planning and Evaluation* (Thousand Oaks, CA: Sage Publications, 2007), p. 1.
18. Ibid., p. 7.
19. Schilling, "From Ineffectiveness to Destruction."
20. G. Yukl, "Leading Organizational Learning: Reflections on Theory and Research," *The Leadership Quarterly* 20, no. 1 (2009): 53.
21. Joseph P. Martino, "The Precision of Delphi Estimates," *Technological Forecasting* 1, no. 3 (1970): 293-299.
22. Dana Mietzner and Guido Reger, "Advantages and Disadvantages of Scenario Approaches for Strategic Foresight," *International Journal of Technology Intelligence and Planning* 1, no., 2 (2005), p. 233. Available at http://www.lampsacus.com/documents/StragegicForesight.pdf (accessed October 16, 2008). They also note the weaknesses associated with the development of scenarios.
23. For a relevant example see Peter Hernon and Laura Saunders, "The Federal Depository Library Program in 2023: One Perspective on the Transition to the Future," *College & Research Libraries* 70, no. 3 (May 2009), forthcoming.
24. James G. Neal, "Raised by Wolves: The New Generation of Feral Professionals in the Academic Library," *Library Journal* (February 15, 2006). Available at http://www.libraryjournal.com/article/CA6304405.html (accessed February 24, 2009).
25. Linda Sue Warner and Keith Grint, "American Indian Ways of Leading and Knowing," *Leadership* 2, no. 4 (May 2006): 225-244.
26. David Gergen and Andy Zelleke, "A Question of Presidential Leadership," *Boston Globe* (June 12, 2008): A13. I collapsed 15 categories into 13 and relabeled one category.
27. Jack and Suzy Welch, "Chief Executive Officer-in-Chief: The President Needs the Same Skills as a Top-notch CEO—Only Sharper," *Business Week* issue 4069 (February 4, 2008): 88.
28. Samuel T. Hunter, Katrina E. Bedell-Avers, Michael D. Mumford, "The Typical Leadership Study: Assumptions, Implications and Potential Remedies," *The Leadership Quarterly* 18, 5 (2007): 440.
29. See Raya Fidel, "Are We There Yet? Mixed Methods Research in Library and Information Science," *Library & Information Science Research* 30 (2008): 265-272.

Leadership and Service Provision in Public Libraries

Niels Ole Pors

Professor in Library and Information Management, Royal School of Library and Information Science, Denmark

Abstract: The intention of this keynote is to present some more or less provocative ideas concerning the development of public libraries.
In USA and Western Europe, we do witness the same types of developments in public libraries and we see very similar themes of discourses independent of the national and local culture in which these libraries operate. Some of the themes concern the management structure and organisation but more important is probably the current think about service delivery in a broad sense. Service delivery concerns the activities. It is areas like collection and collection management, the allocation of resources to the different part of the collection, the interplay and relationship between national internet-based delivery and the local service. Another important theme is the effort concerning the public library and its integration into the community taking up different forms of citizen services, cooperation and partnership with the local community, but also a focus on playing a new and more active role in the cultural scene by for example emphasising learning activities, lifelong learning, internet courses and different forms for events and exhibitions. The ambition is to become a local meeting place, a third room; a common intended to generate social capital.
This discourse and many of the activities resulting from it like 23 thinks, the libraries in the second world and experiments with various forms of social technology appear to how a great appeal in the library profession.
However, both library statistics and numerous studies of users and their preferences give a more differentiated picture. In most countries, the public libraries face economic hardship. They witness stagnating or decreasing numbers of visitors and the issues of traditional materials also tend to decrease. The public appear to value especially the services and products that suffer due to economic pressures and the internal priority setting in libraries. Overall, it appears – at least at the surface – that users do have a rather traditional view of the public library and their stated preferences also seems to be very traditional as they are oriented towards books and information and to a lesser degree towards new services and delivery forms.
It is of course of paramount interest to investigate possible discrepancies between the discourse and the practices in the professions and the users' preferences, priorities and level of satisfaction.
There is probably no right solution to the problem, but it is of both a practical and theoretical significance to investigate which factors influence the development of the discourse and the activities in the professions and in the public libraries and is also important to be able to measure users perception of the significance and importance of the service delivery and to which degree this is connected with measures of satisfaction.

The keynote discusses users' perception of the significance of the various services and presents a model for how it is possible to measure the significance of the single service. This measure is related to measures of satisfaction and what influence that factor.
The keynote further discusses the factors behind the profession's discourse and practices. The concept of an organisational recipe is introduced in relation to organisational culture as two factors that have influence on the way libraries tend to adopt different forms of innovations. Of course, leadership plays an important role and the keynote also introduces measures of the personality traits of library directors and discusses this in relation to the innovation and development process but also in relation to the "sense" or construction the profession is creating of the user.
Finally, the keynote discuss possible consequences and outcomes of the fragile relationship between users and a public service as public libraries.

1. Introduction

In USA and Western Europe, we do witness the same types of developments in public libraries and we see very similar themes of discourses independent of the national and local culture in which these libraries operate. Some of the themes concern the management structure and organisation bur more important is probably the current think about service delivery in a broad sense. Service delivery concerns the activities. It is areas like collection and collection management, the allocation of resources to the different part of the collection, the interplay and relationship between national internet-based delivery and the local service. Another important theme is the effort concerning the public library and its integration into the community taking up different forms of citizen services, cooperation and partnership with the local community, but also a focus on playing a new and more active role in the cultural scene by for example emphasising learning activities, lifelong learning, internet courses and different forms for events and exhibitions. The ambition is to become a local meeting place, a third room; a common intended to generate social capital.

This discourse and many of the activities resulting from it like 23 thinks, the libraries in the second world and experiments with various forms of social technology appear to have great appeal in the library profession.

However, both library statistics and numerous studies of users and their preferences give a more differentiated picture. In most countries, the public libraries face economic hardship. They witness stagnating or decreasing numbers of visitors and the issues of traditional materials also tend to decrease. The public appear to value especially the services and products that suffer due to economic pressures and the internal priority setting in libraries. Overall, it appears – at least at the surface – that users do have a rather traditional view of the public library and their stated preferences also seems to be very traditional as they are oriented towards books and information and to a lesser degree towards new services and delivery forms.

It is of course of paramount interest to investigate possible discrepancies between the discourse and the practices in the professions and the users' preferences, priorities and level of satisfaction.

There is probably no right solution to the problem, but it is of both a practical and theoretical significance to investigate which factors influence the development of the discourse and the activities in the professions and in the public libraries and is also important to be able to measure users perception of the significance and importance of the service delivery and to which degree this is connected with measures of satisfaction.

The paper further discusses the factors behind the profession's discourse and practices. The concept of an organisational recipe is introduced in relation to organisational culture as two factors that have influence on the way libraries tend to adopt different forms of innovations. Of course, leadership plays an important role and the keynote also introduces measures of the personality traits of library directors and discusses this in relation to the innovation and development process but also in relation to the "sense" or construction the profession is creating of the user.

This paper departs from 2 different theoretical perspectives of pertinent interest for management of institutions. One of the perspectives is concerned with the question about how management information and management recipes are adopted and interpreted in organisations like libraries. The other perspective concerns the role of the directors' personality in this context especially how they acquire management information and how they value and use management information in relation to organisational change processes.

This paper is built on several studies into leadership in libraries in Denmark and United Kingdom (Pors et al., 2004; Pors, 2006). The paper also builds on several user studies (Pors, 2008; 2008a). A more detailed analysis of the data collection and the problems involved can be found in the references.

2. Leadership and personality

During the last couple of years, the interest in leadership and management topics has increased very much. This is also the case in library and information science (Hernon, Powell & Young, 2001; 2002; 2007). It is due to the very fundamental changes that takes place overall in the public sector. Many of these changes are connected to requirements concerning accountability, user orientation, outsourcing, quality, information technology and staff-related issues. It is a widespread notion that the requirements in relation to leadership and management have become much more complex.

The complexity is connected to environmental turbulence, change processes and to the amount of vast information that leaders need to deal with. Information in the form of management tools or recipes is one way to confront the organisational problems arising from the changes.

Leadership is an important element in the configuration of organisational culture and both leadership styles and the leaders approach to innovation, change, and competency development are of importance in relation to the directions of the organisation. Leaders are both part of an organisational culture but they also have the possibility to be change agents in relation to the culture. The relationship between leadership priorities and organisational culture are important. One can argue an interesting relationship between the directors' personality and preferences and the direction and change processes in libraries and this is exactly the focus for this paper (Block, 2003; Brown & Dodd, 1998; Kaarst-Brown et al., 2004; Lok & Crawford, 1999, Schein, 1992).

The Revised NEO Personality Inventory (NEO PI-R) is one of the most widespread personality tests based on the Five-Factor model (Costa & McCrae, 1992; 1997; Skovdahl & Mortensen, 2003) and it was employed in this investigation. Besides allowing for both a general and detailed description of personality, the test is also build up in such a way that it takes into consideration the characteristics of the specific test-person in focus. Specific norms for groups of people and profiles have been developed from research to help validate the test-result.

The NEO-PI-R measures five broad personality factors. Each of these is a summary and an average of six facets. Each of the five factors and their associated 6 facets is measured through 48 statements, implying that all 30 facets are measured through 240 statements. The result of the 240 statements is distributed into low and high scores on the 5 factors and the 30 facets, hence demonstrating a personality profile.

We will now turn to a short profiling of the 8 library directors. The profiles of the directors as a whole are very congruent with modern expectations of leaders and managers. They tend to possess emotional stability. They are extroverted and open to change. They all score high on the facet assertiveness. They score high on conscientiousness. Overall, the profiles of the library directors appear to be very far away from the traditional stereotypes of librarians as shy, introverted, a bit old-fashioned, nervous and timid.

The factor named openness is often considered as an important factor in relation to chance processes and it is clear that all directors except one scores high on this factor. One director is distinct from the others, scoring rather low. It is director B that scores low on 3 of the 6 facets. What is more interesting is probably that all directors score high on some of the more important facets related to get things done. All score from middle to very high on actions, ideas and values indicating openness to new ideas.

Common for all the directors have been the fact that they have been involved in change processes. These change processes have focused on both the provision of services and on organisational development implementing more flexible and democratic structures. They have all succeeded to change the libraries both internally and in relation to the users. One of the reasons that change processes have been successful overall can possibly be attributed to the assertiveness of the directors, their overall openness to experience and change and their general high degree of conscientiousness. The organisational culture is a very important mediating factor both in relation to how information in the form of recipes are adopted and translated both also in relation to the actual possibilities the director possess for implementing change. But the style of change management varies. This can be partly explained by situational factors like the local political climate, restrictions due to the building and economy, the organisational culture and other important factors.

The relevant facets or traits that relates to interpretation and adoption of new standards are some of the traits that relate to the factors named openness and conscientiousness. The facets under openness can possibly give an indication of how willing the director is to seek and implement new recipes in the organisation and the facets related to conscientiousness can indicate how through the process of implementation is conducted. These facets will also relate to the directors' sense of the usefulness of own participating in leadership courses and development. We emphasise that it is broad hypotheses.

Another more general aspect is how the directors value innovations or changes. A comparison of D with H indicates the usefulness of analysing behaviour using all the facets and not only the factors. It is evident that the profile of H indicates a person oriented towards actions and change. H also possesses a high degree of impulsiveness and a middle orientation towards ideas. H is more of a doer than a thinker and this is also the way H comes forward in the interview and in interviews with the staff. Things must happen and failures – both own and staff failures – are accepted as inevitable. Some of the change processes are conducted nearly on the spot and many traditional activities are set in motion. In some ways, the change processes runs in a very goal directed manner but there is a high degree of acceptance of a chaotic nature of some of these processes that involves staff very much because the director delegates much based on both trust and on a disposition to take up new challenges. The change processes that have taken place in D's library are conducted in a very different way. They are just as goal directed and strategic but they are much slower and much more deliberated and it is evident that the D places a very high value on bringing the staff along. The disposition for activity seeking is much less here than in relation to H. It results in a "flavour" of the library as a bit more old-fashioned and a bit slower or a bit more cautious in change processes.

The implicit formulated hypotheses about the relationship between personality traits and profiles indicated that the director's openness to especially intellectual experiences or practical innovations and changes influenced the process of implementation of both structures and processes of competences. It also influenced the way the recipes and standards were conceptualised in the organisation. The integration of the recipes was influenced by the perseverance of the director with cultural factors as a mediating factor.

3. Discourses and organisational recipes

These figures contrast to a certain degree to the dominant discourses in the public library profession. The dominant discourses are concerned with modern topics and issues like library as a place and libraries as generators of social capital and societal trust on a more general level. In relation to services the emphasis in the discourses are on issues like lifelong learning, information literacies and integration of the physical library into the digital services. The discourse also contains strong elements of the need for permanent change for example in relation to continuing professional development. There is also much debate on phenomena like 23 things, facebook and other digital services.

A discourse is characterised by dominant themes but is also delimited by themes that do not occur and these absent themes signifies the themes in the discourse. In the 80'ies and 90'ies, the library profession had focus on collections and collection management and especially the concept of immediate availability was a central topic. Today, these themes of discussion are missing from the professional debate.

There existed also a rather interesting debate or discourse concerning the proper relationship between supply and demand in relation to the collection. It is interesting that these topics seldom are covered in the present discussion because the different digital possibilities emphasise new turns of these central concepts. Just to give a few hopefully illuminating examples one can ask questions about the links on libraries' websites and inquire if a link is part of the collection or not. The answer to that question is interesting because if the answer is yes it follows that the libraries have the responsibility for dead links and for the misinformation contained in some of the links. Another interesting question is the transformation of topical needs into specific needs due to the way people search the digital databases. Librarians are not discussing the increase in the selling of books and the reasons behind this interesting fact. Is it because of an increasing affluence in society or is it because of a want for instant gratification?

Many of the elements in a given dominant discourse relates to organisational recipes or standards (Røvik, 1998). A recipe or a standard that becomes a trend has the following characteristics: It often originates in an academic setting but very often it is created in cooperation with the professional world – be it libraries or business. It is blueprinted by leading members of the academic and professional communities and it is taken up also by the consultancy industry. Prestigious firm and companies use it. The recipe incorporates the promise to solve serious problems in the companies and in the institutions they are interesting to work with. They are marketed and they are frameworks for actions but most of all they are interpretable meaning that institutions can adopt them, change them according to the national and organisational culture. They are very often connected to stories of success and the story behind the recipe often takes the form of a drama. Successful recipes tend to hit a trend in the time and use this as a kind of vehicle for its travel across boundaries and cultures. Some recipes like the balanced scorecard have a rather long life. Other – not as successful like for example business process reengineering – have a shorter lifespan. It does not mean that they are not used. It could mean that they are incorporated in the organisational operations but people have stopped talking about it. Finally, all recipes have dimensions of both content and symbolic aspects. It is of course extremely interesting which recipes become dominating themes in the discourse of a profession. It is also of huge interest which recipes a given profession does not include in its arsenal of themes in the discourse.

There is no doubt that the profession as a whole has a very determined focus on change and the need for change. The catch phrase that the libraries stand on a burning platform has been brought forward several times in the discourse and this catchphrase has been used as a kind of rationale for changes. This is of course the consequence of a special or peculiar interpretation of the environment. However, there is no doubt that the ideology of change and the need for change is deeply integrated in the professional identity of public librarians and leaders in the public libraries. It is an interesting question if the interpretation of the environment is in accordance with other indicators of changes in the environment.

4. Users and preferences

One aspect of organisational effectiveness is a system's ability to cope with users and non-users expectations and needs enabling the system to deliver services appropriate to satisfy needs and expectations. Organisational effectiveness has been one of the ultimate goals and objectives for the performance measurements endeavours for many years. Organisational effectiveness is related to processes, products or services and the customer or the user and it is normally seen as an important element in the quality of a service.

The importance or significance for the users of the single services is of course a very important element for the libraries' planning process and assessment of how to proceed. Libqual is a measurement instrument that is often used for this kind of investigation as it specifies the minimal level of service people would like. However, Libqual has not been employed in these surveys. We have simply asked people to attach the significance or importance for themselves on different services. The end result is a kind of ranking that probably is rather robust. The importance or significance is calculated on a scale from 0 to 100 and it forms the basis of the ranking. The ranking of the importance or the perception of the significance of the public libraries' services follows:

Table 1: The users' perception of the significance of different services in two surveys

	High school	rank	Aarhus	rank
A kind and polite service	72	1	90	2
Distance to the library	67	2	91	1
Ambience	64	3	84	3
Collection of non-fiction	62	4	66	5
Quite and peaceful place in the library	59	5	65	6
Collection of fiction	55	6	78	4
Places for relaxation	43	7	51	8
Collection of music	41	8	46	10
Wireless network	40	9	21	14
Collection of film	37	10	47	9
Group work facilities	35	11	15	15
Computers	34	12	28	12
The Library's homepage	34	13	63	7
Study places	33	14	21	14
Exhibitions, lessons	28	15	45	11
N	978		243	

Translated into normal text, one can say that the high school students and the "traditional public library users" prefer a kind and polite service in nice quite rooms in library with ambience not too far away and filled with books.

There are differences between the preferences and significance attached to services among the two groups but rank correlation analysis shows a Spearmans Rho of 0,81 which indicate a very high degree of similarity in ranking the services.

The ranking between the two groups are more or less similar, but there appears to be differences in the importance attached to the service. One explanation for this discrepancy is simple and it is, that the group of high schools students consists of students relying heavily on public libraries and groups or segments that rarely, seldom or never use the public library. This composition of the total group tends to decrease the average figures. In comparison, the respondents from the Aarhus group were all public library users.

In the 2006 investigation in Furesoe (Pors, 2008a), we also asked questions about preferences and significance, but we employed a measurement tool based on forced pair-wise ranking. It is impossible to make a direct comparison, but one can look at the trends and compare these with caution.

The most striking feature of the answers to this question is the similarity in preferences. The respondents were asked on a forced scale where they had to prioritise alternatives. Overall, the users preferred present openings hours more than longer opening hours with less staff service. The preferred more books in favour of longer opening hours or music. The preferred more film than more music. They preferred a broader range of literature more than additional copies of the popular books. We did not find any differences in pair-wise preferences in relation fiction versus non – fiction, computers versus more reading places or more reading places versus more places for relaxation or social interaction.

The conclusion is that users – even the young age group – want more documents. It is a very clear first priority. We do see that this priority and preference increase with age, but it is still a very striking result that young people that rely heavily on and use the library's collection of film and music much prioritise books and documents more if they had to choose. The preferences and the prioritising are probably an expression of the perception of what a public library is – and ought to be. It is obvious that the structure of preferences in relation to public libraries is rather traditional.

The nationwide study of high school students also showed some interesting features of the significance they attached to the services in relation to different demographic factors.

Table 2: The students' perceptions of the importance of services and facilities in relation to demographics. Note: Empty cells imply no significant difference in relation to demographics.

	Type High school			Gender		Study year		
	G	B	T	Female	Male	1	2	3
A kind and polite service	77	69	63	76	66			
Distance to the library	74	61	61	72	61			
Ambience	68	61	59	67	60			
Collection of non-fiction	70	54	52	66	56	56	61	68
Quite and peaceful places in the library	63	55	51					
Collection of fiction	61	49	49	63	44			
Places for relaxation						49	44	36
Collection of music	45	36	38					
Wireless network						45	40	35
Collection of film								

Group work facilities						41	35	28
Computers				32	37			
The Library's homepage	37	28	33			28	36	37
Study places						38	30	29
Exhibitions, lessons								

First of all, there appears to be differences in perceptions of significance and importance dependent on the type of high school. There are 3 types of high schools in the country. The general high school is the classic one. In the table it is called G. There is also a high school oriented towards business topics called B and at last a technical high school called T. The general picture is that the high school students from the general school place more significance on most of the library services than students from the other two hig schools do. We also notice marked differences between male and female high school students. Female high school students tend to value the collection of fiction an non fiction much more than the male students. It is also interesting to note that the students through their study process tend to place less significance to the library as a place to be and work in. However, overall the ranking of the single services is not hugely affected by this segmentation, but the segmentation indicates that the different groups have very different preferences and strength of preferences attached to the single services.

5. Conclusion

It is obvious that the library is a brand associated with books and information. At the same time we can register at least some changes in user behaviour especially related to gender and age. This change is partly due to the new service profile of the library.

In terms of organisational effectiveness it is from a stakeholder perspective and from a user perspective a problem that the priorities of the libraries with regard to document types appear to be out of tune with the perceptions of the users. The public library system as a whole has during the last decade minimised the collection of books quite a lot. The factors behind this situation are an increase in weeding and of course a reallocation of the budget to cover newer media like music, film and PC – games. Another important factor is the system's perceived need for more space to computer areas, meeting rooms and study places.

The discourse of the library profession emphasising new media, the library ad a vehicle in life long learning processes, the library as a thirds place and the like is not really reflected in either the actual use or in the perceptions. The main problem appears to be twofold.

The librarians are constructing user needs that really have not manifested themselves. They are to a certain degree constructing the user. And the users construct or brand a library with perceptions firmly rooted in the past. This discrepancy needs to be remedied if the trust that is so important for public institutions will continue to be at a high level.

There is no doubt that the combination of very change oriented library directors and the increasing amount of organisational recipes interact and speed up the change processes changing the libraries faster than the mental image of them in the users mind.

References

Block, L. (2003) The leadership – culture connection. An exploratory investigation. *Leadership & Organizational development Journal* 24 (6) s. 318-334

Brown, F.W. & Dodd, N.G. (1998) Utilizing organizational culture gap analysis to determine human resource development needs. *Leadership and Organization Development Journal* 19 (7) s 374-385

Cameron, K.S. & Quinn, R.E. (1999) *Diagnosing and changing organizational culture: Based on the competing values framework.* Reading. Addison-Wesley

Costa, P.T & Mccrae, R.R. (1992). *NEO PI-R. Professional manual.* Odessa: Psychological Assessment Resources, Inc.

Costa, P.T & Mccrae, R.R. (1997). Stability and change in personality assessment: the revised NEO Personality Inventory in the year 2000. *Journal of Personality assessment,* 68(1): 86-94.

Hernon, P., Powell, R. and Young, A. (2001) University Library Directors in the Association of Research Libraries: The Next Generation, Part One, *College and Research Libraries*, 62 (March), pp. 116 – 145

Hernon, P., Powell, R., and Young, A. (2002) - University Library Directors in the Association of Research Libraries: The Next Generation, Part Two, *College and Research Libraries*, 63 (January), pp. 73 – 90

Hernon, P & Rossiter, N. (eds) (2007) Making a Difference: Leadership and Academic Libraries. Westport, Connecticut & London. Libraries Unlimited. 2007.

Jackson, C. (1996) *Understanding Psychological Testing*. London. Blackwell.

Kaarst-Brown, M. et al. (2004) Organizational Cultures of Libraries as a Strategic Resource. *Library Trends* 53 (1) s. 33-54

Lok, P. & Crawford, J. (1999) The relationship between commitment and organizational culture, subculture, leadership style and job satisfaction in organizational change and development. *Leadership & Organizational development Journal* 20 (7) s. 365-373

Pors, N.O., Dixon, P. & Robson, H. (2004) The Employment of Quality Measures in Libraries: Cultural differences, institutional imperatives and managerial profiles. Sandra Parker (editor) *Library Measures to fill the void: assessing the outcomes: Proceedings from the 5th Northumbria International Conference on Performance Measurement in Libraries and Information Services.* Emerald. 2004. p. 127 – 135

Pors, Niels Ole (2006) *Mellem identitet og legitimitet. Ledelse, kultur og forandringer i danske biblioteker*. Research rapport. Danmarks Biblioteksskole.

Pors, Niels Ole (2008 a) Trust and Organisational Effectiveness: Discrepancies between users' service preferences and the library system's construction of their needs. Performance Measurement and Metrics 9 (1) 59-68

Pors, Niels Ole (2008) Traditional Use Patterns?: An analysis of high school students' use of libraries and information resources. New Library World 109 (9/10) 431 - 443

Røvik, K.A. (1998) *Moderne organisasjoner: Trender i organisasjonstenkningen ved tusenårsskiftet*. Bergen. Fagbokforlaget.

Skovdahl Hansen, H. & Mortensen, E.L. (2003). *Introduktion. NEO-PI-R.* Paul T. Costa and Robert R. McCrae. Forfattet af Henrik Skovdahl Hansen, Erik Lykke Mortensen og Heidi K. Schiøtz. Kbh. PsykologiErhverv: 5-9. Original title: Revised NEO Personality Inventory (NEO-PI-R) and NEO Five-Factor Inventory.

Libraries and Potential Users: Methodological Approach, the Case of Greek Libraries

Anthi Katsirikou[1] and George Matalliotakis[2]

[1]University of Piraeus Library, Greece
[2]Technical University of Crete, Greece

Abstract: The paper seeks the policies and strategies that Greek libraries apply in order to discover, communicate and attract potential users. Theoretically, every non-user is a potential user of a library and it is common sense that most of the people avoid visiting libraries. Being so, libraries undertake the responsibility to appeal to their clients. The paper:

- ✓ Seeks the communicative methods that libraries apply in order to increase the users,
- ✓ Examines the strategy for appealing new users or new group of people,
- ✓ Seeks the state of the art of Greek libraries, their communication policy,
- ✓ Describes the marketing research on the above theme, and
- ✓ Proposes best practices.

Keywords: Libraries' Communication models; Marketing models; Marketing research; Greek libraries.

1. Introduction

Libraries in the fast communicative environment they live, implement three spaces of interaction:

- ✓ Between librarians who decide the offered services, the resources, the manuals and every necessary equipment for users satisfaction and the exploitation of the service.
- ✓ Among users and librarians who are responsible. The communication aims to identify the users' needs and the relevance of the resources to them.
- ✓ Between Library and users community as a whole. Users receive modified information that can be used to their work. This is the step that library proves its usefulness and illumine its image. (Tamura, 2007)

Libraries are social places, where individuals, teams, social groups interact. Social theories, behaviorism, socio-psychological analyses drive to the recognition of special characteristics of libraries and of every target group they refer. Libraries are also one of the key factors that can impact the development and the prosperity of the social entity they refer. Consequently, we can say that they involve competitiveness and entrepreneurship. They take into account the following factors before decision making:

- ✓ Target focusing,
- ✓ Strategic planning,
- ✓ Efficiency and effectiveness,

- ✓ Resources saving,
- ✓ Cost- benefits analysis.

The coupling of these different options, social and business, designates the communication methods and the policies that libraries choose on occasion.

The synthesis and the identity of the unity that we call "library users" is a continuing changed variable, as it strands upon the dynamic of human mobility, potential individual needs, and behavioral rules of societies. Users can turn into non- users, actually without caution, but not without any cause. Equally non-users could turn into new, enthusiastic users.

2. The research and the methodologies

The questionnaire consists of items that derived from:

- ✓ The subject as come up for discussion in the literature,
- ✓ The marketing plans of business,
- ✓ The adjustment of them to library context.

Needless to say that the findings analyzed by qualitative methods. There is an integrated combination of qualitative and quantitative methods, what is referred as mixing methods (Banwell and Coulson, 2004, Wilson, 2000, Niglas, 1999).

Libraries need to know the synthesis and the characteristics of the population they refer to, in order to successfully appeal them. The major problems on this face the public and the special libraries, which the target groups are fuzzy and random. The social stratification is a matter of research of specialized organizations that collect data on the population structure, family synthesis, economic activities, education, leisure etc. (Wakeham, 2004: 239). The data is completed by using qualitative methods like interviews of opinion leaders, structured observation, discussions with famous public people. The target is to be ensured that the concept, the structure and the procedures of a service are harmonized to the target group.

3. Marketing and libraries

Marketing is the wide range of activities involved in making sure that you're continuing to meet the needs of your customers and getting value in return. These activities include market research to find out, for example, what groups of potential customers exist, what their needs, are, which of those needs you can meet, how you should meet them etc. Marketing also includes analyzing the competition, positioning your new product or service (finding your market niche), pricing your products and services, and promoting them through continued advertising, promotions, public relations and sales. (Conley, Kathleen and Tucker Toni, 2005: 49-50)

Marketing is connected with library's operation itself. Value added works such as cataloguing and classification corresponds to the product packing, embodied also the concept of the product: in this case is knowledge, research, information, entertainment. Shelving, Abstracting and Indexing, bibliography compilation correspond to the promotion. Regarding the users training programs, the location of material in the library correlates with marketing practices, such as study of consumer behaviour, product promotion etc. The mission and the objectives of libraries are modified according to the conditions; services, procedures, rules and operation follow the change. Consequently the Marketing Mix changes too.

To catch the alterations, a marketing plan is necessary in order to define the policies, the promotional practices. On the other hand and because of the 4P balance differs for every target group, it is necessary the research on the groups of population that are the potential clients of the library. 4 Ps of Marketing Mix of libraries (Wakeham, 2004: 237, Hill et al, 2006: 4):

- ✓ Product is the value that librarians add through their knowledge, expertise, and informational, organizational, and retrieval skills (Conley, Kathleen and Tucker Toni, 2005: 50). Product is library's services. Collections consists the basis of the "product", but the main one is an *Idea, an intangible product,* in which the tangible good, the services and the processes are incorporated.
- ✓ Place is the space of the library, either physical or virtual. Place is an important factor that can appeal the potential users. Another factor relevant to this is the location of the building, how easily accessible is it. Relevant to this point is the mention that the place nowadays is both place and space, equally physical and virtual.
- ✓ The Price of library services or products consists of both the staff time spent in ensuring that resources and services are available and accessible and user's time in finding and using resources efficiently (Conley, Kathleen and Tucker Toni, 2005: 50). Libraries do not Price their activities and decisions. However they assess the cost of services, of acquisitions, of operation. The main interest of libraries is the best exploitation of their resources, the advancement of their services, the improvement of their quality, without increasing of their cost.
- ✓ The communicative policy of the library is the Promotion policy and its part of the strategic marketing. Promotion consists every positive action, even the politeness of the staff, but in practice, promotion targets to explain to users and non-users why they need the library in their everyday life.

4. The survey and the results

The questionnaire contains questions for collecting quantitative information, questions for seeking behaviors and attitudes scaled to 4 degrees (the lack of answer means the negative one). The third unity contains questions on the organizational level of the library, its resources (human and economic), its finance and fund raising. The stratification of the sampling of libraries who participated to the survey is analog to the number of libraries that belong to every type. The questions and the analysis follow the structure of a marketing plan (Hill et al, 2006: 271-304).

4.1. Mission and goals of the library. The first two diagrams show the weak idea that Greek libraries have on the strategic management.

- ✓ More than half of the libraries have a fuzzy idea of their mission, and
- ✓ Only 37, 5% has written specific explicit mission. (Fig. 1)

And (Fig. 2)

- ✓ Only 11,4% writes down the strategic plan, shared to the whole staff and,
- ✓ 21,5% of libraries share the plan to employees relevant to the its content.

Fig 1. Library's mission

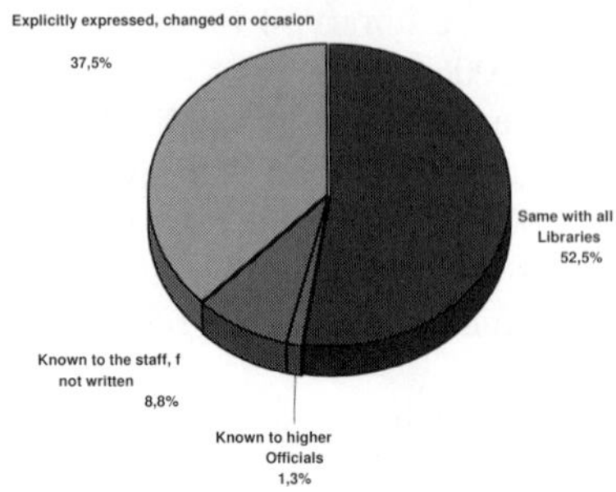

Fig. 2. Means for achieving library's goals as they are ordered by its purpose and strategy :

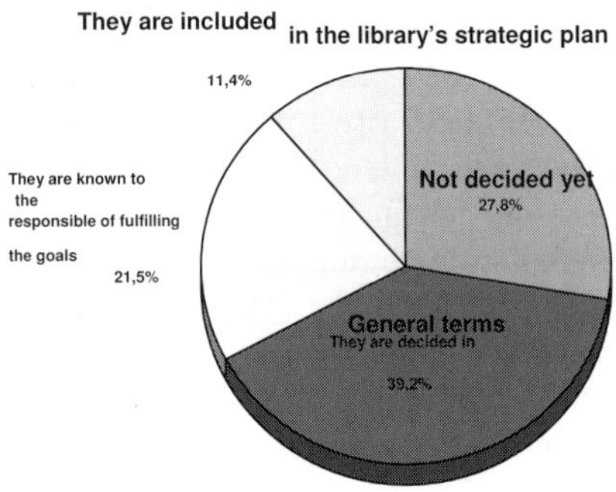

Furthermore, as usual, the 56% of Libraries deny to set economic goals, but the 57, 5% of libraries set non-economic goals, which they achieve and sometimes they overcome. Needless to say that an economic goal is not a business goal: it could be a cost effective goal, or the better exploitation of the resources or the decrease of operational expenses etc. Libraries are negatively biased on economic and public relations actions. Marshall (2001: 117) mentions some causes for academic libraries that seem to be common to every kind:

- ✓ Argument that academic libraries have a captive audience in members of the academic community who need to use the library in order to be successful in their academic areas of teaching and research,
- ✓ Library funding is not a concern because it is linked to overall institutional funding,
- ✓ Promotion is not a part of the library's purpose,
- ✓ Promotion of the library and its services will crate expectations and

demand that are beyond the library's capabilities,

- ✓ Reliance on the university's communication or development office to perform a public relations role will suffice.

4.2. Product (life cycle, new life design). Because of the lack of strategic thought and promotional vision, libraries gave the following answers:

- ✓ 69% declare that the strategic planning is unofficial, and
- ✓ 54, 5% answer that there are no procedures for the creation of new services.
- ✓ Not users but other factors determine the orientation and establishment of new services.
- ✓ The questions on the life cycle of the services reveal that libraries mainly operate as traditional organizations and low communicated.

4.3. Market (target–groups)

- ✓ Most of the libraries (86, 8%) know their population and their mobility.
- ✓ They study the attitude of people, and
- ✓ They try to form a special policy for every group.

The kind of libraries that answered explain it (fig 3):

- ✓ 44,3% does not examine the target group, and
- ✓ 30% systematically focuses on numerous groups of the population.

Fig. 3 Is there any strategy for developing library services?

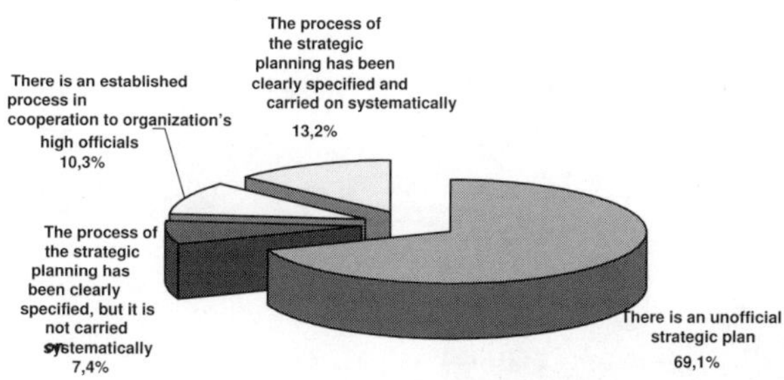

4.4. The library's image and the External relationships.

As it is clear up to now, libraries operation is mainly collection oriented than users -centered. The modernization steps parallel to technology, without harmonizing processes, management, and services. They use technology without innovative processes. The following answers confirm the lack of a strategy for appealing new groups of population and new users.

- ✓ Only 1,4% collects systematically data on users' and groups' behavior, and
- ✓ 7, 8% focuses on the appealing of new target groups (fig. 4).

Fig. 4 Information about users and potential users

External relationships

- ✓ 8,3% agree that strategic alliances increase the users and advertise their services, and
- ✓ 52,8% agrees to evaluate cooperation proposals that could cause the increase of the users.
- ✓ Lack of active, systemic promotion of the library,
- ✓ Uninterested in communication (fig. 5).

Fig. 5 Strategic cooperation for approaching new target groups

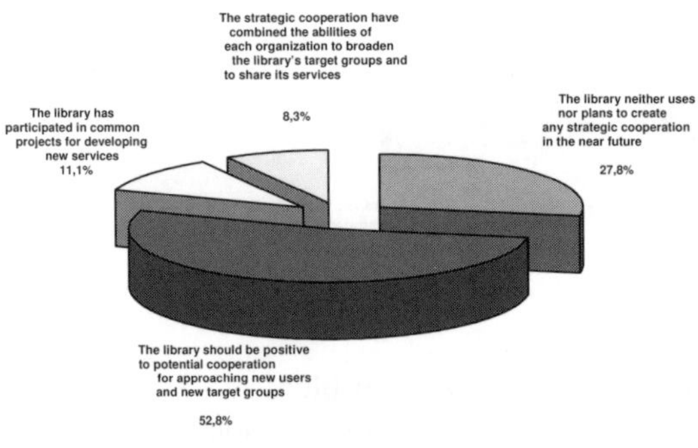

Nevertheless, half of the people that participate to library's events use the library, become members. The opposite valid also: the majority of the members are interested in library's events. That means that users' attitude is positive, but how many people use it? That's the crucial question. That's the main problem of libraries: not the whole people who need libraries use them.

5. Conclusions

It is important to say that the idea that library has for itself is an important factor of its development. It is also important for libraries to realize that they are mainly the space of the community. Users face positively libraries, although the problems exist. Whether or not libraries receive adequate support is strongly influenced by the kinds of relations they have with their public –their total public, including non-reading and non- library using groups. Public relations, “the planned effort of an organization to integrate itself into the society in which it exists”, centers on this problem (Berger, 1979: 180). Libraries need to gain self estimation and to believe to their social service, to their service supply. Only this way exists for finding their users, communicating potential users, promoting their services. Libraries must know their advantages and strengths, their real advocacy.

References

Conley, Kathleen and Tucker Toni (2005): Matching Media to Audience equals marketing success. In *Real life Marketing and promotion strategies in college libraries: connecting with campus and community* (ed. by Barbara Whitney Petruzzell). The Haworth Information press, σ. 47-64.

Berger, Patricia (1979): An investigation of the relationship between public relations activities and budget allocation in public libraries. *Information processing and management,* 15: 179-193.

Marshall, Nancy J. (2001): Public relations in academic libraries: a descriptive analysis. *The Journal of Academic Librarianship,* 27(2): 116-21.

Banwell, Linda and Graham Coulson (2004), “Users and user study methodology: the JUBILEE project” *Information Research,* 9 (2), 13 σ., http://informationr.net/ir/9-2/paper167.html.

Niglas, Katrin (1999), *Quantitative and Qualitative Inquiry in Educational Research: Is There A Paradigmatic Difference Between Them?* Paper presented at the European Conference on Educational Research, Lahti, Finland 22-25 September 1999. http://www.leeds.ac.uk/educol/documents/00001487.htm.

Wilson, T. D. (2000), “Recent trends in user studies: action research and qualitative methods” *Information Research,* 5 (3). http://informationr.net/ir/5-3/paper76.html.

Tamura, S., Miwa, M., Saito, Y., Koshizuka, M., Kasai, Y., Matsubayashi, M. & Ikeya, N. (2007). "Information sharing between different groups: a qualitative study of information service to business in Japanese public libraries" *Information Research,* 12 (2). http://InformationR.net/ir/12-2/paper306.html.

Wakeham, Maurice (2004), “Marketing health libraries”, *Health Information and Libraries Journal,* 21, 237-244.

Hill, Liz, Catherine O’ Sullivan and Terry O’ Sullivan (2006): *Creative Arts Marketing.* Amsterdam: Butterworth Heinemann.

The Quality of Information as Basis of the Library Management Quality

N. Molodtsova and I. Shebalkina

Siberian State Medical University, Scientific Medical Library, Tomsk, Russia

Abstract: In the article the role of document information in the process of library management is indicated. The organization of work with documents is a very important part of the management processes and taking managerial decisions, it influences the efficiency and the quality of management. The development of new technologies implies the system approach to the process of taking decisions on the basis of flexible informational analytical integrated system of management.

The processing project of the service database of regulating information in the scientific medical library of Siberian State Medical University (Tomsk, Russia) is presented.

Keywords: Library management; Document information; Efficiency; Quality; Regulating information; Informational system; Database.

1. Introduction

A great number of scientific, reference, educational, methodical and practical publications is devoted to the quality of library activity in Russia.

One of the most characteristic tendencies is the active interest to management, especially quality management that explains the fact of formation of new management concept in the sphere of library science.

Modern management researches show a great significance of rational information processing for achieving strategic and operative aims.

The quality of inofrmation defines the quality of management because information covers all spheres of management. Being the most important function of management process, information must meet the following requirements: authenticity, accuracy and completeness, efficiency and regularity, its conformity with management level.

Different approaches to management of documentary information are offered by Backland (1994), Larin (2001), Sankina (2002) and other authors.

Management of documentation as function of management is realised in the conditions of decision making process to achieve the aim. That is why documentation management is closely connected with the problems of management, organization structures, the problems of design of information systems management, their implementation and operation, with automation of managerial procedures and processes.

Urgency of the problem consists in support of the processes of documentation information management due to more effective technologies of its processing including analytical components and the connection of management functions with documents, their servicing.

The development of new management technologies plans systematic approach to the decision making process on the base of flexible information analytical integrated management system.

2. Documents management

The organization of work with documents is a very important part of management processes and taking managerial decisions influencing efficiency and management quality.

From the point of view of information technologies documentation information management activity and the management activity itself – as a subsystem of an integrated technological system of library. So, the library management, in Pilko's opinion (2006), is characterised as technological process that supposes regularity of management.

In management activity a document is a tool, means or method of management. The whole documentation is closely connected with the concrete management function for which it is created. It allows, in Larin's opinion (2001), with the help of systematic analysis to identify the content of managerial documents and to connect it with the definite management function.

Optimal system of internal legal regulation helps to provide successfully and realise substantially the local legal regulation of general principles of activity, some decisions and concrete aspects of library operation.

The complex of internal regulated documents, being formed in each library objectively consists of a package of separate interrelated and mutually complementary blocks.

The documents, included, reflect legal organizational and technological sides of professional activity, fix aims, order and conditions of library functioning as informational, educational and cultural institution.

Pilko (2006) suggests to classify the complex of documents regulating the activity of the library for convenience according to the following functions: organizational – administrative documentation, scientific – methodical documentation, normative documentation and technological documentation.

At the present stage in the system of library management the whole range of documents concerning different types and kinds of documentation systems and being a part of documentation support of management.

3. Information management system

The use of information technologies in the sphere of management gives opportunities of more effective and rational organization of information processes, increase of their flexibility and dynamics expansion of the range of analysed factors when making decisions.

"Perfect" information system of management must automate all or the majority of protective kinds of activity in the frames of integrated information space and in interrelation of automated functions. It is more optimal to use the system which is the part of the architecture of the system of complex library automation that implies the use of joint technologies of management automation and documents circulation.

The creation of the system of automated management of documents or service database in the library is a very complicated organizational technical task, administrative office automation being the main, basic platform within information library system.

Designing database, one should orient on the use of standard management system of data and technology "client – server" which allows to combine operative work with archiving documents.

Automated system in the library:

- provides coordinated work of all departments;
- simplifies work with documents, increases its effectiveness;
- increases labour efficiency due to shortening time for creation, documents processing and search;
- increases efficiency of access to information;
- allows to delimit the competence of access of workers to information.

The implementation of such system in the library will optimize the activity of the library in whole, to get analytical information for using and taking important managerial decisions. Without any doubts, the system will influence on effectiveness of library activity as well as on increase of professional personnel training, the culture of the use of modern information technologies.

4. Database of regulating documentation

For solving intersystem tasks of the library one can suggest the module of service database of regulated documentation as foundation of effective library management. Designing technological project of database we relied on methodical basis and regulations considered by Pilko (2006) and Voroisky (1998).

The main source (source data) when forming database is regulated documents of library.

Database supports the main functions of documents processing on-line which include: documents development and custody; search of documents according to different parameters, input, support and custody of any kind of documents; control over implementation of documents; protection and management of separation of rights for access.

Database includes the complex of functional means realised as a program modules helping to plan work, to get interim and resort valuation of separate operations, to control and, if necessary, to correct the plan or process.

The idea of centralised storage of e-documents is also obvious: integrated database in server keeps documents safely, systematizes them and finds necessary information very quickly. Not the least of the features of the system is unification of the most widespread types and kinds of documents in management, development and use of patterns.

Database is corporate storage of regulating documents of the library. In includes the catalogue of organizational efficient, regulatory – methodical and technological documentation, unified forms of documents, documents archive, office documents of departments or separate workers.

Through interface of database, installed in all computers, the workers of the library get access to hierarchy of folders and operations concerning design and search of documents.

The search of documents is realised through folders navigation.

Creating a new document a database offers users to identify its belonging to concrete theme by classifier and to use standard sheet, pattern.

Information, formed by users in the process of selecting data, is displayed as a reference in matrix format, graphic material, fulltext document or pattern.

Different functional and practical tasks are solved by the method of contiguous look of database modules and data selection or seriating. The tasks can be operational analysis of technological processes; valuation of resort support of processes; valuation of work content of library production.

Managers of a library, having full access to all documents, can control the process of creating office documents any time. The analysis of report documents formed in database, gives opportunity to correct the library activity, to improve organizational structure, character and content of implemented works, personnel, provision with financial, material and other resources.

5. Conclusions

It is obvious that documentary information management in the conditions of modern management and development of new information technologies becomes more and more actual.

Automated systems of documents management are directed to be universal information storage, corporate knowledge base, a tool of management of organizational and technological activity.

Independent office database of regulating documentation of the library is considered as organizational technological complex of methodical, technical, program and informational means aimed at support and increase of processes of planning and library management.

Undoubtedly, suggested model of database of regulating documentation will provide the processes of joint training and standardization of documents, integrated informational space and absolutely new level of making operative, managerial and technological decisions.

References

Backland, M., (1994). About fundamentals of documentation management theory. *The American Archivis*t, Vol.57, P. 346-351.

Larin, M.V., (2001). Documentation management: theory and practice. *Office work*, №1, P. 16-21.

Pilko, I.S., (2006). *Informational and library technologies*. Profession Publishing House, Saint-Petersburg.

Sankina L.V., (2002). *Office work*. MTSFER Publishing House, Moscow.

Voroisky, F.S., (1998). *Thesaurus on information science*, Librea Publishing House, Moscow.

3. The Change of Libraries

Change Management in the University Library

Maria Popescu[1], Emilian Corneanu[2], Elena Helerea[3]

[1]Transilvania University of Brasov – Quality Management Assurance Dept. Coord.
[2]Transilvania University of Brasov – University Librarian
[3]Transilvania University of Brasov – University Library Manager
Transilvania University of Brasov, 29, Eroilor St., Brasov, 500036, Romania
[2]Corresponding person, E-mail: emilian.corneanu@unitbv.ro

Abstract: The paper presents a methodology of achieving change management in the university libraries and its application to a case study on *Transilvania* University Library of Brasov. The model discussed in the paper, original in many aspects, outlines two major stages determining the results of the changes upon the organization's overall performance: implementing changes from a strategic point of view and approaching change as a project. The case study includes a synthetic presentation of the library revealing changes done in the last decade and the major deficiencies associated to the changes management approach. The authors present the central priorities of the strategy elaborated by the library management for the coming years and underline the expectation of their achievement with good results, through the professional approach of the change, based on modern management methods and principles, such as team work, staff involving and leadership.

Keywords: Change management; Library management; University library.

1. Introduction

The study aims to establish the key-elements determining the success of the organization's change and to apply the methodology proposed by the authors in achieving changes in the University Library. This research is the first step in the plan of changes that will be developed by the management of *Transilvania* University Library of Brasov in the coming years.

The paper underlines the imperative of achieving some major changes in libraries to increase the flexibility, the quality and the efficiency of the services offered. In the university libraries, these changes assure the fine-tuning of the library's activity with the requirements of the higher education and they contribute significantly to improve the quality of education and scientific research. The studies concerned with this topic outline the elements that impose the change, the major lines of it and several applications in libraries from different parts of the world, including Romania. [Tennant, R. (2006), Troll, A.D. (2001), Wood, E. J. and others. (2007), Doroftei, C.(2005)].

In many cases, the improving actions carried out in university libraries did not lead to their expected results. In Romania the financial constraints faced by the universities and their libraries are often held responsible for the difficulties to achieve changes; in fact, many problems are caused by the mistakes done in managing change.

Differentiation between changes, the use of methods and means leading to a successfully implementation and to an efficient use of human, material and financial resources, as well as the involvement of top management and the setting up of an organizational culture that integrates continuous improvement are the main issues management has to deal with in order to follow up favourable changes. The paper outlines in its first part the stream of thinking and actions to follow in order to increase the effectiveness and efficiency of changes. These elements are concentrated in the methodology of achieving organizational changes proposed by the authors. The second part presents a case-study on *Transilvania* University Library, comprising: an analysis from the change management's point of view of implemented changes in the university library in the last decade; the priority of changes for the next years, taking into account the library's strategy and the results of the diagnosis-analysis of the management system.

2. The methodology of achieving organizational changes

Recent years were for the libraries a period of faster, greater and more dramatic changes than has ever before been experienced. The omnipresence of the new technologies, the ever-increasing cooperation, the globalization as premises of the evolution towards the *Global Information Society,* the emphasis on quality, the diminution of the financial resources are the main agents imposing the change of libraries.

Implementing the necessary changes for the academic libraries is no easy job as it requires a differentiation between changes to ensure the coherence of actions within the available resources. It is also important to use planning and control methods that contribute to reduce the span of the change process and to optimize the use of resources. Finally, it requires suitable structures, staff training and overcoming the resistance to change. All these respects are subjects of change management – a distinct discipline whose key-aspects - in point of increasing the success and the efficiency of organizational changes – we present.

The concept of organizational change, as defined by the management theories, is a significant, extended, important change that affects the entire organization or parts of it. Such changes do not occur naturally, they are changes whose implementation is the task of the management team. The methodology of achieving these changes is one of the main issues of change management and it is treated in very different ways by management theoreticians [Schein, H.E., (1996), Zorlențan, T. et al.(1996), Popescu, M. (2001)].

The best known approach is the one proposed by Kurt Lewin and E. H. Schein (1996) that identifies three essential stages in the process of organizational changes, stages somewhat similar to chemical processes: unfreezing – the trial to create the reasons for change; moving/implementing change – identifying solutions adequate to circumstance and applying them; freezing – a new equilibrium is crystallizing.

From the point of view of implementing changes in the university library, the methodology presented by Popescu, M. (2001) has the advantage of a pragmatic approach that defines two major stages of the process of starting and implementing change: **identifying the need of change** and **achieving change** (see Fig.1).

Identifying the need of change aims to establish the favourable changes that may add value to the organization. In the authors' opinion the important changes must be implemented from a strategic point of view; this means that, when establishing the changes that must be done and their order, the mission and the strategic objectives of the organization are kept in mind. This way one can avoid the risk of starting complex and expensive processes that can not be financially supported or that have little or no effects upon the performances of the organization.

Several studies discussing changes in libraries develop the above idea. Thus, Troll, A.D. (2001) underlines that the evaluation activity usually carried out in libraries is not enough in order to plan changes: without knowing the external and the internal context and the library's strategy, such an evaluation is of no help in understanding what changes are relevant and can assure the accomplishment of the library's mission. It's necessary to define clearly the strategic objectives and the main lines of change that sustain planning changes in the library.

To complete this idea we state that, once the strategy is elaborated it has to be communicated; making public and discussing the mission, the policy and the general objectives of the library are means of communication through which the top management acknowledges everyone concerned its view on the future of the library and obtains their support. Communicating, informing and involving the staff are elements that contribute to overcome the resistance to change which is normal in the case of any major change. The bigger the changes, the greater the resistance to change and ignoring this is the source of many failures as shown in many studies on this topic.

Achieving change, the second stage, is a complex process having clearly stated beginning and ending points and, between, a sequence of three activities:

- the preliminary study or the planning – it's goal is to define change, to evaluate the achieving conditions and the expected results;
- projecting the change – it refers to defining solutions and including them in specific documents;
- implementing and checking the results – it is a stage that, paradoxically, often raises difficulties because of the resistance to change.

These three activities are intricately interconnected: change is achieved progressively, but the process is not linear, solutions adopted in one stage are often rectified in a following one. The amount of innovation the solutions bear, the fact that change by definition involves contouring and implementing new solutions – what causes it to seem unique and risky –, the important quantity of resources involved, the participation of many specialists and actors from different structures are characteristic elements that render complex and difficult the achieving of organizational changes. The solution is to approach them as projects, in the manner proper to project management.

The scheme in Fig.1 synthesizes the methodology for accomplishing the organizational changes, whose application ensures: on one hand – the coherence of the actions, through relating to the strategy of the organization, on the other hand, advantages determined by approaching the change as project, by using the project as "vehicle for the change" [Pellegrinelli, S. and Bowman, C. (1994)], which means, implicitly, applying the principles and methods specific to project management.

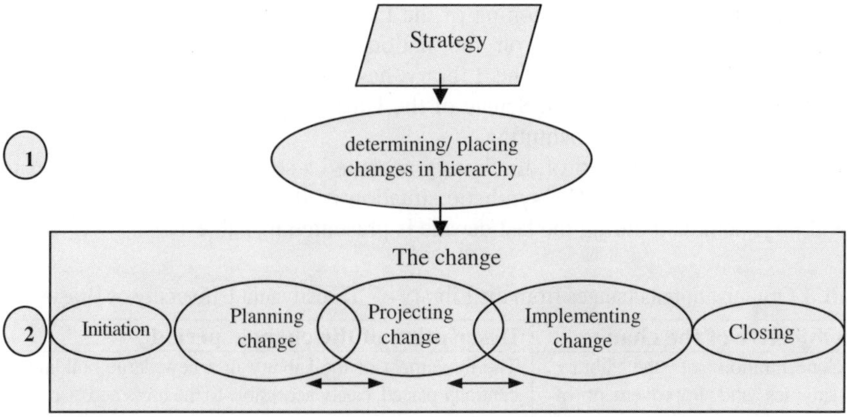

Fig.1 Stages of the process of achievement organizational changes

3. Case study

The case study realized at the Library of Transilvania University of Braşov sets out to analyze the changes made during the last decade within the university library, from the perspective of the change management, to present the change priorities inscribed in the library strategy along the years to follow and to identify the key factors on whom there depends the success of the change projects.

Transilvania University of Braşov is an institution of higher education and research, which enjoys high prestige on the local, national and international level. It is an extended university, with 16 faculties – 8 are of technical profile and 8 of university profile, with more than 22.000 students at the university degree, master's degree and doctorate cycles, full time and distance learning. In the context of globalization, of Romania's integration within the EU, the University achieved important changes in all fields of activity and structures, in view of harmonizing with the new requirements and in view of assuring the quality of the services of education and research. [see the site www.unitbv.ro].

The Library is a structure of *Transilvania* University of Braşov, an entity without its own judicial personality, subordinated to the top management of the university. The mission of the university library is to ensure the documentary and information basis necessary for the education process, to enhance and to communicate them, as well as other services, to the benefit of the information users, facilitating the diversified and rapid access to all categories of sources.

The documentary patrimony of the Library of *Transilvania* University of Braşov includes: books, serial publications, manuscripts, cartographic documents, printed musical documents, audio-visual documents, graphic documents, electronic documents etc. The collections of the Library are constituted and developed through acquisition, transfer, national and international exchange, donations and sponsorship. The endowment is ensured through financing from the university management, as well as through transfers, donations and sponsorship.

The organization and the functioning of the Library observe the provisions of the specific legislation elaborated on the national level, as well as the internal regulations of the university. The Library has its own strategies and plans of activity whose approval by the Senate of the University ensures the integration in the general strategy of the institution.
Like the university it is part of, the library achieved a series of changes in order to improve its performance. The synthetic situation of the important changes within the library, achieved during the last decade is presented in Table 1.

Tab. 1 Organizational changes from the Library of Transilvania University of Braşov

Objective of the change	Description of the change, period
Concentration of the library activities and improvement of the working conditions and of the documentary collection storage	The movement of the Library in a new, large building centrally placed, easily accessible to the users and also to the staff. In 2006 there was set up the new free access room and in 2007 the central deposit for the loan of publications.
Automation of the processes of document management and communication	Provision with computers, linked in network and connected to the Internet (since 1997 and permanently updated); implementation of the Library integrated software Liberty 3, the fourth in chronological order, used since 2007.
Access to digital information: electronic documents, databases, internet resources	The acquisition of electronic documents and the subscription to on-line magazines (since the end of the `90-ies) and databases (after the year 2003).
Improvement of the system of activity evaluation	Making up reports with respect to the publication circulation and to the user frequency at the free access room; Users' statistic evidence and that of the publications made up by the loan service; improvement of the data collection for making up the official statistics required by the local and central authorities. They are realized partly automated, the tendency being of generalizing the automated means of quantitative evaluation.
Development of the human resource in the library	Employment, professional training, life-long education of the staff.
Improvement of the management structure	Redefining the compartments and the posts taking into consideration the new strategy of the library.
Optimization of the processes	Analysis, optimization and description through procedures of the key processes.

Seen from the perspective of the results, the described actions display a series of defaults. For instance:
- the relocation of the library became a strategic objective during the year 2005 after the finalization of a building with another initial destination. The placement of the Library in this building ensured the concentration of the activities and the amelioration of the working environment, however the adaptation costs were high, without ensuring the perfect compliance with the needs of the library;
- the automation of the processes of document management and communication is

likewise questionable under the aspect of the adopted solutions, taking into consideration that the used software requires expensive hardware resources, and the results with respect to the performance of the processes were not up to the expectations;

- the efficacy of the actions undertaken within the library for the access to digital information may be appreciated as reduced, because of the lack of correlation between the equipments in the structure of the informatics system, as well as of the insufficient training with respect to the users' access to these resources. These resources did not benefit from an adequate promotion among the users who, to a too great extent, ignore their informative value and even their existence;
- the modernization of the evaluation system is slowed down by the lack of an adequate evaluation model and also by the generalized delay of the automated means for collecting and processing the data, and the efficiency of the evaluation is also affected by the persistence of the non-trained and disinterested staff in accomplishing this activity.
- the endowment with sufficient, stable and qualified staff is hindered by the still low number of librarians with specialized studies from the geographical area, by the unattractive level of the wages, by the rooting in certain posts of non-efficient employees, refractory to the new.

The outlined deficiencies are, at least in part, determined by the manner in which change management was implemented in the university library, both as regards planning the changes and settling the solutions, and as regards their implementation. It is to be observed especially the neglecting of the social aspects with respect to the staff's training, the resistance to change etc. – as factors which have negatively influenced the efficacy and the efficiency of the change processes.

The university library will continue the process of the qualitative transformations during the following period, but in different ways. The aim is at using efficiently the strategy, as management instrument and at developing mechanisms that should allow the continuous control and improvement of the library performance through systematic actions. To this purpose, in a first stage there was carried out the diagnostic analysis of the management system of the library, whose conclusions are presented as follows, synthesized in strengths and weaknesses.

STRENGTHS

- There is a strategy of the library, harmonized with that of the university. The mission of the library and the system of values are published on the site (http://www.unitbv.ro/biblio/). The objectives are realistic, measurable; the accent is laid on improving the performance, in order to contribute to ensuring the quality of the educational and research services carried out by the university. There was set as priority axis of research the implementation of a system of quality management, through which there is created the framework for the continuous improvement of the quality.
- The university and library management has the capability to professionally approach the changes, evinces competences as regards the ample perspective and its concretization in valid strategies of development, the settling of the plans for further action and the provision with the resources necessary for accomplishing the change projects, the optimization of the structure, the implementation of

modern methods of management.

- Human resources: the library has 52 employees, among which 32 with higher education and 11 with higher education in the field. The staff benefited from training (in IT, quality management) and of mobility exchanges in the country and abroad.

WEAKNESSES

- Control of the performance: the library achieves the assessment of the performance every year; however the criteria and the indicators which are used do not reflect the qualitative aspects of the activity, the effects of the library services upon the educational and scientific research processes. There is no management system that should measure the costs of the services/ activities realized by the library.
- Control of the processes: there has begun to be implemented the management through processes, however the action is in an incipient phase of analysis and description of the key processes through procedures.
- Human resources: staff's evaluation is done in compliance with the law, however the insufficient resources used in this process make the evaluation not always relevant. The participation of the staff in solving the problems is unequal and the rewarding system is non-stimulating.
- Organizational culture: there is no culture of the quality, there are insufficiently promoted values such as team work, staff's implication, opening towards change.

Taking into account the submitted situation, the priority axes for the development of the capability of the library to continuously improve its performance are the following:

- **People**: the continuation of the process of staff training in quality management, with accent on achieving behavioral changes, on raising the degree of implication in solving the problems and on team work.
- **Users**: orientation towards the customers, definition of the requirements and evaluation of their satisfaction. This implies in the first place the improvement of the system evaluating the library performance, through the introduction of criteria and indicators that should better reflect the effects upon the quality of the educational and research processes. The control will be also extended upon the costs of the services and of the activities realized by the library.
- **Processes**: development and implementation of instruments and also of working and control procedures that should ensure the optimization of the processes and their continuous improvement.

The achievement of the change processes will be coordinated by the Management Council of the library. Both the initiation of the projects and their unfolding will be largely promoted in the framework of the library, for obtaining the feedback and for attracting the people in realizing the changes. The financing of the projects will be done from its own funds, but there will be likewise accessed funds from the Operational Programs (POS DRU – for the development of human resources, POS DCA – for the development of the administrative capacity).

4. Conclusions

The existence during the last decades of the university libraries has been characterized by ample changes, a process that will continue. The achievement of the changes is an issue of the management library, whose results may be considerably improved through a professional approach, based on the methods of the change management. The case study developed by the authors presents the first sequences of the change program that will be achieved during the years to follow at the library of *Transilvania* University of Braşov, with reference to the methodology of change elaboration and implementation.

References

Doroftei, C.(2005) *Biblioteca în societatea informaţională. Provocarea schimbării.* Revista Română de Biblioteconomie şi Ştiinţa Informării, Anul 1, nr.2, 2005, pg.42-45, Bucuresti.

Pellegrinelli, S. and Bowman, C. (1994). *Implementing Strategy through Projects*, Lng Range Planning Vol.27, Nr.4, 1994, pg.125-132.

Popescu, M. (2001). *Managementul proceselor de cercetare-dezvoltare*, Editura Universităţii Transilvania din Braşov.

Schein, H.E., (1996). *Kurt Lewin's Change Theory in the Field and in the Classroom.* Systems Practice, Vol. 9 No 1.

Tennant, R. (2006). Academic Library Futures. *Library Journal,* p. 34. Reed Business Information.

Troll, A.D. (2001). *How and Why Are Libraries Changing.* Library Information Technology, Carnegie Mellon, http://www.diglib.org/use/whitepaper.htm

Wood, E. J. et al. (2007). *Beyond Survival: Managing Academic Libraries in Transition.* Libraries Unlimited, Greenwood.

Zorlenţan, T., Burduş, E., Căprărescu, G. (1996). *Managementul organizaţiei.* Editura Economică.

A Small Library with Big Goals - The Library for German Language and Literature, University of Tartu

Kaie Oks

Librarian, Department for German Language and Literature
University of Tartu, Estonia

Abstract: I would like to speak about the Library of the Department for German Language and Literature at the University of Tartu. The University of Tartu is one of the oldest universities in the Nordic countries, founded in 1632. After the collapse of the Soviet Union the situation in our country was changing. We had to build up new society, a new educational system. The example of our library illustrates the developments in Estonia very well. In many areas we had to start from scratch. When learning foreign languages, it is natural that the dictionaries, lexicons and scientific literature are at students' disposal, but in Tartu it was not so. The first German Professor in Tartu – Claus Sommerhage[1] - started establishing a library. Without intensive support of the German and Swiss funds our library would not exist today. Our library is getting better every day, the students and lecturers use it more and more often.

Keywords: Developing process; Importance of financing; Closeness to readers; Supporting the study process; Social gathering place.

1. Introduction

Today I would like to talk about a small library, first and foremost about the advantages of a small library as a librarian sees them. The role of the library has changed and is changing all the time but we cannot forget the main mission of the library – to offer the book and the place for using it. The role of the librarian in a small library is to be a consultant, a source of information and the person who keeps the stocks in order.

2. Brief history of the University of Tartu

I will start my presentation with a small overview of the University of Tartu as our library is a part of the university and it is not possible to observe them apart. The University of Tartu is the oldest university in Estonia and one of the oldest in the Northern countries. On 30 June 1632, King Gustav II Adolf of Sweden signed the Foundation Decree of *Academia Dorpatensis*, which marks the beginning of our university's history.

We can distinguish five periods when we speak about the history of the University of Tartu:

1. The Swedish period 1632-1710
2. The Imperial Tartu University 1802-1918
3. 1919-1940 Tartu University in the Republic of Estonia
4. 1944-1989 Tartu State University (in the Soviet times)
5. 1991 - Tartu University in the newly independent Republic of Estonia

I only describe three of them as the important ones for my presentation.

The first, the so-called "Swedish period", is important while it turned a small provincial town to the university town. The Town Council was interested in having the university here to restore its former prosperity. Tallinn and Riga were big and important centres and not at all interested in the university and the noisy and hectic young men - students.

Sweden in its turn wanted to:

- strengthen the Lutheran religion in the former Catholic country;
- strengthen the presence of the Swedish kingdom.

The students were mostly Swedes and Finns. We are proud that our university is so old but in fact the university, established during the Swedish period, was not one of the best reconized universities in Europe.

The university in Tartu functioned with the Faculties of Philosophy, Law, Theology, and Medicine, enjoying the privileges similar to those granted to the University of Uppsala. The University of Tartu was closed in 1710 after the Swedish army had surrendered to the Russian forces after the defeat in the Northern War.

The second period of the history of the university was 1802-1918 "reopening of the university". This period can be characterized as the prosperity of the university. The Baltic Germans needed the university to educate their children. After the French Revolution studying abroad was not allowed. Russia also needed its own university. So in Tartu the European science and the Russian state met. The Germans wanted to have a small Heidelberg or Göttingen and somehow they succeeded in it. The official language at the university was German and the religion was Lutheran. The 19th century was the period of prosperity of the university, the scientists K. E. von Baer, J. W. Struve and many others show us the level of scientific research in Tartu at that time.

The teaching of Germanic languages also goes back to this period and has long traditions. Already in 1865 the Department for German Language at the University of Tartu was established. The first professor at the department was Leo Meyer[2], a linguist from Göttingen who stayed in Dorpat for 33 years. The number of students increased every day, Rutiku and Kegelmann (2003).

3. Overview of the foundation of German Library

I concentrate my attention on the fifth period which begins in 1991 while at that time our library was established. After the collapse of the Soviet Union the situation in our country was changing. We had to build up new society, a new educational system. The example of our library illustrates the developments in Estonia very well. In many areas we had to start from scratch. When learning foreign languages, it is natural that the dictionaries, lexicons and scientific literature are at students' disposal, but in Tartu it was not so. The first German DAAD-Professor[3] in Tartu – Claus Sommerhage - started establishing a library. Among the many names the DAAD-Lecturer Claus Sommerhage should be emphasized. In 1992-1997 Dr. Claus Sommerhage was Guest Professor at the Department for German Language and Literature, 1997-1999 Extraordinary Professor. He innovated new curricula in teaching German literature, especially Modern German Literature. Since his coming only the overview courses had been taught. He started with analytical literature seminars, Rutiku and Kegelmann (2003). The most important thing he did for the department was establishing our library. He knew that without a library teaching literature was impossible. As Sommerhage had said we had a couple of copies of the novel Aula by Hermann Kant on our shelves.[4] He was right. He started looking for funds in Germany and Switzerland, he used his own connections and personal charm. Without intensive support of the German and Swiss funds our library would not exist today.

4. Financing, programmes, funds

Our library is unique because until 2003 there was no budget for it. Nevertheless, it was increasing with every day. At the beginning many books were donated to our library. Tartu is an old university town and professors and lecturers had their own very good libraries. Many professors and lecturers decided to give their German books to our library.

The theatre "Vanemuine" liquidated its library in 1999 and we received all their books in the German language. From there we have our 23-volume complete works of Dostoevsky from 1922 which is considered to be the best Dostoevsky translation since then.

The oldest book in our library dates back to 1780[5].

We also received books from our German friends. More than 15 years Professor Norbert Nail from the University of Marburg equipped us with every kind of books and journals about the German language and linguistics.

Since 2001 our library is in the project of Gebert Rüf Fund - the Swiss Baltic Net for the Swiss Libraries and Swiss Literature in the Baltic States. We can order German Swiss literature every year for 1000 ChFr. The sum is not big but very valuable for our library. The project also coordinates the work of Schweizer Lesezimmer in the Baltic States. We meet every year in Lithuania, Latvia or Estonia to present our annual work and discuss our problems. These meetings are always useful and interesting. This time the meeting takes place in Vilnius

In 2005-2007 our library was involved in the programme "Menschen und Bücher" (People and Books), an initiative of the Goethe Institute for Central and Eastern Europe. For our library it was a great privilege to be involved in the programme because our financial resources have always been limited. This time we could order books necessary for us and all our lecturers were involved in the ordering process. So we could efficiently enrich our library and every lecturer could order books for his or her course. The budget was 15, 000 EUR and we could also invite a German author to Tartu.

5. Department libraries at the University of Tartu

Since 2003 the University Library has pursued the policy of supporting department libraries. Until then the status of a small department library was obscure. At the Department for German Language and Literature the library policy was always clear. We needed a well equipped library for students and lecturers, we were for the open access. Since 2002 our books are in the library system INNOPAC, which makes every process with books very easy and transparent. Sometimes the department libraries are in a bad state, the books are available for very few readers but our policy was different from the very beginning. When we do have a book, people must know about it, they must have access to it.

6. Importance to the students and lecturers

One of the priorities of our library is its closeness to students and lecturers. We are informed of every need very quickly and for the students it is comfortable that everything about one subject (German language and literature) is concentrated at one place.

Since 1999 the Department for German Language and Literature has its own rooms in the former printing-house in the centre of the town, opposite the university main building. The renovation of the building had been contributed by different foreign embassies. It houses Departments for German, French, Spanish and Scandinavian Languages and is called "Paabel". For our library it gave a possibility to expose all the books better, to create a real library system, to create a room where people like to work. The rooms for the German library in this new building are next to the seminar rooms. The students can use library early in the morning and between the lectures and seminars during the day. Our users are the students of the Department for German Language and Literature, the students of the Language Centre of the University, the Master's course students who study translation and interpretation. Every reader who possesses the university library card is welcome in our library.

Closeness also means that we always consider the requests of the students. In the last years when we received our budget, we have ordered books for the students who need them for writing their Bachelor's or Master's theses. The priority of our library is to be of high scientific quality. This is the direction Claus Sommerhage gave to our library and we still hold on to it. It is sometimes difficult because of our insufficient financing, but we always choose books carefully, ask advice from our German patrons and friends, try to be informed of the newest scientific literature. So we can affirm that our library has been created by professionals and it fulfils its tasks.

One of our main tasks is to support the study process. At the Department for German Language and Literature the main research areas are linguistics, sociolinguistics, contact and text linguistics as well the Swiss literature and the German literature by women writers and the Baltic-German literature. Some subject areas in our library are very well presented, for example German linguistics, literary science, German history, German language history. In the last years the collection of our dictionaries and lexicons is almost ideal. As translation and interpretation are taught at our university, the collection of these books is almost excellent. We also have a good collection of German language textbooks. We have a sufficient number of copies thanks to "LÜKKA" – EU supporting programme. At our department teaching of modern Swiss literature has long traditions. Associated Professor Eve Pormeister has taught it already for 20 years and even wrote her Doctoral thesis on this subject[6]. She has connections with the Embassy of Switzerland, Swiss Funds, Pro Helvetia. Her special interest is the reason why Swiss literature is so well presented in our library.

7. Pleasant meeting place, nice interior

Last but not least, in a small department library, the milieu plays a big role. There are people who never go to the main library of the university. They do not like too big bleak rooms without cosy corners, with too many strange people. Our library is a kind of a social gathering place for the students who study the same subject, have the same problems and pleasures. The nice and comfortable interior (enough place for everybody, computers, open the whole day, exhibitions) plays an important role here. As our rooms have interesting architecture, it is possible to establish exhibitions and that is what we regularly do. The last exhibition is from our student who studies art as her minor. She was happy to have an opportunity to show her paintings to her friends and fellow-students. We all can enjoy her colourful and interesting works.

8. Conclusion

In my paper I want to prove that a small library can be as efficient as the big one if we could use ample opportunities it offers. Small libraries have their advantages if the priorities are fixed and not unreal. Certainly there is a danger to degenerate when the development process stops. When people work together and the thankfulness of the users is the main goal of our work, everything is possible.

References

1. Rutiku, S. and Kegelmann, R. (2003). Germanistik in Tartu/Dorpat. Rückblick auf 200 Jahre,

2. In Memoriam Claus Sommerhage (2005). Tartu University Press in Tartu

Notes

[1] Claus Sommerhage (1950 in Hamm – 2003 in Tartu) 1992-2003 the Professor of German Literature at the University of Tartu

[2]Leo Meyer (1830 in Bledeln near Hannover – 1910 in Göttingen, at the University of Dorpat 1865-1898. The list of his works look: Leo Meyer as University Dozent and Linguist, in : TRÜ Toimetised Nr. 125, Tartu 1962, 74-81

[3] DAAD- Deutscher Akademischer Austauschdienst (German Academic Exchange Service)

[4] In Memoriam Claus Sommerhage (2005),

[5] Versuch eines vollständigen Wörterbuches der Hochdeutschen Mundart in 4 Bänden. – Leipzig: Breitkopf, 1780

[6] Pormeister, Eve , Bilder des Weiblichen in der deutschsprachigen Schweizer Frauenliteratur. Tartu 2003

Sharing Knowledge on Workplace: What Factors Motivate Librarians to Share Their Knowledge?

Garoufallou Emmanouel[1,4], Siatri Rania[1,4], Asderi Stella[2,4] and Balatsoukas Panos[3,4]

[1]Lecturer & Principal Lecturer, Department of Library Science and Information Systems, Alexander Technological Educational Institution of Thessaloniki, Greece
[2]American College of Thessaloniki, Library, Greece
[3]Department of Information Science, Loughborough University, UK
[4]Deltos Research Group

Abstract: The key feature in the development of any organization is knowledge sharing among its employees. There are various factors that motivate people to share their knowledge and managing its flow assists in its dissemination. The aim of this study is to investigate which intrinsic or extrinsic factors motivate librarians to share knowledge in the workplace. To be more specific, a research project was conducted in April 2008 which was based on a questionnaire instrument and semi-structured interviews. The participants were 34 librarians working in four academic and college libraries in Greece. The data collected were analyzed using the SPSS software. Apart from the descriptive statistics, a set of Spearman's correlations were used in order to check any connection between the values under research. The findings revealed that librarians appeared to value more intrinsic rather than extrinsic motivation for sharing knowledge. The mean values showed that the main factors motivating librarians to share knowledge was the fact that it was important for them to do so (6.59) and because they could benefit from other colleagues, by sharing knowledge (6.35). Of less importance was the fact that it might help them get promoted (2.24). The Spearman's correlations were performed in order to test any relationship between any of the four general knowledge sharing attitudes and the factors of intrinsic and extrinsic motivation. One example is that of the attitude "When I have knowledge that might be relevant for others in the library, I do what I can to make it available to them" and the intrinsic motivation factor "I enjoy doing so" ($r_s=0,479$, $N=34$, $p<0.01$, two-tailed). The results of this study suggest that librarians acknowledge the importance of the role of intrinsic motivation in knowledge sharing and thatteam-based culture can benefit the success of knowledge sharing initiatives within libraries.

Keywords: Knowledge management; Sharing Knowledge; Knowledge flow; Motivational factors; Motivation; Academic librarians; Academic libraries.

1. Introduction

Knowledge Management is an organisational practice that manages to balance the human and technological aspects of current organisations into a new management philosophy that values knowledge as an important capital for organisations. Knowledge management establishes the role of knowledge sharing as an important part of a knowledge-centred organisation. Knowledge sharing is an active procedure of constant knowledge transformation (for example, from tacit to explicit knowledge) and generation (from explicit to tacit or from tacit to tacit knowledge) (Nonaka and Takeuchi, 1995). According to Ardchvilli et al (2003) knowledge sharing includes the "willingness to share knowledge" (or contribution of new knowledge) and the "willingness to use knowledge". Knowledge sharing, however, is not just a mechanism for information access and delivery. It is an ongoing procedure of value addition to the organisation's intellectual capital. In addition, it supports the establishment of competitive advantage (Dixon, 2000), the democratization of organisational structures (Huseman and Goodman, 1999) and promotes the idea of a learning organisation (Jashapara, 2004) through the development of sociotechnical networks and communities of practice.

Motivation is an important factor for the successful implementation of a knowledge sharing culture. Several studies have investigated the impact of extrinsic and intrinsic motivation on the development and sustainability of a knowledge sharing initiative both in public and private organisations (for a review of these studies see Balatsoukas, 2005). Researchers have defined extrinsic motivation as the process of engaging employees in knowledge sharing through the use of monetary rewards or the fear of punishment, while intrinsic motivation is based on individual's own interest and satisfaction (Harder, 2008). Although there are several frameworks, such as the SDT that have been used for the investigation of extrinsic and intrinsic motivation in the context of Knowledge sharing (Harder, 2008), these have been most frequently applied in the case of knowledge workers who are occupied in the corporate sector or government bodies. Therefore, there are no studies investigating the role of motivation in the knowledge sharing practices of librarians. Although libraries promote and disseminate information to their customers little is known about how knowledge is shared and disseminated among librarians (Garoufallou et al., 2008).

2. Aim and objectives

The aim of this study is to investigate the factors that motivate librarians to share knowledge in their workplace. The objectives of this study were:

- To examine the impact of extrinsic motivation on knowledge sharing attitudes (contributing and using knowledge);
- To examine the impact of intrinsic motivation on knowledge sharing attitudes (contributing and using knowledge)

3. Methodology

This study is built on a questionnaire instrument and personal interviews with librarians. The questionnaire consists of three sections. The first section collected demographic data about the respondents' gender, educational level, position in the library, type of library and number of years in the job. The second section listed four questions that investigated respondents' perceptions towards general knowledge sharing attitudes. Finally, section three included 16 questions about several factors of intrinsic and extrinsic motivation that could influence knowledge contribution and use. The contents of the questionnaire derived from the motivational matrix for knowledge sharing (Balatsoukas, 2005) and a questionnaire instrument developed by Harder (2008). The items included in the last two sections followed a seven point semantic referential scale (1 = Strongly Disagree, 7= Strongly agree). The population of the sample consisted of all librarians working in four academic and college libraries of the city of Thessaloniki, Greece. The libraries that participated in this study were the central academic libraries of the Alexander Technological Institute of Thessaloniki and the University of Macedonia as well as the libraries of the American Farm School and the Anatolia College of Thessaloniki. A combination of non-probabilistic sampling techniques were employed for the selection of the sample of this study. These were a purposeful and a snowballing sampling technique. The selection of these techniques was based on the difficulty in obtaining or creating a complete frame sample, the exploratory nature of this study as well as for time and cost efficiency. The questionnaire was piloted and then circulated via e-mail to an initial sample that was purposefully selected. Then each recipient of the questionnaire was asked to pass it to other colleagues willing to provide input to it. Although the data collection process is still in progress this paper is focused on the preliminary analysis of the data collected during April 2008 from 34 respondents that is a subset of the data collected so far. The data collected were analysed using the SPSS software. The task of data analysis involved the calculation of descriptive statistics as well as a set of Spearman's correlations. The reliability of this questionnaire was also tested using Cronbach's alpha. The results validated the reliability of the instrument which was above the 0.7 threshold (Cronbach's alpha = 0.809). Finally, respondents of the questionnaire were invited to participate in short structured interviews. These interviews were focused on the collection of further qualitative data about the factors that influenced librarians' motivation and attitudes towards knowledge sharing. The analysis of the data from the interviews was based on the content analysis technique.

4. Results

A total of 34 librarians participated in the study. Twenty eight respondents were females while six were males. The majority of participants in the study was working in a university library (n=21) and the remaining 13 in a college library. Their position in these libraries varied, including library assistants (n=3) library directors (n=4), system librarians (n=4) subject librarians (n=14) reference librarians (n=5) and cataloguers (n=1). Twenty six librarians had a qualification in library or information science. Finally, most participants in this study had been working for less than 10 years in their libraries (n= 20), five respondents had been working between 10–14 years, four respondents between 15–19 years and two for more than 20 years.

Table 1 presents a summary of the mean values of each item of the questionnaire. It is worth mentioning that librarians tended to value more intrinsic rather than extrinsic motivation for sharing knowledge. In the case of extrinsic motivation, they perceived that the evaluation of job performance was the most important factor that motivated them to share knowledge.

Table 1. Attitudes towards knowledge sharing

Knowledge sharing attitudes	**Mean**
When I have knowledge that might be relevant for others in the library, I do what I can to make it available to them.	6.12
When a colleague asks me for help or assistance, I share what knowledge I may have on the subject	6.71
I stay updated by exploring the information I can find on the different knowledge systems and databases	6.03
When I encounter a work related problem, I seek knowledge and help from my colleagues	6.29
Factors of intrinsic motivation	
I share knowledge because is an important value for me	6.59
I share knowledge because I want to find out whether my ideas are relevant	4.97
I share knowledge because I think it is an important part of my job	6.18
I share knowledge because I enjoy doing so	5.76
I share knowledge because the senior management does so	3.58
I share knowledge because I trust my colleagues	5.15
I share knowledge because I am working as a team with other colleagues	5.94
I share knowledge for the pleasure of discovering new insights	6.24
I share knowledge because I can use knowledge from others which is provided to me just in time	6.06
I share knowledge because I can use knowledge of value from other colleagues	6.35
I share knowledge because it is easy to do so	4.06
Factors of extrinsic motivation	
I share knowledge because It may help me get promoted	2.24
I share knowledge because I want my manager to praise me	2.59
I share knowledge because I want my colleagues to praise me	2.97
I share knowledge because it may help me get a salary increase	2.26
I share knowledge because it is important for the evaluation of my job performance	4.85

A set of Spearman's correlation tests were performed to test whether there was a relationship between any of the four general knowledge sharing attitudes and the factors of intrinsic and extrinsic motivation (see Table 1). The findings revealed that the statement "When I have knowledge that might be relevant for others in the library, I do what I can to make it available to them" was positively correlated with two intrinsic motivation factors ("I want to find out whether my ideas are relevant": $r_s = 0.410, N = 34, p < 0.05,$ two-tailed; and "I enjoy doing so": $r_s = 0.479, N = 34, p < 0.01,$ two-tailed) and only one factor of extrinsic motivation ("I share knowledge because it is important for the evaluation of my job performance": $r_s = 0.393, N = 33, p < 0.05,$ two-tailed). Interesting were the findings of the correlations between the statement "When a colleague asks me for help or assistance, I share what knowledge I may have on the subject" and the motivation factors. In particular, this statement was significantly correlated at the 0.05 level with six intrinsic motivation factors but with none of the extrinsic motivation factors. The six factors were: "I share knowledge because I want to find out whether my ideas are relevant", "I enjoy doing so", "the senior management does so", "I trust my colleagues", "I am working as a team with other colleagues" and "I can use knowledge from others which is provided to me just in time". In the case of the third general knowledge sharing attitude: "I stay updated by exploring the information I can find on the different knowledge systems and databases", the results of the Spearman's correlations revealed that there were no significant correlations between this attitude and the motivation factors. Finally, significant correlations were observed between the forth knowledge sharing attitude: "When I encounter a work related problem, I seek knowledge and help from my colleagues" and three intrinsic motivation factors. These were: "I share knowledge because I think it is an important part of my job": $r_s = 0.376, N = 34, p < 0.05,$ two-tailed; "I share knowledge because I am working as a team with other colleagues": $r_s = 0.425, N = 34, p < 0.05,$ two-tailed; and "I share knowledge because I can use knowledge from others which is provided to me just in time": $r_s = 0.442, N = 34, p < 0.01,$ two-tailed.

The analysis of the interviews revealed that librarians perceived knowledge sharing as an important aspect of their work. In particular, the main factors that made them share knowledge with others included: team-working, the production of new knowledge, improvement of job performance, "just in time" delivery of new knowledge, learning and self improvement, effective and efficient problem solving, trust, development of the library's knowledge capital and competitive advantage, sharing of common objectives among the library staff and satisfaction.

5. Conclusions

Despite the small sample size, the results of this study suggest that librarians acknowledge the importance of the role of intrinsic motivation in knowledge sharing. In particular, factors like the 'just in time' provision of knowledge or the development of a team-based culture can benefit the success of knowledge sharing initiatives within libraries. There is a need for research, however, to investigate further the knowledge sharing behaviour of librarians as well as to compare their attitudes with their colleagues in different types of libraries as well as with other professions within the public sector.

References

Ardichvili, A,. Page, V and Wentling, T. (2003). Motivation and barriers to participation in virtual knowledge-sharing communities of practice. *Journal of knowledge management*, **7**, 1, 64 - 77.

Balatsoukas, P., (2005). *From information to knowledge management*. In Proceedings of the 14th Hellenic Conference of Academic Libraries, Athens: TEIA, 63-71. http://eprints.rclis.org/archive/00011871/01/14psab014.pdf, [accessed 14.05.2009].

Garoufallou, Emmanouel, Panos, Balatsoukas, Stella, Asderi, Panagiota, Ekizoglou and Rania, Siatri (2008). *What factors motivate librarians to share knowledge in their workplace?* International Conference of Marketing & Management Systems (ICMMS) 23-25 May 2008, Athens, Greece. http://www.icmms.org/ [accessed 10.5.2009]

Dixon, N. M., (2000). *Common Knowledge: how companies thrive by sharing what they know*. Boston, Mass. Harvard Business school press.

M. Harder, (2008). *How do rewards and management styles influence the motivation to share knowledge*. Social Science research network http://papers.ssrn.com/sol3/papers.cfm?abstract_id=1098881, [accessed 28.04.2009]

Huseman, R. C. and Goodman, J. P., (1999). *Leading with knowledge: the nature of competition in the 21st century*. Thousand Oaks: Sage publications.

Jashapara, A., (2004). *Knowledge management: an integrated approach*. London: Prentice hall.

Nonaka, I. and Takeuchi, H., (1995). *The knowledge creating company: how Japanese companies create the dynamics of innovation*. New York: Oxford University press.

A New Perspective on E-Resource Management

Sanda Bercovici

The Hebrew University of Jerusalem, Israel
E-mail: sandab@savion.huji.ac.il

At the beginning of the 21st century, academic libraries are more and more involved in the creative process of knowledge. New management strategies have been introduced into the reorganization of academic libraries, and they are involved more and more in producing higher performance, in both theory and practice.

The diversity of academic libraries is the direct result of the various types of higher studies institutions, which have different missions, different organizational structures, accents on different academic subjects, and different student populations. Collections content and library services are designed to assist both the educational process and scholarly research in the specific institution. The library must provide answers geared to the specific needs of the patron.

Academic library activity is not static, it has to be sensitive to changes in the external world, which have a high impact on collections, access and services. The continuous changes in higher education and the dissemination of information affect information dissemination, information use and human knowledge. Technological, intellectual and social changes in libraries have a powerful influence on the way libraries inform the community, and also on the way in which library specialists understand their role in higher education and in the educational process as a whole.

The success of an academic library depends on how it understands the dynamism and the complexity of the academic world; this understanding influences its organizational structure, the activity and decisions. The rapid changes taking place at the end of the 20th century and the beginning of the new millennium present a challenge to academic libraries. Analysis of various factors indicates that, to a large measure, library resource allocation influences the organizational transformations and activities of the different services.

Information technology and Information communication (IT and ICT) technology are the factors which have changed the image and the organizational structure of the academic library. It follows that information strategies and their allocation are essential not only for library development, but even for the existence of this subsystem in the university.

The marketing of library services has become primary in information management decisions and in the emphasis placed on library contributions to decisions about the educational process in universities. Although the role of libraries in the information society is better and better understood, it is still not enough.

In many countries, libraries are involved in the process of organizing electronic bibliographies for distance teaching; in others, libraries maintain the electronic resources. In most countries, reference services have been reorganized and extended in order to give immediate answers to the user community. These new phenomena in the academic libraries activity demand an increase in professional staff; as a result, the human resources structure is changing: specialists in information science, in hardware and technicians form some 50% of the library staff. The use of centralized library cataloguing services is the result of the decrease in the number of specialists in technical services (cataloging and classification).

The library plays an important role in the whole information structure of the university. In an era of information dissemination, the libraries deal both with adaptation and with information management (including the management of resources and metadata). The libraries support the research of the local scientific community by the popularization of resources organized by profile and by services on individual alerts, on demand. These activities are allowed by the use of advanced software as SFX, Metalib, Verde, TDOne.

Collection development is still one of the most important roles of an academic library. It satisfies the needs of university users by collecting and preserving all types of relevant resources, but in my opinion, the heart of the profession is user education, while considering user demands.

The progress of IT has affected the integration of different types of documents, influencing the collection development. Collection management includes decisions related to acquisition-sharing policy, to the problematical issues of cataloging or classification of a new typology of resources, to document digitization and archiving and to making them accessible through the Internet.

The concept of "closeness to sources" of the traditional printed collections has been modified, influenced by the multiple access possibilities of a virtual global library, with varied collections of research resources. The information crisis, which caused a need for increased allocations for acquisitions in the academic libraries, has now been affected by the recent financial crisis. Both crises have forced libraries to look for new organizational solutions, based on the features of the new typology of documents and on advanced IT.

. The availability of e-resources challenges libraries to utilize those resources broadly and efficiently and to extract their maximal potential and value. Today's libraries have taken on the challenges of discovery, linking, searching and managing resources, including the management of the back office.

For many decades, the library catalog was the major discovery tool for print collections. In the era of IT, huge developments which have influenced the library collections format, users enjoy the benefits of the e-resources.

E-resources are more dynamic and consequently more volatile; providers, publishers and accordingly URLs and other relevant data change and therefore require discovery tools optimized to support them.

Software programs as SFX and TDNet are important tools for the management of e-resources in the academic libraries, changing the whole concept of work, study and research.

- ***SFX***® is the most widely used link server and the linking solution of choice for over 1,500 libraries worldwide.
- SFX provides users with context-sensitive links to full-text articles and other library-defined resources including the online public access catalog (OPAC) local holdings, preferred document-delivery suppliers, related Web-based resources and services, local information repositories, and a range of other services.
- SFX is in use at the Hebrew University of Jerusalem and the A-Z list is containing not only Latin 1 journals but also a Hebrew A-Z list .

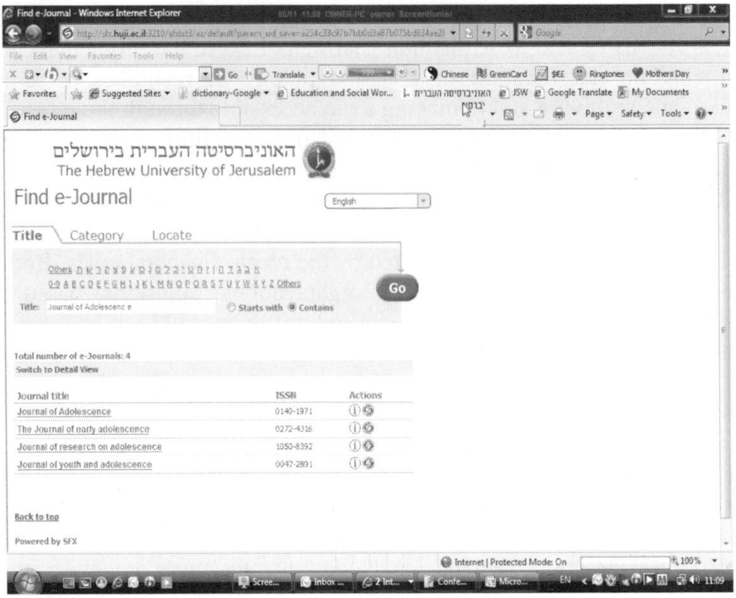

The institution users, with specific IPs may also access the journals on the SFX A-Z list through Google Scholar.

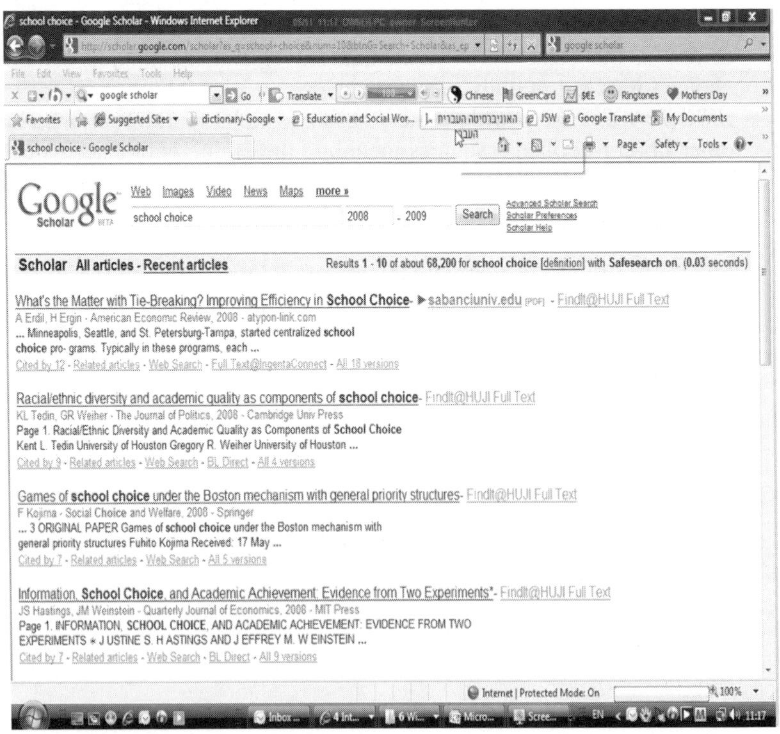

Based on TDNet concept, in the new tool-TDOne discovery layer gathers information of both indexed and federated content.

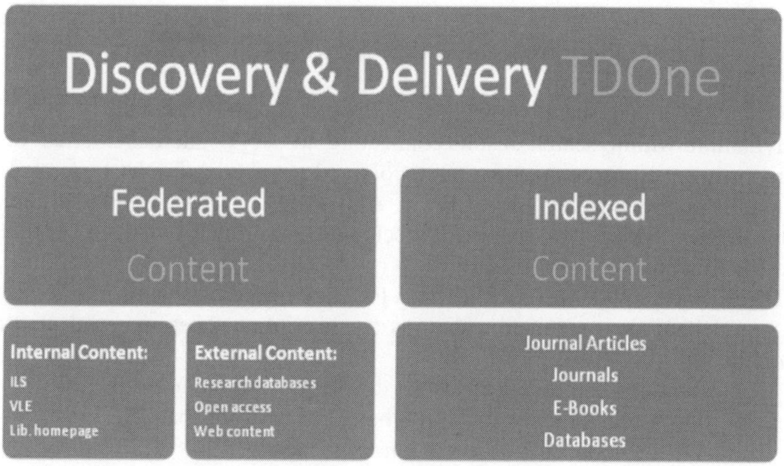

Indexed content means that the content is managed by TDNet and is based on a central knowledgebase and discovered by querying TDNet knowledgebase.

TDNet offers a core solution for *Access, Management, Search and Find*

TDNet is the infrastructure for all linking products

The content – data includes not only the well known traditional library resources, but much more, as:

e-journals (individual / packages),

e-books, conference proceedings , working papers

databases & publisher collections

e-TOC Metadata – title, author, volume, issue, page, date, links, etc.

TDNet is a dynamic tool , providing real-time updating. It also provides an A-Z portal for journals, e-books, databases and collections.

The TDNet TOUResolver is an open URL link resolver,

The TDNet holdings manager is the tool for local catalogue maintenance and data exchange. TDNet provides also a TOC alerting service and an overlap reporting tool.

The federated search is working on the content discovered by querying non TDNet systems, such as the library catalog, digital collections, databases, websites etc.

The A-Z list provides browsing by content type – journals, e-books, databases.

The new service has important advantages such as : the management of comprehensive content, based on a central extensive knowledge base .Through federating, any web-based resource which has a search engine can be integrated relatively easy and fast .

TDOne has a fast and easy setup, based on TDNet existing knowledge base – mostly done by TDNet, saving time and workload for the library.

The TDNet OpenURL resolver – the TOUResolver is based on TDNet extensive knowledgebase, and also on an article level knowledge base. It enables users to complete missing citations, to repair wrong data within citations, provides links from a reference to the most appropriate copy/full text and locates item availability within institutional resources.

TDNet Federated search combines with text analysis technology for efficient navigation within search results,connecting to ANY internal/external resource, supporting various connections protocols and standards. TDNet Federated search supports authentication as LDAP, AD, Proxy etc. It provides a direct and OpenURL linking to retrieved documents, a multi-language support and personalization.

TDNet also provides a set of services for back office management of e-resources. Among them are acquisition data as : subscription dates, renewal alerting and pricing.

As librarians, the SFX and TDNet developers ask themselves:

- Do we really know the user's behavior in cyber space?
- Do we know enough about our users' needs?
- How and what are they looking for?
- How may we help them?

As may be concluded from the analysis of SFX and TDNet tools, they took on three important challenges:

to search any internal and external resources from one point of access,
navigate efficiently within search results,
and provide real-time retrieved document analysis.

4. Digital Resources and New Library Models

Digitizing Library Resources for New Modes of Information Use in Uganda

Helen M. Byamugisha

Makerere University Library P.O. Box 7062 Kampala-Uganda

Abstract: People have become increasingly dependent on digital information and the Internet as a medium for gaining and exchanging information. However, despite promising developments, numerous challenges that are related to digital content and collection, interoperability, standards, knowledge organization systems, users and usability, legal, organizational and social issues, staff education; infrastructure; language barrier and technology remain. This paper concludes that digital libraries are a key technology especially for developing countries. They can assist human development by providing a non-commercial mechanism for distributing humanitarian information on topics such as health, agriculture, nutrition, hygiene, sanitation, water supply and many other areas ranging from disaster relief to medical education. The paper recommends that adapting quickly to new digital technology is vital for success.

Keywords: Information; Digital information; Digital depositories; Digital libraries and technology.

1. Introduction

Libraries are an essential component of a nation's information infrastructure. Historically, libraries have played various key roles in information-oriented societies as the major storehouses of human kind's recorded knowledge. However, the physical media that store the recorded knowledge are constantly undergoing metamorphosis due to continuous technological advancements and innovations. Currently, we live in the so-called "Digital Era" where by information is recorded, stored, retrieved and disseminated in the digital form unlike the past when information was accessed in analog formats. Nowadays information is capable of being stored on specially constructed electronic media and is retrieved whenever required in the most fundamental form, as arrays of zeros and ones (i.e. binary format). Thus, digitization of the library resource materials opens up new modes of use, enables a much wider potential audience and gives renewed means of viewing our cultural heritage with a higher degree of clarity and in a much more compact structure.

2. Why Digital Libraries

The rise of an information economy has brought about an information age that is highly reliant on information and communication technologies (ICTs) (Ngulube,

2004:21). It is an age where the survival and development of human kind are ultimately defined by the use, production and consumption of information. The African Information Initiative adopted the digital agenda in 1996 in order to transform stagnating African economies (ECA, 1996:9). In 2001, the 34th session of the Commission for Africa reaffirmed that ICTs were key to the economic and social development of the African continent (Ngulube, 2004). Digital libraries are organizations that provide the resources, including specialized staff, to select, structure, offer intellectual access to, interpret, distribute, preserve the integrity of, and ensure the persistence over time collections of digital works so that they are readily and economically available for use by a defined community or set of communities (Waters, 1998; Digital Libraries Federation, 2002). The component characteristics of digital libraries are the storage of information in digital form, direct usage of communication networks for accessing, obtaining information, and copying by either downloading or online/offline printing from a master file (Husler, 1996). According to Husler (1996), traditional libraries, which were known as repositories of knowledge, have hence become accessible in database form; the Internet and the Web are making knowledge universal and linked internationally. In summary then, a digital library maintains all, or a substantial part, of its collection in computer-possible form as an alternative, supplement, or complement to the conventional printed and microfilm materials that currently dominate library collections. Digital librarians, including those in Uganda, enable managing very large amounts of data, preserve unique collections, provide faster access to information, facilitate dealing with data from more than one location, and enhance distributed learning environments. Digital librarians also help to perform searches that are manually not feasible and offer to protect the content of the owner's information (Husler, 1996). Some of the forces responsible for digital library development are the changing nature of the book, the patron, the library, standards, information retrieval and metadata.

The changing nature of the book

The book has undergone a series of changes that have made its storage and use more efficient (Koehler, 2004). The changes include transitions in form - from stone slab to papyrus scroll to acid free paper codex to electronic bits. Tables of contents and indexing standards have been developed. More recently cataloguing and classifying standards to describe books in a larger context - the library and later the union catalog were developed. These forms of description and meta-description have allowed librarians to develop organized systems for our information container collections. Koehler (2004) posits that one factor that will affect user-centric models in the libraries of the future is the very nature of information containers. In this case, digital collections provide new additional opportunities for organization.

The changing nature of the patron

Koehler (2001) emphasizes that the future vision of the digital library must include some speculation on potential changes in the kinds of services demands that the library patrons will make on the digital library of the future. The author thinks that it is possible to speculate on how those demands will shape those libraries. The library users do and will want a full array of library services delivered to some point of delivery now at least through some electronic means of delivery-Internet, telephone, and others. Physical objects may be transferred by courier, faxed/scanned and transmitted or accessed online; the popularity of e-books and e-journals will grow. The patrons also expect their libraries to provide different services or rather additional services than once they did before.

The changing nature of the library

The library world has undergone much re-thinking in the last quarter century by embracing the idea of the "library without walls (Birdsall, 1994). The 1990s witnessed the explosion of the Internet and particularly the popularity of the World Wide Web. The Web proved to be both a conduit for and a significant source of an immense amount of information, leading some people to predict the displacement of traditional information institutions like libraries. The patrons' expectations for a distance service delivery across library services have increased. Patrons have come to expect a wide variety of automated push and or pull services form libraries and from a distance. The Internet has led to a redefinition of some but certainly not all library functions. Koehler (1999) however recognized that the Web itself lacks library characteristics. There has been much discussion of variant forms of libraries between "pure traditional" and "pure digital" or the "hybrid library". To understand any aspect of library futures, one must give some consideration to probable changes to the information containers themselves and the institutions in which those information containers may be housed Koehler (2004).

3. The Standards Wars

The establishments of standards of the digital library futures will be dictated by the standardization decisions made now. Koehler (2004) observed that standards have never been more important. Technology, society and systems, are all intertwined and lead to unanticipated consequences. Similarly, changing library standardization and increased universalization of that standardization will lead to unanticipated consequences in the digital library community and in society in general. Consider for example, cataloging and classification and differences among different classification schemes. Many academic libraries in the United States have undergone retrospective conversion from DDC to LCC. Does this suggest that we are treading toward a single standard? The MARC environment has seen the development of a number of different national systems to support local linguistic and stylistic requirements. The MARC standards have evolved. For example USMARC and CANMARC merged as MARC21. Significant limits have already been placed on the content licenses, particularly libraries and their users on their ability to transfer access to or to make copies of the content. If libraries continue to acquire more contemporary and retrospective content in digital under license from second parties, the ability of libraries to continue to serve their users as they have traditionally done may be significantly circumscribed in the future.

Information retrieval and metadata

One of the primary functions of a library is to develop its collection in keeping with the underlying philosophical purpose of the library. What may be appropriate or useful for one patron may not be appropriate or useful for another. Koehler (2004) suggests that expert intermediaries, ultimately human beings, but aided by expert systems provide and will continue to provide those services in the digital libraries of the future. Metadata systems have increased both in number and complexity. The purpose of metadata and metametadata, as with any cataloguing, classification, or indexing system is to provide description in addition to the original or native document. Typically we want improved description to allow for better storage and retrieval of the object and the information contained therein. These systems will span all classes of objects-text, images, audio, and video and multimedia. These will be coupled with expert level search and retrieval systems as well as the end user. Both expert and end user systems will probably have complex human-computer interfaces to facilitate the search and retrieval process.

Higher education needs

The Internet is not a replacement for books, but it is imperative that libraries reposition themselves within their institutions in order to continue to ensure access to information, education, people, services and ICT. Libraries find themselves in a transitional phase, as they adapt to the needs of an innovative higher education sector. The implementation of the strategic vision is not solely the responsibility of libraries and computer centers. Institutions as a whole can and must implement it. Every opposition must be overcome - for example, the library versus the computer center, electric versus printed information, or centralized versus decentralized systems. A sound budget is needed to find some way out of the present fiscal crisis. Schumann emphasized that information provision is an essential factor in research and teaching - for both the natural and the social sciences. He advised that existing institutions and newly created virtual or project-related organizational units must work together in a joined-up way. In the face of reduced budgets, the new challenges must be met with technical innovations, staff training and development, changes to the working environment and by suitable labor and business models. Bundy explained what he thinks it means for libraries to go beyond their traditional role of merely providing information. In his opinion, the academic library is the driving force for change in the area of education. Unfortunately, library budgets continue to be reduced. Bundy calls for a change in the entire system of higher education in order to meet the demands of users. Libraries cannot manage this alone, but they must nevertheless participate in this transition even to the extent of contributing to the curriculum.

Technology push

The focus of most development at present is tools to integrate content that is already being managed by the library. Cox and Yeats (2002) reviewed library-oriented portals solutions and products available in the United Kingdom: This can mean one or all of integrating multiple resources for the user into a comprehensible landscape; allowing cross-searching or searching of many databases with one interface; personalization; behind the scenes authentication; and the enhancement of simple bibliographic records with tables of contents, and dust cover images. Also implied are management tools to customize the gateway for user groups and to consolidate usage statistics. Many of the systems also have a capability to manage the digitization process and local digital collections. Other solutions exist to solve some of these problems and none offer as much control to the library, or such a complete professional solution.

Benefits of Digital Libraries

Digital libraries are a key technology especially for developing countries. They can assist human development by providing a non-commercial mechanism for distributing humanitarian information on topics such as good governance, health, agriculture, nutrition, education, hygiene, sanitation and water supply. Many other areas, ranging from disaster relief to medical education, also benefit from new methods of information distribution. Perhaps even more important than disseminating information originating in the developed world is the need to foster the ability for people in developing countries to build information collections locally.

4. Human Development

Just as industrialization and globalization have increased the gulf between the haves and have-nots, information and communications technology is creating a chasm between the "knows" and "know-nots" (Witten *et al,* 2003). Witten *et al...* (2003) further observed that in the developing world, digital libraries provide perhaps the first really compelling *raison d'être* for computing technology. Five important areas where digital libraries can promote human development include dissemination of human information, disaster relief, preservation and propagation of indigenous culture, locally produced collections of information and then, new opportunities to enter the global marketplace.

Dissemination of humanitarian information

Traditional publishing and distribution mechanisms have tragically failed the developing world (Withen et al (2003). A wealth of essential humanitarian material is produced by various international organizations. Being produced by internationally-oriented, non-profit organizations, funded by all people on the planet, this information is, at least in principle, in the public domain: it could be made freely available in the form of networked digital libraries.

Disaster relief

Natural disasters, such as earthquakes or hurricanes, and man-made ones such as terrorist attacks or nuclear accidents, demand immediate and informed response in an environment where the local infrastructure may be unpredictable or severely damaged. The response to a crisis is characterized by the generation of large amounts of unstructured, multimedia data that must be acquired, processed, organized and disseminated sufficiently rapidly to be of use to crisis responders. Digital library technology allows organized collections of such information, graced with comprehensive searching and browsing capabilities, to be created very rapidly. Intelligence specific to the nature of a disaster, the geographical region and the logistic resources available for the relief effort can be gathered into a built-to-order digital library collection that combines targeted knowledge with general medical and sanitary information. A recent example is the Tsunami wave that killed thousands of people in Asia and left millions homeless.

Preservation and propagation of Indigenous Culture

Information about indigenous culture takes many guises: oral history in the form of narration and interviews; artifacts in the form of images and descriptions; songs in the form of audio recordings, music transcriptions, and lyrics; dances and ceremonies in the form of video, audio, written synopses and interpretations. Multimedia digital libraries allow such information to be integrated, recorded, browsed, and searched, within a uniform user interface. Because language is the vehicle of thought, communication and cultural identity, a crucial feature of digital libraries for culture preservation is the ability to work in local languages. This strengthens individual cultures, promotes diversity and reduces the dominance of only a few languages. Digital library applications in culture preservation have the advantage that the relevant information is readily available locally. But there are countless other scenarios that involve creating and distributing locally produced information collections. Teachers prepare educational material that addresses specific community problems, and adapt published material to employ local examples. Indigenous people have invaluable medicinal knowledge based on local plants or long-acquired knowledge of the cultivation and protection of local species. Such knowledge is vital: more than half of the world's most frequently prescribed drugs are derived from plants or synthetic copies of plant chemicals, and this trend is growing. Local groups assemble information collections that describe and reflect neighborhood conditions, providing new material for socio-cultural studies, fostering cultural exchange while retaining diversity, and increasing international understanding.

New opportunities to enter the global marketplace

The varied demands of digital library development, such as manual metadata extraction, collection organization, cataloging and information presentation, expand the range of tasks that the developing world can undertake, creating valuable new export markets. One of the most important developments of recent years is the establishment of open archives and institutional repositories. Preprints can be found there, as can electronic versions of dissertations, research data, teaching materials, and increasingly also articles that have gone through peer review processes. Rosenberg (2004) also sees the future market for scientific information and education in electronic information repositories. She noted that the repositories are connected with one another over global networks, and since they are based on public standards with digital libraries, the users will be offered more convenient and quicker access to the required information.

5. Challenges of Digital Libraries

The long-term preservation of digital information is a very complex task confronting various challenges, many of which are still subject to profound research. Largely dependent on the primary purpose and the orientation of the project, is the selection of the material the repository shall be composed of. Hereby, the source of the data is determined at first. On the basis of this, a policy has to be declared, whether the material will be handled very selectively, forming a well-sorted collection, or rather gathered in an automatic fashion, resulting in a comprehensive archive. Installing proper storage facilities is a prerequisite for a well working repository. Thereby, a robust and capacious solution is required, but at the same time it needs to be flexible enough to adapt to advances in technology. Digital data is prone to decay. This is not only due to physical deterioration of the storage media used, but to a much greater extent caused by quick succession of ever superior systems replacing hardware as well as software. Because of this evolution, access to digital documents in the long run is at great danger. Strategies have to be developed to counteract this loss of information. Those involve converting data in regular cycles to a subsequent data format that is in use at that time. Another approach sets out to emulate on a future computer then obsolete system environments. However, great effort has still to be put into the research and implementation of such solutions. Ultimately, access has to be provided to the depository. Allowing a convenient and efficient usability of the collections constitute an ongoing task. Furthermore, economics and legal issues demand consideration. Much remains to be done to achieve the realization of such a venture. Yet, steps have to be taken immediately at a high priority taking into account what is at stake. One of the key problems found in the digital library of the present and one that will persist into the future is maintaining the match between the fluid content and its description in the library, digital or otherwise. There is already an emerging literature to point to the complexity and difficulty in maintaining that match, and many conclude, for example, that Web documents, among the most ephemeral of digital material, may be too elusive for serious long-term collecting (Koehler, 2002; Markwell and Brooks, 2002; Nelson and Allen, 2002; Rumsey, 2002). Shiri (2003) identified some of the challenges related to the implementation, development and evaluation of digital libraries to be:

Digital content and collections

This category refers to individual digital objects and collections of objects in repositories encompassing a variety of materials in different digital formats. Shiri (2003) observed that one major challenge with regard to metadata is the diversity of digital information formats. The author noted that there are challenges associated with digital content: for instance conversion of printed materials into digital format and creation of digital- only materials for the purpose of a particular digital library. Digital collections require well-structured metadata schemes to describe digital objects and content at various levels of granularity. Structural and descriptive metadata are two general classes of metadata of particular relevance. Shiri (2003) propounded that one major challenge with regard to metadata is the diversity of digital formats and the ways in which they should be described in different collections with different target audience and uses. In the electronic environment, institutions and individuals license access to content; they do not own the containers that surround that content. Libraries have already found that they are limited in the scope and range of patrons who may have access to their licensed collections. For example, some academic libraries cannot allow people who are not part of their university access to certain licensed electronic content. However, had that information been contained in purchased "paper" journals, under the doctrine of first sale, there would be no issue. Indeed, given copyright and contract provisions, most electronic material cannot be copied and transferred through interlibrary loan (Koehler 2004).

Interoperability and Standards

Interoperability is one of the most heavily discussed issues in digital library research. Shiri (2003) mentioned that the requirement for interoperability is derived from the fact that various digital libraries with different architectures, metadata formats and underlying technologies wish to intellectually interact. The challenge however, is that this can only be done through applying a range of common protocols and standards. Standards within the context of digital libraries encompass all protocols and conventional that has been set for the digital library architecture, collections, metadata formats, interoperability and so forth. For all digital libraries in the world to have common standards is a big challenge particularly for the information scientist.

Knowledge organization systems, users and user ability

This category refers to a range of tools used for knowledge organization, classification and retrieval of knowledge in a general sense. Shiri (2003) acknowledged that one of the challenges is the way in which these interact with each other. Hilt (2002) mentioned that research is under way to investigate issues surrounding mappings and interoperability among various knowledge organization systems. In order to develop usable digital libraries, Shiri noted that researchers have addressed user behavior and user requirements in different contexts including academic environments, schools, government departments and business. One of the challenges is associated with the methodologies and data gathering techniques. He observed that researchers have tried to use a combination of tools and techniques to collect data for user evaluation.

Legal, organizational and social issues

Rights management, intellectual property and copy right issues are all legal aspects of digital libraries. Shiri (2003) intimated that social issues in relation to digital libraries center on the ways in which people view digital libraries and their usefulness; and the extent to which they are integrated into people's lives and social activities. Every government must adopt common laws and procedures so as to eliminate misuse and theft of information. Filtering systems should be used so that genuine users are not inconvenienced. An information product is intellectual property (Thurow, 1997). The protection of intellectual property rights and privacy are the two areas the World Intellectual Property Organization (WIPO) seriously is concerned with. Its December 1996 Diplomatic Conference produced two treaties: the WIPO Copyright Treaty and WIPO Treaty on Performances and Phonograms. The first Copyright Treaty supplements the century-old Berne.

Staff education

Education and training are fundamental to the improvement of the preservation of digital resources (Rosenberg, 2004: vi). Competency and expertise in managing digital resources were identified in a study for the Research Libraries Group as major requirements (Hedstrom & Montegomery, 1998). Kemoni & Wamukoya (2000:134 identified lack of information skills due to inadequate training as one of the impediments to the management of electronic records at Moi University in Kenya. Ngulube (2002a:31) also discovered that expertise in the field of digitization in Southern Africa was very limited. Ngulube (2004) again noted that information studies programs in Africa did not reveal many modules that specifically address preservation of information containers and digital preservation. A survey by Liu (2004) on the subject of digital libraries in the United States, Canada, Europe and Asia revealed that some course contents were not up to date in the field of library and information technology. Ngulube (2004) emphasized that educators should bear in mind that rapid changes in information management technologies and the preservation challenges presented by diverse media require constant upgrading of knowledge and skills so that educators produce graduates who would be comfortable with the demands of the digital age. The answer to this is in giving due emphasis to in-house training.

Infrastructure

Digital libraries depend on Internet and intranet connections, yet there is no foolproof system to prevent virus damage. A more serious obstacle is that network access varies widely across the globe. Differences in technology between developed and developing countries persist. Whereas in 1998 more than a quarter of the US population were surfing the Internet, the figure for Latin America and the Caribbean was 0.8 per cent, for Sub-Saharan Africa 0.1 per cent, and for South Asia 0.04 per cent (UN, 1999). Schools and hospitals in developing countries are poorly connected. Even in relatively well-off South Africa, many hospitals and 75 per cent of schools have no telephone line. Universities are better equipped, but even there up to 1,000 people can depend on just one terminal. The Internet, as Arunachalam (1998) puts it, "is failing the developing world". While global satellite communication networks will eventually bring relief, this takes time and money. The core issue of IT development is the objective of providing universal access, in which libraries play a crucial role. Bringing Internet access to all is a daunting task. Physical distribution of information on recordable devices such as Compact disk read-only memory (CD-ROM), is a very practical format for areas with little Internet access.

Language barrier and technology

Language is the embodiment of a culture and preservation of identity is important. There are about 6,000 languages spoken in the world, and of these nearly 90 per cent are dying out. It is estimated that just over half of the world's population speak one of just five languages: Chinese, English, Hindi, Russian and Spanish. Uganda alone has over 50 languages. In the past libraries came into being at the behest of kings and nobles, and enjoyed aristocratic patronage. With the change to a democratic political system, the responsibility fell on the government. The private sector and the corporate sector especially, were not involved. Any contact was related to their own concerns, not the development of libraries. Now the private sector, particularly in advanced countries manufacturing Internet related equipment, is in a position to extend both material and financial support. Being the major producers of computer technology they are able to set up such industries in developing countries. Developing countries could offer incentives such as tax breaks, investment subsidies and so on. This alone would help in reducing the cost of goods needed for constructing a digital library. Unless this is achieved digital libraries and universal knowledge will be restricted to the elite familiar with one of the major languages of the world. The challenge is to evolve a strategy so as to provide information in the language required by the reader. While installed network software is easily detected, it is difficult to determine whether it is operational. Incorrectly installed or configured software is endemic in developing countries, because computers there are often cast-offs whose software is inappropriate to their present environment, yet system support to rectify the problems is unavailable.

6. Sustainability for Digital Libraries

Sustainability has become a buzzword in the field of new library projects and developments (Hamilton (2004). As McArthur *et al...* (2003) say, in the digital library context, sustainability is a broad term that refers to everything from technical issues about the digital preservation of materials, to the social questions surrounding the long-term accessibility of resources to the public at large. Traditional libraries may not regularly have to justify their existence but most, these days, need to fight to maintain their budgets. The sustainability question arises so frequently in the digital library world because digital initiatives tend to be introduced as special projects (Zorich, 2003). In many cases, insufficient thought has been given at the outset as to how they will turn into long-term developments. And at times of economic pressure, when even the core is questioned, anything else is vulnerable. The key to sustainability, therefore, is to reach a position where the digital library is no longer regarded as an add-on, but as part of this integral core (Zorich, 2003). The answer may include being essential, or an integral, uncuttable part of the organization. This is the status to which digital libraries must aspire (Hamilton 2004). Strategies for achieving sustainability of digital libraries include economic sustainability, finding champions, funding sources and self sustained growth.

Economic Sustainability

Economic sustainability is a softer, more political area than preservation, and consequently solutions are less tangible and concrete. Smith (2003) sums the position up as "the hardest part of sustainability - how to pay for it all". Hamilton (2004) states that there are no easy answers, which is one reason why in the past so many digital library projects have blossomed briefly and then withered. Hamilton (2004) recommended that one view is that more money should be spent on sustaining services and less on initiating projects, but in most cases it is best to start from the premise that external funding obtained to establish a project will rarely be an appropriate source to provide ongoing, unlimited funding for its continuation.

Finding Champions

It is rare that a digital library project is so intrinsically valuable that the host institution is forced to find funds for continuation. Hamilton (2004) suggests that one route towards backing the "withering" trend is to ensure strong branding, linking a successful product with the institution. The author advised that most projects require rallying support through conscious efforts to gain champions beyond the immediate circles and this is where strong, ideally charismatic, project leadership is important.

Funding Sources: the options

Sustainability options are categorized into subscription fees, charges for online courses, sponsorship/endowments, and integration (Hamilton, 2004). He advised that combinations of any of the four might be appropriate. Charging for access will be an option if charges would apply for similar physical information. Charges may also be acceptable for added-value services where basic services are free. Hamilton again stressed that if charges are deemed appropriate there are two approaches: charge from the start or allow free access initially, then charge once the users have been "hooked". The author warned that the availability of so much free information on the Web does create a barrier to payment by individuals who have to be convinced of the value of the particular information you are providing. If the payment will come from institutions rather than individuals, it is important to consider the position of budget holders. For many, payment for a new service will mean something else will have to be stopped. When dealing with academic libraries, the situation is further complicated by the existence of a wide variety of budget control systems ranging from fully devolved to fully centralized, so it can be difficult to target your marketing. Sponsorship and in-kind support can take many forms and creativity may be required to overcome institutional antipathy to and restrictions on advertising. Campbell (2000) gives examples of varied sources of sponsorship for Australian subject gateways ranging from endorsement through free publicity to solid financial support. In-kind contributions are often overlooked. As Zorich (2003) points out, this can lead to problems if the contribution is withdrawn, and it also means that organizations "cannot effectively use this support as evidence when funders seek tangible proof of outside financial commitments to a project". Hamilton (2004) believes that integration is the ultimate goal for many digital library project leaders. But it is hard to integrate a project once its funding has run out. It is also hard to plan for such integration from the outset but this must be the main approach. The formal business plan required by many funders should not be regarded as one more bureaucratic hurdle but the passport to a successful, sustainable digital library.

Self-sustained growth

Libraries in developing countries in particular rely primarily on governmental funding. The resource crisis has affected every field of activity. The problem is further confounded by the increasing cost of books and periodicals in developed countries and the falling value of the currencies of developing countries in the international market. Further periodic increases in freight charges add to the strain on the already low budget allocations. Also, many public and departmental libraries are understaffed. It is clear that relying on the government is not conducive to self-sustained growth. Under these circumstances it is better to explore ways to earn income so as to reduce dependence. This becomes all the more important in the context of globalization. It is therefore essential that adequate thought is given to finding financial resources for digital libraries and their upkeep.

7. Prospects of Digital Libraries

The technological infrastructure

Computers are not so hard to come by in developing countries as one might think. Their extraordinarily rapid rate of obsolescence, coupled with the developed world's voracious appetite for the latest and greatest, makes low-end machines essentially free: instead of clogging landfill sites many (although certainly not enough) find their way to developing countries. A 1998 World Bank survey of developing countries found three to 30 PCs per 1,000 people, depending on the poverty level (World Bank, 2000). With growth predicted at 20 per cent per year, it was estimated that by the year 2000 there were 50 million PCs in developing countries, serving a population of four billion!

Distributed collections

Electronic collectibles have become more commonplace (Koehler, 2004). Vendors, consolidators, and publishers are providing more and more content either directly to end users or to end users through libraries in electronic format. More monograph and serial titles are being offered to institutional and individual subscribers in either electronic format only or in print and electronic format. If the catalog is in digital format, the target object may or may not also be in similar format. Digitized content can be and very frequently is transmitted directly to the end user on demand from the catalog (Koehler, 2004). When libraries and individuals purchase information objects they own the container but not the content. Content ownership resides with the copyright holder. Nevertheless, as owners of the container, we may transfer the title to the container or lend it to others. We also have limited rights to copy the content. In the digital environment, where the concept of container is very different and content is licensed, the rules have changed.

User behavior

Studies have shown that students would like smaller digital portable systems rather than carry too many printed books, although this may be in addition to the printed books. Lynch (2001) predicted that users would carry their digital library in their pocket. In that case, their pocket may actually become a digital wearable system for that purpose. Nokia's research center, for example, had the idea of "virtual pockets" for some time (Lehikoinen, 2000), but the notion has not yet affected libraries. Koehler (2004) observed that the youngest generation of end-users has already learned to search for information independently. They learn and research in groups, move in parallel in diverse virtual worlds and wait impatiently 24 hours a day, all over the world, for immediate unlimited access to relevant information (in full text). Koehler (2004) advised that in order to satisfy these demands, issue-oriented, extremely fast and highly effective, flexible search and retrieval systems are necessary. Librarians can make a contribution here by increasing the information skills of the library users, supporting the process of electronic learning, and by getting involved in creating electronic archives and improving their profile and access.

8. Conclusions and Recommendations

Digital libraries are a key technology especially for developing countries. They can assist human development by providing a non-commercial mechanism for distributing humanitarian information on topics such as health, agriculture, nutrition, hygiene, sanitation and water supply, and other areas, ranging from disaster relief to medical education. The electronic revolution coupled with improvements in communication make it imperative to look beyond today and prepare for tomorrow. In order to promote continuous upgrading of digital libraries in Uganda, there is need for a national information policy to pave the way for the digital library era.

References

Ackerman, M.S & Fielding, R.T. (1995): Collection maintenance in the digital library. Proceedings of Digital Libraries '95, Austin, TX, 39-48, URL: http://www.ics.uci.edu/corps/ackerman.html. (Accessed 20/12/2004)

Borgman, C. (1999): What are digital libraries? Competing visions. *Information Processing & Management,* V. 35, No.3: 227-43.

Borgman, C, (2000): From Gutenberg to the Global Information Infrastructure: Access to information in the networked world, MIT Press, Cambridge, MA. Chen, H, (2000). Introduction to the special topic issue: part 2. *Journal of the American Society for Information Science*, Vol. 51, No. 4: 311-12.

Chowdhury, G. G. (2002). Digital libraries and reference services: present and future. *Journal of Documentation*. Vol.58, No. 3:258-283. URL:http://ninetta.emeraldinsight.com/vl=11085047/cl=17/nw=1/fm=html/rpsv/cw/mcb/00220418/v58n3/s1/p258 (accessed on 28/12/2004)

Digital Library Federation (2002): URL: http://www.diglib.org/ (Accessed 20/12/2004).

Economic Commission for Africa (ECA) (1996): African Information Society Initiative: An action framework to build Africa's information and communication infrastructure. Addis Ababa: ECA.

Frumkin, J. (2004). Defining digital libraries. *OCLC Systems & Services: International Digital Library Perspectives*. Vol. 20, No.4:155-156. http://www.meraldinsight.com/vl=14350097/cl=26/nw=1/fm=html/rpsv/cw/mcb/1065075x/v20n4/s4/p155 (Accessed on 28/12/2004).

Gladney, H.M. (1994): Digital library: Gross structure and requirements. URL: www.csdl.tamu.edu/csdl/DL94/paper/fox.html. (Accessed 21/12/2004)

Goldschmitt, R. (2004): 7th International Bielefeld Conference 2004: Thinking beyond digital libraries - designing the information strategy for the next decade. *Library Hi Tech*. Vol.22, No.4, 347-354. URL: http://ninetta.emeraldinsight.com/vl=11085047/cl=17/nw=1/fm=html/rpsv/cw/mcb/07378831/v22n4/s3/p347 (Accessed on 28/12/2004).

Hamilton, V. (2004): Sustainability for digital Libraries. *Library Review*, Vol. 53, No.8:392- 395; URL: http://ceres.emeraldinsight.com/vl=14350097/cl=26/nw=1/fm=html/rpsv/cw/mcb/00242535/v53n8/s1/p392 (Accessed on 28/12/2004).

Hutchinson Encyclopedia (1997): Digital libraries. Helicon: - London.

ITU (1999): World Telecommunication Development Report: Mobile Cellular. Telecommunication Union, Geneva.

JISC (2002): Funding Council objectives and the JISC strategy 2001-05. www.jisc.ac.uk/curriss/general/#g1. (Accessed 22/12/2004)

JISC (2002): JISC strategy review and progress report. www.jisc.ac.uk/curriss/general/#g1. (Accessed 21/12/2004)

Koehler, W.(2004): Digital Libraries, digital containers, library patrons, and visions for the future. *The Electronic Library,* Vol. 22, No.5:401 – 407

Koehler, W. (1999): Digital libraries and World Wide Web sites and page persistence. *Information Research*. Vol. 4, No.4. URL: http://InformationR.net/ir/4-4/paper60.html. (Accessed 27/12/2004).

Lehikoinen, J., (2000). Virtual Pockets. URL: www.computer.org/proceedings/iswc/0795/07950165abs.htm. (Accessed 28/12/2004)

Lynch, C. (2001): The battle to define the future of the book in the digital world. *First Monday*. Vol. 6, No.6. http:// firstmonday.org/issues/issue6_6/lynch/index.html. (Accessed 23/12/2004).

Marchionini, G. & Fox, E.A. (1999): Progress toward digital libraries: augmentation through integration, Information Processing & Management. Vol. 35, No.3:219-25.

Markwell, J & Brooks, D.W. (2002): Broken links: the ephemeral nature of educational books. *Journal of Science Education and Technology*, 11, 105-8.

Magara, E. (2002): Applications of digital libraries and electronic technologies in developing countries: practical experiences in Uganda. *Library Review* Vol.51, No.5:241 – 255

McArthur, D.J.; Giersch, S. & Burrows, H. (2003): Sustainability issues for the NSDL, Proceedings of the 2003. *Joint Conference on Digital Libraries (JCDL'03)*, Houston, TX: 395. http://csdl.computer.org/comp/proceedings/jcdl/2003/1939/00/19390395.pdf (Accessed 28/12/ 2004).

Nelson, M., &Allen, B., (2002): Object persistence and availability in digital libraries. D-Lib Magazine, 8, 1. URL: www.dlib.org/dlib/january02/nelson/01nelson.html (Accessed 28/12/2004).

Ngulube, P. (2004): A double-edged sword: Challenges and opportunities offered by the digital age to the African information society. ProLISSA 2004. Proceedings of the 3rd biennial DISSAnet Conference:21-40, Pretoria.

Nyamboga M. C. and Ongus W. R. (2004): Incorporating digital libraries module in the curriculum for library and information science education. Paper presented at the SCECSAL XVI, held on 5 – 9, July 2004, Kampala, Uganda.

Oppenheim, C. Smithson, D. (1999): What is the hybrid library? *Journal of Information Science*, Vol.25, No.2: 97-112.

Poll, R. (2004): Informationsverhalten und informationsbedarf der Wissenschaft.Teil 1 der Nutzungsanalyse des Systems der überregionalen Literatur- und Informationsversorgun. *Zeitschrift für Bibliothekswesen und Bibliographie*, 51, 2, 59- 76.

Ramana, P. Venkata and Chandrasekhar, R. V. (2003): Use of information technology in central university libraries of India". *DECIDOC Bulletin of Information Technology*, Vol. 23, No.2:25-42.

Rosenberg, D. (2004): Foreword. In: Chisenga, J. (Ed.). The use of ICTs in Africa public library services: A survey of ten countries in Anglophone Africa. Oxford: International Network for the Availalability of Scientific Publications (INASP): v-vi.

Rumsey, M. (2002): Runaway train: problems of permanence, accessibility, and stability in the use of Web sources in-law review citations. *Law Library Journal*, Vol. 94, No. 1: 27-39.

Rusbridge, C, (1998): Towards the hybrid library. *D-Lib Magazine*. www.dlib.org/dlib/july98/rusbridge/07rusbridge.html. (Accessed 20/12/2004).

Sharma, R.K &Vishwanathan, K.R. (2001): Digital Libraries: development and challenges. *library Review*, Vol.50. N0.1, http://ninetta.emeraldinsight.com/vl=11085047/cl=17/nw=1/fm=html/rpsv/cw/mcb/00242535/v50n1/s1/p10 (Accessed on 29/12/2004).

Shiri, A. (2003): Digital Library Research: Current developments and trends. *Library Review,* Vol. 52, no. 5, p.198-2002. http://ceres.emeraldinsight.com/vl=14350097/cl=26/nw=1/fm=html/rpsv/cw/mcb/00242535/v52n5/s1/p198 (Accessed on 28/12/2004)

Smith, A. (2003): Issues in sustainability: creating value for online users. URL: www.firstmonday.dk/issues/issue8_5/smith/ (Accessed 28/12/ 2004).

Sreenivasulu, V. (2000): The role of a digital librarian in the management of digital information systems (DIS)", In: The Electronic Library, Vol. 18, No.1, 2000, p.12 – 20 http://ceres.emeraldinsight.com/vl=14350097/cl=26/nw=1/fm=html/rpsv/cw/mcb/02640473/v18n1/s1/p12 (Accessed on 28/12/2004)

The Greenstone Software. http://www.cs.waikato.ac.nz/ nzdl/gsdl-docs/Download.html (Accessed 20/12/2002).

Thurow, L.C, (1997): Needed: a new system of intellectual property rights. *Harvard Business Review*: 95-103.
Toffler, A. (1980): Third wave: The classic study of tomorrow. New York: Bantam Books.
United Nations (1997): Universal access to basic communication and information Services, UN Administrative Committee on Coordination.
Waters, D. (1998): What are digital libraries? URL: http://www.clir.org.pubs/issues04.html#dlf (Accessed on 29/12/2004).
William, B.K., Saffady, S. (1995): Digital library concepts and technologies for the management of collections: an analysis of methods and costs. *Library Technology Reports*: 31, 221.
World Bank (1999): World Development Report: *Knowledge for Development*. World Bank, Washington, DC.
World Bank (2000): World Development Indicators 2000, World Bank, Washington, DC.
Yeates, Robin. (2002). Digital library and information systems: where are we heading? *VINE*. Vol. 32, No. 4: 3-18.
Yerkey, A.N. Jorgensin, C. (1996): A course in digital libraries. *DESIDOC Bulletin of Information Technology*. Vol.16, No.1:.31-9.
Varis, T. (1998): Communications in the future UN system. Alger, C.F. The Future of the United Nations System: Potential for the Twenty-first Century, UNU Press, Tokyo, 37.

Paper History and Expertise Provided by the eContentPlus Project Bernstein

Emanuel Wenger

Austrian Academy of Sciences, Donau-City strasse 1, 1220 Vienna, Austria
E-mail: emanuel.wenger@oeaw.ac.at

Abstract: The goal of project Bernstein is the creation of a European integrated digital environment about paper history and expertise. The project connects European watermark databases and thus offers a comprehensive and significant information source about paper. The databases are augmented by specialized image processing tools for measuring, authenticating and dating papers and by a plenitude of contextual data with bibliographical and geographical contents.

This paper presents the results of the project Bernstein. An internet portal allows the multilingual access to all databases connected to Bernstein. Statistical information is extracted from about 120.000 items in the combined databases of the project and presented in numerical form or through powerful diagram visualizations. Data export capabilities forward the statistical information to a cartography tool which can show e.g. the distribution and the trade routes of paper and watermarks.

Keywords: Watermarks; Manuscripts; Paper history; Digital libraries; Cartography; Databases.

1. Introduction

The present project revolves around paper. The significance of paper derives from being the ubiquitous physical carrier for information exchange until the present times. As such, the study of paper is used on the one hand to identify undated paper documents or expertise documents of questioned authenticity. On the other hand, paper studies have also a historical dimension, revealing aspects of technological evolutions, economical infrastructures, state policies, etc. interwoven into human networks across countries. Knowledge of this kind is partly obtained from the physical characteristics of paper, a source of 'hidden information' as opposed to the visible inscription on a paper object. Watermarks visible when holding a bank note against light are an example for such hidden information. They constitute also the most prominent characteristics examined by historians as well as reproduced and documented in catalogues. But a great amount of such and similar paper data with a broad geographical and temporal spread is necessary in order to create a reliable information source.

2. Watermark Terms and Systematics

An essential step for the integration of watermark databases was the adoption of a textual watermark description standard for the project. This textual watermark description standard should achieve two goals: firstly, creation of a common multilingual nomenclature in the form of a vocabulary for all relevant terms for describing watermarks (Bernstein vocabulary for watermark description). Watermarks of the same type can now be described in six languages (English, French, German, Italian, Russian, and Spanish) by the same names and data interoperability like search across all databases which is now imade possible. Secondly, definition of a textual watermark description standard offering a classification scheme for hierarchically organized watermark types which has so far been realized on three hierarchy levels (see www.bernstein.oeaw.ac.at/Bernstein_systematics.pdf).

3. Integrated Workspace

The integrated workspace (http://www.memoryofpaper.eu) is the backbone of the project that provides the digital environment necessary for the integration of resources. Specifically, this is an Internet application interfaced in six languages (English, French, German, Ital-ian, Russian, and Spanish) that gives access to all the Bernstein resources, of which the main components are the catalogue, the atlas, the bibliography, the expertise, and the toolkit (Figure 1).

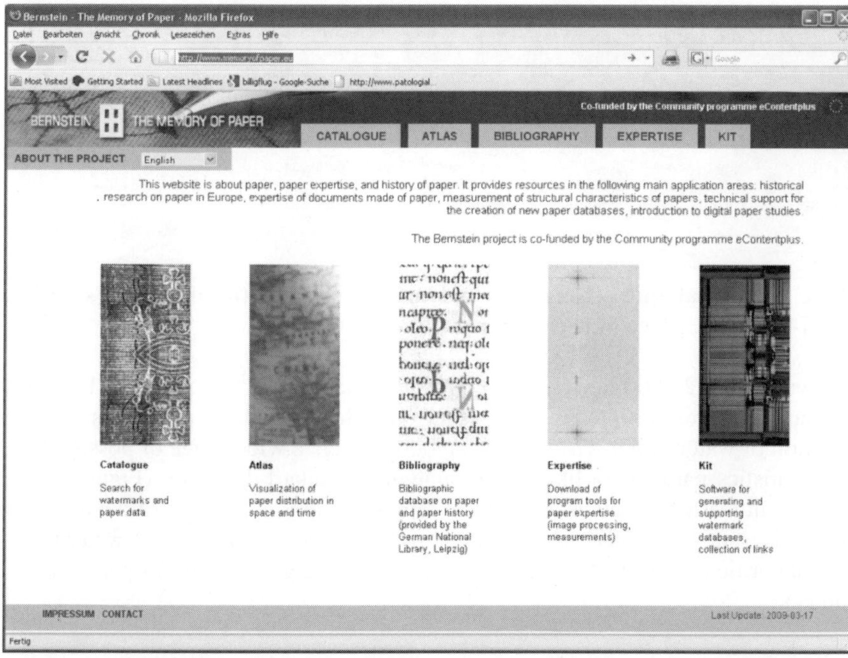

Figure 1: Start page of the integrated workspace (Bernstein web portal)

The main component is the *Catalogue* which allows search in and data retrieval from the various online databases (Figure 2). The search can be formulated in six languages. All search terms are translated automatically into the supported languages according to the Bernstein vocabulary for watermark descriptions. A search in Italian for *sirena* is carried out also for *mermaid* (English) and *Meerjungfrau* (German). Catalogue offers three modes for the search: *simple search*, *advanced search*, and *browse motif*.

Each search is performed within the 'original' databases. The databases were not mirrored but kept at the original locations of the database holders. This provides the advantage that the data is always up-to-date and also avoids copyright problems. The access to the technically different databases is implemented through SRU-gateways. The response times have proven to be satisfactory until now.

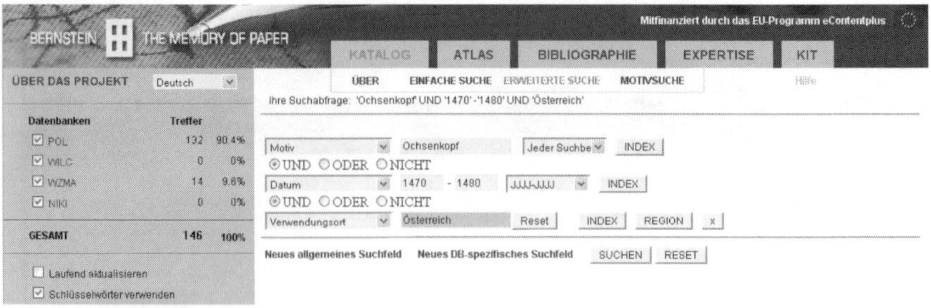

Figure 2: Catalogue (German), advanced search (motif= bull's head, date=1470-1480, place of use=Austria)

With well over 120,000 items in the combined databases of the project, it becomes necessary to provide means for visualising the statistical properties of the collection of watermarks. The statistics module offers a wide range of possibilities. Basic statistics parameters like mean value and standard deviation (Figure 3) are displayed numerically and as a graphical representation in the form of a bar, pie or bubble diagram. Users can analyze single parameters (e.g., number of watermarks per year) or tie and inspect together two parameters (e.g., watermarks per year and country).

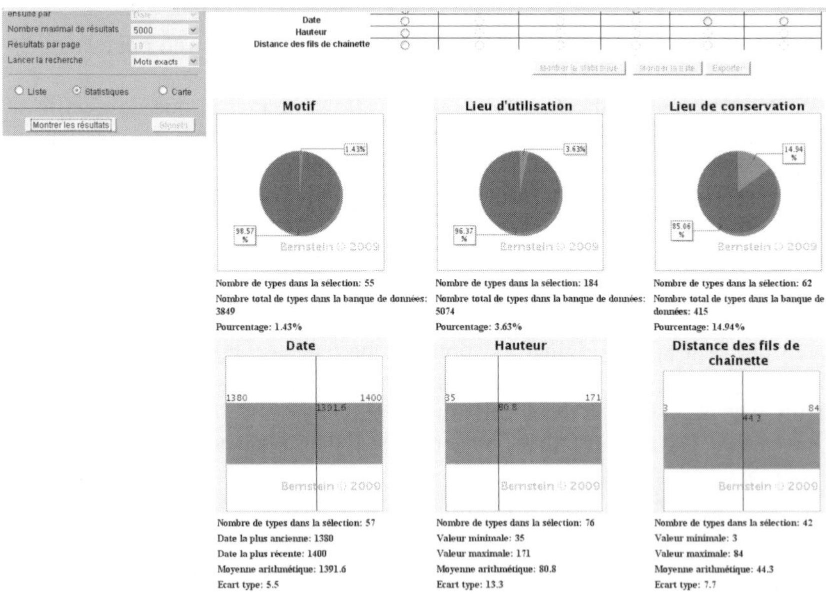

Figure 3: **Statistics (French) – basic statistic parameters (motif=bull's head, date=1380-1400)**

The purpose of the *Bernstein Atlas* is to provide a tool for historical research based on representations of the distribution in space and time of watermarks and other paper characteristics stored in the Bernstein databases and supplemental datasets. Such a dataset of 14,000 place names representing approximately 7,500 unique and identified places with their geographical coordinates was generated. It contains all place names extant in the Bernstein databases, the digitized watermarks and papers repertories, the Bernstein paper bibliography, the incunabula reference works Incunabula Short-Title Catalogue (ISTC, http://www.bl.uk/catalogues/istc), Gesamtkatalog der Wiegendrucke (GW, http://www.gesamtkatalogderwiegendrucke.de), and the plague dataset. The Bernstein databases were augmented with geo-referenced data. This makes it possible to visualize the geographical distribution of a search result in *Catalogue* in regard of the place of use of the paper documents (Figure 4). The field *place of use* can be specified as city or region according to the European standard NUTS (Nomenclature of territorial units for statistics – NUTS, http://ec.europa.eu/eurostat/ramon/nuts/splash_regions.html)

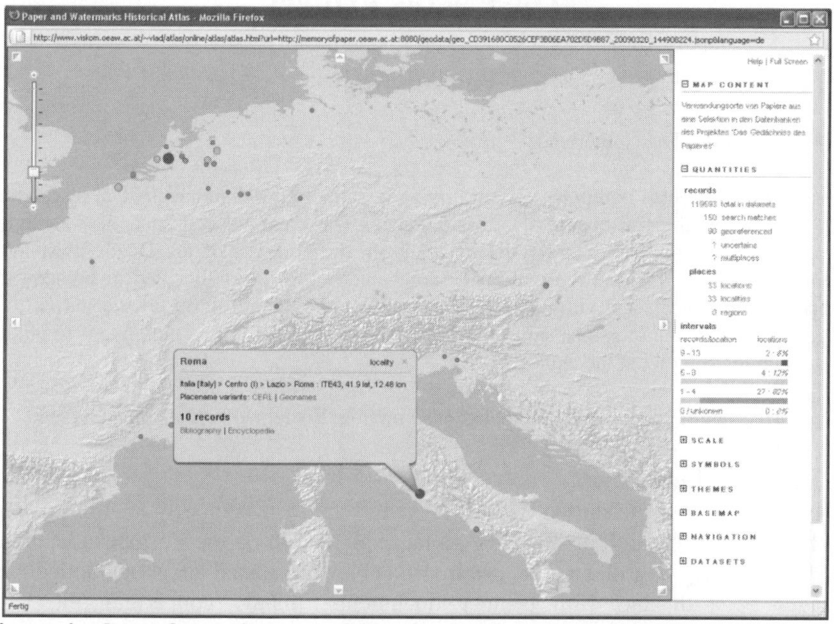

Figure 4: place of use of paper with watermark motif mermaid

4. Conclusions

Project Bernstein offers a European integrated digital environment for paper history and expertise. It connects now all European watermark databases accessible through the Internet at the onset of the project. It offers a comprehensive and unrivalled information source about paper. The databases are augmented by specialized image processing tools for measuring, authenticating and dating papers, and by a plenitude of contextual data with bibliographical, historical and geographical (GIS) contents. A substantial further project goal is the dissemination of the achieved results to a broad audience in the form of a series of exhibitions, a book about paper history and watermarks and an easily installable software package for paper cataloguing.

Further Information
The Bernstein website (http://www.memoryofpaper.eu) which is the Internet 'face' of the project and gives access to its 'body', the integrated workspace.
The Bernstein project presentation as a downloadable Microsoft PowerPoint file (http://www.bernstein.oeaw.ac.at/Bernstein_project_presentation.ppt)
The TWiki development platform (http://www.bernstein.oeaw.ac.at/twiki) serving as a common blackboard and document repository for the project's partners.
The itinerant exhibition, for learning more about watermarks (check locations and order the catalog at http://www.bernstein.oeaw.ac.at/twiki/bin/view/Main/ProjectExhibitions.
The Watermark description standard (www.bernstein.oeaw.ac.at/watermark_terms.pdf).

The Cactus Project

Vincent Mom

DPP Foundation, The Netherlands

Abstract: The Cactus computer system originally supported the archaeological research of a plantation on the Caribbean island of Curaçao. The database consisted of 800 digital images of 17th and 18th century documents from the archives of the Dutch West India Company (WIC). Because the material was so interesting it was decided to broaden the scope of the project, and currently the database contains about 4500 documents (17.000 pages), fully indexed (persons, ships, places and subjects). The current planning is to put the system on the Internet at the end of 2009.

Keywords: Digital documents; Indexing; Data mining; Social networks; WIC; Curaçao.

1. Introduction

The Cactus project started about 3 years ago, in support of the historic archaeological research of San Juan, a large plantation on the Caribbean island of Curaçao (Dutch Antilles). The original database consisted of about 800 digital images of 17th and 18th century documents, mainly concerning the legal possession of a water well, but also deeds of purchase and hand drawn maps with detailed descriptions of the different parcels.

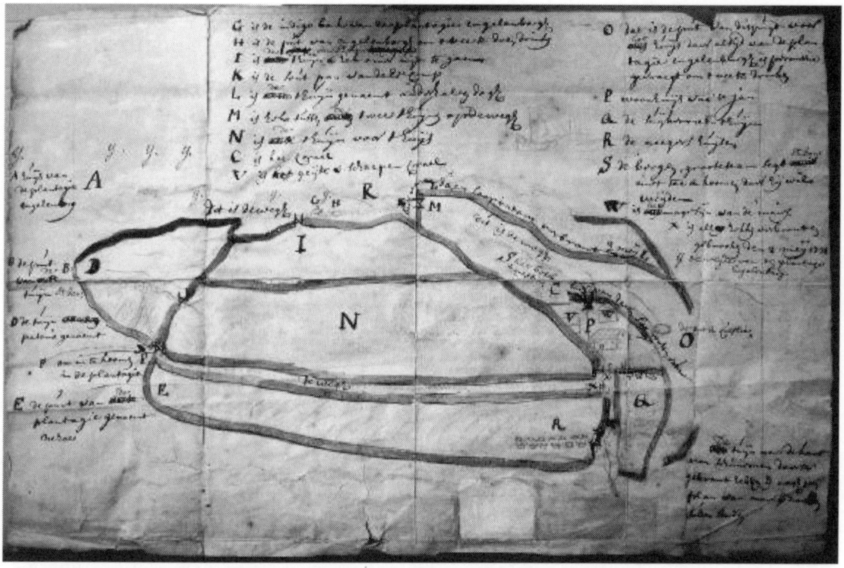

Fig. 1: Map of the plantation San Juan (about 1720)

These documents are a part of the archives (NA 1.05.01.02) of the Dutch West India Company that operated from the early 17th century until 1794 when it finally went broke.

The Cactus computer system was envisaged as a handy tool to guide the user quickly through the available documents. However, the material was so interesting that the scope of the project was broadened (Mom 2007), and currently the database contains over 4500 digital documents (17.000 pages). These have all been indexed (15.000 names of persons, ships, places and subjects. In total about 140.000 index entries). It is probably the largest digital database of WIC documents currently available (Mom and Vautier, 2008).

The documents are letters from the governor and the council of Curaçao to their masters in Holland. But apart from these, there are cash books, legal documents, inventories, reports, witness statements, military orders, official notifications, complaints, application letters, slave death lists, tax documents and much more. The system distinguishes between 85 different document types. Slave trade is one important subject, but also the wars with France and Spain play an important role. Pirates and privateers populate the pages and violence and cruelty are everyday phenomena, clearly reflected in the written material.

The extensive index and the query facilities enable users not only to retrieve relevant documents very quick, but also provide means to generate social networks, based on the fact that if two names appear in the same document, there somehow must be a link between them.

The first phase of the project (document dates between 1700 and 1780) was recently concluded (April 2009) and the system was installed at the Dutch National Archives for a trail period, after which the data will be available through the

Internet. In the next phase, the database will be enhanced with documents from the period 1675 -1700. An additional 2000 pages have already been digitized.

2. The archive's contents

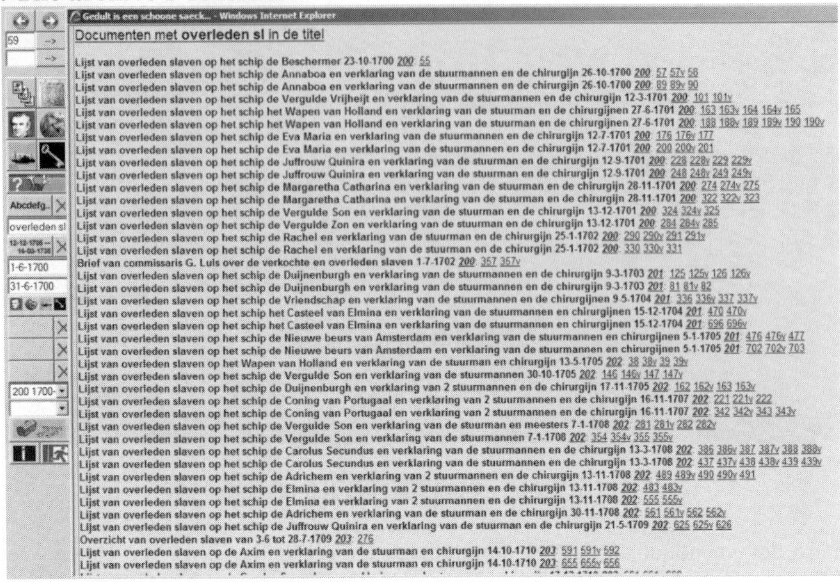

Fig. 2: The death accounts. The Cactus system contains about 100 of these documents, in which the slave traders recorded each slave who died during the journey from Africa to Curaçao.

A proper summary of the contents of the Cactus database requires more pages than the editor would allow, so we must refer to the remarks in the introduction. Therefore to sketch the functionality of the Cactus system we confine ourselves here to one topic only: the death accounts.

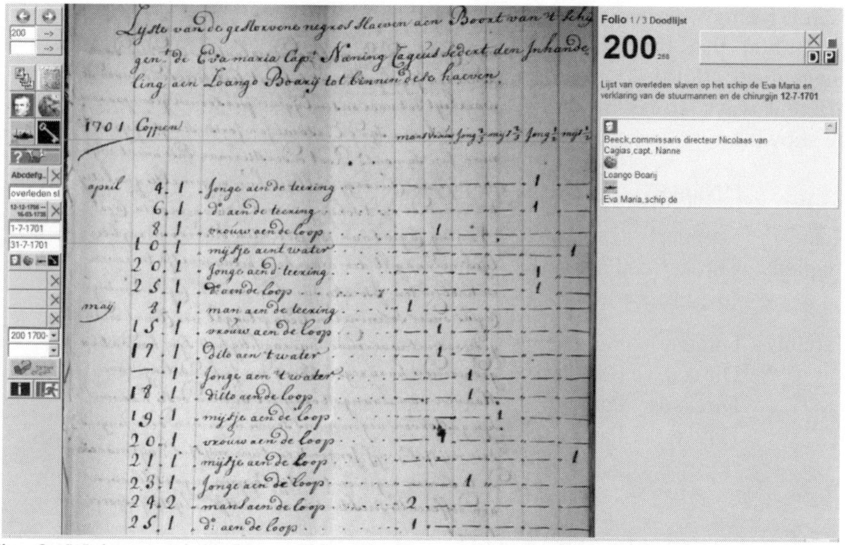

Fig. 3: Main user interface of the Cactus system: in the middle the current page, left navigational buttons and right information regarding the current document and page.

Among the most shocking documents from the WIC archives are the accounting books that were kept by the captains of the slave ships. In fig. 3 an example is shown. The structure is always the same: a standard header, the actual list and at the end the sworn statement of the first steersman and the ship's chirurgeon before the governor that their account was absolutely true, so may God almighty help them. In figure 3 the header reads as follows: 'List of deceased negro slaves aboard the ship called the Eva Maria captain Nanne Cageus since the loading at Loango Boarij until this harbor'. Next follows the actual list. For each entry, the date and the cause of death is recorded. In this list it is mainly 'de teering' (tuberculosis) and 'de loop' (diarrhea). A distinction is made between adults, children '2/3' (age about 9-14) and children '1/2' (age below 9). This journey took 3 months and 29 people in total died. However, another 27 died in the harbor and the woods after arrival (NA 1.05.01.02 volume 200, p. 200-203).
So far this small illustration of what is usually referred to as 'a black page in the history of the Netherlands', which might be considered somewhat of an understatement for a period that lasted almost two hundred years.

3. Searching the data base

Many websites that offer access to large numbers of database records provide unsatisfactory querying capabilities. Often the user is presented with empty text fields in which the relevant search criteria are supposed to be entered. But when proper names from persons, ships etc. are to be searched for, empty text fields are *not* the right way to implement this functionality. In first instance this Google-like approach may look flexible and user friendly but it is not, because it also entails typical Google-like problems: 'Is This All There Is?' and 'Did I Use The Right

Search String?'. Especially with people's names this poses a problem. It was not until 1804 that the first official spelling was introduced in the Netherlands (Siegenbeek 1804) so proper names in the 18th century were often written in different ways, sometimes even within one document. In table 1 some examples are shown.

	Name	Name	Name	Name	Name
Most frequent	Leendert Dircks	Captain Pataccho	Hieronimus Durer	Jacob van Ephraim Jesurun Henriques	Jan Paul George
Variants	Dirckse Dircksz Dircksen Dirkse	Patache Patachio Patacho Patje	Durel Hironimus Jeremias Je:	de Jezurun Jeserun Henriqs	Georgi Georgij

Table 1: Names and variants.

To provide a workable solution, a hybrid approach was chosen. If a new name was encountered, its spelling was copied literally from the document. However, if it appeared later that another spelling variant occurred more frequently, then the most frequent spelling would *replace* the less frequent variant in the index. This approach entails the risk that one name represents more than one individual. But this risk does not appear if all spelling variants of a name are put in the index. For example, in the WIC documents several planters named Jan Dorcas appear, and even from the document context it sometimes is not clear which individual is being referred to. To improve the retrieval results, the user can also choose from a number of simplifications, to be applied to both the search string and the texts to search in. For example, 'c' and 'k' are considered to be equal, or 'g' and 'ch' . Ignoring the 'h' in the texts is another option.
The strength of a retrieval system is defined by 2 parameters, 'recall' and 'precision'. They are defined as follows:

	Relevant	**Not Relevant**	
Retrieved	**A**	**B**	**Precision = A/(A+B)**
Not Retrieved	**X**	**Y**	**Recall = A/(A+X)**

Table 2: Precision and recall. A, B, X and Y are numbers.

An ideal retrieval system would give results with both recall=1 and precision=1 but this goal is seldom reached (Salton and McGill 1983). With our approach we have chosen for a high recall, and a lower precision because we think that the risk to miss information should be minimal with this kind of database system, and for the user it is not difficult to filter out any not relevant data.

4. The subject index

Another interesting activity was the creation of the subject index. The 18th century handwriting of the WIC documents is, in general, very well readable. In the whole database there are only 4 documents which are not readable without in-depth knowledge of old handwriting. These documents are all letters from the reverend minister Theodoris van Cambron, one of the many notorious drunks that populated the island in the early 18th century (NA 1.05.01.02 volume 206 p. 345, 432 and 645v and volume 207 p. 269). So recognizing proper names was not difficult, and could be undertaken on the first reading of the documents. But for the subject index recognizing keywords is not the main issue, but their *relevance* is the question. For each keyword a conscious decision must be made whether to include it, or not. And this is simply not possible without knowledge of the context. So creating the subject index could not be done on the first reading of the documents and therefore the whole indexing process took three steps: On the first reading, all proper names (persons, places, ships) were collected. On the second reading, the index references of the proper names were checked, and at the same time the subject keywords were collected. On the third reading, the subject index was improved, especially regarding consistency as there was a tendency during the second reading to add more and more detail keywords to the index, and therefore especially the first series of documents were re-indexed according to the 'final criteria'.

The subject index is a rather heterogeneous collection of about 3600 individual words, combinations of words, expressions and proverbs. Another possible division is: obsolete or not, in which case the obsolete keywords can be subdivided in 'understandable', 'guessable' and 'unknown'. The last category of course depends individual knowledge of the user/reader and is quite subjective, but this also counts for the creation of the subject index as such, as the sole criterion for entering keywords in the index was: does it concern an interesting topic?

Nevertheless, the category of obsolete (at least in the dutch language) keywords forms an interesting subgroup. In table 3 a small selection is shown which does not require in-depth knowledge of the dutch language. The influence of the Spanish and French languages is obvious.

Keyword	**Meaning**	**Keyword**	**Meaning**
Alphabeta	Booklet to learn to read	Crudo	Some kind of textile
Assientist	Slave trader	Culebra	Bag
Banillas	Unknown	Souvlet	Stroke
Bastron	Battery	Suprineren	To overwhelm
Borico	Some kind of cattle	Trafijgue	Trade
Cabildo	Local governor	Trocqueren	To sell
Cara de oro	Some kind of textile	Ulsisasij	Some medical disorder
Castillano	Unit of weight (Spanish)	Vilipendie	Violation
Comptoir	Office	Vlisirasse	Some medical disorder
Crea	Some kind of textile	Wandevoir	Neglect of duty

Table 3: Examples of obsolete words

5. Data mining and social networks

Although the indexes are not perfect, they nevertheless provide interesting possibilities for data mining and studying social networks. The algorithm used works as follows: first of all, each document represents a certain *value* for each entity (person, place, ship or subject) mentioned in the document, and this value is defined as one thousand, divided by the total number of different entities mentioned in the document. So a letter of recommendation in which only three different names are mentioned provides a value of 333 for the three individuals mentioned, while a taxation list with e. g. 500 names in it will only produce a value 2. In this manner the relative importance of the entities can be established. Below such a ranking is shown.

7534 Beeck,commissaris directeur Nicolaas van
5283 Hansen,equipagemeester weesmeester Lucas
3832 Lamont,secretaris weesmeester Willem
3493 Moijart,koopman reder Juan
3475 Calvo,Jacob
2777 Henriques,koopman factoor Philipo
2685 Luls,commissaris Gerard
2366 Goedvrindt,captein van de burgerij factoor Johannes
1713 Senior,koopman factoor ouderling David
1226 Collen,vendumeester commissaris directeur Jeremias van
1220 Roem,capt. Sijmen Jasperse
1131 Knoppeldoek,capt. Jacob Pieters
1123 Gerves,capt. commissievaarder Pieter
1123 Andrade,administrador generaal Gaspar
1064 Eijck,capt. Michiel Joosten van
1000 Cagias,capt. Nanne
995 Stuart,capt. Hans
993 Visser,capt. Jacob Corse
978 Krans,capt. stuurman Pieter
889 Siewerts,capt. Willem

At the top is the name of Nicolaas van Beeck, in 1700 governor of Curaçao. Then follow the names of civil servants, merchants and ship captains engaged in the slave trade. The Portuguese administrator Gaspar Andrade is a special case: his ship was captured by a privateer from Curaçao, Pieter Gerves. This was illegal, as the Netherlands and Portugal were not on foot of war, but the privateers had thrown all Portuguese documents overboard and planted a Spanish flag aboard the ship, because 50.000 pesos in gold and jewels was not something to let go easily. After a trail which lasted only a few months the WIC confiscated the ship and all its load. Now the weighting algorithm applied for individual entities is easily extended to combinations of entities. So the co-occurrences are ranked in the same way resulting in, for example for Gaspar Andrade, a 'social network' as shown below. We see, amongst others, the names of Philippo Henriques (the shipowner), Pieter Gerves (the privateer), captain Dionisio Coresma (the captain of the seized ship) and the city Cartagena (where the seizure happened).

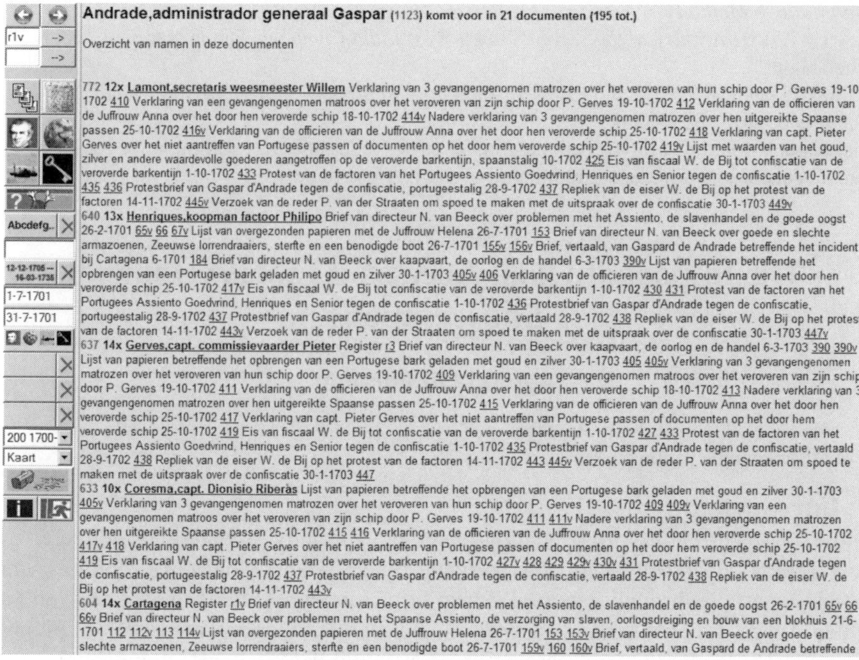

Fig. 4: Social network of the unfortunate administrator Gaspar Andrade

One can immediately jump to a certain document, or navigate through the network by clicking on the names. Networks like these are powerful tools when studying relations between individuals.

6. Conclusions

Phase one of the Cactus project has disclosed a substantial number of WIC documents. Besides, the software developed can also be applied to other digital archives, as the specific WIC data is stored in XML files and all the other components of the system are standard HTML/JavaScript. The second phase of the project (1675-1700) has started but the actual planning is not yet fixed.

Parallel to the Cactus project another one was started, to write short summarizing stories about the most astonishing events, encountered in the archive. These stories are being read by native people from Curaçao and recorded. Currently about 20 subjects are on this list, ranging from council members who try to kill each other and the slave revolt of 1716 to drunk soldiers, the rituals of the pirates and the conquering of Curaçao by the French privateer Jacques Cassard.

References

Mom, V., (2007). The OWINBO (Old Wine In New BOttles) project. *Archäologie und Computer Workshop 11, Kulturelles Erbe und Neue Technologien*. Vienna 18-20 October 2006.

Mom, V. and Vautier, S. (2008). The occupational history of San Juan, a plantation landscape on Curaçao. *Proceedings of the 35th Conference on Computer Applications and*

Quantitative Methods in Archaeology, Berlin 2-6 April 2007
NA 1.05.01.02 *Archive of the second Dutch West India Company*, Dutch National Archives, The Hague.
Salton, G. and McGill, M. J. (1983). *Introduction to Modern Information Retrieval.* Harvard University press, New York
Siegenbeek, Matthijs (1804) Verhandeling over de Nederduitsche spelling ter bevordering van de eenparigheid in dezelfde, Johannes Allart, Amsterdam.

The Impact of Open Access on Library Journal Subscriptions

Ageliki Oikonomou

University of Piraeus Library, Greece
E-mail: oikoang@yahoo.gr

1. Introduction

Most of the current library collection material, especially journal titles, delivered to researchers is a result of a decision made by librarians. Nowadays, libraries can obtain an article through a journal subscription, an aggregated database or even an Open Access archive such as an institutional repository or any other self-archiving archive. These alternative accessing choices would definitely affect the acquisition policies of a library as their main aim is to provide the best and the less expensive purchase options. The potential impact on journal subscription status of open achieves in libraries is considered a highly hot issue among librarians and journal publishers. This matter had become even more serious as over the last decades many research libraries have substantially reduced their subscriptions to print editions of publications where electronic versions are available. Many libraries serving research organizations are increasingly receptive to models that provide Open Access to content published by their affiliated authors in addition to traditional subscription access to journal titles. This kind of model is considered as an alternative option to subscription model to models incorporating author-side payments (ARL, 2009).

2. Scholarly communication and Open Access

Scholarly communication of authors is expressing through journals and monograph publications, though it is not limited to the act of publication. These social processes which are associated with research and publishing, such as informal communication (e.g. telephone, listservs, e-mail, wikis, blogs), attendance at conferences, and formal peer-review journals are all forms of scholarly communication. For almost a century, the relationship between research or academic libraries and the scholarly journals publishers was stable. This was meant that authors offered their papers free to editors; the editors validated the quality of the paper through peer review processes; the journal was published with the peer-reviewed papers, initially only in paper, but lately also online (Sale, 2007). Although, this traditional system of scholarly communication is no longer effective because libraries and many universities are not now able to keep pace with the increasing costs or the plethora of the available scholarly resources and authors tend to communicate with only those of their peers "lucky enough to be at an institution that can afford to purchase or license access to their work" (CreateChange, 2003). Also, readers and library users have access to a smaller amount of any relevant literature, potentially missing vital pieces of information of their interest.

As no research institute or a library can afford to purchase all electronic journals and the subscription model of journal funding is no longer universal, the concept of Open Access publishing model would be an alternative system of dissemination of the scholarly knowledge. What is meant by 'knowledge'? The Berlin Declaration (2003), one the main Open Access initiatives, defines that knowledge is not just the actual research publication, but includes a whole variety of other digital media and objects, as well as research data and a publication should be available as "a complete version with all supplementary materials". There are two basic forms, according to the Berlin Declaration sense of implementation of Open Access practices, with focus on academic journals: 1. The 'green road': deposition of copies (self-archiving of preprint or postprint version of articles) of al-ready published, peer-reviewed research articles in an university or a research institute repository and 2. The 'golden road': a. publication by Open Access publishers or in Open Access journals which are financed either through publishing fees (e.g. BioMed Central)[1] or through public funds (e.g. NIH Public Access Policy)[2] and b. the parallel publication of books in printed form (for a fee) and in an electronic version (with free access) in Open Access publishing houses, or in university publishing initiatives.

3. Potential library journal cancellations

It is common belief that information overload may be the greatest challenge that scholars and librarians have faced in the current era. For instance, 840 papers were published in mathematics in 1870 and by the middle of the 1990s, there were 50,000 new mathematics articles being published per year (Odlyzko, 1995). As a result, a new environment in collection management had emerged in libraries which had led them to have much less buying power than they had in previous decades (Branin, Groen, Thorin, 2000). A comprehensive access to knowledge is one of the major tasks of any library. Open Access may be solution to the 'serials crisis'[3]. In indirect way, as librarians want to help users to find the information they need, regardless of the budget-enforced limits on the library's own collection, they can see Open Access as a supporter to their target

The potential impact of self-archiving of preprint and/or postprint version of articles by authors on journal subscription numbers is one of the current controversial issues of Open Access.

4. Journal cancellations and librarians preferences

Beckett & Inger (2006) indicate that librarians show a trend towards Open Access material as more and more material is available through institutional repositories.

The authors in their international survey between 424 librarians attempted to identify factors that will affect the preferences of librarians in their subscription policies through six attributes: version of article, percentage of a journal articles that are available, reliability of access, how up-to-date is the content, content quality and cost. Their main conclusions are:

a. The strongest influence of librarians in their acquisition policies is the content quality over cost and other attributes,

b. The change in preference librarian from the journal subscription to the same content offered by an Open Access file will be greatest when the only version of this content is the submitted manuscript of the author,

c. The short availability of the content is a determining factor in acquisition policies as the delay reduces the attractiveness of the offered product. Thus, where a supply of an article through an Open Access File (Delayed OA) not exceeding six months, then it is attractive for acquisition,

d. If the content is freely available, all other factors, including the immediate availability offered by the issuer, are treated equally.

In parallel, Ware (2006), through the Association of Learned and Professional Society Publishers (ALPSP), made an online survey in which 340 librarians responded (80% of which came from academic institutions) to record the main factors affecting their decisions on cancellations of journal subscriptions. The members of the association aware of the tendency of authors for self-archiving of preprint and/or postprint articles in repositories, mainly depositary receipts reasonably interested in the potential impact on journal subscriptions for fear of economic losses. The main findings of this research summarised as follows:

1. The process of cancellation of journal subscriptions varies per event, but is a joint decision by librarians and faculty. However, in most cases, librarians are the ones who take the initiative of the agitation of the matter (e.g. based on the analysis of a journal use) and those who eventually decide to cancel.

2. A formal cancellation process includes assessment, consultation, evaluation and financial management of the situation. The consultation-meeting for a final decision may take place by providing data to users of the library of titles proposed for cancellation or provided through research to readers in general.

3. The three main factors determining the cancellation is: whether faculty considered a magazine useful (necessary for their courses or their research), the use and the price of a journal. The next factor is the availability of the content through an Open Access archive. Then the following factors are the journal Impact Factor, quality, significance of a journal and then if the journal is part of special package or if members of the local faculty are members of the editorial board of the journal.

In particular, the price of a journal, librarians, assess the absolute cost and the growth percentage increase.

4. The availability of the contents of a journal through an Open Access archive, librarians argue that it should be done in a very short time (82% believe that, the Delayed Open Access option to dispose should not exceed or be less than 3 months) to be able to compete with the choice of providers through subscription.

5. Those concerning the direct question whether librarians see the Open Access

archives as a good reason to cancel their subscriptions, their responses in descending order are: concerns about the long-term availability of the open archives, about the completeness and integrity of the archives, faculty demand of print journals and pre/postprints are not considered adequate substitutes for the final published articles.

However, 81% of librarians believe that the importance of availability via Open Access articles will increase significantly. In addition, the publishers association worried because the study shows also that the statistical measurements using a well-organized Open Access archive (e.g. in the field of physics) may be a factor in reducing the use the Web pages of their journals.

More recently, Morris (2009), regarding the cancellation of journal subscriptions to her relevant research, cites the views of Rick Anderson, Librarian Acquisitions Officer at University of Nevada, who says: "I can't claim to speak for all libraries, but I can certainly say that at my library, there is no way we could justify an ongoing subscription to a journal the entire, fully edited contents of which are available online at no charge. Actually, no, I'll go further than that: no fiscally responsible library could do so. While I can imagine rare exceptions in the cases of specific journals that might be needed in print, generally speaking there is simply no way to justify the investment of library funds (especially from public coffers!) in the purchase of content that is free to the public…"

From the publishers' perspective, the author states that their concerns are growing about the potential risk of financial viability when copies of a significant proportion of articles in a journal would be freely available elsewhere. Although, the percentage of articles that are freely available, so far, is too low for cancellation subscriptions.

However, studies such as Ware and Beckett & Inger presented above, indicate that librarians expect to cancel subscriptions when "a critical mass of quality-published articles are freely available, then the Authorized version (Accepted version) to be considered adequate alternative to the published version (Published version), provided that is available without delay".

Also, Sale (2007), gives another dimension of acquisition process by saying that the English meaning of word 'acquisition' in libraries has been corrupted as a library is not expected for years to 'acquire' material but actually to obtain the permission to see the included articles. Academic libraries, however, have their journal acquisition budget which exists, according to author, to fund the scholarly publishing industry. Without this budget, "the research peer reviewing process would collapse and something else would have to be invented and funded. Researchers provide their articles free to publishers, most referees provide their services for free too, but the peer-reviewing certification and publishing processes need funding nevertheless". But, as this funding model is beginning to change (due to the Open Access author-pays model, etc.), this expenditure should also change to reflect that shift. Therefore, author makes an experimental thought. He assumes that all journal subscriptions will disappear and all journals have chosen the author-pays or the sponsor-pays model and promote Open Access. Then, primarily and mainly apparently, there are no restrictions on access subscription journals; secondly the potential users (particularly researchers) have access to the entire world literature and thirdly, the money given for journals subscriptions to researchers to read will be consumed for those journals that they publish their research. The budget, then and now (where the author 10% of journals do not charge fees), libraries should meet the challenge. Also, as an increase of Open Access journals, the result will be traditional publishers be forced for competitive reasons to reduce the prices of regular pay. To address these changes, the author suggests the following strategies:

1. Conservative approach. Libraries do nothing. But if libraries continue to pay regular subscription model, the prices will increase due to decreasing subscribers.
2. Activism modest. Libraries to recognize the necessary changes but can not react locally. Then, he proposes to be inverted the known saying: 'Think locally, act globally'. That is, if institutions do nothing to change their behavior, then the libraries to lobby for increases in the number of self-archiving and further increase in authors-pays funding model.
3. Predictive behavior. As a third strategy, the author suggests that the institution has transitional response to the situation. It declares, that payment of author-pays model that is an important requirement and proceeds to a re-alignment of the model 'acquisitions budge' to 'research journal budget'. That is, a proportion of the recurrent budget which will be retained to support alternative forms of financing (such as the model author-pays) to be bound by the foundation for monitoring and adjusting costs in order to combine harmoniously with the changes in the publishing industry and alternative actions for researchers. If this be adopted, author then suggests that libraries should: collect all metadata on an annual basis, analyze this metadata to determine the number of articles by authors from their institution that are published in Open Access journals, compared to toll access journals (subscription journals).

On the whole, King and Alvarado-Albertorio (2008) said that, large commercial journal publishing industry "exercise monopoly or market power, allowing them to charge higher prices, particularly for higher-quality journals". This results in increased journal prices at a much faster rate than inflation over many decades. Open Access publishing would be a solution to the problem but regarding the library journal cancellations is too soon to tell if the free content, from Open Access repositories will lead to cancellations.

5. Conclusions

The survival of libraries is influenced by social, political and economic elements, as the permanently escalated increase of material, acquisition, the unwillingness of the state for sufficient financing, the lack of personnel and the permanent pressure of their editors-suppliers in the control and in the diffusion of information. Accordingly, the analysis and the calculation of cost of their individual operations and the concretely distribution of resources of budget of a library are important processes for its achieved administration. In the frame of the existing economic system, where the competition for the guarantee of economic resources is particularly intense, is observed the acceptance of the opinion that the libraries it is necessary to appear their value with measurable ways. The collections of academic or research libraries, more specifically, even when they have the most generous budgets, cannot cover the increased inquiring needs of instructive personnel of their universities but also their users in general.

Open Access publishing constitutes a new method of diffusion of scientific communication and promotion of government owned, mainly financed research and information. There are certain possibilities, to be a constitute, a viable alternative proposal via its different proposed model in the scientific communication as it can make an essential difference in the saving of budgets of libraries. Nevertheless, there are various questions that require further reflection for its successful application. Between the main questions that occur in the relative international bibliography are the viability of its business model, relevant quality issues (e.g. the existence or the lack peer-review processes), its research impact, questions of subsidy and intellectual rights of authors, the authors unwillingness for deposit and its low or insufficient operation. The present system of publishing and promotion of scientific research possibly will remains prevailing but it will be forced for reasons of competition and survival to proceed in changes.

In regard to the potential cancellations of journal subscriptions, the research proved that do not exist yet stable answers, mainly because of the short-term existence of Open Access. The process of cancellation of subscriptions constitutes a decision that is taken jointly with the total of educational community but librarians are those that take the initiative via analyses of journal use, consultations, economic management and/or collection of data from the users. Librarians show a tendency for future cancellations of subscriptions, when will exist abundance of qualitative freely available scientific articles and when it is realised the convenient availability of article or journal because the delay decreases the validity of their content. Then, the libraries will be called to answer.

References

Association of Research Libraries (ARL) (2009). ARL Statement to Scholarly Publishers on the Global Economic Crisis. February 19, 2009. Accessed October, 30 2009. http://www.arl.org/bm~doc/economic-statement-2009.pdf

Beckett, Ch. & Inger, S. (2006). Self-Archiving and Journal Subscriptions: Co-existence on Competition? An International Survey of Librarians' Preferences. [Internet]. Accessed October, 30 2009.
http://www.publishingresearch.net/documents/Self-archiving_summary2.pdf

Bergman Sherrie, S. (2006). The scholarly communication movement: highlights and recent developments. Collection Building. 25 (4), pp. 108-128.

Berlin Declaration on Access to Knowledge in the Sciences and Humanities (2003). Accessed October, 30 2009.http://www.zim.mpg.de/openaccess-berlin/

Branin, J., Groen, F., Thorin, S. (2000). The changing nature of collection management in research libraries. Association of Research Libraries. Accessed October, 30 2009. http://www.arl.org/bm~doc/changing-nature-coll-mgmt.pdf

CreateChange (2003). CreateChange: new systems of scholarly communication (2003). Accessed October, 30 2009.
http://www.arl.org/createchange/bm~doc/createchange2003.pdf

King, D. W., Alvarado-Albertorio, F. M. (2008). Pricing and other means of charging for scholarly journals: a literature review and commentary. Learned Publishing. 21 (4), pp. 248-272.

Odlyzko, A. M. (1995). Tragic Loss or Good Riddance? The impending demise of traditional scholarly journals. Notices of the American Mathematical Society. 42 (1), pp. 49-56.

Sale, A. (2007). A Challenge for the Library Acquisition Budget. D-Lib Magazine.13 (5/6). Accessed October, 29 2009.http://www.dlib.org/dlib/may07/sale/05sale.html

Ware, M. (2006). ALPSP survey of librarians on factors in journal cancellation. Accessed October, 29 2009.
http://www.alpsp.org/ngen_public/article.asp?id=200&did=47&aid=157&st=&oaid=-1

Notes

[1] http://www.ncbi.nlm.nih.gov/pmc/

[2] http://publicaccess.nih.gov/

[3] For 'serials crisis' see: Bergman Sherrie, S. (2006). The scholarly communication movement: highlights and recent developments. Collection Building. 25 (4), pp. 108-128.

Libraries in the Semantic Web Era

Marek Kopel and Aleksander Zgrzywa

Wrocław University of Technology, Poland

Abstract: This paper focuses on problems with exposing the digital libraries supporting OAI-PMH to the Semantic Web services. The most wanted thing for OAI-PMH metadata is being querable via SPARQL. This means the OAI-PMH formats must be converted and served as RDF. Another important thing is supporting the fourth rule of linked data, which is about interlinking relevant resources. The interlinking can be done by mapping resources across different SPARQL endpoints. But problem arises when the fields to be mapped are not a perfect match. The solution may be some similarity metric with an established threshold.

Keywords: Linked data; OAI-PMH; Semantic web; SPARQL.

1. Introduction

The upcoming era of Semantic Web (SW) domination gives the promise for autonomous machine reasoning. But before the promise becomes reality there are a lot of efforts to make public Web data semantically enriched. The semantic enrichment is believed to allow the Web be readable not only by humans, but also by the machines. As the author of the WWW idea envisioned in Berners-Lee, Hendler and Lassila (2001) the existence of SW would allow the existence of intelligent agents that can process information from the Web autonomously. Autonomously means that unlike today Web browsers these agents would only need a high level of abstraction commands. For example, getting a command "Find a drugstore that is closest to my way home" the agent would estimate optimal way home based on current GPS read, match it to search results for local drugstores and check whether they are open at the time of coming home. It may optionally create an event in user personal calendar with a reminder set after the scheduled work time. That automatic reasoning needs inferencing based on Web data. To make the Web machine readable the data should be described by easy accessible semantic metadata.

As far as libraries are concerned, metadata have always been a part of cataloging. Today in digital libraries it is common to represent metadata using standard ontologies, such as Dublin Core (DC). There is also the idea of exposing the metadata for harvesting in order to create one central database, which would allow to search all the available metadata at once. The protocol for that purpose is Open Archives Initiative Protocol for Metadata Harvesting (OAI-PMH), which is described, along with the whole initiative, in Lagoze and Van de Sompel (2001). The OAI-PMH is RESTful, which means it fulfils Representational State Transfer (REST) principles, as described in Fielding (2000). But even with that architecture, the idea of duplicating the harvested metadata and a central storage is in a way with the SW idea. For the purpose of interoperability of SW services Berners-Lee created and described in Berners-Lee (2007) four rules of linking data on the Web. The main idea of linked data is to make each piece of information identified by dereferenceable URI and available via HTTP. When fulfilling the rules the data can be easily accessed an processed by a query language. The query language used widely for this purpose is SPARQL.

2. Exposing the Data to SW Services

Almost every information system today is using relational database as a storage. Relational database stores data in tables and can be queried using SQL. This is not what SW services can use. SW assumes the data are RDF triples which can be queried via SPARQL. So the simple idea to help SW services gaining traction is to make a transformation interface which would serve the relational stored data as linked data. A tool for publishing the content of a relational database to the Semantic Web is D2R Server described in Bizer and Cyganiak (2006). To describe the mapping between the relational database schemata and the OWL/RDFS ontologies D2R Server uses a declarative language D2RQ. The mapping description is used by the D2RQ Engine, which makes the transformation on the fly and wraps the local relational database into a virtual RDF graph. The graph is then exposed by the server to the RDF browsers, which are enabled to navigate the content of the database. The server also creates a SPARQL endpoint via which SW services can make structured queries. The results can then be retrieved in XML or JSON serialization.

3. Linking the Data

Beside giving object a dereferenceable URI, the other important thing about exposing information as linked data is linking to other resources. The fourth rule of linked data is: "Include links to other URIs, so that they (people) can discover more things". To support that rule D2R Server includes an rdf:seeAlso triple with every resource description that point to an RDF document containing links to other resources. These triples serve as "breadcrumbs" to RDF crawlers and browsers.

However, sometimes the information about other resources that may be useful in context of the retrieved resource is not stored in the relational database or is not available. This is the case with OAI-PMH. One can retrieve metadata records, but there is hardly any information about other useful records. This is because OAI-PMH is about exposing the data to the Web, but it is not the linked data. In Haslhofer and Schandl (2008) authors deal with converting the OAI-PMH endpoint into the SPARQL endpoint. They present the OAI2LOD

Server which is build on the D2R server, but it enables to expose the linked data without accessing directly the relational database. This means the SPARQL endpoint can be set up by anyone, because it only needs an OAI-PMH endpoint as the data source. To satisfy the fours rule of linked data OAI2LOD Server may search and map resources to other linked data resources based on some similarity metric. For example: places or concepts may be linked by name to dbpedia – the linked data version of Wikipedia articles. If a matching entry is found then an owl:sameAs property may be added to the metadata record. In order to make this work the server administrator needs to specify:

1. target OAI2LOD Servers for linking,
2. pairs of source and target fields to be analyzed,
3. a similarity threshold for each pair.

4. The Matching Problem

Using the OAI2LOD Server to expose the DBC digital library metadata records as linked data an unexpected problem emerged . The requirement of linked data fourth rule was supposed to be fulfilled by associating library OAI-PMH records (*http://www.dbc.wroc.pl/dlibra/oai-pmh-repository.xml*) with D2R Server publishing the DBLP Bibliography Database (*http://dblp.l3s.de/d2r/*). The association was supposed to be made by simple matching author names. In this way, when looking up a DBC library record, agent is given a link to other works of the same author in the DBLP database.

It turned out that the exposed OAI-PMH records do not serve author names in any consistent way. Therefore direct matching on the author names could not give positive results. Table 1 shows some examples of author names in DBC library.

Daniłowicz, Czesław [dr hab. inż.], promotor
Dankowska-Żołnierowicz, Bogna
Darboux, Gaston (1842-1917). Wyd.
Daubrée, Auguste (1814-1896)
Dec, Ignacy (1944-)
Dec, Ignacy (1944-). Promotor
Dittrich
Dowojna - Sylwestrowicz, Mieczysław. Red.
Dudziński, Włodzimierz Jan [dr hab. Inż.], promotor
Dudziński, Włodzimierz Jan. Promotor
Dufour, Piotr. Wyd.
Dumas, Jean Baptiste André (1800-1884)

Tab. 1. Example of inconsistency in author names in DBC

On the other hand DBLP database also showed some inconsistency: sometimes giving full first names, sometimes initials and sometimes a combination of the two. In one case the name field was containing a nickname put in quotation marks. Other problems with author field inconsistency concern character encoding, inversing the order of first and last name and occasional notes introduced in parentheses or square brackets. Since the inconsistency is not deterministic cleaning the data is not a solution.

Facing the above problems matching the names with any similarity metric with threshold set to 1 would not give expected results. Thus two questions arise:

1. Which similarity metric to use?
2. To what value set the threshold?

In order to answer these questions an experiment have been carried out.

5. Experiment

For the purpose of an experiment only the author names staring with "D" were taken into account. DBC containing 1700 records stores 56 authors with names starting with "D" in 62 distinct fields. The names were retrieved using SPARQL endpoint with the following query:

```
PREFIX dc: <http://purl.org/dc/elements/1.1/>
SELECT DISTINCT ?uri ?name WHERE {{
 ?uri dc:creator ?name .
 FILTER(regex(?name, "^D")) }
UNION {
 ?uri dc:contributor ?name .
 FILTER(regex(?name, "^D")) }}
ORDER BY ?name
```

In DBC authors are described using DC ontology with two properties: dc:creator and dc:contributor. Authors from DBLP were retrieved in an analogical manner. The DBLP database contains more than 950 000 articles and 570 000 authors. The retrieved authors with name staring with "D" gave 25 876 items stored in a foaf:name and rdfs:label properties.

The author names retrieved from DBLP where tested against each author name retrieved from DBC. This gives over 1.6 million tests for each metric. The tests were based on the following similarity metrics:

1. Block distance or L1 distance or City block distance
2. Cosine similarity
3. Dice's Coefficient
4. Euclidean distance or L2 distance
5. Jaccard Similarity or Jaccard Coefficient or Tanimoto coefficient – Jaccard (1912)
6. Jaro distance – Jaro (1989)
7. Jaro Winkler distance – Winkler (1999)

8. Levenshtein distance
9. Matching Coefficient
10. Monge Elkan distance – Monge and Elkan (1996)
11. Needleman-Wunch distance or Sellers Algorithm
12. Overlap Coefficient
13. Q-gram distance – Gravano et al. (2001)
14. Smith-Waterman distance – Smitha and Waterman (1981)
15. Gotoh Distance or Smith-Waterman-Gotoh distance – Gotoh (1982)
16. SoundEx distance

The open source java implementations of the metrics are available at *http://www.dcs.shef.ac.uk/~sam/simmetrics.html.* They are normalized, which mean when testing 2 strings they return a value from 0 to 1. Value 1 means a perfect match.

	Dziedzic, Andrzej (1957-)	Dziedzic, Andrzej [dr hab. inż.], promotor	Dziedzic, Andrzej. Promotor	Dziedzic , Janusz
BlockDistance	0,67	0,50	0,40	0,50
CosineSimilarity	0,71	0,58	0,41	0,50
DiceSimilarity	0,67	0,50	0,40	0,50
EuclideanDistance	0,68	0,68	0,52	0,50
JaccardSimilarity	0,50	0,33	0,25	0,33
Jaro	0,00	0,00	0,00	0,00
JaroWinkler	0,60	0,60	0,60	0,60
Levenshtein	0,65	0,40	0,63	0,65
MatchingCoefficient	0,50	0,33	0,33	0,50
MongeElkan	0,50	0,54	0,72	0,63
NeedlemanWunch	0,65	0,51	0,63	0,76
OverlapCoefficient	1,00	1,00	0,50	0,50
QGramsDistance	0,72	0,54	0,71	0,54
SmithWaterman	1,00	1,00	1,00	0,63
SmithWatermanGoto h	1,00	1,00	1,00	0,66
Soundex	0,96	0,96	0,96	0,96

Tab. 2. Similarity metrics' scores for testing name "Dziedzic, Andrzej" against 4 examples

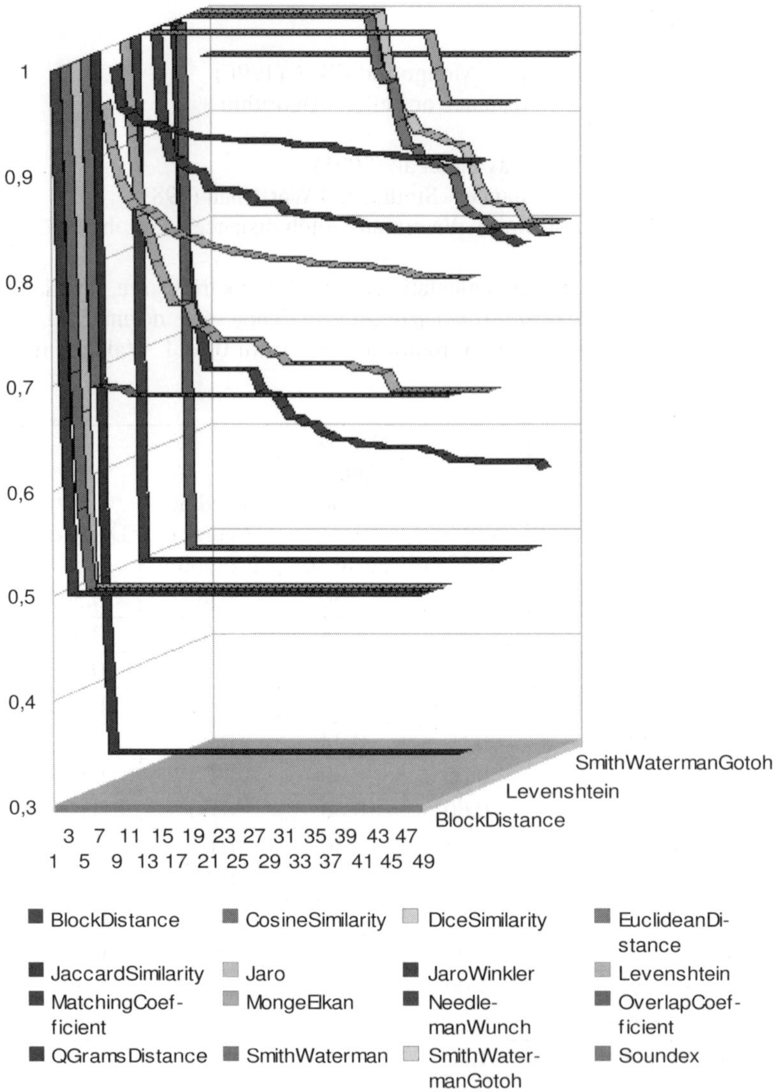

Fig. 1. Monotonicity of top 50 scores for 16 similarity metrics applied to matching author names

6. Discussion

Direct comparison of the names from DBC and from DBLP established only one association. Most of the metrics scored this mapping as 1.0. But, as can be seen on figure 1, three metrics: 6, 7 and 16 didn't evaluated those two names with highest score. Even though they had tested two exactly the same strings. Testing "*Dziedzic, Andrzej*" against "*Dziedzic, Andrzej (1957-)*" and "*Dziedzic, Andrzej [dr hab. inż.], promotor*" got into top 5 scores using metrics: 1-5 and 13. Metrics 12, 14, 15 scored these tests as 1.0. As shown in table 2 metrics' scores in these cases are similar to those from a false positive case: "*Dziedzic, Janusz*".

For overall test results, false positives were given most frequently by metrics: 10 and 16. A true positive "*Danilowicz, Czeslaw*" against "*Danilowicz, Czesław [dr hab. inż.], promotor*" was found in top 100 scores only for measures: 14 and 15.

The example from table 2 shows global characteristic: false positives with some metrics get better scores than true positives and sometimes there is no difference..

Figure 1 show that the range for top scores is quite discrete for metrics: 1-5, 9 and 12. For others, especially: 6, 7, 8, 11 and 13 the score range is more regular.

7. Conclusions

This paper covers problems with publishing digital libraries metadata to the Semantic Web in the form of linked data. Since the relational databases are widely used as a storage the idea is to transform the data and expose them as a SPARQL endpoint. When access to relational database is not possible, library metadata may be accessed vie OAI-PMH endpoint and then transformed to RDF graph. Described in this paper tools for that task are D2R Server and OAI2LOD server. Recently a new tool was developed to make exposing RDF graph even easier for Web developers. The tool is triplify (*http://triplify.org*). The main reason for facilitating users creating Web of data and not only Web of documents is to help SW services gain traction.

Another issue about exposing linked data is interlinking relevant resources. In order to find useful resources to be connected, property values matching must be carried out. Described in the paper experiment verifies matching based on similarity metrics. Experiment results reveal that using one metric does not guarantee positive effects. Using a combination of different similarity metrics for interlinking Semantic Web resources should be further investigated.

On the other hand the Open Archives Initiative Object Reuse and Exchange (OAI-ORE) is the new standard for extending the OAI-PMH with the functionality of creating and sharing aggregations. When widely applied, this may be a better source of connections to relevant resources. Again, reusing the existing connections when exposing metadata records as linked data should be more efficient than staring from scratch with similarity metrics.

References

Berners-Lee, T., Hendler, J. and Lassila, O., (2001). *The semantic Web*. Scientific American, 284(5), 28-37.

Berners-Lee, T., (2007). *Linked Data - Design Issues*. Available at: http://www.w3.org/DesignIssues/LinkedData.html

Fielding, R. T., (2000), *Architectural Styles and the Design of Network-based Software Architectures*. University of California, Irvine

Lagoze, C. and Van de Sompel, H., (2001). *The Open Archives Initiative: Building a low-barrier interoperability framework*. Proceedings of the *1st ACM/IEEE-CS joint conference on Digital libraries*. ACM Press New York, 54-62.

Bizer, C. & Cyganiak, R., (2006). *D2R Server - Publishing Relational Databases on the Semantic Web.* Proceedings of the *5th International Semantic Web Conference*.

Gotoh, O., 1982. *An improved algorithm for matching biological sequences.* Journal of Molecular Biology, 162(3), 705.

Gravano, L. et al., (2001). *Using q-grams in a DBMS for approximate string processing*. IEEE Data Engineering Bulletin, 24(4), 28-34.

Haslhofer, B. & Schandl, B., (2008). *The OAI2LOD Server: Exposing OAI-PMH Metadata as Linked Data.* Available at: http://events.linkeddata.org/ldow2008/papers/03-haslhofer-schandl-oai2lod-server.pdf.

Jaccard, P., (1912). *The distribution of the flora in the alpine zone.* New Phytologist, 37-50.

Jaro, M.A., (1989). *Advances in record-linkage methodology as applied to matching the 1985 census of Tampa, Florida.* Journal of the American Statistical Association, 414-420.

Monge, A.E. and Elkan, C., (1996). *The field matching problem: Algorithms and applications.* Proceedings of the *2nd International Conference on Knowledge Discovery and Data Mining (KDD-96)*. 267-270.

Smith, T.F. and Waterman, M.S., (1981). *Identification of common molecular subsequences.* Journal of Molecular Biology, 147, 195-197.

Winkler, W.E., (1999). *The state of record linkage and current research problems.* Statistical Research Division, US Bureau of the Census, Washington, DC.

5. Focus to Users and User Groups

Users Requirements for Personalised Virtual Digital Libraries

Roberto Caldelli[1], Cezary Mazurek[2], Paolo Mazzanti[1], Tomasz Parkoła[2] and MarcinWerla[2]

[1]Media Integration and Communication Centre Firenze, Italy
[2]Poznan Supercomputing and Networking Center, Poland

Abstract: This paper presents results of the survey which was performed in the frame of the European project named ENRICH (ECP-2006-DILI-510049), funded under the eContent*Plus* programme. The aim of the survey was to acquire users' preferences regarding various aspects of two essential digital library functions: individual collections (static and dynamic) and individual virtual documents. Overall number of the survey responses reached 459 responses gathered from digital library users from 12 European countries. The image of users' preferences formed on the basis of responses lead to the definition of requirements for the creation of personalised virtual digital libraries. In this paper we present adopted procedure for performing the survey, analysis of the responses and final conclusions regarding personalised virtual digital libraries.

Keywords: Digital library; Personalised virtual digital library; Individual collection; Individual virtual document; ENRICH project; Digital objects aggregation; Virtual research environment.

1. Introduction

The European project ENRICH, funded under the eContent*Plus* programme, aims at creation of the virtual research environment for study of historical cultural heritage documents gathered from various European cultural institutions. The project builds on the Manuscriptorium portal, initially developed by the National Library of the Czech Republic and AiP Beroun in scope of Memoria programme described in Knoll (2004). Such an environment needs a clear set of requirements regarding particular features it will provide. In case of user personalization area of the ENRICH project there are two major features to be focused on: individual static and dynamic collections and individual virtual documents. It was decided that in case of these two major features the requirements will be specified by the end-users which are to be the final beneficiary and most interested party. A survey was conducted to elicit requirements.

The survey prepared within the ENRICH project was composed of five basic parts including: an explanation of the survey form structure and rationale, basic questions about the respondent and detailed questions about particular functions of the two personalization features given under analysis. Additionally, ENRICH partners translated the text of the survey into their native languages to receive more results and with better accuracy. The survey was filled in by over 450 respondents from 12 European countries participating in the ENRICH project. This gave a reasonable amount of data to be analysed and interpreted with respect to the final requirements. The percentage of filled surveys by respondents from particular countries is presented on Figure 1.

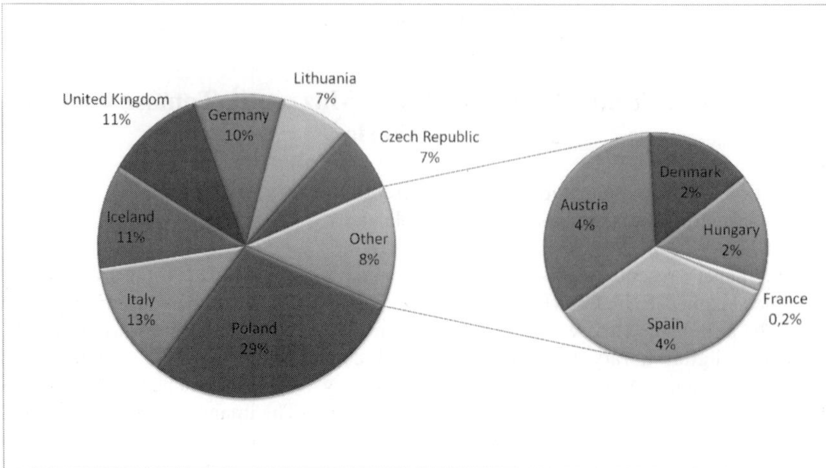

Figure 1 Percentage of filled surveys by respondents from particular countries.

This article gives an overview on the scope of the survey, results analysis and final conclusions; in particular section 2 describes the survey structure, section 3 presents the most important analysis and section 4 includes final conclusions and advices regarding analysed features.

2. The questionnaire structure

According to the MINERVA EC (2003) *Handbook for quality in cultural websites: improving quality for citizens*, "A user is a professional person or not, a specialist or not, who casually or with specific aims, occasionally or systematically uses the Cultural Web Application. User identity is extremely variable depending on cultural profile, aspirations for cultural growth, professional aims and even momentary curiosity" (see also in MINERVA EC (2008)). Therefore, a quality website in general or a quality digital library in particular, must be user-centred, "taking into account the needs of users, ensuring relevance and ease of use through responding to evaluation and feedback" (5th MINERVA Quality Principle, in MINERVA EC (2003-2004)).

In order to realize a high quality European Digital Library, really user-centred, based on his/her needs, tasks and behaviours, the Enrich Questionnaire was a strategic method of investigation of the users requirements for personalised virtual digital libraries. The survey is globally composed by 23 structured multiple questions, easy and quick to be completed.

The access to the questionnaire consists of a specific on-line webpage that presents the "*Digital library readers demands/needs survey*" in many European languages for the different users, to ease questionnaire understanding also to people not very familiar with English. Primarily, in order to fill in the questionnaire, the user can select his/her specific country in a reference table for the choice of the language. The introduction is structured to explain the questionnaire as a part of the European ENRICH project and the user is invited to take time to complete the survey and notified that this will help the ENRICH project to address the issues s/he is interested in and ensure that the developed technology meets his/her needs.

The first part of the survey consists of 3 questions, specifically created and formulated in order to collect information about the user experience. In particular, information about the type of respondent as well as his/her experience, that may help to better interpret the survey results. Firstly, it is asked which group of digital library users the user belongs to, in order to identify the user in the following macro categories: researcher, teacher, student and other. Secondly, it is required information about the level of user's experience with digital libraries: a regular user, occasional regular user, a rare user. Finally, it is analyzed the level of user's experience with Manuscriptorium digital library: regular user, occasional user, rare user, never used before.

The second part of the survey, questions 4-23, concerns with individual collections (IC) and virtual document (VD). In order to design the functionalities on the basis of the user needs, the questions ask how the user, as a digital library reader, considers the static and dynamic IC and VD (necessary, useful, neutral, not useful, redundant) and where s/he would need to keep them for further usage (digital library reader account locally, personal computer's hard drive, not need to save IC/VD for further usage). Another important aspect of the personalisation is to grant an interaction of the user with the digital library environment, for this reason it is asked if the user is interested about the possibility to receive a notification (e.g. e-mail notice or RSS feed) about new documents in his/her dynamic IC and VD, to have personal notes about any of his/her IC/VD, or files with additional information to any of his/her IC/VD. The goal of the questionnaire is also to prepare the basic architecture of the search inside the Digital Library, so it is asked if the user is interested to have the possibility to search his/her IC/VD and if s/he is interested to share (not edit) own IC/VD with other readers. In this field is also useful to know who can see the shared IC/VD and is asked to whom the user prefers to make visible his/her individual shared collection and virtual document. User can select one of the following answers: all readers and I do not need the possibility to hide any collection/document, all readers and I have the possibility to hide/unhide any collection/document, selected readers only. Other specific questions are about the possibility to give a copy of the IC/VD to any other reader and what information to share in regard to the IC/VD (the documents list only, the documents list notes and the additional information attached, the documents list and, depending on his/her decision, notes and additional information).

It is necessary to provide to the users the capability to interact with the digital library and by this survey they can say how the services should be improved, so that their expectations can be better met. That is why a question analyzes the importance of the media types within the virtual digital library. User can select one of the following answers for images, texts, audio and video: necessary, useful, neutral, not useful. At the end of the questionnaire, the user has the possibility to write additional comments in a dedicated form, that allows the user to provide further interesting indications on the matter that s/he thinks are not completely covered by the survey. S/He can also write the e-mail address, to receive a copy of the final report with the interpretation of the survey results. In order to give a service user centred, usable and accessible, it is basic to remind that below the reference table of the questionnaire there was an additional link for accessing "the digital library readers demands/needs survey statistics", where the users can directly see and check the survey results, divided by Country, Number of filled surveys, Number of distinct IPs.

3. Analysis of results

The survey was basically directed to researchers, teachers and students. Researchers form the primary group of users, interested in new functionality connected with research environment being built within the ENRICH project. For researchers, the digital content available in the research environment will need appropriately adjusted features, which will allow performing specific research activities. Teachers may not only be interested in finding and using educational materials already available in the system, but also in using the functions allowing them to prepare course-focused materials for their students. Students will benefit from all the materials (e.g. prepared by their teachers) and will have the opportunity to use the environment to raise their skills and enhance knowledge. Naturally, beside these three basic groups, other interested users were also invited to fill in the survey. These are usually users interested in discovering cultural heritage documents such as manuscripts, early printed books, archival papers, etc. and are mainly amateurs, which would like to take a look at the most impressive documents and discover some interesting facts.

The results from the first part of the survey which was used to obtain basic information about the respondents show that the final requirements should be reliable and representative for the target users as majority of respondents was familiar with digital libraries and also convergent with survey target users group. It also appeared that the researchers are the most experienced group of respondents with digital libraries. On the other hand students are the least experienced respondents group.

The most important parts of the survey queried users about individual collections and individual virtual documents features. Users were given a detailed explanation of these two terms in order to interpret the questions appropriately.

Individual collections allow any reader to create and maintain his/her own set of documents within his/her profile and to share it with other readers. Documents grouped in individual collections are always easily available to the reader for instant usage. There were two types of individual collections given under analysis:

- static individual collections – created by readers by adding directly selected documents;
- dynamic individual collections – created by readers by specifying criteria for the collection membership. For example, a dynamic individual collection may be specified as all the documents created before 1450 and related to alchemy. As the content of the digital library changes, the content of the dynamic collection may also change.

More information about the implementation of such collections in distributed environments can be found in Mazurek (2006).

Virtual documents are documents created manually with parts (e.g. selected pages) of other digital library documents. For example a reader can build a virtual document demonstrating the art of illumination for a selected period (e.g. from the most representative parts of illuminated documents for this period). Additional information may be also attached to the virtual document by its creator.

The basic question in regard to individual collections was about the necessity of this feature. Overwhelming majority of respondents stated that both dynamic and static individual collections would be either useful or necessary when working with digital library. For individual documents the initiating question investigated the importance of the media type to use for individual documents. There were four possible answers: text, image, video, audio. It appeared that text media type is the most necessary media type to work on. The image media type situated just after the text. Video and audio media types received very similar marks – useful and neutral, but not necessary. Figure 2 depictures responses concerning the necessity of individual collections and Figure 3 the importance of the media types for virtual documents.

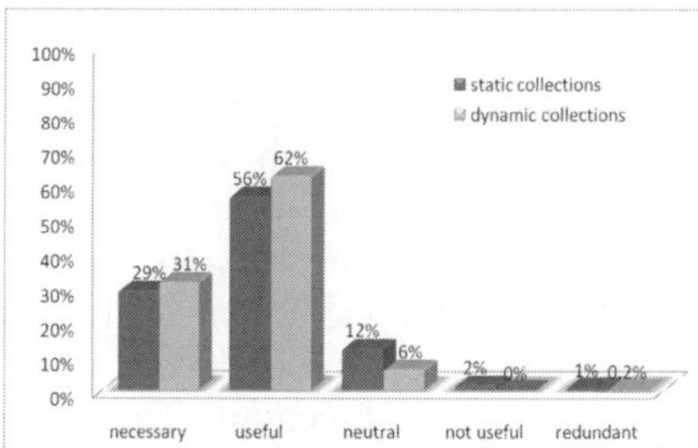

Figure 2 The necessity for individual collections feature

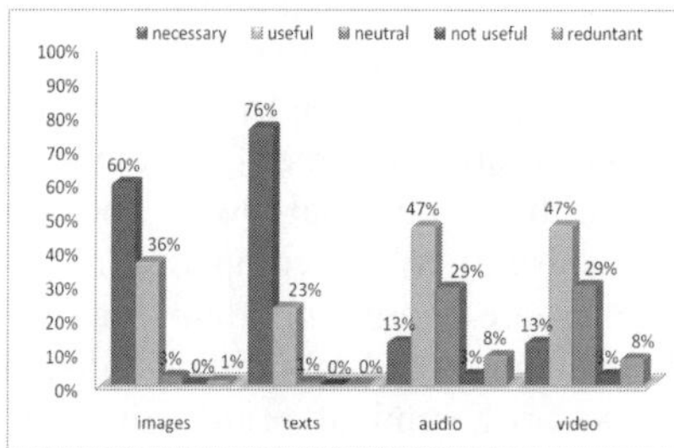

Figure 3 The importance of the media types for virtual documents feature

Second part of questions concerned interaction of the user with the digital library environment; in particular respondents were asked about the storage place for individual collections and documents, changes notification for dynamic individual collections and search mechanism for static individual collections. Both for individual collections and documents respondents preferred to store information about them in the on-line facilities (e.g. reader account) rather than in the local storage facilities (e.g. hard drive). Changes notifications in the dynamic individual collection (to which changes notifications may only apply) were evaluated as a useful function. In this case group of users identified as students was the one which mostly voted for this function. This is probably because of a higher popularity of notification tools (e.g. RSS feeds) among young people. The last, but a very important function evaluated within the interaction part of the survey concerned the search mechanism. It appeared that it was rated by most of respondents as necessary. Major part of remaining respondents recognised this function as useful. It is interesting to note that this function was evaluated as the most necessary in respect all functions connected with individual collections. Therefore the results prove that search function is a very important function connected with individual collections. We may also indirectly conclude that users are willing to create individual collections containing many documents therefore they require search functionality for them.

Third part of questions concerned individual collection and document notes functionality and was investigating not only the possibility to textually describe particular individual element, but also attach to it additional items (e.g. files) which are related to the source material. There were questions asking respondents for their opinion about textual personal notes connected with: an individual collection, a whole document and part of a document. There were also questions about necessity for attaching personal files to: individual collection and whole document. Results for all these questions are presented on Figures 4 and 5. According to respondents, possibility to have personal notes and personal files connected with individual collections is useful. When comparing results for these two functions it appears that personal notes are more important for users than personal files. When analysing gathered results in regard to individual documents it appears that respondents created by their answers a kind of priority list for three investigated functions. The most needed function is the one that allows users to add notes about the whole individual document, the second one is a function for adding notes to particular parts of document, and the less required function is the one that allows users to attach files with additional information to individual virtual document. The results are quite natural because they prioritise functions from the most simple one (notes to the whole document) to the most advanced one (attaching files to documents).

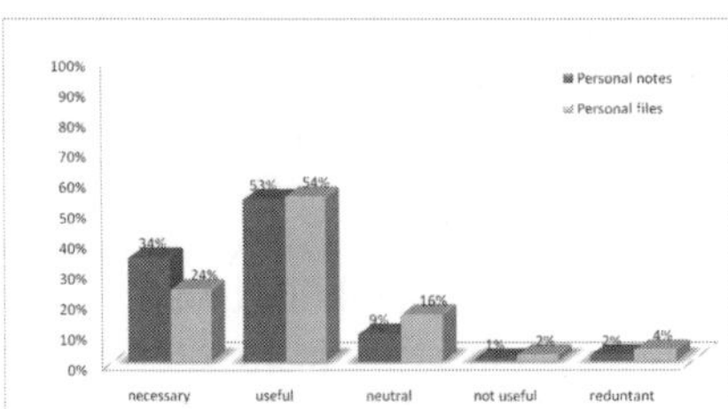

Figure 4 Personal notes and files necessity for individual collections

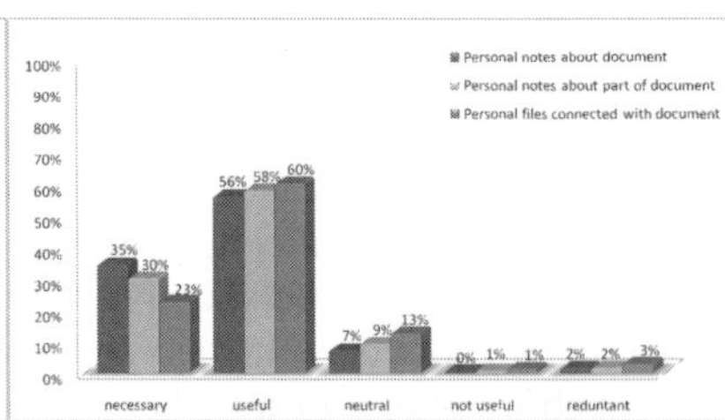

Figure 5 Personal notes and files necessity for individual documents

The last set of questions investigated community building functionalities such as sharing individual collections and documents with other users, controlling visibility of particular parts of shared content and even giving a copy of particular collection or document to other users. Functionality which would allow users to share individual collections and documents with other users was evaluated by most of respondents as useful. Around one-tenth of respondents stated that these are necessary therefore these functions are not mandatory and should be introduced only when other, more important functions are ready. Three additional questions were investigating specific aspects of the functionality for sharing individual collections and documents.

First aspect was connected with the visibility of shared collections and documents to other users (results are depicted on Figures 6 and 7). It appeared that most of respondents would prefer to choose which individual collections and documents will be available to all other users and which will be hidden from them. Majority of reminder respondents would prefer more restrictive access to their individual collections and documents (grant access to selected users only). Additional analysis of relations between the question concerning sharing function and the question about visibility of collections and documents show that the more respondents were sceptic about sharing their individual elements the more they wanted to secure their elements from other users (by selecting visibility option giving them more advanced possibilities). This fact suggests that responses are quite consistent therefore more reliable.

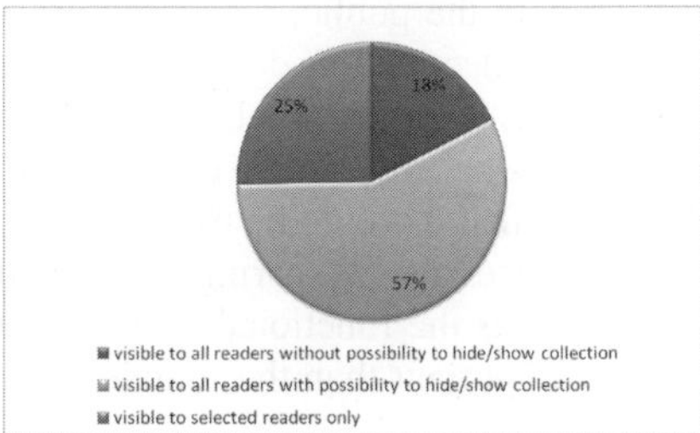

Figure 6 Results for visibility function for shared individual collections

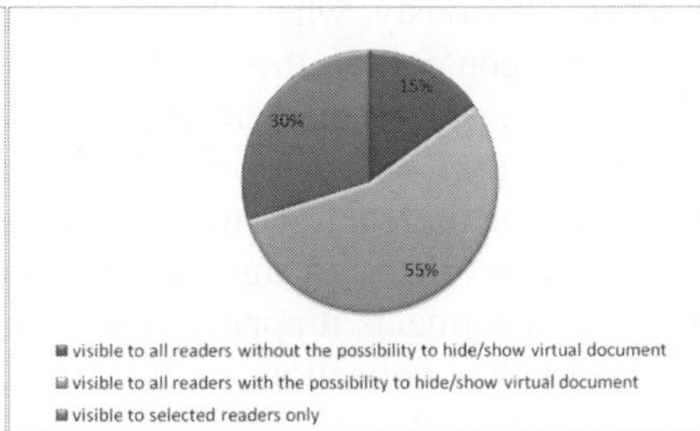

Figure 7 Results for visibility function for shared individual documents

Second aspect concerned the issue of additional elements (notes, attached files) which should be shared with other users (results are depicted on Figures 9 and 10). Both for individual collections and documents most of respondents selected the option to have the full configuration possibilities regarding the elements to share. Only minor part of respondents would share the document and additional information without any constraints.

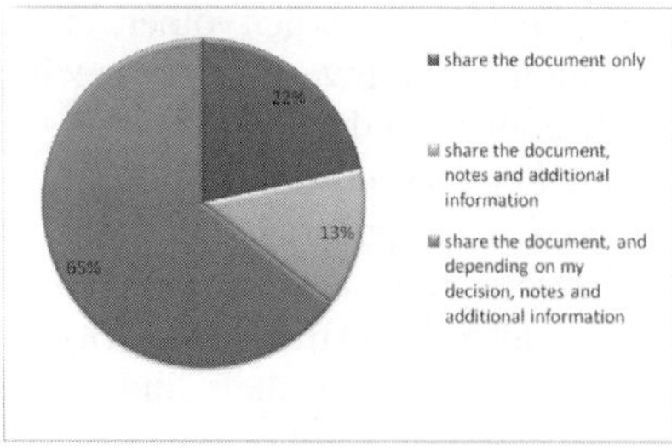

Figure 8 Individual documents sharing function

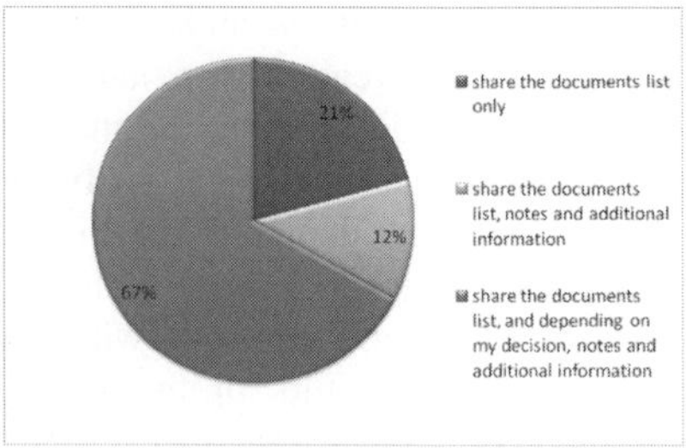

Figure 9 Individual collections sharing function

Third investigated aspect was about giving a copy of personal collection or document to other users. Obviously, when sharing a collection with the public, registered users cannot edit the content of the element (individual collection or document). The purpose of copying of an element is to create a new instance of the element and to enable a selected user so he/she can start to use it as his/her own. Answers given by most of respondents in regard to this functionality show that it would be useful. When comparing these results with the question about the necessity of sharing individual collections and documents it appeared that for respondents the functionality to give a copy of an individual collection or document is more important than the functionality which allows to share it.

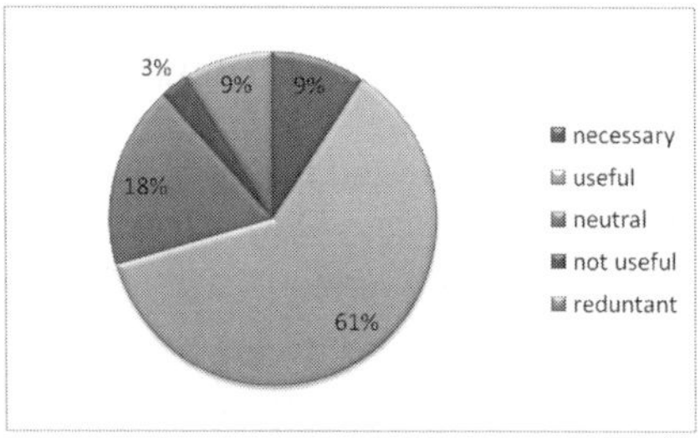

Figure 10 Functionality for giving a copy of individual documents

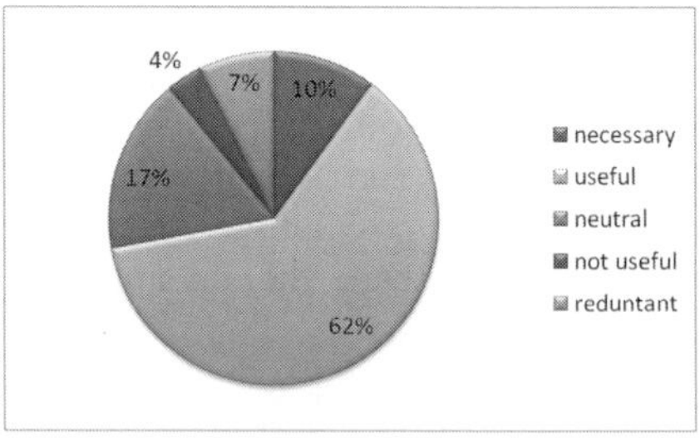

Figure 11 Functionality for giving a copy of individual collections

4. Conclusions

Results of the survey performed in frame of the ENRICH project gathered opinions of experts, professionals, students and hobbyists from 12 European countries. The analysis based on the results gave reliable overview of the users requirements concerning user personalisation features in digital libraries. The survey investigated two basic personalisation features for digital libraries: static and dynamic individual collections and individual virtual documents. The results, as interpreted in the previous section, proved the correctness of the intentions to implement the new features. Full analysis of the survey is available as the ENRICH project deliverable D 4.1, Caldelli (2008).

At the very basic level the results proved that investigated features for user personalisation in scope of digital libraries are reasonable to be introduced. In particular, further activities should be focused on providing individual collections functionality and virtual documents functionality with a special reflection for processing and manipulating text documents and providing community building facilities.

The textual form of documents in digital libraries seems to be the most attractive one for research and other types of use. It also appeared that respondents prefer to use on-line services for storing collections and documents they will work on, which is quite natural because of the convenience for the users. Change notifications for dynamic collections and searching mechanism for individual collections also received positive marks from respondents and seem to be useful.

Personal notes and files for individual collections and documents were evaluated as valuable. In case of individual collections respondents preferred personal notes over personal files. In case of individual documents respondents created a priority list where particular functions were ordered as follows (starting from the most required function): personal notes about whole document, personal files connected with part of a document and personal files connected with whole document.

Community building functionalities were evaluated as useful with some sceptic attitude for opening all individual elements to the public. Respondents would rather keep the visibility of their elements in control and grant appropriate rights to selected elements or users only. What is interesting, the functionality to give a copy of individual collections or documents higher marks than the functionality which allows sharing individual collections and documents.

Based on the survey results, the most important subset of investigated functions will be introduced in the virtual research environment which is built in scope of the ENRICH project. Further activities should be also focused on providing the remaining, positively evaluated functions.

Acknowledgements

Works under the ENRICH project funded by eContent*Plus* programme (no. ECP-2006-DILI-510049; „European Networking Resources and Information Concerning Cultural Heritage"). Project website: http://enrich.manuscriptorium.eu/

References

Caldelli, R., Kligiene, R., Mazzanti, P., Parkoła, T., Psohlavec, T., Werla, M., (2008). Definition of requirements for the creation of personalised virtual digital libraries. ENRICH project deliverable D4.1.
http://enrich.manuscriptorium.com/files/ENRICH_WP4_D_4_1_final.pdf

Knoll, A. (2004). Digital Access to Old Manuscripts, *Linguistica Computazionale*, 2004, Vol. XX-XXI, Digital Technology and Philological Disciplines, 277 – 286.

Mazurek, C., Stroiński, M., Węglarz, J., Werla, M., (2006). Metadata harvesting in regional digital libraries in PIONIER Network, *Campus-Wide Information Systems,* 2006, Vol. 23, No. 4, 241–253.

MINERVA EC, (2003) *Handbook for quality in cultural websites: improving quality for citizens, Identity* http://www.minervaeurope.org/publications/qualitycriteria1_2draft/cap1.htm

MINERVA EC, (2003-2004) *Cultural Website Quality Principles* http://www.minervaeurope.org/publications/tenqualityprinciples.htm

MINERVA EC, (First edition September 2008) *Working Group Handbook on cultural web user interaction* - Quality, Accessibility and Usability http://www.minervaeurope.org/publications/handbookwebusers.htm

Qualitative Approach and Grounded Theory for Assessing User Evaluation of Library Services: City Library Network of Perugia - A Case Study

Chiara Faggiolani

Scuola Speciale per Archivisti e Bibliotecari, Sapienza Università di Roma, Italy
Phd in Library and Information Science

Abstract: This paper presents the aims, the methodology and the preliminary results of an in-progress investigation into the users of four libraries belonging to the City Library Network (one main library and three satellite public libraries) in Perugia, a city in the centre of Italy with 160,000 inhabitants. The main aim of the investigation is to explore the degree of satisfaction, the needs, the motivation and the perceptions of both real and potential users, by means of quantitative and qualitative research methods. It also aims to be a reflection on the methodology used, accepting that the dichotomy "qualitative versus quantitative" has long been set aside and considers the two approaches in fact deeply complementary. On an operational level, the investigation foresaw the use of questionnaires to evaluate user satisfaction, and face-to-face interviews and focus group sessions aimed at examining specific issues raised by the questionnaires, enquiring not only into the "how much" of the incidence of certain variables but more interestingly into the "why". Finally, the paper examines the relationship between empirical research and theoretical speculation. The investigation has attempted to ascertain the validity of the application of Grounded Theory Methodology and to establish whether the ATLAS.ti program is able to guarantee greater objectivity when applying qualitative research techniques.

Keywords: Grounded Theory; Qualitative method; Interview; ATLAS.ti; Advocacy; Interpretation.

1. Introduction

This paper presents the objectives, methodologies and research of an on-going investigation into the users of four libraries belonging to the City Library Network of Perugia, a central Italian city with 160,000 inhabitants.

The research, which aims at investigating the degree of satisfaction, the motivation and the perceptions of both real and potential users of the libraries, by means of qualitative research techniques, also intends to be a reflection on methodologies and on the relationship between empirical and theoretical reflection in biblioteconomy.

The concept of "fluidity" of the individual is one which is perceived at the present time even within the sphere of biblioteconomy and, as such, requires that the user be considered from a *holistic* point of view, recuperating the notion of interpretation as a new research instrument and not as an obstacle to the objectivity of the investigation. This instrument can be used in order to reach a deeper awareness of the user's needs, whether he expresses them or not, and to understand the motivation behind his use of a library and his perceptions of the experience. "An evaluation of an information service may be subjective or objective. Subjective studies based on opinions are not without value because it is important to know how people feel about a service. But an evaluation is of most value if it is *analytical* and *diagnostic*, seeking to discover how the service might be improved, and it is difficult to base this type of study on opinion alone" (Lancaster, 1993). This means that the aim of research is to demonstrate the reliability of data collected through qualitative investigation techniques in order to prove that the qualitative approach can be indeed "analytical" and "diagnostic".

It is more than evident that evaluation has previously been directed more towards the service rather than its users and that the techniques employed until the present day have been valuable in measuring the rate of usage and the number of users, but not in creating an accurate profile of who these users are, nor in discovering why they are making use of the service. In this light, quantitative research techniques, however vital for the management of libraries, do not allow full comprehension of the relationship between a library and the environment it is set in, nor the unexpressed needs of library users, thus leaving some important aspects of the service totally in the dark.

This does not mean that qualitative techniques should be considered instruments capable of drawing a complete picture of the issues in discussion – quite the contrary – putting into practice a qualitative approach means abandoning the prospective of exhaustivity and being aware that "the qualitative prospective, due to its subjectivity and its low level of formalization, is more difficult to transform into schematized procedures…." (Corbetta, 2003).

The belief behind this investigation is that qualitative and quantitative research, although profoundly different, are, however, profitably complimentary: "There is no one act, no single decision taken in research which is not an inextricable mix of quality and quantity […] Each one constitutes aspects which, though mostly indistinguishable, are in co-presence in every single phase of an investigation: the ying and yang, as it were, of every effective operation of investigation […] There is, thus, an essential tension between quality and quantity in every data collection and analysis technique" (Campelli, 1999).

This research is in step with a new trend in Italian biblioteconomy, which until recently, has given ample space to quantitative evaluation based on performance indicators and which is now attempting to integrate this approach by investigating subjective aspects of users' motivation, their requirements and their perceptions of the quality of the service.

This territory seems to be the most fertile for the implementation of qualitative techniques as it is the kind in which the results of a certain type of research which steps outside the usual schemes, favouring a direct contact with the users, listening to them and being willing to reflect on any points raised, can actually be substantial and significative: "Quantitative research finds what it looks for but we will never know anything about what it did not look for. Qualitative research finds what it finds but we will never know what it does not find" (Lucidi, Alivernini, Pedon, 2008).

2. Definition of the Method: Grounded Theory Methodology

The Grounded Theory Methodology has been chosen as a methodological support and reference theory in order to ensure that a correct approach to the investigation was followed in accordance with qualitative logic, in respect to the data and the categories which must not be heterodox, but rather, founded on the data itself: the Grounded Theory is the construction of a theory which does not originate in a logical deduction process, nor in an abstract speculative procedure which takes inspiration from pre-existent theoretical reflections, nor even does it confer the value of empirical proof to data in order to verify and illustrate the aforementioned suppositions. This is because the approach views the data as the source for a theory which can make sense of the data itself, explaining in this way the origin and the reason for the theory and granting the data a theoretical statute which goes well beyond that of mere elements useful for the verification of theories based on non-data sources" (Strati, 2009).

This new concept of data, as a *generator of theory,* has determined the need to approach the investigation without narrowing down research design into excessively detailed questioning, but rather, prefers using a generative "*What's going on here*?" style of enquiry (Glaser, 1998), which embraces the full complexity of the issue, rather than attempting to reduce its elements to a few controllable variables. The choice of methodology, if on one hand, is a reflection of the paradigm of reference, more significantly, is dependent on the type of object one wishes to investigate and on the viewpoint from which one intends observing each specific issue. It is not a coincidence that Grounded Theory has become widely used in fields of application of practical disciplines (e.g. marketing, medicine, management, etc.) which are faced with tangible problems requiring operative solutions. One of the main characteristics of the Grounded Theory, the fact that "*it fits and works*", makes it particularly suitable for application in all those disciplines in which research and theoretical reflection are defined as the basis for the development of operative indications and strategies directed at carrying out change (Tarozzi, 2009).

It can be easily understood how biblioteconomy, which perceives library service evaluation as one of the keys to improving libraries, is inexorably drawn to a research methodology which gives priority to investigating input supplied by users who are, or should be, the ones served by such institutions, thus allowing for the generation of useful theories based on a practical foundation.

Analyzing motivations, expressed or unexpressed needs and user satisfaction, whether the individual is already a user or is only a potential one of library services, obliges us to face the reality that every library is a world within itself and that the territory in which it operates is highly complex, the perimeter of which cannot easily be defined, in as much as the issues under examination are dynamic and imbued with an

enormous quantity of variables, the most important of which being the attitude with users approach libraries with, which is in turn dictated by their personal perception of such institutions.
Reference to the Grounded Theory in this context appears extremely useful since the objective of the research is to identify processes associated with phenomena, beginning with those articulated by the users themselves, and the development of an interpretive theory able to integrate and conceptualize empirical data in order to supply answers which are useful and valuable in the planning of library services. Reflection on the method, moving from *linear* (quantitative approach) to *circular* (qualitative approach) and from circular to *recursive* (Grounded Theory), must move forward hand in hand with the development of the field work, and should not be allowed to wane during the initial phase, but should be alimented by a continuous and profitable comparison with the observed reality.

3. Case Study: The City Library Network of Perugia

Given the initial premises, a case study has been chosen as the most suitable instrument for the *holistic* approach which characterizes this research, and the most effective strategy to explain the "*how*" and "*why*" of the phenomena to be examined, never losing sight, however, of its inaptness to shed light on frequency and rate (the "*where*" and "*how much*") (Yin, 2003).
With a case study, the phenomenon is investigated as it occurs, making it impossible to detect the demarcation between the phenomenon itself and its context: "The entire research design in a case study is heavily conditioned by the way in which the unit of analysis is defined. "*What is my case*?" is the question a researcher should always be able to answer. In more clearly defined situations, such as clinical research, the case coincides with the individual. In other environments, rather than an individual, it may involve a group, an organization or an event. The definition of the unit of analysis is closely connected to the way in which the initial research questions and the study hypotheses have been defined" (Lucidi, Alivernini, Pedon, 2008).
It is noteworthy to see how in this investigation, the unit of analysis (library users), which is the specific "social object" our attention is focused on, does not coincide with the unit of data collection, which in our case, is the individual user. The case study, as already mentioned, is highly adapt for the qualitative approach as in both contexts one cannot be satisfied with a generalization of the results but should aim at a acquiring more detailed understanding.
The City Library Network of Perugia was chosen for the case study for characteristics which belong to this particular institution and for the impression it gives of being a "modular" system, therefore able to be broken down and analyzed in its individual parts from different points of view. It is a small yet complex network, which although being composed of a small number of libraries gives a picture of a relatively differentiated system. The fact that it is collocated in the small city environment of Perugia allows the dynamics of cultural consumerism to be easily observed. Furthermore, the nomination of a new director just a few months before the beginning of the investigation indicated that a change of direction in the management of the network was already underway – one which has revealed itself to be more dynamic and more attentive towards the needs of the public, showing a greater propensity to

enquire about its expectations. Included below is a brief presentation of the individual libraries which make up the Perugia network with the aim of highlighting the main criticalities through SWOT Synthesis.

Augusta Library

Strengths	**Weaknesses**
- Historical patrimony; - Located near the University; - Has roots in the *collective imagination;*	- Located within the town's limited traffic zone; - The premises themselves and the interaction with the public are not user-friendly; - Low percentage of material and open bookcase;
Opportunities	**Threats**
- Opening of a deconsecrated Church to free up the reading room, thus no longer using library space for other services and activities;	- Possibility it could be perceived as a conservation library; - Users are mostly academics and students;

Sandro Penna Library (San Sisto)

Strengths	Weaknesses
- Immediately recognisable; - Premises are young and dynamic; - Large open spaces and nearby theatre; - Spacious children's section;	- Service management and usage is very "traditional", static; - Children's section is not completely adapt for its purpose;
Opportunities	**Threats**
- Coordination with the theatre; - Located close to many schools; - The district is undergoing a phase of expansion;	

Biblionet Library (Ponte San Giovanni)

Strengths	**Weaknesses**
- Location: Ponte San Giovanni is a young district, the library is centrally positioned within it and near commercial activities;	- Inadequate design of the layout of the children's section; - Difficult to recognize; - Lack of patrimony in relation to the social context (foreigners);

Opportunities	Threats
- Better re-design of interior spaces;	- Possibility that it becomes identified as only a local library;

Multimedia Library

Strengths	Weaknesses
- Deep roots in the local community; - The building has a spacious garden and terraces;	- Interior spaces are small; - Low external visibility;
Opportunities	**Threats**
- Re-opening of the children's section; - Terrace can be covered; - Garden can be used to a greater advantage;	

The case study (Users of the Library Network) was divided into two macro-units (actual users and potential users), then divided again into sub-units (users of the four libraries analyzed individually: the Augusta Library, the Biblionet Library of Ponte San Giovanni, the Sandro Penna Library of San Sisto and the Multimedia Library), in order to isolate and examine single aspects of the global context depending on the specific questions one wished to pose, aiming at "reassembling" the pieces at the final stage of analysis, whilst keeping in mind that reconstructing the identity of the Library Network usage goes well beyond a simple summary.

4. Qualitative Interview: An Explorative Technique and Effective Instrument for Advocacy

Field-work began in December 2008 and in its first phase took the form of a series of meetings with the library director and staff members, with the aim of sharing the objectives of the investigation and verifying that the library could indeed sustain the process.

The motivation of the staff and its full involvement, it should be remembered, are determining factors if one wishes a library to be closely connected to the reality in which it operates, and to be open to dialogue, dynamic, able to read and interpret its cultural context of reference and to find the most successful solutions to meeting the requirements directly and indirectly expressed by the users. These first meetings, in line with the Grounded Theory perspective, can be considered an initial part of the field-work: in this way we can consider the director and the library staff as expert witnesses who can offer a natural vision of the issue, in as much as they are carriers of a "focalized" point of view. The research design, fully approved and accepted, foresaw two different usage profiles in its first phase of implementation:

- Real Users: 800 questionnaires were distributed within the libraries (Augusta Library: 312; Multimedia Library: 136; Biblionet Library of Ponte San Giovanni: 136; Sandro Penna Library of San Sisto: 216) in a two-week sample period from 20th March to 3rd April, with the objective of evaluating user satisfaction;
- Opinion Leader: a series of qualitative interviews were arranged and carried out with a selection of Opinion Leader citizens with an explorative and advocacy finality (began 14th March and still in progress).

As far as the purely quantitative part of the investigation is concerned, for reasons of synthesis, we will avoid, at the present moment, dealing with all the details connected to the creation of the questionnaire and the sampling design used for their distribution which, although deserving of an adequate examination, will have to be sacrificed in order to leave space for the description and details of the technique used for the qualitative interviews which are the focus of this investigation. Due to the aforementioned particular characteristics of the Library Network and the specific moment of dynamism which it is experiencing, and also to the uniqueness of the city context which made it possible, we felt it useful to involve a small group of citizens, considered to be Opinion Leaders, with whom the technique of the Qualitative Interview was applied.

This was in line with the objective of investigating in greater depth how the Library Network is perceived by people who are directly involved in the organization and management of different aspects of city life and this in itself turned out to be a powerful instrument of advocacy.

The interview which undoubtedly represents the most highly privileged form of data collection in social sciences, is an instrument which can be used in a significant way in the context of the participation which characterizes qualitative research and which, unlike interviews with questionnaires, places the interviewer and the interviewee in a position in which their verbal exchange and sense of reciprocity contribute to the building of knowledge.

The selection of the Opinion Leaders used a *theoretical sampling* design, reasoned and not probabilistic, in which the representativity of the subjects interviewed was established not on a statistical basis but on one of typology in order to ensure they represent diversified social situations, thus reflecting the social complexity of the issue being investigated (Cicognani, 2002).

In this type of sampling the definition of the sample is not finalized before the data collected is underway, but continues throughout the collecting and elaboration phases, in that cyclical process which constitutes the DNA of qualitative research: "the choice of cases takes place progressively throughout the research process, based on what potential they might have in offering a contribution to the *in fieri* theoretical interests of the researcher".

The small number of the samples is justified by the intensity of the technique in which "one single case of an interviewer being able to create a pleasant feeling of empathy with the interviewee can often be more useful than dozens of questionnaires in understanding certain social dynamics" (Corbetta, 2003).

The aim of the interviews was to identify crucial issues and highlight those which require further study – in other words, listening to the description of each individual's concept of what they imagine a library should be, listening to their "library stories", one can "explore" the collective imagination and paint a general picture of the expectations people have of libraries, ultimately achieving the identification of the issues affecting the library network in examination. Finally, it is important to highlight the attention this operation received within the city itself – hardly a matter of secondary importance and one which fully covers the *advocacy* function. "Library advocates have their own stories about how the library has made a difference in their lives....One library asked library school students to spend a Saturday interviewing library users. Every library should have cards placed strategically to make it easy for patrons to share their "success stories". Some people thanked ALA for sponsoring its "Libraries Change Lives" contest and giving them an opportunity to share their stories. Sharing these stories in testimony before governing bodies, interviews with reporters or conversations with the college president, school principal and other leaders is one of the most powerful ways to make the case for library support" (ALA 2008).

5. VISE Logic Data Analysis with ATLAS.ti

Over the last few years there has been a lot of talk about the marriage between computers and qualitative research, with the effect, on a methodological level, of increasing the precision and the reliability of a researcher's classifications, improving the rigorousness of his reasoning and guaranteeing an audit trail of his claims, which has long been considered one of the main weaknesses of qualitative research. Among all the software "at the service" of this type of analysis, ATLAS.ti, software CAQDAS (Computer Assisted Qualitative Data Analysis Software), is generally considered the one best able to highlight innovative methodological approaches. "ATLAS.ti was designed to facilitate the development of a theoretical model firmly based on text, that is to say, to produce scientific knowledge by permitting the categories of analysis of the researcher to interact with the meanings constructed by the subjects in the discourse. Furthermore, the network structure of the program recalls the logic of recursivity and interconnection which is the basis of the Grounded Theory (Milesi, Castellani, 2002). Although it was not designed exclusively to respond to the needs of research based on the theoretical and methodological perspective of Grounded Theory, it contains explicit reference to it.

The analysis procedure foresees, as a first move, the creation of a *Hermeneutic Unit:* "it can be likened to a file we have in our computer and it contains not only references to files to be analyzed but also to sets of other objects which illustrate the route of conceptual analysis the researcher is following. One can visualize documents for analysis whether they be text documents, images, videos, and audio registrations: in ATLAS.ti language these are called *Primary Documents* (PD)" (Chiarolanza, De Gregorio, 2007).

Once PDs (in our case, transcriptions of the qualitative interviews) are placed in the files, one can begin the first operation of *open coding* which consists of linking a selection of words, phrases or paragraphs (*quotations*) to emergent and sensibilizing conceptual categories (*codes*). In our case, the decision was taken to favour an operation of codification which did not follow the *line-by-line* rule, but which gave codes as much to entire paragraphs as single words, assigning a general sense to parts of the text in their entirety, thereby avoiding setting ourselves limitations according to standards of "quantity".

Despite the fact that the job of interpretation is absolutely supported by ATLAS.ti, whose help must be recognized as a determining factor, the effort has been made never to lose sight of the fact it is an instrument, and must continue to be regarded as such. In this way, the codification operations have been carried out following GT logic: "These acts of research have distinguished themselves by their continual activity of conceptualization, occurring right from the very earliest stage of the research, its planning. How does this happen? Isolating an image or a written field-note and highlighting the part of the image or of the text which captures our attention, we find a denomination – generally speaking a verb, as it valorizes the procedural aspect – which appears to represent that which caught our attention and interest in the first place. The denomination gives us a sense of what we ought to note in those empirical data, without summarizing the notion. Glaser and Strauss state that the kind of concepts which must be generated will have two essential interconnected characteristics. In the first place, the concepts will be *analytic*, or rather, sufficiently general to outline the characteristics of concrete entity and not the entities themselves. Furthermore, they should be *sensitizing*, and produce a "significant" photograph, supported by images capable of evoking features of one's own personal experience" (Strati, 2009). Also in line with the GT conceptualization concept is the notion that the network model is the best representation of a text: ATLAS.ti, functioning according to VISE logic, allows for cyclical and reiterated process of analysis, comparison and interpretation, which supplies a high precision yet creative approach to textual data. VISE logic is fulfilled in the successive operations of codification, until the Core Category is identified and at that point it is possible to visualize the properties of objects and the relationships between them (visualization), without losing the global meaning of the text even as you work on a specific level (integration), whilst still maintaining an intuitive and innovative approach to the research (serendipity, exploration) (Milesi, Castellani, 2002).

References

Campelli E., (1999). *Da un luogo comune. Elementi di metodologia delle scienze sociali*, Franco Angeli, Milano.

Campelli E., (1991). *Il metodo e il suo contrario. Sul recupero della problematica del metodo in sociologia*, Franco Angeli, Milano.

Chiarolanza C., De Gregorio E., (2007). *L'analisi dei processi psico-sociali, lavorare con ATLAS.ti*, Carocci Editore, Roma.

Cicognani E., (2002). *Psicologia Sociale e ricerca qualitativa*, Carocci Editore, Roma.

Cicognani E., (2002). *L'approccio qualitativo della Grounded Theory in psicologia sociale* in *Metodi qualitativi in psicologia sociale*, a cura di B. Mazzara, Carocci Editore, Roma.

Corbetta P., (2003). *La ricerca sociale: metodologia e tecniche, Vol. 1 I paradigmi di riferimento*, Il Mulino, Bologna.

Corbetta P., (2003). *La ricerca sociale: Metodologia e tecniche. Vol 3: Le tecniche qualitative*, Il Mulino, Bologna.

De Gregorio E., Mosiello F., (2004). *Tecniche di ricerca qualitativa e di analisi delle informazioni con ATLAS.ti*, Kappa, Roma.

Glaser B., (1998). *Doing Grounded Theory. Issues and discussions*, Sociology Press, Mill Valley (CA).
Lancaster F.W., (1993). *If you want to evaluate your library...*, Library Association Publishing, London.
Library Advocate's Handbook,(2008). American Library Association, Chicago.
Lucidi F., Alivernini F. Pedon A., (2008). *Metodologia della ricerca qualitativa*, Il Mulino, Bologna.
Milesi P., Castellani P. (2002). *L'analisi qualitativa di testi con il programma ATLAS.ti* in *Metodi qualitativi in psicologia sociale*, a cura di Bruno M. Mazzara, Carocci Editore, Roma.
Strati A., (2009). Introduzione all'edizione italiana di Glaser B.G., Strauss A.L., *La scoperta della Grounded Theory. Strategie per la ricerca qualitativa*, Armando Editore, Roma.
Tarozzi M., (2009). *Conversazione con Barney G. Glaser: "A quarant'anni dall'uscita di The Discovery of Grounded Theory",* in B.G., Strauss A.L., *La scoperta della Grounded Theory. Strategie per la ricerca qualitativa*, traduzione italiana a cura di A. Strati, Armando Editore, Roma.
Yin R. K., (2003), *Case study research, design and methods*, Sage, Newbury Park, California.

Tartu University Library as a Medium between Different Patrons

Krista Lepik

Research Fellow, University of Tartu Library, Estonia
PhD Student, University of Tartu, Estonia

Abstract: 12 semi-structured interviews with faculty members of the University of Tartu have been conducted in order to start generating a grounded theory about the academic library's communication with different patrons. What is the meaning of the academic library for faculty members and how they perceive the issue of availability of reading materials proposed for students are the main research questions discussed in this paper. Additionally, some attention has been paid at current alternatives of making compulsory reading materials available for students.
Keywords: Academic libraries; Faculty-library collaboration; Collection development.

1. Introduction

The paper is about the relationships between the various university faculty members – teaching and research staff and – university library. Besides being a supporting facility for University of Tartu, the University of Tartu Library (UTL) should also be viewed as a medium between two important patron groups: faculty members and students.
In this paper I will at first take a glance at theoretical aspects and previous studies concerning faculty-university library relationships. I will proceed, paying attention on methods of ongoing research. Last but not least I'll introduce the faculty members' attitudes towards university library and explore the integration of compulsory reading materials into particular courses.
The theoretical axis of this work is relying on symbolic interactionism (Blumer 1969): *i.e* how faculty members perceive the meaning of university library while interacting with other people and how they build up their „communication strategy" with library according to this meaning. The communication strategy of faculty members itself is

analysed by looking at how faculty members select compulsory and recommended literature for students.

According to Osgood and Schramm circular model (McQuail & Windahl 1993: 19) the communication process between acting parties is understood as an endless array of identical functions, namely encoding, decoding and interpreting. The communication between faculty members and librarians presupposes same functions (of the university library, see figure 1). It is the mutual nurturing of the meaning „university library“ that takes place every day even if we all (faculty members, students, librarians) don't notice it.

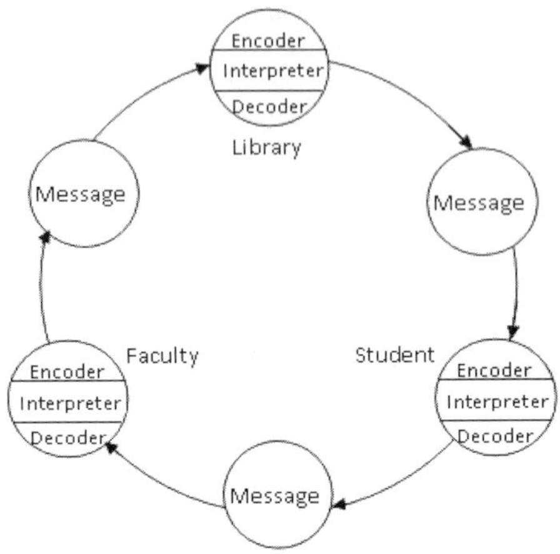

Fig. 1 Further development the Osgood and Schramm circular model

Lots of publications concern the (changing) role of librarians and information literacy – these are subjects that also may deal with faculty-librarian *or* student-library relationships and that are been very widely discussed (some of the most recent ones include Ghosh (2009), Saunders (2009), McAskill (2008), *etc.*). But what happens if we deal with those parties simultaneously, positioning the university library between faculty members and students?

A thorough overview on faculty-librarian relationships by Paul O. Jenkins (2005) has been issued, concerning also the role of faculty members in collection development and working together in information literacy. Also a few years ago, in 2006, on IATUL Conference, Peter Stubley introduced activities performed under aegis of „New Partnership“ in the University of Sheffield Library. Those works prove that the academic libraries have taken a new course – from service provider to a partner. But this is the point of view of the librarians. As Jenkins referred, faculty members are needed to be „convinced of the importance of information literacy“ (2005: 64). If the faculty members do not take information literacy for granted as librarians do and their views of participating in university library's activities is somewhat different than librarians', then maybe there's sometimes a need to take one step back and look back on the meaning of the academic library from the point of view of a faculty member.

Current research context is looking at University of Tartu Library (founded in 1802) that is the largest academic library in Estonia. Additionally, there are over 30 specialized libraries of different faculties, institutes, chairs and research centres of

University of Tartu.

According to the philosophy of collection management in UTL, one circulating copy of a textbook or a monoghaph used as a textbook is acquired for every five students (Rahvusteavikute eksemplaarsus..). „Nevertheless the needs of faculty and students are taken into consideration. If a new curriculum or research area is emerging, the library has to react to the changes flexibly and provide the needed information. At the same time, interdisciplinarity makes the situation complicated as acquisition guidelines based on Universal Decimal Classification (UDC) cannot cover all needs of library users.“: Schwede (2006).

2. About the research

The first goal of my research is to study the meaning of university library through the eyes of faculty members. The second goal is to explore the availability of compulsory and recommended literature for students of University of Tartu. Further empirical section will be organised through the research questions and will first look at how much are faculty members counting on university library while providing students with lists of reading materials. I will conclude looking at how integrated is the compulsory reading material into particular courses; can or cannot students manage without it.

Gathering data for my paper took place in the beginning of February until the beginning of March as 12 semi-structured interviews were conducted with faculty members of 4 different subject areas: *realia*, *humaniora*, *medicina* and *socialia*.

Respondent	Subject area	Number of courses (in Fall 2008/Spring 2009)	Total time (in years) of being a faculty member and giving lectures
R1	*Medicina*	6	44
R2	*Socialia*	6	16
R3	*Socialia*	16	3
R4	*Medicina*	17	14
R5	*Humaniora*	10	20
R6	*Socialia*	7	16
R7	*Realia*	8	9
R8	*Medicina*	7	17
R9	*Humaniora*	5	8
R10	*Realia*	1	2
R11	*Realia*	12	17
R12	*Socialia*	13	10

Table 1 Brief descriptions of respondents (Data about the number of courses is obtained from the Studies Information System ÕIS)

The selection from the population of faculty members based on the representative characteristics (so the faculty members were not selected randomly). Embracing different subject areas was first of the criteria for finding appropriate respondents for interviews. Another important aspect was whether the respondents taught students or

not: it helped to include different faculty members from research fellows to professors. During the respondents' selection process another criterium, experience, also emerged – so the total time of being a faculty member was also taken into account.
The transcripts of interviews are analysed to start generating grounded theory (Strauss & Corbin 1998). For providing more reliability to this research, the outcomes of the interview are complemented with juxtaposition of lists of compulsory reading materials (with permission from all respondents) with data from:

- Estonian online public access catalogue called ESTER,
- ÕIS (Studies Information System of University of Tartu where some digitized articles and chapters are preserved) and
- available scientific databases for University of Tartu.

3. The results

In the context of University of Tartu, the university library is perceived as an important supporting facility. In case a faculty member has had some kind of contact with any research fellow from UTL, he or she also payed little attention to UTL as research & development facility. The main building of the library is seen as a studying and meeting place, but mostly useful for students. Some faculty members had lots of nostalgic memories about UTL (from times they were students of University of Tartu) but today they all have remained at a distance from the main building. However, the specialized libraries either of faculty member's faculty, chair, institute or research center are used often (due to proximity, specialized collections, librarians familiar with same research area) and University of Tartu Library is seen as an invaluable access provider to databases of scientific, technical, medical and social science literature.
While preparing a list of compulsory reading the faculty members are generally keeping in mind the accordance of reading materials to the curriculum and if possible, are relying on their decades-long experiences – but the availability of the publication (in library, on one's own shelf) is also a noteworthy issue. One cannot include publications that are not available for students, to the compulsory reading list: it is obvious, *matter of the competency of faculty member* (R2) or *even unethical* (R8), they say.
A paradox in case of bachelor students was emerging: although the faculty members may want to provide them with best available reading materials that are often also used in "high-ranked" universities, the susceptibility of a student may set its limits. Students are not used to read or they have not got much time to read (as lots of them also have a job) so they prefer to rely on conspectus that is provided during a lecture – fortunately in relatively many courses it *is* sufficient. There are so called fans, of course, young enthusiasts, but according to interviews they form a minority among others. For bachelor students, the extent of lectures and independent reading may also vary in different curricula. Students in open university, master students or PhD students seem to have higher motivations for studying and for them the proportion of additional reading materials (be they compulsory or recommended) is also considerable. The issue of lack of time seems also to be less problematic in case of elective courses – as choosing these courses bases on the free will of students and the

faculty members are usually providing students recommended reading materials rather than compulsory reading lists.

Without question, the faculty member is seen as the compiler of the reading list. Some of the faculty members I've interviewed showed interest towards possible assistance from librarian in matters concerning information distribution: like making photocopies or electronic files in PDF format, looking for publications that some of patrons have forgot to return, retrieving books from repositories to the "shelf of course pack" or gathering and notifying about relevant offers of new books from publishers to the faculty members. The latter is especially useful *if a librarian* (mainly in the specialized library) *is familiar with the "profile" of the faculty member* (R12) and can therefore identify publications that might be relevant to the faculty member. Being alumnus or alumna of particular research area (but not necessarily of library and information sciences) might be also an advantage, but about the level of education the opinions of faculty members again varied. Some proposed that the librarian should have at least bachelor degree, some faculty members, on the contrary, would prefer a librarian who is at least a PhD student in relevant field.

Tasks of a librarian mentioned in previous paragraph might refer to downgrading the role of a librarian to a position of an assistant or secretary. But it is necessary to emphasize that these were the activities that were considered supportive while preparing a reading list. Discussing about the general concept of "competence of a librarian", the faculty members pointed to different skills and virtues that have been almost traditionally valued among librarians as well. It is important that a librarian had professional knowledge about librarianship: that includes orienting in bibliographic records, skills of using *different programs* (R3) and databases and quick response to queries (that was the quality mentioned most often). Kindness, helpfulness, empathy and generally good communicating skill were mentioned as virtues of a librarian as a good partner for the faculty member. From librarians of specialized libraries, well-orienting in home library's collections is also expected.

While conducting and analyzing the interviews, an issue of the extent of following marketing rules in a university library became important question. On one hand university library should be an active service provider *that pays attention at different target groups* (R2) and acts as a *meeting place rather than sanctuary* (R3). But there's also the *status of a university library* (R4) as universities have always had libraries. It may happen, as one of the faculty members claimed, that *if the library is seen among faculty as a customer service provider rather than equal partner with mutual goals, this concept may start spreading also on the university as a whole as in some sence the students perceive the university library and university as an integral whole* (R12).

Before dealing with availability of reading materials I would also like to introduce shortly practical suggestions of faculty members that were revealing during interviews. Some of these were quite personal or perhaps even hardly practicable like maintaining a *small gymnasium in library* (keeping in mind that "*Mens sana in corpore sano*")(R3). But *keeping university library opened all summer long* (UTL has usually been closed in July)(R5) or *collecting links of open access video lectures* (R7) are undoubtly worth (re)considering.

It is obvious that a university library cannot provide necessary copies of printed textbooks or monographs for each student. Therefore faculty members have proposed either through the cooperation with library or without it different ways to make textbooks' contents available for students:

- lectures and in case of lack of time, additional conspects (handed out or e-mailed),
- rotaprint editions,
- „course packs“ that include relevant books or copies of chapters and articles (making copies and retrieving books from repositories has usually been a task for librarians as mentioned earlier) have proven to be very useful before implementing Studies Information System ÕIS some years ago and are used in some institutes,
- photocopies „on demand“ (usually initiated by students in case of lack of printed textbooks or rotaprint editions),
- scanned chapters (or saved e-articles) in Studies Information System are most often used today. ÕIS enables faculty members to make reading materials available either for users of ÕIS (that is for Tartu University students and staff) or for subscribers of particular course. It is also possible to remove the reading material from ÕIS (or make it inaccessible) when the particular course is over,
- web-based courses in the Blackboard learning environment,
- video lectures (service provided by the Multimedia Center of Tartu University) were found especially useful in case of technology-oriented courses or guest lecturers.

When students start to work on their research projects, they are also introduced different databases of scientific literature. In some cases it is done by faculty member as supervisor of the research project, but seminars and courses about using different electronic information sources (relevant web pages and free databases in the Internet, databases accessible in computer network of Tartu University) were also mentioned. Those courses were prepared and lectures were delivered by faculty members not librarians although there is also a web-based course „Basics of information literacy“ developed by subject librarians of UTL (my colleague Vilve Seiler will introduce it on QQML 2009).

It is necessary to note that there is a considerable difference between compulsory and recommended reading materials. It is found sufficient if there are at least 1-2 items of a publication from recommended reading list in the specialized library. As some faculty members are experts who teach specific disciplines for smaller groups of students, the problem of interdisciplinarity mentioned in the introduction is not acute for them. If necessary, they also apply strategies mentioned earlier. So the juxtaposition of curricula with OPAC is a relevant issue in case of interdisciplinary courses where compulsory reading materials are proposed.

Juxtaposition of syllabi and OPAC ESTER, Studies Information System and databases available for University of Tartu has shown that at the particular time of year (before the exams sessions) the compulsory reading materials are well available. There are plenty of copies either for loan a book for use outside the library or at least some for local loan. But by default every academic librarian can predict that the need for some books will be increasing during the exams session. So – to the contrary to my tentative assumption a further analysis of the loans of compulsory reading materials is needed, using data from the circulation mode of ESTER.

4. Conclusions

The interviews lead to an assumption that although the faculty members generally value the role of university library they are not always ready or interested in sharing same enthusiasm about „new partnership“ with librarians as their attitude towards university library may be formed during long years when the ideas of meeting faculty members' needs from behalf of university librarians were also in development. A faculty member creates her or his own strategies for coping with current situation and if these ways work sufficiently well, there is seen no need to change the strategies. Therefore, while proposing ideas (like personalized bulletin of new books, leaving a trace about scarce item in OPAC *etc.*) the librarian should have a pretty good argumentation on behalf of these.

As if upon a hidden agreement, during the interviews the faculty members also commenced to reveal their attitudes towards books. Although there is not much space to discuss this observation, it might affirm the notion that the roles of the library and librarian are perceived in connection with the importance of books and other printed materials. It is somewhat threatening as important electronic information resources (especially for faculty members) are mediated to patrons via university library. It as a sign of quality if information is made available as if using a magic wand, but it shouldn't mean undervaluing the role of the academic library or competence of academic librarians.

An advantage of conducting semi-structured interviews was that the author could interview faculty members herself, without using any assistance and pose additional question according to the „path“ of the conversation. According to expectation it helped to collect data rich in nuances.

Research activities introduced in this paper have so far focused mostly on faculty members' perceptions of university library and the availability of the reading materials (be these compulsory or recommended). In order to gain as realistic picture as possible of the meaning of the university library, views of its librarians (especially subject librarians and acquisition librarians of UTL) and other patrons – students need to be added. As already mentioned, additional analysis, using circulation mode of ESTER needs to be conducted in order to reveal the availability and loan frequency of different publications proposed by the faculty members. The analysis would be useful for detecting „bottle-necks“ perhaps even at the level of a particular publication.

Acknowledgements

The author wishes to thank all 12 faculty members of University of Tartu who agreed to participate on interviews, the colleagues from UTL for comments about the research and Pille Pruulmann-Vengerfeldt, my PhD thesis's supervisor in University of Tartu for encouragement and advice. This paper has been prepared with the help of Estonian Science Fund Grant No 8006.

References

Ghosh, M., (2009). Information Professionals in the Open Access Era: the competencies, challenges and new roles. *Information Development*, Vol. 25, No. 1, 33 – 42.

Jenkins, P., (2005). *Faculty-Librarian Relationships*. Chandos Publishing, Oxford.

McAskill, W., (2008). Information Literacy: The Leadership Role of the Academic Librarian.

College Quarterly, 2008, Vol. 11, No. 1, 1 – 15.
McQuail, D. and Windahl, S., (1993). *Communication Models: for the Study of Mass Communication*. Longman, London.
Rahvusteavikute eksemplaarsus Tartu Ülikooli Raamatukogus: Tartu Ülikooli Raamatukogu direktori korraldus Nr 00005-230407-1-9/RT. 2007
Saunders, L., (2009). The Future of Information Literacy in Academic Libraries: A Delphi Study. *Portal: Libraries and the Academy*, Vol. 9, No. 1, 99 – 114.
Schwede, K., (2006). Kogude hindamine ja komplekteerimine. *Raamatukogu*, 2, 8 – 11.
Strauss, A. and Corbin, J., (1998). *Basics of Qualitative Research: Grounded Theory, Procedures and Techniques*. Sage, Thousand Oaks [etc.].
Stubley, P., (2006). The Politics of Embedding: Library as Partner not Support Service. Proceedings of the *IATUL 2006 Conference*. Available at http://www.iatul.org/doclibrary/public/Conf_Proceedings/2006/Stubleypaper.pdf; checked 29 April 2009.

Information Behaviour of University Students

Eva Ortoll-Espinet[1], Aurora González-Teruel[2] and Esther Gilabert-Ros[2]

[1]Universitat Oberta de Catalunya, Information Science and Communication Sciences Department, Spain
E-mail: eortoll@uoc.edu
[2]History of Science and Documentation Department, University of Valencia, Spain
E-mail: agonzal@uv.es

Abstract: This work presents the preliminary results of an information behaviour study of students in two Spanish universities. A qualitative methodology was adopted and the results analysed following the grounded theory. The results were classified according to the reasons that motivated the information seeking behaviour, the means used for their resolution and the results of the search process. The use of a qualitative perspective allowed us to obtain a general picture of university students' information problems. Future lines of research are determined, and the results include a future research agenda.

Keywords: Information behaviour; Qualitative methodology; University students.

1. Introduction

European universities, and among them Spanish universities, began a convergence process toward a European Higher Education Area (EHEA) in 1999, through the *Bologna Accords*. This process will conclude in 2010 with a new university model. This model envisages management structures configured around an education focused on students' learning processes. Information technologies will play a fundamental role in those processes.

This direction change presupposes that the main organizations providing information should consider designing services focused on the students, who are to be the main focus of university activity. This direction change will therefore affect the bibliographic supplier and information services and also those aspects of administration which, although related to non-pedagogical information, are necessary for the academic management of the students.

For the planning and design of these services, research into and study of students' information behaviour is required. It is of vital importance to take this into consideration at an early stage, especially in the early phases of information system development, for two reasons. First, because it enables the integration the information needs of future users into the definition of the mission and the goals of the information system. Secondly, because involving these future users in the process of change will help to reduce their reticence to that change.

We should not forget, moreover, that part of the EHEA philosophy is focussed on the importance of multiple subject competences. This not only facilitates useful interaction with the information systems but also the autonomy of information management for all aspects of professional and personal life.

Literature review

According to a recent survey of bibliographical sources, an average of 9.8% of research reported in the field of information needs and uses in Spain in the period 1990-2004 is centred on the university context (González Teruel and Abad García, 2007). In general, these works study the use of a service (Perea Vega, 2002), the use of an information resource (Ferrán Ferrer, N, *et al* 2007), the use of the information (Urbano Salido, 2000) or satisfaction with the use of an information system (Villarejo Sánchez, 2004).

However, a system-centred perspective, focused on a quantitative methodology, with a partial view of the information search process, although useful for the evaluation of those systems, is not adequate for its planning and improvement. More recently, in a study of undergraduate student information behaviour, with EHEA already envisaged, Pinto and Sales (2007) adopted a perspective more focused on the user. In this case, for students studying translation, the objective is the design of learning programmes rather than the planning of information systems. Also, we found one work (Arquero Avilés, et al, 2007) focused on planning CRAI (Learning Resources Centre) at the Universidad Complutense de Madrid. This work has as its objective the incorporation of information needs in the process of mission definition, goals and objectives.

Finally, in the Spanish context, we can cite the more inclusive work of Cobarsí *et al* (2008) on campus information systems at Spanish universities. The perspective proposed in this research is to seek a broad vision of the information services used by university students. In this work, the authors present the operative definition of the Campus Information Systems for students in the following way: *an interrelated group of information resources, accessible by computer through the campus institutional web support, both internal and external, that a university places at the disposal of its users to enable them to consult it and/or provide a selection of significant and relevant data, in the broad context of their university life in its academic, administrative and social senses, in order to improve students' knowledge base*" (pp. 52).

At an international level, it is possible to find more works centred on the study of information behaviour of university students during their academic activities. These works are undertaken from a user perspective and with a qualitative methodological focus. For example, the work of George, *et al* (2006), carried out by means of semi-structured interviews, demonstrated the need for teachers and librarians to work together. Similarly, Lee (2008) adopts a qualitative methodology to investigate the way that undergraduate students look for information by means of diverse university structures.

a) Methodological approach

In 1977, in the INISS study, one of the most important and significant in the field of Information Behaviour, Streatfield and Wilson chose the use of investigation-action methodology because the overall result of previous research in this field was that: "..*much information-behaviour research had proved to be sterile and unimaginative*..". In addition, they used observation and interviews (methodological triangulation) to obtain relevant information that resulted in specific actions related to the information systems of the environment studied.

It can now be seen that this was an early example of a critical position with regard to previous studies centred on users. In these studies, a quantitative position that sought to quantify the transactions between a user and the system had prevailed. Also, sampled and generalised results had been used, usually using self-administered questionnaires. In this sense, Wilson (1999) stated that quantitative research methods were adopted that were inappropriate to the study of human behaviour.

It comes to seem indisputable that there is a need to adopt a holistic perspective of the information seeking process through the use of a qualitative methodology or methodological triangulation (quantitative-qualitative). Thus the qualitative approach or methodological triangulation has had an increased presence in papers presented to ISIC (Information Seeking in Context), the main international conference in this field (Vakkari, 2008). The grounded theory is also of increasing importance in this field. According to Strauss y Corbin (1990), the grounded theory is used when there is a need to go out into the field in order to understand a phenomenon and when the experience is continuously evolving. In this regard, the work of Ellis (1993) is important, the results of which, in terms of contributing to and advancing the study of the information behaviour, lead to one of the most important models of information seeking behaviour. More recently, the work of Razavi and Iverson (2006), centred on the role of personal space in students' learning.

2. Objectives

This investigation addresses the following objectives:

a) To validate the use of a qualitative and inductive approach, the grounded theory, in the study of the information behaviour.
b) To describe the information behaviour of the students of two Spanish universities in two different contexts: a virtual campus (Universitat Oberta de Catalunya - UOC) and an on-site campus (Universitat de València – UVEG) in order to extract practical recommendations for information systems planning according to the user's information needs.
c) To analyse if the university campus characteristics (physical or virtual) have an effect on the students information behaviour.

3. Procedures

Study location

The data was collected from two Spanish universities between February and April 2009. The first, the UOC (Universitat Oberta de Catalunya), uses a virtual learning environment. In this context, the students are trained in the efficient use of the virtual campus. This training is conducted in academic (didactic resources) and administrative environments. The second, the UV (Universitat of València) develops its academic activities on an on-site campus. In recent years, this university has developed various programmes to introduce technology into the learning and academic environment, although academic activities follow a traditional model.

Study subjects

The objective of this research was not to obtain generalised results, but rather to collect detailed information. That is, this research aimed to discover the various different situations of the university students' information seeking behaviour during their academic life, but did not aim to discover which are the most frequent. Therefore, to obtain the maximum diversity of possible situations, the selection of participants was carried out by means of a purposive sample. Thus, two variables were used to select the cases used: type of studies and credits obtained.

Data collection

In depth, semi-structured interviews were conducted with university students representing most of the disciplines from UV and UOC. The interviews were carried out in person in the UV and by post in the UOC. The interviews were designed to cover occasions in which there was a need for more information to resolve a situation or problem. Specifically, information was collected related to the following situations: the beginning of university life, carrying out administrative procedures, studying a subject, the use of the university's technological resources, extra-curricular training, seeking grants, seeking employment and participation in extra-academic activities.

Data analysis

For data analysis, the grounded theory approach was employed (Strauss y Corbin, 1990). This inductive approach facilitates knowledge of the phenomenon studied without theoretical or previous classifications and aims to construct theory based on observation. This approach is useful in information behaviour as a means of initiating the research. To this end, in the preliminary phase, the following tasks were carried out: a) a review of interview results; b) each of the researchers made a proposal of the topics to be analysed by reading and analysing of the data; c) the various categories and the proposed topics were discussed and the researchers agreed on the final classification; d) the collected data was analysed and categorised into three areas: the situation that motivated an information behaviour, the means used for their resolution and the results of the process.

4. Results

From the 26 interviews, 83 incidents or information problem situations were gathered, an average of 3 situations per interview. We present below the data analysis results for the two universities studied. The data is analysed together, except in those cases where there are significant differences.

Our analysis enabled us to identify situations that initiate an active process of information seeking and use, and how the students resolved them. The two main important findings that emerged from our analysis were that the key factors affecting the user's information behaviour were interaction with information systems and service expectations.

4.1 Situations that required an active process of information seeking and use

4.1.a. Information problems that required an interaction with Campus Information Systems

Following the analysis of the 83 situations, we can put the information problems into three categories: a) academic issues related to the courses being taken (22 incidents); b) administrative issues to enable the courses taken to be followed properly (46 incidents) and c) social issues, including in this group problems related to activities such as email connection or other facilities provided by the university, but not linked to courses (21 incidents).

Situations related to courses being taken produced data which reflected concerns in three areas: 1) extending the content specific course; 2) course assignment or project; and 3) pedagogical materials for courses.

The problems related to administrative issues produced the greatest variety of incidents described. The students reported problems related to: 1) general administrative office information; 2) starting university; 3) course credit recognition; 4) course enrolment; 5) physical location of classes; 6) timetable; 7) free courses; 8) scholarships and grants; and 9) practicum administration.

Problems related to social issues produced a variety of different situations: 1) campus electronic connection and email management; 2) transport cards and university card; 3) free subject courses or languages courses; and 4) employment seeking.

4.1.b. Information required

Analysis of the data suggests that two kinds of information are required to solve the problems in the three areas described above a) academic and bibliographical information related to a course subject and b) organisational information provided by the university and related to their administrative procedures and services.

a) Academic and bibliographical information.

The first type of information is that required to solve the problems identified in the "Academic Issues" category. The information required for each problem concerned:

1) Content extension for a specific subject course: the information required was bibliographical.
2) Course assignment or project: the information required was bibliographical.
3) Course and pedagogical material: the information required was bibliographical and included class notes or other documentation generated by professors.

b) Organisational information.

The second type of information needed was that required to solve the problems identified in the "Administrative Issues" and "Social Issues" categories. The information required for each problem concerned:

1) General administrative office information.
2) Starting university: students described initial disorientation in the first semester at the university and their information problems were related to identifying university services and their location.
3) Credit course recognition: procedural information.

4) Course enrolment: various types of information problems were described, and were associated with the stages in the procedures: general lack of knowledge about course enrolment process, with special focus on specific situations in the process (payment confirmation, etc.).
5) Physical location of classes: in this situation, although the problems were basically the same, we found some differences between the two kinds of university. The physical university students had problems with class locations, and the virtual university students had problems with the physical location of examination rooms.
6) Timetable: as with the previous situation, we observed a small difference in the kind of problems. The physical university students described problems with the general timetable, and the virtual university students described problems with specific dates in the classroom timetable.
7) Free courses.
8) Scholarship and grants.
9) Practicum administration.
10) Campus electronic connection and email management: procedural information and information required to change passwords.
11) Transport cards and university card, etc.: procedural information.
12) Free subject courses or languages courses: procedural information and information about the courses offered by university.
13) Employment seeking: procedural information.

It is interesting to note that no significant differences were found between the two kinds of universities studied in relation to information problems and the information required to solve them.

4.2 Information problem resolution

Our results show that the strategies employed to resolve the information problems were similar in both universities and that the reasons for electing formal or informal information sources depended on which of the three information categories described above were concerned.

a) Academic issues.

The preferred sources described by students when trying to resolve academic information issues were the same in both universities, although there was a difference in the procedure used to obtain pedagogical material: in the virtual university the students have a specific virtual space for that purpose, in the physical university the preferred channel is personal contacts.

The Internet was the preferred means to obtain additional or complementary bibliographical information for a course. The reasons, as previous research has demonstrated, is speed and ease of use. The students are aware of the information quality and credibility of that resource.

Nevertheless, the library and Internet are used equally to find bibliographical information. The motivation to use it is less, however, and the students said they use the Library because they know it is the formal way to obtain information, but they are not comfortable with it. Most students perceive the Library as less useful and use it when no other means is possible.

The most frequently cited barriers associated with Library use are related to the structure of information resources, and the perception that the contents are not sufficiently up to date. Interface barriers are cited by only one student. This shows that the information retrieval process is not the problem, and that the question is more associated with content management and quality criteria.

b) Administrative issues

The reasons for selecting specific means of solving administrative information problems are again linked to the speed and ease of use. But in this case, the perception of speed and ease of use is associated with informal channels such as other students and, less frequently, the tutor. The CIS Administrative Office is used only when students perceived it as the only available resource.

The major problems associated with course enrolment were the lack of precise information about the process in the case of the physical university, and on difficulty in understanding the information at different stages of the individual process in the case of the virtual university. This shows that information accuracy and information visualisation is two important features of information systems. One student said that lack of precise information "leads you to enrol in a course you don't really want".

The time spent in finding the correct information is clearly a problem when interacting with SIC, and that expenditure of time produces a lack of confidence in the source. The web information structure is also cited by students as a barrier.

c) Social issues

Curiously, most of the problems related to the Social Issues category were solved by the use of the corresponding SIC. The majority of problems in this category were those linked to electronic campus connection and email management, and also obtaining university cards. The most important reason to select the SIC as the preferred means is that the various procedures involved and the information about them is clear. When information problems are more abstract (job seeking or free courses) other students, the tutor and Internet are the preferred channels.

The principal barrier for this information resource category was the lack of awareness of the information need: "if you don't look for something you don't know that it exists".

4.3 Grounded theory findings: Campus Information Systems: Interaction and expectations as concerns of university students' information behaviour

As we noted previously, two main concepts emerge from the data analysis, interaction with and expectations of the Campus Information Systems. These are the fundamental concerns that affect university students' information behaviour. We will proceed to describe how these concepts are reflected in the three categories we defined previously in relation to information problems and resources.

a) Academic issues.

The principal feature for good interaction with CIS is related to better information architecture, with special emphasis on the reduction of web hierarchies. Secondly, content analysis made by university staff, both academics and librarians, is viewed as a value added feature when interacting with the systems, enabling students to have more content abstracts, comments on specific resources, integration of information, information in digital formats and a more detailed evaluation and selection of their utility and contents. Thirdly, students expect a more personalized service.

In general the search process is viewed as a waste of time, insofar as they don't perceive it as important, even if the institution offers instruction on information seeking. As one student said, "the important thing nowadays is not the search process, it is the analysis". In this sense, the data shows that students have a high level of self-confidence to remember the strategy they have used to obtain information and in their ability to repeat the process in futures uses.

So, we can state the following propositions:

P1- The greater the effort invested on a user centred design for the information structure of Campus Information Systems, the more useful the resources will be perceived to be by students.

P2- The more added value processing with regard to resource contents and formats made by librarians and teachers, more students would use those resources.

b) Administrative issues

In general, CIS - Administrative Office interaction is expected to be more personal, both in aspects such as direct feedback to students and in information visualisation. Another important feature is the time needed for carrying out an interaction with the system. In the virtual university, students have the expectation to obtain information by different means for each specific problem.

CIS - Administrative Office interaction is affected by the degree of accurate information processing. Only one student indicated their role as information provider when engaged on administrative formalities.

The principal expectations of this CIS are again related to information architecture, more accurate information and better information visualisation.

So, we can affirm the following propositions:

P3- The more personalised the information given in relation to Administrative issues, the more user friendly would be the interaction of students with CIS Administrative Office

P4- The more effort made on information accuracy in the CIS - Administrative Office and on the visualisation of personal administrative data information, the less time students would spend doing administrative transactions, and the information service would therefore be perceived as more useful.

c) Social issues

The problems linked with social issues category are, unexpectedly, much more focused, as the information resources are less abundant and clearer. The information process is viewed as more accurate than in the other to CIS categories, except when students are seeking job information.

The interaction with CIS-Social is described as correct and useful, except on those issues related with security features of email or campus electronic connection.

The expectations in this category are concentrated on the accuracy of information related to extra academic activities. Finally, students in the virtual university reported that their expectation was to increase the possibilities of incorporating and making available more formats to manage their personal information with email.

So, we can establish the following proposition

P5- The less abstract is perceived the information needed to solve a problem, the more frequently students use formal channels to access it.

5. Conclusions

– Using an inductive qualitative approach in this information behaviour study of the university students allowed us to obtain an overview of problematical situations related to searching and the use of information in academic life. This information will be the starting point of future research into aspects related to the information seeking process of university students. These lines of future research will be developed using concepts from the context observed, without recourse to pre-conceived ideas, theories or previous classifications.

- More research is required in the field of administrative problems. It becomes clear that the personalisation of information, in both a virtual and actual environment, is a key element of information systems. The students usually search for information about administrative procedures through personal channels. They uses the SIC only to formalise the procedures.

- In spite of the enormous investment universities have made in the purchase and maintenance of information resources, most students do not perceive the library as a useful service. They prefer the Internet as an information resource. It will be possible to develop a project on this issue related to the implication of the librarian's services with regard to the process of teaching-learning, specifically, on all aspects related to the planning and development of repositories of learning materials. The success of an information system does not depend only on its financial cost or on its technological sophistication, but on its adaptation to the user.

- In summary, in the early phase of this study, results have emerged on various aspects of descriptive and theoretical propositions that can continue to be developed through grounded theory procedures, specifically, open coding and theoretical sampling.

References

Arquero Avilés, R., Caballos Villar, A., Cáceres Zapatero, M. D., García-Ochoa Roldán, M. L., Horta García, C., Ramos Simón, L. F., Zornoza Boy, J., (2007): Planificación de Centros de Recursos para el Aprendizaje y la Investigación (CRAI's): un estudio de caso. *Boletín de la ANABAD*, vol. 57, nº2, 335-357.

Cobarsí, J., Bernardo, M., Coenders, G., (2008): Campus information system for students: classification in Spain. *Campus-Wide Information Systems,* vol. 25, nº 1, 50-64.

Ellis, D., (1993): Modelling the information-seeking patterns of academic researchers: a Grounded Theory approach. *Library Quarterly*, vol. 63, nº4, 469-486.

Ferrán, N., Casadesús, J., Krakowska, M., Minguillón, J., (2007): Enriching e-learning metadata through digital library usage analysis. *The Electronic Library*, vol. 25, nº 2, 148- 165.

George, C., Bright, A., Hurlbert, T., Linke, E.C., St. Clair, G. Stein, J., (2006): Scholarly use of information: graduate students' information seeking behaviour. Information Research, vol. 11, nº 4, paper 272 [Available at http://InformationR.net/ir/11-4/paper272.html]

González Teruel, A., Abad García, M. F., (2007): Information needs and uses: an analysis of the literature published in Spain, 1990–2004. *Library and information science research*, vol. 29, nº 1, 30-46.

Lee, H. L., (2008): Information structures and undergraduate students. *The Journal of Academic Librarianship*, vol. 34, nº 3, 211-219.

Razavi, M. N., Iverson, L., (2006): A Grounded Theory of Information Sharing Behavior in a Personal Learning Space. In: *Proceedings of the ACM CSCW '06 Conference on Computer Supported Cooperative Work*, Banff, Alberta, Canada, November 4 - 8, 2006.

Perea Vega, G., (2002): La biblioteca de la Universidade da Coruña. Estudio con los alumnos.

Revista española de Documentación Científica, vol 25, nº1, 29-48.
Pinto Molina, M. and Sales, D., (2007): A research case study for user-centred information literacy instruction: information behaviour of translation trainees. *Journal of Information Science*, vol. 33, nº 5, 531 – 550.
Strauss, A. and Corbin, J., (1990): B*asics of qualitative research: Grounded theory procedures and techniques*. Newbury Park, Calif: Sage Publications.
Urbano Salido, C., (2000): Tipología documental citada en tesis doctorales de informática: bases empíricas para la gestión equilibrada de colecciones. BiD-*Textos universitaris de Biblioteconomia i Documentació*. 2000, nº5. [Available at http://www2.ub.es/bid/consulta_articulos.php?url=http://www.ub.es/biblio/bid/05urban2.htm]
Vakkari, P., (2008): Trends and approaches in information behaviour research. *Information Research*, vol. 13, nº 4, paper 361. [Available at http://InformationR.net/ir/13-4/paper361.html]
Villarejo Sánchez, N., (2004): Evaluación del grado de satisfacción de usuarios fomentado por el OPAC de la biblioteca de la UNED de Talavera de la Reina (Centro Asociado). *Revista general de información y documentación*, vol. 14, nº1, 193-198.
Wilson, T. D., (1999): Models in information behaviour research. *Journal of Documentation*, vol. 55, nº3, 249-270.
Wilson, T. D. and Streatefield, D. R., (1977): Information needs in local authority social services departments: an interim report on project INISS. *Journal of Documentation,* vol. 33, nº4, 277-293.

Public Libraries in the Information Ecology System of the Local Community (Focus Group Interviews with the Information Ecology Mapping – Approbation of the Method and the First Results)

Daina Pakalna

University of Latvia, Riga, Latvia

Abstract: The aim of the research "Municipal Public Libraries: Value, Trust and Satisfaction with the Services" is to evaluate the value of services provided by the public libraries in the level of local community.
According to the first results obtained, the resources and places to gather information differ from cities to the country, depend on the age group of the inhabitants, their information literacy, the financial position, accessibility to the internet and some other factors.

Keywords: Local community; Municipal public libraries; Library users and non-users; Focus group interviews; Information ecology.

1. Introduction

Public libraries are institutions established by the society providing the functions of information, education, culture and serving as the public centre. Berryman (2005) point out thet the Libraries are financed by the state and the local municipalities – they are maintained and developed making use of the tax payers' money hence it is essential to prove that the funds are disposed rationally with the tangible benefit to the society.

Activities of public libraries can be examined in different levels:

- making use of the library statistics (number of members, visitors, figures on handing out and circulation of library stocks etc., showing the activities of libraries);
- inquiring into the opinion of library users;
- studying the influence of the library activities on the local community.

The first two levels of research are implemented within the library, studying the activities of public libraries and the quality of their services. Researches, usually in the form of questionnaires, are carried out at the library – respondents are the library users. However these studies do not provide a complete outlook on the information and services required by the local community in general including the potential library users.

The third level of research is much more complicated and related with the study of information needs at the local community.

The first two levels of research are represented by the approach oriented to the system but the third level represents the approach of contextual studies. (Durrance and Fisher-Pettigrew, 2002).

The contextual approach of studies is used in the research by the title "Public Municipality Libraries: Value, Trust and Satisfaction with the Services", implemented in the framework of the project of municipal public libraries "Father's Third Son" co-funded by the Government of Latvia and the Bill & Melinda Gates Foundation (from January till June, 2009 it is carried out by the Institute of Social and Political Researches under the University of Latvia).

The aim of the research is to evaluate the value of services provided by the public libraries in the broader context – in the level of local community. There will be two methods of research used – the opinion survey of the adult population and the focus group interviews with the information ecology mapping.

A focus group interviews with the information ecology mapping is done to find out:

- What information is needed for people;
- What are the habits of searching for information;
- What sources of information are used the most frequently;
- What are the access points for information;
- What is the role of the public library in the information ecology system of the local community?

2. Theoretical Basis

Information ecology is the so – called the new paradigm of information management. Texas University professor Thomas H. Davenport can be considered as the founder of the concept. In 1997 the book "Information Ecology" by him and Laurence Prusak was published. (Davenport and Prusak, 1997).

They relate this concept with the information environments of organizations. Information ecology as the interdisciplinary course of research was developed by the scientists of the Anthropology Department at the Georgia University. (Stepp, 1999).

Information ecology approach includes not only the information technologies, but also the strategy, politics of information, information behavior, and information environment forming the united system.

Davenport and Prusak (1997) focuse on the four main aspects that can be marked out:

- integration of diverse types of information;
- recognition of evolutionary changes;
- emphasis on observation and description;
- focus on people and information behavior.

There are two theories of information science employed in the research:

- Ecological Theory of Human Information Behavior;
- Everyday Life Information Seeking (ELIS).

Ecological Theory of Human Information Behavior was defined and depicted in the form of a model by Williamson (2005) from the Charles Sturt University (CSU) in Australia.

As it is characteristic for the information ecology approach – a human being – the user of the information – is in the centre of the model. Processes, from the formulation of information requirements till the usage of information, are depicted in the model. The model also describes all factors affecting these processes, e.g. social and cultural values, lifestyle, physical environment, emotional factors, and social – economic conditions. During the research this model can facilitate to understand the formation of the information ecology model in the local community determined by the information behavior of people – the users of this information and understand the role of each library as an institution in the information seeking model. This model helps to define the sources of information available in the community, their accessibility, understand the requirements of information seeking, their habits and the factors of affection.

Everyday Life Information Seeking (ELIS) model was developed by Savolainen (2005) to demonstrate the social and cultural factors affecting the usage of information sources on the daily basis. The preferred sources of information are determined socially. The ELIS model combines both the social and psychological factors.

The way of life or "the order of things" based on the habitus idea by Pierre Bourdieu is the starting – point in the ELIS model. The habitus can be defined as the system of thinking, perception and evaluation determined socially and culturally. The habitus is a relatively solid system; one can ground on experience and make selection, e.g. of information sources and channels.

According to both of these theoretical models the matrixes of information ecology mapping, separately marking out the points of information seeking in columns, are formed.

3. Methodology of Research

Methodology of research was developed and actively approbated by the Master studies students from the Department of Information and Library Studies at the Faculty of Social Sciences at the University of Latvia. They simulated the course of discussion in the focus group and put themselves in the roles of both researchers and the inhabitants of provincial towns (the mayor of a town, the owner of a café and a shopkeeper, a sawmill worker, a housekeeper, a pensioner, a new teacher, a games – mistress, and a veterinarian).

There were 10 focus groups planned – 5 of them in the towns and 5 in the rural municipalities covering all areas of Latvia. Librarians, who know the community people very well and who are familiar with the social demographic situation in the community and the economic activities (largest enterprises, sectors, etc) were the coordinators of all focus groups.

Participants (from the age of 15 up to 74) were selected based on their place of residence including both the users and non-users of library services *(see table 1).*

Table 1. Participants in first eight focus groups'

Participants	Male	Female	Total
Libray users	10	23	33
Library non users	22	25	47

Discussions are lead by a moderator; the technical assistants file (record or photograph, record in the dictaphone) and map the information ecology in the community during the discussion.

In the beginning the participants of a discussion are asked to put down 3 – 5 questions on the cards they have looked for the answers. These questions are summed up in the thematic groups and the most frequently mentioned topics are chosen for discussion (3 pending matters for each focus group).

Information ecology mapping is performed based on the topics using the initially prepared matrixes with the information seeking points (home, other places, place of work, institution, library) put down. The sources of information (persons, the internet, the traditional mass media (radio and TV), newspapers, magazines, and books) are labeled with colored stickers.

Participants of the discussion are asked to talk about the way of seeking answers for the particular question – where the information was sought, what sources of information, if the search was successful. Later a separate map is drawn for each topic depicting the most commonly mentioned places and sources of information seeking. Each technical map is discussed with the participants of each discussion.

The combined information ecology map joining the places and sources of seeking information, putting down the number of mention, stating whether the information was found, partly found or not found, is drawn at the end.

4. First Results

Summing up the results of the first eight focus groups' interviews it is possible to conclude that the most sought topics people have searched for information on are: employment and career (discussed by 7 focus groups), housing/maintenance, education, transportation, culture, recreation, sport, politics and laws, health *(see table 2).*

Table 2. The rank order of major information topics

Most frequently mentioned topics	**Focus groups**
Employment and career	7
Housing/maintenance	4
Education	3
Transportation	3

Culture, recreation, sport	3
Politics and laws	2
Health	1

In order to obtain some information people usually talk to other persons – they can be either family members, colleagues or other specialists. When it comes to the sources of information the Internet is the most wildly used source of information followed by newspapers and magazines, traditional media and books. The majority of respondents had the Internet access at home but it was used also at the work place and libraries.

Table 3: The total number of mention for the sources of information and places in the first 8 focus groups

Source of Information and Place	**Number of Mention** (*F - found, P -partly found, N – not found*)
Internet	**129 (F113; P4; N12)**
Internet - home	78 (F68; P2; N8)
Internet – workplace	23 (F23)
Internet – other place	
Internet - institution	
Internet - library	30 (F22; P2; N4)
Persons	**110 (F103; P1; N6)**
Person - home	26 (F24; P2)
Person – workplace	30 (F26; N4)
Person – other place	66 (F62; P1; N3)
Person - institution	40 (F37; N3)
Personas - library	8 (F7; N1)
Traditional mass media	**23 (F22; N1)**
Mass media - home	19 (F18; N1)
Mass media – workplace	1 (F1)
Mass media – other place	1 (F1)
Mass media - institution	1 (F1)
Mass media - library	
Newspapers, magazines	**46 (F40; N6)**
Newspapers, magazines - home	19 (F15; N4)
Newspapers, magazines – workplace	12 (F11; N1)
Newspapers, magazines – other place	4 (F4)
Newspapers, magazines - institution	3 (F2; N1)
Newspapers, magazines - library	13 (F12; N1)
Books	**23 (F23)**
Books - home	11 (F11)
Books - workplace	
Books – other place	2 (F2)

Books - institution	3 (F3)
Books - library	9 (F9)

A student from Zalenieki rural municipality draws attention to the fact that the quality information needed for one's studies is not always easy obtainable in the Internet: "*When it comes to the serious matters, unfortunately the Internet resources are not sufficient and it is required to pay money. The problem is that there is much information and one has to know how to cut out dead wood. I do not always succeed so I prefer books*".

Despite the presumption that elderly generation hardly uses any PC and Internet, there were people of pension age – active users of Internet in several focus groups. An elderly lady at the age of 69 at the rural municipality library in Ulbroka told us that she uses her PC to process photographs; she also scans the slides and digitalizes the sound records.

Each focus group also discussed the importance of library at the local community. Libraries serve not only as the place of seeking information but also as the educational and cultural establishments; they are places people like to spend their time at and meet other people.

The librarian of the Zlekas rural municipality organizes trips to theatres, concerts, calls together the ladies club. There is a church service performed on Sundays at the library of Viksnas rural municipality because the church is far away from the centre of the rural municipality and it is difficult to get there for the elderly people.

There are free training courses organized in many libraries. A 68 years old pensioner from the focus group at the Zalenieki rural municipality told us that she has finished training on the development and implementation of projects organized in co-operation with the library. Then she completed training on the financial reports required by the State Revenue Service because she owns a small farm. There was a very good training on the communication she completed in the premises of the local library. She also learnt the Internet at the library. Now she can come to the library but she also has the Internet connection at home. She is very satisfied and grateful that she can study and is not lagging behind with the rest of the world.

5. Conclusions

In order to provide the local community with the appropriate library services it is not enough to study the satisfaction with the services among the library visitors. It is essential to understand the information requirements, information seeking habits and the ways of obtaining information in the community in order to come up with some new services. A focus group discussion with the information ecology mapping is an appropriate method to find it out.

According to the first results obtained, the resources and places to gather information differ from cities to the country, depend on the age group of the inhabitants, their information literacy, the financial position, accessibility to the internet and some other factors.

Public municipality libraries have not only the informative function but they also serve as the local cultural and educational centers. There are various cultural

happenings and training courses organized by libraries.
All public municipality libraries in Latvia have free Internet access points. This opportunity is used not only by pupils and young people but it is popular for all citizens, even if they have an Internet connection at home. Librarians are well trained and able to consult the PC and Internet users.

References

Berryman, J., (2005). *Sustaining Communities: Measuring the Value of Public Libraries* [online]. Available: http://www.sl.nsw.gov.au/services/public_libraries/docs/sustainingcommunities.pdf

Durrance, J. C. and Fisher-Pettigrew, K. E., (2002). Toward Develping Measures of the Impact of Library and Information Services. *Reference & User Services Quarterly,* Vol.42, No. 1, 43 - 53.

Davenport, T. H. and Prusak, L., (1997). *Information ecology: mastering the Information Knowledge Environment,* New York, Oxford.

Stepp, J. R., (1999). Prospectus for Information Ecology, *Georgia Journal of ecological Antropology*, Vol.3, 39-73.

Williamson, K., (2005). Ecological Theory of Human Information Behavior. *Theories of Information Behavior*. Medford, New Jersey, 128 - 132.

Savolainen, R., (2005). Everyday Life Information Seeking. *Theories of Information Behavior*, Medford; New Jersey, 143 - 148.

User Profiles: From a Qualitative Case Study Approach to Providing a Better Service

Paula Sequeiros

Associate Researcher to the Instituto de Sociologia, Porto University, Portugal

Abstract: User profiles were designed through a qualitative approach to a case study of a public library, starting from an analysis of space social relations, of how the building's design shaped reading practices and of how space was actually being used.

Keywords: User profiles; Case study; Space relations; Building, architecture and qualitative methodology; Public libraries; Portugal.

Acknowledgement: my special gratitude to Silvia Grünig, architect and lecturer, with whom I did a comparative study of this and another library (unpublished) and who generously contributed with her critical vision to the final form of this paper.

1. Introduction

Library buildings are artefacts that shape reading practices, allowing for or inhibiting the appropriation of space and the creation of particular reading atmospheres. We relied on previous theory on how space and social relations interact in the production and reproduction of space, Lefèvbre (2000), and on how users appropriate and practice it, eventually circumventing constraints, Certeau (1990).
An integrated, intensive approach was used in order to analyse and interpret - Geertz (1973, 3), Blumer (apud Becker, 1996) - not only those practices but also their wider context of relations and processes, as well as the socially constructed meanings

attached to them by subjects, for a comprehensive understanding of the whole social reality, Blumer (apud Donmoyer, 2000, 49).

An interesting, rich case was picked and a theoretical sample constructed according to the perceived diversity in that library - gender, age, social class, ethnic origin, disabilities: 28 users, one library manager, one assistant librarian, the maintenance supervisor, and the architect were interviewed.

An empirical research was designed, focusing on users' real practices, and taking into account social inequalities as well as power relations. Within a qualitative framework, and with a strong ethnographic support, observation - Seale (2004) - and interview - Kvale (1996) - techniques, were used focusing on users actual practices and discourses, as well as on those of librarians, staff and architects, along side with the building analysis. An analysis of children's drawings was also used to supplement their interviews.

Envisioning public reading as a public service, I assume the favouring of the provision of democratic spaces, Calhoun (2005), to be enjoyed as places of encounter and discovery, be it for cultural, leisure, information or learning purposes, as well as a compromise with the intentionality of the constructed object and of the purposes of the research, Haraway (1991).

2. The Almeida Garrett Public Library

Inaugurated in 2001, the library is inserted within the largest public park in the city of Porto, dated from the 19th century. Its romantic design includes rose gardens, lakes, gigantic trees, a magnificent view over the river, hosting a sports pavilion, a restaurant, and a children's park. The area is well served by public transportation, half way from both city centres. The library is an attractor: only a half of the interviewed resided in the metropolitan area.

According to the architect, José Manuel Soares, his wish was to bring the garden into the library, while not imposing a building on it and to control the incoming light without blocking a relation with the surroundings or veiling the particularity of the place. Conceptually, the architectural programme stressed the importance of free access to stacks, and demanded a library for "those who are about to have a first contact with books", as well as for students, where one could walk in or out freely, in continuity with the public space. His main concerns were to conceive a space "ready to be used in different ways", "according to each time period", but "still able to go on being adapted", allowing for small spaces to be appropriated and preventing dispersion, a space that could be "clearly put under questioning". He also remarked how all departments, the Culture councillor and the National Book Institute cooperated in the project, and on how European funding allowed for high quality materials and innovative solutions.

The library occupies two of the four levels, an art gallery and a hall the others. There are separate areas, although not completely isolated, for general reading, for children, series, multimedia and Internet. The architect tried to avoid a hierarchical distribution of services by the different floors, the hierarchy of spaces was strategically used in creating decreasing noise levels as one progresses in the building, but still allowing for a vision of the whole space.

3. How space, in general, is evaluated and sensed

Feeling the space

Users took some trouble in reflecting and defining how that space made them feel. Further to the initial difficulty in referring to something simultaneously abstract and concrete, Lefèbvre (2000, 100), they unanimously praised the light and transparency and the integration in the park. The surrounding garden was frequently mentioned to state how the building's insertion was very positively valued, although just the children stated to use it frequently. Adults felt that it transmitted, nevertheless, a calming atmosphere.

The location was also appreciated, almost all the interviewed readers use public transportation to get there, some living nearby go on foot.

We could observe how readers weaved their "reading cocoons", perhaps lighter than the front glass façade, but still encapsulating their activities. Their gazes abstracted – by an *absent impertinence*, Certeau (1990) – desensitized from the surroundings: two peacocks paced along the the windows sills during one of the interviews, no one seemed to notice them.

Emotionally, although indulging in diverse activities, they collectively weave a reading climate, a product of the social relations reflected in a practiced space Lefèvbre (2000). Tranquillity, organization, concentration, the possibility of integrating a stimulating intellectual labour ambiance, all were signalled out as valued characteristics - a climate they don't get if staying home.

And going to the library is not necessarily an individual act: children are always accompanied by adults, some adults and adolescents come in pairs or groups. At times a certain small talk goes on, maybe around the latest news headlines, as was the case with the raise in the price of bread. Co-presence is valued, even when not addressed to, familiar faces are registered and discreetly followed.

The need for privacy is differently felt, seeming to vary according to living habits, at work, home, according to gender or social class: a young woman dislikes being stared at "in an unpleasant way" by men; the homeless reader thinks it's only natural that others try to peep into the Sites he's visiting, "they're not going to take any bite out of me!"; the sole idea of a lack of privacy in the library made the young couple, sharing an apartment with twelve other family members, laugh out loud. Almost all referred to this co-presence as a tacit agreement – a *relational contract*, Certeau (1990): being in a public space presupposes some concessions over the space personally reserved.

Personalization, privacy, surveillance

«I need my private space and live amid a lot of people», a therapeutic community. In this library reading "is never-ending, is finding the words for things, resting and reflecting […,] very pleasurable". "If I stopped leading this life I'm used to in public spaces, I'd be surely loosing a certain pleasure and harmony I long for".

The need to socialize is clearly felt by many. *Proximity without propinquity* - according to Park's expression, apud Tonkiss (2005) - the withdrawal inherent to reading overlaps with the need for privacy characteristic of urban lives.

Personal, private space created by reading is like a bubble, soft but protecting. The rules of co-reading are passed along with learning to read: this practical knowledge – the habitus of Bourdieu (1979) – entitles one, "naturally" not expect to be disturbed. The most annoying intrusion appeared to be cell phones ringing, which might draw users to require staff intervention.

Surveillance activities by security guards and the installation of cameras – which nobody had spontaneously noticed – are felt as protective: the library is felt as a safe space. And so is the surrounding garden, except for a blind reader who has trouble in circulating through its winding paths and reach the entrance, or for an elder reader with mobility issues who keeps alert while crossing it.

For a few readers, with personal histories of surpassing barriers to become library users, their present situation was felt as an accomplishment: a woman, daughter of manual workers who toiled to get their children educated, and who became blind; a retired male reader, attending the Senior University, who rejoices for seeing young people studying, a chance he didn't get in his days.

Now let's have a look at how different users appropriate this space. Keeping in mind the library's insertion in the park, some metaphors Haraway (1988) arose when aggregating and classifying them.

4. User profiles identified

Bees - Occupational users

To actively occupy their time in a useful way inside the library, presently working for a salary or not, is this group's purpose.

They may stay for the whole day, several days a week: "I leave when the lights go off, [when] I have no choice!… Now my day ended, I may focus on something else" (male reader, 34, unemployed). A female assiduous reader belongs to the so-called *residents*, the local librarians' nickname. "The day goes by more quickly, it's more productive" (female, 28, unemployed). Their stronger motivations: to profit from an environment favouring their study and free resources. Their common feature: to actively be occupied in tasks, organized and planned in detail, from subjects to schedules. They research and write on matters according to their education or curiosity, shape up for job competitions. Unemployed or retired are words avoided in their personal narratives, surely avoiding the social stigma; but their disposition and a work ethics, adapted to their present situation, seem all to shape their practices. Were they at an office or university, we would not hesitate to state they *are* working.

They are six young adults, half hold a degree – they come to enjoy the company of others and the togetherness, Bakardjieva, (2004), of like-minded that helps discipline their work; one is an elderly citizen, strolling from one continent to another, who profits from Internet access to update his biographical Site. For half of them using the Net is the main purpose of the visit, two brought their portables, and listen to music with earplugs. Two others referred the Net as a secondary resource. Other main activities vary: reading newspapers, writing pieces on the city's History, a female reader is a multiple user (varied resources); one studies, another borrows books and trains computing and language skills, profits from an enticing studying environment, considered more stimulating than the therapeutic community she lives in.

Their activities stay anchored to the tables; exteriorizing their doings when writing, plugging laptops, changing belongings from one place to another. They occupy the same zones as *students* and *scholars,* referred to further on.

Butterflies - Strolling readers

Unlike occupational readers, they have no specific activity or interest in mind, just want to stroll around and spend time in a pleasant and a accompanied way, although generally not interacting - resembling Wirth's (1964) urban strollers. And strolling take glances at newspapers and magazines, records, Internet pages, books, heading for multiple resources. Less qualified (secondary school or less), they are manual workers, retired, unemployed with different ages.

Most used areas are multimedia, couches, circulating zones. "When I feel low, I get here and it seems I reinvigorate. Crossing that door, this is as if it were my house, my family" - former typographer, 34, unemployed and homeless, comes in one or two hours every day. He enjoys the age diversity, seeing new faces. His homeless companions persuaded him: "you watch a movie and when you go out you feel quite another person!". Watching everything, including cartoons, sometimes peeps in whatever film is already being displayed. And, above all, enjoys reading the newspaper, specially the one he used to work for.

Another 50 year old stroller, former car mechanic, acknowledges that others come in seeking "not to be alone", which he himself doesn't admit to be doing. Used to read intensely, "maybe it was a refuge", nowadays has an eye condition, reason why he turns to the Internet, which he can't afford at home.

A 9 year old girl comes every Saturday in the company of an adult sister and an elder brother. Regretting she can't stay longer for the Story Hour – her sister must cook lunch – she reads a little at home; her brother reads a lot, especially before falling asleep and always borrows a film before leaving.

And yet another interesting case: a very young couple comes pushing two baby charts. Both 22 and under the minimum educational level, the mother is enrolling as a reader, he guides her as an experienced user (here and abroad where he was raised). They live in a single room, in an apartment of twelve, several of them unemployed or working in underqualified jobs. They plan to come every Saturday, all four, to use the Internet, which they value for the information they gather on nursing babies, "more than the doctor says", to look for baby games and send SMS. She reads very little, only aloud for the babies. He prefers films and music. They value this wide, clean, ordered space, quieter than a cybercafé, where they find more privacy than at their crowded home. Petit (2001, 118) states: «intimacy, interiority, worrying about oneself, all that was not for [the poor], it was a heritage of people with means. [...] The absence of intimacy is perhaps the best poverty indicator, even more than income».

***Sparrows* - Recreational readers**

For this other group the library is mainly a recreational and conviviality space. All multiple readers, sometimes they bring their own toys in, attend events, aloud reading. They may meet and join other children in games, or take part in school visits. Most used zones are the children's area and the multimedia.

"I read grownup books on trucks, at school I only read teaching books, I borrow and play in the computer", where he created his own profile to play regularly – 8 year old boy, coming with his parents from a neighbouring town.

"Here above it's more for reading, down there [multimedia] it's more for leisure, to be more relaxed" - African immigrant, in his forties, comes to the library to profit from his several days of rest. This international truck driver added another library card to those collected in European cities where he lived for short periods of time. He intends to email friends and relatives scattered all over the world, and to spend time enjoying whatever the media (CDs, DVDs and Youtube, magazines, borrowed books). He's the only adult in this group.

As a note we would draw the attention to the fact that, in spite of the promises of a "leisure society" - a never attained reality – or the fact that a growing number of people are being left without paid work, leisure activities still carry the burden of stigma under a dominating productivist ideology. While alienating or consumerist leisure activities are well envisaged, that may not be the case with some activities, which are more tolerated than supported – as a user said you should not do in a library «things libraries aren't meant for».

All the others are children who burst in accompanied by relatives and teachers. We spoke with several of them, aged 4 to 8, and used their drawings to understand what they think a library is and what they like doing there.

They draw, play computer games, read books or listen to reading aloud. Almost all of them have books at home. They use chairs, cushions or lie on the floor. They know what they're not allowed to do: scribble books – «you must grow up first» – step on top of the tables. They laugh and move at ease, sometimes run. Some are scolded for going up a ramp that leads to the top of the stacks.

On Saturdays, during Story Hour, the reading room becomes too narrow to accommodate all of them and their parents, grandmothers. The temperature rises, books and sheets turn into fans to drive the heat away.

The majority prefers to play with the computer. A 7 year old boy, a multiple reader, draws a library using several crayons at the same time: «books are multicoloured»; several small squares get filled with the alphabet, resembling the computer game he used before, all topped by the word Library; in a corner a small character uses a computer, and above "I read" is inscribed. Outside a smiling bright sun, some stars, and his football club symbol.

Almost all of them also take a walk in the garden or go to the children's park when visiting the library.

***Ants* - Student readers**

They come to study, sometimes in groups or couples; a great part is still attending their degree classes, one is a taking a Master's, a few already graduated and go on studying themes in the areas they specialized.

They're motivated by conviviality, companionship, a relaxed but still attracting environment – joining others equally occupied stimulates them. The choice for this library and their reading is instrumental: university libraries don't usually allow group study, titles are associated with their courses, don't use much other bibliographic resources. They come mostly after lunch, carrying the books they need, sometimes laptops, some use mobile audio to create an aural privacy – the earplugs also signal that they don't want to be disturbed (Bull, 2006); the isolation propitiated by reading is thus reinforced by this creation of personal, individualized atmospheres. Ages range from 24 to forty something.

They mainly occupy individual tables, the workstations with Internet access on ground floor or inferior, and eventually the vacant tables on the extreme end. Sometimes use tricks, Certeau (1990) to create extra space: clothes, bags, books are scattered to occupy more than one place, signalling that they are not willing to share coupled tables; they sometimes frown at people chatting, signalling their labour is being disturbed. They compete for space silent but actively, assumptions on adequate uses (and users) seem to protect their presence before any others, their work being a «natural» enough and sufficient credential. Some express their contentment for an environment that has no complete silence, which would bother them, preferring this light hush-hush as a background.

Owls **- Scholar readers**

A small group in this library, they indulge in researching some theme of personal choice or to complete a formal education. They study autonomously, on their pace and appreciate conviviality. As experienced users know every corner and their presence is discrete. Frequently take notes from their readings, write essays. Local History is a common topic among them. Their presence is highly regarded both by other users and staff. They're very likely *residents*.

An elderly scholar states how it pleases him to find answers for the «doubts that trouble» him, and how he enjoys watching younger people at study.

The residents, a subgroup

Resident readers behave like *habitués*, concentrating in the tables surrounding the mezzanine: a privileged spot to control visually the whole space.

This subgroup is composed mainly of scholars but also of occupational readers.

Some elder male readers benefit from the special care of a very attentive female librarian: noted absences may trigger further need to be informed about their health. In her words: "this is their second home", "they get accustomed to us and we to them". We noticed that they use the complaints book, a resource scarcely known to others. An extreme case may, in spite of its particularity, depict how they feel entitled to this special attention: an elderly male reader once knocked on the staff entrance carrying his special sofa and asking to have it placed for him besides his usual table.

This long acquaintance, the frequency and duration of their visits, their competition for personal attention, all facilitate that they may act as a pressure group. Counteracting this, we may still hear some commentaries from less skilled personnel, judging them for "not doing a thing in life, besides going there", associating negative values to this form of leisure.

A single note on a particular kind of readers: the loners – we could trace the activities of a lot of lonely people, people to whom a collective, common space like this is probably the only chance to get some company and get the feeling of people moving around them.

5. Differences and inequalities

Another note to stress that the most economically dispossessed revealed a unique capacity to reflect (and cherish!) the opportunities offered by a public library, revealing also that their particular perspective was closely tied to their social positioning, what Haraway (1988) names the *vantage points of the subjugated*. They were also very concerned of hypothetical cuts in services, due to an ongoing privatization of public services.

When recently talking to a friend (male) librarian he expressed some concern for the fact that reading was progressively feminised. We could not find evidence to support this assumption. Although girls presently tend to qualify with higher classifications, and education is tightly tied to reading habits, both genders seemed represented during our field observations. On the other hand, a clear gender difference was perceived on the absence of middle-aged or elder women: unlike men and younger women their leisure is probably still strongly confined to domesticity. A single exception was a woman who lived for many years abroad where she got into the habit of visiting libraries.

Nor did we find evidence of segregation on account of ethnic differences; curiously a noisy and large group of African adolescents used to enter to access the Internet during lunch time. They came in during our stay and we tried to get to talk to them; in spite of our demand, the guards in the entrance did not signal them to us, when leaving; they just went out unnoticed, like any other users.

The workstation for the blind and amblyopic was appreciated, in spite of having a low use. A wide publicity and the elimination of physical barriers when crossing the garden should be taken into account.

Although, we did find some aspects that call for improvement: occasional visits by homeless men were triggering some fears of insecurity by users. We were told that some of them used to bath in the restrooms. As this is a municipal facility, users in need of special care or attention should be forwarded to social workers for advice and care but not be excluded from the a library. Our view is that these urban figures may embody the fear of the *outcast* and *stranger*, that is, subjective insecurity feelings are really fantasizing and amplifying real insecurity situations, Fernandes (2003). Symptomatically no real danger situation was ever reported in the premises, apart from the episode with the contours of an urban myth– an often told story of a fight with a gun between two immigrants, which the security staff assured had really never happened.

Some librarians told us that the homeless began constituting a problem from the moment they began entering in groups to watch movies, leading some users to complain about couches being used to sleep in and TV sets being occupied for too long. We could whiteness users sleeping in the (comfortable!) couches. But these «normal» users were not disturbed for that, the staff usually ignored it. As a consequence one TV set was removed from the multimedia area, another is used for documentaries, only two are left for feature films. We would advise a different approach, as watching a film is as good an activity as reading a book: to reinstall that TV set and have it play programmed and scheduled films, announced in advance. Conflicts around titles choices could be avoided and still have the room and used to its maximum capacity.

In spite of the architect's wish not to discriminate by floor height, signs of differentiation can traced attached, not to space, but to supports: multimedia requires less *cultural capital*, Bourdieu (1979), attitudes, body postures, are clear markers of a *corporal hexis*, Bourdieu (1977, 87) tied to social class.

6. Concluding remarks

Almeida Garret Public Library is being used as a civic centre, beyond a traditional role, no cultural or leisure activities should, *a priori,* be set aside. These new needs are to be best understood in the context of the city and present housing and life conditions. Some valued dimensions of the library, from the users' point of view were: propitiation of a space fostering study and work through the provision of a stimulating collective environment, of order and tranquillity, the availability of collective free resources. Other positive characteristics were noted. As the allowed relaxed atmosphere and the possibility of coming in and out at one's ease is a clear advantage and existing surveillance does not curtail this. Readers cherish free public resources like this; most deprived users were, as might be anticipated, the most sensitive to this economic advantage.

The urban location is also facilitating, although we'd say not determinant, judging by the number of readers that are driven in from neighbouring localities; easiness of public transportation, though, seems to be much appreciated. The library building is finely integrated in the surrounding garden, standing side-by-side in a good dialogue and nice reciprocal mingling.

The Library provides enough differentiation and flexibility for personal or group appropriation of space and resources for readers of different social conditions and differentiated expectations. Space provides at the same time privacy and conviviality, without imposing restrictions on group work, on social interchange and on collective enjoyment.

This atmosphere, welcoming for its scale, spatiality, light, materials and transparencies, while cultured in its balance and sober style.

Activities here should be faced not only as profiting from public but also from Commons goods: services, equipments, skills, cultural and informational resources are shared in a rational and sustainable way, as an example opposing the individualization which characterizes (and de-characterizes…) our daily lives. The possibility of housing a large diversity of uses must be deepened and cherished in order to stimulate the participation in a democratic public sphere that fosters the co-presence and the connection of these differences.

References

Bakardjieva, Maria, (2004),. Virtual togetherness: an everyday life perspective. In: Feenberg, Andrew, Ed. & Barney, Darin, Ed. **Community in the digital age: philosophy and practice**. Rowman & Littlefield. ISBN 0742529592.

Becker, Howard, (1996). The Epistemology of Qualitative Research. In: Richard Jessor, Anne Colby, And Richard A. Shweder. **Ethnography and human development: context and meaning in social inquiry**. Chicago: University of Chicago Press, p. 53-71. Also available from:
<http://www.rnd.ncnu.edu.tw/hdcheng/research/quali/The%20Epistemology%20of%20Qualitative%20Research.htm>.

Bourdieu, Pierre. 1979. **La distinction: critique sociale du jugement de goût**. Paris: Les Éd. de Minuit. ISBN 2-7073-0275-9.

Bourdieu, Pierre (1977) **Outline of a Theory of Practice.** Cambridge: Cambridge University Press. p. 87

Bull, Michael, (2006). Investigating the culture of mobile listening: from Walkman to iPod. In: O'HARA, KENTON & BROWN, BARRY. **Consuming music together: social and collaborative aspects of music consumption technologies**. Dordrecht: Springer, p. 131-149. ISBN 1402040318.

Calhoun, Craig, (2005). **Rethinking the Public Sphere: Presentation to the Ford Foundation.** [online]. Social Science Research Council. Also available from: <http://www.ssrc.org/programs/calhoun/publications/Rethinking_the_Public_Sphere_05_speech.pdf>.

Certeau, Michel de, (1990). **L'invention du quotidien: art de faire**. 2nd ed. Paris: Gallimard. ISBN 2-07-032576-8.

Donmoyer, Robert, (2000). Generalizability and the single case study. In: Gomm, Roger, Hammersley, Martyn & Foster, Peter. **Case study method**. Sage, p. 45-68. ISBN 9780761964148.

Fernandes, Luís, (2003). A imagem predatória da cidade. In: **Etnografias Urbanas**. Oeiras: Celta, p. 53-62.

Geertz, Clifford, (1973). **A interpretação das culturas**. Rio de Janeiro: Zahar.

Haraway, Donna, (1991). A manifesto for cyborgs: science, technology and socialist feminism in the 1980s. In: **Simians, cyborgs and women: the reinvention of nature**. New York: Routledge, p. 149-181.

Haraway, Donna, (1988). Situated knowledges: the science question in feminism and the prrivilege of partial perspective. **Feminist Studies**, vol. 14, no. 3, p. 575-599.

Kvale, Steinar, (1996). **Interviews: an introduction to qualitative research interviewing**. Thousands Oaks: Sage. ISBN 0-8039-5820-X.

Lefebvre, Henri, (2000 [1974]). **La production de l'espace**. 4ème ed. Paris: Anthropos. ISBN 2-7178-3954-2.

Petit, Michèle. 2001. **Lecturas: del espacio íntimo al espacio público**. México: Fondo de Cultura Económica. ISBN 9681663799 9789681663797.

Seale, Clive, ed., (2004). **Researching Society and Culture**. 2nd ed. Los Angeles: London. ISBN 9780761941972.

Tonkiss, Fran, (2005). **Space, the city and social theory: social relations and urban forms**. Cambridge, MA: Polity. ISBN 9780745628264.

Wirth, Louis, (2001 [1938]). Urbanismo como modo de vida. In: FORTUNA, CARLOS. **Cidade, cultura e globalização**. 2ª ed. Oeiras: Celta, p. 45-65.

Users' Image Seeking Behaviour in Multilingual Environments: Experience in Combining Qualitative and Quantitative Data

Evgenia Vassilakaki[1], R. J. Hartley[1], Frances Johnson[1] and Dave Randall[2]

[1]Dept. Information & Communications, Manchester Metropolitan University, UK
evgenia.vassilakaki@student.mmu.ac.uk
E-mail: r.j.hartley@mmu.ac.uk
E-mail: f.johnson@mmu.ac.uk
[2]Dept. Sociology, Manchester Metropolitan University, U.K.
E-mail: d.randall@mmu.ac.uk

Abstract: The volume of information available on the Web in various languages and the growing number of the non-English native speaking users generate a need for developing and providing Cross Language Information Retrieval (CLIR) systems. The efficient development of such systems depends greatly on gaining a better insight into users' interactions and search behaviours in multilingual environments. In this context, the decision about which method/s to employ is considered essential. This study reports on the reasons why a mixed methods research was adopted; the decision for implementing questionnaire, observation, retrospective thinking aloud and interviews; the way in which they were combined and the values and limitations posed by such an implementation.

Keywords: Multilingual information retrieval; Mixed methods research; Qualitative/ quantitative methods; CLIR systems; User image seeking behaviour.

1. Introduction

The increasing amount of information accessible on the Web in various languages and the rapid growth of non-English native speaking users demonstrate a need for developing systems in Organizations, Libraries, Archives for supporting Cross Language Information Retrieval (CLIR) and Access (CLIA). A variety of different techniques for implementing and organizing different linguistic resources and achieving better retrieved results have been tested and cross-evaluated. All these efforts aimed to provide the best possible system for the average web user to search and retrieve the desired information regardless of the language written. In this process, little attention has been given to user interaction and behaviour with these systems which are considered to be essential if we are to develop CLIR systems that support effective search behaviour and performance.

In this context, the decision on the specific methods to be used and the way in which they are to be implemented is considered important to obtain insights into users' search behaviours when developing a CLIR system. In particular, this study intends to report on the specific four methods employed, the reasons why these have been chosen, the way they were implemented and the value and limitations that these posed when developing CLIR systems that support effective search behaviour and performance.

The remainder of the paper is structured as follows: a brief description of the way that the study was set and carried out is given in section 2. We report on the reasons why a mixed methods research was adopted in this study in section 3. A description of the way the four different methods were implemented and the strengths and weaknesses of each are reported in sections 4, 5, 6 and 7 consequently. A discussion on the strengths and weaknesses in regards of the generated findings is followed in section 8. Finally, we conclude summarizing the way that these methods could be used from a managerial perspective of decision making to provide efficient CLIR systems and services to users in section 9.

2. Study's Description

This study aims to draw insights on the value and limitations posed by the employment of both quantitative and qualitative methods when exploring users' information seeking behaviour in multilingual environments. As this study focuses on methods, the description of the way this study was executed will be kept brief. The full length on the findings on users' image seeking behaviour reported can be found in Vassilakaki et al. (2008).

This study adopted the FlickLing Interface, a multilingual search interface for the well-known web application Flickr as the test object. FlickLing was developed and offered by the organizers of the CLEF2008 (Cross Language Evaluation Forum (CLEF) http://www.clef-campaign.org/) to enable user behaviour experiments for the interactive track (iCLEF2008) to be performed Clough et al. (2008). FlickLing uses the Flickr collection to provide a realistic multilingual search setting for carrying out cross-language user behaviour experiments. Additional information can be found in Clough et al. (2008) and Peinado et al. (2008).

The task assigned to the users was to search across languages for the given three known, non-annotated images in FlickLing after login. The users did not know in advance, in which of the six languages supported by FlickLing (English, German, Dutch, Spanish, French, Italian) the images were described. As a result, users were forced to use all the features and functionalities of FlickLing to search for the images across languages.

Finally, a sample of ten (10) users, three male and seven female, aged 20 to 40, was used for the purposes of this study. All ten users were in some way or another related to Manchester Metropolitan University (MMU). Users were all coming from different cultural backgrounds, speaking a variety of native languages and having a different level of comprehension for a variety of foreign languages.

Each user on arrival was given general instructions regarding the study and the assigned task. They were then asked to fill in a questionnaire enquiring on personal details and prior experience and engage on completing the task. A system recording software was used to capture users' search behaviours while performing the task. The video produced was then played back to users asking them to describe their actions focusing on why they were behaving in this way and what they were thinking in retrospect. At the end, a brief, semi-structured interview was run with each user. All sessions were run individually, in the same lab and lasted approximately two hours each.

3. Mixed Methods Research

The use of different methods for collecting data and answering research questions arose due to a strong debate concerning the adoption and implementation of only qualitative or only quantitative methods. The idea of implementing methods from both categories has been initially faced with doubt and controversy in various disciplines. In the social and behavioural sciences, a number of reasons have been identified regarding the implementation of mixed methods in carrying out research with the same quality and validity as with the mono-method research. In particular, three areas can be identified in which mixed methods appear to be superior to single method approaches (Tashakkori and Teddi (2003): a) mixed methods research can answer research questions that the other methodologies cannot, b) mixed methods research provides better (stronger) inferences and c) mixed methods provide the opportunity for presenting a greater diversity of divergent views.

In this context, a variety of ways of combining qualitative and quantitative methods to address research questions have been defined. We are taking the view of Bryman (2008a) and (2008b), who identified the following ways based on a content analysis of empirical articles in the social sciences using mixed methods research:

Triangulation or greater validity: is a way in which quantitative and qualitative methods are combined to triangulate findings in order to be mutually corroborated. The idea of triangulation was initially evolved from the work of Campbell and Fiske (1959) and later expanded by Denzin (1978) introducing four different types of triangulation methods, including data triangulation, investigator triangulation, theory triangulation and methodological triangulation.

Offset: this way suggests that both quantitative and qualitative methods adopted to address the research questions have their own strengths and weaknesses, so the researcher by combining them can offset the weaknesses and draw on their strengths.

Completeness: in this way the researcher uses both qualitative and quantitative methods to form a more comprehensive account of the research area.

Process: qualitative methods provide a sense of process lacking from quantitative methods which focus on the structures in social life.

Different research questions: it is based on the argument that different methods (quantitative/ qualitative) address different questions as expressed by the authors themselves.

Explanation: when one of the two methods is used to explain the other method's findings.

Unexpected results: it is suggested that a combination of quantitative and qualitative methods could help to explain unexpected results generated by one method by employing the other.

Instrument development: when qualitative methods are employed in order to gather necessary data for formulating the final questionnaire and scale items in order to achieve better wording of both questions and answers provided.

Sampling: when one method is used to enable the sampling of respondents of cases.

Credibility: it is based on the suggestion that employment of both methods (quantitative and qualitative) could enhance the integrity of findings.

Context: refers to situations where qualitative methods are used to provide contextual understanding enabling at the same time the generalisation or identification of relationships among variables.

Illustration: the use of qualitative methods to illustrate quantitative findings.

Utility or improving the usefulness of findings: the combination of both methods could be more useful for practitioners and others.

Confirm and discover: the use of qualitative data to form the research questions and quantitative methods to test their applicability in a specific case.

Diversity of views: the combination of researchers and participants perspectives by employing quantitative and qualitative methods and identifying variables through quantitative method and meanings through qualitative.

Enhancement or building upon quantitative/qualitative findings: the use of quantitative or qualitative methods to build on already obtained quantitative or qualitative data.

Other/ unclear: no clear way of using mixed methods research was identified in some of the empirical articles in the social sciences after conducting a content analysis.

Not stated: no specific or stated way of using mixed methods research was identified in some of the empirical articles in the social sciences after conducting a content analysis.

The decision to adopt and apply a mixture of quantitative and qualitative methods in this study falls in the offset and completeness categories. In particular, four different methods both qualitative and quantitative have been employed: a) questionnaires, b) observation, c) retrospective thinking aloud and d) interviews. These methods have been chosen for the following reasons: a) they extract different data (quantitative/ qualitative), b) they overlap ensuring that no relevant data will be lost and c) they enable the collection of both concrete and difficult to misinterpret data.

Apart from the mixture of the different methods employed, the order of these also proved significant in both collecting and verifying the data. In particular, the questionnaire and the observation sheet were providing the facilitators with hints on users' information seeking behaviour while retrospective thinking aloud and the interviews were clarifying the reasons why users were behaving in this way. In addition, the stress put on the users was kept in balance throughout the study minimising the possibilities of users feeling tired early or uncomfortable in the study.

An extended description of the way the four methods have been applied will follow, focusing on: a) the way they have been designed, b) the main reason for having been designed in this way and c) how these methods contributed to the collection and final analysis of the data. Moreover, for each method a series of strengths and weaknesses will be described based on the way these were applied and on the data collected and analysed.

4. Questionnaire

This study applied a questionnaire mainly for two reasons: a) to gather information about the user sample and b) to enable the formulation of questions to be asked during interviews regarding users' search behaviour and habits adopted in the specific study. It was employed more as a supplement to the main method of the study (retrospective thinking aloud) for collecting data and contributing to their further analysis.

In this context, the questionnaire was designed to extract data on the following distinct areas of the user sample: a) users characteristics, b) users' previous experience in searching on the web for images across languages and c) users' familiarity with Flickr web application. In particular, it contained mainly a set of closed questions and a few open questions when it was needed to justify further users' answers.

Users were asked at the beginning to specify both their native language and their level of comprehension for each of the six languages (English, German, Dutch, Spanish, French, Italian) supported in FlickLing and/or state their knowledge for any additional languages. These were important to establish if they are monolingual, bilingual or multilingual and their level of comprehension for each of these languages for reasons of competency in searching in these languages.

Moreover, it enquired after users' experience in: a) searching images on the web and b) searching for images across languages. These enabled us to form an idea of their level of experience and focus on the reasons why they search for images in other languages.

In regards to prior usage of Flickr application, our interest focused on knowing how familiar users were with Flickr. It was thought that experience in Flickr would be a variable affecting users' image seeking behaviour since FlickLing was based on and using Flickr's image database.

Finally, three questions were included regarding users' demographic details such as age, gender, education to further identify the characteristics of the user sample of this study. In addition, these were placed at the end so that users felt more comfortable answering them rather than thinking why their personal-demographic details were requested at the beginning of the study.

This questionnaire was also used to form questions during interviews. In particular, the facilitator would go through the questionnaire when the user would have answered it and if any of the user's answers were contradictory to his search behaviour then the facilitator would ask why was that so. For example, when a user with a basic knowledge in French as stated in the questionnaire would receive a French annotated image and would not search in French or use the provided translations, the facilitator would ask to find the reason of this behaviour.

The employment of the questionnaire enabled the definition of the user sample characteristics and users' previous experience in each of the sections of interest. This questionnaire was kept as brief, concrete and easy to fill in as possible, mainly: a) to minimize the hassle to which users had to go through in completing it, b) to relieve the overload from carrying out the whole experiment (employment of four different methods) and c) to constrain the time spent on full-filing the various elements of the study. At the same time, it enabled the credibility of the data gathered.

On the other hand, users were left alone to complete the questionnaire and as a result some of them did not answer all questions, withhold some information or provided contradictory data because they had either misunderstood, misinterpreted the questions or did not pay attention and filled it in very quickly.

5. Observation

The method of observation was also employed to form an overview of the users' information seeking behaviour while performing the given task. In this context, the facilitator would be able to follow up users' discussion and explanations during the retrospective thinking aloud process and could form the necessary questions during the interviews based on the observations made.

A specific form was designed to assist the work of the facilitator in forming specific questions during interviews regarding pre-selected research areas of the test object and the study. This was done in an attempt to shed light on specific users' behaviours on specific occasions. This form was categorized according to the areas that were to be examined. These were defined in accordance with the main aim of the study. Every category had a set of predefined questions/ remarks that the facilitator had to complete according to the user's behaviour each time and write additional comments. A set of three forms was assigned to each user, one for each image. These forms were coded according to the number assigned to each user and the order of the images (e.g. 01/01, 01/02, 01/03). These were to be used for forming the questions during individual interviews in order: a) to verify users' saying on retrospective thinking aloud, b) to shed more light in the provided answers and the reasons stated and c) to bring users' thoughts on the surface.

The observation sheet designed proved to be a very valuable tool for the facilitator to extract data and formulate questions on users' behaviours and actions during interviews. In particular, it helped the facilitator to focus on specific areas, write comments, remarks and relevant questions for each user. In addition, the facilitator would note down users' expressions while searching for the images that the facilitator would use during interviews to engage users in conversation asking him/her to explain why the user made that comment. On the other hand, the facilitator could miss the overall user interaction because he/she was focusing on specific elements of users' behaviour. In addition, the quantitative data gathered though concrete would have no meaning or could easily be misinterpreted without users' further comments and justifications of these actions. Finally, the users may have altered their search behaviour because they were observed, as a result this may have affected the data gathered though all possible precautions have been taken to avoid it.

6. Retrospective Thinking Aloud

Retrospective thinking aloud belongs to Think Aloud Protocols and it is a widely used method for usability testing of software and interfaces Ericsson, K.A., and Simon, H. (1985) and Haak, M., de Jong, M., and Schellens, P. J. (2003). This study employed retrospective thinking aloud aiming to derive findings entirely on users' thoughts, comments and search behaviours rather than depending on data gathered through only quantitative methods and facilitator's observations, interpretations and questions. This method required that users would complete the given task with the testing object and describe their thoughts and actions afterwards which were screen captured using camtasia.

This method comes with many benefits for both the users and the facilitators. The users were left alone to work on the given task in their own way and at their own pace, with no time constraints and interact with the test object. This practice proved beneficial for the non-English native speakers since they could search thinking in their own language as they do in their daily lives. Most importantly, afterwards during retrospective thinking aloud they could elaborate more and explain better their actions because they had the necessary time and they were relieved from the stress of completing the task assigned. In addition, the users had the opportunity and time to feel comfortable with the environment, test object and the facilitator. In this way, the focus was on peoples' cognitive processes after having completed a specific task.

In addition, retrospective thinking aloud enabled the facilitator to gain insights on users' information seeking behaviours, identifying the reasons why users were behaving in this way and asking relevant questions during interviews. These were used for verifying what the users stated on their own or to enquire more details and justifications. In addition, the users rather than the facilitator pointed out the problems concerning the test object.

The use of a screen capture software in system recording users actions and playing it back to them in real time also contributed to the study. In particular, the users could easily reflect back to their thoughts and explain their actions leaving no room for misinterpretation. In this context, the users were providing information on their general search behaviour in an attempt to justify their actions.

On the other hand, the users were feeling tired during the retrospective thinking aloud because as a process it was time consuming since it was taking as much time as the users have already spent on fulfilling the task. As a result, they were expressing unease and tiredness with describing everything in detail because of the time already spent on the task. In addition, the majority of the users were trying to justify as clearly as possible why they were failing to find the image because the recording of their performance was making them feel uncomfortable. The users were thinking that they did not employ the necessary search mechanisms based on what they were seeing on the screen. They were even trying to find ways of how they could have search differently and how this could have affected the final outcome.

7. Interviews

The last part of the study consisted of small scale individual interviews with every user after the completion of the retrospective thinking aloud. The main goal of these interviews was to clarify: a) the answers provided in the questionnaires, b) the specific actions of the user's image seeking behaviour during the search session and c) the users' expressions during retrospective thinking aloud.

The interviews carried out were semi-structured and the questions asked derived from the questionnaire, the observation sheets and the retrospective thinking aloud process. As a consequence, the questions asked to the users varied but they were all focused on users' image seeking behaviour when searching across languages.

The interviews enabled the verification of specific sayings of the users during retrospective thinking aloud and of the users' answers in the questionnaire. In addition, the data gathered through observation were able to be interpreted as users were asked to provide explanations on specific actions noted on the observation sheet. On the other hand, the interviews were kept brief because users were already tired and they were not willing to spend a long time on answering additional questions.

8. Discussion

The development of effective CLIR systems depends to a great extent on exploring and recording users' information seeking behaviour and the reasons which trigger these behaviours. The identification and employment of the most suitable methods to monitor these behaviours are essential in generating the necessary findings. This study employed a mixed methods research drawing from the view of Tashakkori and Teddlie (2003) that mixed methods enable better (stronger) inferences and can answer questions that single methods cannot.

In this context, a combination of four different methods, both quantitative and qualitative have been adopted to generate findings. These methods were employed bearing in mind that all of them entail both strengths and weaknesses in regards to the way developed, implemented and data gathered. Nonetheless, these were adopted falling in the offset and completeness ways of combining qualitative and quantitative methods as identified by Bryman (2008a) and (2008b). As a result, a combination of methods was used to offset the weaknesses of the methods employed and draw on the strengths of both. Questionnaire was used as a mean to easily define users' characteristics but it could only provide hints on users' search behaviour, which could be further exploited during interviews. In addition, observation enabled the identification of specific search behaviours and actions on specific occasions and the formulation of relevant questions but without the users' explanations during retrospective thinking aloud and interviews would be meaningless. Moreover, the retrospective thinking aloud enabled the collection of data entirely on users' explanations of their actions and description of their thoughts in retrospect rather than on facilitator's observation. On the other hand, it was as a process exhausting for the users because each session lasted approximately an hour and a half. Finally, interviews though they were kept short in length provided the chance to verify further users' answers in the questionnaire and specific actions noted during observation and clarify users' expressions during retrospective thinking aloud.

The notion of completeness was also important in identifying users' information seeking behaviours and reflecting on the development of CLIR systems. Taking the view of Bryman (2008a) and (2008b) on completeness, we employed four different methods coming both from quantitative and qualitative methods in order to form a more comprehensive account of users' information seeking behaviour in multilingual environments. In particular, we were able to define our sample and discover hints on our users' searching behaviour of which to verify on retrospective thinking aloud and/or ask during interviews. In addition, observe users' behaviour and clarify their actions accompanied by their thoughts, expressions and justifications during retrospective thinking aloud and interviews. The adoption and combination of these four methods enable the generation and gathering of diverse data on different aspects of the same research area, users' image seeking behaviour in multilingual environments. The data that was gathered would have been extremely difficult if not impossible to gather by using any other method(s) alone or in combination.

In addition, this notion of completeness was reinforced by the specific order in which the four methods have been applied. It provided the facilitator with the possibility of gradually accumulating data on users' search behaviour. In the beginning there would be only hints about users' general search characteristics, then notes on specific actions and finally users' own words and explanations regarding their actions and thoughts. Finally, the facilitator would only need to form questions clarifying, verifying and justifying users' actions during interviews. Therefore, the data gathered was providing a full and comprehensive account of users' image seeking behaviour in multilingual environments. Data extracted based on users' own comments rather than facilitators observations and assumptions.

9. Conclusion

The investigation and monitoring of users' interaction and search behaviour with multilingual environments is considered to be one of the most important factors in developing efficient and effective CLIR systems. As a consequence, the decision on which methods (qualitative and/or quantitative) to employ in order to gain a better insight to users' behaviours and thoughts is also essential. This study used a mixed methods research understanding that mixed methods enable better (stronger) inferences and can answer questions that single methods cannot. In particular, four methods both quantitative and qualitative have been adopted such as questionnaire, observation, retrospective thinking aloud and interviews. These methods have been designed and implemented to draw insights on different aspects of users' characteristics and/or search behaviours. The defined order of their implementation was used to gradually gain a better and more comprehensive insight into users' actions and thoughts and to enable the formulation of relevant questions. In addition, the offset and completeness way of combining the chosen methods have been adopted in order to offset their weaknesses and draw on their strengths enabling the better and a more comprehensive understanding of users' image seeking behaviour in multilingual environments.

References

Bryman, A. (2008a). *Social research methods*. Oxford University Press, Oxford; New York.

Bryman, A. (2008b). Integrating qualitative and quantitative research: how is it done?. In *The mixed methods reader.* V.L. Plano Clark and J.W. Creswell (eds). University of Nebraska-Lincoln, California.

Campbell, D.T., and Fiske, D.W. (1959). Convergent and discriminant validation by the multitrait-multimethod matrix. *Psychological Bulletin,* Vol. 56, 81-105.

Clough, P., Gonzalo, J., Karlgren, J., Barker, E., Artiles, J. and Peinado, V. (2008). Large-scale Interactive Evaluation of Multilingual Information Access Systems: the iCLEF Fickr Challenge. Workshop on *Novel Methodologies for Evaluation in Information Retrieval,* 30 March 2008, Glasgow, Scotland, pp. 1–5.

Denzin, N.K. (1978). *The research act in sociology: a theoretical introduction to sociological methods.* Butterworths, London.

Ericsson, K.A., and Simon, H. (1985). *Protocol Analysis: Verbal Reports as Data.* MIT Press, Cambridge, Mass. ; London.

Haak, M., de Jong, M., and Schellens, P. J. (2003). Retrospective vs. Concurrent Think-aloud Protocols: Testing the Usability of an Online Library Catalogue. *Behaviour & Information Technology,* Vol. 22, No. 5, 339 – 351.

Peinado, V., Gonzalo, J., Artiles, J. and Lopez-Ostenero, F. (2008). UNED at iCLEF 2008: Analysis of a Large Log of Multilingual Image Searches in Flickr. In Peters et al (eds): Evaluating Systems for Multilingual and Multimodal Information Access 9th Workshop of the Cross-Language Evaluation Forum, CLEF 2008, Aarhus, Denmark, September 17-19, 2008, Revised Selected Papers, Springer LNCS (to be published).

Tashakkari, A. and Teddi, C. (2003). *Handbook of mixed methods in social and behavioral research.* SAGE, London.

Vassilakaki, E., Johnson, F., Hartley, R. and Randall, D. (2008). A Study of Users' Image Seeking Behaviour in Flickling. In Peters et al (eds): Evaluating Systems for Multilingual and Multimodal Information Access 9th Workshop of the Cross-Language Evaluation Forum, CLEF 2008, Aarhus, Denmark, September 17-19, 2008, Revised Selected Papers, Springer LNCS (to be published).

Communicating with Difficult Customers

Noemi Somorjai[1] and Csilla Raduch[2]

[1]M.A. Lib.Sci., Semmelweis University Budapest Institute of Behavioural Sciences Library, Hungary; Ph.D Student Eotvos Lorand University Budapest Department of Library and Information Sciences, Hungary

[2]B.A. Semmelweis University Budapest Institute of Behavioural Sciences, Hungary

Abstract: Librarians regularly meet customers who have various behavioural problems or experience stressful life situations (unemployment, divorce, loss of a beloved, bereavement, etc.) As librarians we often encounter library users who are upset, anxious or extremely frustrated. How should we handle such customers?

Librarians should be aware of the fact that it is not the librarian who is the cause of frustration in library users. Customers are usually categorized into four behaviour types, two dominant and two submissive subtypes. Librarians should also be aware of the subtype to which they belong.

When communicating with difficult customers we should stay calm and maintain composure. Allowing people to have their say without being interrupted and to ventilate their feelings can be most beneficial. When replying we can use plural ('we can try to...') We should also try to avoid using denial. It is better to use affirmative sentences and offer some solutions. Politeness and determination are advisable.
Psychologists assume that such difficult customers may have suffered early childhood traumas. They tend to re-enact a traumatic experience because at the time they have not been able to express and verbalize their feelings in the respective situation. As a result of these traumas they tend to alternate between the roles of aggressor and victim.
Surveys show that the more optimistic librarians are, the more leisure in speaking style and dressing, and the more often they refer to work related experience, the more successful librarians will be in communicating with the difficult customer.
Keywords: Librarian–user communication; Communication with difficult custmers; Defusing aggression.

1. Introduction

Why and who is a difficult customer angry with?

There are several possible reasons why a customer can be angry or frustrated. They may be members of a discriminated group or belong to less privileged social classes who suffer disadvantages in society. Other causes are more common, and may apply to any of us, e.g. accumulating anger, failure in asserting ourselves or standing up for our rights, being late or short of time in general, experiencing difficult life situations, suffering from an illness, or a close relative being ill, suffering from pain, exhaustion, depression or anxiety.

In such situations library customers eventually give vent to their frustration or anger at the information desk in the library. The librarian should always be aware that s(he) is NOT the cause of the patrons' feelings. In the position of a helper they are often expected to diffuse the angry patron and deal with the customer's frustration. (Rubin, 2000)

Experts categorize the patrons' behaviour in seven types (Smith, 1993). The scale is wide, it goes from simple frustration through anger to intolerable behaviour. (Frustrated, upset, angry, complaining, blaming, furious, intolerable behaviour)

2. Behavioural types

In psychological literature we also can find references to types of human behaviour. There are two dominant and two subdominant types of behaviour as defined in literature.

Type-A behaviour: Manager

You are lucky if you can meet or belong to this type of behaviour. Manager-type men and women are independent, they work in teams. Problems are merely challenges to them. They are realistic in assessing their personal capabilities. They can ask for help without feeling envy or humility. They plan, set priorities, struggle and help others to do the same. They are assertive and respect the aims of colleagues and others.

Type-B behaviour

Type-B persons are similar to type-A managers in many aspects. They are task-oriented, they like independence and self-reliance. Their wish is to control their environment. They tend to behave in an aggressive, impolite way. They are not so willing to take into consideration the aims and wishes of others. When their goal attainment is threatened it becomes more important for them to control their environment. In communication they express their opinion but do not listen to others.

Type-C behaviour

They are just the opposite of type-A and type-B persons. They are not in control, they place the 'locus of control' outside themselves. They feel they haven't got enough power or authority. They are continuously looking for care and trying to avoid any refusal. They would rather give up than fight for their rights. Type-B persons can intimidate type-C, therefore type-C persons flatter Type-B. Type-C seeks acceptance and support and likes to be considered good at caring and supporting others.

Type-D behaviour

They feel they lack personal power and the ability to build relationship with others. They are very vulnerable, self-defensive. They like routine tasks, they prefer to avoid making decisions, rules, develop a process or organise work. They don't like to be bothered by others. If their personal security is threatened they retreat to their silent world. They hardly communicate anyway. Their manner can be frustrating to type-A and type-B persons.

How to communicate with difficult customers?

So we examined different kinds of human behaviour. It is important to decide which group we ourselves belong to. If we are aware of this, we can proceed to develop a coping strategy for dealing with difficult clients.

First of all, it is advisable to stay calm and relaxed. Refrain from interrupting the client, as that would only be adding fuel to the fire. It helps to breathe deeply in and out, slowly exhale through the mouth and inhale through the nose. Deep breathing enhances recognition of feelings and resists the fight-or-flight reaction triggered by the event. An imaginary or actual step back may be helpful in finding the most adequate solution.

If the client can't find the requested item you can say 'I will do my best so we could find the requested item.' Refrain from using negative sentences. Instead of saying 'We never lend any reference books' you can say 'Reference books are often used in the reading room so we can make photocopies or scan the requested pages.' (Rubin, 2000) Be polite and determined. The library user should feel they are talking to a highly experienced professional.

It is important that librarians should do their best to fulfil the request of the patron - even if it is against the regulations of the library. Experts claim that changes in research, in access of internet, in databases etc. are rapid and unexpected and due to these recurrent changes library regulations are hardly able to follow these perpetual processes. The library profession and services are moving from printed material to electronic versions. We are able to supply our customers with less limited electronic information. The information we present today may be out of date tomorrow.

So if we did our best to fulfil the request of the patron librarians should leave the reference desk for a short time to relax. Thus, watching some relaxing photos, a brief walk in the open air, smelling some flowers, or visiting a nearby fountain would be most refreshing. (Fescemyer, 2002). Talking to a friend or colleague, jotting down a note for our boss could also be beneficial. You can just put it down or hand in to the library director if necessary.

What can we learn from other helping professions?

Psychologists deal with difficult clients all their life. How can it be they are still satisfied with their job? Berne, the famous psychiatrist defined difficult clients as persons who seek help with the purpose to refuse it. Difficult behaviour depends on the acceptance of the therapist: their level of tolerance, their needs and experiences. Librarians should recognise: a difficult customer is not an objective category.

Difficult clients may suffer from early childhood traumas. In adulthood they seek help but they are reluctant to accept it. They are afraid of repeated rejection, hurt or becoming defenceless. Psychologists assume they try to re-enact those early childhood traumas because they are not able to verbalize the feelings they experienced in the respected situation (Quinn, 2002).

Due to these traumas these clients may often identify themselves either with the victim or the aggressor. They will expect librarians to take part in this game. AVOID this trap! You must not reply as an aggressor or a victim. Instead, the librarian should stay calm and relaxed in order to show to the client that there are other ways to behave, it is not necessary to stay in the role of a victim or aggressor. Do NOT let the client disturb you in exercising your role of a helper. The target of the behaviour of the difficult customer is not the librarian, they generally behave this way in life.

3. Conclusion

The best communication strategy is to accept the behaviour of the client. The task of the librarian is to accept rather than avoid, escape or judge library patrons. Arguing and debating with the clients would only heighten their resistance. The paradox of agreeing with the client can neutralize this process.

When library users act in a bad manner the best thing the librarian can do is to stay calm, speak and move slowly and gently. Thus the librarians can communicate to the client that the situation is controllable and there is no reason to panic or become hysterical. Surveys show the more optimistic librarians are, the more leisure in style of speaking and dressing, and the more often they refer to work related experience, the more successful librarians will be in communicating with difficult customers.

References

Fescemyer, Kathy: Healing after the unpleasant outburst: recovering from incidents with angry library users. In: Reference Librarian 2002. No.75/76.

Quinn, Brian: How psychotherapists handle difficult clients: Lessons for librarians. Reference Librarian 2002. Bo.75/76.

Rubin, Rhea Joyce: Defusing the angry patron. New York: Neal-Schuman 2000.

Smith, Kitty: Serving the difficult customer. New York: Neal-Schuman 1993.

6. Information Literacy

Measuring Information Literacy Policies

Carla Basili

Consiglio Nazionale delle Ricerche, Italy
Lumsa University, Rome

Abstract: Information Literacy is still largely absent from the priorities of national information and education policies. A need for a systematic body of evidence on the strategic role of Information Literacy is recognised and leads to the identification of a set of variables, which can be useful to provide a first picture of the Information Literacy polices in Europe, with a particular focus on Higher Education. The set of variables constitutes the theoretical framework supporting the European Observatory on Information Literacy Policies and Research*.
*European Observatory on Information Literacy Policies and Research - *http://www.ceris.cnr.it/Basili/EnIL/gateway/gatewayhome.htm*

Keywords: Information literacy; Policies; Qualitative variables; Higher education; Europe.

1. Introduction

Information Literacy (IL) is increasingly becoming recognised as an enabling factor for a full exploitation of the opportunities offered by an Information Society. According to Abid (2004) – a voice among many:

Information Literacy is part of the basic entitlement of every citizen, in every country in the world, to freedom of expression and the right to information and is instrumental in building and sustaining democracy (Abid, 2004).

This pivotal role in public participation, even if so largely recognised in the research literature, does not seem to have a counterpart in the mental map of policy makers.

Elsewhere (Basili 2008) we have underlined how Information Literacy comes under the jurisdictional sphere of both education and information policies and this "sharing" certainly does not work in favour of a focus on the problem.

2. Policy studies and analysis: The need of evidence

Policy making is a complex activity since it derives from the interpretation and combination of myriad facts and events. Two different positions emerge about how the best decision-making takes place: by intuition - an innate personal ability of the policy maker – or by a careful evaluation of all available and relevant information.

The latter is the case of data-driven policymaking, which – according to Esty-Rushing (2007) – includes the following key features:

Collection and analysis of data to spotlight problem areas and potential solutions;

Development of quantifiable measures to assess policy performance and draw comparisons across similar circumstances or peer groups so that "best practices" can be identified and expanded; and

Public dissemination of data and metrics on policy results, so those outside government can hold public officials accountable for their performance.
According to the American Political Science Association, policy studies area branch of the Political Science (http://www.apsanet.org/) and informs policy by analysing trends and developments. Policy making about complex phenomena, in fact, usually relies on policy studies and guidelines derived from the combination of myriad facts.

Indicators are among the most powerful tools providing objective criteria by which complex phenomena can be analysed. They are forms of evidence of the *status quo*, but can also be used for evaluation of trends and goals.

According to the Oecd (1993), indicators are parameters that give information on some phenomenon and reduce complexity in order to make problems quantifiable and communicable. Averch (1980) conceives indicators as tools "to shape lines of arguments and policy reasoning".

So simple and effective descriptions, nevertheless, do not correspond to simple procedures for indicator production, since an indicator is made up of a definition, a value, a measurement unit, and needs to be. collected on a regular and systematic basis. Defining indicators is therefore a very time-consuming process and for this reason it is afforded for measuring dimensions of quite a large applicability.

On the contrary, Information Literacy policies in Higher Education is so much a specific issue as to be absent from most of the authoritative sources of education and information indicators[1]. This is the reason why we decided to start a research project – the European Observatory on Information Literacy Policies and Research - aimed at providing a first evidence of what we call the *IL-readiness* of the different countries in Europe[2].

3. Stratifying the Information Literacy discourse

A first step of our research agenda has been the identification of a three axes IL model, according to which it is possible to articulate reasoning on the multidimensional Information Literacy discourse, discourse that is still largely open in the literature from a definitory point of view. The IL model relies on the distinction among three different perspectives of analysis, corresponding, in our vision, to three different denominations:

- ✓ Information Literacy as a discipline (Culture of Information),
- ✓ Information Literacy as a socio-political goal (Education to Information);
- ✓ Information Literacy as a cognitive development (Information-skill).

A detailed explanation of the arguments supporting such a distinction is illustrated in (Basili 2008a). Here just a summary of the main points is given below.

The original coin of the term *Information Literacy* by Zurkowsky in 1974 set definitely the concept as a *policy* issue, as emerges from the following parts of his report:

I-PROLOGUE The goal: achieving information literacy

[…] the work of the Commission[3] should be viewed in terms of achieving total information literacy for the nation. This paper seeks to:

Provide indicators of the broad range of services already being offered by non-government, non library-based business firms.

Identify the policy questions that need to be resolved in order to maximize the pluralistic structure of the information economy already in place in order to achieve information literacy for our entire population, and

Suggest priorities which the Commission should consider in attaining the goal of information literacy. (Zurkowsky, 1974)

Zurkowsky's voice seems to be unheard for fifteen years, until the release in 1989 of the ALA definition, where information literacy is conceived mainly as a *skill* to be spread worldwide by libraries.

During the '90s, a major focus have been devoted to IL as a *discipline* implicating curriculum re-design, according to various types of configurations: parallel, integrated, embedded.

The three axes of reasoning are of course interrelated: the Education to Information goal cannot be independent from a realistic expectation of what the information skills to be achieved consist of; in turn, both the policy goal and the skill have to be supported by specific disciplinary contents to be imparted. Nevertheless, the distinction among three different axes – policy, disciplinary, cognitive – constitutes a first categorisation useful to identify different threads of reasoning about IL and, in turn and mainly, leads to the identification of different sets of variables.

4. IL-readiness: How to measure it?

The EnIL research agenda is focused on a number of basic questions about IL policies and research, summarised below.

Policy awareness: to what extent is IL a national policy issue in the different European countries?

Higher Education Policies: What are the academic policies related to the integration of IL into university curricula?

Best practices: what is the best implementation model of IL in Higher Education?

Barriers: what are the main barriers to an effective integration of IL into academic curricula?

Literacy status: what is the level of IL competency among university students in Europe?

Each research question corresponds in our vision to a *qualitative* variable and the whole set of variable is aimed at depicting a first evidence of what we call the *IL-readiness* of a country.

The activities in the EnIL network have been inspired to the above main questions and, consequently, articulated into two main courses of action:

- a multilingual questionnaire to be addressed to European university students in order to get comparable data about the Information Literacy status of students in the different European countries. To date the questionnaire is available in twelve languages on the EnIL website[4].
- the European Observatory on IL Policies and Research.

From now on our discussion will be focused on the EnIL Observatory and its design criteria, which can be distinguished into: purpose-oriented, geographical, and research-sensitive criteria.

Purpose-oriented design criteria match the scope of the EnIL Observatory and therefore draw attention to the policy and research facets of the IL discourse and to the Higher Education context. This means that initiatives of a political matrix or in the academic environment are mainly considered.

Geographical criteria comply with the regional focus of the Observatory: Europe and European countries. This implies that the Observatory is hierarchically organised on a country-basis and includes European countries. A section related to the European Union initiatives is included, even if the Observatory is not limited to European Union Member States.

Research-sensitive criteria comply with our vision of what contributes to the IL-readiness of a country. Only what can be considered a factor supportive of the IL-readiness condition of a country is included in the Observatory.

To date the Observatory has been established for Austria, Denmark, Estonia, Finland, Germany, Italy, Latvia, Lithuania, Poland and Spain, and consists of more than 600 web pages.

The above described criteria have been implemented in the framework of the Observatory, consisting – for each country - of the following sections:

Policy initiatives
Survey reports
Research projects
Campus initiatives
Events
Special Interest Groups
Academic library initiatives
Tutorials
Learning resource Centers
Public library initiatives

Fig. 1 *Sections of the EnIL Observatory for each country*

The framework in fig. 1 is the matrix into which the different IL initiatives in a country are arranged. In other words, each initiative constitutes an entry in a specific section of the Observatory and the general format of each entry includes the following fields:

Title and network address:
Body responsible:
Start date:
End date (if applicable):
Typology:
Textual description:
Keywords:

Fig.2 *Format of each entry in the EnIL Observatory*

Each field in the entry has been identified and included in the format because it has been considered functional to a variable which must be observed.

The "*age*" of the IL discourse in the country is indicated by the earliest "start date" of its initiatives: the age, in turn, expresses the *timeliness* of the country in affording the IL problem.

The "*degree of the involvement*" is represented by the field "body responsible" of the initiative: the wider jurisdiction of the body indicates the wider involvement of the country (the government, a university, a faculty, a library).

The "*perception of the IL nature*" is represented by the operative field of the body responsible (Education or Technology or Culture or Telecommunications or Innovation Ministries; the disciplinary field if academic institutions, …)

The "*scale of the initiative*" is represented by the field "typology"(national policy document, library tutorial, research project, report, academic policy document, …) , which expresses the potential of both the impact of the initiative and the value attributed to IL in the country.

Each initiative described in the Observatory has been assigned a set of keywords, denoting its subject content. To date, the keywords have been freely attributed, due to the lack of a controlled vocabulary for the field of IL policies. This is among the future tasks to be performed in the EnIL Observatory, in order to achieve better indexing of the documents and allow for comparative searching among the various countries[5].

5. Conclusions

A policy commitment is the great absent in the Information Literacy discourse at European level. In a time of competition for scarse resources, policy attention can be gained only on the basis of evidence of problems and needs.

The European network on Information Literacy (EnIL) is a research project with three main *foci*: Europe, IL policies and research, Higher Education.

A preliminary step in the EnIL research agenda was the recognition of three axes along which to articulate reasoning about Information Literacy: policy, disciplinary and cognitive. The three axes model can be used to distinguish among different variables to be taken into account when attempting to implement the Information Literacy goal in a community (citizens in a country, students in a campus, pupils in a school, knowledge workers, etc..).

The European Observatory on IL Policies and Research is among the results of the EnIL project and is a first step towards comparing European countries with respect to IL-readiness. A first set of qualitative variables have been identified, which can be combined to represent the concept of IL-readiness. They are: policy awareness, timeliness, degree of involvement, nature of IL perception, scale of the IL phenomenon, potential impact. The identified variables have been conceived as the basic framework of the EnIL Observatory, and used to establish the various sections of the Observatory and the format of each entry. Further work is in progress in order to expand and modify this initial set of variables.

References

Abid, A. (2004). Information literacy for lifelong learning. Proceedings of the *70th IFLA General Conference and Council. http://archive.ifla.org/IV/ifla70/prog04.htm*

Averch, H. (1980), Science Indicators and Policy Analysis, *Scientometrics*, 2 (5-6), 339-345.

Basili C. (2008a) *Theorems of Information Literacy* in: *Information Literacy at the cross-*

road of Education and Information Policies in Europe/ Basili C. 33-52

Basili, C. (Ed.) (2003) *Information Literacy in Europe. A first insight into the state of the art of Information Literacy in the European Union*. Rome: CNR.

Basili, C. (Ed.) (2008) *Information Literacy at the cross-road of Education and Information Policies in Europe*. Rome: CNR.

Basili, C. (Ed.) (2009) *The Observatory on Information Literacy Policies and Research in Europe* . Rome: CNR.

Esty, D.C. – Rushing, R. (2007) *Governing by the numbers. The Promise of Data-Driven Policymaking In The Information Age*, Center for American Progress

Hambrick, R. Jr., (1998) Building the policy studies enterprise: a work in progress, *Public Adm. Rev*. 58 (6), 533–539.

OECD (1993), *OECD Guidance on Safety Performance Indicators: A Companion to the OECD Guiding Principles for Chemical Accident Prevention*, Preparedness and Response. <www.oecd.org/dataoecd/60/39/21568440.pdf>

Reggiani, L. (2009*) Implementing the Observatory: towards a controlled language*. In *The Observatory on Information Literacy Policies and Research in Europe/ Basili C.* 13-32

Zurkowsky, P.G. (1974) *The Information Service Environment Relationships and Priorities*. Related Paper No.5

Notes

[1] UNESCO-UIS/OECD (2005) *Education Trends in perspectives. Analysis of the world education indicators*. Unesco institute for Statistics, Organisation for Economic Co-operation and Development, World Education Indicators programme - Mejer, L. – Gere, E. (2008) *Education in Europe - Key statistics 2006*, Eurostat, *Data in focus*, 42/2008 - Policy Indicators for Higher Education: WICHE States, *http://www.wiche.edu/policy/Factbook/* - OECD - Working Party on Indicators for the Information Society (2007). *Information Economy – Sector definition based on yhe International Standard Industry Classification (ISIC 4)* – Commissione delle Comunità Europee (2007). *Un quadro coerente di indicatori e parametri per monitorare i progressi nella realizzazione degli obiettivi di Lisbona in material di istruzione e formazione*. COM(2007)61 definitivo

[2] The European Observatory on IL Policies and Research was established in 2006 and is among the results of the European network on Information Literacy (EnIL - *www.ceris.cnr.it/Basili/EnIL/index.html*), a research project started in 2001 by the author and supported by the Italian National Research Council, with the aim of adopting a common research agenda and sharing results among IL researchers in Europe .

To date the network includes IL experts from research and academic institutions in: Austria, Belgium, the Czech Republic, Denmark, Finland, France, Germany, Greece, Ireland, Italy, the Netherlands, Portugal, Slovenia, Spain, Sweden, and the United Kingdom. Enlargement of the network is in progress, in order to include all European countries.

[3] the National Commission on Libraries and Information Science

[4] www.ceris.cnr.it/Basili/EnIL/index.html

[5] for a detailed account of the need of a controlled vocabulary in the field, see Reggiani (2009)

New Technologies, Citizen Empowerment, and Civic Life

James Rettig

University Librarian, University of Richmond and
President, American Library Association (2008-2009)
Boatwright Memorial Library
University of Richmond, USA

Abstract: Information literacy and civic literacy intersect in ways that are important to society and that demonstrate the value of librarians and publishers. Librarians and publishers play an important role in cultivating information literacy in the populace so that citizens can carry out their civic responsibilities in an informed and responsible way. The spread of the Internet and the challenges it poses to traditional information providers creates new challenges for publishers and librarians.

Keywords: New media; Information literacy; Civic literacy; Publishers; Librarians; Mass media.

1. Introduction

Gutenberg's introduction of movable type made the printed book era possible in the fifteenth century. Once printing and paper production became industrial processes, mass media developed. Multiple copies of books produced at acceptable prices allowed increased, albeit far from universal, ownership of books. Newspapers and magazines also emerged as economically viable means to record and distribute information. Mass media yielded varied social dividends. Where ecclesiastical or government censorship did not interfere, the mass media allowed expression and dissemination of varied points of view. This enriched and enlivened civic discourse. One can legitimately question whether or not the American revolution in 1776 would have occurred had it not been for newspapers and pamphlets that spread new ideas and ideals and united the colonies in opposition to England.

Information technologies have improved continuously and new information technologies have emerged. The rate of increase of new knowledge and discovery accelerated century after century. Except for the most politicized and sensational newspapers and journals, mass media also became de facto authorities and trusted sources of knowledge and information. The exception, of course, has been in societies with state controlled media that functions as a propaganda tool as much and perhaps more than its functions as an information source. In such cases disbelief is many citizens' response to the state controlled media's messages.

With the development of mass media, information became more abundant and more accessible. However producers and distributors of information and the consumers of information played distinctly different roles. Publishing a newspaper, a magazine, or books or launching and maintaining a television or radio station all require significant start-up capital. This has limited the number of actors in these mass media industries. For this reason, that limited number of publishers and broadcasters have enjoyed significant social influence. They have also acted as gatekeepers, choosing which creative works to publish, broadcast, and disseminate and which works to ignore. There have always been exceptions, e.g., vanity publishers catering to authors whose books cannot find a publisher. Underground publication, another exception, have played an important role in repressive societies, e.g., the samizdat publishing system in the Soviet Union. However the social influence of alternative media enterprises has rarely been a match for the dominant media.

The most successful media enterprises have been able to shape public opinion and at times have even created something approximating social consensus. This has not always been for the good—e.g., the McCarthy era in mid-twentieth century in the United States had a chilling effect on free expression. Because these enterprises have, however, seen themselves as having a responsibility to society, they have generally valued fidelity to fact and reality. Many of them have become trusted sources of information. There have, of course, been and continue to be mass media organizations that play fast and loose with fidelity to fact. Overall, however, for much of the twentieth century in American society and other developed countries the mass media has enjoyed significant social influence. In part this has been due to the relative scarcity of the means of producing and dissemination information and the concentration of this power in those established media organizations.

2. New Technologies and Changing Roles

That has changed dramatically over the past 15 years with the astronomical growth of the Internet. Reasonably priced personal computers and access to powerful networks has changed the costly scarcity of media production into an affordable abundance. Free software allows individuals to set up a blog and become publishers. It has empowered the individual citizen and called into question the mass media's authority. In the era of the print-only newspaper, an individual could write a letter to the editor. The editor would decide whether or not to publish that letter, either in full or part. If published, the letter would reach a portion of the newspaper's readers.

Compare that narrow dissemination to today's opportunities. Now blogs and other even more dynamic, interactive social software allow individuals who once would have reached only a limited audience to reach a much larger and more geographically dispersed audience. This has undermined the authority of the mass media.

American comedian and satirist Stephen Colbert ironically used the mass medium of television to illustrate how authority has eroded. He did it with a concept he called "truthiness." The American Dialect Society named "truthiness" its word of the year for 2005. Truthiness, the ADS explained, "refers to the quality of preferring concepts or facts one wishes to be true, rather than concepts or facts known to be true." As Mr. Colbert said, "I don't trust books. They're all fact, no heart." (Truthiness Voted 2005 Word of the Year 2006) Yet how quickly this word has dropped from use!

Perhaps truthiness has lost favor because it requires effort. To establish the truthiness of the so-called "fact" that the population of African elephants had tripled, Steven Colbert had to ask the viewers of his *Colbert Report* television show to modify Wikipedia's article on elephants. People recognized this as satire and placed no stock in the false statement about elephants' sudden population boom. Nonetheless they rushed to edit the Wikipedia article to misstate the status of the African elephant population. Truthiness requires action. It also requires consensus, something that can come about without the overt effort necessary to establish the "truthiness" of a so-called fact.

Take, for example the ease with which millions of Americans during the U.S. 2008 presidential campaign accepted the falsehood that Barak Obama is a Muslim. This claim often cited his middle name—Hussein--as proof, even though there is no if-then connection between one's name and one's religious affiliation. Take as another example from that campaign the ease with which many, including some librarians, accepted at face value the bogus claim that as mayor of Wasilla, Alaska Sarah Palin tried to remove a long list of books from Wasilla's public library—even though some books on the list hadn't yet been published at the time. Has rumor displaced truthiness?

Or perhaps opinion, undisturbed by fact, has replaced both truth and truthiness. On October 2, 2008 CNN in the United States announced results of a viewer poll: 85% of the respondents said that cyclist Lance Armstrong has never been involved in doping. This poll result was presented on the air as if the numbers reported the truth the same way the final vote total in an election identifies the winner. The point of the story was that the French anti-doping agency AFLD wanted to retest Armstrong's 1999 Tour de France urine samples. Apparently AFLD places more faith in science than in quick polls of CNN viewers. Perhaps majority opinion has come to supplant accurate, trustworthy information.

In the pre-Internet era, because economic factors limited the number of media outlets, people who wanted information were at least exposed to ideas that might run contrary to their own. As they paged through a newspaper they might read an op-ed article or an editorial that took a stand different from their own. This clash of ideas would stir debate, or at least encourage a reader to consider a conflicting point of view. Where once the mass media had the opportunity to generate debate and foster social consensus, today individuals can use information media to insulate themselves from ideas and influences they do not agree with.

Right-wing talk radio in the United States, personified by Rush Limbaugh, illustrates the way that an individual can isolate himself or herself from debate and conflicting views. Guests are invited on the show because their opinions agree with the host's opinions. Callers call in to express their agreement and to attack those they disagree with. This tautological process creates a fortress mentality in which truth can easily be sacrificed for unanimity of opinion and for affirmation of a group's shared beliefs and values. Surrounded only by like thinkers, no new ideas penetrate the fortress and only old ideas abide within it. Ideology doesn't matter; left-wing talk radio has the same invidious narrowing effect.

The Web and social networking software can intensify this intellectual isolation. One can join only those Facebook and Yahoo groups, subscribe only to those online discussion groups, and read only those blogs that affirm and never challenge one's own opinions. Such narrowing and hardening of opinion, outlook, and attitude intensifies political conflicts. They lead to accepting as a political scorecard of wins and losses for one's faction as the measure of society's health, a measure that in its narrowness is in itself actually a measure of dysfunction in civic discourse. Compromise and collaboration become very unlikely, perhaps impossible. And in the quest for reinforcement of personal acknowledgement and affirmation, acceptance of truth and fact loses importance.

In *China Road: A Journey into the Future of a Rising Power* Rob Gifford describes how in Shanghai

> One shiny new office tower…has become a huge TV screen, with advertisements and government propaganda alternately lighting up the entire side of the building, one message replaced five seconds later by another.
>
> *Welcome to Shanghai. Tomorrow will be even more beautiful.*
> *1,746 more days until the Shanghai World Expo.*
> *Sexual equality is a basic policy of our country.*
> *Eat Dove chocolate.* (Gifford 2007)

Even discounting a sweet tooth, the citizens of Shanghai undoubtedly place greater stock in ads for chocolate than in the ruling party's nostrums. They have learned through experience how to judge the source of a bit of information, just as viewers of the *Colbert Report* know how to evaluate satire.

Libraries play many important roles in our communities. We help the members of those communities—elementary and secondary students, citizens, college students, etc.—learn to recognize the need to find and evaluate information and how to do so. School and academic librarians work with faculty to teach these concepts and competencies to students. Public librarians strive to do the same, albeit for much more diffuse communities. These opportunities open to librarians when people recognize that they need information, for example, when they want to test the truth of a claim about a candidate for public office or when they want to know what options are open to them after they receive a foreclosure notice that may force them from their home.

3. Information Literacy and Civic Literacy

Information literacy intersects with civic literacy. A Web search on "civic literacy" turns up myriad definitions. The Partnership for 21st Century Skills defines it in part as "Participating effectively in civic life through knowing how to stay informed and understanding governmental processes." (Partnership for 21st Centruy Skills 2004) In preparation for last fall's national election in the United States, public and academic libraries posted information on special election Web pages, created book displays, and hosted public forums about the issues. Elections come and go; but issues abide, as do our roles to promote information literacy and civic literacy.

Librarians and publishers have a vital role to play in increasing civic literacy. Because of our profound commitment to intellectual freedom we vigorously defend the American classic *The Adventures of Huckleberry Finn*, J.K Rowling's tales of a young wizard in training, and a children's book about two male penguins who care for an egg. (Richardson and Parnell 2005) We present programs on controversial subjects, inviting proponents and opponents to share their views in a trusted public forum. We make our meeting rooms available without prejudice to groups whose own prejudices we may well find repugnant. The library is the Ellis Island of ideas. We welcome ideas from all and provide a place where they clash, meld, morph, and synthesize to challenge and energize society and its public discourse.

When Stephen Colbert misused Wikipedia to foist upon its users bogus information, he called into question the validity of Wikipedia's social editing methods and its premise that collaborative social knowledge will correct individual errors. At one extreme we have mass movements that negate this premise—for example, the rise of the National Socialist German Workers' Party in the 1930s, the sectarian conflicts in

Iraq, and the new vigor that white supremacist groups have felt since Barack Obama's election as president of the United States. Many have questioned Wikipedia's premises, usually citing the lack of authority among many, perhaps even most, of its self-appointed authors.

On the other hand, there are many testimonials to the success of the Wikipedia editing process. In the September 2006 issue of *The Atlantic*, Marshall Poe, an academic historian who studies and writes about Russia discussed the article about him in Wikipedia. (Poe 2006) One of Wikipedia's many anonymous editors nominated that article for deletion. Others, none identifiable by name, responded. The discussion ended with a strong assertion by "Tupsharru" who had searched the Library of Congress's catalog and cited Poe's strong record as a published Russian historian. "Tupsharru" concluded his argument by writing, "I don't know why I have to repeat this again and again in these deletion discussions on academics, but don't just use Amazon when the Library of Congress catalogue is no farther than a couple of mouse clicks away." (Poe 2006)

Three years ago Poe predicted that Wikipedia's future was secure, that it had become "the place where all nominal information about objects of widely shared experience will be negotiated, stored, and renegotiated. When you want to find out *what something is*, you will go to Wikipedia, for that is where common knowledge will, by convention, be archived and updated and made freely available." (Poe 2006) Collaborative social knowledge about "what something is" can be and, as Wikipedia has demonstrated, is very useful to the worldwide readership Wikipedia has attracted. The Library of Congress has asked for help from the collective knowledge hive to identify what some of the things in its collections are. Describing its "Photos on Flicker" project, the library "invite[s] you to tag and comment on the photos, and we also welcome identifying information—many of these old photos came to us with scanty descriptions!" (Library of Congress 2008) This is another good use of social knowledge, even when only one person can identify the subject or date or place captured in a photograph. By sticking to describing "what something is" and by responding quickly to attacks such the one Stephen Colbert launched on its article on elephants, Wikipedia has established its credibility within that limited scope of conveying what things are. That does not prevent Wikipedians from trying to exceed those limits and explain what things mean—things such as the Israeli-Palestinian conflict, the presidency of George W. Bush, global warming, or euthanasia.

These topics touch on civic life at the international level. History has shown through incidents such as the ethnic cleansing in the Balkans in the 1990s and the unpunished lynchings of blacks in the United States in the nineteenth and early twentieth centuries that the knowledge of the hive can be dangerous and deadly when it claims to explain what things mean.

4. Roles of Publishers and Librarians

Librarian and publishers have a special role and responsibility in civic life at every level—the village or city, the state, the nation, and the world. Through books, periodicals, and other media that analyze things to explore their meanings, publishers and librarians enrich civic life and promote civic literacy. Citizens can stay informed an educate themselves about the issues of the day and explore varied interpretations of what things that affect their lives and the world mean. Publishers and librarians and Wikipedia share responsibility for helping people know what things are. When it comes to understanding what things mean, our role complements Wikipedia and other collaborative social knowledge projects.

This latter role presents special challenges. Understanding what things mean usually requires an extended explanation and a carefully structured argument that organizes and interprets relevant evidence. The shelves of our college and university libraries brim with books written to explain the meanings of myriad topics. These books require from their readers a commitment of time and attention and a willingness to examine the evidence and the author's interpretation of that evidence's meaning.

The scarcest commodity today in every developed society is attention. Each day thousands of stimuli vie for our attention. The 2008 U.S. presidential campaign illustrates the effect of this on civic life. In September the *New York Times* reported on

> one of the most frustrating challenges that Mr. McCain and Mr. Obama are facing going into the final weeks of this campaign: the ways in which the proliferation of communications channels, the fracturing of mass media and the relentless political competition to own each news cycle are combining to reorder the way voters follow campaigns and decide how to vote. It has reached a point where senior campaign aides say they are no longer sure what works, as they stumble through what has become a daily campaign fog, struggling to figure out what voters are paying attention to. (Nagourney 2008)

The McCain and Obama campaigns weren't trying to make carefully structured arguments that organize and interpret relevant evidence. They were simply trying to get attention—preferably positive attention—for their respective candidates.

Getting attention for a message is only the first step. The message needs to be presented in a way that engages attention. And then there is the biggest challenge for publishers and librarians—presenting information about what things mean, not just coherently, but also concisely. The dominant medium for information dissemination and access today is the Web. It seems that attention spans for information delivered electronically has shrunk to the size of a single Web page, preferably one that requires only a small bit of scrolling.

5. Conclusions

The challenge publishers and librarians face in carrying out their mission in democracies to assure an informed citizenry has three components:

- First, to attract the attention of readers/viewers/listeners—for the multimedia aspects of the Web allow for all three of these modes simultaneously
- Second, after attracting a reader's/viewer's/listener's attention, engaging it so that the individual doesn't click away to some other information source
- Third, conveying information about complex issues succinctly

Libraries depend to a great extent, but not exclusively on publishers to create information resources that meet these three criteria. The greatest challenge will be the third. Thus far the electronic book has mimed the printed book, generally mirroring its appearance in PDF format. Neither e-books nor printed books make it easy for empowered citizens, an synonym for readers, to respond to let alone interact with an author the way they can by commenting on a blog post. Authors and publishers need to experiment with electronic book forms that are transformative—forms that integrate information in forms other than just linear text and that encourage conversation among the books' users. Ideally these new creations will engage people in vigorous, informed debate about public policy issues and lead to greater civic literacy.

Librarians will continue to play a familiar role with these new creations. First, we must accommodate them in our collections and devise ways to describe them that make them accessible very soon after they are published. New electronic forms of publishing will not wait for old cataloging codes to catch up to them. We must also encourage their use. Most importantly, we must continue to help readers/viewers/listeners appreciate the need to look at all information resources critically and to evaluate them using familiar criteria such as the authority of the creator, the source's factual accuracy, the creator's biases, etc.

Every new information medium poses challenges. In the United States newspapers are struggling with these issues as the immediacy and ubiquity of online access displaces static daily ink-on-paper delivery of information. The plight of newspapers illustrates the necessity for publishers of other current genre to experiment more. Librarians need to embrace new media and help users understand these new media's strengths and limitations. As information technologies and delivery systems continue to change, both publishers and librarians need to find ways to continue to provide resources that explain not just what things are, but what things mean. There is danger in not taking these risks—not just the danger of being considered an irrelevant institution or profession, but the graver danger that society will organize itself in such ways that people are never exposed to a range of competing ideas and will receive only information—factual or erroneous—that consistently reinforces but never challenges their thinking.

References

Gifford, R. (2007) *China Road: A Journey into the Future of a Rising Power.* New York: Random House.

Library of Congress. (2008) *Prints and Photographs Reading Room* . June 3, 2008. http://www.loc.gov/rr/print/flickr_pilot.html (accessed November 16, 2008).

Nagourney, A. (2008) "Carefully Shaped Message Now a Campaign Relic." *New York Times*, September 16, 2008, section A, p. 22.

Partnership for 21st Centruy Skills. (2008) *Civic Literacy.* 2004. http://www.21stcenturyskills.org/index.php?option=com_content&task=view&id=258&Itemid=126 (accessed November 16, 2008).

Poe, M. (2006) "The Hive." *The Atlantic.* September 2006. http://www.theatlantic.com/doc/200609/wikipedia/6 (accessed November 16, 2008).

Richardson, J, and P. Parnell. (2005) *And Tango Makes Three.* New York: Simon & Schuster Books for Young Readers.

Truthiness Voted 2005 Word of the Year. (2006) January 11, 2006. http://www.americandialect.org/index.php/amerdial/truthiness_voted_2005_word_of_the_year/ (accessed May 2, 2009).

Challenges in Teaching Information Literacy in Online Courses

Vilve Seiler

University of Tartu Library, Estonia, Subject Librarian

Abstract: This paper discusses the models of teaching information literacy at the University of Tartu. The library offers two general e-learning courses: *Fundamentals of information literacy* as an optional subject for baccalaureus and master's students and *Introduction to information research* as an elective subject for doctoral students. Based on the basic course, subject librarians offer discipline-specific online courses which are taught as a part of some subjects and are compulsory for students.

Keywords: Information literacy; Academic libraries; Teaching library; e-learning.

1. Introduction

During recent years, the amount of literature on information literacy has been growing, different approaches to information literacy education have been discussed and information literacy has become an issue at many academic libraries.

There are many definitions of information literacy. The definition presented in this paper is the one provided by the American Library Association, which has been most cited: "To be information literate, a person must be able to recognize when information is needed and have the ability to locate, evaluate and use effectively the needed information" (ALA, 1989).

Information literacy is topical right now because, in relation with the reforms of higher education, ongoing in European countries, the learning outcomes are very important and outcomes-based curricula are being designed everywhere. Teaching of information literacy has a direct effect on the stu-dents' study results, as these skills support such outcomes as critical thinking, solving of problems and lifelong learning. Information literacy enables to improve the quality of studying and helps the students to become life-long learners. People who can search for information and evaluate and organise information are more successful in their studies and later, in their career; they are self-directed learners, much valued by society. (Rockman, 2004).

This paper discusses the challenges of implementing information literacy education at the University of Tartu, Estonia (www.ut.ee). First, the conception of the stand-alone e-learning course *Fundamentals of information literacy* is described, then the teaching and learning approaches are discussed; the paper ends with examples of the students' responses to the course.

The design and implementation of the information literacy course was a challenging task that was meant to find an answer to the questions whether such a course, developed at the library, could find positive response at the university, whether it would attract students and whether the students would appreciate the knowledge acquired during the course and, last but not least, whether librarians would be able to teach such a course. We also wanted to find assurance whether an e-course as a form of teaching and learning would be suitable for teaching information literacy.

Our experience could be useful for other academic libraries who wish to use e-courses in teaching information literacy and to formalise information literacy education.

2. Initiative of teaching library – stand-alone information literacy e-learning course

The mission of the University of Tartu Library (www.utlib.ee) is, by developing its collections, to offer the best library and information services and be a trustworthy partner to the members of the University of Tartu and other library users in supporting their teaching and learning, research and professional careers.

To facilitate access to information, the library licences to valuable and expensive digital resources. In order to benefit from these resources at their fullest, the students have to obtain information literacy. Very often the librarians can see that students do not know professional databases relevant for their specialities and are not familiar with the ways of information search.

The university library as a provider of information resources feels the responsibility to offer students and university staff knowledge of information resources in their subject field, to enable the students to find the information they need and to improve the quality of their assignments. The aim is to teach how to use their own library and its resources, but also to provide information literacy education considering the ALA definition, according to which information literacy education is wider than teaching of specific information resources – it also includes critical thinking skills and the evaluation of the information sources.

Numerous discussions on how information literacy should be taught have been held in librarians' professional publications. The majority of participants of these discussions believe that teaching of information literacy should be integrated or embedded into the subjects of the curricula and the importance of cooperation between the faculties and the library is much stressed. Some authors, such as Johnston and Webber (2003) and Owusu-Ansah (2004), argue that information literacy could be a subject in its own right and it can be taught in the form of stand-alone courses. Owusu-Ansah (2004: 12) is convinced that "the library should offer an independent credit course in information literacy, one that offers in depth engagement with issues inherent in and skills attendant to information literacy".

In order to demonstrate the need for information literacy at the university and to draw attention to it as a possible curriculum subject, and to give students the opportunity to develop more in depth information literacy skills and abilities, we decided, first, to design a basic course in information literacy and later, to use all possible means to integrate the teaching of this course into different curricula and subjects. In 2006, we developed a web-based course *Fundamentals of Information Literacy*. It is a credit-bearing optional course, giving two credit points (3 ECTS). The course is suitable for all specialities, as it is related with the virtual subject area libraries of the University of Tartu Library and it is taught by the subject librarians of the library, who supervise the students of their specialities. The learning modules were designed bearing in mind the needs of both the beginners and advanced learners and all students receive individual tutoring. The course is especially suitable for Bachelor's and Master's students, who already have their own research subject and specific information needs.

In 2008, a continuation course was designed for the target group of advanced learners, which has been included into all curricula of doctoral students of the university. The curricula of doctoral studies prescribe for all-university key competence subjects, in the amount of eight credit points; information literacy as an essential key competence has been included among them.

Why e-learning?

E-courses allow teaching of a large number of students and offer a more extensive programme than a traditional course, restricted by time limit, usually requested from the library. As the participants come from different faculties, the flexibility of an e-course is a great advantage and all participants can study at their most suitable time and place. At a web-course, it is easier to consider the needs of both the beginners and the advanced learners; the chapters of the course are built in gradation and the learner can choose which part of it he/she wants to study more thoroughly. Information search is a process and the result can be achieved by different paths. Feedback from the forum of the course allows drawing attention to different possibilities in such a way that all participants can benefit from it.

3. Teaching and learning approach

The course programme was designed in accordance with the ACRL-developed information literacy standards for higher education. (ACRL, 2000) These five standards, together with performance indicators and learning outcomes, cover the whole range of information literacy and present possible spheres of activities, where libraries can participate in the teaching of information literacy.

Learning modules

In e-courses, the good structure of materials – so that they were comprehensive and quick to learn – is of essential nature. Material is thematically ordered, but it is not necessary to read the chapters in a rigid order. – they are structured and necessary parts can easily be reread when doing the exercises. We did not aim at compiling detailed materials on the use of specific databases, but wanted to introduce the types of different databases and general search principles so that the graduates of the course would in the future be able to search new databases on their own.

The course consists of 13 modules, discussing types of information sources, principles of information search, types and structure of databases, advanced search in different search environments accessible for the University of Tartu Library, possibilities for searching scientific information on the Internet, as well as the evaluation of information sources and the avoiding of plagiarism.

Study process

The whole course is carried out in the virtual learning environment Blackboard, where the students can find the materials, submit their homework, communicate with the tutors and with each other, and get feedback. E-course can succeed only if the whole study process has been carefully planned.

At the beginning of the course, a week is set aside for getting familiar with the environment and the course and for the students and tutors to get acquainted with each other in order to support the forming of a group. Starting from the second week, the participants practice information search on their subject according to the course plan and submit their work to respective forums, where they can get feedback. For example, in the first exercise, the students have to find, with the help of virtual subject libraries, the EBSCO and CSA databases that are relevant to their subject, get acquainted with them, describe in detail and analyse their search strategies for keyword and subject heading search and compare the suitability of both searches for their subject. Next exercises contain searches in other professional databases; by the end of the course, the students have obtained an overview of all databases and learned how to collect database entries which are relevant for their subjects. During the last week of the course, they write a review of all of their searches and analyse and reflect upon their learning process and successes, and submit a bibliography, formulated according to the system of referencing that they had chosen.

Pedagogical approach

The course is based on the constructivist treatment of learning that positions the student in the centre of the learning process. While choosing the activities for the course, we paid much attention to the activating methods and problem-based learning. Self-directed learning is the most important activating strategy for the web-based learning, making the learner responsible for his/her motivation and awareness (Pitt and Clark, 2006).

In our course model, we also applied elements of the relational frame for information literacy education, introduced by Bruce, Edwards and Lupton (2006), who underline that reflection and planning of the search process are the key aspects of the searching experience and that search planning and active searching reflection influences the quality of the search performance.

We also drew from the action research model for Reflective Internet Searching, presented by Edwards and Bruce (2002), which shows online searching as a circle of continuous planning, acting, recording and reflecting. In all information search exercises of the course, the students give detailed records of their searches, describe different versions of the searches and analyse, which search strategy gave the most relevant results, and in the final review, reflect the whole of their learning process.

Studying at the information literacy course is flexible and the learners can control their learning process. They can choose when and what to learn, selecting just the materials they want to study and centring upon them. Practical exercises are flexible as well, meaning that certain conditions have to be fulfilled, but the subject and the information sources can be chosen by the learner and thus, the learners have greater freedom and responsibility of interpreting the course. The exercises submitted by the students can be read by all participants of the course and checking of other learners' ideas together with the feedback from the tutor can add value to learning. In such a way, all learners create new content for the course, which is accessible for all of their fellow students.

The learners mostly work independently; the developing of independence and critical thinking has an important role in the course. Information search skills are developed by practicing different searches and in interaction with the tutor. In order to support other ways of learning, we have, in some exercises, used collaborative learning.

Giving feedback is a time-consuming activity, it has to be constructive and support the learner. Advisory feedback is especially valuable during the learning process, as it motivates the learners and helps them to get better results. Usually, one tutor supervises 10-15 students during the course, which is the optimal number. The tutor is not an expert in certain specialities, but he/she knows databases, has a vast experience of information search and can offer valuable suggestions. The role of the tutor is, rather, that of an advisor and moderator in learning and information processes, according to Ingraham, Levy, McKenna and Roberts (2006: 166), “it shifts away from direct instruction towards strategies that will facilitate those dialogical interactions between learner and tutor, and between learners, that are the heart of constructivist and relational pedagogies”.

In order to reduce the workload of tutors, it is possible to use peer-tutoring. However, when using peer-tutoring, the students need to be given precise criteria and guidelines for their activities. We first used this method at an advanced course, and the concentration of doctoral students onto the subjects and search processes of their fellow learners exceeded our expectations. This method also helps to unify the learners into a group, it motivates and activities them and develops their critical skills in evaluating their own, as well as their fellows’ work.

Students’ perceptions

In order to get evaluation of the course, we asked the participants to express their thoughts about the materials, exercises, schedule and the activities of the tutors in an anonymous forum, and to state, whether the course met their needs and expectations. The students wrote free text about what the course had given to them. Many participants expressed their views about the course in the review of the final week, where they analysed their learning process. Of 215 students, who passed the course *Fundamentals of Information Literacy*, 107 gave feedback about the course and all of them were sure that it had been necessary and useful, were happy that they had chosen the course and several of them admitted, that such a course would have been vital for them already earlier. 37% of them said that they found information about new databases and services they had previously not been aware of. Many students admitted that, prior to the course, they had used only the library e-catalogue and the Internet. 21% of the participants mentioned that during the course, they much improved their knowledge of different search methods and search skills. During the course, it was well visible how the participants’ skills in planning their searches improved. 28% of the participants said that due to the information literacy course, they have better chances in writing a good bachelor’s or master’s thesis, as they are much better able to search for and choose information sources. Some of the participants said that the acquired skills help them in their career as well.

The structure of the course was praised by 36% of the participants. They said that the course is flexible and student-friendly and well suitable for self-study, as it allows for studying whenever it is convenient. “Independent searching and analysis were the most important parts of the course, as this is the best way of learning something.” The reading of works of fellow learners was also considered important, as “it gives you the feeling that you are not alone in taking the course.” Individual and quick feedback is much appreciated by the students, who repeatedly used the words quick, efficient, practical, positive, advancing, supporting, and useful in their commentaries. The experience of studying on the Internet and using Blackboard was appreciated as well. The participants expressed the idea that the teaching of information search should be included in the curriculum of the 2nd and 3rd year bachelor’s studies.

A participant of the course drew the following conclusion, "Fundamentals of Information Literacy = new and interesting knowledge + well compiled and clear study materials + specified criteria concerning the passing of the course + friendly tutors."

Suggestions received from the feedback have helped to continue developing the course every year. A model of such a course that centres on independent active work and furthers the development of learners' critical thinking is very time-consuming and considerably increases the tutors' workload. At the same time, students appreciate such courses where they can receive quick individual feedback; positive feedback from students, in its turn, motivates the organisers of the course and the tutors to improve the course.

In 2008, this course was given a special award in the field of *socialia* at the competition The e-Course of the Year of the Estonian e-University. Information of this successful course is spreading at the university and at several specialities a wish has been expressed to include it into the curriculum as an elective course.

4. Courses integrated into different subjects

In addition to stand-alone general information literacy course, some students have the opportunity of developing their information literacy within courses in their speciality. As a large part of the basic course is similar for all specialities, subject librarians can use its modules for fitting in speciality-based information literacy courses by adding speciality-specific content. Earlier, subject librarians organised seminars, requested by teaching staff, for introducing information sources and information search; the duration of these seminars was only 90 minutes. Now, it is possible to offer much more exhausting courses. Much depends on the subject librarian – if he/she is able to convince the lecturers in the benefits of such courses for the students, the opportunities for cooperation can be found.

At present, such courses, compulsory for students, are held within individual subjects at the Faculties of Law, Exercise and Sport Sciences, Education, and Social Sciences. They are carried out in the environment of e-learning face to face with the main course, they have in different ways been integrated into specialty courses, and the content and practical activities of the course are agreed upon with the lecturer of the subject. As a rule, the number of participants at these courses is large (in 2008, the total of 1270 students participated in five different courses), and it is not possible to use exercises with individual feedback. Instead, tests with automatic feedback have to be used. However, students can still elect a separate course in information literacy if they need it.

We hope to attract attention to such courses at other faculties as well and we can tailor the programme of the course according to specific needs of different faculties. E-learning gives a huge advantage here, as the faculties do not need to find special classroom time.

5. Conclusions

We can conclude, based on our observations of the student learning as well as on feedback from the students that both the basic and advanced courses in information literacy were successful. The courses fulfil their objective of drawing attention to information literacy at the university. This allows the library to address its objective of integrating information literacy into the university curricula. Specialty-centred information literacy courses have already been adopted at four faculties.

Not all subject librarians had had some previous experience in teaching information literacy. According to the conception of the basic course, all subject librarians had to supervise the students of their faculties, thus not only students learned from each other's exercises and commentaries – the tutors had to learn as well. As a result of the course, even those subject librarians, who were not so comfortable with teaching, have become information literacy specialists and tutors.

Preparation and management of an e-course is extremely labour-consuming; the forwarding of materials, communication and grading require full responsibility of the organisers. E-learning suits information literacy courses very well just for its flexibility, as the participants can plan their time, but it also requires self-discipline and motivation. Due to e-learning, it is easier to integrate information literacy modules into courses of different specialities, as the students do not need to come to the library for lectures and no special classroom time is needed.

The library continues to offer a general basic e-course *Fundamentals of Information Literacy* as an optional subject for students in the autumn semester, and doctoral students can elect a course *Introduction to Information Research* in each spring semester. The content and form of both of these courses constantly need updating.

References

ACRL (2000). *Information Literacy Competency Standards for Higher Education.* Available at http://www.ala.org/ala/mgrps/divs/acrl/ standards/ informationliteracycompetency.cfm; accessed 26.03.09.

ALA (1989). *American Library Association. Presidential Committee on Information Literacy. Final Report.* Available at http://www.ala.org/ala/mgrps/divs/acrl/publications/ whitepapers/presidential.cfm; accessed 4.04.2009.

Bruce, C. S., Edwards, S. and Lupton, M. (2006). Six frames for information literacy education: a conceptual framework for interpreting the relationships between theory and practice, *Italics,* Vol. 5, No 1. Available at http://www.ics.heacademy. ac.uk/italics/vol5-1/pdf/sixframes_final%20_1_.pdf; accessed 4.04.2009.

Edwards, S. L. and Bruce, C. S. (2002). Reflective Internet Searching: an action research model, *The Learning Organization,* Vol. 9, No 4, 180-188.

Ingraham, B., Levy, P., McKenna, C. and Roberts, G. (2006). Academic Literacy in the 21st Century. *Contemporary Perspectives in E-learning Research: Themes, Methods and Impact on Practic*e, 161-173.

Johnston, B., and Webber, S. (2003). Information literacy in higher education: a review and case study, *Studies in Higher Education,* Vol. 28, No 3, 335-352.

Owusu-Ansah, E. K. (2004). Information literacy and higher education: placing the academic library in the centre of a comprehensive solution, *The Journal of Academic Librarianship,* Vol. *30*, No. 1, 3-16.

Pitt, T., and Clark, A. (2006). *Creating Powerful Online Courses Using Multiple Instructional Strategies.* Available at http://www.emoderators.com/ moderators/pitt.html; accessed 26.03.2009.

Rockman, I. F. (2004). Conclusion: Continuing the Dialogue. *Integrating Information Literacy into the Higher Education Curriculum: Practical Models for Transformatio*n, 237-251.

7. Quality

Quality Management in Academic Library: A Case Study of the Science and Technology Area in Spain

M. Pinto[1], V. Fernández-Marcial[2] and C. Gómez-Camarero[3]

[1]Universidad de Granada, Spain
[2]Universidad de La Coruña, Spain
[3]Universidad de Málaga, Spain

Abstract: This paper presents partial results of a research developed during the year 2002 to 2006. Population analyzed was Science and Technology teachers of Spanish universities. The investigation has worked with sample academic users, distributed among 19 Spanish universities. The main contribution of this study is to present a BIQUAL tool. It is useful for the evaluation of the quality services in university libraries and especially of Science and Technology. This tool is created using the user's point of view. Results identify behaviour of these users and the aspects that concern the quality of the service in this environment. We also discuss about some problems and difficult experimented in this research. We analyzed the use of quantitative methods, in special, survey as well as it effectiveness to library quality management.

Keywords: Quality management; Academic library; Science and technology area; Spain; Survey.

1. Introduction

The movement towards improved quality in higher education has engendered an extensive and systematic process of evaluation in all areas included academic libraries. In 1999, the European Association for Quality Assurance in Higher Education (ENQA) was created to lead these processes. This European agency has paved the way for national agencies to be established in member countries.

The process of evaluating quality in Spanish academics libraries began in 1998 with the implementation of the First National Evaluation Plan, in which the academics libraries in Catalonia, Valencian Community and of the University of Salamanca were comprehensively examined. The Catalonian libraries collectively participated in a transversal evaluation to improve quality (1999-2002), led by the Consorci de Biblioteques Universitàries de Catalunya and the Agència per a la Qualitat del Sistema Universitari de Catalunya. Since 2003 a transversal evaluation was carried out in all universities libraries within the framework of the 2nd University Quality Plan and the Andalusia Plan for Quality in Universities. To develop quality evaluation process some different models have been used, such as:

a) The SERVQUAL model, based on the work of Parasuraman, Zeithmal & Berry (1985), was developed in the eighties for the private sector to measure quality service through five dimensions: tangibles, reliability, assurance, empathy and responsiveness.

b) Contributions from the LibQual instrument, developed by the University of Texas and applied experimentally in North American university libraries from the North American Association of Research Libraries (ARL) (2008), and later extended to various libraries both in North America and other countries, now with more than 1000 participating institutions.

c) Contributions from the European Foundation Quality Management (EFQM) models. Based on it Spanish Library Evaluation Guide has been designed (2006).

All these models have a general scope. We though it is necessary to work with specialized models that attempt a particular of diverse knowledge areas. For this research we selected a Science and Technology area. We choose this knowledge area because it is the economic and innovation engine of a society.

Our research hypothesis was that a science and technology academic researchers and teachers have particular information behaviour different from other areas. A better knowledge of the behavior patterns and preferences shown by science and technology researchers in their use of library services will thus allow libraries to tailor their services to the characteristics of these users. It is in order to provide them with a better service and obtain higher levels of satisfaction.

With this ideas the purpose of our investigation[1] was designed a quality management tool for Science and Technology academic library.

[1] (The project entitled Design of the BiQual instrument for the Evolution and Continuous Improvement of Information Systems: Application in the Area of Science and Technology, was carried out in the period 2003-2006 and held by Science and Technology Ministry.)

2. Methodology

A specific tool, BiQual, was designed to find out users' opinions on service quality in university science and technology libraries, and to inquire about the specific information needs of this particular group. The questionnaire had 44 items divided into three sections:

- The first section made a comparative appraisal of the level of importance and perception attributed to 16 aspects, taking into account that perception of quality depends on the degree of importance attributed to the aspect appraised. In this section a 5-point scale was used, in which 1 denoted not at all important and 5, extremely important. Perception was also measured on a 5-point scale where 1 denoted null and 5, very high.
- The second section, comprising 13 items, reviewed the use of various library services, bearing in mind that level of use and experience are decisive factors in service evaluation.
- The third section measured their attitude about trends in university libraries, and thereby inter-related quality service with users' information behaviour. In this block, respondents were asked to evaluate 11 items.

BiQual was designed with the idea of providing a specific library quality service tool for the science and technology area. Initially, the idea of adapting the Libqual survey to this area was mooted, but it was found to use a different conceptual approach. BiQual is inspirited on the SERVQUAL model and it is use the following five quality service dimensions:

- Service accessibility: the library's capacity to provide access to its collections, products and services in any format. Both physical and remote access possibilities were included, for example the size of the digital collection.

- Functionality: this dimension measures the physical, technological and environmental conditions that guarantee optimal library use, such as via remote access.
- Communications: this mechanism measures the information flow between the library and its users, from librarian skills to channels to evaluate service quality.
- Use: the aim of this dimension is to identify the current use of the academic library.
- Value added services and trends: Many new products, facilities and services adapted to the needs and expectations of science and technology users were suggested to respondents.

In relation with sample, we selected 19 universities from a total of 69 institutions existed in 2003, the year the project began. It is clear that main prerequisite to selected this institutions was that every one of them should offer science and technology degrees. Other criteria were also applied: a) all the Spanish Autonomous Communities (Autonomous Communities are the socio-political division of Spanish territory) should be represented, b) the widest possible range of areas should be represented and universities with a high reputation in those areas included, c) there should be a balanced mix of older and newer universities, d) each university should be representative in terms of the number of students and variety of degrees offered.

Following the sample selection process, we endeavored to identify different knowledge areas in order to create a map of the subjects covered within the broad field of science and technology. Once we had established this classification, and attempted to identify the university departments with these categories, we realized that designation of structures varies greatly from one university to another. Nonetheless, we divided the total area into three large standardized blocks.

The final sample was of 564 surveyed people. Even our first intention was to work with 10.200 teachers distributed by different areas and universities. But we only obtained a 5.5% of response. In terms of statistical significance we get our objectives because we work we a sampling error of +/- 5% and a confidence interval of 95.5%.

The research was carried out in various stages. We can define it as pilot and final phase. The pilot phase involved both qualitative and quantitative methods. It provided us with experiences and key information to design the final study, in terms of sample, method and survey. The first sample comprised both faculty and students. In fact, we started to work with science and technology students. The results of the analysis of this stage showed the students' information behaviour to be very poor. In general, students use the academic library as a place to study, but with their own documentation. They rarely use the libraries' books, electronic journals or databases. There is obviously a direct relation between experience and evaluation: if people do not use a service, they cannot evaluate it. Consequently, students were excluded from the second stage of the study reported in this paper.

The method we used in the pilot study consisted of 25 interviews and 6 focus groups. We also administered 400 questionnaires in different universities. To carry out it we contact made with faculty through colleagues known to the research team. But applied personal surveys required us to arrange a date and time for the survey to be administered and also to travel to the selected universities. This arrangement complicated the research for two basic reasons. First, the research team had to travel to the universities; second, the teaching staff had to have sufficient time available both to participate, and to encourage their students to take part in the study. As a result, we implemented in final phase an electronic questionnaire.

A second lesson learned from the pilot stage was to try and see things from the user's perspective, an essential starting point in quality management and in information services in general. We had initially designed the BiQual survey on the basis of qualitative results, bibliography and our experience in undertaking surveys. However, the quantitative pilot phase revealed that the technical terminology we had used was confusing to respondents. For this we must to re-written questionnaires in more accessible language to make the items more easily understood by the users, both faculty and students. This problem was illustrated most clearly by the use of the term inter-library loan. We assumed that users would be familiar with the term, but we realized that although they used this service, they did not always refer to it by this name. We eventually used the expression "Ease of obtaining documents not found in the library". Also we verified that some questions were irrelevant or repetitive and the number of items was therefore reduced from the initial 47 to 41, thus modifying the style of the questionnaire.

The second stage, as we indicated previously, was developed throughout electronic survey. We sent emails to faculties of selected universities. We found theirs contact on institutions websites. After compiled all fulfilled questionnaires we analyzed results using SPSS software.

3. Results

The results are presented for the three main questionnaire blocks. First, the two variables, importance and perception, are examined. Second, the level of use of the service is described. Finally the trends defined by the user are explained.

An independent analysis of the Satisfaction and Perception values reveals that the most highly valued dimension is collection accessibility. Journals emerged as the most significant information source, with a rating of 4.74 in importance and 4.66 in the case of variety and suitability of electronic journals. This results contrast with consideration about printed format journals, which obtained a rating of 4.29. Coinciding with the efforts made by university libraries in recent years to maximize Web accessibility, ease of website use obtained the highest value of 4.79. When we asked about the importance of instruments to measure quality service, which scored a low 3.60 on a 5-scale.

The analysis of the perception section reveals that the mean level of satisfaction is lower than importance (3.85 and 4.35, respectively). Also we noted that the parameter with the lowest satisfaction rate is "Scope and existence of the audiovisual collection". The importance value is also low for this parameter. These results indicate the scant impact this kind of collection has among these users.

A comparison of the levels of importance and satisfaction shows that one of the most deficient points is also one of greatest interest to the surveyed population: while a high level of importance is attributed to journals, the level of satisfaction expressed with them tends to be low. Inter-library loan shows a low level of quality, since there is a difference of 0.56 between Satisfaction and Importance. Despite efforts to improve OPAC user friendliness, it has a low level of quality, rated 4.55 in importance, whereas satisfaction with this service drops to 3.99.

An appraisal of the behaviour of the variance shows that the five aspects with the lowest satisfaction ratings are those with the most disparate scores. From this result, we can conclude that different levels of quality service exist, depending on the university evaluated, and that these services have a higher degree of evolution and development in some universities than in others.

In relation with library use we check a highest percentage in online document access. This result can be regarded as a trend: university faculty prefer to access documents on line and only visit the library occasionally. This is seen in the result for use of the library reading room; visited on a low 5.9% of occasions, and the researchers' room, 11.2%.As expected from this type of user, access to databases is very high, contrasting with the slight use of the library OPAC service. Researchers are well aware of where to find the books in the library, and consequently they go directly to the corresponding section to find out about new additions and access these documents; the same applies to printed journal.

The results from this section were very different from what the research team had anticipated: the picture obtained on the surveyed population's behavior was quite the opposite of the initial hypothesis. While the research team had assumed that the user would largely accept the trends already shown in the most advanced university libraries, the users outlined a series of activities that they would prefer to take on themselves, for example filtered information, rather than delegating them to the librarians.

In the third block of the questionnaire, the survey respondents were given the opportunity to make suggestions for improvements to the academic library. From a systematization of their responses, the following data emerged and was organized into various sections:

a) The first section refers to holdings, and identifies the need to improve the printed book collection, followed by interest in improvements in both electronic and printed journal holdings.

b) The second section, referring to the library's physical space, elicited only a few recommendations: the need for a spacious periodicals room and improvements to the researchers' room.

c) In the section referring to technologies, the main recommendation focused on adapting the library to the new technologies, with a resulting interest in improving access to electronic documents, better access to electronic journals and more digitization of holdings.

Other recommendations noted were for improved loans, library staff training and increased budgets for library acquisitions.

4. Conclusions

Academic library role for science and technology faculties continuing to be important for them. We check a paradoxical approach in relation traditional and modern services. User prefers electronic information access but they show their desire for an increase in the library's printed collection. Users still prefer to consult, read and browse books with their own hands.

As we refer before, the use of electronic information is one of the most consolidated trends among these library users. The growing use of electronic information is particularly obvious in one specific type of information source, namely electronic journals, which according to other studies is one of the most popular formats among researchers. The status of electronic journals is elevated higher still if we compare the demand for electronic journals with other types of document such as audiovisual material (4.85%) or multimedia (0.97%) . This growth increases as technological changes are incorporated into researchers' information behaviour and the initial technological barriers to electronic information access gradually disappear.

These explanations underline some very important aspects from the perspective of scientific communication. First, they confirm the fact that scientific journals are the most important channel of communication for researchers for many reasons, including currency, content quality, and the specific characteristics of electronic format journals such as ease and speed of access to information and its retrieval, and the convenience and values added by their digital nature: text searching, hypertext links between articles, data and commentaries, incorporation of multimedia, audio, and so on. The level of consideration for these electronic journals in the scientific academic and research sphere is beyond doubt, as can be seen in the following comment taken from our survey:

"My own experience has convinced me that access to digital format journals is a decisive, important and vital step in keeping up to date and increasing productivity in both research and teaching activities. "

Thus, the need to consult this type of information source electronically is acutely expressed, and vindicates the claim to this type of access as a requisite service of any academic library that values its reputation, extending the possibilities to consult electronic journals from outside the library or even the university campus, as expressed by the following survey respondent: "On-line access to all scientific journals from home or from the university is important."

Our research remarks a deficient in quality library services. There is an electronic resources and services demand higher than library offers. This results linking with Missingham's ideas (1999).

Moreover, the increase in access to electronic journals attests to the need for knowledge on how to access the information they provide. Some users highlight this need as an urgent priority: "Clear, detailed information is needed on accessing electronic journals." This comment reflects the demand for more efficient diffusion mechanisms to inform the whole university community—faculty and researchers specifically—about the electronic journals the university library subscribes to.

Almost at the same level as increased subscriptions to electronic format scientific journals (both issues are generally dealt with in the same response) is the demand for greater access to specialized databases: "Greater access to and availability of electronic journals and scientific databases."; "More bandwidth and more accessible databases or a larger number of on-line accessible journals."; "Increase the digital content of the library's materials and the availability of scientific databases that allow rapid searches of research and teaching subjects."

From these responses on access to electronic format scientific journals and specialized databases, we can infer a need for training courses designed to provide this user group with the skills to retrieve information from the different information retrieval systems used by the main providers of access to electronic journal content.

However, the answers to this issue take a different approach, since very few explicitly mention the need for this type of training (4.85%). Furthermore, the third block of our questionnaire indicates a clear tendency among scientists towards autonomy in their search for information, expressing, rather, a need for skills training for their students: "I think both communication with users and training activities should be increased. I particularly believe it would be useful to address training to first, second and third cycle students."; "The librarian should master catalog tools and be more dynamic in guiding students, showing a personal willingness to explain and transmit what he or she knows about the use of computer and printed tools."

This user attitude to training courses could be linked to a possible confusion they may have about the librarian's knowledge and functions. According to Ha-Lin Chiu (2000), the limited inclination of library users towards using reference services is not because they do not need help, but rather because many of them do not consider that librarians can be a valid information source in solving their specific, specialized needs. In other words, it seems that in general, they do not believe the librarian has the right knowledge to solve a specific information need.

The training of librarians is an issue that arises in some of the respondents' opinions, directed not at the tasks traditionally attributed to librarians (custodian or lender of books...), but particularly concerning the tasks librarians should undertake in relation to the new challenges. Of particular note, these tasks include the preparation of new products such as: guides to specialist resources, the librarian's collaboration in creating electronic resources for teaching and research, periodic canvassing of faculty's information needs, information about projects, selective diffusion of information.

The increased consumption of digital information in university libraries consequently demands an adequate and sufficient infrastructure, the need for which is also indicated in the users' responses. This is shown by demands for more computers available for use in the library itself, improvements in tailoring the library to new technologies, wireless access and access to holdings from places other than those defined as academic or university locations.

Users also comment on improvements in the library buildings. In addition to opinions that the physical spaces of the library should be improved in general, others focus their criticisms on the lack of sufficient workspaces for researchers. Mark Powell (2002) expresses the need to reform library space as follows, "Modern academic libraries must rationalize and respond to pedagogical and technological changes and foster changing and continuing forms of student learning to enable students to achieve their best work and ready them for their post-qualification vocation. To achieve this, librarians must consider remodeling existing library space...".

A further service noted for improvement is that of lending, Some comments in relation with this are: "Improve lending management (notification by electronic mail, etc.)", but also referring to extending the types of documents that can be borrowed, as the following user remarks: "I would particularly like to be able to borrow research journals, and not to have to photocopy them in the library itself".

Respondents raised the original question of coordination of European library policies to allow the smooth and efficient exchange of information sources between European university libraries, an issue that would have significant repercussions for European convergence.

In summary, library quality management means to attempt user's expectations. Besides academic library try to improvement continuously theirs services, users requirement are modifying faster than library offers. Quality library service experiment a lack because there is not a very close relationship between quality expectative and quality designed. Our research remarks the urgent necessity of quality management in science and technology libraries due to impact of their research results on Spanish develop society.

References

AGENCIA per a Qualitat del Sistema Universitari a Catalunya (AQU) (2006). *Guía d'avaluació dels serveis bibliotecaris i de la seva contribució a la qualitat de l'aprenentatge i de la recerca.* Available: http://www.cbuc.es/cbuc/content/download/3493/20939/version/1/file/GuiaSB_cat.pdf (April 4, 2008).

Chiu, H.L. (2000). Seeking help in Hong Kong's academic libraries, *OCLC Systems & Services,* Vol. 16 , No. 4, 181–188.

Consejo de Coordinación Universitaria (2008). *Áreas de conocimiento.* Ministerio de Educación y Ciencia. Available: http://www.mec.es/educa/jsp/plantilla.jsp?id=1031A&area=ccuniv&contenido=/ccuniv/html/habilitacion/area_conocimiento.html (Mars 23, 2008).

LIBQUAL+ (TM) (2008). *Charting Library Quality service.* Association of Research Libraries/ Texas A&M University. Available: http://www.libqual.org (January 7, 2007).

Missingham, R. Science and technology: a web of information: impact of the electronic present and future on scientists and libraries. Proceedings of the Ninth Australasian Information Online & On Disc Conference and Exhibition. Sidney: Information Science Section, Australian Library and Information Association. Available: http://www.csu.edu.au/special/online99/proceedings99/205a.htm (Mars 3, 2006).

Parasuraman, A.; Zeithaml, V.A. & Berry, L.L. (1985). A conceptual model of quality service and its implications for future research, *Journal of Marketing,* Vol. 70, No. 3, 201–230.

Powell, M. (2002). Designing Library Space to Facilitate Learning: A Review of the UK Higher Education Sector, *Libri*, 52, 110.

Multi-Faceted Measuring of the Quality as a Tool for Quality Improvement in the Kuopio University Library, Finland

Jarmo Saarti, Arja Juntunen and Aino Taskinen

Kuopio University Library, Finland

Abstract: From the beginning of the 1990's, different types of quality management and evaluation systems have become integrated into higher education institutes in Finland due to the creation of the European Higher Education Area (EHEA). At the same time, an overhaul of the higher education legislation and structures was instigated in Finland. This has meant that the university services, e.g. libraries have had to integrate more efficiently into the core processes of the universities. The paper describes the building of the quality management system in one library and especially how different types on quality measurement systems - statistical analyses, benchmarking, surveys - are used in order to improve the quality of the library services. A major emphasis is in the involvement of management at both the strategic and everyday level.

Keywords: Quality management; Evidence based management; University libraries; Finland.

1. Introduction

The Finnish academic world consists of 20 state owned Universities and 30 Polytechnic high schools. In 2006, the Finnish Ministry of Education published the principles for the structural development of Finnish institutes of higher education (OPM, 2006). The main aims were to reduce the number of Finnish higher education units, especially by merging smaller units into larger ones. In addition it was intended that the autonomy of the Universities should be increased in order to improve the competitiveness of Finnish higher education and research (see also Saarti 2008).

From the beginning of the 1990's, different types of quality management (QM) and evaluation systems have become integrated into higher education institutes in Finland. One impetus for these systems, especially for the evaluation process, was the decision by the member states of the European Union to create a European Higher Education Area (EHEA), a process that was initiated in Bologna in the summer of 1999. This led to the establishment of pan-European policies and decisions on how these should be implemented in the member states. The Finnish Ministry of Education has listed the aims for quality control in Finland (Korkeakoulujen laadunvarmistus, 2004, also see ENCA, 2005) as follows:

1. Universities and polytechnics will establish quality systems that will cover all of the processes undertaken within the institution.
2. To meet the goals set in the Communiqué of the Conference of Ministers responsible for Higher Education in Berlin on 19 September 2003 (2003) in Finland, evaluations or auditing of the universities and polytechnics will be implemented.

Thus the higher education institutions have the responsibility for quality control on their campuses. The auditing is carried out by the Finnish Higher Education Evaluation Council (FINHEEC) (see FINHEEC, 2004). The timetable for these evaluations is such that all the higher education units are intended to have been evaluated at least once by the year 2010.

The University of Kuopio, Kuopio, Finland (http://www.uku.fi/english/) has an international reputation in the fields of health, environmental science and well-being, with particular strengths in biotechnology, life sciences and biomedicine. It is one of the 20 universities in Finland and has about 6,200 students, 1,800 staff members and an annual budget of about m€ 100.

Kuopio University Library is an academic library which is open to everyone. The library was established in 1972. Its library collections and expertise are focused on health sciences, pharmacy, biosciences, environmental sciences, information technology, business, and social sciences. The annual budget of the Library is about m€ 3. There are 35 staff members in the Library. The collections consist of approx. 143,000 monographs, 800 printed journals (subscriptions), 14,500 electronic journals, 50,000 electronic books, and 5,500 audiovisual sources and other material. Each year, information literacy teaching is provided for a total of 1,000 student credits.

As part of the above structural changes, two Finnish universities - the University of Joensuu and the University of Kuopio will merge to form the University of Eastern Finland to be launched from the beginning of the year 2010. This poses new challenges for the management as well as for the quality management of the library's services. In the following section we will discuss the building of the QM system of the library and especially the creation of the feedback system that we have been developing in order to gain evidence-based facts on which to base decision making.

2. Managing quality in an academic library

In the year 2003, the University of Kuopio set a goal to adopt an ISO9001:2000 based quality management system in order to support the management and continual process of improvement throughout all University activities. The goal was to pass the Higher Education Evaluation Council audit (objective achieved in 2006) and the acquisition of an international certification of the teaching quality management system (target achieved in 2006).

The University Library initiated its quality management system construction at the same time as the university (see Saarti & Juntunen 2007). The library's designated quality manager has participated in all the University's quality network meetings. The aim has been to ensure that the library's activities are an integral part of the University's core functions: teaching, research and social function.

Kuopio University Library is defined as a service unit within the University. It is part of the Centre for Information and Learning Resource Services; the other units are the Learning Centre and Information Technology Centre. The Centre for Information and Learning Resource Services share a joint quality manual, which includes definitions of the management system, core processes, resources and follow-up. Cooperation of the service units has been useful, because the activities are mutually reinforcing: for example, from the library's point of view the cooperation with the information technology professionals has made it possible to create better services, especially when so much of the information sources are currently available through computer networks. Cooperation with the Learning Centre has provided access to experts who offer support in the library's information literacy instructional courses.

Also in addition to the previously mentioned quality manual, the library's quality management system contains our terms of reference. They are divided into two parts: the library's web site describes the services which are offered to the customers. The library's intranet contains the terms of reference created for the staff to ensure the quality of services. These include detailed manuals for lending library materials and how to manage the reference service. They also ensure that the patrons receive the service promised in the quality management system.

So how has the situation improved within our library, due to this the quality work which has been systematically conducted for more than five years? First, the organization has become more coherent. The separation between departments has been substituted with operational teams that take responsibility for the planning, organizing, and reporting their operations. This affects each individual worker; they can now perceive how their input contributes to the totality of the library's functions. In addition the information flows more freely between individual employees working in teams.

The goal of the organization's management is to ensure that there are adequate resources, as well as, empowering, motivating and maintaining the skills of the staff and finally the management group monitors the activities undertaken by the organization. In our library, implementing QM-system has led to a remarkable growth in staff training as well as ensuring effective communications for both to our customers and staff.

The library has clearly changed during the quality work; it is now customer-friendly in all library core processes; i.e. the acquisition and organization of electronic and print collections, information literacy tuition and reference work, as well as lending and copying services.

It has been decided that the QM-system for the new University of Eastern Finland to be launched at the beginning of the year 2010 will be built on the principles of the University of Kuopio's QM-system. It also has been decided that the first internal audit is to be held during the year 2009.

There will be new challenges to be faced when building the QM system for our new University Library, e.g.:

- distance between the campuses is about 140 km
- University of Kuopio's faculties' disciplines make extensive use of electronic material; in Joensuu they use more printed material
- in Joensuu, the University has not carried out a systematic QM implementation: there is a notable need for the training of personnel and restructuring old ways of thinking
- the increase of the number of the staff to a total of 80 persons when joining Kuopio's 35 and Joensuu's 45 persons
- managing of the communications and a more complex unit; building community with the aid of modern virtual technologies.

3. Creating tools for the evidence based management within the library

The past decades have seen a revolution in the social sciences and there is a vigorous debate on which are the optimal methods for gaining a better understanding of human and social behaviour. A type of triangulation has been applied in this type of approach where both quantitative and qualitative methods have been used in gathering and combining data in the analysis of the behaviour of the target groups.

Since the library and its services are about people, their needs and their actions, this triangular approach is most useful when building the feedback toolkit of one's QM system. In the Kuopio University Library, we have used the following methods:

-collecting and analyzing statistical data
-monitoring user actions
-undertaking user surveys
-conducting user interviews
-gathering feedback from our services, especially IL teaching
-analysing ones own actions in a yearly self evaluation and self assessment of teams' and staffs' achievements
-collating knowledge from the outside world of the ideas to the library service improvement including benchmarking
-conducting systematic management reviews

The most important statistical tool for our QM system is KITT – Research Library Statistics Database (https://yhteistilasto.lib.helsinki.fi/index.jsp). It was developed and is maintained by the National Library of Finland. The database follows the international ISO 2789 library standard. It contains statistical information about all the Finnish university libraries, polytechnic libraries and about twenty special libraries since the year 2002.

The KITT database provides the basic information about frame organisations, library collections, library use and users, opening times and facilities, finances and staff. It is a good tool for benchmarking library resources by using time series and analyzing the data trough the key numbers and basic key figures that are automatically calculated by the system.

It is possible to obtain statistical data directly from the library system about catalogued collections, registered borrowers and home loans. The Finnish National Electronic Library, FinELib, gathers financial and statistical information about acquisition and the use of the electronic library resources. All the libraries have their own ways of collecting the other needed statistical data, using the common national guidelines.

Our user surveys can be divided into two categories: regular and case-specific. In particular, we have monitored our patrons' needs and actions in the acquisition and use of the library collections. We have found that tri-annual survey suits us best with respect to our own and our patrons' schedule. As a result of our regular surveys, we have been able to make strategic decision, e.g. make a shift from printed journals into e-journals over the past 10 years as well as changing our library premises ideology from being book oriented to a customer oriented. (See Juntunen & al. 2005 and Kananen & al. 2006.) Case-specific surveys and user-interviews have been conducted in order to test the effectiveness of these new services and their functionality.

One important tool that has been implemented into our managerial tool box as a result of the building our quality system has been the decision to undertake systematic management reviews. We have taken a two-level approach here: at the beginning of the year we look at the coming year and at the end of the year we conduct the actual management review that combines all the data and feedback collected from our patrons and services. In addition to the reviewing of statistics and survey results we also have annual reports from our service teams that concentrate on the analyzed user feedback of our services and how the services have been developed based on this feedback.

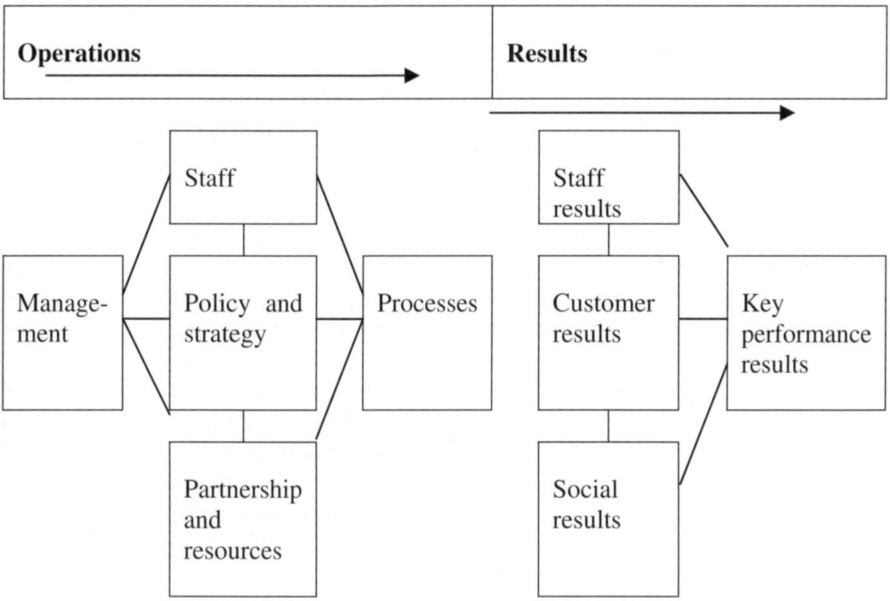

Figure 1. EFQM based facets for key figures

We also have become acquainted with the EFQM (European Foundation for Quality Management) model. The EFQM model was created to help to understand and review the connections between an organisation and its results. By using the model as an evaluation tool, it is possible to identify problems and develop the organisation's capabilities and resources. The central features of the results are the staff results, the customer results and social performance results.

The EFQM model is not yet in active use in Kuopio University Library, we have only made some tests to see how it should work. In order to make it a useful tool for the QM system, we have to develop our statistical methods to gather and analyze the data needed. The KITT database does not include all the required indicators to describe all the operations and results we want to exploit. At the present, we have defined the set of key figures to be followed and we are implementing their analysis according to the EFQM division shown in figure 1.

4. Conclusions

So has the implementing of our QM-system been worth the effort? The answer is unequivocal: yes. At the staff level, there clearly can be seen a better motivation for the work as well as a desire to improve one's skills. At the management level, we have been able to move towards a more evidence based leadership that has evoked quite drastic changes in how we see our role and our services within our university. At the service providing level, we have been able to rethink and re-evaluate all our services as well as being able to implement a culture of continuous improvement.

The QM-system clearly needs a well-designed and a functional system for gathering facts on which the management as well as other staff within the library can base their decisions. Here we have found out that the triangulative approach is useful: we need statistical data and its analysis and we need surveys and other more qualitative methods that provide us on the other hand a clear picture what is happening but at the same time represent tools to identify the apparently minor changes that might revolutionize our future within a few years.

This data when analyzed appropriately and communicated in a compact manner also helps the library in its internal and external lobbying. This enables us to stress our contribution to the university's research and tuition as well as in helping us to convince those holding the university purse-strings why we need adequate resources in order to fulfil the needs of our customers.

The most rewarding experience that provided proof of our success has been the internal and national surveys (see e.g. Nummela 2008) where we have been able to demonstrate that we have actually improved continually our library: as well as regarding the image of the library and the grade that our customers award for the services provided. Another rewarding experience has been benchmarking other Finnish university libraries; our library have been placed within the "top five" service providers in our field.

Acknowledgements:
The authors are grateful to Dr Ewen MacDonald for revising the English.

References

Communiqué of the Conference of Ministers responsible for Higher Education in Berlin on 19 September 2003 (2003). Realising the European Higher Education Area. Berlin: European Union. [Last visited 3rd June, 2008.] Available from: http://europass.cedefop.eu.int/img/dynamic/c1400/type.FileContent.file/Berlin_en_US.PDF

ENCA (2005). *Standards and Guidelines for Quality Assurance in the European Higher Education Area.* Helsinki, European Association for Quality Assurance in Higher Education. [Last visited 3rd June, 2008.] Available from: http://www.bologna-bergen2005.no/Docs/00-Main_doc/050221_ENQA_report.pdf

FINHEEC (2004). *Plan for Action 2004-2007.* Helsinki, FINHEEC. . [Last visited 3rd June, 2008.] Available from: http://www.kka.fi/pdf/muut/muut_julkaisut/KKA.Net1_04Toim.eng.pdf

Juntunen, Arja and Ovaska, Tuulevi and Saarti, Jarmo and Salmi, Liisa, (2005). Managing library processes: collecting data and providing tailored services to end-users. *Library management* 26(8-9):487-492.

Kananen, Jukka and Ovaska, Tuulevi and Saarti, Jarmo, (2006). Collection policy management for the Kuopio University and Kuopio University Hospital, Finland: detecting the needs of users and developing high-quality collections. *Health Information and Libraries Journal* 23(3):179-188.

Korkeakoulujen laadunvarmistus [Quality assurance of higher education] (2004). (Opetusministeriön työryhmämuistioita ja selvityksiä 2004:6). Helsinki: Ministry of

Education. [Last visited 3rd June, 2008.] Available from: http://www.minedu.fi/export/sites/default/OPM/Julkaisut/2004/liitteet/opm_226_tr06.pdf?lang=fi.

Nummela, Maria (2008). *Kirjastojen kansallinen asiakaskysely 2008* [National libraries' usersurvey 2008]. Helsinki, National Library. [Last visited 24th April, 2009.] Available from: http://www.kansalliskirjasto.fi/attachments/5zwmHi8F9/5AIXw7VEj/Files/CurrentFile/Kansallinen_asiakaskysely_raportti.pdf.

OPM (2006). *Korkeakoulujen rakenteellisen kehittämisen periaatteet* [The principles of the structural development of the higher education institutes]. Keskustelumuistio 8.3.2006. (Opetusministeriön monisteita 2006:2.) Helsinki, Ministry of Education. [Last visited 3rd June, 2008.] Available from: http://www.minedu.fi/export/sites/default/OPM/Julkaisut/2006/liitteet/opm_31_Korkeakoululaitoksen_rakenteellinen_kehittaminen.pdf?lang=fi

Saarti, Jarmo and Juntunen, Arja, (2007). From the Rhetoric of Quality Management to Managing Self-Organizing Processes: A Case Study on an Expert Organization. In: *Advances in Library Administration and Organization*, editor James M. Nyce, 25, 97-112.

Saarti, Jarmo, (2008). The structural development of Finland's higher education institution libraries as a part of the universities' renewal. *The National Library of Finland bulletin* 2008. Accessed via: http://www.kansalliskirjasto.fi/extra/bulletin/article2.html.

Quality Metrics in Academic Libraries: Striving for Excellence

Leoné Tiemensma

Midrand Graduate Institute, South Africa

Abstract: Quality in academic libraries is a multi-dimensional construct. Quality management and quality assurance is part of measuring performance excellence. Libraries are services. To improve service quality, stakeholders' needs and expectations should be monitored and measured, shortfalls should be identified and addressed.

Some basic principles are common to all measurements, but quality metrics will focus on the unique nature and factors that could affect quality of academic library services. Measuring quality includes the resources, resource delivery, the service environment, the management and staff, and the different stakeholders. In the digital environment, the academic library also moves from collection to connection, with new demands and performance indicators. Both quantitative and qualitative measurements are required to evaluate the overall performance of the library. The ultimate goal of measurement is improving the "fitness for purpose" of the library.

Keywords: Academic libraries; Academic libraries – User satisfaction; Academic libraries – Evaluation; Performance assessment; Quality management; Quality assurance; Service quality.

1. Quality management and quality assurance in academic libraries

Understanding academic libraries requires understanding of higher education issues and needs. Academic libraries have a unique nature. The academic library functions in a larger context and it is necessary to determine how the library contributes to achieving the overall objectives of the parent institution.

Quality management involves the processes, activities and measures that contribute to the management of the quality of the products, service or other outputs from the organisation (Roberts & Rowley 2004: 158). Quality assessment of the academic library is part of the total quality management (TQM) of the institution. TQM acknowledges that there is always room for improvement, that all organisations can and do fail, that employees make mistakes, and that we could all do better (Brophy 1997: 75). Quality management includes quality assurance and quality enhancement.

Quality assurance refers to the processes associated with ensuring that quality adheres to externally or internally set standards (Roberts and Rowley 2004:159). Quality assurance is a part of accrediting an institution. Education in South Africa is strictly monitored by the Department of Education, the South African Qualifications Authority (SAQA) and the CHE (Council for Higher Education). In South Africa the HEQC (Higher Education Quality Committee), a sub committee of the CHE, is responsible for this issue. One of the audit criteria of the HEQC, is "Academic support services (e.g. library and learning materials, computer support services, etc.) adequately support teaching and learning needs and help give effect to teaching and learning objectives" (Blake 2008). Quality assurance in academic libraries is part of measuring performance excellence.

One of the objectives of the Bologna Declaration, a joint declaration of the European Ministers of Education, is the "Promotion of European co-operation in quality assurance with a view to developing comparable criteria and methodologies" (Bologna Declaration 1999), and the *Standards and Guidelines for Quality Assurance in European Higher Education Area* followed.

In the United Kingdom, the Research Assessment Exercise (RAE) assesses research quality. Researchers in the UK examined the relationship between library funding at UK universities and RAE ratings and found that higher funding of an academic library was associated with higher RAE ratings (Haddow 2007: 32). Strong research universities had well-supported libraries.

In Australia, a new funding model for research in Australian higher education institutions, the Research Quality Framework (RQF), impacts on academic libraries (Haddow 2007: 26-29). This model creates high demand for assistance from library staff on various levels.

Quality management in academic libraries thus has various dimensions:

- Accreditation by external bodies. Academic libraries are subject to formal quality audits and quality assurance processes;
- Achieving a quality of service that contributes to the institution's mission, vision, aims and objectives;
- Achieving a quality of service that satisfies the research and information needs and expectations of academic and non-academic staff, undergraduate and postgraduate students, and university management;
- Library management – *How* the service is provided. Operating in an effective manner with regards to, for example, staff, space and facilities, resources, acquisitions, access, availability, circulation, finances and information technology.

Quality management operates at different levels of the institution and the purpose is quality enhancement and providing accountability. Information managers need to prove the worth of their services so that the parent institution acknowledges the impact of library and information services. The quality of the academic library could affect the overall quality of the institution.

2. Service quality

Libraries are services and they exist to provide a service to the users who need it. Some basic principles are common to all quality measurements of services and also to library and information services. Quality of service is defined by the organisation's or customer's perception of both the quality of the product and the service providing it (Zeithaml, Parasuraman & Berry 1990). Quality is linked to customer satisfaction, although quality for one customer or group of customers does not necessarily mean quality for another customer or group. A Working Group of IFLA on performance measurement agreed that "we must start performance assessment from the viewpoint of the user…" (Te Boekhorst 1995: 278).
Zeithaml, Parasuraman and Berry (1990) developed the Gap Analysis Model (Figure 1), based on substantial research amongst service providers. This model shows how a perceived service can diverge from actual delivered service and this can assist to identify gaps and causes of poor service, which could affect quality.

Figure 1: Gap Analysis Model: Factors affecting service quality

Gaps model of service delivery

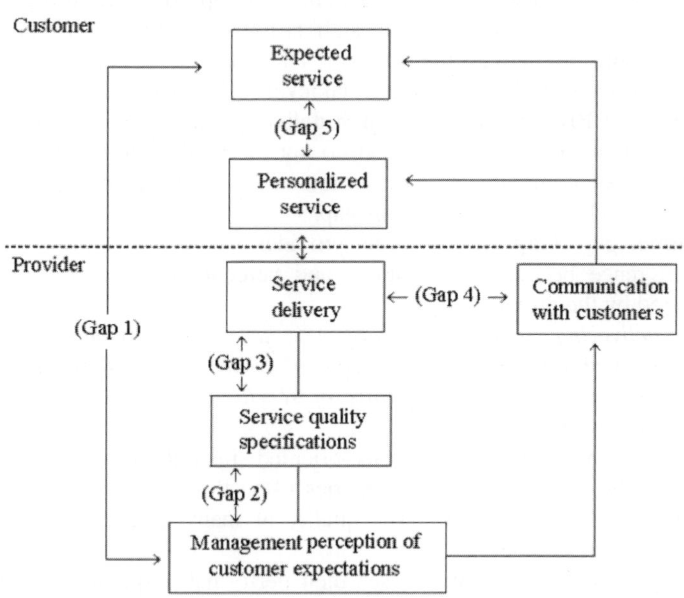

(Zeithaml, Bitner & Gremler 2006: 46)

This model highlights five gaps in service delivery (Zeithaml, Parasuraman & Berry

1990; Zeithaml, Bitner & Gremler 2006: 32-46):

1. Provider Gap 1: Not knowing what customers expect and desire. The key reasons for this gap, are a lack of marketing research, inadequate upward communication, and too many levels of management. To close these gaps, customers' expectations should be researched, marketing research findings be used effectively, interaction between management and customers be increased, upward communication from contact personnel to management be improved, and the number of levels between contact personnel and management be reduced. Managers should understand what are the most important to customers. Communication from management to employees and between staff and customers is necessary to obtain relevant information on the service.

2. Provider Gap 2: Wrong service quality designs and standards. This gap occurs when there is inadequate commitment to service quality, a lack of perception of feasibility, inadequate task standardisation and an absence of goal setting. Quality service requires commitment and strong leadership from top management, as well as from middle management levels. Staff should believe that customer's expectations are feasible - the organisation or institution should have the capabilities to meet requirements for service in terms of finances, operating systems, resources and staff. Operating procedures and standardising some aspects of the service tasks can provide consistent service quality. With clear and specific goals for customer service, performance can be measured against these goals. These goals should be based on customers' requirements and expectations.

3. Provider Gap 3: Service-performance gap. This gap arises when organisational policies and procedures are in place, but staff is not following them. Staff may be unable or unwilling to deliver the service. This gap is the difference between organisational service specifications and actual levels of service delivery.

4. Provider Gap 4: Promises do not match delivery. Customers will perceive low-quality service when the service promised do not match the service that is actually delivered. Inadequate communication on various levels (for example advertising and public relations) can be responsible for this gap.

5. The consumer gap (Gap 5): These four provider gaps contribute to the consumer gap - the difference between expectations and perceptions of customers and the service delivered by the provider.

"The key to delivering high quality service is to continually monitor customer perceptions of service quality, identify causes of service quality shortfalls, and take appropriate action to improve the quality of service (close the gaps)"(Zeithaml, Parasuraman & Berry 1990).

Measuring quality in non-profit, service-oriented institutions is not as highly developed as in the profit sector, and libraries often do not attend to performance measurement (Petr 2007:170, 174.). The quality of many libraries has never been really measured or questioned.

Although many libraries have not assessed their performance quality explicitly, they have often evaluated their services and user satisfaction on a small scale.

3. Quality metrics in academic libraries

There is no universal definition of what quality is. The ISO 9000 (2005) standard describe quality as "the consistent conformance of a product or service to a given set of standards or expectations". According to the ISO Standard 11620 *Performance indicators for libraries,* "quality" is the "totality of features and characteristics of a product or services that bear on the library's ability to satisfy stated or implied needs" (ISO 11620, 1998). Quality and effectiveness often implies the same.

In the 20th century the focus was strongly on quantitative measurements such as the number of items in stock, the use thereof, number of visitors and reference requests. Measurements were traditionally library-focused rather than institutionally focused. A paradigm shift characterises the 21st century, as user's expectations, technology, measurements, and many other library scenarios have changed. The library has a more expansive role and measuring quality is broader. The focus is strongly on user expectations and needs. The shift is "from measuring what you can count to measuring what counts" (De Jager 2004). This implies qualitative measurement, which is fundamentally subjective.

According to Phipps (2001: 365), the purpose of gathering service quality data should be to identify what is working well and what is not and to increase knowledge of customer requirements.

The Northumbria International Conference on Performance Measurement in Libraries and Information Services is a highly successful biennial conference organized since 1995 within Northumbria University, Newcastle upon Tyne, United Kingdom. The focus is on librarians, information professionals, museum curators and records managers leading and developing the measurement and monitoring of performance in their institutions.

Various research studies were carried out to assess performance in academic libraries, with the aim to highlight different factors that could affect the perceptions of quality of academic libraries services, to name a few:

A number of studies have been done in the United Kingdom and Europe. In a report on assessment of academic libraries, "The effective academic library" the Higher Education Funding Council for England (1995), provided a model for the assessment of performance:

- *Integration* level between the mission, aims and objectives of the institution and those of the library
- *User satisfaction* with overall service provision and specific key services
- *Delivery:* Objectives of the specific institution met and volume of output
- *Efficiency:* Relating service provision to resource inputs
- *Economy:* Overall costs, operating costs.

(Winkworth 2001:722).

Snoj and Petermanec (2001) investigated Slovenian academic libraries and identified the following dimensions that could affect the perceived quality of library services:

- The library collection;
- the physical surroundings of the library;
- equipment and information technology;
- library and information services;
- library staff.

According to a report on Malaysian agricultural libraries, Majid, Anwar & Eisenschitz

(2001), the factors that affected the perceived quality are:

- The provision of current literature;
- the adequacy of the library collections;
- the involvement of the respondents in selecting material for the library;
- the adequacy of library equipment;
- the adequacy of the physical facilities in the library;
- library skills of the users;
- frequency of library visits;
- the location of the library;
- the adequacy of the library promotion;
- the availability of needed materials;
- the availability of library assistance.

A project in Poland "Performance analysis for Polish research libraries" is focused on the development of methods and standards for the evaluation of quality of research and academic libraries (Derfert-Wolf, Gorski & Marcinek 2005).

A project to evaluate Croatian academic library services (Petr 2007), is a good example of using both quantitative and qualitative measurement, although they did not include library users. A short questionnaire for library staff, an extended questionnaire for library directors or chief librarians, interviews with library directors or chief librarians, and the analysis of library documentation are the survey instruments.

In the United Kingdom, the Standing Conference of National and University Libraries (SCONUL) initiated a User Satisfaction Project to develop a standard nationally used user satisfaction assessment method (Winkworth 2001: 729). It is an easy to use questionnaire composed entirely of tickboxes to permit machine reading, with questions on how successful users were in using particular services, how satisfied they were, how important particular services were, whether expectations had been met, use of other libraries, and satisfaction and importance overall.

The most important international set of performance indicators and standards are the ISO standard on library performance indicators - ISO 2789 (2006) and ISO DIS 11620 (2006) and the IFLA guidelines for performance measurement in academic libraries. These IFLA indicators are: resources and infrastructure, use, efficiency, and potential and development (Poll & Te Boekhorst 2007):

A. Resources, infrastructure: What services does the library offer?

Library as place for learning and research	A.1. User area per capita
	A.2. Seats per capita
	A.3. Opening hours compared to demand
Collections	A.4. Expenditure on information provision per capita
	A.5. Availability of required titles
	A.6. Percentage of rejected sessions
	A.7. Ratio of requests received to requests sent out in interlibrary lending
	A.8. Immediate availability
Staff	A.9. Staff per capita

Website	A.10. Direct access form the homepage

B. Use: How are the services accepted?

General	B.1. Market penetration
	B.2. User satisfaction
	B.3. Library visits per capita
Library as place for learning and research	B.4. Seat occupancy rate
Collections	B.5. Number of content units downloaded per capita
	B. 6. Collection use (turnover)
	B.7. Percentage of stock not used
	B.8. Loans per capita
	B.9. Percentage of loans to external users
Information services	B.10. Attendance at training lessons per capita
	B.11. Reference questions per capita
Cultural activities	B.12. Attendance at events per capita

C. Efficiency: Are the services cost-effectively?

General	C.1. Cost per user
	C.2. Cost per visit
	C.3. Cost per use
	C.4. Ratio of acquisitions costs to staff costs
Collection costs	C.5. Cost per document processed
	C.6. Cost per download
Processes - speed	C.7. Acquisition speed
	C.8. Media processing speed
	C.9. Employee productivity in media processing
	C.10. Lending speed
	C.11. Interlibrary loan speed
Processes - reliability	C. 12. Reference fill rate
	C.13. Shelving accuracy

D. Potentials and development: Are there sufficient potentials for future development?

Electronic services	D.1. Percentage of acquisitions expenditure spent on the electronic collection
	D.2. Percentage of library staff providing and developing electronic services

Staff development	D.3. Attendances at training lessons per staff member
Budget	D.4. Percentage of library means received by special grants or income generation
	D.5. Percentage of institutional means allocated to the library

Quality in academic libraries can have many aspects. Measuring service quality in academic libraries could thus include the following areas:

1. **Resources (information content):** The quality of the collection could determine the quality of information support to teaching, learning and research.
   - Relevance of documents and items available in the library
   - Access to information sources – document delivery, catalogue
   - Access to accredited academic journals - subscription or licensing
   - Electronic document delivery: Electronic materials and electronic access to information
   - Balance between holdings and access, and balance between print and electronic materials
   - Open access
   - Institutional repositories, for example technical reports, theses, dissertations and academic articles can be an indication of the research input and output of the institution
   - Special collections and rare items
2. **Management and Organisation (service environment and resource delivery).** Commitment of the library management team to create an encouraging work environment. Management should be prepared to change decisions and procedures in order to improve service quality.
   - Information strategies: Policies (for example a collection development policy) and procedures to the provision and management of information. According to the Follett Committee in the United Kingdom (Brophy 2000: 31), this would include the acquisition, creation, management and use of information, as well as information relationships with external agencies.
   - Space and space management: buildings and facilities (such as printing and photocopying,), storage and study space, reading areas.
   - Information technology and network connections available to users, as well as library management systems for basic operations like acquisitions, cataloguing and circulation.
   - General appearance - notices, signage, posters, tidy shelves, furniture, appearance of staff – should be inviting. (You never have a second chance to make a first impression)
   - Marketing of the library and its services – what the library has to offer. (marketing = visibility)

- Professional involvement in selection and acquisition.
- Library expenditure, although it is not so easy to measure costs, for example how do you measure "value for money"? The total library budget - for example library materials, electronic access, network infrastructure, buildings, personnel, other overhead costs - should be measured to determine return on investment.
- User education
- Retrieving of information
- Reference and enquiry services
- Liaison between the library staff and teaching staff
- Co-operation between libraries, for example consortia.

3. Staffing and staff management: Staff is responsible for delivering services to the users. They are on the front line with customers. Strong management and leadership play an important role in delivering services. However, every employee in the institution must share the responsibility to contribute to quality. Improved service performance could be the result of staff commitment to service quality.

- Staff attitude - knowledgeable, enthusiastic, approachable, helpful staff - is a key ingredient of performance Staff skills, qualifications, training and development, further education, workshops and conferences
- Performance management and reward systems to provide feedback on performance
- Staff involvement in planning and decision making. Teamwork encourages shared responsibility.

When measuring quality in academic libraries, the needs and expectations of all the different stakeholders and users should be taken into account. The majority of users are full-time academic and non-academic staff, undergraduates and postgraduates. There are multiple stakeholders with different priorities and performance measure requirements: end-customers (students), service purchasers (academic departments, institutions), funding institutions (funding councils, government), guardians of quality (professional bodies), service managers, and staff (Winkworth 2001: 722).

Benchmarking between academic libraries is a means of assessing performance, apart from quality measurement in one's own institution. Benchmarking usually involves the following, according to Roberts and Rowley (2004:169):

- Regularly comparing performance with standards or best practices;
- Identifying gaps where performance falls below standards and comparators;
- Seeking out different approaches that can achieve improvements in performance;
- Implementing improvements;
- Monitoring progress with improvements and reviewing the benefits.

By comparing yourself with others, one can understand how they operate effectively and apply practices to one's own organisation.

4. Quality and the digital environment

With the development of information and communication technologies in the digital environment of the 21st century, users have other needs and expectations from library services. (Who needs the library anymore? We have the Internet!). There is a move from collections to connections.

Since the mid-1990s, scientific publications began the transformation from print to electronic resources and libraries began to invest in e-resources. Users are often more interested in access to information than physical materials. Additional measures to evaluate the performance of digital library environments need to be developed, for example transaction logs on Weblogs reveal search strategies and use of digital documents.

The United States Association of Research Libraries (ARL) developed performance indicators for digital library environments, including accessible electronic resources, expenditures for networked resources, use of networked resources and services, and library digitization activities (Roberts & Rowley 2004: 174). A number of other projects are working on e-metrics. The EQUINOX project combines a set of twelve electronic indicators with a software package which demonstrate the linkages between each indicator and library objectives (Winkworth 2001: 722). A study at the University of Illinois investigated the library's return on investment and the benefits of using electronics resources (Kaufman 2008). In this study more than 80% of respondents identified the following ways in which digital access had a positive impact on their work: Digital access allows them to dedicate less time to physical visits to the library, digital access allows scholarly information to be better integrated into their research workflow, and digital access allows them to make better use of literature in interdisciplinary and emergent fields of study.

5. Methodology of quality measurement

Quality assessment of an academic library includes products, services, individuals (users, staff, management), as well as the institution. Quality metrics of the service will have to include evaluations at an individual, service, and organisational level. Quality measurement means collecting statistical and other data that describe the performance of the library and analysing these data in order to evaluate the performance quality. Quality criteria are determined by the institution's requirements and the library's goals and objectives, as well as the users' needs and expectations.

To measure quality in academic libraries, one needs to investigate a common framework of reference, an agreed set of standards, performance indicators, evaluation criteria and methodologies. It is, however, important to take local conditions into account, as libraries have different missions and goals, collections and services, and countries may have different standards. Performance indicators will be determined by the specific institution and purpose of the specific measurement.

- Both qualitative and quantitative methods are necessary for measuring the library and its services.
- Quantitative as well as qualitative data can be collected through questionnaires. A combination of closed (precoded) and open (free response) questions can be used. Quantitative data is easy to analyse, but open questions - qualitative data - need content analysis.
- Quantitative statistical data - expressed in numbers - can show the state-of-the-art of the library, for example user data, collection size, management

data, transactional usage data and financial expenditure.

- Qualitative measures evaluate expectations, views, opinions, suggestions and are largely subjective. Methods for qualitative measures include surveys, interviews and discussion groups.
- A simplistic summary of quantitative versus qualitative characteristics:

Quantitative	**Qualitative**
Breadth/mass data	Depth/smaller samples
Objective	Subjective
"Scientific"	"Non-scientific"
Highly structured approach	Looser approach
Answer "how often"/"how much" - statistical	Answer "why" - causative
Less helpful with complex topics	More helpful with complex topics
Emphasis on neutrality	Emphasis on the actor's perspective
Usually clear-cut precise results	Useful for preliminary work

(Morgan 1995: 138)

- Performance statistical reports, monthly and annual reports, and other library documentation can be analysed.
- It is important to involve different user groups in the academic library in performance evaluations. Different evaluations, expectations and perspectives are needed to measure the quality of the library and information services.
- Specific surveys on a large scale can measure user satisfaction directly, although they can be time-consuming and costly. Instruments such as SERVQUAL and LibQUAL are valuable tools in measuring library service quality.

  Zeithaml, Parasuraman & Berry (1990) developed SERVQUAL, a general instrument for measuring customer's perceptions of service quality. They identified five general service quality dimensions which contribute to consumer expectations and perceptions of service quality (Zeithaml, Parasuraman & Berry 1990: 26):

  - *Tangibles:* Appearance of physical facilities, equipment, personnel, and communication materials;
  - *Reliability:* Ability to perform the promised service dependably and accurately;
  - *Responsiveness:* Willingness to help customers and provide prompt service;
  - *Assurance:* Knowledge and courtesy of employees and their ability to convey trust and confidence;

- *Empathy:* Caring, individualized attention the firm provides the customers.

Many libraries adapted SERVQUAL as instrument to measure service quality.

LibQUAL is a joint project of Texas A&M University and the Association for Research Libraries in the United States that enables institutions to address service quality gaps and to enhance responses to user needs. The dimensions of LibQUAL are:

- *Affect of service:* The human side of the institution – empathy, accessibility and personal competence;
- *Personal control:* The extent to which users are able to navigate and control information that is provided;
- *Access to information:* The adequacy of the collections themselves and the ability to access needed information on a timely basis;
- *Library as place:* Comprising utilitarian space for study and collaboration. (Roberts & Rowley 2004: 16)

- Services can be rated formally through surveys, meetings and interviews with library staff and users. Academic libraries often have formal library committees to advise library management.
- Services can also be rated more informally through a suggestion box, complaints box, electronic channels and informal communication with library staff and users. Staff can keep record of informal complaints or suggestions that users make. Staff at the front-line of service delivery will be aware of gaps in the service and user dissatisfaction.
- Ongoing liaison between library staff and groups of users could monitor user satisfaction (Brophy 2000: 65). An annual user satisfaction survey on a smaller scale can give users the opportunity to comment on the service.
- Performance measures may rate the overall performance of the service, or certain aspects of the service.

It is necessary to review performance measures from time to time and to make adjustments and other changes when needed.

6. Conclusions

Quality in academic libraries is a multi-dimensional construct. Performance measurement is part of a broader quality framework. Quality assessment is done from the perspective of different groups of people. Both quantitative and qualitative measurements are required to determine the quality and effectiveness of the library. Quality measurement is a recurrent process and quality metrics in academic libraries should be done with appropriate frequency in order to keep up with constant change, new demands (e.g. post-graduates), trends and developments (e.g. electronic resources and technology).

According to a project in Croatia to measure quality in public and academic libraries, "Insufficient awareness to library service quality affects all library processes, and ultimately leads to deterioration of that service quality" (Petr 2007: 174).

It is of utmost importance that all stakeholders are aware of the value and importance of quality metrics as a tool to strive for excellence and to enhance quality. What are we doing? Why are we doing that? What matters? Where are we failing and how can we close the gaps?

The ultimate goal of measurement is improving the "fitness for purpose" of the library and to enhance quality. The academic library is a role player in higher education effectiveness. Leadership and good management are needed, as well as involvement and commitment by all employees. Libraries are services and they need to re-examine the ways in which services are delivered continuously. It is the task of the academic library to move from a passive service provider to an active and vital force in the institution.

References

Blake, J. (2008). *Education and quality metrics.* Midrand: Midrand Graduate Institute.

Bologna Declaration of 19 June 1999: Joint declaration of the European Ministers of Education. European Higher Education Area. (1999). Available at: www.bologna-bergen2005.no/Docs/00 Main_doc/990719BOLOGNA_DECLARATION.pdf_(Accessed 15 April 2009).

Brophy, P. (1997). Total quality management. In: *Resource management in academic libraries.* London: Library Association Publishing.

Brophy, P. (2000). *The academic library.* London: Library Association Publishing.

De Jager, Karin. (2005). *Counting what matters: To measure what counts.* Paper: Getting beyond the starting blocks: Quality assurance issues in academic libraries. Stellenbosch: University of Stellenbosch.

Derfert-Wolf, L., Gorski, M.M. & Marcinek, M. (2005). *Quality of academic libraries – funding bodies, librarians and user perspective: a common project of Polish research libraries on comparable measures.* Proceedings: World Library and Information Congress: 71th IFLA General Conference and Council, August 14th-18th, Oslo, Norway. Available at: www.ifla.org/IV/ifla71/Programme.htm (Accessed 16 April 2009).

EQUINOX. Library performance measurement and quality management system. (1998-2000). Available at: http://equinox.dcu.ie/index.html

Haas, Andrine J. (2006). Assessment of library resources and services as part of the college program review process. In: *It's all about student learning: Managing community and other college libraries in the 21st century.* 2006. Edited by David R Dowell & Gerard B McCabe. Westport: Libraries Unlimited.

Haddow, G. (2007). Academic libraries and the research quality framework. *Australian Academic and Research Libraries,* 38 (1): 26-37.

Higher Education Funding Council for England. (1995). *The effective academic library: a framework for evaluating the performance of UK academic libraries.* Bristol: HEFC.

ISO 11620. (1998). *Information and documentation. Library performance indicators.* Geneva: International Organization for Standardization.

ISO DIS 11620. (2006). *Information and documentation. Library performance indicators.* Geneva: International Organization for Standardization.

ISO 2789. (2006). *Information and documentation. International library statistics.* Geneva: International Organization for Standardization.

ISO 9000. (2005). *Quality management systems, fundamentals and vocabulary.* Geneva: International Organization for Standardization.

Kaufman, Paula T. (2008). The library as strategic investment: results of the Illinois return on investment study. *Liber Quarterly,* 18 (3/4). Available at: http://liber.library.uu.nl/publish/articles/000269/article_content.htm. (Accessed 16 February 2009).

LibQUAL+TM. Available at: http://www.libqual.org/

Majid, S., Anwar, M.A & Eisenschitz, T.S. (2001). User perceptions of library effectiveness in Malaysian agricultural libraries. *Library Review,* 50 (4): 176-187.
Morgan, Steve. (1995). *Performance assessment in academic libraries*. New York: Mansel.
Petr, K. 2007. Quality measurement of Croatian public and academic libraries: a methodology. *Performance measurement and metrics,* 8 (3): 170-179.
Phipps, Shelley. (2001). Beyond measuring service quality: learning from the voices of the customers, the staff, the processes, and the organization. *Library Trends,* 49 (4): 635 – 661.
Poll, R. & Te Boekhorst, P. (2007). *Measuring quality: performance measurements in libraries.* The Hague: International Federation of Library Associations (IFLA).
Pritchard, S.M. (1996). Determining quality in academic libraries. *Library Trends,* 44 (3): 572-595.
Roberts, S & Rowley, J. (2004). *Managing information services.* London: Facet Publishing.
Snoj, B. & Petermanec, Z. (2001). Let users judge the quality of faculty library services. *New Library World,* 102 (1168): 314-325.
Te Boekhorst, P. (1995). Measuring quality: The IFLA guidelines for performance measurement in academic libraries. *IFLA Journal,* 21(4): 278-281.
Winkworth, Ian. (2001). Innovative United Kingdom approaches to measuring service quality. *Library Trends,* 49 (4): 718-731.
Zeithaml, Valarie A., Parasuraman, A. & Berry, Leonard L. (1990). *Delivering quality service: Balancing customer perceptions and expectations.* NewYork: Free Press
Zeithaml, V.A, Bitner, M.J. & Gremler, D.D. (2006). *Services marketing: Integrating customer focus across the firm.* Boston: McGraw-Hill.

Approaches to and Perceptions for Quality: Empirical Evidence for the Public Libraries in Greece

P.A. Kostagiolas[1], A.P. Margiola[2] and St. Zimeras[3]

[1] Lecturer, Dep. Archive and Library Science, Ionian University, Greece
E-mail: pkostagiolas@ionio.gr
[2] Librarian, Central Library and Information Center, University of Ioannina, P.O. BOX 1186 GR - 451 10, Ioannina, Greece. E-mail: anmargiola@cc.uoi.gr
[3] Ass. Prof., University of the Aegean, Department of Statistics and Actuarial – Financial Mathematics, Karlovassi, Samos, 83200, Greece. E-mail: zimste@aegean.gr

Abstract: Public Libraries can surely play a significant social, cultural and economic role. Improvements on quality however are a necessary prerequisite. On the other hand, quality is a complex and subjective concept, which should incorporate at any given time the true (expressed and implied) needs of all interested parties. This paper investigates and empirically assesses the current perceptions for quality in Greek public libraries in order to suggest a way forward for quality management implementation. For that purpose a survey based on semi-structured interviews with the directors of Greek public libraries has been constructed and the results are presented.

Keywords: Public libraries; Quality management; Perceptions; Survey; Greece.

1. Introduction

Public Libraries play a significant role providing information services to the community. Public libraries worldwide face new economy and societal pressures on a wider as well as on a local level (Kostagiolas and Korkidi, 2008). Nowadays, the role of the public libraries is to constitute the key factor in satisfying user needs and the promotion and fulfillment of the information society. Libraries however confront to a novel information environment in which technology advents are rather unique to human history (Kaane, 2006). Public libraries need to search for new methods in order to incorporate the users into the philosophy of services they offer. The application of a quality management system may contribute to the libraries development of activities at all sectors and focuses on the user needs with an effective and efficient way (Barbêdo and Turrioni, 2003). At the same time, a significant reason for applying modern management methods is the increasing competitive rather international environment they operate (Lilley and Usherwood, 2000). This competitive environment affect directly or not the financing of the public libraries (Barlow and Morris, 2007; Audit Commission, 2002).

Within this rapidly changing and competitive environment additional pressure is applied to libraries all over the world. Public libraries in Greece in particular face significant problems including lack of financial resources, lack of staff and rather obsolete organizational structure (Kostagiolas and Korkidi, 2008). Greek Public Libraries during the last twenty years have made considerable efforts to improve quality and to develop new services; in the majority of the cases through the use of financial support from the European Community. Some of the most significant projects were the Hellenic Public Libraries Union Catalogue, the bookmobile units of the Greek Central Public Libraries and the ARGO project which can provide access to the library catalogues via internet etc.

In Greece there are three types of "public" libraries, the ones that are financially supported by the Ministry of Education, the municipal libraries which are under the responsibility of the local authorities and the children's libraries which are also financed by the Ministry of Education (Papazoglou and Semertzaki, 2001). There are 46 public libraries in Greece, with the 29 of them characterized as Central (Metropolitan) public libraries serving a rather extended geographical area, the 9 of them are characterized as historical because their collections include old and rare documents. Moreover, it was found in 2008 that there are also 194 "active" municipal libraries (Kostagiolas and Korkidi, 2008) and about 25 children's libraries (Papazoglou and Semertzaki, 2001).

This paper initially provides an overview of the distinct approaches for quality management in public libraries in order to show that the apprehensions of all those involved in applying a specific quality management system should indeed be tuned to the nature of each quality approach; while no approach should be conceived as a panacea (Kostagiolas and Kitsiou, 2008). Also, issues for quality management in public libraries and the results of a survey which was conducted during the second quarter of 2008 through semi-structure interviews are presented. The survey includes 46 public and 45 municipal libraries directors in Greece and studied their perceptions regarding: their intention for the implementation of quality management systems; the reasons that may lead to the decision to apply quality management systems and the results expected from the implementation of quality management systems.

2. Approaches for quality management in public libraries

Improving service quality in the consolidated organizational daily routine in libraries might in the end become a complex challenge (Kostagiolas & Kitsiou, 2008). That is because the various groups of interested parties involved, both within the local community and outside of it, do not necessarily perceive quality in the same way. Therefore, the quality itself should not be perceived as unique, since each interested party such as management, employees, users, regulation authorities etc. perceive quality in a rather distinguished way according to their viewpoint. The above mentioned suggestion significantly influence the way investments are made for quality management in various types of libraries (Kostagiolas & Kitsiou, 2008). The different aspects of quality for academic libraries has been studies by Derfert-Wolf et al. (2005) where it was assumed that the different stakeholder groups users, management and personnel have different priorities. Indeed the priorities of the users are access, delivery, speed, work premises, personnel response, trustworthiness of service; while the priorities of management include cost, effectiveness, quality of planning, positive results for the users, collaboration with other organizations – reputation); and the priorities of the personnel for quality management includes good working conditions – quality of planning – reputation – systematic personnel development.

Diachronically public libraries have a significant cultural, social and economical role and empowered the expansion of the reading audience and the reading development. In the beginning of the 21rst century public libraries do indeed play a significant role and over the last decades they have strived to satisfy user emerging needs and to exploit a number of new opportunities. Nowadays, new opportunities may be exploited and new capacities promoted in order to gain the appropriate funding. One such opportunity is the digitalization of the public libraries collections and the creation of information centers with free access to the internet for the users. On line catalogues and other services have created new conditions and have altered the profile of public libraries. More recently, bookblogs are sometimes structured and used by public libraries in order to inform and encourage especially young people to be members of and visit the library. Moreover, public libraries require access to consortiums as strategic opportunities arise more steadily for the consortium than for the stand alone library. Competencies and skills of librarians are redefined and the role of information specialists must adjust to the new environment.

There is a surplus of definitions at the bibliography referring to quality in libraries. Although, quality management is a multidimensional activity directly related to specific organisational goals that should be looked on as a never –ending upward spiral (Chim, 2007). As far as the public libraries are concerned, *quality management is both an underpinning philosophy and the variety of tools and techniques, which focus the organizational structure, its resources, the people within in and the views of all relevant stakeholders on attaining and continuously improving measurable organisational objectives informed by the preferences and needs of the end-user.* (Milner, et al., 1997). Furthermore, according to the ISO 11620, quality in libraries is defined as “the totality of features and characteristics of a product or of a service that bear on the library’s abilities to satisfy stated or implied needs”. The variety of approaches that the literature reveals, shows that for libraries the quality maze' has not yet been solved (Usherwood, 1995).

During the last decades, organizations, both national and international, have been cultivated and introduced several approaches that regard to the implementation of process-oriented management systems, quality assurance standards and to the development of accreditation models and/or total quality management (TQM) programmes (Kostagiolas and Kitsiou, 2008). An approach similar to this is ISO 9001:2000 series of standards which together form a coherent set of quality management system standards that may create the basis on which a library can certify a quality management system (Fontana and Sardelli, 2005; Kiran et al., 2006; Valls and Vergueiro, 2006; Chim, 2007; Garratt, 2007; Sacchetti, 2007; Turk, 2007).

Another approach include the Total Quality Management (TQM) which according to BS 7850 is defined as the "*management philosophy and company practices that aim to harness the human and material resources of an organization in the most effective way to achieve the objectives of the organization*". In other words, TQM focuses at the constant improvement of service and the satisfaction of internal and external customers (Butterwick, 1993; O'Neil, 1994; Siraj Nissa Begum, 2003). In addition, quality awards have a set of detailed criteria for self-evaluation. To be exact, the Deming Prize, which was established by the Union of Japanese Scientists and Engineers in 1950, under W. Edwards Deming's influence (Deming, 1986), consists of certain criteria that are divided into ten categories. These criteria are mostly based on Deming's ideas and more specifically on the application of quality control and statistical process control (Brophy and Coulling, 1996). Moreover, the European Quality Award (EQA) has been developed within the framework of the European Foundation for Quality Management (EFQM) and is based on nine criteria and thirty-two sub-criteria, equally divided between enablers and results. Furthermore, the Malcolm Baldrige National Quality Award, set up by the US Congress in 1987, was composed of seven categories, each with a quantitative weighting, which are reviewed each year.

The Library and Information Sector Improvement Model (LISIM) is an especially designed model for self–assessment in public libraries which has been distinguished in the literature as well as in the library practices all over Europe. LISIM summarizes ten core management practices in six stages of achievement which offer direction on how the library and information service might ameliorate its current approach (Kinnell Evans et al., 1999). Two additional approaches for the public sector are the Quality Framework of Stewart and Walsh (1989) and the Democratic Approach of Pfeffer and Coote (1991). The former, proposed a foundation in order to be begun the development of the quality management in the public sector (Kinnell Evans, 2000), while the latter, presented a further comprehension between the public and the private sectors (Pfeffer and Coote, 1991).

Over the last years, quality assessment and performance evaluation is based on groups of library indicators that cover the full range of the stakeholder views (Brophy, 2008). The assessment processes include the collection and the analysis of the elements which portray the library performance. For example, EQUINOX has developed indices for performance measurement in libraries. This has being achieved by employing international standards for library performance indicators including indicators for electronic libraries services (Bowden, 2000; Brophy, 2001). In addition, CAMILE is considered to be a concerted action on management of information for libraries in Europe and it brought together experiences and expertise in library management through the partnership of four existed libraries programmes projects:

DECIDE, DECIMAL, EQLIPSE, και MINSTREL. More specifically EQLIPSE project's aim was to produce and test an open software system containing quality management and performance measurements tools based on ISO 9000 and the draft ISO 11620 standards respectively, which could support decision making in libraries of all types (MacDougall, et al., 1997) Over the last years in Greece, a coherent set of quality indicators and standards have been recognized and followed annually for the academic libraries by MOPAB.

Finally, another approach include the benchmarking which is defined as the comparison and review of libraries' service performance and its aim is to detect and implement feasible areas for amelioration (Wilson and Town, 2006). There are two key types of benchmarking: the comparison of results and the comparison of processes (Kinnell et al., 1999). Likewise, qualitative and quantitative methods as far as the user satisfaction is concerned, have been used in order to assess the quality in libraries worldwide (e.g. Crawford, 2003; Sadeh, 2007; Sadeh, 2008). Methodologies of this nature embody also the SERVQUAL (Parasuraman et al., 1988; Parasuraman, 2004) and the SERVPERF models (Cronin and Taylor, 1992). Indeed, the first (SERVQUAL) defines service quality as the difference between library users' expectations and perceptions; while the second (SERVPERF) directly captures users' performance perceptions in comparison to their expectations of the service experience. An important alteration is the LibQual protocol which has been introduced for the academic libraries worldwide.

Evidently, the pathway to quality is not unique due to the wide number of the distinct approaches that can be followed. Indeed it is quite different an investment based on the implementation of a quality assurance models than one based on Total Quality Management or quality performance evaluation. For us it is important to study the perceptions and the expectations of library administration in order to balance the perceptions of and the approaches to quality management. This may improve the top management commitment to a certain approach and indeed support an informed decision regarding a specific quality management approach.

3. Empirical evidence for quality management in the Greek public libraries

Nowadays, the uncertainty of the environment is perhaps as high as ever. Quality management may be seen as a methodological useful way for handling the threats and taking advantage of the opportunities imposed by the external environment. Quality comprehension expresses the library´s organizational and management culture as well as the professionalism of its employees. It is also true however that more initiatives and financing is required in order to empower and really boost the current efforts towards quality management. Public libraries that respond to the modern challenges should operate as open, essential, educational and cultural points indissolubly linked to the users' needs, ameliorating the internal relations inside the domain and the external with the community (Kumbar, 2004).

For libraries in Greece quality management systems implementation becomes increasingly popular either through the ISO 9001:2008 standard or through a number of other approaches including other quality programs such as the Libqual. Indeed, the Municipal Centre for Historical Research and Documentation in Volos-Greece was awarded with the commitment of excellence in European Quality Award (EQA) and a number of academic libraries have been certified their quality management systems (Kostagiolas & Korkidi, 2008). However, only limited work has been made available for quality management implementation in public libraries. In this work a survey is presented for the studying a. the perceptions of the library directors for developing a quality management system and; b. the expectations of the library directors for the potential improvements through the implementation of quality management systems.

3.1 Methodology and questionnaire development

The qualitative empirical study conducted was based on the development of a semi-structured questionnaire for conducting the interviews. The questionnaire follows Kostagiolas and Kitsiou's methodology (adapted to the public libraries), who conducted research in Greek academic libraries in 2007 but with certain adaptations made during a preliminary pilot phase. Firstly, the directors of public and municipal libraries were conducted, the research aims were explained to them and they asked to participate in the research.

The questionnaire comprises questions of open and closed type. For the closed type questions a five-step Likert scale was used, ranging from 1 ="total disagreement" to 5 = "total agreement", so that those participate in the research would express the degree of their agreement. The questionnaire was arranged in three sections and comprises three questions of the open type and 32 of the closed type. The research questions in section A aim at recording the basic information about the library and the participants and the perceptions of those participated as to the existence of a quality system, the intention for developing a quality system. Moreover, the library directors were asked to choose from a sequence of quality definitions those which represent their opinion. This was done in order to study the way the library directors perceive quality; and the definitions provided are the following:

- Quality is customer satisfaction through product or by service (Siraj Nissa Begum, 2003).
- The very concept of quality in the library, namely providing the needs of users with the available resources (Valls, Vergueiro, 2006).
- Public services operate within a context which requires special consideration [and] the quality of the surroundings and the service relationship would influence customer perception and satisfaction as much as the service which was received (Stewart and Walsh, 1989).
- Quality management is both an underpinning philosophy and a variety of tools and techniques, which focus the organizational structure, its resources, the people within it and the views of all relevant stakeholders on attaining and continuously improving measurable organizational objectives informed by the preferences and needs of the end-user. (Milner, et al, 1997).
- The totality of features and characteristics of a product or of service that bear on the library's ability to satisfy stated or implied needs (ISO 11620).
- Quality (…) means that a service is "good" as well as "cheap" (Poll, 2006).
- The total composite product and service characteristics of marketing, engineering, manufacturing and maintenance through which the product and service in use will meet the expectations of the customer (Feigenbaum, 1983).

The research questions of section B aim at examining the perception of those questioned as to the reasons or motivations for applying a quality management system in their library. The research questions in section C aim at examining the perception of those questioned as to the expected consequences or benefits from the implementation of a quality system. Each of the sections A, B and C is accompanied by an open type question (a total of three open questions). The research did not aim at formulating generalizable results, despite the fact that according to Behrakis (1999) the results and the analysis produce indicative results based on the opinion of the experts, i.e. the directors of Greek public and municipal libraries.

3.2 The profile of the survey conducted

The qualitative survey conducted during the second quarter of 2008. Contact information for the Greek public and municipal libraries was mainly collected from the Ministry of National Education. Overall the directors of 91 prominent libraries (public, metropolitan and municipal) were approached from all over Greece. From these the 46 are directors of public libraries, of which 23 (50 per cent) responded positively to the research project, while from the 45 selected municipal libraries only 21 responded (46.6 per cent). The final overall number of directors participated in the research was 44 library directors, which represents a response rate of 48.4 per cent.

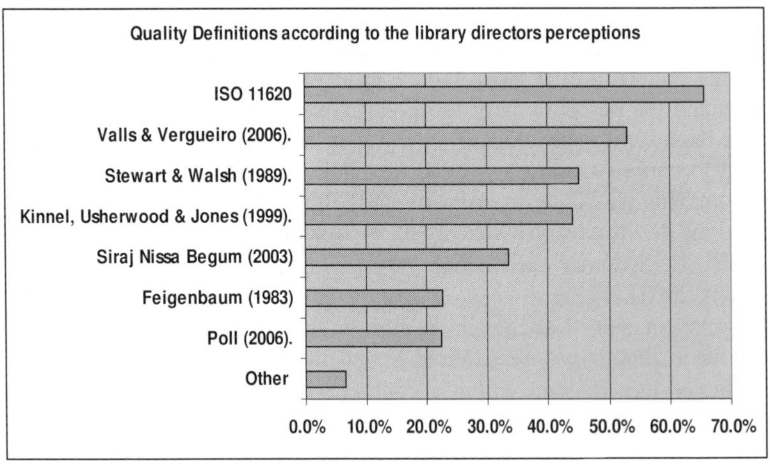

Figure 1: The actual percentages of the answers given by the library directors for the quality definitions.

3.3 Results and discussion

The actual percentages of the library directors' choices regarding the definitions of quality are presented in Figure 1. As can be noted from Figure 1, the definition given by the ISO 11620 seems to be the one wider accepted by the library directors while the ones by Valls and Vergueiro (2006) and Stewart and Walsh (1989) follow. The definitions received more attention are primarily focused on user satisfaction and therefore quality according to the library directors' perceptions should mostly be defined upon this viewpoint. Therefore, other approaches such as the application of quality performance indicators and/or quality control and/or quality assurance systems, although are quite significant for the public libraries, do not directly perceived to express the concept of *library quality*. In the following questions of Section A, the library directors were asked to state whether they have implemented a formal quality management system in their libraries and whether they believe that formal quality management implementation will be necessary in the near future. In fact one library director has stated that a formal implementation of a quality management system has taken place and about one third of the library directors stated that they would definitely invest or they would probably invest in the near future in implementing a quality management system. It seems that library directors are mostly concerned with the library users' satisfaction and are less interested for other rather technical aspects of quality assurance and quality management.

Section B of the questionnaire investigates the perceptions of library directors regarding ten significant motives/reasons for implementing a formal quality management system. The motives are presented in a hierarchal order in the first column of Table 1, and thereafter the mean score and the sample size are exhibited. The mean score for each of the motives is indicative to the degree this particular motive is perceived as important for implementing a formal quality management system by the public library directors which participated in this research, in the scale from 1 "lowest importance" to 5 "highest importance". Higher mean scores were given to three motives he improvement of user satisfaction, the library processes, and as a competitive advantage.

A hierarchy of the motives for quality management	**Mean Score**	**N**
Information services	4.51	41
Library processes	4.07	41
Competitive advantage	4.00	43
Communication	3.88	42
Entrance to new markets	3.88	42
Future demand	3.82	44
TQM implementation	3.77	43
Expansion tendency	3.65	43
Certification of others	3.63	43
Current demand	3.15	41

Table 1: Results of the closed ended research questions of Section B regarding the motives behind a potential implementation of a quality management system.

Section C of the questionnaire investigates the perceptions of the library directors for seventeen expected consequences (results) after the development and the implementation of a quality management system. In Table 2 the mean scores are presented in a hierarchical order for each of the expected results examined. The mean score is indicative to the degree to which the library directors perceive as possible each of the results included in the questioner. The majority of those surveyed agree that the development of quality management systems will bring about an improvement in library services together with improvements of user satisfaction levels. Indeed below are the five expected consequences with the highest scores:

(1) overall improvement of the information services provided;
(2) improvement of the user satisfaction level;
(3) improvements of digital services;
(4) improvement of library processes; and
(5) improvement of users's service provision

The library directors took part in the survey ascribe especially high percentages to consequences related to the users and lower percentages to "quality culture", "improvement of teamwork", "improving relations with suppliers", etc. The directors anticipate that a quality management system implementation will amend the library's processes, operations and productivity.

The results may be compared to the ones produced in a similar study conducted for the academic library directors in Greece in Kostagiolas and Kitsiou (2008). For Section B, regarding the motives for implementing quality management, the first four as well as the last three motives in the hierarchy created are the same; while only small differences are noted in between. Moreover, for the expected consequences for a potential implementation of a quality management system, only slight differences can be noted. Indeed, the first two expected results in the hierarchy are the same for both academic and public libraries; while the "Digital services", and the "Teamwork and cooperation" expected results come little higher in the public library directors expectations.

A hierarchy of the results from quality management implementation	**Mean Score**	**N**
Improving information services	4.55	42
Users' satisfaction	4.30	43
Digital services	4.26	43
Library processes	4.23	40
Users's service experience	4.19	42
Teamwork and cooperation	4.05	41
Service' indications	4.02	43
Communication	3.98	43
Quality culture development	3.95	42
Productivity	3.83	41
Competitive position	3.74	42
Personnel and management relationship	3.68	41
Acquisition	3.65	43
Classification	3.60	43
Cataloguing	3.60	43
Time and finance losses reduction	3.59	39
Improvement of relationship with suppliers	2.98	42

Table 2: Research results of the closed ended research questions, Section C, for the expected benefits when implementing a quality management system

In Greece, there seems to be a growing level of awareness regarding quality issues and quality management, although the library directors participated in this research are still rather reluctant about the implementation of formal quality management approaches. Also quality management seems to be "future demand" than a "current demand". As far as the open-ended question is concerned, the directors of the Greek Public Libraries bring forward the problems of financing, the need for qualified personnel, the lack of infrastructure and sometimes the lack of modern technological equipment. The study results provide an overall picture for the perceptions of the directors of Public Libraries in Greece for both the motives and the expected benefits from the development and the implementation of a quality management system such as ISO 9000:2000. Overall it is our impression that *quality* is mostly conceived by the library directors participated in the research as an issue concerning the satisfaction of user needs. Hence, under this general attitude, the management of quality mostly relates to actions for measuring the level of users' perceptions, needs and expectations. Therefore, quality is perceived to be a pathway for bringing the public libraries closer to the communities they serve.

4. Conclusion

The implementation of quality incorporates the modification and the shifting of the "established organizational system" from its current form (structure and/or operation) to an enhanced state in order to keep library at the center of the city's activity. In this changing era, in Greece, we should counter the complex systems of the "problems" with equally complex systems of "solutions". Investments towards achieving quality in Public Libraries may include a number of different approaches and would expect greater benefits if it is based on creative changes rather than on a series of continuous small modifications. The question is not whether "quality" is of interest, but which "quality" may provide the best approach for the Public Libraries at the present and in the future. Quality Management may allow one to follow developments, but not to outdistance current uncertainties.

References

Audit Commission (2002), *Building better Library services: learning from Audit inspection and research*, London: Audit Commission.

Barbêdo, S.A.D., Turrioni, J.B. (2003), "Sistema de Gestão da Qualidade e um modelo de integração estrutural em bibliotecas: análise comparativa em dois estudos de caso", in *Simpósio de engenharia de produção, 10, Unesp, Bauru*, http://www.simpep.feb.unesp.br/anais10/gestaoqualidprodutividade/arq01.PDF

Barlow, A., Morris, A. (2007), "Usability of Public Libraries: perceptions and experiences of new users", *World Library and Information Congress: 73rd IFLA General Conference and Council*, Durban, South Africa (available at: http://www.ifla.org/iv/ifla73/index.htm).

Behrakis, Th. (1999), Multi-dimensional Data Analysis. Methods and Implementations, Livani, Athens.

Brophy, P. (2008), "Telling the story: qualitative approaches to measuring the performance of emerging library services", *Performance Library and Metrics*, Vol. 9 No. 1, pp. 7-17.

Brophy, P. (2001), "Assessing the performance of electronic library services: the EQUINOX project", *The New Review of Academic Librarianship*, Vol. 7, pp. 3-18.

Brophy, P., Coulling, K. (1996), *Quality management for information and library managers*, London, Aslib.
Butterwick, N.B. (1993), "Total quality management in the university library", *LibraryManagement*, Vol. 14 No. 3, pp. 28-31.
Chim, W. (2007), "The quest for excellence: one library's experience", *Library Management*, Vol. 28 Nos 6/7, pp. 323-36.
Crawford, J. (2003), "Reviewing a programme of evaluation in an academic library: the case of Glasgow Caledonian University", *Performance Measurements and Metrics*, Vol. 4 No. 3, pp. 113-21.
Cronin, J.J. Jr and Taylor, A.S. (1992), "Measuring service quality: a reexamination and an extension", *Journal of Marketing*, Vol. 56 No. 3, pp. 55-67.
Deming, W. E. (1986), *Out of Crisis*, Cambridge, Cambridge University Press.
Feigenbaum, A.V. (1983), *Total quality control*, New York, McGrow-Hill.
Fontana, A.I. and Sardelli, A. (2005), "Managing quality in a national library: the case of the national central library of Florence, Italy", Proceedings. World Library and Information Congress: 71th IFLA *General Conference and Council. Libraries – A Voyage of Discovery, Oslo*, www.ifla.org/IV/ifla71/papers /o77e-Fontana_Sardelli.pdf.
Garratt, O.G. (2007), "ISO 9001: 2000 and change management", *7th Northumbria International Conference on Performance Measurement in Libraries and Information Services*, www.lib.sun.ac.za/northumbria7/Programme.htm
Kaane, S. (2006), "Marketing reference and information services in libraries: a staff competencies framework", *World Library and Information Congress: 72nd IFLA General Conference and Council, Seoul, Korea,* http://www.ifla.org/IV/ifla72/index.htm
Kinnell, Evans M. (2000), "Quality management and self assessment tools for public libraries", *Proceedings. 66th IFLA council and General Conference*, Jerusalem, http://www.ifla.org/iv/ifla66/papers/112-126e.htm
Kinnell, Evans M., Usherwood, B., Jones, K., (1999), *Improving Library and Information services through self-assessment, a guide for senior managers and staff developers,* London, Library Association.
Kiran, K., Pauziaah, M. and Sossamma, G. (2006), "Quality management service at the University of Malaya Library", *Library Management*, Vol. 27 Nos 4/5, pp. 249-56.
Kostagiolas, A. P., Kitsiou, B. M. (2008), "Issues and perceptions for ISO 9000 implementation in Greek academic libraries", *Library Management,* Vol. 29 Nos 6/7, pp. 583-589.
Kostagiolas, A. P., Korkidi, M. (2008), "Strategic planning for municipal libraries in Greece", *New Library World*, Vol. 109 Nos 11/12, pp. 546-558.
Kumbar, R. D. (2004), "The importance of Marketing and Total Quality Management in Libaries", *Electronic Journal of Academic and Special Librarianship,* Vol. 5 No. 2/3, http://southernlibrarianship.icaap.org/content/v05n02/kumbar_r01.htm
Lilley, E., Usherwood, B. (2000), "Wanting it all: the relationship between expectations and the public's perceptions of public library services", *Library Management* Vol. 21 No. 1, pp. 13-24.
MacDougall A., Ofarrell J., Williams J. (1997), *EQLIPSE Evaluation and Quality in library performance: System Europe, final report and final specification (deliverable report 7)*, Dublin City University, Dublin Ireland.
Milner, E., Kinnell, M., Usherwood, B. (1997), Quality management and public library services, in *Quality management and benchmarking in the information sector,*Bowker-Saur.
O'Neil, R.M. (1994), *Total Quality Management in Libraries*, Libraries Unlimited, Englewood, CO.
Papazoglou A., Semertzaki E. (2001), "Changes and developments in Greek Libraries", *The Electronic Library*, Vol. 19 No. 3, pp. 158-167.
Parasuraman, A. (2004), "Assessing and improving service performance for maximum impact: insights from a two decade-long research journey", *Performance Measurement and Metrics*,

Vol. 5 No. 2, pp. 45-52.
Parasuraman, A., Zeithaml, V. and Berry, L.L. (1988), "SERVQUAL: a multiple-item scale for measuring consumer perceptions of service quality", *Journal of Retailing*, Vol. 64, pp. 12-37.
Pfeffer, N. and Coote, An. (1991), *Is Quality Good for You?, a critical review of quality assurance in welfare services,* London, Institute for Public Policy Research.
Poll, R. (2006), "Quality measures on a National Scale – comparison of projects", *World Library and Information Congress: 72nd IFLA General Conference and Council, Seoul, Korea* http://www.ifla.org/IV/ifla72/index.htm
Sacchetti, L. (2007), "ISO quality as a driver of continuous improvement", *Library Management*, Vol. 8 No. 2, pp. 88-97.
Sadeh, T. (2007), "Time for a change: new approaches for a new generation of library users", *New Library World*, Vol. 108 Nos 7/8, pp. 307-16.
Sadeh, T. (2008), "User experience in the library: a case study", New Library World, Vol. 109 Nos 1/2, pp. 7-24.
Siraj Nissa Begum, S. (2003), "Total Quality Management in the Academic Library", *Library Philosophy and Practice*, Vol. 5 No. 2, www.uidaho.edu?~mbolin/lppv5n2.htm..
Stewart, J., Walsh, K. (1989), *The search for quality*, Local Government Training Board.
Turk, N. (2007), "Building a culture of quality assurance in the libraries of the University of Ljubljana", *New Library World*, Vol. 108 No. 3, pp. 177-82.
Usherwood, B. (1995), "Quality Management and Public Library services", *International Conference on Performance Measurement in Libraries and Information Services*, Northumbria.
Valls, V.M. and Vergueiro, W. (2006), "Quality management on information services according to ISO 9000", *New Library World*, Vol. 107 Nos 1230/1231, pp. 523-37.
Wilson F., St. and Town J. (2006), "Benchmarking and library quality maturity", *Performance Measurement and Metrics*, Vol. 7 No. 2, pp. 75-82.

Library Investment Index -- Why is it Important?

Brinley Franklin[1], Colleen Cook[2], Martha Kyrillidou[3] and Bruce Thompson[4]

[1]University of Connecticut, USA
[2]Texas A&M University, USA
[3]Association of Research Libraries, USA,
[4]Texas A&M University and Baylor College of Medicine, USA

Abstract: The Association of Research Libraries(ARL) has engaged in the implementation of the Task Force on New Ways of Measuring Collections' recommendations and developed a new index, the Library Investment Index, originally called 'Expenditures-Focused Index' which was published in the *Chronicle of Higher Education* for the first time in 2007. The Expenditures-Focused Index was renamed in 2008 to the Library Investment Index to better reflect the notion that money spent on libraries is reflective of investments in intellectual, scholarly, and community capital. This paper offers a closer examination of the implications of the Library Investment Index (formerly known as Expenditures-Focused Index) and discusses its importance for the research and wider library community. It addresses both the methodological advantages and limitations as well as the political significance of the development of this index.

1. Introduction

In an environment where collections are morphing into terabytes, petabytes, exabytes, zettabytes, and yottabytes of information, it is questionable whether the units of volumes held, volumes added, and serial subscriptions can continue to offer the utility they had in the past. The challenge of measuring collections in new ways gave rise to the work of the Association of Research Libraries (ARL) Task Force on New Ways of Measuring Collections which engaged into a two year process and moved from debate on these issues into action. The Task Force was convened in December 2004 and built in much of the earlier work and debates that were engaging the ARL directors during the 1990s.[1] During its two-year investigation, the task force systematically collected qualitative feedback through one-on-one interviews with each ARL library director. During the second year of its operation, the task force deployed two top researchers in qualitative and quantitative methodologies, Yvonna Lincoln and Bruce Thompson. Two reports were produced for the ARL community: "Research Libraries as Knowledge Producers: A Shifting Context for Policy and Funding,"[2] documenting the results of the qualitative inquiry, and "Some Alternative Quantitative Library Activity Descriptions/Statistics That Supplement the ARL Logarithmic Index," documenting the results of the quantitative inquiry.[3]

2. ARL Task Force on New Ways of Measuring Collections: Interview Results

During the in-person interviews of the Task Force members with more than 100 ARL directors in the spring and summer of 2005, a number of key issues surfaced that needed to be addressed. Themes from these interviews highlighted that:

- Data is not expressing uniqueness of materials;
- Relevance to teaching, learning, research is not adequately reflected;
- Collections go beyond printed volumes;
- Research library is more than collections—it includes its services and ARL is not telling the story with the ARL Membership Criteria Index;
- Increase in expenditures for electronic resources is changing collections;
- Ownership and access are not contradictory approaches;
- Consortial relationships/cooperative collection development is increasingly important;
- Shared storage facilities are a necessity;
- Duplicate serials based on bundling is a huge problem for research libraries since quality control issues vary from product to product;
- Special collections are not reflected in our current statistics; and
- ARL Membership Committee does not use the Membership Index exclusively like it used to in the past as it takes into account qualitative indicators now.

Many directors recognized the historical significance of the long standing ARL Statistics[4] dataset to show trends, as a way of accounting for university investments, and its importance for comparison and benchmarking. But the voices expressing serious concerns with the ARL Membership Criteria Index were clear in that the Index is misunderstood, misleading, and unhelpful.

During the second year of the investigation, Bruce Thompson was engaged and did an exhaustive and thorough analysis of the ARL Statistics data attempting to identify additional patterns in the data though factor analysis. In his analysis, he confirmed the statistical validity of the ARL Membership Criteria Index and suggested an improved alternative, what came to be known as the Library Investment Index (or Expenditures-

Focused Index).

3. Task Force Recommendations

In February 2007, the result of the two year investigation of the Task Force resulted in the formation of an action agenda approved by the ARL Board of Directors, the ARL Task Force on New Ways of Measuring Collections, and the ARL Statistics and Assessment Committee. The action agenda has a number of R&D components but it stands as a practical approach to support research libraries as they are transforming their operations from what has been a 20th century approach into a 21st century approach. The practical and political readiness of different research libraries to adopt new ways of describing their operations varies and is presented in Figure 1. The action agenda offered a wise compromise that keeps what is valuable from the past and also helps libraries move boldly into new territory. A conscious decision was made to maintain the ARL Membership Criteria Index for institutional purposes but not publicize it in the Chronicle as it contains variables like volumes held, volumes added gross and current serial subscriptions that are volatile to transformative changes. For a stable way of describing libraries, the Task Force relied on the expenditures variables, and promoted and published it in the Chronicle of Higher Education the Library Investment Index.

Figure 1. New Ways of Measuring Collections: An Action Agenda Adopted February 2007

1. Reserve use of the current membership criteria index for those occasions when it is needed for consideration of membership issues.
2. Implement an expenditure-focused index.
3. Use the new expenditure-focused index for any public reports, such as in the Chronicle of Higher Education.
4. Begin to develop a services-based index that combines the following three factors: collections, services, and collaborative relationships.
5. Revise definitions for collections-related data categories currently collected and experiment with a variety of new measures, including usage data, strength of collections, and service quality measures to develop a richer set of variables for potential inclusion in the three-factor alternative index (see above).
6. Collect qualitative data to develop a profile of ARL member libraries.

Figure 2 presents the variables that are comprising the ARL Historical or Membership Criteria Index and the Library Investment Index. A special note is made here regarding the naming convention of the ARL Historical or Membership Criteria Index. Although the ARL Membership Criteria Index was historically used to determine membership, this is not the case any more as the membership criteria have been supplemented with qualitative indicators. Currently, the ARL Membership Criteria name is more a reflection of the history of the old practice of determining membership based on the index. Currently, it is used as only one indicator among many others to be taken into consideration when identifying potential candidate institutions for membership to ARL. Thus, we interchangeably refer to the ARL Membership Criteria Index as the Historical Criteria Index in this paper. The indicators that supplement the Historical Criteria Index are qualitative in nature and to date they have not been tested in an affirmative way as ARL has not accepted any new member libraries based on the combined (qualitative and quantitative) criteria. The new Library Investment Index is yet another way to supplement these criteria with an objective approach when considering potential members.

Figure 2. The Story of Two Indices

Historical Criteria Index or Membership Criteria Index	Library Investment Index (previously named Expenditures-focused Index)
• Volumes Held • Volumes added gross • Current Serials • Total Expenditures • Professional plus support staff	• Total Expenditures • Salary Expenditures • Materials Expenditures • Professional plus support staff

4. The Library Investment Index

As noted by Thompson in his report, the two indices correlate highly but there is a distinct advantage in using the Library Investment Index: "The use of a measure of total expenditures versus the use of some combination of (a) volume counts (historically part of the older statistics) and (b) expenditures on digital resources (only recently measured as part of the supplementary statistics) could (1) finesse the difficulty of distinguishing these two resources (2) while at the same time recognizing the changing face of the library in an increasingly digital world."[5]

Figure 3. Correlations between the ARL Membership Criteria Index and the Library Investment Index (formerly known as Expenditures-focused Index)

Correlations

		index03	rindx03 Rank of index03	expind03	re03 Rank of expind03
index03	Pearson Correlation	1	-.955**	.903**	-.911**
	Sig. (2-tailed)		.000	.000	.000
	N	113	113	113	113
rindx03 Rank of index03	Pearson Correlation	-.955**	1	-.785**	.943**
	Sig. (2-tailed)	.000		.000	.000
	N	113	113	113	113
expind03	Pearson Correlation	.903**	-.785**	1	-.817**
	Sig. (2-tailed)	.000	.000		.000
	N	113	113	113	113
re03 Rank of expind03	Pearson Correlation	-.911**	.943**	-.817**	1
	Sig. (2-tailed)	.000	.000	.000	
	N	113	113	113	113

**. Correlation is significant at the 0.01 level (2-tailed).

In Figure 3, we report the correlations between the two indices and their ranks for the 2002-03 ARL Statistics showing that all correlations coefficients are very high. The same analysis was performed for every year between 2002-03 and 2006-07, and shows strong correlations.

Figure 4 demonstrates the regression line between the ranks of the two indices based on the 2004-05 ARL Statistics data and shows that the relation between these two is again very strong (R-square =.88).

Figure 4. Regression of Rank of the Library Investment Index and the ARL Membership Criteria Index

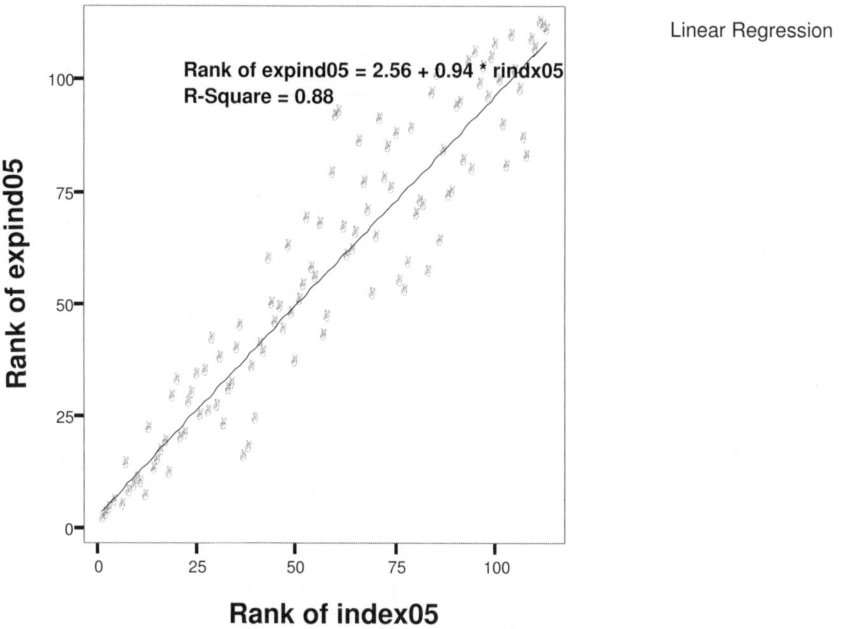

So, why is the Library Investment Index a better choice? As can be seen from Figure 5, the ARL Historical or Membership Criteria Index as calculated using the Principal Component Analysis Method every year has an eigenvalue that is lowering over the last few years year after year. The underlying factor is undergoing a gradual transformation primarily due to the serial subscriptions, volumes held and volumes added gross data.[6] As collections are transforming, the Historical Criteria Index is capturing this evolution alas resulting in a less robust indicator over time. Over time, the variance explained has been lowered from 90.5% in 2002-03 to 81.7% in 2006-07 (Figure 5). The Principal Component Analysis of the Library Investment Index on the other hand explained more than 92% of the variance and is stable over the same time period.

Figure 5. How Is the ARL Membership Criteria Index Changing?

ARL Historical Criteria Index (previously named ARL Membership Criteria Index)		
Variance Explained from Principal Component Analysis		
	eigenvalue	% of Variance
2002-03	4.53	90.50
2003-04	4.46	89.23
2004-05	4.40	87.94
2005-06	4.39	87.94
2006-07	4.08	81.7

External research also confirms that library expenditures relates to factors like institutional reputation. Sharon Weiner, Dean of Library Services, University of Massachusetts Dartmouth, published "The Contribution of the Library to the Reputation of a University"[7] where she explores the relationship between a peer-assessed reputation rating for doctoral universities with cross-institutional performance indicators for universities and their libraries, using the ARL Statistics among other sources. Weiner finds that library expenditures is the only consistently significant variable in this relationship. These findings are supportive of the ARL direction to make publicly available the Library Investment Index (formerly known as Expenditures-Focused Index).

5. Conclusion

Clearly 'measuring the size of library collections cannot be what it used to be.'[8] The continued work of collecting profile descriptions from ARL member libraries[9] as well as the potential of developing a three-factor index[10] hold promise for richer and more fulfilling ways of capturing the value of research libraries. Currently, we have a rich array of assessment tools which continues to be supplemented with new efforts and explorations describing effective and successful library services.

References

1. M. Kyrillidou and W. Crowe, "In Search of New Measures," *ARL: A Bimonthly Report* 197 (1998): 8-10, http://www.arl.org/bm~doc/newmeas-2.pdf; M. Kyrillidou, "Research Library Trends: ARL Statistics," *Journal of Academic Librarianship* 26 (2000):427-436; M. Kyrillidou, "To Describe and Measure the Performance of North American Research Libraries," *IFLA Journal* 4 (2001): 257-263; M. Kyrillidou, "From Input and Output Measures to Quality and

Outcome Measures, or, From the User in the Life of the Library to the Library in the Life of the User," *Journal of Academic Librarianship* 28 (2002): 42-46; and M. Kyrillidou, "Library Assessment as a Collaborative Enterprise," *Resource Sharing and Information Networks* (special issue of on the theme "Creative Collaborations: Libraries Within Their Institutions and Beyond") 1/2 (2005/2006): 73-87, http://www.libqual.org/documents/admin/kyrillidou_haworth_sept72004.pdf.

2. Yvonna Lincoln, "Research Libraries as Knowledge Producers: A Shifting Context for Policy and Funding: Final Technical Report to the Task Force on New Ways of Measuring Collections, Association of Research Libraries," Presented at the ARL Membership Meeting, October 18, 2006, http://www.arl.org/bm~doc/lincoln.pdf.

3. Bruce Thompson, "Some Alternative Quantitative Library Activity Descriptions/Statistics That Supplement the ARL Logarithmic Index," Presented at the ARL Membership Meeting, October 18, 2006, http://www.arl.org/bm~doc/bruce_3mk.pdf.

4. K. Stubbs, "University Libraries: Standards and Statistics," *College and Research Libraries* 42 (1981): 527-538; K. Stubbs, "On the ARL Library Index," Paper presented at the 108th meeting of Research Libraries: Measurement, Management, Marketing, Minneapolis, MN," 1986; K. Stubbs, "Lies, Damned Lies . . . and ARL Statistics?" Paper presented at the 108th meeting of Research Libraries: Measurement, Management, Marketing, Minneapolis, MN, 1986; K. Stubbs, "Apples and Oranges and ARL Statistics," *Journal of Academic Librarianship* 14 (1988): 231-235; K. Stubbs, "Access and ARL Membership Criteria," Proceedings of the 125th Meeting of the Association of Research Libraries, 1993, 117-122, http://www.arl.org/bm~doc/stubbs93.pdf; and M. Mekkawi, "The ARL Library Index as a Decision-making Tool," *College and Research Libraries* 43 (1982): 396-401.

5. Thompson, 19.

6. Martha Kyrillidou, "Reshaping ARL Statistics to Capture the New Environment" *ARL: A Bimonthly Report* 256 (2008) http://www.arl.org/bm~doc/arl-br-256-stats.pdf; Martha Kyrillidou, "The Impact of Electronic Publishing on Tracking Research Library Investments in Serials" *ARL: A Bimonthly Report* 249 (2006), http://www.arl.org/bm~doc/arlbr249serials.pdf.

7. S. Weiner, "The Contribution of the Library to the Reputation of a University." *Journal of Academic Librarianship* (2008), doi:10.1016/j.acalib.2008.10.003.

8. Kyrillidou, "Reshaping ARL Statistics to Capture the New Environment."

9. Lincoln.

10. Thompson.

8. Using Qualitative and Quantitative Methods in Digital Library Education and Research

Digital Library Education from the Information and Knowledge Management Perspective: Action Research Approach

Sirje Virkus

Tallinn University, Institute of Information Studies, Estonia
E-mail: sirvir@tlu.ee

Abstract: Preparing students to work in the digital environment is an important responsibility of library and information science (LIS) schools. While most LIS schools offer courses or modules related to different aspects of digital information management, there are few dedicated digital library programmes in Europe. This paper discusses an action research strategy used to examine the relevance and methods of teaching/learning information and knowledge management (IKM) within the Digital Library Learning (DILL) joint international master curriculum at Tallinn University.

Keywords: Action-research; Diagnostic analysis survey; Digital library education; Estonia.

1. Introduction

Preparing students to work in the digital environment is an important responsibility of library and information science (LIS) schools. While most LIS schools offer courses or modules related to different aspects of digital information management, there are few dedicated digital library programmes in Europe. This paper discusses an action research strategy used to examine the relevance and methods of teaching/learning information and knowledge management (IKM) within the Digital Library Learning (DILL) joint international master curriculum at Tallinn University (TU).

The paper is divided into four sections. The first section gives an overview of the Digital Library Learning curriculum at TU. The second discusses the origins and theoretical foundations of action research and pragmatic reasons for the use of this research strategy for improvement of the DILL programme at TU. The third provides an example of the diagnostic analysis survey as a method within the action research strategy to implement change in course development in the digital library educational programme at TU. Finally, some selected findings of the diagnostic analysis survey are presented in this paper.

2. International Master in Digital Library Learning

A joint international master programme on Digital Library Learning (DILL) is a two-year programme for information professionals who intend to work in the complex world of digital libraries. It is a joint programme between Oslo University College (Norway), Tallinn University (Estonia) and Parma University (Italy) which was supported in the framework of the European Union (EU) Erasmus Mundus programme. The students will acquire a joint Master's degree (120 ECTS) which is recognised by all three partners.

The learning objectives of the programme as follows:

- to develop knowledge and skills of digital librarianship through studying the cutting edge of digital library research as well as real world applications and best practices;
- to develop research skills through independent, yet supervised, research projects within the digital environment, applying relevant methods and analytical approaches;
- to understand the impact of digital environments on the role of information professionals in the knowledge society.

DILL is delivered on campus, and the students spend one term at each partner institution. The first three terms consist of six modules, each amounting to 15 ECTS. In the first semester at Oslo University College in Norway two modules are offered: (1) Research Methods and Theory of Science and (2) Digital Documents. In the second semester at Tallinn University in Estonia the following modules are offered: (1) Information and Knowledge Management and (2) Human Resource Management. In the third semester at Parma University in Italy two modules are offered: (1) Access to Digital Libraries and (2) Usage of Digital Libraries: Quantitative and Qualitative Evaluation. In the last term the students write their Master's Thesis amounting to 30 ECTS. Students can choose to write their Master's thesis at either of the three partner institutions; this depends on the topic and the location of the main supervisor.

There is a growing interest in the DILL programme; 101 applications were submitted in 2007; 204 applications in 2008 and 247 applications in 2009. Students from third-countries can apply for European Commission (EC) Erasmus Mundus scholarships.

The dominant paradigm that informs learning and teaching at the Institute of Information Studies (IIS) at TU is constructivism. The central principle of constructivism is that knowledge cannot be transmitted to learners but must be "individually constructed and socially co-constructed by learners based on their interpretations of experiences in the world" (Jonassen 1999, p. 217). The IIS has also experimented with ICT-based teaching and learning methods and tools since 1994 and recently social software has been used to support the learning process (Virkus, 2008). Therefore, teachers focus more on coaching and tutoring activities rather than delivering lectures and the functionality of ICT as well as social software are used to support the learning process. This also applies to the DILL programme.

As stated earlier, one of the modules offered in the DILL programme by the IIS at TU is *Information and Knowledge Management* (IKM). IKM is quite a wide area of study. There are many Information Management (IM) programmes and several

Knowledge Management (KM) programmes at master's level and many IM and KM courses within various library and information science (LIS) programmes. Widen-Wulf et al (2005) evaluated IM modules in nine different programmes and KM modules in ten different schools in Europe; from the KM programme descriptions 64 different topics and from the IM programmes 36 different topics were identified. Therefore, offering the IKM module consisting of 15 ECTS was a real challenge.

3. Action Research Approach

An action research (AR) strategy was chosen in order to examine the relevance and methods of teaching/learning IKM within the DILL programme at TU. The AR strategy is particularly suited to research in the field of education as it helps researching teachers to resolve their own teaching challenges. This strategy was well suited to our goal of developing an IKM module for DILL students and improving the module to respond to the needs of the diverse student body. The researcher was at the same time the designer of the module, as well as a lecturer delivering content in the module.

The present research addresses the following questions:

- How can the IKM module be implemented in the DILL programme?
- What are the barriers to implementation?
- What are the potentials for implementation?
- How might they be overcome/implemented?

There are a number of AR definitions available in the literature. Carr and Kemmis (1986, p.162) provide the following definition of AR:

> Action Research is a form of self-reflective enquiry undertaken by the participants (teachers, students or principals, for example) in social (including educational) situations in order to improve the rationality and justice of (a) their own social or educational practices, (b) their understanding of these practices, and (c) the situations (and institutions) in which these practices are carried out.

Elliott (1991, p.69) put it in this way: AR is "the study of a social situation with a view to improving the quality of action within it." Mills (2003, p.4) defines the AR the following way:

> Action research is any systematic inquiry conducted by teacher researchers to gather information about the ways that their particular school operates, how they teach, and how well their students learn. The information is gathered with the goals of gaining insight, developing reflective practice, effecting positive changes in the school environment and on educational practices in general, and improving student outcomes.

According to Robson (2002) the purpose of the AR is to influence or change some aspect of whatever is the focus of the research. It adds the promotion of change to the traditional research purposes of description, understanding and explanation. Improvement and involvement are central to AR. AR is not only about research but also about action. Its aims are the improvement of a practice of some kind, the improvement of the understanding of a practice by its practitioners, and the improvement of the situation in which the practice takes place (p.215). Thus, AR is "learning by doing" - the researcher aims to identify and gain a better understanding of real world problems, find solutions for them, see how successful their efforts were, and if not satisfied, try again (O'Brien, 2001). AR is a participatory research; collaboration between the researcher and those who are the focus of the research are seen as central to AR (Robson, 2002, p.215).

Kemmis and Wilkinson (1998, p.21) refer to AR as a spiral or cyclical process. There are four basic steps in the AR cycle: planning, action, observation, reflection/review/change. What separates this type of research from general professional practices is that "the researcher studies the problem systematically and ensures the intervention is informed by theoretical considerations" (O'Brien, 2001). Riding et al (1995) note that AR methodology also offers a systematic approach to introducing innovations in teaching and learning.

AR is used in real situations, rather than in experimental studies, and in situations which require flexibility, the involvement of the people in the research, or where change must take place quickly or holistically (O'Brien, 2001). Educational AR has its foundations in the writings of John Dewey, who believed that professional educators should become involved in community problem-solving. Therefore, it is not surprising that many practitioners operate mainly in educational institutions wishing to improve their practice and focus on development of curriculum, professional development, and applying learning in a social context (O'Brien, 2001, Dick, 2006).

However, AR has a long history. Kurt Lewin, a German social and experimental psychologist, was the person who first used the term 'action research' in his 1946 paper *Action Research and Minority Problems*. He viewed AR as a way of learning about organizations through trying to change them (O'Brien, 2001). Eric Trist, Lawrence Stenhouse, John Elliott, Stephen Kemmis, David Hamilton, Dave Ebbutt and Jack Whitehead have contributed significantly to this methodology. By the mid-1970s, four main 'streams' had emerged: traditional, contextural (action learning), radical, and educational AR (O'Brien, 2001). However, this paper does not propose to trace the history of AR as this has been done by several authors (e.g. McNiff, 1992; Greenwood and Levin, 1998; Reason and Bradbury, 2001). AR is also known by many other names, including participatory research, participatory action research, collaborative inquiry, emancipatory research, action learning and contextual action research (O'Brien, 2001).

AR is considered to be a form of qualitative research and methods used are those which are generally common to the qualitative research paradigm. However, within the AR strategy there are a wide variety of research methods and techniques: document collection and analysis, participant observation, questionnaire surveys, structured and unstructured interviews. The triangulation of viewpoints and methods is also important in AR.

The main concern designing the IKM module within the DILL programme was that students had very diverse backgrounds, education, culture and experiences and their levels of preparation was not uniform. Early intervention was necessary so that we were able to identify deficiencies, obstacles, preferred teaching and learning methods and media, and make adjustments early in order to help students to gain the required competencies.

Different methods were used to decide how to deliver the IKM module as well as improving the module within the DILL programme: a literature review, a web survey of course and programme descriptions on the sites of LIS schools, expert interviews, a diagnostic analysis survey, observations, a course evaluation survey, and focus group interviews were all undertaken.

On the basis of the literature review, the web survey of course/programme descriptions on the sites of LIS schools and expert interviews the core topic areas were selected and were divided into the five meta categories - contents, context, process, people, and information technology - suggested by Widen-Wulf et al (2005). The learning outcomes were developed and divided into the five categories: knowledge and understanding, cognitive/intellectual skills, practical skills, key/transferable skills and intercultural competencies.

The constructivist approach where learners actively construct their knowledge based on their own experiences and learning is regarded as a social process provided the pedagogical basis for the IKM module. There was less focus on the acquisition of facts and on teaching and more on learning processes, knowledge generation, meta-cognition, self monitoring and on guided support.

The pedagogic approach used at IIS also advocates the use of variety of technology and media for curriculum delivery and student support. Students attending face to face seminars in campus are using the virtual learning environment IVA which is used to facilitate academic community building, the practice of communication skills and to provide resources and tools to support the learning process (Virkus, 2008).

The IKM module also attempts to provide different perspectives and views on IKM by inviting experts to contribute to the DILL programme on campus or via ICT tools. Robert M. Hayes, Michael E. D. Koenig and Ronald E. Day from the United States, Abdus Sattar Chaudhry from Singapore, Gillian Oliver from New Zealand, Peter Ingwersen from Denmark and Tom Wilson from the United Kingdom are just a few examples of experts who contributed to the IKM module.

The IKM module makes use of a range of different learning materials and resources and different ways of learning. In this module both formative and summative evaluation techniques were intensively used. The major final assignment is a collaborative problem-based group project.

However, while different methods were used in this AR strategy to develop and improve the IKM module, this paper focuses only on the diagnostic analysis survey. This is for two reasons: firstly to demonstrate the use of this particular tool in an educational setting, and secondly to use findings from the survey to show why AR is appropriate and necessary.

4. Diagnostic Analysis Survey

Few studies have discussed the methodological approaches of diagnostic analysis (DA) in any depth. These studies are mainly from the field of medicine or organisational development. A diagnostic analysis requires gathering information prior to the implementation of change, and is designed to identify the barriers and facilitators within a programme or course that may frustrate or facilitate the uptake of change (Hamilton et al, 2007).

The goal of the DA survey in this study was to clarify the needs and expectations of the learners for the IKM module with regard to the content and delivery options. It was expected that it would enable us to tailor the IKM module in the best way to suit students' requirements within the framework that had been set.

The objectives of the DA survey were:

- To gain information about the students' existing knowledge about IKM, prior to the commencement of the module so that the module can be delivered at the right level.
- To identify which topics and components of the module, as set out in the original specification, are the most enthusiastically regarded by the participants, and which are likely to be the most useful for them in their future work.
- To identify students' preferences concerning course organisation and delivery methods.
- To gain specific information about access to and familiarity with the technology available to the participants.

The data was collected during both the 2007/2008 academic year and the 2008/2009. Eighteen DILL students in the 2007/2008 academic year and twenty one DILL students in the 2008/2009 academic year formed the target group. In 2007/2008 the diagnostic analysis survey was carried out during an orientation week in February, one week before the IKM module started at Tallinn University. In 2008/2009 it was conducted two months before the IKM module started (in the period when students studied in Oslo) which gave more time to implement change.

The data collection tool was a questionnaire. The questionnaire included qualitative free text responses and a limited number of quantitative tick boxes. The DA questionnaire was divided into five sections: (i) Background Information, (ii) Course Content, (iii) Learning and Teaching Process, (iv) Technical Support and Skills, and (v) Media Preferences.

The *Background Information* section requested demographic information including name, gender, age, country and previous job of the student.

The *Course Content* section asked questions about previous experiences with IKM, the main authors who had influenced students' thinking about the IKM field, familiarity with IKM topics, the most relevant topics for them, and suggestions for module content.

The *Learning and Teaching Process* section asked questions about students' learning experiences; for example, this section included the following questions: Which methods of training and support would you find most suitable? How would you rate the barriers in affecting your participation in courses? What are the main obstacles you regularly encounter in learning? What kind of training could help alleviate these? What experiences (negative and positive) you have had with different learning methods? How do you prefer to learn (learning style)?

The *Technical Support and Skills* section asked questions about the familiarity and usage of ICT tools and social software.

The *Media Preferences* section tried to find out what is the preferred way of distributing learning materials for them, what file formats do they prefer for

electronic learning materials, and what is, according to their experiences, the most effective communication channel during the course.
At the end of the DA questionnaire respondents were asked to provide additional comments under the question 'Is there anything else that you'd like us to know?'

5. Examples of Selected Results

The examples presented in this section are just some selected results from the DA survey. This data has been selected in order to demonstrate the suitability of action research in this setting.

Background Information

The demographic information requested included name, gender, age, country and previous job of the student. In the 2007/2008 academic year there were eighteen students from 16 countries; students were from Australia, Canada (2 students), Colombia, Ethiopia (2 students), Ghana, India, Indonesia, Italy, Kenya, Kosovo, Kyrgyzstan, Laos, Maldives, South Africa, Tanzania and Thailand. In the 2008/2009 academic year twenty one students from 15 countries studied the programme: from Bosnia and Herzegovina, Botswana (2 students), Ethiopia (2 students), Ghana (2 students), Indonesia, Iran, Italy, Kenya, Nigeria (2 students), Taiwan, Thailand (2 students), Uganda, USA, Venezuela and Vietnam (2 students). In 2007/2008 there were eleven female and seven male students, in 2008/2009 fourteen female and seven male students studied the programme. The youngest student was 22 years old and the oldest student 52 years old with an average age of 34 in 2007/2008. In 2008/2009 the youngest student was 24 years old and the oldest student 44 years old with an average age of 30. In 2007/2008 ten students had worked as a librarian, two students as a lecturer in a university and six students had other jobs. In 2008/2009 thirteen students had worked as a librarian, three students as a lecturer in a university and five students had other jobs.

Table 1: Student demographics

2007/2008	*2008/2009*
18 students from 16 countries	21 students from 15 countries
Sex: 11 female and 7 male students	Sex: 14 female and 7 male students
Age: 22<52 (average age 34)	Age: 24<44 (average age 30)
Previous job - Librarian - 10 - Lecturer – 2 - Other - 6	Previous job - Librarian - 13 - Lecturer – 3 - Other – 5

Course Content

This section asked questions about previous experiences with IKM, the main authors who had influenced students' thinking about the IKM field, familiarity with IKM topics, the most relevant topics for them, and suggestions for the module content.
The main authors who had influenced students' thinking in the IKM field were

Thomas H. Davenport, Ikujiro Nonaka, Hirotaka Takeuchi and Tom Wilson. However, only a limited number of students answered this question.
Students were asked to indicate their familiarity with the IKM topics on the scale where 1 was 'no clue' and 10 'it's my research area'. Familiarity with the proposed IKM topics varied considerably among students in the academic year 2007/2008 as well as 2008/2009. There had some students who assessed their competence level highly (it's my research area), but the majority of students assessed their competence level from 1 to 3 on the proposed scale. Table 2 illustrates the results of the 2008/2009 academic year. The first number illustrates the lowest competence level and the last number the highest competence level indicated by students within this topic area.

Table 2: Students familiarity with the IKM Topics in the 2008/2009 academic year

IKM Topic Area	*Familiarity*
Development of IKM	1-2
Key Concepts of IKM	1-10
Dimensions & approaches towards the nature, role & value of IKM in organizations	1-4
Historical traditions that have informed IKM theory and models	1-5
IKM and organizational culture	1-6
IKM Cycle: Knowledge Codification, Coordination, Transfer & Sharing	1-8
IKM Process: Knowledge creation, information storage & retrieval, information seeking, tools & techniques for information dissemination	1-10
IKM Technologies. Information systems and design	1-10
IKM tools and projects in practice	1-10
Strategic and planning issues, ideas of intellectual capital	1-3
Information use through learning processes, networking and collaboration. Individual and social learning	1-10
Learning and digital library	1-10
Information-related competencies in education & in the workplace	1-10

Students were asked to choose five out of the afore mentioned areas which were the most relevant for their studies. The most relevant topics in 2008/2009 were:

- IKM Process: Knowledge creation, information storage and retrieval, information seeking, tools & techniques for information dissemination (mentioned by 13 students).

- Learning and digital library (13 students).
- IKM Technologies. Information systems and design (12 students).
- IKM Cycle: Knowledge Codification, Coordination, Transfer & Sharing (9 students).
- Information use through learning processes, networking and collaboration. Individual and social learning (9 students).
- IKM tools and projects in practice (9 students).
- Information-related competencies in education and in the workplace (7 students).
- Key concepts of IKM (6 students).
- IKM and organizational culture (6 students).
- Development of IKM (5 students).
- Dimensions & approaches towards the nature, role & value of IKM in organizations (5 students).
- Historical traditions that have informed IKM theory and models (3 students).
- Strategic and planning issues, including ideas of intellectual capital (2 students).

At the end of this section students were asked to provide additional comments under the question 'Anything else you would like to know in the field of IKM?'. The areas suggested by students in the academic year 2008/2009 included, for example, evaluating reliable and accurate information resources, evaluation of good management practices, knowledge mapping in digital environments, best practices in digital libraries, community practices, issues in third countries and in government organizations, and e-learning solutions.

Learning and Teaching Process

The students were asked for their opinions relating to the most and less suitable methods of training and support. In 2007/2008 the most suitable methods of training and support were seminars, lectures (listen and learn), discussions, practical 'hands on' and case studies. In 2008/2009 the students favoured demos/experiments, practical 'hands on', case studies, a field work and coaching/mentoring/one-to-one learning. In 2007/2008 the less suitable methods of training and support were role play, coaching/mentoring/one-to-one learning, group work, demos/experiments and multimedia (video/ computer-based) learning. In 2008/2009 the less suitable methods of training and support were assessments, discussions/sharing of experience, group work, lectures and seminars.

However, there were quite different opinions relating to the most and less suitable methods of training and support among students in 2007/2008 and in 2008/2009. For example, demos/experiments were the most suitable methods of training and support in 2008/2009, but the less suitable in 2007/2008.

The main obstacles encountered in learning in 2008/2009 were lack of previous experience, lack of good English language skills, lack of ICT skills, too long and intensive courses, too many readings in electronic form, poor communication and teaching skills. The following answers illustrate some of these obstacles:

> "If the course is a totally new area/field and the lecturing of such course is of high speed it might constitute an obstacle"
>
> "My English writing skills. I spend a lot of time to write an essay"
>
> "When the lecturer does not explain particular concepts well. That is when he or she just mentions a point but does not explain it"
>
> "Well, I prefer reading the print text because of my eyes condition. Reading about three hours on the system gives my eyes problems".

Students were asked for their opinions of what kind of training could help alleviate their learning obstacles. The following answers in 2008/2009 suggest that the teacher/tutor has an important role to play to support students:

> "Starting from the simple areas then gradually proceed to the complex ones"
>
> "More attention and simplified methods"
>
> "By giving a guidance to tell us which one is basic and suitable to start and which ones are advanced"
>
> "Give practical example. Interaction with the students and teacher relationships"

Students were also asked to describe negative and positive experiences they have had with different learning methods. One student notes:

> "Lectures, only listen to lectures; have no chance to feedback. This method makes students negative in learning and understanding"

Other students answered:

> "I like to have assignments throughout the course. Too much pressure to have the whole grade dependent on 1 project or exam! Also, I don't care for presentations…"
>
> "Negative – I can't understand what lecturers' saying because they talk too fast. Positive – I'm starting to like to work in a group (previously I really hate to work in a group)"

Some answers from the DA survey in the academic year 2007/2008 illustrate the way DILL students' prefer to learn:

> "Individually – I like to study in my own. I like to complete assignments throughout the course and to get feedback, NOT have 1 huge assignment or exam that determines my whole grade. Constructive feedback is very important – helps me to gauge my progress. I feel like I learn better this way – I know that the instructor and I are on the same pace"
>
> "I would like to try new and different ways because in my country we have a tradition of memorizing and listening to long lectures, I'm not opposed to it, but I would like a mixture of styles"
>
> "I'm very serendipitous, I like taking different and sometimes original topic to explore. Sometimes this approach leads me in fields that I don't understand, in which I have few competencies. I always like someone who can drive me on relevant topics, questions, issues, documents. I like to cultivate my personal knowledge, but at then sometime have the opportunity to have someone that drives me, and doesn't make me be lost".

Technical Support and Skills

The survey also aimed to determine the students' familiarity with several ICT applications and social software tools. This was vital because having a clear idea of the individual practices of students using various applications would inform any future decisions about how to use these applications effectively within the IKM module.

The majority of students in the academic year 2007/2008 and 2008/2009 knew how to use MS Excel and PowerPoint applications. Fewer students know how to design a webpage, use the audio/video conferencing tools and create databases using MS Access. Only two students out of both groups of students know how to use javascript.

Table 3: Students' familiarity with ICT applications

	2007/2008 N=18	*2008/2009 N=21*
I know how to use Microsoft Excel	17	17
I can use PowerPoint for making presentations	18	19
I know how to design a webpage	11	9
I can create databases using Microsoft Access	11	7
I can use the audio/video conferencing tools	9	10
I know how to use javascript	1	1

The majority of students in the academic year 2007/2008 and 2008/2009 were familiar with Skype. Fewer were familiar with other social software tools and only four students out of both groups of students had experiences with Second Life.

Table 4: Students' familiarity with social software tools

	2007/2008 N=18	*2008/2009 N=21*
Skype	17	20
Blogs	13	17
Wikis	10	15
Tagging	11	14
Flickr	10	9
Podcasts	4	6
Second Life	2	2

Media Preferences

The purpose of this section was to find out what students preferences were with regard to the distribution of learning materials, what file formats they prefer for electronic learning materials, and what they have found to be the most effective communication channel during the course.

In the 2007/2008 academic year printed textbooks, photocopies (readers etc) and publicly available electronic documents on the WWW were the most preferred learning materials for students. In the 2008/2009 academic year electronic documents in the virtual learning environment or learning management system were the most favoured document format. Learning materials on CD-ROMs were not preferred by either group of students. Table 5 illustrates students' media preferences; 1 means highly preferred and 5 less preferred.

Table 5: Student preferences with respect to distribution of learning materials

	2007/2008	*2008/2009*
Printed textbooks	1	2
Photocopies (readers etc)	1	5
On CD-ROMs	4	6
Electronic documents in the LMS/VLE	2	1
Publicly available electronic documents on the WWW	1	3
E-mails (or attachments)	3	4

One student also noted:

> "I'd prefer open format, because I use Linux, I like to act and annotate documents. So I prefer printed one but leaving them online is fundamental, too. We can always print them".

However, there were some differences relating to preferences for some of the formats. For example, photocopies were a highly preferred form in 2007/2008, then in 2008/2009 photocopies were less preferred.

6. Conclusions

Action research has proved to be a very valuable method in educational settings. AR is about analysing and reflecting about your professional practice and going through a cycle of change. It is believed that teachers are more effective in educational practices if they are active participants in educational research.

The diagnostic analysis survey proved to be a useful tool in IKM module improvement and enabled us to tailor the module in the best way to suit students' requirements and improve the quality of the student learning experience. However, AR should be a continuous process in the educational institutions to better serve the needs of a varied student population. The differences in the data collected for these two cohorts of the DILL programme have clearly demonstrated that we cannot assume one homogenous approach to course delivery of the IKM module can be developed and implemented for all subsequent intakes. On the contrary, ongoing review, flexibility in design and evaluation of course delivery are essential, so an action research strategy provides the ideal framework to achieve these objectives.

References

Carr, W. and Kemmis, S. (1986). *Becoming critical: education, knowledge and action research.* London: Falmer Press.

Dick, B. 2006. Action research literature 2004-2006: themes and trends. *Action Research,* 4(4), 439-458.

Elliott, J. (1991). *Action research for educational change.* Milton Keynes: Open University Press.

Greenwood, D. J. and Levin, M. (2007). *Introduction to action research: social research for social change*. 2nd ed. Thousand Oaks, CA: Sage.

Hamilton, S., McLaren, S. and Mulhall, A. (2007). Assessing organisational readiness for change: use of diagnostic analysis prior to the implementation of a multidisciplinary assessment for acute stroke care. *Implementation Science* [online], 2 (21). URL: http://ukpmc.ac.uk/articlerender.cgi?artid=1052478 [accessed 20.5.09].

Jonassen, D. (1999). Designing constructivist learning environments. In: C. M. Reigeluth, C. M. (ed.). *Instructional design theories and models: a new paradigm of instructional theory*. Marwah: Lawrence Erlbaum Associates, Publishers, pp.15-240.

Kemmis, S. and Wilkinson, M. (1998). Participatory action research and the study of practice. In: B. Atweh, S. Kemmis, and P. Weeks (eds). *Action research in practice: partnership for social justice in education*. London: Routledge, pp. 21-38.

McNiff, J. (1992). *Action research: principles and practice*. London: Routledge.

Mills, G. E. (2003). *Action research: a guide for the teacher researcher*. 2nd ed. New Jersey: Merrill Prentice Hall.

O'Brien, R. (2001). Theory and Practice of Action Research [online]. URL: http://www.web.ca/~robrien/papers/arfinal.html [accessed 20.5.09].

Riding, P., Fowell, S. and Levy, P. (1995). An action research approach to curriculum development. *Information Research* [online], 1(1) URL: http://InformationR.net/ir/1-1/paper2.html [accessed 20.5.09].

Robson, C. (2002). *Real world research: a resource for social scientists and practitioner-researchers*. 2nd ed. Oxford: Blackwell.

Reason, P. and Bradbury, H. (2008). Handbook of action research: participative inquiry and practice. 2nd ed. London: Sage.

Virkus, S. (2008). Use of Web 2.0 technologies in LIS education: experiences at Tallinn University, Estonia. *Program: Electronic Library and Information Systems*, 3, 262 - 274.

Widen-Wulf, G. et al. (2005). Knowledge Management/Information Management. In: L. Kajberg and L. Lorring (eds.) *European curriculum reflections on library and information science education*. Copenhagen: The Royal School of Library and Information Science, 2005, pp. 121-132.

The Role of Open Access in Fostering Knowledge Sharing and Collaboration in Ethiopia: A Case Study

Getaneh Agegn Alemu

Institute of Information Studies, Tallinn University, Estonia
International Master in Digital Library Learning
E-mail: getaneh@gmail.com

Abstract: Only science, technology and research would alleviate the intertwined social and economic challenges of developing nations such as Ethiopia. This study adopts a qualitative approach and uses the case study method. Fourteen researchers and librarians were interviewed in four organizations in Addis Ababa, Ethiopia. This study reveals that the current scholarly communication system in Ethiopia is faced with technological and social challenges. Open access is undoubtedly a viable alternative to Ethiopia. It is viable because it has been proved so in many developing countries. Ethiopian universities and research institutions should adopt open access policies and strategies that would improve the access and dissemination of scientific research results. A concerted effort is required from administrators, librarians, researchers, funding agencies and government to implement and fully harness open access in Ethiopia.

Keywords: Open access; Scholarly communication; Institutional repositories; ETD; developing countries; Ethiopia.

1. Introduction

As a distinctive resource, knowledge favours openness and expands through sharing, use and re-use. As pointed out by Arunachalam (2008:7) "knowledge wants to be free". In an earlier article, Arunachalam (2003:pp.16) said "*The quest for exploring unknown territories – the loneliness of a long-distance runner – is the personal aspect. But aggregation and advancement of knowledge takes place by collective efforts of researchers around the world.*" This quest for sharing and openness in science in fact led to the flourishing of new disciplines, professional associations, and communities of practice in which all led to scientific discoveries and innovations. Most of these discoveries and findings have been communicated through journals, conference proceedings and other kinds of formal and informal communication outlets. Especially journals have served as main means of scholarly communication mediums.

The history of journal publishing goes back to 1665 when Henry Oldenburg, the secretary of the Royal Society of London, began to compile and distribute the correspondences of the members of society in a journal named "*Philosophical Transactions of the Royal Society of London*" (Willinsky, 2006; Swan, 2006; & Solomon, 2008). Before 1665, scholars used to communicate using hand written letters and had to make a copy of each correspondence and distribute it to other scholars (Solomon, 2008).

Currently there are more than 25,000 journals and they publish 2.5 million articles per year (Dewatripont at al., 2006; Canessa & Zennaro, 2008). Most of these journals are subscription-based (toll-access) where the reader or his/her institution has to pay a fee to access to the contents. This model has served scientists well until the prices of journals began steeping to a level where even richer universities such as Harvard were unable to afford to subscribe all or most of these huge numbers of journals. Exorbitant journal prices have forced academic institutions and libraries to cut journal subscriptions. Open access is a response to what is known as the "serials crisis". Solomon (2008) claims that the serials crisis covers the time between1970s to the present and it has left many researchers with limited access to peer-review scholarly literature (Chang, 2006; Salo, 2008; Pappalardo, 2008).

While the digital divide continues to widen, the disparity in access to scientific publications between the scholars from developed and developing countries also continues to expand. Ondari-Okemwa (2007) conducted an empirical study by extracting articles indexed from 1997-2007 by the Science Citation Index, the Social Sciences Citation Index and the Arts and Humanities Citation Index and compared developing countries research output with that of developed countries. The findings were rather staggering. From the years 1997-2007, only 235 articles from DR Congo and only 2747 articles from Ethiopia had been indexed. As one may expect, South Africa leads Sub-Saharan countries with 51,738 indexed. On the other hand, in the year 2006 alone, USA and UK produced 100,000 and 97,904 records of scholarly publications respectively. While margins of error for such research remain possible, the figures are a perfect example of the knowledge divide between the developed and developing countries.

Open access is claimed to be one of the solutions to bring scientists on a relatively equal footing in terms of access to knowledge hence researchers in developing countries can disseminate and access scholarly knowledge. The question which open access scholarly model suits to these countries and how open access can be best harnessed remains to be explored. There exists no research on open access in Ethiopia. This research will illuminate the practicalities and procedures of how open access scholarly communication models could foster and support knowledge sharing and collaboration among Ethiopian researchers. Based on the findings, the recommendations will delineate steps that can be taken by university academics and librarians in Ethiopia to best harness and contextualize open access initiatives to their needs.

2. Methodology

2.1. Case Study as a Method

A case study research method is employed in order to obtain information and understand the awareness about open access and explore how open access would improve the research uptake, collaboration and knowledge sharing among researchers in Ethiopia. According to Yin (2003) case study is a preferred strategy to address the how and why research questions. A case study is a well-suited strategy to empirically investigate "contemporary phenomena" such as open access and its context Ethiopian universities and research institutions. The research problems lend themselves for a case study research because of the need to answer the how and why. Observation and literature showed that there has been little or no effort made to implement open access in Ethiopia. It was therefore a new phenomenon.

Qualitative: The study is qualitative because this approach suits best for a new phenomenon which has not penetrated the daily activities of subjects. If open access had been fully implemented; it would have been much easier to answer the research questions using quantitative research methods. It would have been for example possible to answer the number of articles submitted, accepted, published, the download rate, impact factor and type of software used, standards implemented, and related questions which would easily provide quantitative figures. However, open access has not been implemented in Ethiopia hence qualitative data analysis was preferred.

The case: the case in this case study is "open access". In this research, open access is assumed as contemporary a phenomenon that has been initiated by and for researchers, librarians, and funding agencies. Case study, as a research strategy, is best suited to investigate such interventions (Yin, 2003; Pickard, 2007). Semi-structured interview technique is chosen to collect data from researchers and librarians about open access within their respective institutions.

Controlling bias: Qualitative research and analysis is shaped by both the subject's and researchers' characteristics such as experiences, qualifications and even biases (Warden and Wong, 2007). The researcher of this study has been exposed to several discussions, workshops, lectures and readings about open access and its impact in research. There is a possible bias towards the benefit of open access to developing countries. Some biases are unavoidable. Care has, however, been taken to avoid unnecessary bias.

Interpretive: qualitative data analysis is interpretive (Ezzy, 2002). In this research the case is open access. Open access is considered as a phenomenon that would affect the subjects of this research who are mainly academic researchers and librarians working within a university or research institution context. In fact, whether open access has made significant effects or not, will be seen in this study. The subjects of the research and the researcher's interaction will create an interactive and iterative environment that will enable to collect enough evidences about the case.

Sampling: a purposeful sampling technique was adopted for this research. According to (Ezzy, 2002), a purposeful sample is selected by convenience and ease of use. In this case study, 4 librarians and 4 academic staff members (researchers) from Addis Ababa University; 1 librarian from the International Livestock Research Institute (ILRI) InfoCentre; 2 staff members of Ethiopian Development Research Institute (EDRI) (1 librarian and 1 researchers); 1 staff member of the Ethiopian Ministry of Science and Technology (EMOST), and 2 Ethiopian academics writing their PhD thesis in the UK were interviewed. The information gathered from interviews, websites, reports and secondary sources from these mix of institutions is believed to be representative to inform about the Ethiopian scholarly communication systems.

Context: Warden and Wong (2007, pp.6) argue that because of the context of a qualitative analysis, "meaning is tied to a specific setting and population and it will change over time". The questions asked for this research would bring a different answer over time ones for example a specific technology has changed or a new training has been offered about open access. The awareness of open access by researchers would certainly be different over the next year or so because of possible training interventions in that regard.

Iterative process: Warden and Wong (2007) mention that qualitative analysis is iterative. In the context of this research, the researcher used such approach in order to verify facts or fill gaps that has been forgotten or uncovered during the initial investigation. According to Srivastava and Hopwood (2009: pp.1) argue that an iterative process or qualitative data analysis should be considered "not as a repetitive mechanical task but as a reflexive process, is key to sparking insight and developing meaning". Hence, for Srivastava and Hopwood (2009) the visiting and re-visiting of the facts helps to verify it and also gain a new insight and helps to refine the focus of the research. Additional meetings, phone calls, email exchanges were made. Websites were revisited to verify information that was vague during interview transcriptions and to provide more context to it hence gather meaning out of it.

2.2. Data Collection

Interview method was chosen to collect data from researchers and librarians about open access within their respective institutions. The interview method was therefore preferred from questionnaire as it provides richer information that may be arisen out of the face-to-face conversations. The researcher has observed and read that open access in Ethiopia has not really been a focus of attention. Considering the fact that the awareness about open access is very low in the country, asking researchers and librarians what open access models and strategies they prefer, what kind of software they use for institutional repositories, and which open access journals they use to publish would only provide with limited or no relevant information for the research. Hence the interviewer has to first define and explain about open access. Interviewees were first contacted via email or telephone and asked to cooperate to share their views about open access to scholarly research in Ethiopia. The consent of interviewees was asked in order to voice record the responses and discussions arisen out of the interview and were digitally recorded. All but one of the interviews was conducted in Amharic.

2.3. Limitations of the Study

There exists no research on open access in Ethiopia, hence supporting it with evidence from related literature on the topic was difficult. Due to time constraints, it was not possible to include the regional universities and research institutions in Ethiopia. Only 14 interviewees were selected by convenience.

3. Findings and Recommendations

This section reports and discusses the results obtained through interviews. The responses and observation revealed that the scholarly communication system in Ethiopia is very weak. The research that has been produced does not reach its intended user. Open access initiatives have not made any significant inroads in Ethiopia. There are no institutional repositories to archive research results. There are no open access journals either. The low open access uptake is attributed to both social and infrastructural challenges. Based on the findings, this research provides recommendations on how to implement open access in Ethiopia.

3.1. Access to Electronic Resources (e-journals)

The government of Ethiopia funds public universities and research institutes to subscribe to books and journals. This budget is however very limited. The limited budget does not allow universities to subscribe to international journals. Most of the interviewees reported that their respective institutions do not subscribe to peer-reviewed journals. The results of the interviews revealed that over the last few years Ethiopian universities and research institutions have been involved in projects that aim to provide access to electronic resources. Many of the interviewees (lecturers and librarians) are aware of INASP/PERI project. Some also mentioned HINARI and AGORA projects which provide access to health and agriculture journals respectively.

AAU is a national coordinating institution for the above initiatives and facilitates the registration of institutions to have a negotiated and free access to electronic journals and databases. Some of the electronic databases that are available to Ethiopian libraries and research institutions through the INASP/PERI project are Ebsco Host, Blackwell Synergy, AJOL, Cochrane Library, Cambridge University Journals, JSTOR, and Emerald Insight. EDRI, ILRI and regional universities have also access to such journals. Librarians reported that the usage rate for such journals is very low. The initiatives by INASP/PERI, HINARI, and AGORA to provide access to scientific scholarly articles have not been matched by adequate access to bandwidth to download articles. In addition, there is lack of awareness about the availability of resources and it is also reported that the academic staff and researchers lack information literacy skills to use such resources. Hence, this mismatch has slowed the use of electronic journals.

3.2. Dissemination of Ethiopian Research Results

The findings of this study showed that the dissemination outlets for Ethiopian research are mainly print publications and conferences. Many of the publications have limited circulation. There are very few journals and publications to disseminate research. The results from the interview indicate that Ethiopian journals and publications are hardly available online. The interviewees reported that researchers are forced to go to a library in order to find out what has been done on specific topic and in many cases even the libraries do not have list of research works. One respondent underscored that there exists a big gap between the knowledge community and policy makers in Ethiopia.

3.3. Electronic Theses and Dissertations at AAU (AAU-ETD)

AAU-ETD is operational since January 2009. It uses the Dspace software. The system supports to deposit items in English and Amharic languages. The AAU-ETD currently hosts only 1669 items of theses and dissertations which is very few for a university that has tens of thousands of theses and dissertations produced over the years. As it is indicted on the summary given above, the data, content, submission, and preservation policies are not properly defined. The Faculty of Law, Institute of Ethiopian Studies, and Institute of Educational Research have not added a single collection to the repository. This is mainly the lack of action and commitment from staff of the respective faculties.

AAU should extend its ETD; include other types of research works, teaching materials, and conference proceedings. It should also define institutional policies of submission, access and preservation. But most of all, AAU should also create an environment where content can be populated to its ETD smoothly. Jones, Andrew and MacColl (2006, PP.111) exclaimed that "*an empty institutional repository is analogous to a library with empty bookshelves. Even though a lot of time and effort has been spent in setting up the optimal technological infrastructure, the success of the initiative will be ultimately measured by the usefulness to users, and thus, by proxy, the depth and richness of the body of content contained within.*"

3.4. The Need to Change the Status Quo: Towards an Open Access Scholarly Communication Model in Ethiopia

Excepting ILRI, which uses its website to link to some of its research results, AAU and EDRI rely only on print publications to disseminate their research results. According to the findings of this study, AAU lacks clear institutional policies and strategies to disseminate its research results. Both AAU and EDRI have no institutional storage/repository for their research outputs. Consequently, their researchers' visibility to the outside world is very low. Researchers, students, industries and the general public have no access to most of the research that has been done within AAU, EDRI.

The current scholarly communication model in Ethiopia is dysfunctional and does not address the needs of the country. The government has embarked on expanding public universities and the number of student intakes increases every year, post graduate education is on the rise, industries are booming, research institutions are being instituted and their number is growing steadily and yet the scholarly communication outlets are very limited and out of date. Many students who are studying abroad and researchers across the world may need to access research work that has been investigated in Ethiopia and yet there are no institutional repositories, electronic journals, and properly designed websites to provide such services. These problems call not for an evolutionary transformation of the Ethiopian scholarly communication model but a revolutionary one. Embracing open access models would help achieve such a complete overhaul of the current print-based and limited distribution model.

Institutions such as AAU should overhaul their research dissemination system. They need to recognize that Ethiopian research is obscured from use by policy makers, scholars, students and industries. As pointed out by Swan (2007) developing countries are hard-hit by the subscription-based scholarly communication model as researchers in these countries cannot simply afford to pay for access. While open access has become a talking point for many researchers and librarians in the developed world and has been embraced by wealthy institutions which recognized they cannot afford to subscribe to the ever increasing number of journals, developing countries are slow to uptake such initiatives. It is therefore essential for countries like Ethiopia to design open access strategies that is contextualized to the needs of researchers.

3.5. The Ethiopian Ministry of Science and Technology (EMOST) should take the Lead

It is apparent that in order for open access initiatives to succeed it should get government support. In order to implement open access and promote open access, the Ethiopian government through its Ministry of Science and Technology should develop a policy in consultation with universities, research institutions, libraries, funding agencies, and renowned researchers. EMOST should coordinate the adoption of an open access policy. Lessons can be learned from South Africa and other countries who have successfully implemented open access. The following recommendations are contextualized from (Suber, 2007).

- The Ethiopian government through EMOST should adopt a national policy that makes it a requirement for government research grantees to provide open access to the research results;
- When research grants are offered to Ethiopian researchers, the grant should made to include money for publication of the research results in author-pays open access journal models;
- Annual government budgets for Ethiopian universities and research institutions should include budget lines for setting up institutional repositories;
- Ethiopian universities and research institutions should include in their contract for employment that any research work conducted by salaried staff members should be made open access;

- EMOST in collaboration with universities, research institutions and other responsible government bodies should work to develop a national open access repository of research. Such online service should be able to harvest those repositories which are located elsewhere in the country and provide a single search interface to browse and search for content from those repositories and to do so the repositories should use OAI-PMH compliant software and appropriate metadata standards such as Dublin Core;
- EMOST should mandate the deposit of a copy of the research conducted through its Local Research Grant (LRG) to institutional archives of the researchers. The ministry should also develop a national science and technology repository which can be accessible freely to everyone through an open access license;

3.6. Awareness about Open Access is Crucial

Awareness about open access is very low among Ethiopian researchers and librarians. Many could not distinguish between free and open source software and open access. As per the interview discussions held with academic staff, researchers and librarians of the various institutions involved in this study, open access has not made any strides in Ethiopia. In relative terms, however, librarians are better informed about open access initiatives. This awareness by librarians is a result of half-day workshop participation on December 22, 2008. The workshop entitled "*Open Access: How to improve accessibility, visibility and impact of your research outputs for librarians and researchers*" was organized by eIFL.net and AAU.

Ethiopian universities and research institutions should have an open access advocates selected both form the researchers and librarians who would organize events to create awareness about open access. This awareness creation can also be done using the institutions' websites, brochures, notice boards and local staff meetings. With support from administrators, librarians should take up the responsibility of creating awareness about open access. Especially, AAU has experienced and well trained library staff than other regional universities and research institutions, so AAU should organize national workshops on open access and should choose open access advocates.

3.7. Institutional repositories: Ethiopia's Green Road to Open Access

None of the organizations involved in this study have institutional repositories. None have institutional policies to mandate depositing or self-archiving. Most of them, especially government organizations, do not have properly designed and maintained websites. In the course of few years, even AAU, the biggest and oldest university in the country, has changed its website from one interface to another. The website's content lacks consistency. It does not have links to many of its faculties, institutes and programs. As reported by the interviewees they cannot possibly see what other research institutes of AAU have investigated/researched as there is no accessible list of researches.

The discussion held with the interviewees, indicated that the problem for not having a website or having a poorly designed and badly maintained one is not technical or even economical. Both AAU and EDRI have qualified ICT staffs who are versatile with advanced web technologies. Both have cutting-edge servers and relatively stable Intranet network infrastructure. The main problem, however, is lack of action and commitment from the responsible people mainly ICT centers and faculty administration. One respondent mentioned that AAU's problem is mainly cultural and attitudinal.

Many major universities and research institutions use their websites as major outlets to disseminate research, promote their activities and reach stakeholders including students. AAU research institutes, the EDRIand other Ethiopian universities and research institutions should not underestimate the power of well-designed and processional websites which are updated and maintained regularly. AAU, EDRI, and ILRI should ensure that their institutional research products including peer-reviewed literature, conference proceedings, and research reports, teaching materials, theses and dissertations are stored, organized and made accessible to anyone in an open access repository.

3.8. Mandating Self-Archiving: the Prophylaxis against Zeno's Paralysis

The results from the interview showed that researchers and librarians believe that self-archiving of research results would benefit themselves and their institutions. However, they also mentioned their fears. Some respondents indicated that they fear that open access would infringe their copyrights and expose their work to plagiarism.

Currently, none of the institutions involved in this study require their researchers to deposit their final research e-prints. The major reasons for this are the absence of institutional repository systems, absence of institutional policies and mandates, and lack of willingness to take such initiatives form both the side of the libraries and university management and researchers themselves. Many experiences of other countries and institutions show that mandating self-archiving is an effective strategy (Guedon, 2006) hence EMOST, AAU, EDRI and ILRI should devise mechanisms to make it a mandatory requirements for researchers to deposit especially public funded research results to an institutional repository designed for such purpose. Suber (2009) recommends that "*if you're serious about achieving OA for the research you fund, you must require it*".

3.9. The Need for National and Institutional Open Access Policies

We recommend that Ethiopian Universities and research institutions should embrace open access as their model for scholarly communication. We also recommend that they should mandate the submission and self-archiving of research results especially those theses and dissertations, research that has been done with public-funding. Public funding here refers those research projects funded by government funds such as the LRG of EMOST. In fact open access can be embraced without national and institutional policies and strategies. Hence, EMOST as a national government body should initiative a national open access policy. Institutions such as AAU, EDRI and ILRI should also adopt institution wide policies. Lessons can be learned from other developing countries and institutions which have adopted open access policies.

Suber (2009) suggests that funding organizations and universities should require not request self-archiving. In many institutions in Ethiopia, there are no electronic repositories. Until that is in place, authors should be required to submit the last PDF version of their research results (theses, dissertation, pre-prints, post-prints, and reports) to their respective libraries. Libraries will therefore be required to develop digital repositories and make such works accessible to all.

As also suggested by Suber (2007), the open access policies should require (not only encourage) the archiving of research articles and pre-prints. Such a requirement should, however, be rewarded with promotion and training opportunities. The policies should stipulate that when authors publish in non-OA journals, they should retain their rights to self-archive in their institutional repositories. Peter Suber also recommends that when funding agencies do not cover publication costs, author institutions should cover such costs. Post graduate students should be required to submit final copies of their theses and dissertations. Besides, conference proceedings need to be open access (Suber, 2007).

3.10. Use of Licenses in Institutional Repositories

Authors and librarians need to know about the Creative Commons (CC) licenses and other alternative licenses. Librarians need to advise researchers on the use of CC licenses and continually consult SHERPA's RoMEO website to check the publisher's copyright & archiving policies. Institutional repository managers in consultation with authors and university managers should customize the CC licenses to their interests and make sure that the authors understand these licenses and submit their contents.

In customizing CC licenses, Ethiopian universities and research institutions should ensure libre open access instead of gratis open access. While the first type of open access removes only price barriers, the second removes both price and permission barriers. In other words, the licenses should allow optimum flexibility in the use, adaption, and even commercial use of content. The license should ensure the works should be used with integrity and proper attribution.

3.11. Free and Open Source Institutional Repository Software

It is important to note that highly scalable, tried and tested software for institutional repository development is free and open source. One such software is Dspace which is being used at AAU. There are also other major software such as E-print, CDS Invenio, and Fedora. Ethiopian universities and research institutions should develop technical capacity and form online software communities to support the customization, installation, configuration and maintenance of such systems. Such communities should customize and contextualize the Free and Open Source software to the needs of Ethiopian researchers. One obvious need is having Ethiopian languages interface software. AAU may take such initiative to organize trainings to regional universities.

3.12. Federation of Ethiopian Institutional Repositories

Jones, Andrew and MacColl (2006) argue that setting up federating institutional repositories than a central one offers more scalability and the feeling of ownership by the institution and also the scholars who provide content to the repositories. They recommend distributed and grid storage mechanisms.

Ethiopian universities and research institutions should therefore work towards a federated digital repository where content can be harvested using OAI-PMH compliant architecture where standardized metadata such as Dublin Core is used. Such architecture offers the ability for users to search all systems in one interface.

3.13. Institutional Repositories Should Use OAI-PMH Compatible Software

Institutional repositories should fulfil some minimum technical requirements in order to be harvested and used optimally. Jones, Andrew and MacColl (2006) specify that institutional repositories should use software that which is open and interoperable. The institutional repository needs to be interoperable with other repositories. To this end, it needs to be OAI-PMH compatible. The OAI-PMH protocol is a technical solution using HTTP, XML and Qualified Dublin Core and enables to harvest metadata and provide cross searching of repositories.

3.14. One More Value Proposition for Institutional Repository Investment: Preservation

Digital information is more fragile than paper. Due to the fast pace of technological changes, the medium for digital objects obsoletes. If institutional repositories do not adopt viable preservation strategies (such as migration and emulation), it is highly probable that the content within such repositories will not be accessible within a short time frame. Institutional repository advocates and developers can cite preservation of the institution's research cultural heritage as one of the major value propositions.

3.15. Open Access Journals: the Golden Road towards Open Access to Ethiopian Knowledge

In choosing the golden road to open access what AAU, EDRI and ILRI should consider starting an online open access journal while continuing with the print subscription-based journals. Such a hybrid model would allow them to continue the subscription-based print journals while allowing converting these journals to electronic forms and made them accessible as open access journals. Open source software such as the Open Journal Systems (OJS) may be used to run and manage open access journals.

3.16. Incentives will drive open access forward

It has been noted that mandating self-archiving is an essential strategy of open access. However, the mandate to self archive should be motivated by well-planned incentive mechanisms. Such incentives should be inclusive to benefit all. It is also recommendable to take a carrot and stick approach to reward those who deposit or self-archive or to penalize who fail to do so. These incentives should be in the form of both tangible(salary increment, research grants, promotion, etc) intangible benefits such as promotion on one's academic career, prestige, and authority that also comes through the impact of making one's research visible.

4. Conclusion

Ethiopia should embrace the opportunities presented through open access initiatives. Funding agencies, universities and research institutions should take bold actions in adopting open access policies and strategies in a concerted fashion. Ethiopia should learn lessons from Southern African countries that have successfully lied down visions and strategies for an open access to knowledge. Ethiopian universities, research institutions and funding agencies should mandate self-archiving especially for research that has been carried out through public-funded money. Open access journal publishing models should also be embraced with strategic viable plans that take into account the challenges of setting up and running journals. With the availability of open source journal management software, existing print journals of

AAU and publications of ILRI and EDRI should start OA journals.

Open access offers alternatives to the current dysfunctional scholarly communication system in Ethiopia. It is dysfunctional because it has not addressed the needs to researchers, industries and the general public. It is dysfunctional because it has made Ethiopian research invisible and consequently researchers have lost the research impact that they should have gained through the use of their works by others. Open access is an alternative model of scholarly communication and should be considered as a double edge sword: it improves access to research and provides an opportunity to disseminate own research. It maximizes research usage and consequently optimizes research impact. It allows South-South and North-South knowledge sharing and collaboration. Ethiopia should not miss this golden opportunity to leapfrog the knowledge divide that has persisted for so long.

References

Arunachalam, S. (2003). Information for research in developing countries- information technology, a friend or foe?. *International Information & Library Review*, 35, 2, 133-147.

Arunachalam, S. (2008). Open Access to Scientific Knowledge. *DESIDOC Journal of Library and Information Technology*. 28, 1, 7-14.

Canessa, E. & Zennaro, M. (Eds.) (2008). *Science Dissemination using Open Access, A compendium of selected literature on Open Access*. Trieste: ICTP.

Chang, C. C. (2006). Business models for open access journals publishing. *Online Information Review*, 30,6, 699-713.

Dewatripont, et al. (2006). Study on the Economic and Technical Evolution of the Scientific Publication Markets in Europe. *Directorate-General for Research, European Commission*, available at: http://ec.europa.eu/research/science-society/pdf/scientific-publication-study_en.pdf (accessed 08 December 2008).

Ezzy, D. (2002). *Qualitative analysis: Practice and innovation*. London: Routledge.

Guedon, J. C. (2006). Open access: a symptom and a promise. In N. Jacobs (Ed.), Open access: key strategic, technical, and economic aspects (pp. 27-38). Oxford: Chandos Publishing.

Ondari-Okemwa, E. (2007). Scholarly publishing in sub-Saharan Africa in the twenty-first century: challenges and opportunities. *Presented at the PKP Scholarly Publishing Conference*, 11-13 July, 2007, available http://ahero.uwc.ac.za/index.php?module=cshe&action=downloadfile&fileid=81806115511849201275250

Pappalardo, K. (2008). Understanding open access in the academic environment: A guide for authors. *Open access to Knowledge (OAK) Law Project*, available at: http://www.oaklaw.qut.edu.au (accessed 5 October 2008).

Salo, D. (2008). Innkeeper at the Roach Motel. Library Trends, Vol. 57 No. 2, available at: http://minds.wisconsin.edu/handle/1793/22088 (accessed 28 October 2008).

Solomon, D. (2008). *Developing open access journals: a practical guide*. Oxford: Chandos Publishing.

Suber, P. (2007). What you can do to promote open access. *The SPARC Open Access Newsletter* http://www.earlham.edu/~peters/fos/do.htm (accessed 07 April 2009)

Suber, P. (2009). Open access policy options for funding agencies and universities. *The SPARC Open Access Newsletter*, issue130, available at: http://www.earlham.edu/~peters/fos/newsletter/02-02-09.htm#choicepoints (accessed 07 April 2009)

Swan, A. (2007). Open access and the Progress of Science. *The American Scientist*, available at: wwvv.americanscientist.org (accessed 17 October 2008).

Swan, A. (2006). Overview of scholarly communication. In N. Jacobs (Ed.), *Open access: key strategic, technical, and economic aspects* (pp. 3-12).Oxford: Chandos Publishing.
Willinsky, J. (2006). *The Access Principle*. Boston: MIT Press, available at: http://mitpress.mit.edu/0262232421 (accessed 22 October 2008).
Yin, R. K. (2003). *Case study research: design and methods*. 3rd ed., London: Sage.

Ghanaian Library and Information Science Professionals' Conceptions of Digital Libraries: A Phenomenographic Study

Eric Boamah

Institute of Information Studies, Tallinn University, Estonia
International Master in Digital Library Learning

Abstract: The purpose of this research is to identify Ghanaian LIS professionals' conception of DLs and how knowledge of DL has impacted on LIS education in Ghana. Various high level librarians and lecturers from the main library school in Ghana were interviewed using the phenomenographic research approach to discover variations in perceptions leading towards identification of qualitatively different conceptions of DLs. The findings identify 7 categories of Ghanaian information professionals' conceptions of the digital library and show them to be both similar to, and in some part different from conceptions described or exhibited in previous research by their counterpart professionals in the developed world. The research implies that as a new concept that thrives on Information and Communication Technologies (ICTs), knowledge about DLs is very useful for its full development and operations. It is even more important to find out people's knowledge about the concept in areas where there is inadequate and unavailable ICT as well as other socio-economic situations which pose real challenges. The research project contributes knowledge to the LIS field in Ghana. It is believed that a common basic understanding on the DL phenomenon can help solve some of the challenges and make the development of DLs in Ghana possible. Once academic libraries manage to establish their digital collections, it will not be difficult to have a national digital collection and then to think of digitally preserving the rich cultural heritage of Ghana for lasting preservation.

Keywords: Digital libraries; Library and Information Science professionals; Conception; Library education.

1. Introduction

It is clear today that Digital Libraries (DL) are well established in many institutions of higher education and by various countries (Passos, Santos & Ribeiro, 2008). Digital libraries are new, and investment in them is fraught with unknowns. Consequently, librarians and library directors are looking for information about different institutional experiences, including what digital library investments are considered good, meaningful and cost-effective, and what influences have helped shape successful digital library programs and projects.

Library and Information Science (LIS) education in Africa started in 1944 in Ghana (Boye, 1996; Gupta, 1993; Mammo, 2007). As a developing country, Ghana is saddled with some technological and other problems that have prevented her from extending the glory to establishing additional library schools, let alone developing a digital library (Alemna, 1994). Ghana has neither a digital library nor a national library. Public library services in Ghana are provided by the Padmore Library on African Affairs, also known as the Ghana Library Board (GLB). (A. A. Alemna, personal communication, April 24, 2009).

The reseacher is a student of an international master programme in Digital Library Learning (DILL). His two year experience in the programme brought him into contact with fellow students from over 16 different countries across the world and over 20 lecturers (both local and visiting) who are experts in the LIS field from Europe, America, Australia and Asia. Discussions on DLs with both students and lecturers throughout these two years of study suggested to the researcher that there are varied understandings of the concept as well as implementations of digital libraries. It is believed that the different understandings are also influnenced by a persons background (professional, cultural or beliefs). Coming from a developing country (Ghana), the researcher was interested in studying how LIS professionals from Ghana perceived the DL.

2. Statement of the Problem

There is a greater concentration of discussions on DLs in the developed world than in developing countries. The concept of digital libraries has been given different meanings and definitions by different professionals even in the areas of high concentration of discussions on the concept. Some scholars even doubt the veracity of the concept. For instance, David Weinberger argues convincingly that online libraries are not libraries at all (Weinberger, 2008 pp. 18).

DL thrives on computer technologies and systems. Developing countries like Ghana are still struggling with these technologies. The majority of the people do not have access to computers and the Internet. Libraries and other related institutions are saddled with technological problems (Alemna, 1999). Knowledge of computer technologies and their usage is low in Ghana comparing to the developed world (Martey, 2004). There is very low bandwidth for Internet connectivity. High bandwidth is extremely expensive and few organizations in Ghana can afford it. There is also unstable electricity supply. The cost of running generator plants to supplement power supply, for the few who can afford, is also high (A. A. Alemna, personal conversation, April 23, 2099; H. Asomah-Hassan, personal communication, April 1, 2009).

In November, 2008, the first batch of the International Master in Digital Library Learning programme (DILL 1) had a workshop at the University of Parma, Italy, where each of the 20 students [the actual number of students in DILL1 was 18, but 2 other Erasmus students from Estonia and Germany joined the group at Parma University making the number 20] were asked to do a short presentation on their countries and the state of their national libraries. It was observed at the workshop that most of the developing countries did not have a DL and even worse, a national library at all in Ghana. Students from Africa and other developing countries on the programme presented projects other than DLs in their countries.

This calls for the need to acknowledge the phenomenon of DL as well as strengthen the education on DLs in developing countries, with particular reference to Ghana. It is hoped that creating awareness of DLs in developing countries can motivate governments and institutions as well as library associations to redirect resources to developing their own DLs. So that, in spite of their technological and other challenges, developing countries can take long strides in the development of DLs. This also can help bridge the wide gap between the developed and developing worlds in terms of Information technology (IT) and DL development and use.

The central questions to this study are:

- What are Ghanaian LIS professionals'conceptions of DLs?
- How has knowledge about DLs impacted on LIS education in Ghana?
- What challenges face LIS education in Ghana?

3. Definitions and Perceptions on Digital Libraries

In his book, "Understanding Digital Libraries", Lesk (2005), gives a precise explanation of the digital library concept. Lesk believes that IT is the platform upon which DLs are built. According to Lesk, a digital library is a collection of information which is both digitized and organized and which gives us power we never had with traditional libraries. He further explains that a digital library can be searched for any phrase; can be accessed all over the world; and can be copied without error. He believes that digital libraries are going to change the social system by which information is collected and transferred. A digital library is not just a collection of disk drives; it will be part of a culture (Lesk, 2005).

Lesk's mention of digital libraries as being part of a culture, brings to mind what Hagedorn-Saupe et al. (2008) said about digital libraries in their work on the Ministerial Network for Valorising Activities in Digitization – European Commission (MINERVA EC) project [working on quality, usable and accessible cultural websites]. According to Hagedorn-Saupe et al. (2008); "a digital library is a library in which collections are stored in digital form (as opposed to print, microform, or other media) and accessible by computers" (Hagedorn-Saupe et al., 2008, p. 15).

Both the physical and the digital libraries offer a service to their users, in that they both make collections available through specific kinds of search and retrieval systems. The digital content is normally accessed remotely via computer networks. A digital library, from the ICT point of view, according to Hagedorn-Saupe et al., is a type of information retrieval system. Librarians may consider a digital library as another space of cultural mediation and conversation, similar to a library but in a digital environment (Hagedorn-Saupe et al., 2008, p. 15).To Hagedorn-Saupe et al. (2008) there are three fundamental components in a digital library: a) the collection, b) access services and c) the user.

According to the Digital Library Federation (DLF, 1998) a consortium of libraries and related agencies that are pioneering the use of electronic-information technologies to extend collections and services, "Digital libraries are organizations that provide the resources, including the specialized staff, to select, structure, offer intellectual access to, interpret, distribute, preserve the intergrity of, and ensure the persistence over time of collections of digital works so that they are readily and economically available for use by a defined community or set of communities".

The Network of Excellence on Digital Libraries (DELOS, 2007) defines a digital library as: "An organization, which might be virtual, that comprehensively collects, manages and preserves for the long term rich digital content, and offers to its user communities specialized functionality on that content, of measurable quality and according to codified policies" (DELOS, 2007).

Digital Library is defined by Greenstein and Thorin (2002), as a library in which collections are stored in digital formats (as opposed to print, microform, or other media) and accessible by computers. The digital contents may be stored locally, or accessed remotely via computer networks. a digital library is a type of information retrieval system (Greenstein & Thorin, 2002).

According to International Fedration of Library Associations Institutions (IFLANET, 2000), The World Digital Library (WDL) will make available on the internet, free of charge and in multilingual format, significant primary materials from cultures around the world, including manuscripts, maps, rare books, musical scores, recordings, films, prints, photographs, architectural drawings, and other significant cultural materials. The objectives of the WDL are to promote international and inter-cultural understanding and awareness, provide resources to educators, expand non-English and non-Western content on the internet, and to contribute to scholarly research (IFLANET, 2000).

From the definitons and explanations above, it becomes clear that the concept of DLs is quite complicated (and sometimes confusing). Professionals look at it from their different professional standing. However, there are certain common elements that run through the definitions. For instance, almost all the definitions agree that it is an organization, it collects digital materials, stores and makes these materials available to target users, etc. It therefore behoves professionals to strategize and intensify the education on DLs. Other authorities are working seriously on the education about DLs.

4. Research Approach

To answer the research questions in order to achieve the objectives of this study, the qualitative research strategy has been chosen because the central aim of this study is to gain a comprehensive understanding of how library and information professionals in Ghana perceive DL phenomenon and how has knowledge of DL impacted on LIS education in Ghana.Since this does not involve any quantification and measurement, the qualitative strategy seems appropriate. The study is in the perspective of the interpretivist paradigm.

Research Strategy

There are varied methods within qualitative research. However, to be in line with the purpose of this study which is to find out how library and information professionals in Ghana have experienced the DL phenomenon, and their subsequent perceptions of this phenomenon, it becomes imperative for the researcher to choose a suitable method. It seems that, the phenomenographic method used in the qualitative research will suit most for the purpose of this study.

Sampling Strategy

For the purpose of this study, non-probability, purposive sampling was chosen to generate data for the research. The research population has been assumed to be LIS professionals in Ghana. LIS professionals are defined as persons with first and higher degrees and LIS graduates as well as other degree holders with rich experience working in the library and other information field. It was from this population that the sample has been drawn for this study.

The phenomenographic approach is effective with interviews on a "fewer" sample of respondents who have expert ideas on the topic under discussion, (L. Limberg, personal communication, March 20, 2009). To be in line with the logic of purposive sampling, which was employed for the selection of the sample and size, information-rich cases were considered. In this sense, information-rich case refers to individuals within the population who have indepth knowledge, expertise and experience which they have acquired by working for at least two years in library and information science field in Ghana.

Data Collection Process

The main instrument used for collecting the data was the interview technique. The interview questions were designed following the research questions and with the aim of helping to achieve the objectives of the study. The questions were tested in pilot interviews with three master's students in Europe.

The researcher resided in Estonia, from where the study was conducted. All the respondents resided in Ghana. To get to the respondents, the researcher first contacted two persons whom he used to get the contact details for the rest. One of these two contact persons was a lecturer at the Information Studies Department of the University of Ghana. His role was to talk to lecturers in the department about the intentions of this study, which he had already been briefed on. He managed to get the consent of three (3) well experienced lecturers from the department, and the librarians from KNUST, UCEWK, CSIR and Accra public library. They all, with the exception of the librarian at Accra public library, agreed to grant the interview on phone and then forwarded their contact numbers and e-mail addresses to the researcher in Estonia, through e-mail. The librarian at the Accra public library, upon contacting him, requested to have his view written. The one from UCEWK library, after several calls and rescheduling of times for the interview, eventually could not get a suitable time. So she was not interviewed. The other contact person was a reference librarian at the Balme Library, UG. He also talked to other librarians in the university and forwarded to the researcher in Estonia, a list of professionals totalling eleven.

The Interview Process

In all, 18 professionals were gathered through the process, from the population of LIS professionals in Ghana. The researcher decided to contact all the 18 people for the interviews. Two out of the 18 never responded at all to the several calls made by the researcher to their contact numbers nor replied to the emails sent to them. Sixteen professionals responded to the researcher and accepted to take part of the study. Six out of the sixteen indicated that they would prefer to write their ideas instead of verbal interviews. Only one kept this promise with very little information.

Ten expert views were therefore used for analysis. Most of the interviews were conducted between March 23 – April 9, 2009. Time period for an interview was from 25 - 30 minutes. All interview sections were recorded using skype call graph software with the consent of respondents.

The interview questions were grouped in such a way that some questions were aimed at only lecturers at the LIS school and another group, aimed at the librarians. Each interview question was evaluated with respect to both thematic and dynamic dimensions: thematically with regards to its relevance to the research theme, and dynamically with regards to the interpersonal relation in the interview. A good interview question should contribute thematically to knowledge production and dynamically to promoting a good interview interaction (Kvale, 1996).

Data Analysis Process

The data that resulted from the interview was analyzed manually. All the recorded interview sessions were transcribed. Similar ideas were identified and grouped into categories. To identify various themes, the researcher used a word processor, where he used one colour to highlight texts under a theme and a different colour to highlight text of other themes. The researcher used the categories to refer to terms around which data was grouped. The categories were then regrouped under bigger ones and merged into themes. As a phenomenographic study, this analysis was modelled along studies conducted in phenomenographic approach by experts like Andretta (2007); Boon et al, (2005) and Limberg (1998).

Limitations of the Methodology

The phenomenographic method is quite new in the scientific research fratenity. Limited studies have been conducted using this method. The researcher therefore had fewer examples to follow. The interview was very appropriate for this research. However, it would have been less difficult if the researcher was in Ghana personally. Some important experts, whose ideas would have been very useful for this study, were missed. They would have agreed to take part in the study if the researcher was in Ghana himself. The Internet connection which was used to make the calls was not always constant.

5. Analysis of Research Findings and Discussions

In this section, discussion of the findings of this study is presented. It presents the analysis of the data obtained through the interviews. It is worth noting that not all of the issues discussed in the interviews are presented but only those that have relevance to the research questions.

Demographics

As has already been indicated in the methodology chapter, results from the interviews with 10 LIS professionals are presented and analyzed. There were 3 females and 7 males. Out of the 10, 2 were only lecturers and 4 were only librarians. The remaing 4 were both Lecturers (L) and Librarians (L) at the same time. In Ghana, a University Librarian (UL) refers to the senior-most librarian at a university library who is in charge of managing the operations of the library. Out of the 8 librarian respondents, 3 were University Librarians. Another 3 were Academic Librarians (AL) working in a university library, but they were not in charge of the library. The remaining 2 librarians were a Public Librarian (PL) [Public Library in this context refers to libraries meant for the public and not attached to any particular institution, be it academic or not] and an Institutional Librarian (IL) respectively. [Institutional Library in this context refers to a library attched to institutions other than academic ones].

The least number of years of service among the respondents was 2 years and the highest numer of years of service was over 30 years. Two of the respondents who worked as lecturers only, had served for 10 and 5 years respectively. Two respondents had served for 2 years as librarians only. Another two had also served for over 30 years as librarians. An (AL) had served for 16 years as a librarian and 8 years as a lecturer in the library school. An (IL) had also served for 5 years as a librarian and 3 years as a lecturer in the library school. The UL 1 and PL 1 had served for 9 and 8 years respectively. Below, Table 2 displays demographic information about the respondents.

Table 1: Information about respondents

Respondents' code	Category	Gender	Length of Service (Years)	Qualification
L1	Lecturer	Male	10	PhD
L2	Lecturer	Female	5	Mphil
UL1	Librarian	Female	9	MA
AL1	Librarian	Female	2	BA
AL2	Librarian	Male	2	BA
PL1	Librarian	Male	8	MA
ULL1	Librarian/lecturer	Male	Over 30	MA, Mphil
ALL3	Librarian/lecturer	Male	16 & 8	Mphil
ILL1	Librarian/lecturer	Male	5 & 3	Mphil
ULL2	Librarian/lecturer	Male	Over 30	PhD

Findings: Ghanaian LIS Professionals' Conceptions of DLs

The section describes DL as it is conceived amongst LIS professionals from Ghana who participated in this study. The descriptions are outcomes of the data gathering and analysis strategy reported above. Taken together they represent the phenomenon of DL as has been uncovered in this investigation. The products of a phenomenographic analysis are outcome space categories of descriptions which detail each conception and include quotations which illuminate the conceptions (Boon et al, 2005).

Categories of Conceptions of DLs

In all 7 categories of conceptions of DLs were identified. Table 3 below illustrates the various categories of conceptions as identified by the Ghanaian LIS professionals. Following the table is an explanation of the various categories of conceptions

Table 2: Categories of conceptions and their descriptions

Conceptions of Digital Libraries	Description
Resource and Content Conception	Accessing and retrieving information
ICT Conception	Tool for providing better access to information
Collaboration Conception	As a collaborative endeavour
Complementary Conception	Complementing traditional library
Challenge Conception	Needing resources, infrastructure, training
Educational Conception	As a tool for improving academic work
Preservation Conception	As a tool for preservation and extension

Category 1: **Resource and Content Conception**

In this category, DL was conceived as an information resource with content and functionality that enhance easy access and retrieval of information. Professionals perceive the content of a DL to include both locally generated materials as well as those produced from outside the country. At the heart of this conception are the benefits DLs give to users by providing easy access to content in a fast multi-modal way. Thus, the key purpose was to access and retrieve of information. Below are quotations from some of the views expressed by respondents as to how they perceive DL to be in terms of resource and content.

> I think the digital library is a huge (accessible and retrievable) database made up books, journal articles, preprints of prints, remote and relevant databases and any other information that the clientele of a particular library may need for research and academic work [ULL1].

The resources and content becomes an institutional repository when they are generated within and for an institution or institutions.

> There are different definitions for DLs But what I think is, when in a setting you don't have any book at all and when all these books have been put in electronic formats and a database is created for all the books, which is very impossible, I know. All the books in the library cannot be put into electronic formats. You'll not be allowed to put all of them in electronic formats without permission. But you can do institutional repository. [ULL 1]

As can be seen from respondents' statements, the contextual dimension within this conception is the use for which the content of the resource may be retrieved. What you want to use the information for, will be influenced by which content to retrieve.

The time or temporal focus is how quickly they perceive the DL will bring the resultant materials. This conception indicates that Ghanaian professionals attach importance to the contents of DLs. What is contained in the DL will influence what will be retrieved given the appropriate functionality and tools.

> There should be content for the DL. If you do not have content, then what is the ICT for? The important thing is to generate the content. Like most of us, we didn't do ICT in school, but we have the content. So now it is easy for us to apply it. If even I do not do it directly, I employ someone with an ICT background to convey that content to help me do it [PL 1]

Category 2: **Information Technology Conception**

In this category of conceptions respondents saw DLs as using ICT as a tool for information accessibility and retrieval. At the core of this conception lies the importance of ICT for information access and sharing. Personal networking through ICT and providing equal access to information for all users, irrespective of their background or conditions (whether physically fit or challenged), was the focus of this conception. Ghanaian universities have identified the need for ICT to deliver DL service. One respondent noted:

> ...if you have tools or any technologies that will enable fast and easy information delivery, go for it. That is DL.... that is the'what, the 'how' is a different matter [ULL 1]

Another respondent stated:

> [The library] launched its automated online catalogue on March 26, 2009. We are almost there. There are only a few things to do; we need to put the barcodes in the books and then we are almost there with our OPAC. Equipments, software, etc are all ready we are using the Alexandra software, which is different from what others are using. It is already installed just that we need few things in place. But, I hope by the end of this year ... will also go online [UL1].

The central focus of perceiving ICT as a tool to access and retrieve information was on the speed with which the 'tool' makes this access and retrieval possible. This conception shares a similar purpose with the previous conception (Resource and Content Conception). The two go hand-in-hand. It was perceived that putting more emphasis on ICT at the expense of content is not the best.

> ..... We believe that ICT is good, but it is just a vehicle. The content is more important. It is the vehicle of getting the content available to people quickly, evenly and several people simultaneously. That is what we see. We don't want them to put more emphasis on ICT and forget about the real information aspects [UL 1].

Respondents also noted, when talking about LIS education, that the library school in Ghana puts more emphasis on IT at the bachelor degree level and less on library contents. But at the diploma level they teach more about library contents and have less emphasis on IT. Employers are not happy about this and would prefer that the library school puts emphasis on content too.

> I have said it within myself that is two people apply for a job in my library with a diploma and a degree qualifications; I will employ the diploma holder. This is because; the diploma holder knows more of library works

> than the BA information studies holder. So this is something we are also telling the library school [UL 1].

Category 3: Collaboration Conception

In this category, DL was conceived as a collaborative means of satisfying the information need of users. The focus of this conception was to illuminate the idea that DLs do not function as separate entities to achieve needed results. This means that information needs can be met by the synergy of different efforts by people, content and tools and services such as training. It is not the work of one person or library or a service.

This collaboration can be seen as a group of libraries pooling resources together to make subscriptions for digital materials which they would not be able to get access to, individually.

> In Ghana, we have a consortium called the Consortium of Academic and Research Libraries (CARL). It is this consortium which subscribe to electronic journals and electronic databases. We have not gotten into e-books yet. So together, each of the universities has about 19000 online journals available for use. [UL1].

Through collaboration many user needs can be met, which would have been difficult for a single library to achieve. Even though these libraries are not always DLs or do not have digital collections, they are able to provide electronic journals to their users as a results of the collaboration.

> ....so it looks like now we are serving a lot of people. All the public universities are members and several of the private universities are also members of the consortium. I must say it's been very useful and helpful, making current information available to people [UL1].

Category 4: Complementary Conception

In this category, DL is conceived as a unit that requires the complementing qualities of other entities to make its work complete. At the core of this conception is stressed the important idea that even though DL was borne out of traditional libraries, the two have quite different features but together form a useful combination of skills, qualities and physical features that work together to satisfy users' needs. The point here was that traditional libraries need DL qualities to perform better and DLs need qualities of traditional libraries to exist, rather than one taking over the other. This means the idea that DL will soon take the place of traditional libraries was not the perception in this category.

> I don't think DL libraries can totally replace the traditional libraries. That would render some people jobless.Eg in our part of the world with our economic problems, it will take a long time. In my opinion that wouldn't be good. I think DL is a good thing, even though I do not appreciate the idea of it taken over the traditional library completely [AL1].

The complementary conception of DL becomes important with the problem of the digital divide and other problems facing developing countries. There can be better results if traditional and digital libraries complement each other.

> We believe that DL is very important, but with our own peculiar situation, our environmental and economic situation, we might not serve our people if we decide to go 100 percent digital. That is why we believe that it is good

> to go digital but it's better to use print side by side [UL 1].

To complement each other, there can be electronic databases, created to ease access in place where accessibility to available information resources is difficult.

> ...so the DL that I am envisaging for the distance learners is that since some of them are in Wa, Navorongo, Tamele and spread all over the country, and there are no good libraries to serve them, I thought something must be done for them. If you are in Accra or Kumasi or in any of the big cities, you can visit the libraries, but if you are away from the cities, it becomes difficult to get access. If you are doing a degree course and you don't have access to information, I said that a database of what can be put in electronic formats should be put and made available to these students. Now at worse, you can put bibliographic details and then show the person where he can obtain the documents. So you see what I mean by DL, it might not be like what others think of DL [ULL1].

The complementary conception can be seen clearly in the use of information resources. Professionals find the use of both the electronic as well as physical libraries, useful. They may need to supplement the information they get from one source with those obtained from the other.

> I use the internet to look for information a lot, but I am not satisfied with its use. The information it provides is not adequate. You need to get information from other sources like the library to supplement [AL 1]

Complementatary conception can help to prevent problems that may arise with the use of only one information resource. For instance, when one has problems with the use of an electronic resource, physical resources might be used as a supplement.

> I would liked to use the internet to look information because it is efficient. But sometimes there are problems with the computers. So I would use the two [AL1]

Category 5: Challenge Conception

DL is conceived as a challenge. This conception points out issues identified to be various challenges that come to test the abilities of a DL, its developers or users. The focus indetifies these challenges and once they are identified there can be possible solutions to address them in order to enhance processes that will lead to the development of DLs. The challenges of DL comes in many forms, more so, as Ghana is coming from the developing world and is affected negetively by the digital divide. The development of DLs needs funds, equipment, expertise as mentioned by several respondents. Ghana faces a big challenge in terms of funds for education and ICT as well as possible DL development.

As the respondents noted:

> Equipments are very expensive to acquire, when they break down cost of maintenance is also high [ULL 3].

Libraries as well as the library school lack infrastructure. As one respondent explained:

> There is high cost of infrastructural development. There are very few lecturer room but many students [L 1]

Another respondent also indicated how identified the challenge of inadequate equipment;

> In the advance countries they just get rid of these computers when they are about 5 year of use. But this is not the case of Africa. People can use a pc for over 10 year or more and most of the time these are acquired second-hand [ULL 2]

DLs are based on electronic gadgets and function with electricity. There is inconsistent electricity supply in Ghana.

> .As a result of the electricity problems I have acquired a standby generator plant to supplement power supply. But cost of maintaining the generator and fuel is very high [ULL3].

The need for adequate training and expertise was also frequently mentioned; where equipment is acquired, there is the challenge of expertise operation.

> I think I need some training before I can use the DL, especially on the job training [AL 2]

It was stressed by several respondents that education on libraries and for that matter DLs is inadequate in Ghana. One respondent noted:

> I think many people including the professionals themselves are not aware the information policy in Ghana and many library issues [AL 1]

In adequate LIS educate education can also be a challenge.

> People do not visit the public library. There is very little interest in reading in Ghana, I think there should be more education about libraries to create and sustain people's interest [PL 1]

Category 6: Educational Conception

In this Category, DL is conceived as a tool that can be used to improve academic work and education in general. The essence of this conception is to illuminate the idea that DL can be used as a tool to make teaching and learning better. Many of the respondents connected the DL with LIS education in Ghana and found that the curriculum needs changes. Respondents indicated that DL theoretical and practical aspects should be better integrated into LIS education in Ghana.

> We need to educate our people right from the school system for them to be aware of how the world is moving towards [ILL 1].

As a result of knowledge about DLs, lecturers are taking up training courses to upgrade their skills and knowledge in order to be current in their delivery. Also DLs can enhance the access and retrieval of relevant information with very little effort, time and cost. This will make course delivery and learning easier.

> People have gone for training and all that so when they come back things will change. Hopefully by the begining of the academic year most of them would have returned from training and start to teach [ULL 3].

There is an attempt to incorporate courses that include not just learning, but practical learning about DLs in the library school in Ghana. In view of this the lecturers are revising the curriculum. This is an attempt to improve LIS education in Ghana.

> Lecturers at the library school met at Dodowa for a retreat to deliberate on the need for a revision of the curriculum where we plan to put in much electronic content. The revised curriculum will include course on DLs [L 2].

As an improvement tool, DL, through the "ICT as a tool for providing better access to information"conception, different student groups can get equal access to information for their academic work.

> There are two categories of students on our campuses 1) the abled body, the sighted and the on-campus 2) the physically challenged, the visually challenged and the disabled. All educational training have so far favoured the first group. But as a result of the idea of DLs through the provision of ICT, coverage is now for all students in my university [ULL2].

Data from the interview however indicated that students do not take lectures on ICT seriously.

> ... there was a course on information retrieval. I expanded it by making it possible for student to come to the ICT centre and have for it. We took them in groups and then we'll teach them how to look for information on the Internet. But students were not serious with it. Those who came too were not attentive [ULL 1].

Ghanaian professionals are aware of all these problems. They are doing what they can to provide their duties and responsibilities in the challenges. One respondent explained:

> [We] will want to do something about the digital divide and so there have been series of workshops, seminars and conferences on digitization, automation and institutional repository inside and outside Ghana [ULL 1]

Respondents expressed numerous challenges. Those relating to this study are what have been presented. The interview data suggest that professionals want to do something about these challenges. But they can only do what they can, as the data indicates.

Category 7: Preservation and Extension Conception

In this category, DL is conceived as a tool for preserving and expanding resources. As a digital platform DL is perceived to provide an easy, safe and lasting medium for preserving resourses.

> It is a novel concept which is very necessary for us especially the third world countries, which will help us expand our resources and also preserve them [ULL 2].

The resources can be seen in the areas of education and culture which are now preserved in libraries and other information resource institutions.Materials in these libaries are physical books and other physical materials. But with the DL these materials will be digitized and made into electronic forms.When these materials are digitized and the services automated, they provide an extension of these resources and were viewed as providing lasting preservation for the content. One respondent noted:

> There is a vast difference between the automated library and the manual one. Before the automation of this library, users always needed to come to the library to check to see if a particular material was available or not. However, after automation one can check the availability of the material in the library before coming here in person to use it [AL 2]

So with the automation of the library, the services are now not only confined to the library building. It has been extended to the users, wherever they might be.

> At the moment we have an electronic library in. So we have totally automated our services now and the library can be accessed from anywhere

> on campus here, from the halls, offices or from any part of the world. So things are now changing in the country. This is the first of its kind in Ghana and we are hoping that the other university libraries would also go electronic similarly or emulate [ULL 2].

DL as a tool of extending resources can also be seen in LIS education where attention is on a particular group of students. But with "ICT as a tool providing better access to information", educational resources could be extended to all different target groups. As quoted in conception 2.

> I said to myself, why don't we do something for the disadvantaged. So I said to myself, the only way we can do that will be to find out what ICT or DLs can do for these students so that we give coverage to all students and not some of them. So I set up automating the whole library [ULL 1].

In fact, many services are provided without taking into account the disadvantaged in Ghana, particularly physically challenged persons. This is seen even in our schools, including the library school. Facilities and infrastructure are provided with only the normal persons in mind. But as can be seen from the respondent's comment above, ICT made it possible to extend resources to all students.

Discussion

In this section, the findings of this study are presented by comparing them to the data from the literature review. There hasn't been any study on conceptions of DLs in the literature. There were however several studies conducted on conceptions in Information Literacy (IL) by Boon, et al, (2005), Limberg (1998), Andretta (2007) and Bruce (1999). They also used the phenomenographic approach so the style of dicussion of this study could therefore be modelled to relate to some of these studies. The results were also compared to the framework of ICT and DLs as explained by Martey (2004) in his article about ICT use in Distance Education in Ghana.

In relation to the first conception, "DL as seen as an information resource and content", the findings are consistent with the literature cited previously. Regardless of the absence of, and limited experience in DLs and electronic information resources, professionals from Ghana see the phenomenon as a huge source (database) to obtain accessible and retrievable information in the form of electronic books, articles, online journals and other resources, to satisfy the information needs of their clientele. Even though several of them indicated that they have not used a DL before, they perceived the phenomenon to be a great source of information with useful content with functionality that enhances easy access to and retrievale of the content.

> I will say that yes it is a DL because now one can access the holdings of the library through the library's OPAC from even outside Ghana [AL 2].

Some definitions from the literature also see DLs from the resources and content perspective just as conceived by the Ghanaian LIS professionals. For instance the definition given by Hagedorn-Saupe et al. (2008) and also Greenstein and Thorin (2002) approach. According to the handbook on cultural web user interraction, prepared by Hagedorn-Saupe et al. (2008)

> a digital library is a library in which collections are stored in digital form (as opposed to print, microform, or other media) and accessible by

> computers. (Hagedorn-Saupe et al., 2008, p. 15).

Digital Library is defined by Greenstein and Thorin (2002) as;

> ..... a library in which collections are stored in digital formats (as opposed to print, microform, or other media) and accessible by computers. A digital contents may be stored locally, or accessed remotely via computer networks. a digital library is a type of information retrieval system (Greenstein and Thorin, 2002).

But there are many other definitions which look at DLs in a much broader perspective like the definition given by DLF and DELOS;

> Digital libraries are organizations that provide the resources, including the specialized staff, to select, structure, offer intellectual access to, interpret, distribute, preserve the intergrity of, and ensure the persistence over time of collections of digital works so that they are readily and economically available for use by a defined community or set of communities (DLF).

The DELOS Digital Library Reference Model defines a digital library as:

> "An organization, which might be virtual, that comprehensively collects, manages and preserves for the long term rich digital content, and offers to its user communities specialized functionality on that content, of measurable quality and according to codified policies" (DELOS, 2007) .

The comparison indicates that Ghanaian professionals have similar perceptions as their counterparts in the developed world, but there are also significant differences. An important difference comes as a results of the digital divide. Most of the professionals from Ghana discussed DLs as they have heard or read about it, and not so much as they had used it or seen it used.

> I have never used a DL before. I don't think the Internet is a digital library because I don't think that DL is the information that we provide using the Internet connectivity [PL 1]

The conception that DL can be recognized as ICT being used as a tool to provide better access to information can also be related to the data in the literature. Professionals believe that any tool that helps in information delivery must be embraced by whoever takes the helm of affairs.

ICT is not mostly used in Ghana because the country is affected by the digital divide. In the absence of DLs ICT is used to provide digital library services. By this conception it is being stressed that DL is not just about the software but requires a technology to link the resources, just as one respondent noted;

> A DL is different from the software that is used to develop it. The softwares are used as the means to get the DL done, they are not DL per se [ILL 1]

From the literature, the ICT conception can be supported by Lisk (2005)'s assertion that IT is the platform upon which DLs are built (Lesk, 2005).

A comparison of the view by Lesk (2005) and the views by professionals from Ghana indicates that perhaps ICT oriented view to DLs is quite strong in Ghana because people associate DLs with technology, because they do not have appropriate training. Also it may be the lack of possibilities to experience DLs which has come about as a result of weak ICT infrastructure. This also results from challenges caused by the digital divide.

The conception of DL as complementary to the traditional library is supported by data from the literature. The change from traditional to digital library takes time and these must work hand-in-hand. The interview data suggest that digital libraries are not going to take over traditional libraries completely.

Inferences that can be made from the various definitions and explanations of DL suggest that they are not only talking about purely digital artefacts. For instance the explanation given by Hagedorn-Saupe et al. (2008); the DL has three components a) the collection, b) access services and c) the user (Hagedorn-Saupe et al., 2008, p. 15).

> There are three fundamental components in a digital library: a) the collection, b) access services and c) the user

This explanation show that the DL is not totally digital but complementary to the traditional library or other elements.

The Educational Conception is very important to this study because it provides data to answer the second research question. This category of conception identifies DL as a tool for improvement in academic work as well as education in general. Responses from LIS professionals indicated thet they believe that development of DLs as well as knowledge of DLs has impacted on LIS education in Ghana.

Professionals therefore believe that early and intensified education about DLs in our schools and making policy makers aware of library developments will help.

When students are trained in the use of ICT, they are able to use it as a tool to look for information in a fast and easy way to improve their academic work. However, several respondents especially from library school, indicated that students do not take ICT education seriously enough.

The importance of the Preservation Conception of DL as a preservation tool to this study can not be over emphasised. As the name suggests, DL means that its contents are digital. This means any material stored in such a library will have to be digitized. These materials contain all kinds of valuable information, records and even scientific and cultural heritage. Turning these into in digital form and storing in the DL means ensuring continued and long lasting access. This is the essence of digital preservation. Using the DL to do this agrees with the assertion that indicates the use of the DL as a tool for preservation. All the DL definitions discussed in the literature and cited again in this discussion part support the view that DL can be conceived as a preservation tool. Greenstein and Thorin (2002 can be seen as one example illustrating this view.

> ... as a library in which collections are stored in digital formats (as opposed to print, microform, or other media) and accessible by computers. The digital contents may be stored locally, or accessed remotely via computer networks. a digital library is a type of information retrieval system (Greenstein and Thorin, 2002)

The Challenge Conception provides data to answer the third research question of this study. This category of conception identifies DL as a challenge that requires resources, infrastructure, training and services, in order to operate as a DL. Professionals perceive many challenges facing DLs as well as LIS education in Ghana. Most of these challenges are in the areas of ICT as a results of the digital divide. Other challenges include economic problems, such as inadequate funds, cost of equipment, expensive bandwidths, inconsistent electricity supply, just to mention a few.

6. Conclusion

Ghanaian LIS professionals conceive DLs as an Information Resource and Content; as an ICT tool for better access to information; as a collaborative endeavour; as complementary to traditional library; as a challenge needing resources, infrastructure, training and services; as an educational tool to improve academic work and education, and as a preservation tool.

The library school in Ghana is revising its curriculum to include courses that will result in students learnings about DLs. Lecturers are taking training courses in ICT and DLs to upgrade their skills in order to be in a better position to teach DLs related concepts. This is a positive impact on LIS education in Ghana. Libraries in the country are trying to automate aspects of their collections. It also implies that LIS professionals in the country are doing their best even in the midst of the problems, most of which are beyond their control.

Professionals in Ghana see many challenges facing LIS education and DL development in the country. In their view, it is only when there are serious attempts to overcome these challenges that there can be DLs in Ghana. The challenges are seen in the areas of inadequate funds, high cost of equipment, inadequate lecturers, unstable electricity supply just to mention a few.

Most of the problems the LIS field is facing in Ghana and Africa at large are as a result of the lack of interest in the field by the people. The basic challenge that underlines all other challenges is the lack of funds. Inadequate equipment, lecturers, high cost of maintaining generator plants to supplement electricity supply and high cost of greater bandwidth all require funds. The government of Ghana allocates very little funds to support libraries. This is because there is woefully the lack of interest in libraries which has been there for long. Time has come for the government, students and staff and individuals to develop interest in reading and the use of the library so that adequate resources will be channelled to the development of the libraries and the subsequent development of DLs. Library associations in Ghana should also be more vibrant in their activities in order to create positive awareness of the field by the Ghanaian public. The various universities should support their libraries by allocating equal resources from their overall budgets just as to other departments in the university. This can help the libraries to undertake more projects and workshops that can help them move towords developing DLs. In view of this, (digital) library literacy should be taken seriously both in schools and in the libraries when users come to use the services. In the school, library literacy should start early to create positive affection for libraries in the children. In various libraries, there can be programmes and services organized for their users so that they can also learn about digital libraries and its services.

It is a positive step that the library school is now reviewing its curriculum to include courses that will teach about DLs. This should be implemented rapidly for many students to benefit from it. There should be more programmes and workshops for lecturers and librarians to take
advantage of them, to upgrade their skills in the field of ICT, so that they can be in a

better position to teach students about DLs and assist library users respectively.

Reference

Alemna, A. A. (1999). The impact of New Information Technology in Africa. *Information Development*, 15(3), 167-170.

Alemna, A. A. (1994). Recenet changes in library education in Ghana. *Journal of Education for Library And Information Science*, 35(4) 348-53.

Andretta, S. (2007). Phenomenography: a conceptual framework for information literacy education. *Aslib Proceedings*. 59(2) 152-168. doi: 10.1108/00012530710736663

Boon, S., Johnston, B. & Webber, S. (2007) A phenomenographic study of English faculty's conceptions of information literacy. Journal of Documentation, 63(2). pp. 204-228

Boye, M. I. S. (1996). Fifty years of library education in Ghana and the Challenges of restructuring. *Education for Information*, 14(1), 31-45. Retrieved from Academic Search Premier database.

Bruce, C. (1999). Phenomenography: opening a new territory for library and information science research, *The New Reeview of Library and Information Research*, 1, 31- 47.

Greenstein, D. & Thorin, S. E (2002). The Digital Library: A Biography. Retrieved, March 29, 2009, from Digital Library Fedration, Council on Library and Information Resources Web site: http://www.clir.org/PUBS/reports/pub109/pub109.pdf

Gupta, S. (1993). Development of the library profession and education in Ethiopia. *International Information & Library Review*, Vol. 25, pp. 73-83.

Hagedorn-Saupe, M., Arpiainen, H., Desaive, P., Latour, N. D., Ermert, A., Feliciati, P., Froeschl, G. Et al,(Eds.) (2008). Handbook on cultural web user interaction (1st ed.). Europe, MINERVA EC project. Pp. 15-16

International Federation of Library Associations and Institutions (IFLANET, 2000). In the Digital Environment. Retrieved, March 23, 2009 from http://www.ifla.org/en/publications/the-ifla-position-on-copyright-in-the-digital-environment

Lesk, M. (2005). Understanding Digital Libraries. San Francisco: Elsevier Inc.

Limberg, L. (1998). Experiencing information seeking and learning: A study of the interaction between phenomena. Department of Library and Information Studies. Abstract retrieved Retrieved, June 24, 2009 from http://www.ped.gu.se/biorn/phgraph/civil/graphica/diss.ab/limberg.html

Mammo, W. (2007). Demise, renaissance or existence of LIS education in Ethiopia: Curriculum, employers' expectations and professionals' dreams. *The International Information & Library Review,* 39 145-159. doi:10.1016/j.iilr.2007.02.004

Martey, A. K. (2004). ICT in Distance Education in Ghana. *Library Hi Tech News*, 21(5) 16-18. doi: 10.1108/7419050410546356

Network of Excellence on Digital Libraries (DELOS, 2007). A Reference Model for Digital Library Management Systems. Retrieved June 23, 2009 From http://www.delos.info/index.php?option=com_content&task=view&id=345&Itemid=

Passos, R., Santos, C. G., & Ribeiro, M. C. (2008). Education digital libraries management; Sharing the experience of UNICAMP educational faculty. *International digital library perspectives*, 24(4), 219-226. doi: 10.1108/10650750810914229

Weinberger, D. (2008, April). Online libraries are not libraries at all. *Knowledge Management in Practice: Connections and Context. KM World;* Information Today Inc. p. 18, 29.

Using a Free Online Questionnaire to Determine the Skills, Competencies and Knowledge Required to Work in a Digital Library Environment in Australia

Katherine Howard

Tallinn University, Institute of Information Studies, Estonia
International Master in Digital Library Learning

Abstract: This paper discusses the data collection technique used to determine the skills and knowledge required of academic librarians working in a digital library environment in Australia. The research was undertaken as part of the researcher's master's thesis conducted at Tallinn University. The data collection instrument used was a freely available online survey tool, and its advantages and disadvantages are discussed in terms of the desired outcomes and circumstances surrounding the thesis project. Decisions regarding the design of the questionnaire are also discussed.

Keywords: Digital libraries; Skills; Knowledge; Online survey; Australia.

1. Introduction

Library and Information Science (LIS) education in Australia - like many other countries around the world – has been and is moving through a period of change, as the educational and skill requirements for librarians and information workers of the future are discussed. In Australia, this is evidenced by the activities of the Australian Library and Information Association (ALIA), including the Education and Workforce Summit held in March 2008 (ALIA, 2009a) and the National Advisory Congress (NAC) held in July 2008 (ALIA, 2009b). Amongst other things, the summit explored issues surrounding library and information services education, whilst the NAC discussed what needs to be done to ensure information workers possess skills for a future workforce from a professional development perspective.

The study investigates what is perhaps the newest facet of the Library and Information Science field - that of the digital library. The stimulus for this study was the realisation that LIS schools in the US and Europe were offering dedicated digital library programs, often at masters level, yet there did not see to be the same level of development from their Australian counterparts.

<u>Research Question</u>

The research questions of the study are:

1. What are the skills and knowledge required of today's information professional to work in a digital library environment, in the opinion of both LIS educators and practitioners?
2. What elements should be included in an LIS programme in Australia in order to facilitate the development of such skills and knowledge to work in a digital environment?
3. Is there a need for a dedicated digital library programme to be introduced in Australia?

<u>Scope/Limitations</u>

The study was conducted within the following guidelines:

- Only Australian practitioners and educators were included in the target groups surveyed. The practitioners were from academic libraries only.
- Educational aspect was undergraduate and postgraduate only – Continuing Professional Development (CPD) and/or Summer Schools/short courses were not considered.
- The discussion about whether LIS education in Australia should be at undergraduate or postgraduate level was not included
- Teaching methods/pedagogy/modes of delivery have not been taken into consideration in the study
- English language references/literature only was reviewed

2. Methodology

The study is a post-positivist approach to Survey Research which uses an online questionnaire as the data collection method. The questionnaire consists of both closed and open ended questions, thus yielding both quantitative and qualitative data. A descriptive analysis (also called descriptive statistics) has been applied to the quantitative data, while the qualitative data will be analysed using content analysis. This paper specifically looks at the advantages and disadvantages of using an online questionnaire as data collection instrument as used in this research project, along with decisions that were made regarding the design of the questionnaire.

Online questionnaires

The rise in internet usage and computer-mediated communication has also had an impact on the research community (Wright, 2005). An increasingly popular data collection tool is the online questionnaire, but like any data collection tool it has its advantages and disadvantages. Some of them are the same as paper-based questionnaires, but some are unique to the online environment.

Advantages of Online Questionnaires

Perhaps the most apparent advantages for using online questionnaires are cost, time and the removal of geographical and temporal boundaries (Wright, 2005; O'Neill, 2004). Online questionnaires do not incur the costs of paper, printing and postage that paper-based ones do. They also have the potential to collect a large amount of data in a relatively short time frame, but perhaps one of the biggest advantages of online questionnaires is that results are collated by the programme used and basic statistical information provided so that the analysis can start immediately after the data collection phase has ended. According to O'Neill (2004), there is evidence to suggest that online questionnaires obtain a higher number of responses than paper-based questionnaires. She also cites the reduction in respondent errors as an advantage to online questionnaires (O'Neill, 2004). As it is possible to format questions to be answered in a certain way, or mark questions as compulsory, incorrect or incomplete answers can be highlighted with an error message, requesting the respondent to complete the answer before moving on.

Disadvantages of Online Questionnaires

One of the major disadvantages of using online questionnaires is the element of bias that is introduced (O'Neill, 2004). Perhaps the most basic of these is that not everyone has access to the internet. While this is perhaps more pertinent in developing countries, the sheer size of Australia means that many of our rural communities do not have internet access. There are also populations with varying degrees of what may be termed "digital literacy" – knowing how to use a computer and access internet. These two concerns were not problematic for this study because of the targeted respondent groups – Australia has no academic library or rural LIS department, so access to the internet was not a concern. It was also expected that digital literacy (or lack thereof) would not be an issue with this group of respondents. Technical problems such as non-delivery of messages and messages going to spam folders can also pose problems when using online questionnaires. In the current study, this was avoided by sending a link to the questionnaire via email or e-list, rather than utilising the 'invitation' functionality of the online programme (where the invitation to respond to the questionnaire is sent from the online questionnaire site itself). Additionally, as messages were sent to e-lists where respondents have had to subscribe, it was unlikely that messages from this list would go to a spam folder.

Issues of response rate will almost always be problematic for online questionnaires. According to O'Neill (2004), "[a] response rate cannot be determined unless the target audience for a web-based survey is a known and finite group" (para 5). However, the number of respondents can be determined.

Appropriateness of an online questionnaire for the current study

An online questionnaire was selected for the data collection method as it was believed to be the most effective means of collecting data from Australian respondents when the researcher was based in Europe. Interviews were considered, but it was believed that a greater number of respondents could be reached via an online questionnaire than could be interviewed. As the researcher desired geographical coverage of the six Australian States and two Territories, this was also a determinant in selecting the online questionnaire method. If interviewing both practitioners and educators, it would be possible to interview perhaps only one of each from each State/Territory (a total of 16 interviews), given the time limit imposed on the research. As the study intended to identify any potential trends or consensus amongst respondents, a questionnaire was deemed to be the most beneficial technique to achieve this aim, as a broader perspective could be gained. A further benefit and time-saving factor of the online questionnaire is that results are automatically collated and summarised, ready for analysis.

As highlighted, the circumstances of the current study minimised any disadvantages inherent with using an online questionnaire. The advantages of no geographical or temporal boundaries, the potentially larger number of responses and the time-saving advantage of automatic data collation were the prime reasons for selecting an online questionnaire as the data collection tool for this study.

Online Questionnaire: Tools Available

Seven free online survey tools were evaluated to determine which would best suit the needs of this study (refer Appendix). Many had limits on the number of questions that could be asked; the number of responses that the survey creator had 'free' access to (although all responses are saved in a database – but payment is required for access to any that go over the maximum number); and time limits which started when the questionnaire was first created – not particularly helpful when surveys go through many transformations and pilot testing.

The evaluation criteria applied to these tools was quite flexible, but nonetheless there were some minimum criteria that needed to be met. First and foremost, to fulfil ethical obligations, the data collected needed to be secure. Secondly, it was preferable that the service be free, however, if the tool deemed most suitable had a cost, then this would have been met. Functionality was also of high importance – the number of questions that could be asked; the types of questions (i.e. multiple choice, free text, Lickert-scale type rankings); and the level of freedom available in the formatting (although it was acknowledged that complete personalisation would not be possible with a free service). The availability of the data needed to be as flexible as possible to allow the researcher unlimited access throughout the research process. Finally, there could not be restrictions on the number of responses received, nor limits on the time that the questionnaire was available for respondents to complete, notwithstanding limits imposed by the researcher. The eSurveysPro.com (http://www.esurveyspro.com/) programme offered the most flexible service, with all of the aforementioned criteria being met and none of the limitations discussed.

3. Questionnaire Design

The questionnaire was designed to gather information about skills and knowledge required of today's library and information professionals to work in a digital library environment. The education requirements to facilitate the development of such skills were also explored. The demographic information requested included gender, age, location, position title and number of years experience in the LIS discipline. Position title was considered important, particularly for practitioners, as it would assist in identifying those working in specifically digital positions. Gender, age and number of years experience were included as it would be interesting to note if there were any differences between those in positions with digital responsibilities and those in more "traditional" positions. Being an area with a higher focus on IT, it was thought that perhaps the gender distribution might be more in favour of males in a younger age group. Location was requested to determine what level of coverage of the six states and two territories was achieved.

As there were two populations that would be receiving the questionnaire (Educators and Practitioners), two versions were created to suit the two groups. The information requested of each group remained the same, but the wording of some questions changed slightly to reflect the intended audience. For example, the educators were asked: "Please rate the following skills from the perspective of what ***you*** [emphasis added] believe is required of a Library and Information Professional in a digital role within an Academic Library." The Practitioners were simply asked: "Please rate the following skills as they apply to your job."

Inclusions on the skills list from which respondents were required to make selections were drawn from the existing scholarly literature. Throughout the literature, 'skills' are often separated into two broad areas – 'professional skills' which encompass the professional knowledge required of one's field; and 'generic skills' which, according to Bridges (1993) incorporates skills which can be applied "across different cognitive domains or subject areas [and] across a variety of social and [.....] employment situations" (para. 13). Many other terms are used interchangeably with 'generic skills' and include 'transferable skills' and 'core skills' (Bridges, 1993); 'personality traits' (Tennant, 1998); 'personal qualities' (Goulding, Bronham, Hannbuss and Cramer, 1999; Andrews and Ellis, 2004); 'generic personal skills', 'personal skills', 'personal factors' and 'personal attributes' (Goulding et al., 1999); 'generic capabilities' (Partridge and Hallam, 2004); 'personal transferable skills' (Ashcroft, 2004); 'personal attributes' (Marion, 2001); 'behavioural traits' and 'behavioural characteristics' (Marion, 2001; Lynch and Smith, 2001) and there are more. To confuse matters further, some studies use different terminology within the same study. For example, Marion (2001) uses 'personal attributes', 'behavioural traits' and 'behavioural characteristics'; Lynch and Smith (2001) include 'behavioural traits', 'behavioural characteristics', 'behavioural skills' and 'behavioural requirements' and Goulding et al. (1999) as mentioned above use 'generic personal skills', 'personal skills', 'personal factors' and 'personal attributes.'

For the current researcher, what was covered in the term 'generic skills' was considered too broad and all encompassing, so the 3 level distinction made by Orme (2008) was utilised. Orme retained both 'professional skills' and 'generic skills', but added 'personal qualities'. For consistency, 'personal skills' was used in place of 'personal qualities' in the questionnaire in this study.

Definitions for Generic Skills and Personal Skills given in the questionnaire were based on the distinction made by Khoo (2005, p. 6) and are as follows:

Personal Skills: appropriate attitudes, values and personal traits
Generic Skills: skills which cut across disciplines. Also referred to as transferable or 'soft' skills

As a means to clarify some skills which could possibly belong to both Personal Skills and Generic Skills, consideration was give to whether the skill could be 'taught' or not. For example, it is rather difficult to "teach" someone a sense of humour, but skills such as leadership or communication – whilst often a somewhat 'natural' ability – can often times and to a certain level, be taught. Such skills were then placed in the Generic Skills list, as it was believed that these skills could be encouraged and developed through various initiatives in the teaching and learning process (e.g. setting of group assignments to develop teamwork skills).

It could be argued that there is extant literature which covers these Personal and Generic Skills and that including them in this questionnaire was therefore superfluous. However, it was decided to retain this aspect for three reasons. Firstly, to ensure that coverage of the skills required is comprehensive; secondly to ensure that respondents didn't feel the need to add skills such as 'Communication' and 'Teamwork' when asked to list 'any other skills required'; and finally, due to the age of some of the literature utilised (e.g. Goulding et al., 1999), to confirm if these Personal and Generic Skills are still relevant today and in a digital library environment.

The word 'specific' was added to Partridge and Hallam's 'discipline knowledge' (2004) to highlight the fact that this is "knowledge over which the profession claims unrivalled expertise" (Kennan, Cole, Willard, Wilson and Marion, 2006a). The explanation given in the questionnaire was:

Discipline Specific Knowledge: knowledge that is learnt in a Library and Information Science university programme (either graduate or postgraduate) or that has been learnt since graduation (for example through CPD or on the job).

All skill lists were presented in the questionnaire in alphabetical order, as this was considered the most neutral order. The inclusion of skills on the three lists, plus the curriculum suggestions, is discussed in the following sections.

Personal Skills

The skills listed under Personal Skills on the questionnaire were derived from Goulding et al. (1999). A more recent list was searched for - Orme (2008) was taken into account, but it was considered that the list provided by Goulding et al. was far more comprehensive. However, Goulding et al's list of 34 skills was reduced to 28 skills as it was found that some of what was considered personal qualities were actually better placed in the Generic Skills category, in light of the definitions given above. For example, 'written communication' and 'articulate' were both encompassed within 'communication' which was included in the Generic Skills list.

Generic Skills

The Generic Skills list was based on a compilation of Fisher (2004), Partridge and Hallam (2004) and Orme (2008). The skills from each list were compared and analysed with any duplicates removed. Those skills which were deemed not suitable for an Australian environment (e.g. languages) were also removed along with skills such as first aid qualification and full driving license which appeared in Orme (2008). Orme's study was the result of a content analysis of job advertisements, and whilst the skills mentioned might be important and necessary to demonstrate when applying for a job, they were not considered to be relevant here. A list of 16 Generic Skills was presented on the questionnaire.

Discipline Specific Knowledge

The list of Discipline Specific Knowledge was derived from the study of Choi and Rasmussen (2006b). A combination of the most important areas of knowledge identified, along with areas that participants in the study felt were lacking, were utilised to obtain the list of Discipline Specific Knowledge for the current study. Choi and Rasmussen also identified skills such as communication in their results, but as previously discussed, these skills belonged to the Generic Skills list in this study. A total of 19 selections representing Discipline Specific Knowledge formed this part of the questionnaire.

Curricula for Digital Library Education

Two programmes in digital library education and one project concerning digital library curricula were selected to provide indicative content for potential elements to include in a digital library curriculum, in order to facilitate the development of the skills and knowledge required to work in a digital library environment. They were:

- International Masters in Digital Library Learning (Oslo University College, Parma University and Tallinn University joint master programme)
- Masters in Digital Library and Information Services, University of Borås, Sweden
- The Digital Library Curriculum Project (Chapel Hill/Virginia Tech collaboration)

These three options were selected for their geographical diversity (two from Europe, one from America); the fact that they are quite recent developments in the field of digital library education; and because of the current researcher's intimate knowledge of the International Masters in Digital Library Learning programme. Again, the content was analysed and consolidated into broad categories of topics, with a total of 16 options presented on the questionnaire.

4. Conclusions and Future Research

An online questionnaire was appropriate for the circumstances surrounding the current study. However, to gain a more in depth understanding of the requirements to work in a digital library environment, it would be beneficial to conduct focus groups and interviews. Conducting a similar project within different library sectors such as Special, Government and/or Corporate libraries would also give a broader overview of the skills and knowledge required to work in a digital library environment, thus providing a consensus or highlighting differences in sectors.

An analysis of current LIS programmes offered in Australia to determine if they meet the requirements as indicated by the data obtained in this study could also be seen as a next step. This could potentially lead to decisions regarding curricula inclusions to ensure the future generations of LIS practitioners are well equipped to work in this ever changing digital environment.

References

Ashcroft, L. (2004). Developing competencies, critical analysis and personal transferable skills in future information professionals. *Library Review, 53*(2), 82–88. doi: 10.1108/00242530410522569

Australian Library and Information Association (ALIA) (2009a). ALIA Education and Workforce Summit 2008. Retrieved February 17, 2009 from http://www.alia.org.au/education/summit08/

Australian Library and Information Association (ALIA) (2009b). Your Voice. The ALIA National Advisory Congress 2008. Retrieved February 17, 2009 from http://www.alia.org.au/governance/nac/2008/

Bridges, D. (1993). Transferable skills: a philosophical perspective. Studies in Higher Education, 18(1), 43-51. doi: 10.1080/03075079312331382448

Choi, Y. and Rasmussen, E. (2006b). What Is Needed to Educate Future Digital Librarians: A study of current practice and staffing patterns in academic and research libraries. *D-Lib Magazine 12*(9). Retrieved March 20, 2009 from http://webdoc.sub.gwdg.de/edoc/aw/d-lib/dlib/september06/choi/09choi.html

Fisher, B. (2004). Workforce Skills Development: The Professional Imperative for Information Services in the United Kingdom. Paper presented at the ALIA Biennial Conference, Gold Coast, 21-24 September. Retrieved March 24, 2009 from http://conferences.alia.org.au/alia2004/pdfs/fisher.b.paper.pdf

Goulding, A., Bromham, B., Hannbuss, S. and Cramer, D. (1999). Supply and demand: the workforce needs of library and information services and personal qualities of new professionals. Journal of Librarianship and Information Science, 31. doi: 10.1177/096100069903100405

Kennan, M.A., Cole, F., Willard, P., Wilson, C.S. and Marion, L. (2006a). Changing workplace demands: What job ads tell us. Aslib Proceedings 58(3), 179-196. doi: 10.1108/00012530610677228

Khoo, C. (2005). Educating LIS professionals for Singapore and beyond. In J. Tan et al.

(Eds.), Celebrating 50 years of librarianship in Malaysia and Singapore (pp. 26-37). Singapore: Library Association of Singapore; Kuala Lumpur: Persatuan Pustakawan Malaysia. Retrieved March 24, 2009 from http://www3.ntu.edu.sg/home/assgkhoo/papers/Khoo.LIS_education_for_Singapore.2005.pdf

Lynch, B. and Smith, K.R. (2001). The changing nature of work in academic libraries. *College and Research Libraries, 62*, 407-420. Retrieved April 15, 2009, from http://www.lita.org/ala/mgrps/divs/acrl/publications/crljournal/backissues2001b/september01/lynch.pdf

Marion, L. (2001). Digital Librarian, Cybrarian, or Librarian with Specialized Skills: Who Will Staff Digital Libraries? in ACRL Tenth National Conference Denver, Colorado, 143-149. Retrieved April 11, 2009 from http://www.lita.org/ala/mgrps/divs/acrl/events/marion.pdf

O'Neill, B. (2004). Collecting research data online: Implications for extension professionals. *Journal of Extension, 42*(3). Available from http://www.joe.org/Joe/2004june/tt1.php

Orme, V. (2008). You will be.... a study of job advertisements to determine employers' requirements for LIS professionals in the UK in 2007. *Library Review, 57*(8), pp. 619-633. DOI 10.1108/00242530810899595

Partridge, H. and Hallam, G. (2004). The double helix: a personal account of the discovery of the structure of [the information professional's] DNA. Paper presented at the ALIA Biennial Conference, Gold Coast, 21-24 September. Retrieved March 14, 2009 from http://conferences.alia.org.au/alia2004/pdfs/partridge.h.paper.pdf

Tennant, R. (1998). The most important management decision: Hiring staff for the new millennium. *Library Journal, 123*(3), 102. Retrieved April 13, 2009 from http://web.ebscohost.com.ezlibproxy.unisa.edu.au/ehost/pdf?vid=5&hid=116&sid=903d34f7-3627-4c3b-806b-5e6b117d0bde%40sessionmgr8

Wright, K. (2005). Researching Internet-based populations: Advantages and disadvantages of online survey research, online questionnaire authoring packages and web survey services. *Journal of Computer-Mediated Communication, 10*(3). Available from http://jcmc.indiana.edu/vol10/issue3/wright.html

Appendix: Online Questionnaires

A list of the online questionnaires evaluated:

Survey Monkey: http://www.surveymonkey.com/
Poll Daddy: http://www.polldaddy.com
Survey Gizmo: http://www.surveygizmo.com
Pollograph: http://www.pollograph.com/
Survey Pirate: http://surveypirate.com/
Free Online Surveys: http://freeonlinesurveys.com
eSurveys Pro: http://www.eSurveysPro.com/

Intellectual Capital and Public University Libraries: A Knowledge Sharing Perspective

Reuben Mushi

Institute of Information Studies, Tallinn University, Estonia
International Master in Digital Library Learning

Abstract: Knowledge economy is resulting into competition which increases the demand for innovation. The wave has urged libraries which faced no competition before to think of ways to add and show more value to its users. The coming of digital libraries and other information providers challenges traditional libraries to improve its practices before becoming obsolete. This paper is based on the findings from the research for the Master thesis focused on establishing the relationship between intellectual capital and knowledge sharing. It is an explanatory survey addressing the issue of intangible assets as unseen value in public libraries. The research intended to use both a questionnaire and interview to ensure validity. A questionnaire was designed in such a way that key questions were asked alternatively in the same questionnaire to compensate the interview which its feasibility was constrained by time and distance. The questionnaire was then administered to six different universities to ensure reliability of the findings. As a consequence of distance and difficulties in selecting respondents, snowball sampling was used. Descriptive narrative and mapping were then used to explain the findings. Due to time and distance constraints the research focused only on the aspect of human capital and structural capital and leaves such aspects as customer capital, renewal capital and process capital to be covered by other researchers.

Keywords: Knowledge management; Intellectual capital; Knowledge sharing; University libraries; Questionnaire.

1. Theoretical framework

As the consequence of ongoing globalisation, organisations found themselves in confrontation with worldwide competition. This in turn has pushed organisations toward thinking of a more effective use of the knowledge and expertise owned by their employee as a strategic resource and a way to build and sustain their competitive advantages. Early 1990's, the business communities realised that knowledge is an important resource for the organisation and need to be sustained and nurtured. This marked the beginning of the use and the proliferation of the term intellectual capital.

Intellectual capital refers to different things to different people depending on how it is used. This paper however adopts the definition from Stewart. Stewart refers to intellectual capital as the sum of everything everybody in a company knows that gives it a competitive advantage (Stewart, 1999: xix).

This paper holds that Intellectual Capital is an umbrella term to incorporate but not limited to such things as brands, goodwill and intellectual property, corporate culture, peoples' ability and talents and organisations corporate memory. Depending on the settings to which it is applied, Intellectual Capital may be divided into Human Capital, Structural Capital and Customer Capital. *The definition provided below are derived from (Kok, 2007).*

1. Human capital: includes experience, capabilities, skills, and expertise of the human force of an organisation.
2. Structural capital (or organisational capital): includes the systems, networks, policies culture and any other processes that allow individual knowledge to be used to add value to the organisation.
3. Relational (customer) Capital: includes the connections that people outside the organisation have with it, their loyalty, the market share, the level of back orders, and similar issues.

Knowledge Management, Intellectual Capital and knowledge sharing are three key concepts of this paper. At some point their relationship is somewhat of a conundrum. The perspective in this paper is that both intellectual capital and knowledge sharing are part of the broader term Knowledge Management. Intellectual Capital focuses on such initiatives by an organisation to explore and use the tacit and explicit knowledge to add value whereby knowledge sharing can be one initiative under it. In the practical world, some practitioners regard knowledge management as misnomer and prefer to use knowledge sharing. However in this paper I do stress that not only knowledge Management deals with knowledge sharing but it indeed concerns itself with the whole process of creating, distributing, applying and evaluating the results of the knowledge in question. I suggest that "management" is not necessarily meaning "control" it may as well mean the skilful handling or use of something such as resource and this is the definition underpinning this paper. *See more about this definition in Oxford advanced learners dictionary of current English (7th ed.) (2007).*

Many ways for the discussion of the intellectual capital exists. This paper focuses on how Intellectual capital can bring about the positive results on knowledge sharing in Public University Libraries. It oversees the aspects of Human Capital and Structural Capital to suggest better ways to which knowledge sharing will be improved by the former and the latter resulting improved performance.

The relationship between intellectual capital and knowledge sharing is indeed binary. Intellectual capital may improve knowledge sharing and knowledge sharing may as well result in the formation of intellectual capital. If through sharing knowledge staff get to know what they did not know before, their intellectual level is improved and their performance may improve as well. However, the focus of this paper is to see how human capital and structural capital may lead to better knowledge sharing. It looks at such things as motivation, incentives related to knowledge sharing, creativity, library values, competences and social skills as factors pertaining to Human Capital which may help improve knowledge sharing. It looks at such things as library structure, technological infrastructure and policies to mention but a few as part of structural capital which if they are managed better improvement in knowledge sharing may be achieved. In this paper I hold that, human capital is the most valuable component and efforts for enhancing knowledge sharing through intellectual capital should start with human capital. The workforce's ability to share is first enhanced then the infrastructure to enable sharing is laid. *See the model below proposed for the theoretical framework to underpin this paper.*

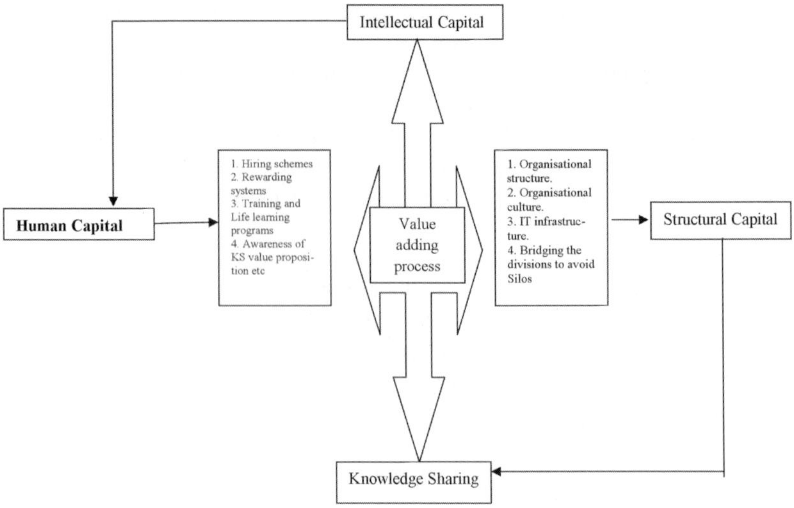

Source: Concepts and diagram designed by researcher.

2. Theoretical perspective

This paper seeks to explain how knowledge sharing will add competitive value to Tanzania Public University libraries. Through the use of adequate sample size, the purpose of this paper will be to generalise the results of the findings. It is therefore with this effect that the paper is developed under the perspective of a postpostivistic. According to Lincoln and Guba, the purpose of positivistic research is to generalise the findings. Postpositivism is rooted under the premise that any perception of the reality cannot be an objective picture but is drawn from the empirical observation and existing theory (Pickard, 2007). According to Lincoln and Juba (as quoted by Pickard, 2007) a postpostivist believe in the social reality and accept that knowing this reality will always be inhibited by imperfections in detecting its nature. The imperfections are the results of human fallibility (Lincoln and Guba, 1985).

3. Methodology

This paper is based on an explanatory survey research whereby a sample is studied to draw conclusion about the population. It seeks to establish the relationships between knowledge sharing and Intellectual capital. Burns (as quoted by Pickard, 2007) states that the explanatory survey seeks to establish cause and effect relationships but without experimental manipulation; for example, the effects on teacher's motivation of merit scheme, the effect of social climate on adolescent values (Burns, 2000).

4. Research design

The paper employed both qualitative and quantitative methods. Largely the paper used qualitative methods to collect descriptive and detailed data. The qualitative method was characterised by open ended questions to give respondents more space to air out their view. To make it possible to generalise the result of the findings, the research at some point employed some quantitative techniques such as the use of statistics and comparison based on likert scales and percentages.

5. Scope of the study

The phrase Intellectual capital takes on different meaning depending on the discipline in which it is used. However there is a common agreement among many interested parties that Intellectual capital includes three components named human capital, customer capital and structural capital. [See for example Sveiby (1997), Saint Onge (1996), and Bontis
(1998).]. Skandia, a Swedish based insurance company, has developed one of the well established models for measuring intellectual capital which includes renewal and development capital on top of the three mentioned earlier. Other will add innovation capital and process capital. [See Evidsson and Malone model (Edvinsson & Malone, 1997)]. To do justice to the topic it would be wise to discuss these aspects all together in this paper but as one can predict each of them may be a research project in its own respect. Considering this fact, this paper will limit itself to Human Capital and structural capital and its relationship to knowledge sharing only. The study covered Tanzania Public University Libraries.

6. The use of Intellectual Capital to improve knowledge sharing

6.1. Human Capital perspective

The dynamics in the social, economic and technologies require libraries to rethink how they approach their day to day work. Even though different libraries faces unique challenges depending on their social, economic and technologies surrounding them, the value of human capital is more now than ever if positive result is to be achieved. The need to compromise with the changing environment comes with the high demand to improve the quality of employees in our libraries. To effect this, library policies guiding the hiring and upgrading the employee skills need to reflect the awareness of the changing environment. Performance incentives and training programs are essential to empower and motivate employees. Modern Human Capital policies will provide libraries with a means to improve their performances and lead to efficiency as a way to effectively serve their users. The notion terming training as cost need to be changed to viewing it as an investment. Staff is the key asset in libraries whose value can be enriched through investments.
The following discussion aims at suggesting how Intellectual Capital can be used to improve knowledge sharing. It discusses the issue of human capital and structure capital to suggest how the former and the latter can help libraries excel in knowledge sharing. Such aspects as leadership, hiring schemes and training are explored under Human Capital. Later the discussion on how Structural Capital can be used to improve knowledge sharing concludes the discussion.

6.1.1. Leadership

As Bob Buckman suggests the culture is indeed important for knowledge sharing to succeed. Buckman insist that leaders play a key role in shaping the culture which will have an impact on the organisation's ability to share knowledge across time and space *see (Buckman, 2004).* As noted with the responses from the field, seventeen out of twenty one respondents agreed that their libraries have a vision. Even though it was beyond the scope of the research to investigate any strategies for updating Library visions, the mere fact that majority of responses agreed that the vision is often shared, allows us to postulate that, if sharing is emphasised in their visions the situation could have been better. Libraries need leaders who will work as a team to convey a clear and consistent understanding of the vision not only through their words but as exemplars through their deeds. The visions can become an obstacle to achieving a sound knowledge sharing strategy. This research was conducted in six public university libraries with long history some dating as early as 1970's (i.e. University of Dar es salaam). This suggest that if leaders come and go and still use the same vision, then chances are high that none of the visions are anywhere close to promoting knowledge sharing.

The data collected suggests that knowledge sharing has not been very successful. The keys leading to its success depends much on what initiatives taken by leaders. Once the importance of knowledge sharing is known to Tanzania Public University libraries, the first step will be for them to audit the skills libraries holds. Then the second initiative will be to develop a vision on what is to be achieved then to identify the competences needed to achieve the vision. Things pertaining to intellectual capital are somewhat difficult to evaluate, to assess the progress, they will be a need to point out key indicators for success, *see more in Malhotra, 2000* on how this model was used in Israel.

Trust has been among the issues mentioned to be critical for knowledge sharing. If knowledge sharing is to happen, then the trust environment should be available. No one stand a better chance to create the environment for the trust to build in than a leader. No matter how good rewarding and compensation systems are integrated within the knowledge sharing strategy, if there is no trust, the efforts to promote sharing are wasted. Whatever be the case, studies suggest that leadership can influence how knowledge is shared both positively and negatively *see for example* (Cruz, Henningsen & Smith, 1999; Henningsen, Henningsen, Jakobsen, & Borton, 2004; Larson, Christensen, Franz, & Abbott, 1998; Worford, Colabro, & Sims, 1975). Leaders and how they manage and what they value, their attitudes with regard to knowledge sharing will always have an implication on shaping the culture which determines how individuals will share their knowledge.

"Information is power" is perhaps one of the very common slogans on par with the proliferation of networked computers. Knowledge sharing culture will start with leaders who seek information. Once leaders are connected from the world outside their own organisations, they get access to best practices in leadership and on top of that they share and receive new knowledge from different perspectives. Connection power is thus important to enable leaders to create new knowledge and share the knowledge with others. Once they know what others are doing and assess how relevant to their situation, they are likely to take what is useful, leave what is not useful and modify it to fit their own settings as a result new knowledge is formed. This is an example how leaders can be examples of knowledge creation and sharing.

6.1.2. Hiring schemes

The issue of hiring and recruitment has been enough challenging for libraries.

Tanzania Public University Libraries are not isolated by such challenges. The changing environment calls for Tanzania Public University Libraries to forecast the need for the future and incorporate them in the hiring schemes. Some challenges suggested by Cribb include such questions as; do we hire for today's needs or tomorrow's? How can we hire for the future needs of the library? How do we go about providing human resource development for the needs of the organisation as a whole, not just for the specific jobs people perform? These issues are not confined to libraries. Many other organisations are also trying to deal with these challenges, *see (Cribb, 2005).*

As Peter Drucker put forward that the most valuable asset of a 21st century institution will be its knowledge workers and their productivity, libraries need to switch from hiring for skills mode. Increased competition demand strategic thinkers. Attributes are outweighing skills in the knowledge economy. It is possible to train skills, but no school can train attributes. You can train someone to be a classifier or a cataloguer or computer specialists, but how do you train learning agility? Studies done in Australia libraries and presented in the report "*Preparing for demographic change*" emphasises the importance of library staff being "strategic thinkers" in other words being able to see and understand the 'big picture' and the environment within which libraries operate. Other attributes considered essential for the library workforce include: Multi-skilled, Diverse backgrounds, Good interpersonal skills and committed to lifelong learning, *more suggestions can be found in Cribb, 2005.*

Even though knowledge sharing allows sharing of experts and reuse of valuable information, Tanzania Public University Libraries need to have a recruiting and hiring strategy that is targeted to fill short and long term human capital needs and, specifically, to fill gaps identified through its workforce planning efforts. One way to achieve this is to ensure that recruiting and hiring programs are overseen and proved to be fair and unbiased based on the demographic profiling maintained by Libraries over time. The successful recruiting and hiring programs will ensure that training and hiring is based on what those who are subjected know and not who they know.

6.2. Structural Capital perspective

No matter how much staff are ready to share, once there is no infrastructure to facilitate the sharing, it will be difficult for sharing to happen. This section discuss the issue of structural capital and propose how such things as organisational culture, structure, technological infrastructure and knowledge sharing strategy can help facilitate knowledge sharing. While the previous section discussed about the opportunities, incentives, training, and other aspects pertaining to enhancing employees ability to participate in knowledge sharing, this section discuss how to support those who are enhanced and ready to share their knowledge to add value to an organisation.

6.2.1. Organisation culture

Culture has been one of the most well known obstacles to knowledge sharing. The minimal scale of knowledge sharing revealed by data collected suggests one of the two things. It either suggests the absence of sharing culture or the failure of existing sharing culture. Whether the answer is A or B, the message is very clear that Tanzania University public Libraries need overhauling their organisation culture to support knowledge sharing practices. Trying to promote knowledge sharing within the same organisation culture may lead to the devastating consequences including waste of time and resources and likely the same efforts in the future even with a right strategy may receive a negative welcoming.

Most major change efforts in the past have failed due to the ignorance of the importance of cultural change, *see more in* (CSC Index 1994; Caldwell 1994; Goss et al. 1993; Kotter and Heskett 1992). This is not exceptional with libraries not either with knowledge sharing, the demand to rethink library's culture to accommodate knowledge sharing initiatives is important. The burgeon of knowledge sharing in Tanzania University libraries relies on cultural changes. The new culture should advocate creating and maintaining an environment whereby employees are willing and able to collaborate easily. Cooperative culture should be fostered to allow problems being solved together that way staff gets opportunity to learn from each other and contribute, and raise the trust level.

When asked whether knowledge is not shared because staff holds the knowledge hoarding for power perception, none of the respondents believed that. They pointed out that staff are often willing to share their knowledge. What can be derived from these responses is the fact that libraries lack a culture that supports collaborative works and that library staff is not encouraged shying from personal ownership of knowledge. If staff are willing to share, yet the magnitude of knowledge sharing is still below average, then chances are high that leaders are still happy with the routine culture. Unless there is a certain level of discontent among leaders with the current situation, it is likely that the state of knowledge sharing will not improve.

As non profit organisations facing a serious challenge of justifying their relevance, Tanzania Public University libraries need to add more value to their practices. They will be a need for libraries to create a culture that understands what knowledge is important to support the changing environment and put that knowledge into action. Little knowledge added to the routines will have a significant impact. As pointed out in *Malhotra, (2000)* knowledge assets are governed by the law of increasing returns which make it different from the traditional view of diminishing returns. A culture should not be to be contented with accomplishing daily routines, but what should we do to add value to the routines. Tanzania Public University libraries should aim at adding value to their users through the acquisition, creation, sharing, and reuse of any aspect of knowledge relevant to their environment, internally and externally. They need to think outside the boundaries of current practices and services in order to keep up with the more rapid pace of change.

When Drucker speaks about knowledge residing in the heads of employee as the most valuable asset of a 21st Century organisation, he refers to tacit knowledge. It is not procedural knowledge that is contained in manuals and protocols that libraries need to share to add value. Libraries need a culture that promotes informal knowledge sharing to facilitate capturing of tacit knowledge. Because tacit knowledge is communicated indirectly through human interaction, Nonaka and Takeuchi emphasize the importance of organizational culture in determining whether or not the exchange and communication of tacit knowledge will occur, *see* (Nonaka & Takeuchi, 1995). Findings suggest that informal strategies for knowledge sharing are not used at all in Tanzania Public University libraries. Of 21 respondents filled the questionnaires not a single respondent suggested any of informal strategies listed in the choices. When they were asked to suggest other strategies apart from the list of choices given, the answer was still the same, none suggested any informal strategy.

6.2.2. Organisation structure

The success of knowledge sharing in Tanzania Public University libraries will be very much influenced with the structures which support sharing. The investigation done through the websites of all the libraries but one which are covered under the research reveals that they are configured in hierachirchal structures. Even though the researcher could not find any data about the last library in the website, it took the respondent four visits to this library to have the questionnaires answered as library staff waited for the consent from the director. This allows us to predict that, this library configuration is also hierachirchal. Communication is the most important factor to facilitate knowledge sharing. Studies show that hierachirchal structures hinder the smooth floor of information between staff and between staff and their supervisors see for example (O'Dell & Grayson, 1998; Creed and Miles 1996).

Knowledge sharing is well promoted by more flexible structures than hierarchical structure. In general, organic structures stand a better chance to enhance knowledge sharing than hierachirchal one. In those cultures which maintain hierarchies, knowledge holder may be discouraged by the long communication channel they have to go through to deliver the information they wish to. Tanzania Public University libraries need more of participative structures if they are to enhance knowledge sharing. This is supported by the research done by (Ahmed, Lim& Loh, 2002).

Suggesting changing of the whole structure is likely to cause more problems than it can solve. Alternatively, libraries should opt to modify the same existing structures to allow more flexibility and participation. Nonaka and Takeuchi (1995) indicate that a combination of a formal organizational structure and a non-hierarchical, self-organizing organizational structure would improve knowledge creation and sharing capabilities. The combination of the two structures will promote innovation through cultivating a more cooperative climate. More social interaction which is indeed essential for exploring tacit knowledge is likely to happen when the organisation structures are less formalised and decentralised.

Cooperation should go beyond the limit imposed by departmentations. When the researcher visited different sites for the libraries in questions to see how the divisions are made, it was found that three departments were most common in almost all libraries. These were identified as reader's services, technical services and information services even though there were slight differences in the labels. This suggest that, if there is no way to bridge these departments to allow knowledge flow irrespective of employees attachment and job functions, then silos may be created and competition is the likely consequence than cooperation. At this juncture departments may concentrate in their own department accomplishment than collective problem solving.

Tanzania Public University libraries need to turn into learning organisations. This suggests the need to adjust their structures to put more emphasis in learning through knowledge creation and sharing than reinventing the wheels. Restructuring involves distribution of power where library leaders need to be more as facilitators than directors. This goes along side with culture change where the core values and visions of the organisations are restructured to reflect the importance of creating and sharing knowledge. Among other things job descriptions should help libraries to relate skills and support communities of practices. Working in groups needs to be encouraged to facilitate interaction and collaboration in attending work related to the groups.

Learning organisation is promoted by technological infrastructure. Knowledge workers need to be connected with other knowledge workers and most important to be connected with the information. Knowledge transfer and dissemination is well promoted by well laid IT infrastructure. It may not be feasible to suggest the acquisitions of new IT infrastructures such as high speed computers and collaborative work tools such as videoconference tools and projectors in not for profit organisations like libraries. Even worse university libraries which depend on the university budget wise. However, there is a strong need for the available infrastructure to be put into use effectively. Findings suggest that only 3 respondents admitted passing information to others in workplaces through internet.

Knowledge economy requires library to realise the increased need to create structure which will allow the more use of the valuable knowledge in the heads of their employee. Networks of teams should replace traditional hierarchies and knowledge should become the main organizational resource. This way libraries are likely to use their employee's talents as part of a competitive strategy to create, share and utilize information created to gain more competitive advantage.

7. KS strategy

To secure a strategic advantage, libraries need to generate more value in the services they offer. This is achieved once there is a strategy which allows staff and processes in libraries to generate and use more knowledge. This section discuss some strategies which Tanzania Public University Libraries may use to facilitate knowledge sharing and thus create new knowledge and better reuse the available knowledge to add more value.

7.1. Creation of knowledge bases and communication networks

Knowledge management practices is expected to help libraries engage in effective research and development of knowledge, creation of knowledge bases, exchange and sharing of knowledge between library staff. One strategy which is likely to enhance knowledge sharing between library staff and between libraries is the creation of knowledge bases. This involves the creation of best practice databases, directories of expertise, procedures and discussion forums. Not only this will facilitate knowledge sharing but it will also enhance organisation memory and improve decision making processes.

In the previous section, the essence of better structures to facilitate knowledge sharing is outlined. Knowledge sharing is enhanced by the ability to create a strategy which allows information to be easily accessible and circulated through computers and communication networks. Communication networks need to extend to knowledge holders within and outside the libraries and should allow the retrieval of information in an efficient way and quickly. As suggested in the previous paragraph, maintenance of expertise directories can be one way to determine where the connection must reach. Effective communication is essential to promote learning and innovation which will improve the quality of knowledge sharing. Flexible structures will allow easy information flow and compensation systems will encourage knowledge sharing.

7.2. Awareness of new value proposition for knowledge sharing

Knowledge is power only when is used. Tanzania Public University Libraries need to find a way to show staff how knowledge will benefit them. Leaders should take the initiative now to address the issue of the new value proposition for knowledge so that the essence of distributing knowledge will be justified. It is important to stress on the rapid change and make staff aware that what work today may not work tomorrow and that new knowledge is important for the value adding process. At this point is crucial for leaders to use best practices example to show how access to others' knowledge can improve their performance and how sharing what they know makes their knowledge more valuable.

British Library is given as an example whereby they conducted staff skills audit with the aim of starting a consultancy service, *see more about this staff audit in* (Dakers, 1998). Tanzania Public University libraries may start a program whereby the competence audit is handled. This starts by mapping competences found in library staff and then compare them with the requirements of their positions. This being a starting point, then the development program is started to help employees acquire the skills necessary for the libraries to achieve their objectives. Once everyone knows what the library expect, and once everyone is trained to achieve these objectives then sharing becomes easy as employee will be working together to achieve one goal. It will be one way to overcome the silos created by functional subdivision attached to employee due to their attachments to specific departments.

7.3. Technological infrastructure

One strategy to put into effective use the IT facilities in Tanzania University libraries is the introduction of online message boards or online forums. Through the use of a moderator a discussion of particular topics in an ongoing basis will facilitate knowledge sharing among participants and allow cooperative problem solving culture. It will bring awareness of knowledge in particular subjects make it easy for staff to know who to ask for help and save their time while promoting informal knowledge sharing.

Online message boards can then be facilitated by email listservs. Listservs refers to electronic mailing list software application which are normally organised around a shared interest. Once there is cooperation among libraries then it is easy to identify different skills that way whenever someone find a content somewhere he or she can predict to whom it may be useful and send it. Not only listserv are accessible to large number of people but discussion forums capabilities are integrated in listservs and their design fosters interactivity and archiving of messages. However in such a situation, it should not be taken for granted that all users are likely to use the listservs accordingly, they should be the administrator who is empowered by policies on how to handle those who abuse the facility. The benefit of discussion boards and listservs suggest that it worth training or hiring a good facilitator to be able to rip full advantage.

Training regarding employee familiarisation of new IT systems and processes will improve their abilities to create and share knowledge. Some applications may seem so familiar and basic and it is taken for granted that people know how to use them. Knowledge sharing goes further beyond basic application of the IT systems. It needs proper training especially on how technology can facilitate the retrieval of information and its distribution. Staff needs to be aware of the recent technologies, what new capabilities have been added and what IT can achieve and what it cannot achieve. Training should cover demonstration of all advantages of any new system over existing ones. With the absent of more sophisticated technologies, staff perceptions may go further beyond what the IT can deliver and make staff reluctant to explore the existing systems due to underestimation.

Technology has come now to help libraries improve their practices. What was not possible before the introduction of computers is now possible with computers. Technology can facilitate Tanzania Public University libraries to use multimedia for adding video clips or voice to databases or problem and solution databases whereby librarians can interact online with users helping them solving their problem or finding their way to the mass information in libraries. Traditional library practices can be very much enhanced through computers were by a limited card catalogue for instance may be enriched with more information through annotations and qualifiers. Technology provides easy access to experts just by a click one may be able to send an email and receive feedback from an expert. The transfer of tacit knowledge is made easy through technology. When people see how something is done then it is easy for them to understand. Programs come with help manuals and make their use a little bit easy and effective. Computer networking has facilitated interaction not just between people but between people and machines.

8. Conclusion

This paper addressed the issue of Intellectual Capital. It concentrated on how such elements of Intellectual Capital named Human Capital and Structural Capital may help Tanzania Public University Libraries improve knowledge sharing practices. It was found that knowledge Sharing in Tanzania Public University Libraries is done but in a marginal scale. Such things as organizational structure, culture and IT infrastructure were found to be among the causal factors of the situation. Hierarchical structures and lack of compensation schemes were identified to have profound effects in knowledge sharing while the issue of awareness on the current value proposition for knowledge sharing and lack of cooperative problem solving culture affecting the knowledge sharing culture in the Libraries. It was identified from the responses that the use of IT to facilitate knowledge sharing needs more emphasis. Further studies are needed in developing models for measuring Intellectual Capital (Intangible assets) in libraries. There is a strong need for libraries to learn what works better and unlearn what didn't work. Alvin Toffler, an American writer and futurist postulated that "*the illiterate of the 21st century will not be those who cannot read and write, but those who cannot learn, unlearn, and relearn.*"

References

Bontis, Nick (1998). *Intellectual Capital*: An Exploratory Study that Develops Measures and Models, *Management Decision*, 36(2), 63-76.

Buckman, R.H. (2004). *Building a knowledge-driven organization*. New York: McGraw-Hill Professional

Burns, R.B (2000). *Introduction to research methods* (4th ed.). London: Sage

Creed, W.E. & Miles, R.E. (1996). *Trust in organisations*: a conceptual framework linking organisational forms, managerial philosophies and the opportunity costs of control. California: Sage

Creed, W.E. & Miles, R.E. (1996). *Trust in organisations*: a conceptual framework linking organisational forms, managerial philosophies and the opportunity costs of control. California: Sage

Crib, G. (2005, August 14). *Human Resource Development*: impacting on all four perspectives of the Balanced Scorecard. Paper delivered at the World Library and Information Congress: 71st IFLA General Conference and Council, Oslo, Norway.

Cruz, M.G., Henningsen, D.D., & Smith, B.A. (1999). The impact of directive leadership on group information sampling, decisions and perceptions of the leader. *Communication Research*, 26(3), 349-369.

CSC Index. (1994). *State of Reengineering Report* (North America and Europe). Cambridge, MA: CSC Index.

Dakers, H. (1998, August 18). *Intellectual capital*: auditing the people assets. Paper presented at a workshop of the section on Management and Marketing at the 64thIFLA General Conference, Amsterdam

Edvinsson, L. & Malone, M.S. (1997). *Intellectual Capital*. New York: Harper Collins Publishers.

Goss, T., Pascale, R., & Athos, A. (1993). "The reinvention roller coaster: Risking the present for a powerful future". *Harvard Business Review*, 71(6), 97-108.

Henningsen, D., Henningsen, M.L., Jakobsen, L., & Borton, I. (2004). It's good to be a leader: the influence of randomly and systematic selected leaders on decision making groups. *Group dynamics*, 8(1), 62-76.

Kok, A. (2007). Intellectual Capital Management as Part of Knowledge Management Initiatives at Institutions of Higher Learning. *The Electronic Journal of Knowledge Management,* 5(2), 181-192

Kotter, J. & Heskett. J. L. (1992). *Corporate Culture and Performance*. New York: The Free Press.

Larson, J. R., Jr., Christensen, C., Franz, T. M., & Abbott, A. S. (1998). *Diagnosing groups*: The pooling, management, and impact of shared and unshared case information in team-based medical decision making. Journal of Personality and Social Psychology, 75(1), 93-108.

Lincoln, Y.S. & Guba, E.G. (1985). *Naturalistic inquiry*. London: Sage.

Malhotra, Y. (2000), *Knowledge Assets in the Global Economy*: Assessment of National Intellectual Capital. *Journal of Global Information Management*, 8(3), 5-15.

Malhotra, Y. (2000a). *Knowledge Management and New Organisation Forms*: A Framework for Business Model Innovation, Knowledge Management and Virtual Organisations. Pennsylvania: Idea Group Publishing.

Malhotra, Y. (2000b). *Knowledge Management and New Organization Forms*: A Framework for Business Model Innovation, *Information Resources Management Journal*, 13(1), 5-14

Nonaka, I. & Takeuchi, H. (1995). *The knowledge creating company*: how Japanese Companies Create the Dynamics of Innovations. Oxford: Oxford University Press.

O'Dell, C. & Grayson, C. J. (1998). If we only knew what we know. Identification and transfer of internal best practices. *California Management Review,* 40(3), 154-74.

Pikard, A.J. (2007). *Research methods in information*. London: Facet Publishing.

Saint-Onge, H. (1996). *Tacit knowledge*: the key to the strategic alignment of Intellectual Capital ", *Strategy and leadership*", 24(2), 10-14.

Stewart, Thomas (1997). *Intellectual Capital*: the new wealth of organisations. New York: Doubleday.

Sveiby, K.E. (1997). *The New Organizational Wealth*: Managing and Measuring Knowledge-Based Assets, San Francisco: Berrett-Koehler.

Toffler, A. (1980). The third wave. New York: William Morrow.

Wehmeier, S. (Ed.). (2007). *Oxford advanced learners dictionary of current English* (7th ed.). Oxford: Oxford University.

Wofford, J.C., Colabro, P.J., & Sims, A. (1975). The relationship of information sharing norms and leader behaviours. *Journal of Management*, 1(1), 15.

The Use of Online Synchronous Interviews as a Data Collection Technique

Le Dieu Tran

Institute of Information Studies, Tallinn University, Tallinn, Estonia

Abstract: The viability of the use of instant messaging (IM) clients (e.g. Skype and MSN Messenger) to conduct online synchronous interviews is debatable due to the limitations inherent in computer-mediated communication. This data collection technique was utilized in the researcher's master's thesis project, which explored the concepts of trust and risk in the online hospitality network, The CouchSurfing Project. Semi-structured interviews were conducted over Skype and MSN Messenger with respondents from five different countries. Various challenges and benefits of IM were experienced by the researcher and the respondents. In the opinion of the researcher, it was found that the advantages had outweighed the disadvantages due to the circumstances of the thesis project.

Keywords: Online synchronous interviews; Instant messaging; Chat; Computer-mediated communication; Semi-structured interviews.

1. Introduction

This paper examines the use of online synchronous interviews as a method of collecting data for the researcher's master's thesis project. More specifically, the advantages and disadvantages of using instant messaging (IM) clients to conduct interviews are explored in this paper.

IM clients such as Skype, MSN Messenger, ICQ, Google Talk, and others enable real-time communication via the Internet. Text-based messages are sent back and forth between the parties, mimicking a conversation in a telephone call or face-to-face interaction. Many IM clients also have the capability to conduct chats with audio and/or video.

The aim of the researcher's thesis project was to acquire a deeper understanding of the concept of interpersonal trust in an online community, namely, The CouchSurfing Project (www.CouchSurfing.org). CouchSurfing is an online hospitality network whose purpose is to connect travellers and local hosts offering free accommodations and more importantly, a chance for cultural exchange. CouchSurfers complete online personal profiles that allow other members to search for and make requests for accommodations based on information on these profiles. In the discombobulated virtual environment, online personas might not reflect reality. Issues of trust and the perceived risks associated with CouchSurfing were explored in the study. Semi-structured interviews were conducted with 6 CouchSurfing members and 6 non-members via text-based chatting on Skype and MSN Messenger.

2. Advantages and Disadvantages (Interviewer)

For both interviewer and respondent, there are various advantages and disadvantages of using instant messaging to conduct interviews. The advantages and disadvantages from the perspective of the interviewer are discussed in this section.

Firstly, an advantage of using IM to conduct interviews is that the sample could theoretically consist of people from anywhere in the world with a reliable Internet connection. Hence, geography and time would not be an issue since the interview could be conducted in the comfort of the respondent and interviewer's respective workspaces. This was particularly relevant in the case of the researcher's thesis project. The researcher was not limited to recruiting local participants (i.e. compared to conducting face-to-face interviews) and was able to draw upon the global nature of the CouchSurfing community, which comprises of members from over 200 countries around the world. Incidentally, the 12 respondents who were interviewed for the study come from five different countries.

Furthermore, conducting interviews via IM was fairly cost-effective since the researcher did not have to obtain equipment to record or video tape the interviews as well as search for a meeting venue. Additionally, the researcher did not need to spend money to travel to an actual venue for the interviews.

Since the interviews were text-based, a written transcript was generated as each interview was being conducted. Thus, it was not necessary to spend time transcribing face-to-face/audio/video interviews. With the time constraints of the 5-month thesis project, not having to transcribe interviews was quite beneficial for the researcher. The data analysis process (i.e. coding of the interviews) was able to commence promptly after each interview was given. Furthermore, the ability to see a written record as the interviews were conducted provided the opportunity for the interviewer to quickly go over the responses and ask follow-up or clarifying questions during the interview if needed. As well, any errors that would have resulted from a transcriber misinterpreting or mishearing an audio recording would be eliminated since the respondents typed out their own responses. In addition, since the respondents provided their own punctuation, they had greater control over how they would like their messages to be exactly presented.

Although not an issue with the researcher's thesis project, an additional advantage of using IM is that the researcher is able to reach populations that were likely once not easily accessible. For instance, if a researcher is studying a sensitive topic that involves individuals who would like to keep their identities hidden (e.g. studies involving same-sex individuals, people who have been afflicted with a particular disease, those who have been physically/emotionally/sexually abused, are just a few examples), IM interviews offer a certain level of anonymity to the participants (Couch & Liamputtong, 2007). For example, participants could be recruited online in forums and message boards and they would only be required to provide their IM alias, which is often a pseudonym, in order to engage in an IM interview.

If participants are not obligated to reveal their true identities, they may be more willing to chat freely about their opinions and experiences that might be considered risky or deviant (Markham, 2004). However, the researcher would have to take the participants' word that they indeed are who they purport to be. For example, a researcher who is doing a text-based IM interview with a teenage girl who has been battling bulimia assumes that she is who she says she is and not a middle-aged man pretending to be one.

Consequently, the lack of visual cues in computer-mediated communication is a disadvantage of interviewing via IM. For example, subtle, non-verbal cues such as body language or even verbal cues such as tone of voice or inflection (which help contextualize what the respondent is trying to express) are absent in a text-based IM interview. As well, the lack of visual cues makes it difficult to build rapport between the interviewer and respondent. For example, the researcher was not able to nod or smile at the respondent to demonstrate empathy or to encourage him/her to elaborate on an interesting point. Thus, emoticons such as :) for "smile" or :(for "frown" were often used to explicitly convey the mood or tenor of a phrase.

Another possible disadvantage of using IM is the need for the researcher to become familiar with the jargon and emoticons that are often used while chatting. For example, LOL to indicate "laugh out loud", BTW for "by the way", IMHO for "in my humble opinion" and so on and so forth. However, this was not a problem for the researcher as she uses IM daily and is familiar with the chat language.

Lastly, the researcher is not able to assess whether the attention of the respondent is fully focused on the interview. It is quite possible that the respondent could be doing other things while the IM interview is taking place. For example, one of the respondents admitted that she was preoccupied with another task during the IM interview and so she was unable to devote her complete attention to the interview.

3. Advantages and Disadvantages (Respondents)

For the purposes of this paper, in order to get a sense of how the participants of the study had felt about being interviewed via IM, they were invited to respond to a brief online survey that was created using SurveyMonkey. Ten out of the total number of 12 participants of the study responded to the survey.

The results of the survey indicated that 3 of the respondents are novice IM users and 7 are experienced IM users. When they were asked their frequency of IM use, 5 respondents use IM 5-7 days a week, 1 uses it 2-4 days a week, 2 use it once a month and 1 rarely uses it. All of the respondents use IM to keep in contact with friends, while "communicating with family" came in second (4 of the respondents selected this), and 1 respondent uses IM for educational purposes. Text-based chatting was the most popular form (8 respondents), followed by both audio-based chatting (1 respondent) and video-based chatting (1 respondent). Thus, this form of communication was not foreign to most of the participants of the study.

When the respondents were asked to indicate their level of hesitancy towards being interviewed via IM, 8 replied that they were "not at all hesitant", 1 was "hesitant" and 1 was "very hesitant". The respondent who was hesitant commented after the interview that she enjoyed the experience and appreciated the time to think and compose her responses instead of just uttering the first things that came to her mind. For the respondent who was very hesitant, the interview was conducted via audio-based IM because the respondent preferred to have a verbal conversation instead of a text-based one. This provided the researcher with the opportunity to compare interviewing via text-based IM with audio-based IM. In brief, the duration of the audio-based IM interview was shorter than the text-based one (i.e. the audio-based was about 1 hour, the text-based interviews were 2 hours on average) because it is naturally faster to speak and listen than read and type. As well, from the researcher's perspective, it seemed easier or at least quicker to build rapport with the respondent in a verbal conversation than a written one.

The respondents were asked if they preferred to have been interviewed using a different interviewing method. Six replied "no", while 4 indicated "yes". All 4 said that they would have preferred a face-to-face interview instead of doing it via IM. These findings suggest that more than half of the respondents were comfortable being interviewed via IM, however, there was a strong preference towards face-to-face interviews.

The respondents were given a list of advantages and disadvantages of using text-based IM as an interviewing tool, from the perspective of the interviewee. The list was compiled from literature (O'Connor, 2006; Couch & Liamputtong, 2007; Opdenakker, 2006) as well as from the researcher's experience of conducting and being interviewed via IM in the past. The respondents were asked to select their top three choices from each list. The results are indicated below in bold, with the order indicated in parentheses.

Advantages of being interviewed via IM:

- Ability to clarify interviewer's questions
- **Ability to do the interview in the comfort of my own workspace (e.g. school/home) (2)**
- **Ability to think and compose my responses before sending them (1)**
- Ability to interact in a familiar communication medium
- Ability to see a written record of my responses during the interview
- **Time lapse between messages allows time for reflection (3)**
- Other

The respondents also suggested other interesting advantages:

- The ability to do other things at the same time (such as eat or surf the Internet)
- If the interviewer asks a question about topics or terms that are unclear to the respondent, s/he can do a Google search during the interview
- If the respondent speaks with an accent or is not confident with his/her English-speaking skills, s/he might be more comfortable communicating via text-based IM

Disadvantages of being interviewed via IM:

- Difficulty building rapport with the interviewer
- **Necessity to read and type my responses rather than say them out loud (2)**
- **Length of time it takes to do the interview (3)**
- Being distracted by other things online (e.g. reading my emails)
- Not being able to see the interviewer (i.e. lack of visual cues)
- **Potential for misunderstandings to occur because the context and reference of messages are unclear (1)**
- Difficulties with using the technology
- Other

Other disadvantages suggested by the respondents included:

- Difficult to maintain focus because it was necessary to find something else to do during the time lapses
- Depending on the part of the world, there might be a lack of reliable infrastructure (e.g. internet service, electricity, etc.) to support the technology
- IM is considered a social tool used to chat with friends and family instead of a tool for school or work purposes

Lastly, the respondents were asked if they would be comfortable conducting an interview via IM (i.e. as an interviewer). Nine of the respondents said "yes" while 1 replied "no" because s/he stated that s/he did not like to write. The reasons given by the respondents who said "yes" included:

- Interviewing via IM is a major time saver because the interviews do not need to be transcribed
- Offers wide geographical access
- It is a fairly cost-effective method since the researcher should already have the necessary equipment (e.g. computer, IM client)
- The researcher might not get as much information compared to a face-to-face interview, but one would still get more info than from a questionnaire
- Responses contain less "noise" or chatter since the interviewees have already filtered them (i.e. the interviewees have time to reflect and focus their responses instead of rambling)
- IM is a medium that the respondent uses daily so it would feel absolutely natural to conduct an interview via IM
- It is useful to be able to go back and read parts of the transcript during the interview just in case the interviewer forgets to ask something or needs more clarification
- One respondent stated that if face-to-face interviews were not possible then interviewing via IM would be a second choice since certain aspects that can only be captured in a face-to-face interview would be lost (e.g. body language, social cues, etc.)

Incidentally, it was primarily due to many of the reasons suggested above that IM was chosen as the data collection tool for the researcher's study.

4. Conclusions

Although interviews conducted via IM do not offer a full picture compared to face-to-face interviews, there are many advantages to using this method, which have been described in this paper. Accordingly, there are challenges as well.

In any case, the decision to use IM as an interviewing tool should be based on the study's budget, timeframe and perhaps more importantly, the type of participants needed in the study; in particular, whether ensuring total anonymity is crucial. If so, IM would be a suitable method to achieve this. As well, if visual/social cues such as observing body language or tone of voice are important, then interviewing via IM is likely not an appropriate method.

In the case of the researcher's thesis project, the advantages seemed to outweigh the disadvantages, although the disadvantages are veritable concerns. However, due to the time constraints of the five-month thesis project, interviewing via IM was the most convenient, effective and affordable way to obtain the necessary research data.

References

Couch, D., & Liamputtong, P. (2007, Sept.). Online dating and mating: Perceptions of risk and health among online users. *Health, Risk & Society, 9*(3), 275 – 294. doi: 10.1177/1049732307312832

Markham, A. (1998). *Life online: Researching real experience in virtual space*. Walnut Creek: Altamira Press.

O'Connor, H. (2006). *Advantages and disadvantages of online interviewing.* Retrieved on May 5, 2009 from http://www.geog.le.ac.uk/orm/interviews/intads.htm

Opdenakker, R. (2006, August). Advantages and disadvantages of four interview techniques in qualitative research. *Forum Qualitative Sozialforschung / Forum: Qualitative Social Research, 7*(4). Retrieved from: http://nbn-resolving.de/urn:nbn:de:0114-fqs0604118.

9. Evaluation

Assessment of Library Instruction using Performance Based Software

Gayla Byerly and Cindy Batman

Instruction Assessment Coordinator, University of North Texas, Willis Library, USA
E-mail: gayla.byerly@unt.edu

1. Introduction

At the University of North Texas, the curriculum has a mandatory second semester of English for all students named English 1320. The students write a required research paper for the English1320 course. The UNT librarians, collaborated with the English faculty to include a library orientation. We wanted to teach skills included in the Association for College and Research Libraries Information Literacy Competency Standards for Higher Education (http://www.ala.org/ala/acrl/acrlstandards/informationliteracycompetency.htm) into the library instruction. The library orientation takes place in the Willis Library in a computer room. During the library orientation, a librarian instructs students how to do research using the UNT Libraries website. Including how to find help from a librarian, do a subject search in the online catalog, and how to search in Academic Search Premier. Other instruction includes where to find materials in the library, how to print in the library, and other information to help make the research process easier. Librarians deliver all of this information in one class period to about 80 English classes per year.

The English faculty was very satisfied with the collaboration and we librarians considered the collaboration successful. However, we began to wonder how much the students actually learned in the library orientations. The paper surveys distributed in library orientations only measured how satisfied the students were with the instruction and what the students report they think they have learned. We wanted to assess actual student learning and not what students think they have learned. After a thorough search, we found two tools that test information literacy skills. The two tools we found were the Standardized Assessment of Information Literacy Skills (SAILS) and ETS's Information and Communication Technology (ICT) Assessment test student skills. Both Project SAILS and ICT work to test institutional initiatives of information literacy skills (Rockman, 2005). However, both these tools require a large amount of time to administer. The library orientation is only one class period and we needed something to assess learning in a short time. Our dilemma is one most academic librarians face. According to an ACRL survey in 2001, 95% of library instruction is done in only one class period (Merz &Mark, 2002). Library administration assisted us by providing time with a computer programmer, Frank Gosnell. Mr. Gosnell worked with us to create and develop software that was performance based. After several months of development, the software looked like the UNT Libraries website with the steps of the assessment on the left side. After getting the Institutional Review Board approval, we began using our assessment software. We named the software Library Instruction Software for Assessment, LISA.

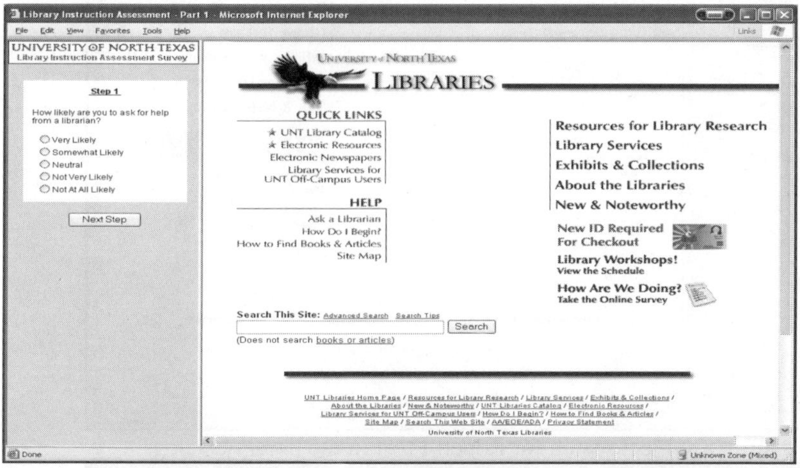

Step 1 of LISA: How likely are you to ask for help from a librarian?

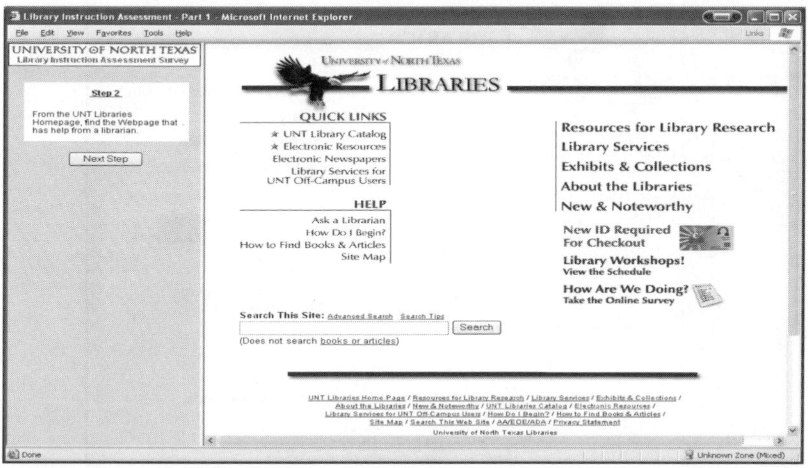

Step 2: From the UNT Libraries homepage, find the page that has help from a librarian.

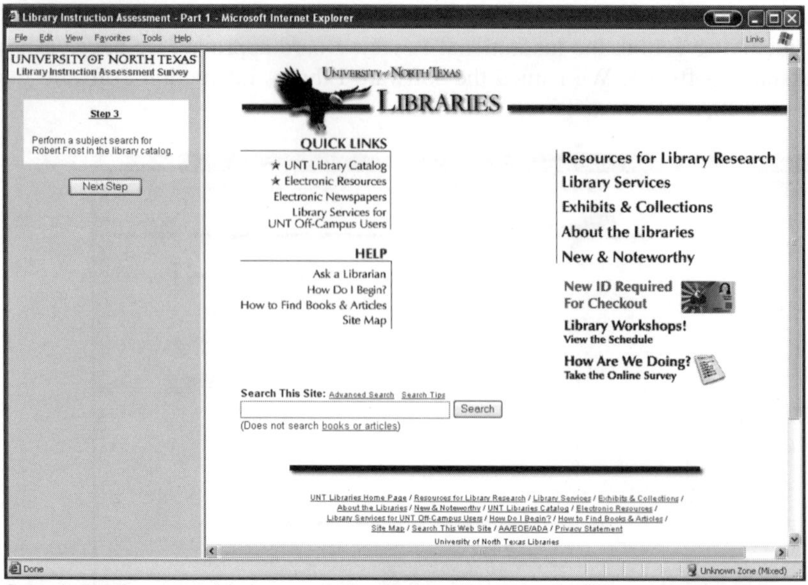

Step 3: Perform a subject search for Robert Frost in the library catalog.

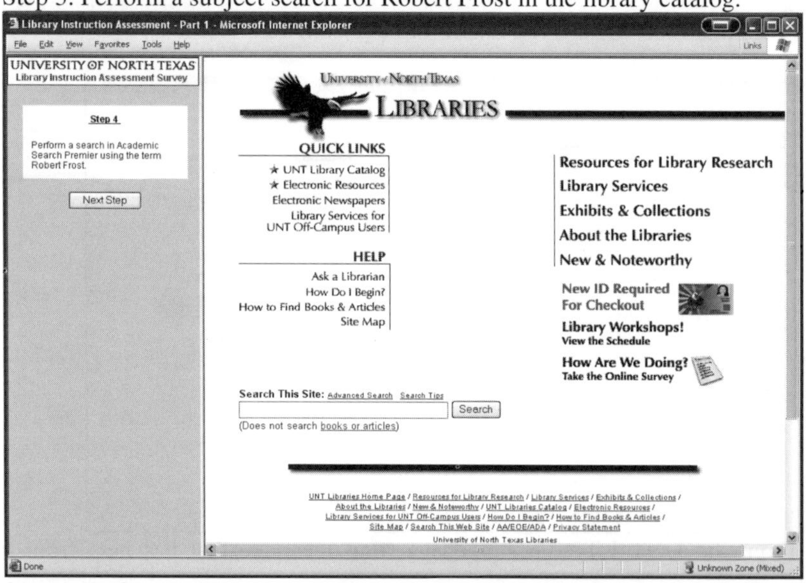

Step 4: Perform a search in Academic Search Premier using the term Robert Frost.

We administered a pretest of at the beginning of the library instruction session for a baseline of student knowledge. At the end of the library instruction session, we administered the posttest to assess whether students learned the library skills taught in the library instruction sessions. As soon as the class began, students took the pretest that consisted of four steps. The first step was a simple question asking the students how likely they were to ask for help from a librarian using a Likert scale.

The next three steps asked students to perform a search on the UNT Libraries website to find help from a librarian, perform a subject search in the online catalog, and to perform a search in Academic Search Premier. After taking the pretest, the librarian taught the students all the steps that appear on the posttest. The posttest is a repeat of the pretest with demographic information and comments added. We asked some classes to come back at the end of the semester to take a post posttest. The post posttest was a repeat of the posttest to discern whether students retained the skills taught in the library orientation.

2. Quantitative Results of LISA

The first step of LISA measured how likely students were to ask for help from a librarian as a measure of library anxiety. We found that 70.72% of students were either somewhat of very likely to ask for help from a librarian. In the posttest, 84.19% were somewhat or very likely to ask help from a librarian.

With Step 2, we found the results helpful in correcting library instruction. Step 2 asks students to find the Help From A Librarian webpage. To keep the flow of the instruction, librarians showed students how to get to the Help From a Librarian webpage from a webpage other than the UNT Libraries homepage. The percentage of students able to find the Help From A Librarian webpage went down in the posttest. Once we corrected our instruction and showed students from the UNT Libraries homepage, the statistics from the posttest went up. In the pretest, 68.04% found the Help From A Librarian webpage. Posttest, 58.56% found the correct page and the post posttest, 73.7% were successful.

Step 3 asked students to perform a subject search in the catalog using the author Robert Frost. Students sometimes have an author such as William Shakespeare as the author. If they perform a keyword search for William Shakespeare, the results are far too many and not helpful. A subject search is an essential skill for the research paper assignment. The first results of LISA found 1.24% of students successfully performed a subject search in the pretest. The posttest results were 11.13% and post posttest 7.8% were successful. The next academic year we used LISA, but added an active learning component to the catalog instruction. As a result, our posttest results shot up to 38%.

The last step in LISA asked students to perform a search in Academic Search Premier (ASP). First, students had to find ASP, which is located three pages deep from the UNT Libraries homepage. 16.49% of students performed successfully in the pretest. 49.69% were successful in the posttest, while in the post posttest 47.43% were able to perform the search.

3. Qualitative Results of LISA

The posttest of LISA included the question: "What did you learn that you didn't know before this library instruction?" LISA collected 439 responses. Since the question was optional, not all of the 575 students responded to this question. Students responded in a variety of ways. Only 12 students responded that they did not learn anything new. Two of the responses were incomplete or incoherent.

One hundred eighty-two students reported on satisfaction with the UNT Libraries services and resources. Many of the students in this group reported positive feelings learning about Academic Search Premier, the full text articles from ASP, how to access ASP remotely, and the ease of searching in ASP. A significant number of students mentioned databases in general. In addition to comments about databases, students commented positively on the ability to access library resources remotely.

While a majority of students mentioned one or two resources or services they learned about in the library instruction session, eighty-nine students reported that they learned "everything." One student wrote, "I learned basically everything about the library." Another student's comment was "I learned how to do just about everything. I had no clue how to use this website what so ever and now I know how to find things that will help me on my research paper. Thank you very much for your time and help."

The third largest group of student comments expressed their satisfaction with the part of the instruction that taught them how to narrow results to a manageable number. Forty-one students specifically mentioned the librarian's instruction about how to limit search results. One student reported they learned "How to specify your search so that you don't have 2398473294823 different things to look through." Most mentioned they were happy to learn how to narrow results because it would save them time.

Students mentioned the library website thirty-one times. Some students write that they had no idea that the library website had so much information to help them with research. Here is a typical student response: "I also learned a wealth of knowledge on how to search for books, periodicals, etc. on the website."

Thirty students wrote comments about learning out to get a help from a librarian. Some students mentioned the webpage that detailed such librarian services as the hours of service, locations of the reference desks, toll free telephone number, librarian chat room, and librarian email. One student reported learning, "That the librarians were so willing to help."

Interestingly, twenty-four students mentioned that they did not know that the university had five library buildings. In their comments, they seemed surprised to learn that we had so many and many different kinds of libraries, such as the Science and Technology and the Media Library. Five students commented on the coffee house addition of the CyberCafe in the Willis Library.

Twelve students specifically mentioned the citation help from the library website and Academic Search Premier. In addition, eleven students said they learned about the library catalog and how to use it effectively.

4. Conclusions

A majority of academic librarians in the United States struggle to teach information literacy skills to students in a single library session. While clearly one class period is not nearly enough time to teach the range of skills identified by the ACRL Information Literacy Competency Standards, librarians continue to try to teach the skills with as much time as is allowed. Librarians need to have a tool to assess how well the students understand the materials taught in the library instruction sessions. The tool needs to be performance based, easy to use, and take little time in the session.

We used the LISA results to change instruction for the catalog. The results proved that students struggled to learn the catalog. We added an active learning component to our catalog instruction. The results went up 38% of students successful in a subject search from 11%. Good assessment tools aid librarians to do better instruction, which results in better student learning.

References

Association of College and Research Libraries *Information Literacy Competency Standards for Higher Education* (2000), available at: http://www.ala.org/ala/acrl/acrlstandards/informationliteracycompetency.htm

Merz, L.H. & Mark, B.L. (2002) Association of College and Research Libraries—College Libraries Section, *Assessment in College Library Instruction Programs*, ALA, Chicago, IL, p.4

Rockman, I. & Smith, G.W., 2005, "Information and communication technology literacy: New assessment for higher education," *College & Research Libraries News* Vol. 66 No. 8, pp. 587-589.

Self-Efficacy: An Alternative Approach to the Evaluation of Information Literacy

Serap Kurbanoglu

Professor, Department of Information Management, Hacettepe University, Ankara, Turkey

Abstract: Information literacy is the key skill required for lifelong learning, however, acquiring information literacy skills is not enough by itself for success; individuals should also develop confidence in these skills. Low self-efficacy beliefs may be a significantly limiting factor for individuals to use their information literacy skills effectively. Determining the level of self-efficacy beliefs for information literacy will enable individuals 'at risk' to be identified. Therefore, it is suggested to use self-efficacy scales as additional assessment tools while mixing and matching assessment methodologies to gather usable information for the evaluation of information literacy instruction programs.

Keywords: Information literacy; Self-efficacy; Evaluation; Assessment

1. Introduction

Societies of information age need independent learners equipped with lifelong learning skills. Information literacy – the ability to find, use and communicate information - is the keystone of lifelong learning. Information literate people are critical thinkers, effective consumers of information, and self-directed learners who use and communicate information effectively and responsibly. Members of information society should be equipped with information literacy skills to be able to succeed in a world where change is the basic driving force of the daily life. However, acquiring information literacy skills is not enough by itself for success; individuals should also develop confidence, in other words strong self-efficacy beliefs in these skills.

Libraries, in all sorts, play a central role in teaching information literacy skills. Creating and maintaining information literacy programs that will support lifelong learning has become a mission for almost every library. In order to increase the quality and the success of information literacy training programs, instructors develop assessment strategies. There are many of tools and techniques which can be used for the assessment of information literacy training programs. In this paper, self efficacy beliefs for information literacy will be examined as an additional assessment strategy in the overall evaluation of an information literacy program.

2. Assessment & Evaluation: Key Components of Instruction Programs

Assessment, collection and the analysis of data about learner's performance, and evaluation, the interpretation of that assessment (Grassian & Kaplowitz, 2001), should always be seen as part of teaching process to find out how well the goals and objectives of an instruction program have been met. The main aim of assessment is continual examination of both teaching and learning for improved learner performance. Assessment results can be used in monitoring learner's progress, improving instruction, carrying out program evaluation, defining program's strengths and weaknesses, modifying or improving the program and motivating learners (Gage & Berliner, 1991). According to information gathered through the assessment process, adjustments can be made in methods, techniques and material. Furthermore, the results of assessment contribute to the decision making about the future of the program.

In order to increase the quality and the success of information literacy training programs, instructors should plan evaluation and assessment strategies. Assessment strategies and techniques vary along several parameters. They can be formal or informal; formative or summative; qualitative or quantitative. Furthermore, different techniques vary as to their reliability, validity, and usability. Evaluation and assessment strategies and methodologies should be selected according to their relevance to the learning outcomes or performances to be measured. Selecting an appropriate technique depends on having a through understanding of the strengths and weaknesses of the various techniques. Mixed data collection and triangulation (a combination of methods) are increasingly being used for the evaluation. However, practical constraints such as time, money, and available expertise should also be considered before taking decisions on which techniques to use (Grassian & Kaplowitz, 2001).

Interest in developing strategies and tools to assess information literacy is growing. The number of librarians introducing assessment of information literacy into their organizations is increasing along with the number of assessment tools developed by these librarians. Librarians, most often, attempt to assess information literacy skills by using tests based on multiple choice, fill-in-the-blank, and matching questions. However, there has been a debate about inefficiency of these tests to evaluate higher order skills and information literacy skills in real life situations (Walsh, 2009; Dunn, 2002; Scharf et al, 2007). Open ended questions, essays, portfolios, self-assessment scales, interviews and observations are other assessment tools being used.

This paper neither attempts to provide an overview of assessment methods and tools nor to determine the best methods for assessing information literacy. It points out instead that information literacy instructors should be more critical and flexible in the use of assessment tools and techniques than ever and should consider mixing and matching methodologies and tools to gather the greatest amount of usable information for the evaluation.

3. The Concept of Self-Efficacy and Sources of Self-Efficacy Beliefs

The concept of self-efficacy has been developed primarily in the discipline of social psychology by Bandura (1977; 1986; 1997). Self-efficacy refers to a belief in one's ability to successfully perform a particular behavior or task (Cassidy & Eachus, 1998). Bandura (1997) defines self-efficacy as a belief in one's own capabilities to organize and execute the course of action required to attain a goal.

There is a close link between attitudes and experience, and the attainment of self-efficacy. Research by Bandura (1986) shows that efficacy perceptions develop from a gradual attainment of skills and experience over time. Within the construct of perceived self-efficacy, the motivation of behavior is one's belief in the capability to perform an act (Bandura, 1997).

According to Bandura self-efficacy beliefs are influenced by four principal sources of information namely mastery experiences, vicarious experiences, social persuasion, and physiological and emotional states (Bandura 1986; Koul & Rubba, 1999; Pajares, 2002)

Mastery experiences: Individuals form their self-efficacy beliefs by interpreting information primarily from their previous experience. Individuals interpret the results of their actions and use the interpretations to develop beliefs about their capabilities to engage in subsequent activities (Bandura, 1994; 1995; Pajares 2002; Koul & Rubba, 1999) Typically, successes raise self-efficacy while failures lower it. On the other hand, as Bandura (1986) indicates, after a strong sense of self-efficacy is developed through repeated successes, occasional failures do not effect it easily.

Vicarious experiences: Self-efficacy appraisals are partly influenced by "vicarious experience" of observing others perform tasks. The influence of the vicarious experiences on self-efficacy beliefs is weaker than the mastery experience. Individuals become especially sensitive to vicarious experience when they have had insufficient familiarity with the task in their hands. Vicarious experience is particularly powerful when observers see similarities between themselves and the model. Observing the successes of such models contributes to the observers' beliefs about their own capabilities. On the contrary, failures of such models can undermine the observers' beliefs about their own capability to succeed (Bandura, 1986; 1995; Pajares, 2002).

Social persuasion: Verbal persuasion which individuals receive from others can also contribute to the development of self-efficacy beliefs. Positive persuasions may empower, negative persuasions may weaken self-efficacy beliefs. People who are persuaded verbally that they possess the capabilities to master given tasks are likely put more effort when difficulties arise. It is usually more difficult to strengthen self-efficacy beliefs through positive encouragement than to weaken it through negative appraisals (Bandura, 1986; 1995; Pajares, 2002).

Physiological and emotional states: Physiological state also influences self-efficacy beliefs. People gauge their degree of confidence by the emotional state they experience as they contemplate an action. Strong negative emotional reactions, such as anxiety, stress, and fear can lower self-efficacy perceptions (Bandura, 1986; 1995; Pajares, 2002).

4. The Importance of Self-Efficacy for Information Literacy

Self-efficacy beliefs provide the foundation for human motivation, well-being, and personal accomplishment. In other words, self efficacy beliefs influence the totality of human behavior. People have little incentive to act or to persevere if they believe that the task in their hands exceed their capabilities, but they undertake and perform activities if they believe that their actions can produce the outcomes they desire (Bandura, 1977; 1986; Pajares, 2002; Koul & Rubba, 1999; Cassidy & Eachus, 1998).

According to Bandura (1977) success is not only based on the possession of necessary skills, it also requires the confidence to use these skills effectively. Hence, besides learning information literacy skills individuals of today's societies must also develop confidence in the skills that they are learning. Attainment of strong sense of self-efficacy beliefs becomes as important as possessing information literacy skills.

Self-efficacy beliefs determine how long individuals will persevere and how resilient they will be in the face of difficulties and how much effort they will expend on an activity. Individuals with a high self-efficacy perception expect to succeed and will persevere in an activity until it is completed. On the contrary, individuals with low self-efficacy perception anticipate failure and are less likely to persist doing challenging activities. The higher the sense of efficacy, the greater the effort, persistence, and resilience (Pajares, 2002) which are two factors crucial for information problem solving, self-regulated learning and lifelong learning. Bandura underlines that individuals who develop a strong sense of self-efficacy are well equipped to educate themselves when they have to rely on their own initiative (Bandura, 1986). This is why developing a strong self efficacy perception for information literacy becomes necessary to accomplish lifelong learning.

Self efficacy is a factor which influences human functioning. Although the knowledge and skills they possess play critical roles on the choices they make, people's level of motivation, and actions are based more on what they believe than on what is objectively true (Bandura, 1997; Pajares, 2002). Because high level of self-efficacy leads to a desire and willingness to act and to risk trying a new behavior, it becomes important for the use of information literacy skills for lifelong learning. If individuals feel themselves competent and confident about their information literacy skills they will willingly undertake and solve information problems. Otherwise, it is more likely that they will avoid and hesitate to try solving information problems in their hands.

Self-efficacy has generated research in areas as diverse as medicine, business, psychology, education and computers (O' Leary, 1985; Lev, 1997; Schunk, 1985; Koul and Rubba, 1999; Delcourt and Kinzie, 1993; Karsten and Roth, 1998; Compeau and Higgins, 1995). The number of the research regarding to self-efficacy for information literacy, however, are only few in number (Akkoyunlu and Kurbanoglu, 2003; Kurbanoglu, 2003; Kurbanoglu, Akkoyunlu and Umay, 2006). As Neely (2002) has indicated sociological and psychological factors involved in the development of an information literate individual are neglected. Perceived self-efficacy can be considered as one of the psychological factors which has an impact on information literacy.

5. Measuring Self-Efficacy

Because self-efficacy is based on self perceptions regarding particular behaviors, the construct is considered to be situation specific or domain sensitive. That is, an individual may exhibit high levels of self-efficacy within one domain while exhibiting low levels within another one (Cassidy & Eachus, 1998).

Perceived self-efficacy refers to an identified level and strength of self-efficacy. The strength of self-efficacy is measured by degrees of certainty that one can perform given tasks (Zimmerman, 1995). Therefore, although self-assessment is considered as a rather subjective method, self-efficacy demands to be measured directly (rather than indirectly) by the use of self-report scales (Cassidy & Eachus, 1998). Preparation of self-efficacy scales requires time and patience. One must be certain to measure the self-efficacy beliefs relevant to the behavior in question (Pajares, 2002).

The necessity for the measuring self-efficacy for information literacy relates to the impact information literacy is having on many aspects of life and in particular on lifelong learning. Increasingly individuals of information societies are expected to be proficient users of information. Low self-efficacy may be a significantly limiting factor for individuals exploring information problem-solving skills vital for lifelong learning. The development of an appropriate measure of self-efficacy for information literacy will enable individuals 'at risk' to be identified.

6. Conclusions and Suggestions

Low self-efficacy beliefs may be a significantly limiting factor for individuals to use their information literacy skills. Reducing anxiety and increasing learners' confidence in their own information literacy skills should be valid and important goals of information literacy instruction. Measurement of self-efficacy for information literacy will enable learners who might need additional help to be identified. Therefore, it is recommended that, in addition to assessing individuals' actual knowledge and skills on information literacy, methods have to be developed to assess the level and strength of their self-efficacy beliefs regarding to these knowledge and skills. Admittedly, assessment of self-efficacy beliefs does not provide all the necessary information to be used for the evaluation of instruction programs by itself. It should be considered as a part of an overall evaluation strategy while mixing and matching variety of methodologies and tools to gather usable information for the evaluation.

References

Akkoyunlu, B. & Kurbanoğlu, S. (2003), Öğretmen adaylarının bilgi okuryazarlığı ve bilgisayar öz-yeterlik algıları üzerine bir çalışma. [A study on initial teacher training students' perceived self-efficacy for information literacy and computers], *Hacettepe Üniversitesi Eğitim Fakültesi Dergisi,* 24, 1-10.

Bandura, A. (1977). Self-efficacy: toward a unifying theory of behavior change. *Psychological Review,* 84, 191-215.

Bandura, A. (1986). *Social foundations of thought and action: a social cognitive theory.*

Englewood Cliffs, NJ: Prentice Hall.
Bandura, A. (1994). Self-efficacy. In V. S. Ramachaudran (Ed.) *Encyclopedia of Human Behavior* (Vol.4, pp. 71-81). New York: Academic Press.
Bandura, A. (1995), Exercise of personal and collective efficacy in changing societies. In A. Bandura (Ed.). *Self-efficacy in changing societies.* New York: Cambridge University.
Bandura, A. (1997). *Self-efficacy: the exercise of control.* New York: W. H. Freeman and Company.
Cassidy, S. & Eachus, P. (1998). Developing the computer self-efficacy (CSE) scale: investigating the relationship between CSE, gender and experience with computers. *Journal of Educational Computing Research, 26*(2), 133-153.
Delcourt, M., & Kinzie, M. (1993), "Computer technologies in teacher education: The measurement of attitudes and self-efficacy", *Journal of Research and Development in Education,27,* 31-37
Dunn, K. (2002). Assessing information literacy skillsin the California State University: A progress report. *Journal of Academic Librarianship, 28*(1/2), 26-35
Gage, N. & Berliner, D. (1991). *Educational psychology* (5th ed.). New York: Houghton Mifflin.
Grassian, E. S. & Kaplowitz, J. R. (2001). *Information literacy instruction: Theory and practice.* New York: Neal Schuman Press, (pp. 1-45).
Compeau, D. R. & Higgins, C. A. (1995), Computer self-efficacy: Development of a measure and initial test, *MIS Quarterly, June,* 189-211.
Karsten, R. & Roth, M. R. (1998), The relationship of computer experience and computer self-efficacy to performance in introductory computer literacy courses. *Journal of Research on Technology Education*, *31*(1), 14-24.
Kurbanoglu, S. (2003). Self-efficacy: a concept closely linked to information literacy and lifelong learning. *Journal of Documentation,* 59, 635-646.
Koul, R. & Rubba, P. (1999). An analysis of the reliability and validity of personal internet teaching efficacy beliefs scale. *Electronic Journal of Science Education.* September. Retrieved May 29, 2009 from http://unr.edu/homepage/crowther/ejse/koulrubba.html
Kurbanoglu, S., Akkoyunlu, B. & Umay, A. (2006). Developing the information literacy self-efficacy scale. *Journal of Documentation, 62*, 730-743.
Lev, E. L. (1997), Bandura's theory of self-efficacy: Applications to oncology. *Scholarly Inquiry for Nursing Practice, 11*(1), 21-42.
Neely, T. Y. (2002), *Sociological and psychological aspects of information literacy in higher education.* Lanham, Maryland: The Scarecrow.
O'Leary, A. (1985), Self-efficacy and health, *Behavioral Research & Technology, 23*, 437-451.
Pajares, F. (2002) *Overview of social cognitive theory and of self-efficacy.* Retrieved May 29, 2009 from http://www.des.emory.edu/mfp/eff.html
Scharf, D., Elliot, N., Huey, H., Briller, V. & Joshi, K. (2007). Direct assessment of information literacy using writing portfolios. *Journal of Academic Librarianship, 33*(4), 462-478.
Schunk, D. H. (1985), Self-efficacy and classroom learning. *Psychology in the Schools, 22*, 208-223.
Walsh, A. (2009). Information literacy assessment: Where do we start? *Journal of Librarianship and Information Science, 41*(1), 19-28
Zimmerman, B. J. (1995). Self-efficacy and educational development. In A. Bandura (Ed.). *Self-efficacy in changing societies.* New York: Cambridge University Press, (pp. 202-231).

Knowing the Needs. A System for Evaluating the University Library

Ane Landøy[1] and Angela Repanovici[2]

[1] University of Bergen Library, Norway, Dept. of Fine Mechanics and Mechatronics,
E-mail: Ane.Landoy@ub.uib.no
[2] Transilvania University of Brasov, Romania
E-mail: arepanovici@unitbv.ro

Abstract: In the light of the digital library development and of the online communication development, the university education develops in its turn new educational instruments and at the students' disposal to improve their professional skills and their individual studies. The university libraries, which have traditionally been focused on supporting the scholars' needs in research, have begun to play a more active role in this changing the educational system, as a result of the Bologna process. Incorporating the new technologies in the didactic process, accessing the electronic informational resources, using the web space for communication, all these imply qualitative research so as to determine and to optimize the students' learning methods, and we see a movement in the library world of libraries actively pursuing this. However, to be able to play an active role in the students' acquiring of scholarly skills, libraries need to implement systems for uncovering the gaps in students' knowledge. We find that theories and practices from the fields of market research and marketing analysis provide a helpful perspective. In this paper we will present a system for an university library to gain knowedge about their student's needs. This consists of several parts, and we will use examples of surveys, questionnaires and structured interviews. Also, we will present an analysis of data that have been acquired as part of our collaboration in European projects between the university libraries of Brasov, Romania and Bergen, Norway

Keywords: Marketing; University library; Electronic resources; Library assessment.

1. Introduction

As a result of the Bologna process and the changes in technology, one can see a digital library development. This is in tune with a development of the university education towards new educational instruments put at the students' disposal in order to improve their professional skills and their individual studies. University libraries, which have traditionally been focused on supporting the scholars' needs in research, have begun to see the need for playing a more active role in this changing educational system.

There have been many different solutions to the challenges of incorporating the new technologies in the didactic process, accessing the electronic informational resources and using the web space for communication. All these imply qualitative research so as to determine and to optimize the students' learning methods. Libraries in the world are actively pursuing this.

The theories and practices from the field of Market research and Marketing analysis may provide a helpful perspective in providing systems for uncovering the gaps in the student's knowledge. This "uncovering" is vital for the University libraries, for them to play an active role in helping students acquire scholarly skills.

2. What is necessary for a library to know?

The first step in a system for gaining knowledge is deciding what one wants to know. Is it the student's actual information behaviour when it comes to finding information for solving an assignment? Is it the choice between printed or electronic sources for students? Or what the university staff prioritizes? Is it the results from the library's teaching of information literacy? These are just examples of different questions a library may want to ask itself. This will be vital; as determining where the focus of the system of gaining knowledge is have a major influence of how to successfully design the methods.

A special part of relevant information is to be found in different kinds of statistics. This may be the library's own statistics, of visitors, books borrowed, downloads of electronic resources; or it may perhaps be the university statistics of age and geographical composition of students.

3. How to find out?

For each of the "questions" that wants answering under Part One, there will be one or several preferred methods of extracting that information. For the student's actual information behaviour one can use different kinds of observation methods, or use a survey for controlled questions. For the choice between printed or electronic resources one may look at the statistics for down loads vs the ordinary loans, or use interviews with different groups of users. For the results of the library teaching, one may have separate questions in the exams, or ask the examinators for their views.

4. Experiences from Bergen and Brasov

Since 2005 the University of Brasov and the University of Bergen Library have cooperated within the European Union Framework. As one of several projects, there has been planned and implemented a small survey of the student's use of electronic vs. printed material for their information gathering. The survey was developed in Brasov, after in-depth interviews and a pilot, and then translated into Norwegian and used. The results from both libraries can then be compared.

As a background for the survey it is hypothesized that:

1. Students who have more computer experience will be more likely to use the library's electronic resources and have higher self-efficacy.
2. Students who use the library's electronic resources from home have higher self-efficacy.
3. Students who frequent the library more often are more likely to use the library's electronic resources.
4. Students who use the library's electronic resources will be able to discriminate them from information from the Internet.
5. Students who express interest in learning about the library's electronic resources will have higher self-efficacy.

The survey examines some factors that correlate with students' usage of the library's electronic resources. While examining the relationship of age and gender to usage, we also focused on the concept of self-efficacy, a person's belief in their ability to attain desired outcomes

5. Methods

A pilot survey was conducted in the spring semester of 2008. That survey had a number of open-ended questions that were used to determine the close questions we asked in the fall survey. Although helpful in some areas (for example, to determine what students came to the library for), some of the open-ended questions had a very low answering rate and therefore were not helpful in focusing our final survey's questions (in particular, students did not answer open-ended questions relating to which electronic resources they used.)

Our fall 2008 survey contained two distinctive parts: a self-efficacy standard measuring instrument and a library component.

The self-efficacy survey made use of a Likert scale. Seventeen statements were presented to the students, and they could agree or disagree with them on a five point scale, from 1=Strongly Disagree to 5=Strongly Agree. Thus. a total numerical value can be calculated from all the responses.

The library section consisted of 31 questions. Questions one through six were concerned with gathering demographic data. Questions seven to 12 focused on whether or not the student used the Internet and what for. Questions 13 to 26 dealt with how the students used the library and its electronic resources. Questions 26 to 31 focused on the how students gather necessary information for their research. Most questions were closed-ended, although some were open-ended.

Survey responses were coded and input into the SPSS statistical package for analysis and the hypotheses presented above were tested using analysis of variance (ANOVA). The ANOVA is used to uncover the effects of independent variables on an interval dependent variable. This procedure employs the statistic (F) to test the statistical significance of the differences among the obtained means of two or more random samples from a given population. The statistic (F) is a ratio, which, if sufficiently larger than 1, indicates that the observed differences among the obtained means are statistically significant. It is important to note here, however, that the samples were not random, which reduces the generalization of our results.

Students' demographics

Demographics often yield important clues as to what factors contribute to undergraduates' use of electronic resources. There is a correlation between background characteristics such as gender, race, and initial critical thinking scores and library use during the freshmen and sophomore years, although these played less of an important role in the junior year.

Age

Age is one variable that correlates with comfort with computers and use of electronic resources.

Gender

Gender is another relevant factor in examining use of electronic databases. In a study of high school students, it was found that their attitudes towards computers and their computer use tended to vary by gender. This difference, however tended to diminish with computer experience.

Frequency of computer use

Computer anxiety is another contributing reason that discourages users from taking advantage of library resources and services

Library use

Students' library use is another variable influencing the use of electronic resources. It is reasonable to assume that the more an undergraduate uses the library, the more familiar the student will be with its resources, including its electronic resources.

Self-efficacy

The degree of self-efficacy is another variable that appears to influence use of the library's electronic resources.

6. Results and Discussion

Computer and Internet use

Computers are definitively present in students' lives in that 94% reported having access to a personal computer at home, with 93% saying they own one. For this population of incoming students there is no digital divide. Perhaps because so many students have access to a computer at home, they do not seem fully aware of the computing resources available to them: only 34% said they had access to computers at school, although there are student computer laboratories on campus.

Our incoming students are also very familiar with the Internet: 73% say they access the Internet daily, and an additional 25% at least once a week. In other words, over 97% of students access the Internet weekly or more often. When surfing, 44% look for educational information, 42% for entertainment information, 30% for news, 25% check for sports information, 9% for health information, and 70% report using e-mail often.

Library use.

Data revealed that 67% visit the library weekly, and only 1% has never been to the library. Asked what they did at the library, 80% reported studying, 38% to do research, 33% to sleep, 30% to socialize, 24% to use the library's electronic resources, 22% to check books out and 21% to e-mail or chat .

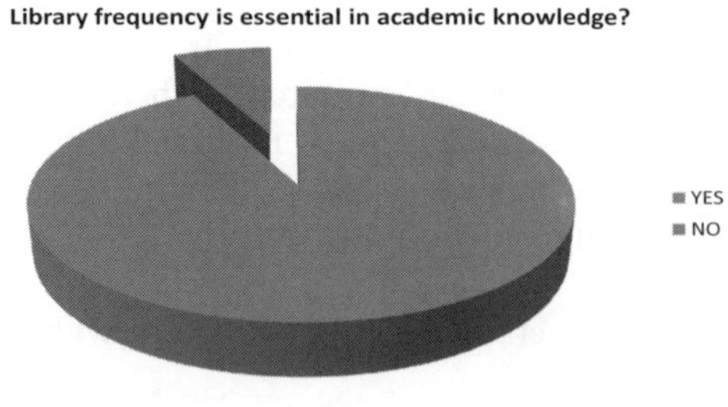

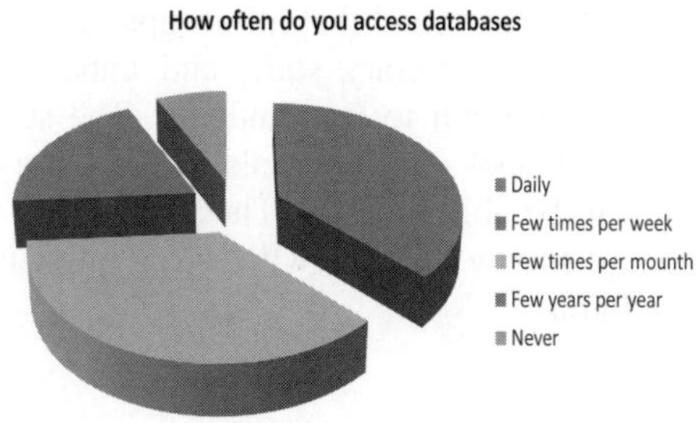

Even though some of these areas overlap (research and use of electronic resources, for example), it is clear that these students are mostly using the library as a place, not to make use of the library's resources or services.

It is interesting to note that although only 24% responded that they use the library's electronic resources when at the library, 81% responded that they have used those resources, and 30% said they use them at least weekly.

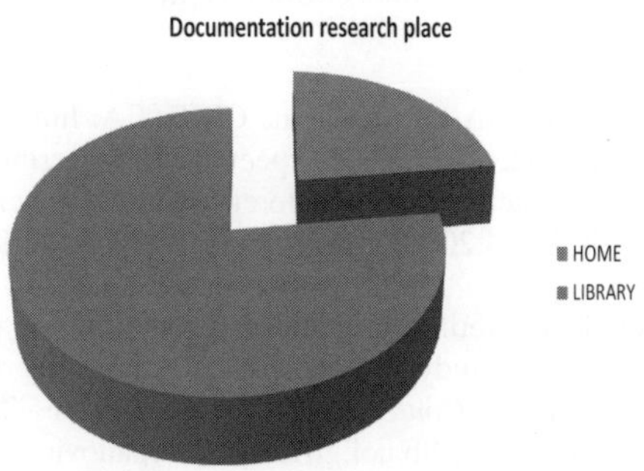

LibQual

The survey described above is a smaller specialized survey. A library may also use a larger, more general survey to cover (or rather uncover) the "customers" view of library services in more general terms. One such survey is LibQual. When the University of Bergen Library in the spring 2009 joined other Norwegian University libraries to use this survey, it was found that all groups of "customers" were happy with the service rendered by the library staff, and unhappy with the electronic resources, finding them too difficult to find and use. The scholarly staff was less pleased with the selection of books and journals in the library, while the students wanted more quiet zones to be able to work. These are just a few examples of the preliminary findings, and a survey like this will give a lot of information about the needs of the users of the library

7. Conclusion

In this paper we have given some examples of different kinds of information-gathering tools that a library may use in order to uncover needs among the users. The tools shown include examples of interviews, focus groups, specialized surveys and general surveys. In accordance with marketing research theories, these different kinds of tools can be systematized and put together in a system for providing a better knowledge. Further, this evaluation-system will make it possible for a library to improve its performance in accordance with the needs of the users.

Finally, research could also explore, in more depth, what makes students decide to use the Internet as opposed to the library's electronic resources, and what kinds of incentives would encourage students to use more of the library

It's ascertained that the Internet and the library are the most important informational resources.

The students rather make use of electronic informational resources.

The library services are considered by the patrons to be well organized, but the students prefer booklets containing instructions regarding the use of resources.

References

1. Angela REPANOVICI, Ion BARBU, Luciana CRISTEA: Information Literacy Learning Model for Engineering Students In New Aspects of Engineering Education, Proceedings of 5th WSEAS/IASME International Conference on Engineering Education (EE'08), Heraklion, Greece, July 22-24,2008, ISBN 978-960-6766-86-2,ISSN 1790-2769, pag.73-78.
2. Angela REPANOVICI: Marketing research for promoting the products and services of the university library. Case study at Transilvania University Library of Brasov, 17th *Greek Academic Libraries Conference*, 24 September *2008,Ioanina*, INVITED SPEAKER,pag.13, www.17conf.lib.uoi.gr/files/a7.Repanovici.ppt
3. Angela REPANOVICI, Ane LANDOY: Marketing research in internet resources: user need analyses, CONFERENCE SPEAKER Internet librarian International, Translating 2.0 technologies for tangible benefits & transparency, 16-17 October 2008, London, Information Today, Inc., ISBN 978-1-57387-364-2, Pag.143-151. http://www.internetlibrarian.com/2008/speakers.php?speaker=AngelaRepanovici
4. Angela REPANOVICI: Information Technology implication in Student Behaviour for Information Literacy skills, in Education and New Educational Technologies, Proceedings of the 4th WSEAS/IASME International Conference on educational Technologies (EDUTE'08)
Corfu, Greece, October 26-28,2008, PLENARY LECTURE, pag.9-10, pag.81-86 ISBN 978-960-474-013-0; ISSN 1790-5109

Portuguese School Libraries. The Design and Implementation of a Self Evaluation Model

Elsa Maria Quelhas Conde and Rosa Maria Mira Canhoto Martins

School Libraries Network, Ministry of Education, Portugal

Abstract: This paper contextualizes and describes the design and implementation of the Portuguese school libraries Self Evaluation Model. This instrument, inspired by evidence-based practice, contributes to assess the impact of school libraries in teaching and learning, whilst raising their profile at the heart of educational communities. Created by the School Libraries Network, it is aimed at collecting objective information on how school libraries develop and operate, how they contribute for effective student learning and success and for the goals of lifelong learning.

Keywords: School libraries; Self evaluation; Evidence-based practice; Value; Impact on learning; Portugal.

1. Introduction

The School Libraries Network is a programme created by the Portuguese Ministry of Education in 1996, aimed at establishing and developing school libraries in basic and secondary schools.

The principles underlying its inception identify the school library as an essential resource of the education system, with a decisive impact on skills and competence development, and on the preparation of the lifelong learner in the information-rich society. School libraries focus on student achievement by providing students with access to resources that stimulate intellectual growth and the development of critical thinking skills. As an integral part of the school curriculum, school libraries create a rich learning environment and play an effective role in supporting students and educators in the development of teaching and learning.

The delivery of a quality school library media program must be enhanced and is a priority to the School Libraries Network, which now faces a new operational stage after having completed the development of a significant number of school libraries and student reach: 100% of the basic schools' student population benefit from a school library. The percentage is of 92% for secondary education students and of 35% for primary school students who can use the school library of their own school. However, there is a larger percentage of smaller schools benefiting from the school library services of a library located at the group of schools' headquarters.

Helping school libraries to make a difference and achieve effectiveness and assisting them to measure impact and performance became, in this context, a priority. The construction of a school library Self Evaluation Model is the necessary answer to provide school libraries with a tool that will help them move forward by continuously seeking improvement.

2. Evaluating school libraries performance. How big is their impact?

Today, the impact of school libraries and the transformational action they bring along to the schools within which they operate is growingly acknowledged.

Traditionally, the assessment of this impact was centered in inputs (size of the collection, staff, budget) and outputs (number of loans, number of visits, number of sessions with students) measurements. This cost-efficiency paradigm has been replaced by a new logic, focused on the impact and benefits of school library's services for its users. Value and interest are now placed in measuring how successful services are and the approach is centered on results as the ultimate outcome of the services school libraries provide. At the end of the day, this shift means moving from assessing service efficiency to assessing service efficacy.

Cram (1999) describes this value-driven process: "[...] libraries have no inherent objective value. Value is (subjectively) assigned and is related to perception of actual or potential benefit. Rather, libraries create value by leveraging intangible assets in such a way as to add value and create benefits. They do not manage value. They manage processes and activities and they make decisions that might lead to production of value to the users of the library and to the parent organization".

The social context, the wide technological dissemination and the growing economical pressure underscore the need to demonstrate the value of school libraries. Evaluation plays a fundamental role in offering evidence of that value, as a validation exercise, but also as goal setting instrument, aimed at discovering how far we want to go and what the added value of our service is. This role is thus summarized in two fundamental questions: how do school libraries function and deliver their services? and what is their real impact in schools and in students' success?

3. Key concepts of the School Libraries Self Evaluation model

The School Libraries Self Evaluation Models aims at answering those questions, as part of a global development strategy for Portuguese school libraries. Several objectives grounded the decision of creating and implementing this instrument:

- the establishment of an instrument tailored to facilitate good management practices and continuous improvement cycles. As it is stated by the Model, "schools are to face this process as a self-identified need and not as an externally imposed instrument. The school as whole will benefit from the analysis and resulting reflection. It is expected that the self-evaluation process mobilizes the entire school community and that it can improve the wide range of possibilities offered by the school library", even if ruptures with rooted practices are required. (School Libraries Network, 2008)
- meeting the priorities established in the governmental agenda, centered around evidence-based policies and *what works* policies, and identification of value-generator services. The assessment of public administration services and programmes and the development of evidence-based policies has become a reform pathway conducted by the Portuguese government, materialized in instruments such as SIADAP - the public administration perfomance evaluation integrated system; schools' external evaluation; and, more recently, teaching staff assessment. Services are invited to evaluate performance and by doing it, they become more transparent and effective in their quest for continuous quality;
- following up on the education system reform (changes at management level, creation of new departments and internal structures of power, school and teaching staff assessment) with the achievement of a greater role for school libraries and the generalization of library-inclusive politics of recognition;

- answering to ICT driven change and to the possibilities introduced by new digital environments, which have challenged traditional school library service offer. There is now a generalized sense of urgency pushing services to identify weaknesses and change attitudes and practice.

The concepts and core units of meaning that sustained the elaboration of the model are introduced in the following sections.

3.1 The concept of value

The Self-Evaluation Model provides a reference framework for pedagogical regulation and action, offering a set of critical success factors to guide schools in delivering quality and reaching best performance throughout the different domains of school library activity. Value is a transversal concept, understood by the Self Evaluation Model as "an inner feature of objects but as something related to experiences and to the benefits we can extract from them. No one will contest that pleasant, well equipped libraries are important, but more important than that is the use we make of them, consistent with its very mission and leading to performance results which meet school's programmed objectives". (School Libraries Network, 2008)

Value is moreover inherent to good management practices and to continuous improvement cycles: based on the identification of strong and weak points, a new development plan must be forged. This plan, informed by an evidence-based understanding of the school library and the context within which it operates, is paramount to elaborating realistic objectives and priorities.

3.2 The concept of evaluation in organizational context

In the organizational context, the literature defines evaluation as a quality seeking process, a way of "systematically assessing effectiveness against a predetermined norm or standard" (Cronin, 1982), a comparison between "what is" and "what out to be for the purpose of exercising judgment (Van House et al., 1990:3), a systematic reality check, confirming the "extent to which a system (for example a library) has achieved its objectives in a certain period of time". It is also described as a "systematic process of determining value (in terms of benefit gained) and "quality" (as reflected in customers' satisfaction) of a system. (McKenzie, 1989: 156).

3.3 The concept of evidence-based practice and action-research

The concept of evidence-based practice is operationalized by the systematic collection of evidence related to the daily functioning of a service. The quantity and quality of the evidence collected must inform practice and provide valuable information that answers a specific question or effectively contributes to finding a solution or improving a malfunctioning situation.

Several experts have explored the concept. Ross Todd (2008) applies it to school libraries, considering that they must make a difference in the school they serve, while demonstrating their impact in teaching and learning: "EBP combines professional wisdom, reflective experience, and understanding of students' needs with the judicious use of research-derived evidence to make decisions about how the school library can best meet the instructional goals of the school. In order to accomplish this, school libraries need to systematically collect evidence that shows how their practices impact student achievement; the development of deep knowledge and understanding; and the competencies and skills for thinking, living, and working. […] A holistic approach to evidence-based practice in school libraries involves three dimensions: evidence for practice, evidence in practice, and evidence of practice".

Great emphasis is placed in determining how processes contribute to the achievement of a larger goal, which should be confirmed by the accomplishment of specific quality-embedded outcomes. Resources and processes are important only in the measure of their added value and contribution to developing teaching and learning.

The Self Evaluation Model is also an example of an action-research process, as it endeavors the establishment of a relationship between processes and the impact or value they generate. Typically, such a process comprehends: (1) identification of a problem; (2) evidence collection; (3) scrutiny, evaluation and interpretation of evidence; (4) knowledge generation to guide future action. (Markless and Streffield, 2006:120)

3.4 A new concept of school library: impacting teaching and learning

The renewed concept of the school library as a hub for innovative and collaborative ways of teaching and learning encompasses new strategies to approach and apprehend knowledge and reality, based on permanent questioning, research and inquiry (inquiry based learning). It reflects a global modification of the social structures as a result of the ICT dissemination, networks development, and emergence of new information diffusion and knowledge construction environments, which call for new literacies and lifelong learning.

Moreover the school library needs to cope with change and reinforce its role by researching evidence of its impact in student's attainment and performance and by investing in the development of its critical success factors.

4. Fitting the Self-Evaluation Model with the school

The self evaluation process must develop harmoniously within the heart of the school as an organizational structure, with which it interacts. Those structures or clusters have variable interests and levels of intervention: there is the executive board, which must be included in the assessment development at a very early stage, acting as a process facilitator; but there are also teachers, students, families, tutors and other agents whose participation will be requested.

The organic relation of the school library with the school's greater ecology and organizational context determines its success or failure. This process is deeply related to how management structures are able to engage in integrative, collaborative work solutions. If this practice fails, the opportunity for success is undermined. That is normally the case for schools with a restricted participative culture, little innovativeness, resistance to embrace chance, and lack of staff with a goal-oriented vision.

A good interaction, reflective organic embeddedness of the school library happens when:

- ✓ The school library action plan is part of the school's strategic and operational plan and there is an alignment of goals and teaching and learning objectives;
- ✓ The teacher librarian is no longer merely seen as an information manager and becomes a key actor with an active role in students' training, curricular

development and literacy and digital literacy promotion and advancement;

- ✓ Cooperation is reinforced through planning of collaborative activities with the teaching staff of all subjects;
- ✓ The teacher librarian is a catalyst for the school's enhanced performance and success;
- ✓ The teacher librarian seeks permanent questioning and improvement of management practices and is concerned with how they impact school and students' success;

The teacher librarian is a leader, able to demonstrate the school library's value, using evidence and exploring continuous communication flows with different school actors and stakeholders. (Eisenberg e Miller 2002)

Leadership and the ability to set a goal and vision and strategically implement them are paramount to the success of the self-evaluation process. It entails:

- ✓ Having a conciliating attitude and the capacity to react and counter problems:
- ✓ Grabbing the opportunity and being keen on managing the agenda of hot issues and on presenting strategies to the executive board;
- ✓ Articulating priorities and discussing objectives, programs and projects with the school;
- ✓ Developing a culture of evaluation. Managing evidence adequately to better communicate the school library value and correct gaps;
- ✓ Continuously communicating and cooperating with the school structures and with community stakeholders.

As exposed above, the Self Evaluation Model is intertwined with the school library's strategic planning and must respond adequately and timely to the school's identity characteristics and objectives. Meaningful decision-making is therefore grounded in the evidence collected, in a state of permanent dialogue with the school library's internal (structural conditions) and external environments. Setting priorities, acknowledging threats and strengths, and adjusting action to greater teaching and learning objectives is possible only if these aspects are taken into consideration.

5. The Self Evaluation Model structure

The school libraries Self Evaluation Model comprises 4 domains, divided in sub domains. This structure was devised to fully capture the critical aspects of school libraries' activity as facilitators of multimodal structures – material, human, financial, informational – and teaching and learning resources connected to the curriculum, reading promotion and literacy development within school and at the wider community:

A. Supporting Curriculum Development:

A.1 Articulating the School Library with the Curriculum, Pedagogic Structures and Teaching Staff; A.2 Developing Information Literacy Skills;

B. Promoting Reading and Literacy.

C. Projects, Partnerships, Open-ended and Community-oriented Activities: C.1 Supporting Open-ended, Extra-Curriculum and Curriculum-Enrichment Activities; C.2 Projects and Partnerships;

D. School Library Management; D.1 Co-operation with the School/ Groups of Schools. Access and Services Provided by the School Library: D.2 Staff, Equipment and Resources for Service Provision; D.3 Collection Management.

The model is implemented yearly, with schools selecting one particular domain, which will constitute the core of the self-evaluation procedure. The departure point may emerge from several triggers: an initial scoping and diagnosis exercise; the selection of an area identified as critical by previous assessments; the selection of a priority domain following the school's goals and needs-based assessment; the empirical knowledge derived from the library's functioning.

The operationalization of the model must be acknowledged as an intrinsic process, internalized within the library's normal activities, practices and routines.

After a period of 4 years all domains must have undergone the self-evaluation procedure. This time frame matches every school's management and strategic planning cycle.

Each sub domain includes a set of indicators, which address nuclear aspects of its effective functioning. In turn, indicators unfold into critical success factors - examples of situations and actions which successfully operationalize a given indicator, contributing to the attainment of a better assessment qualification.

The model is purposefully ambitious in the definition of these factors to stimulate excellent performance and simultaneously avoid that schools portray commonly developed activities only. This way, good practice is fostered, combined with a training and professional development component.

Evidence reveals the depth and scope of activities and sustains the appreciation of results. For each indicator the model provides potential evidence collection instruments, which will support evaluation and the determination of a performance level.

Within the model's structure, the last table contains examples of improvement measures, whenever specific needs or debilities pertaining to a specific indicator are detected in the library's performance and call for action.

Performance levels are also part of the Model, defining what the school library is expected to deliver in relation to each sub domain. School library provision can be described as being at one of four performance levels: excellent, good, intermediate, and poor. This scale serves the purpose of reality check, performance assessment and awareness of what is at stake to achieve higher performance levels.

Different levels of the scale are attached to descriptors, which are related to indicators and critical success factors considered for each domain or sub domain. A level of service provision is attained when the library's services correspond to the descriptors listed in a proportion of 4/5, 5/6, 6/7, etc., depending on the number of items under the typical description of a school library at each level.

This assessment demands a systematic investigation and is sustained by evidence obtained through a battery of both quantitative and qualitative methods, as well as through various information collection techniques, amongst which are:

- ✓ Policy and strategic planning documents regulating school (PEE, PCT) and school library's activities (Activity Plan, Rules and Regulations, etc,);
- ✓ Meeting logs, records of meetings, views and perceptions about school library-led activities;

- ✓ Routine planning documents, schemes of work, lessons plans, promotion materials;
- ✓ Statistics and records;
- ✓ Work produced by students at the library and in co-operation with the library;
- ✓ Data generating instruments specifically designed to collect evidence: observation logs, questionnaires, interviews.

The Self Evaluation model is accompanied by a Data Collection Tools booklet, comprising several instruments: teaching staff questionnaires, students questionnaires, family/ tutors questionnaires; observation grids for curriculum-related school library activities and reading and literacy competencies: Checklists, etc.

Evidence collection instruments can be tailored to each school library's specificities: modifications are welcome if considered necessary, for instance as it is the case for primary schools and pre-schools. The use of these instruments is directed at allowing uniformity in the type of data gathered, making benchmarking exercises feasible without denying the possibility of contextual adjustments.

It is suggested that evidence collection instruments are administered to 20% of the teaching staff and 10% of the total student population – students of all school years to ensure balance and representativeness.

6. A methodology for implementing the model

Implementing self evaluation requires the previous accomplishment of several steps:

- ✓ Motivation and institutional commitment of the school's executive board and pedagogical structures towards the school library self-evaluation process;
- ✓ Teaching staff and executive board induction and training on self evaluation procedures to enhance engagement and burden-sharing;
- ✓ Participation of the school library in extended or restricted meetings with teaching staff for data collection;
- ✓ Flexible and pro-active attitude of the teaching staff in the provision of data and documentation;
- ✓ Establishment of evidence collection strategies targeting students, in cooperation with teachers;
- ✓ Wide and full acceptance and acknowledgement of results;
- ✓ Engagement in the promotion of an improvement and development plan.

Conducting the evaluation plan is a process made of different stages:

- ✓ Diagnoses;
- ✓ Choice of a Domain to undertake self evaluation;
- ✓ Defining which evidence to collect, suitable collection instruments, limitations and needs assessment;
- ✓ Defining populations and samples to administer instruments;
- ✓ Establishment of a time frame;
- ✓ Data collection and analysis;
- ✓ Identification of strengths and weaknesses and positioning of the school library in a performance level ranking, according to benchmarks provided;

- ✓ Interpretation and description of assessment results. Definition of improvement measures;
- ✓ Communication of assessment results and foreseen improvement measures, which will integrate the school' Internal Evaluation Report.

The School Library Self Evaluation Report is a document containing the description of the assessment results. It is aimed at sensitizing the management boards, promoting the diffusion of results and building a bridge to the fulfillment of future planning needs.

The fact that the self-assessment procedure focuses, every year, exclusively on one domain does not mean that all other domains and areas of intervention of the school library are to be neglected and eliminated from the School Library Self Evaluation Report. Quite on the contrary, this document is useful in providing a holistic vision of the school library's functioning. Section A of the report shall include detailed, well grounded information pertaining to the domain under analysis; but section B exists to report information related to all other domains, which must remain active and monitored.

A final grid summarizes the self-evaluation global process, developed during a 4 year time frame, corresponding to schools' management cycles. A Profile fact sheet also accompanies the Annual School Library Self Evaluation Report, providing additional relevant information, updated yearly, concerning the contextual situation of each school.

7. The implementation pilot

The implementation pilot of the Self-evaluation model is a two-year phase initiated in 2008 and it is still ongoing.

This experimental period started with an introductory meeting held at the 5 Regional Directorates of Education. These meetings officially launched the Model and were attended by teacher librarians and heads of executive boards. As a rule of thumb only schools staffed with full-time teacher librarians were invited.

Throughout the year, the process was followed-up locally by the School Libraries Network staff based in schools and monitored centrally by the School Libraries Network headquarters.

From September to December 5 online training courses on the Self Evaluation Model took place, targeted at teacher librarians coming from all 5 Regional Directorates of Education. More than 120 teachers participated. As part of these training sessions, the School Libraries Network held a Seminar in Lisbon with international experts Ross Todd, Kathy Lemaire, Peter Streatfield and Nancy Everhart.

Last year a total of 119 school libraries have tested the Model: 12 primary and schools and pre-schools; 8 integrated basic schools (providing the three cycles of basic education in an *integrated* form); 69 second and third cycle schools; and 30 secondary schools, all geographically spread around the country.

The School Libraries Network obtained feedback from 98 of the total universe of schools that implemented the model: 19 school libraries tested Domain A; 45 tested domain B; 7 tested domain C; and 27 tested domain D.

Almost all of these schools attained level 2 (Intermediate) or 3 (Good). Three school libraries attained level 4 (Excellent) and one school library attained level 1 (Poor), which somehow denotes problems with the conduction of the self evaluation process.

8. Structural constraints and facilitating factors

The implementation pilot was pivotal for extracting conclusions and detecting difficulties in applying the model. It is necessary to understand these difficulties in light of the recent existence of school libraries in Portugal – they are mainly the result of the lack of evidence—based assessment practice and of the entrenchment of an evaluation culture excessively focused in inputs and processes rather than in outcomes in impacts.

Many school libraries experienced difficulties in the identification of an array of evidence potentially collectable through the use of suggested instruments. This resulted in poor, vague descriptions and in the omission of relevant information. Observation grids for competence assessment were especially difficult to use and there were also problems with analyzing, interpreting and deriving weaknesses, strengths or conclusions from data. Few schools experienced problems with logging and computerizing data.

A great number of schools found it hard to self-rate and define a performance level, poorly articulating results, standards, critical success factors and scenarios. This last difficulty, especially evident for collaborative work dimensions, is most likely due to the distance that still separates best performance scenarios from reality, making it difficult for libraries to achieve learning improvement and students' attainment goals.

Throughout 2009, the School Libraries Network carried the implementation pilot forth, opening the testing phase to more participants. There is now a total of 300 participating schools and a solid acceptance and understanding of the instrument, now used in its manifold contributions for planning, execution and assessment of school libraries' activities. This growing recognition by schools' executive boards and by the General Inspection of Education contributes to raising the Model's profile and to its wider promotion and implementation.

9. Future development perspectives

After running the two-year implementation pilot, the School Libraries Network will promote the generalized use of the model throughout previously assessed and not yet assessed schools, which will expectably benefit from the allocation of a full-time teacher librarian.

The pilot will contribute to problem detection and further revision, after which the model will reach a stabilized version. We anticipate this process will be finalized by the end of this school year, after completion of the following steps:

- ✓ Simplification of the Model's features, thriving for the definite construction of a clear cut, transparent instrument, free from unnecessary information;
- ✓ Create information collection instruments and techniques specifically tailored for primary school and pre-schools and new instruments (interview scripts, focus group interviews, questionnaires for the school/ group of schools executive board, etc.) and improve existent instruments (i.e. observation grids);

- ✓ Create an application package using Excel, Access, SQL or SPSS, accompanied by a user guide, to introduce schools to data processing and analysis;
- ✓ Promote the diffusion of good self-evaluation practice amongst schools;
- ✓ Apply ISO standards to the statistical analysis of school libraries' services and activities;
- ✓ Produce guidelines on how to adjust the school library evaluation results to the school' self-evaluation procedure, establishing links with external evaluation promoted by the General Inspection of Education;
- ✓ Continue the advocacy and promotion initiatives, as well as teacher professional development and training for model implementation;
- ✓ Consider new aspects of school libraries offer such as service provision for new audiences, several schools or group of schools.

10. Conclusion

It has now been a year since the Self Evaluation Model implementation pilot was initiated. This phase, still ongoing, was crucial to determine the Model's sense of opportunity and adequacy for school libraries and to perfect it and more consistently adjust it to the school and the library's needs. Despite some predictable constraints, the model is frequently referred to as an instrument at the service of continuous improvement and appropriation levels are encourageably high. Next phases comprehend adjustments based on information collected from the pilot and further extension of the Model to a vaster universe of schools.

Bibliography

Brophy, P. (2006). *Measuring library performance; principles and techniques*. London: Facet Publishing.

Cram, J. (1999). "Six Impossible Things Before Breakfast: A multidimensional approach to measuring the value of libraries". Third Northumbria International Conference on Performance Measurement in Libraries and Information Services, 27-31 August. <http://www.alia.org.au/~jcram/six_things.html> [20/05/2009]

Cronin, B. (1982). Performance Measurement and Information Management. Aslib Proceedings, 1982, 34 (5), 227-36.

Eisenberg, M. & Miller, D. (2002). This Man Wants to Change Your Job, *School Library Journal*. 9/1/2002 <http://www.schoollibraryjournal.com/index.asp?layout=article&articleid=CA240047> [20/05/2009]

School Libraries Network (2008). *School Libraries Self Evaluation Model* <http://www.rbe.min-edu.pt/np4/np4/31.html> [20/05/2009]

Markless, S. & Steatfield, D. (2006). *Evaluating the Impact of your library*, London, Facet Publishing.

Mackenzie, G. 1990. Performance measurement. In: Maurice, L., ed. *Academic library management*. London: The Library Association: 196–205.

Scholastic Research (2008) "School Libraries Work! Scholastic Research & Results". <http://librarypublishing.scholastic.com/content/stores/LibraryStore/pages/images/SLW3.pdf > [20/05/2009]

Todd, R. (2008) "The Evidence-Based Manifesto for School Librarians". *School Library journal*. <http://www.schoollibraryjournal.com/article/CA6545434.html> [20/05/2009]

Van House, N. et al. (1990). *Measuring academic library performance: A practical approach*. Chicago: American Library Association.

10. Impact Assessment

IFLA, Sustainability and Impact Assessment

Fiona Bradley

Programme Coordinator ALP, International Federation of Library Associations and Institutions (IFLA), The Netherlands

Abstract: As an international organisation dedicated to improving access to information through libraries, IFLA has a number of core activities in place to achieve this goal. The Action for Development through Libraries Programme (ALP), and the Freedom of Access to Information and Freedom of Expression (FAIFE) Committee are two such activities that have in recent years benefitted from substantial funding from the Swedish International Development and Co-operation Agency (Sida). Through Sida's funding IFLA has been able to undertake training and education activities for librarians in all areas of librarianship – from cataloguing to Internet access in libraries.
Sida's funding for IFLA ends in December 2009. What do libraries and library organisations do when the money for activities runs out? How do they best persuade funders, potential funders and other stakeholders that the activities they carry out offer value for money, and have an impact beyond the numbers of people trained? How can libraries show exactly how important they are to their users and wider society? This paper talks briefly about IFLA's experiences with funders' evaluation requirements and the difficulties of finding an evaluation methodology that is appropriate for the type of international activities IFLA engages in. It discusses the need for success stories and best practice in IFLA's advocacy work, and suggests that impact assessment offers a way to show the real value of library work to key partners and stakeholders.

1. About the International Federation of Library Associations and Institutions (IFLA)

IFLA is the global voice of the library profession, with more than 1600 members in 150 countries. IFLA represents the interests of more than 700,000 information workers worldwide, and has regional offices and language centres across the globe representing diverse cultural and library practices (IFLA, n.d.).
IFLA works to advocate for free access to information, to demonstrate the value of libraries, and to promote high standards in the profession. Training programmes are one of many ways that IFLA carries out this work. IFLA committees, such as the Committee on Copyright and Other Legal Matters (CLM) develop policy, which is implemented by the Action for Development through Libraries Programme (ALP) and the Committee on Free Access to Information and Freedom of Expression (FAIFE) via workshops, training programmes, and guidelines.
IFLA currently provides training to librarians in a wide range of areas. These include policy-based workshops on IFLA manifestos, including the Internet Manifesto (IFLA/FAIFE, 2002), Manifesto on Transparency, Good Governance and Freedom from Corruption (IFLA/FAIFE, 2008a), and the IFLA/UNESCO Public Library Manifesto (IFLA/UNESCO, 1994). Another important training programme

is Access to Information on HIV/AIDS through Libraries (IFLA/FAIFE, 2008b). IFLA uses a variety of training models, one model comprises a team of core trainers who provide cascade, or train-the-trainer, delivery in countries around the world that have expressed a need for a particular training programme. IFLA's trainers are located world-wide and work on behalf of IFLA to deliver training to colleagues in their region.

IFLA has a large and diverse array of activities beyond these training programmes, from individual workshops in-country to setting standards for the whole profession. This gives IFLA an advantage in reaching library and information workers across the world. However this can also make administering, reporting on, and evaluating its activities challenging.

2. Activities, Funding and Impact Assessment: Activities and Funing

ALP and FAIFE received grant funding from the Swedish International Development and Co-operation Agency (Sida) from 2004-2009 to provide training in areas including professional development and human rights. Reporting on these activities has tended to be quantitative, which does not necessarily reflect the outcomes of the training after the programme. In 2008 IFLA Headquarters gained more capacity with the creation of the role of Senior Policy Advisor Role and an advocacy unit. As a result, IFLA decided to increase the emphasis on evaluating the impact of its activities. IFLA is now actively investigating the use of impact assessment. The method is being used as a trial in 2009 to evaluate FAIFE's activities.

Impact assessment is a process that aims to identify the consequences of an action (Markless & Streatfield, 2008). Actions can take many forms, but in IFLA's case this may include training programmes, new services, or the introduction of a new policy. For IFLA, Impact assessment offers the means to:

- evaluate our diverse activities using methods that work in different situations, countries and cultures.
- show value to funders, potential funders and other stakeholders.
- complement some of the work of IFLA's strategic partners, some of whom are already using this methodology. For example, the Global Libraries programme of the Bill and Melinda Gates Foundation uses impact assessment to measure their programmes.
- show the importance of libraries to users and society: moving beyond statistics about door count and circulation to success stories and case studies that vividly illustrates IFLA's work.
- demonstrate sustainability: libraries are worth funding. Impact evidence provides the basis for better advocacy for libraries.

Impact Assessment will enable IFLA to set indicators and benchmarks more closely tailored to programme objectives, to capture the difference that training makes to the librarians who participate and ultimately, library users. Impact assessment provides a framework to ensure that the goals of a programme are met, and more broadly to answer the question "does this programme make a difference?" The technique will also be used to develop a method for evaluating training that can be carried out by trainers in-country to find out what happened after the training has ended – did it change the skills or knowledge of the librarians who were trained? This gives IFLA the ability to distribute the work of collecting impact data to regions around the world and to ensure that measurement is designed with the needs of different countries in mind.

It also provides a mechanism for improved reporting on progress to funders, programme participants and other stakeholders. The technique will be used to enhance IFLA's reporting to Sida in 2009, in addition to the measures that are currently collected. Data collected in 2009 will give IFLA the ability to measure progress across the whole year. Although this is a relatively short timeframe, it will help to evaluate how well the new assessment techniques have worked.

When designing and collecting measures of impact, it is important to collect data from all points of view, and not just data that supports a positive outcome. Understanding how programmes can be improved, and in some instances, knowing what went wrong, is essential to improving programmes in the future. Yet, designing impact measures can be difficult. Analysing whether a change was the result of your action alone is not easy to determine (Poll & Payne, 2006). Any number of other factors may havec ontributed to a librarian's knowledge and skills as a result of training, such as seeking advice from colleagues or reading about new services. For this reason, it is important to design impact measures that are instead representative of change, what Streatfield and Markless call "surrogates" (Markless & Streatfield, 2008). Only with this comprehensive approach to collecting and reporting on impact can the technique be used as a tool for advocacy.

3. IFLA and Impact Assessment

IFLA is using impact assessment in 2009 as a trial to evaluate FAIFE's activities. An example of this is cascade training delivered in Peru, Russia and the Philippines. Impact indicators are identified at the start of the project, followed by four impact phases;

- Phase 1: IFLA trains core trainers in programme material and collecting evidence for impact assessment
- Phase 2: Core trainers return to their regions to train colleagues, and collect stories for evidence
- Phase 3: Stories gathered during training are analysed
- Phase 4: IFLA evaluates evidence against indicators to measure impact

All projects using the technique in the trial in 2009 are currently at stage 2. IFLA will evaluate its experience of using impact assessment in 2009, and if it is a positive one will strongly consider using the method in appropriate projects in the future.

In the future, impact assessment may be used by IFLA to demonstrate success in implementing its projects and to obtain additional funding for projects. Funders want to see that organisations have the capacity to successfully carry our programmes and ensure their sustainability. More broadly, funders want to know, "are libraries good value to invest in?"(Poll & Payne, 2006). Impact assessment can provide a strong body of evidence for funders that can be illustrated with success stories and case studies. In turn, the evidence that IFLA generates with impact assessment can be used to support IFLA's advocacy goals of freedom, equity and inclusion. IFLA has introduced an Advocacy Framework to guide a strategic approach to training and activities (IFLA Headquarters, 2009), impact assessment is one of the ways that this new approach will be measured.

4. Evidence, funding and sustainability

Funders are increasingly interested in evaluating the sustainability of programmes, to ensure that they will be able to continue past the period of initial funding and to maintain quality control. Preparing sustainability plans at the start of funding is a useful way to consider the long-term costs of running programmes, how they will be evaluated, and if and when they should. Some funding organisations such as The Global Libraries programme of the Bill and Melinda Gates Foundation are already using impact assessment. It is important for libraries to become familiar with, and to use, funders' assessment methods to satisfy grant conditions and to assist with securing future funding. Demonstrating the success and sustainability of a project is essential to the long-term funding of libraries.

Impact assessment has the potential to provide richer information about the success of IFLA's projects, that goes beyond attendance figures. It is hoped that it will be able to provide a more detailed picture of how IFLA's work brings positive change to library staff and their communities by using stories and narratives. In turn, it will assist in advocating for libraries, by being able to build on evidence, case studies, and success stories to more clearly describe the difference libraries make.

References

IFLA. (n.d.). More about IFLA. Retrieved from http://www.ifla.org/en/about/more

IFLA Headquarters. (2009). 2008 IFLA Annual Report. Annual Report, IFLA. Retrieved from http://www.ifla.org/files/hq/annual-reports/2008.pdf

IFLA/FAIFE. (2002). The IFLA Internet Manifesto. Retrieved from http://www.ifla.org/en/publications/the-ifla-internet-manifesto

IFLA/FAIFE. (2008a). IFLA Manifesto on Transparency, Good Governance and Freedom from Corruption. Retrieved from http://www.ifla.org/en/publications/ifla-manifesto-on-transparency-good-governance-and-freedom-from-corruption

IFLA/FAIFE. (2008b). Learning Materials for workshops on Access to information on HIV/AIDS through Libraries. Retrieved from http://www.ifla.org/en/publications/learning-materials-for-workshops-on-access-to-information-on-hivaids-through-libraries

IFLA/UNESCO. (1994). IFLA/UNESCO Public Library Manifesto 1994. Retrieved from http://www.ifla.org/en/publications/iflaunesco-public-library-manifesto-1994

Markless, S., & Streatfield, D. (2008). Supported self-evaluation in assessing the impact of HE libraries. Performance Measurement & Metrics, 9(1), 38-47.

Poll, R., & Payne, P. (2006). Impact measures for libraries and information services. Library Hi Tech.

What is Impact Assessment and Why is it Important?

David Streatfield

Information Management Associates, UK;
Sharon Markless, Senior Lecturer in Higher Education, King's College, London, UK

Abstract: This paper offers a definition of impact assessment and discusses some of the implications of this and other definitions. A particular approach to impact assessment is introduced, as developed for use in a variety of library and information service settings (Markless and Streatfield, 2006) and the principles underpinning this approach are described. This approach has been adapted by the Bill and Melinda Gates Foundation's *Global Libraries Initiative* when providing impact planning and assessment support to grantees through their '*IPA Road Map*'. The approach was also adopted by the International Federation of Library Associations (IFLA) in devising its impact assessment strategy for evaluation of its future *Free Access to Information and Freedom of Expression* (FAIFE) work. The importance of impact assessment in a variety of settings is outlined: from school libraries to university researcher support and from public libraries to electronic information services. Some 'unofficial' observations are offered on the relationships between impact assessment, advocacy and service sustainability, particularly in relation to major service development programmes such as the Global Libraries Initiative.

---

*Although this paper draws on and quotes from the **IPA Road Map** developed by the Global Libraries Initiative, all the comments and opinions expressed are those of the authors and should not be interpreted as representing an official GL viewpoint.*

---

1. Defining impact

In preparing our book on *Evaluating the impact of your library* (Markless and Streatfield, 2006), we borrowed a definition of impact from the educational evaluation literature (Fitz-Gibbon, 1996), as:

" … any effect of the service (or of an event or initiative) on an individual or group." This definition acknowledges that the impact can be positive or negative and may be intended or accidental. When using this definition, measuring impact is about identifying and evaluating change.

These broad precepts were adopted by the Bill and Melinda Gates Foundation in relation to the Global Libraries Initiative (GL) work in various countries, some aspects of which will be described in more detail in later papers in this seminar. The GL Impact Planning and Assessment (IPA) *Road Map*, which is intended to help grantees to engage with impact assessment (and which we helped to write), again emphasises change, but in more specific ways:

> "The essential element of impact is change: the ways in which individuals, groups, communities or organizations are changed through your country grant program; the results of the program. We may therefore define impact as: any effect of your country grant program on an individual, group or community."

The GL definition repeats the caveats about negative impacts and about intention but adds a dimension about the breadth and depth of change. An impact:

- may be wide ranging, affecting many stakeholders from library staff to library users; from local government officials to local community groups, or
- may be more specific, directly affecting only one group of stakeholders
- can occur on levels from the superficial to the life-changing.

For a large-scale programme such as the GL, it is important to strike a balance between the different levels and types of impact, as well as between short and longer term effects. As the GL *IPA Road Map* says,

> "Too much long term, far reaching impact will be difficult to achieve and monitor; too much short term, limited impact will not allow you to use the full potential of your country grant program".

The main levels at which a major programme can have an impact are summarised in the diagram below:

Global Libraries Initiative *IPA Road Map*, 2008

Clearly some of these areas of impact would require long-term attention but collecting evidence of impact about others could be accommodated within an annual planning cycle.

2. Evaluation or assessment: implications of the definitions

Working in a UK and European context, we have readily adopted the nomenclature of impact evaluation, which we have interpreted as largely dependent upon qualitative research evidence about effectiveness and as broadly complementary to 'traditional' performance measurement, seen as quantitative and largely focused on monitoring service efficiency. In this broad context, assessment is primarily a term used in gauging educational performance of students.

In strong contrast, the GL Program reflects wide (but not universal) US research usage in distinguishing between ***impact planning and assessment*** and ***impact evaluation***. In this view, IPA is seen as the entire process of gathering both qualitative impact evidence and performance metrics and applying them through advocacy to secure sustainability of services. The term impact evaluation is reserved to describe systematic causation or attribution studies (using a rigorous approach to collecting evidence that shows whether and how an intervention is directly responsible for particular changes or benefits). Causation studies seek to answer such questions as 'How much better off are beneficiaries *as a result of* the intervention?' or 'Does the intervention have a different impact on different groups?'; 'Did the intervention *cause* the impact?' and 'What would have happened if the intervention had *not* taken place?'

Although this distinction is important (and reflects the wider impact evaluation concerns of the Bill and Melinda Gates Foundation) the IPA *Road Map* stresses that:

> "GL does *not* expect grantees to undertake attribution studies. In the context of Global Libraries, IPA concentrates on planning to make a difference through the country grant program; on assessing implementation (what has been put in place); and on gathering evidence of benefits that have accrued or changes that have been made since the country grant program began. We can reasonably assume that the country grant program has *contributed* to the changes identified and has 'added value' but there may be other influences involved so we do not seek to prove a causal relationship."

3. An approach to impact assessment

Over the past ten years we have developed an approach to impact assessment[1] that is specifically designed to help managers of libraries and information services to get to grips with the impact of their services. This work emerged from recognition that although most library service managers are comfortable with collecting traditional performance data to monitor the efficiency of their services, many found it hard to step back and address the deeper effects of their services on users and their communities. The book referred to earlier sought to distil our experience of running impact evaluation workshops and consultancies for library and information service managers of all kinds (including public, health, education, government, law and business LIS managers). In essence, this approach encourages LIS managers to

- carefully articulate the impact objectives of that part of the service under review (so that you know what you are trying to achieve)
- consider which impact indicators will be most useful to tell whether that element of the service is succeeding or not

- then, to decide what evidence will be collected to illuminate the chosen impact indicators and how to collect it, and
- decide how to use that evidence to enhance services and secure service sustainability.

In working through this process, we encourage participants to:

- maintain a clear focus on what is manageable and achievable within available resources
- base choices about where to focus on what is known from the research evidence about where libraries ***can*** make a difference
- align library themes for impact assessment with wider organisational/national objectives and priorities
- approach impact objectives by asking what will tell you that change has occurred
- recognise that most impact evidence is qualitative in character, calling for rigorous application of social science research methods based on observation, asking questions and inferring change from review of the products of people's activity (e.g. student assignments)
- see the need for baseline impact evidence to enable judgements to be made about progress over time
- recognise that impact assessment timetables may not readily fit into the library annual planning cycle.

The impact indicators generated through this type of process can be as broad or as narrow as the vision of the participants. For example, strategic impact objectives for a library service might range from more community involvement in local government decision making to individuals use information to: make better business decisions.

The main principles underlying our approach to impact assessment are that:

- staff should be empowered to understand and conduct impact assessment work
- key decisions about the scope and focus of this work should be influenced by those directly involved, including service users where feasible
- impact indicators should be appropriate for the service and not imposed by an outside agency for political purposes
- flexibility is needed in conducting impact assessment but based on rigorous application of appropriate evidence-collection methods
- given the relative novelty of impact assessment for most library service managers, impact assessment should be viewed as a process of managing organisational change.

Applying this approach globally

Again, these principles were adhered to when this broad approach was adopted by the Global Libraries Initiative in developing the 'IPA Road Map' to support grantees. The IPA journey for grantees is presented in four stages:

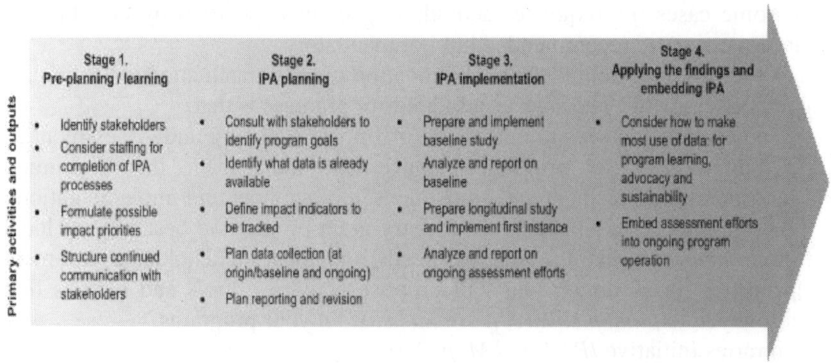

Global Libraries Initiative *IPA Road Map*, 2008

Grantees are encouraged to identify the most relevant impact areas for their own countries; themes where the country grant program can potentially have a large impact on individuals, organizations and communities. The main areas suggested where public access to information in libraries can make a difference are:

Education
Health
Culture and Leisure
Economic development
Communication
E-government

A matrix is provided in the *IPA Road Map* covering each of these impact areas in greater detail and showing outcomes for libraries and librarians, short-term impacts on communities and users, and longer term impacts on the community and society. This matrix is designed to offer ideas to grantees when holding local discussions and making decisions to create their own impact framework. Grantees are encouraged to ask themselves which of these elements are most relevant to their community, government and other stakeholders and what their objectives should be in each of these areas of activity. They are also advised to avoid spending unnecessary resources on assessing elements that will not add much to the picture.

As well as presenting short and longer term impacts on users and their communities, the matrix gives examples of how implementing a country grant program can build capacity within libraries themselves. The library can be enhanced to provide equal and unhindered access to information, be a center for the community, and give access to relevant local content; librarians can develop knowledge and expertise to support each of the areas of activity.

When grantees have decided on the locally-relevant impacts that they want to achieve through their GL Program they are encouraged to formulate impact indicators to provide information on program effectiveness in meeting impact goals. Help is then offered for the other stages in the impact assessment process.

In addition to their own impact evidence, grantees also have to collect required performance metrics intended to help monitor progress of the GL program as a whole. In some cases the requisite methodology is also specified by GL. Further performance metrics are recommended but not mandatory.

Why does the Bill and Melinda Gates Foundation give so much attention to impact planning and assessment? The answer provided for grantees is that:

> "The Foundation sees the inclusion of Impact Planning and Assessment as a commitment to program management that, from the beginning, incorporates assessment and adjustment into planning and implementation. As a grantee, you will design a country grant program to best fit your local environment, targeting audience needs and local stakeholder/government priorities. In so doing, you will propose activities, tools and metrics that allow you to *plan, measure, learn* and *sustain* your programs."

Global Libraries Initiative *IPA Road Map*, 2008

Our general approach to impact assessment was also adopted recently by the International Federation of Library Associations (IFLA) in devising its impact assessment strategy for evaluation of its future Free Access to Information and Freedom of Expression (FAIFE) work. The only essential difference was that the planners chose to focus their impact indicators on the effects of the programme training on the library staff who took part rather than on the users of their services. This choice of focus was dictated by the limited resources available for evaluation work.

4. From global to local: why impact assessment matters

Impact assessment of LIS services is important whether the work is undertaken on a global, national or local scale. The Global Libraries Initiative identifies three main reasons for collecting impact evidence; to show:

"1. Whether projects are being conducted effectively, in order to learn from and improve project activities;
2. Whether the program is making a difference to people, groups, organizations or communities; and lastly
3. To use that evidence of impact to advocate for continued support and/or funding from relevant stakeholders."

Global Libraries Initiative *IPA Road Map*, 2008

Similar principles apply at a national or local level, but other elements may also come into play. Confining ourselves to projects with which we have been directly involved:

- For IFLA, there is an additional incentive of being able to meet the changing impact evidence requirements of potential project funders;
- *The School Library Self-Evaluation* process and materials commissioned by the then Department for Education and Skills (England) gives school library managers a basis of comparison for their library with others, as well as a framework for developing the chosen aspects of their service (Markless and Streatfield, 2004; Streatfield and Markless, 2004);
- For the 22 university library teams participating in the *Impact Initiative* the incentive was primarily to gather evidence to inform the development of their services at a time of rapid change in teaching and learning, information literacy provision and support and e-information provision

(Markless and Streatfield, 2005; 2006). Their work also provided a model and evidence-gathering materials for other universities (see http://vamp.diglib.shrivenham.cranfield.ac.uk/impact/impact-initiative);

- The main issue for health libraries is to meet organisational priorities requiring that services should have a positive impact on patient care (see Weightman and Williamson, 2005);
- As for public access to ICTs, there is still much to do. The recent literature review by the Center for Information and Society found that

    "there is limited conclusive evidence on downstream impacts of public access to ICTs. The evidence that does exist suggests that the public access ICT model is not living up to the expectations placed on it. This is not necessarily because public access has had no impacts, but because its impact is particularly difficult to identify and measure. As a model, public access to ICTs has experienced success and failure, leading to both reinforcement of the belief that the model should be expanded and strengthened; as well as claims that public access ICTs are ultimately ineffective or even counter-productive from the development perspective."
    (Sey and Fellows, 2009)

5. Impact assessment, advocacy and service sustainability

There are clearly an important series of relationships between impact assessment, advocacy and service sustainability, especially in relation to major service development programmes. The GL Initiative makes this explicit:

"The impact planning and assessment process can assist grantees, program officers, and other strategists and policy makers with impact planning and assessment [and] with this evidence, advocate for continued development of libraries, computer use, and financial sustainability."

Our experience suggests that there are three significant potential pitfalls in using impact assessment evidence to make the advocacy case and secure sustainable services. We have noted some tendency amongst national organisations to conflate impact assessment and advocacy, even to the extent of commissioning the collection of impact evidence to support the advocacy case.

There is also a tendency to 'cherry pick' only the most positive evidence in making the advocacy case. In our view, impact assessment should be seen as an independent process that may or may not give rise to evidence of success and should lead to a 'warts and all' approach to the presentation of findings for advocacy purposes. Most politicians at local or national level can readily identify the 'good news only' approach to presenting evidence and any such approach will rapidly undermine the case being presented.

Finally, although we confidently assert that rigorous impact assessment combined with lucid advocacy will lead to service sustainability, there is comparatively little evidence to suggest that this is how key decisions are usually made. Evidence-based strategic decision making may be highly desirable, but are our societies ready for this? Or are we still at the stage of development characterised by the Irish dramatist George Bernard Shaw, when he said that "Reformers have the idea that change can be achieved by brute sanity"?

References

Fitz-Gibbon, C.T. (1996) *Monitoring education: indicators, quality and effectiveness* London: Cassell

Global Libraries Initiative (2008) *IPA Road Map. This Road Map is part of the GL Toolkit (closed website) provided to help grantees in relation to the Global Libraries Initiative.*

Markless, S. and Streatfield, D.R. (2004) *Improve your library: a self-evaluation process for secondary school libraries and learning resource centres* 2 vols. London: Department for Education and Skills www.teachernet.gov.uk/schoollibraries

Markless, S. and Streatfield, D.R. (2005) 'Facilitating the Impact Implementation Programme' in Library and Information Research 29 (91) (Spring) 10-19. The whole of this special issue of LIRN is devoted to the Impact Implementation Programme.

Markless, S. and Streatfield, D.R. (2006) *Evaluating the impact of your library* London: Facet Publishing

Markless, S. and Streatfield, D.R. (2006) 'Gathering and applying evidence of the impact of UK university libraries on student learning and research: a facilitated action research approach' *International J. of Information Management* 26; 3-15.

Streatfield, D.R. and Markless, S. (2004) *Improve your library: a self-evaluation process for primary schools* London: Department for Education and Skills www.teachernet.gov.uk/schoollibraries

Sey, A. and Fellows, M. (2009) *Literature review on the impact of public access to information and communication technologies. CIS Working paper no. 6* Washington, Seattle: University of Washington, Center for Information and Society.

Note

[1] Although 'impact evaluation' is our preferred term (as rehearsed earlier in this paper), we have used 'impact assessment' throughout in the interests of clarity.

Real Life Impact of Public Access Computers' Centres in Global Libraries Romania

Marcel Chiranov

IREX Romania
E-mail: mchiranov@irex.ro

Abstract: After about five months of operations some of the Global Libraries Public Access Computers Centres started to show positive impact on people life. Building an Impact Assessment Framework and implementing it in an effective and efficient way is looking like a tough and rewarding challenge.

Keywords: Metric; Interview; Result oriented approach; Customer focus.

1. Introduction

The Global Libraries program in Romania is being implemented by the International Research and Exchanges Board (IREX). This program started in November 2007, with 12 pilot sites; the learning from these will be rolled out to much more extensive country implementation. Over 1,500 public libraries are expected to receive computers, software, intensive training and assistance in delivering customers focused services. During the pilot phase, IREX tested several implementation mechanisms and one of the most important was the Impact Planning and Assessment (IPA) process. Several important questions for full-program roll-out are now closer to being answered:

- What will a successful Public Access Center (PAC), in a public library, look like? What does 'satisfied users' mean? What metrics should be used to track progress?
- What topics are most important for public library users, which can be addressed through tailored services in public libraries?
- What tools and processes to use in order to collect this information? How the management of information will look like?
- How to ask librarians to cooperate in impact related data collection, in order to not to ask too much of them, and help them feel comfortable with data collection? How much is 'too much' when asking librarians to collect impact related data on PAC activity?

In order to answer these questions IREX organized a Library Capacity Analysis in a sample of 208 Romanian libraries, and Citizens Needs Assessment through interviews with 1,066 citizens. Both were done by a professional survey company. Together with the survey company we decided to select samples for the two surveys based on next criteria:
1. Library Capacity Analysis to be implemented only in localities under 15,000 inhabitants. About 97% of Romanian public libraries are located into such localities. All the Internet providers agreed in localities with higher inhabitants' number the broadband infrastructure is present. Also Romanian Librarians Association confirmed localities over this threshold most probably have adequate resources to contribute to program implementation.
2. Citizens Needs Assessment to be implemented all over Romania being, focused on topics of interest for citizens. Library users and non users were equally important for the survey. IREX considered is important to understand non users' needs, with the hope will succeed to attract new customers for public library services.
The main conclusions from the two surveys are as follows:

- 99% of the interviewed communities considered that they need a PAC
- Citizens reported interest in the following topics: (% out of total options)

1. Healthcare for all (medical advice, finding the closest practitioner, clinics, pharmacies) - 94.6%
2. Information regarding local government - 94.1%
3. Information as to how to access funds or credit for small businesses - 90.8%
4. Job placement 88.2%
5. Funding sources for community development - 87.5%
6. Communication on-line: creating an email address, talking on Skype - 86.9%
7. Developing a business plan - 85.8%
8. Information regarding accessing EU funds - 85.6%

9. Banking information - 85.6%
10.How to write a CV, and job interview skills - 85.6%

Those conclusions have been helpful to design results oriented activities and to draft the representative metrics to be observed during implementation.

In parallel with the Citizens Needs Assessment survey, Global Libraries Romania ran community meetings with all pilot sites to better understand their priorities and expectations. Those findings were checked against the Citizens Needs Assessment, and the overlap was almost perfect. Also from the statistical data is known about 8% of Romanian citizens are using public libraries services. This figure has been confirmed through Citizens Needs Assessment. This has been used as a triangulation method to control risk in assessing target group needs.

2. Metrics measurement: tools and processes

IPA for pilot phase tested several methods and processes for data collection in order to better understand how to have a customer focus and results oriented approach. The metrics tested were either quantitative or qualitative in order to have relevant controls on processes.

Some of the most important metrics which were tested during the pilot phase:

1. Number of PAC individual users (registered users, active over a period of time)
2. Number of PAC total visits
3. Number of PAC users which reported personal objective achievement after using services
4. Librarians' confidence with the new PAC related responsibilities
5. Customers' satisfaction with new PAC services

During 2008, Global Libraries Romania organized quarterly meetings with the 12 pilot library sites. Each contained IPA sessions which were organized based on some simple criteria:

1. To use only friendly terms (plain Romanian) and customer focused approach in order to help librarians understand data collection

2. To introduce the librarians step by step into data collection and reporting, allowing gradual learning and making a tight connection between new PAC services, data collection and satisfying user needs

3. To try to collect only relevant data for the PAC activity and avoid data 'over-collection'

4. All sessions were planned and delivered through informal sessions/brainstorming rather than formal training. Everyone was asked to offer opinions and their feedback was always positive and constructive.

The whole group felt they actively participated in the data collection design.

The first quarterly meeting was focused on what data should be collected and how, including carefully defining with the libraries what successful PAC services would look like. Now it was brainstormed possible definitions for 'satisfied user' to be used during future measurements.

The second quarterly meeting focused on questionnaires to be used in data collection. The assembled librarians commented on questionnaire strengths and

weaknesses, and greatly improved the data collection tools. The main focus was to define metrics following pretty similar logic with actual libraries metrics.
During the third quarterly meeting, Global Libraries Romania heard the first successes! A citizen in a rural area, with difficulty accessing specialized medical practices, had successful kidney surgery. A lady found out about a good Urology practice in a big city, and made an appointment with the help of the librarian within the PAC. Also, we learned about the first people who asked for librarian help to fill out an on-line CV and complete a job application, and some of these later obtained new jobs. Hearing these success stories helped us define how often and with what content librarians would report back to Global Libraries Romania on the PAC services.
After this meeting Global Libraries Romania decided that it is useful to have a separate Librarian survey after one year of pilot project and also a further survey (handled by the librarians) to collect PAC users feedback. This was supposed to collect mainly qualitative data in order to understand how PAC helped users and how Global Libraries Romania affected librarians professional and personal life.

3. Impact evidence and information for future action

The last quarterly meeting offered the opportunity to analyze the above-mentioned surveys, and describe how the data collection and IPA work will be done in future.
At this point we had a good understanding of what a satisfied PAC user can look like, what data the librarians can collect and how they will report. We also learnt about other PAC success stories: people finding good information and guidance for themselves or for their kids; a driving licence test passed after practicing with on line tests; IT small business development using a PAC; or communicating with relatives abroad. The user survey questioned 1,217 PAC users, who answered questions relating to their perceived PAC benefits, see Fig.1.

4. Lessons learned from the user surveys

- There is a lot of interest in PAC
- There is a group of library patrons ready and eager to use more sophisticated services
- There is a group of library patrons able to take action based on information they receive from PAC; probably we should pay more attention to encouraging this proactive attitude
- Content management, or delivery services, proved to be very helpful
- Success stories of users solving personal problems using PAC services appeared very soon after PAC services were implemented
- In some places library patrons volunteered to assist librarian or other patrons with hardware/software issues; this is a great resource for program implementation.

5. Lessons learned from the librarian surveys

- Librarians easily surpassed implementation barriers if they understood the final objectives
- Librarians are eager to modernize their services
- Most of the librarians understand that they have to create alternative services in

order to keep their patrons' interest and maintain public funds for their activities
- Not all librarians easily leave their comfort zone to do new activities (travel, attend training, interact with new people)
- Some of the librarians need to see a more structured process in operation in order to consider implementing it themselves
- Some of the librarians seem to be very effective and efficient in data collection and reporting; if we explained the use of the information and provided them with conclusions, the process ran very smoothly.

28 librarians working in the 12 pilot sites answered the survey after one year of pilot implementation. They were asked only two questions:
"What were Global Libraries Romania strong points?", and "What were Global Libraries Romania weak points?" See Fig. 2 and Fig.3
This data was helpful to design the **Librarian Satisfaction Index** which will one of the important metric to follow. It will include details on how comfortable is the librarian in new PAC job, what further assistance needs the librarina have, what are the most important topics addressed by users questions, what other services PAC can offer

6. Conclusions applicable to broad program roll-out

1.IPA should be handled in cooperation with librarians, using easy to understand terms and processes that are simple to manage
2. Satisfied PAC users (success stories) can appear in as short time as six months of efficient PAC management; this provides important early advocacy opportunities
3. If IPA is developed based on librarians' and users' needs, and results are consistently shared, librarians will take ownership quite fast. Is important to always use real-life examples to describe the connection between data collection and processing and the PAC activity
4. The Romanian Librarians' Association (ANBPR) has already expressed a wish to add the IPA indicators that Global Libraries Romania is collecting into their official data collection practice
5. Early Global Libraries Romania success stories look exactly like some of those from the Martin Luther King Public Library in Washington DC: there is a strong focus on finding employment and on education/alternative education methods (observation done during study visit in March 2009).
6. All these qualitative and quantitative findings are useful for advocacy purposes, to design new customer focused services within PAC or public libraries, or to improve the present services.

Acknowledgments
Thank you all partners which made this team work possible. Lots of appreciation for all librarians in pilot sites (Bucuresti, Hunedoara,Iasi,Tulcea and Zalau) for being enthusiastic, and pro active in testing our data collection tools. Thanks to Liviu Dediu and Dragos Neagu of ANBPR for long Skype discussions on libraries statistics, before we ever met first time! Thanks to Paul Baran, Global Libraries Romania Director, which constantly supported IPA planning, ideas, research, understanding the long run benefits of having a good IPA strategy to successfully manage the program.

Fig. 1 PAC users reporting personal objective achievement and their weight into users looking for corresponding subject

Subject	%	No of users
National minorities issues	4.76%	2
Flight reservation	6.67%	3
Project funding	7.61%	4
Environment	9.09%	7
Online tax payment	18.57%	8
Find a job	18.91%	45
Business development	23.33%	28
Bank loans	23.46%	19
Agriculture	23.91%	22
Working with government	27.18%	28
Tourism	28.23%	35
Professional training	33.02%	35
E-commerce	41.30%	38
Legal information	48.11%	89
Education	63.93%	358
Health related	65.05%	67
Communication with abroad relatives	76.99%	358

Based on these findings IREX identified the metrics and processes to be used for performance measurement during broad program implementation. It will be a **Customer Satisfaction Index** which will include: field of interest, success in finding the right information, success in achieving a professional or personal goal by using PAC services, how supportive is the librarian operating PAC, what other information or service can be delivered through PAC, what other information or service can be delivered through the public library, how easy is to find a free computer within PAC.

Fig. 2 What did you appreciated during Global Libraries Romania pilot phase implementation? (max score 5)

Internet based services	4.96
New services for library patrons	4.96
We learnt how to create a modern library	4.90
Computers donation	4.82

Knowledge acquired	4.79
Advocacy training	4.72
Relationship with IREX team	4.47
Better image within community	4.44
PAC Management	4.40
Networking with other librarians	4.38
IT training	4.36
Improved relationship with local organizations	4.28

Fig. 3 What was your biggest challenge during Global Libraries Romania pilot phase implementation? (max score 5)

Long time to receive software	2.91
Whole process too bureaucratic	2.88
Too much travel	2.74
Long time to receive hardware	2.59
Too many trainings	2.53
Unclear working procedures	2.44
Too many persons asking information	2.29
Not enough networking with other librarians	2.18
Bad communication with IREX team	1.61
Library's users not interested on complex services	1.39
IREX team not prepared well enough	1.24

11. Information and Communication Technology Services

Exploring the Level of Information and Communication Technology Services and Use in Secondary School Library Media Centres in Kuwait: An Interpretive Case Study Research

Hasan Buabbas and Benachir Medjdoub

Research Institute for the Built & Human Environment University of Salford, UK

Abstract: The purpose of this study is to investigate the provision of information and communication technology (ICT) services and applications in secondary school library media centres (SLMC) in the state of Kuwait. This study focuses on the school community (teachers and pupils) and their skill at using, and knowledge of, ICT. There has been no previous research which has investigated the use of ICT in secondary school library media centres, so this study aims to fill the gap. In order to thoroughly understand the phenomenon, an interpretive case study approach has been adopted, and multiple qualitative and quantitative data gathering techniques have been utilised. In order to research the subject within context, pertinent literature was reviewed from both developed and developing countries. Initially, data gathering instruments showed remarkable findings. Both qualitative and quantitative data analysis approaches were used to produce valid and reliable results. The findings indicated that there was a significant lack of ICT related services in Kuwaiti school libraries. The results also showed that integration of ICT services into SLMCs was strongly advocated by teachers and pupils alike. To conclude, the results highlighted the need to better understand the importance of new environments in education. The findings of this research also highlighted the need for Kuwaiti policymakers to review and improve the current situation.

Keywords: School library media centre; ICT in school libraries; Qualitative and quantitative study; Case study.

1. Introduction

The school library media centre (SLMC) is a core component of a school. A typical library has the capability to inspire teachers and students alike (Barrett and Douglas, 2004). Clark (2006) stated that in recent years, the emergence of Information and Communication Technology (ICT) has considerably changed not only the educational theory and process, but also the SLMC services and facilities. The potential of ICT in the school is such that it can help sustain the quality of teaching and reinforce the relationship between learners and curriculum. The ICT applications within an SLMC also provide school communities with a wide range of information resources and stimulate their perception of information (Garner, 2006;, Papazoglou, 2001). Evidence suggests that technology has granted access to a broader range of knowledge beyond the school (CILIP, 2001). Developed countries, in particular, have integrated and deployed the ICT applications into their education system and their SLMCs.

Developing countries, however, still struggle and endeavour to embed the new technology tools into their education system. Recently, the state of Kuwait realised the importance of ICT in schools and the significance of the new environment. The Ministry of Education in Kuwait has not shown a particularly strong initiative in incorporating the ICT applications within its schools. The new technology that has been supplied to the secondary schools and its SLMCs has been poorly integrated and falls short of harnessing its huge potential (Al-Sayer, 2001). There is a need to evaluate and understand the new phenomenon from different angles. Therefore, this paper focuses on investigating the level of ICT applications and services available in Kuwaiti secondary schools and their libraries, as well as exploring school community skills and maturity towards ICT.

Research is any conscious premeditated inquiry and investigation which seeks to increase one's knowledge of a given situation. The research method technique varies according to the subject under investigation (Goldhor, 1972). This study adopted an interpretive multiple-case study approach including a qualitative and quantitative method. Qualitative and quantitative data gathering instruments were utilised to collect data which was pertinent to the research in question.

Ultimately, the paper is part of a broader project. This study focuses on the integration of ICT applications in the secondary school libraries of many developed and developing countries, the roles the libraries play, and their significance and services. In addition, the researcher endeavours to demonstrate the school community's perception towards ICT-based services in the SLMCs. Therefore, to clarify the proposition, and to answer the study questions below, we focused on the use of qualitative and quantitative methods and instruments throughout the research. The study makes use of an interpretive philosophical stance in order to factor in the researcher's own views, references, and experience, and provide an in-depth analysis and understanding of the phenomenon under investigation. Furthermore, the paper adopts an interpretive multiple-case study approach and, to gain knowledge and data, combines qualitative and quantitative multiple data collection instruments including interviews, direct observation, documents and questionnaire.

2. General Rationale for the Study

The Kuwaiti government has been concerned with establishing libraries in each school since the 1950s (Zehery, 1994). Moreover, the Ministry of Education has attempted to supply their schools, and indeed their SLMCs, with proper resources. This is in order to provide various information resources to enhance teaching and learning processes (Al-Musalam, 1988). However, a qualitative and quantitative study conducted by Haidar (1974) and another study carried out by Al-Terkait and Rezg (1987) indicated that the SLMCs in Kuwaiti secondary schools were still far from ideal and had inadequate facilities to serve school communities. Traditionally, Kuwaiti school libraries have limited information resources and are mainly used as a place to store outdated books (Zehery, 1994).

The accession of ICT has persuaded the developed countries to integrate the new technology into their educational organizations, and indeed, their SLMCs (Birch et al., 2003). Thus, it is felt that the current SLMCs in Kuwait should effectively implement the new technological environment, as SLMCs already exist in many developed countries. Realising the significance of ICT, the Ministry of Education in Kuwait has endeavoured to diffuse the ICT into their SLMCs for the last two decades. This is in order to enlarge the traditional school libraries services, as well as to encourage school communities to use SLMCs (Al-Tammar and Badawi, 1994).

The purpose of this study is to investigate the secondary SLMCs in Kuwait regarding the availability of ICT services and applications. The study explores teachers' and students' perception, maturity and skills in the use of ICT services. Furthermore, it determines whether the harnessing of the new technology encourages the school communities to use the SLMCs, and whether the ICT in schools improves educational theory and practice.

The central research questions this study seeks to answer are as follows:

1. What are the perceptions of students and teachers in relation to the importance of the ICT services in schools and SLMCs?
2. What is the effective level of usage of ICT facilities in the SLMCs by students and teachers?
3. What are the barriers and enablers for effective integration of ICT services within the SLMC in Kuwaiti secondary schools?

3. Literature Review

Various factors have been discussed during the review of the literature in this paper, enabling the reader to understand the theme. However, the researcher briefly identified two main propositions. The first, to review various researchers' perspectives on the significance of the use of qualitative and quantitative methods in librarianship terrain. The second, to display the pertinent literature on the efforts of integrating ICT into SLMCs.

3.1 Qualitative and quantitative approach

Qualitative and quantitative research is associated with a number of different approaches and is utilised in many social researches (Bryman, 1988). A number of IS researchers, for example, advocated that qualitative and quantitative dimension may be used in any research (Paré, 2001). In addition, Powell (1991a) revealed that qualitative research focused on disclosing people’s experiences. It has had a positive influence on the information science researches by viewing library users’, librarians’ and administrations’ perspectives. In recent years, the qualitative method has been predominantly used in librarianship studies. Powell (1991a) argued that "qualitative research tends to apply a more holistic and natural approach to the resolution of a problem than does quantitative research. It is also give more attention to the subjective aspects of human experience and behaviour" (Powell, 1991a, p.47).

Qualitative and quantitative researches can be used in different research strategies, besides survey and experiment researches. It is employed by positivist researchers, and also very often by interpretive and critical researchers (Oates, 2006; Gay, 2006). Denzin and Lincoln (1998) argued Powell's standpoint that both qualitative and quantitative researchers are concerned with an individual's perspective. Moreover, Light (2003) revealed that qualitative data is concerned mainly with meaning (materials), whereas quantitative data with that of measurement (data). The qualitative data can be analysed through quantitative numerical analysis procedure (Oates, 2006). Powell (1991b) revealed that qualitative researchers can be considered qualitative research.

In relation to this study, the qualitative and quantitative data techniques used can effectively cover and clarify all questions and contexts addressed in the paper. The qualitative and quantitative data techniques allow the explanation of an individual's point of view, and the observation of realistic life surrounding the phenomenon. Moreover, from this approach the researcher is able to foster rich information from documents, and gain valuable data from a large population (Denzin and Lincoln, 1998; Light, 2003). Therefore, the data pursuit in this study requires qualitative and quantitative approaches.

As a form of gathering data and materials, qualitative data is a collection of non-numeric data, analysed and interpreted in order to gain insights into a particular phenomenon of interest (Gay et al., 2006). This type of data technique is crucial for interpretive multiple-case study researches (Oates, 2006). Janesick (1998) suggested that qualitative design "requires the researcher to become the research instrument. This means the researcher… must sharpen the skills necessary for observation and face to face interview" (1998, p.42). Qates (2006) claimed that qualitative researchers were unsatisfied regarding the information that they gather about data analysis. While Gay et al (2006) asserted that quantitative data is a "collection of numerical data in order to explain, predict, and/or control phenomena of interest" (2006`, p.9), it is stated elsewhere that qualitative data derive directly from the fieldwork (McClure, 1991).

There are six sources of qualitative evidence that can be employed in the case study research, including: documentation, interviews, direct observation, archival records, participant observation and physical artefacts (Yin, 1994`; Myers`, 1997), while the main quantitative data source method is survey and questionnaire (Zayton, 2004). Powell (1991b), in addition, declared that qualitative data gathering such as direct observation and interviews are correlated with quantitative data instruments in many librarianship researches. Through interviews and observation, the qualitative researcher has the opportunity to be close to the participant. Goldhor (1972) argued that the investigator influenced the qualitative data gathered, and to avoid this the researcher should prepare himself before implementing these techniques. As the quantitative investigator is dependent only on questionnaires to gather data, this means that the interaction between the researcher and participant is superficial (Denzin and Lincoln, 1998). Many previous librarianship researches encountered difficulties when using the questionnaire: the instrument often gave inappropriate answers which consisted of opinions rather than evidence. Moreover, the questions sometimes are ambiguous and the participant does not know what the researcher means (Goldhor, 1972). However, qualitative and quantitative data is significant for librarianship to measure and improve its policies and its services. It is critical that the data and statistics found should be clearly defined, accurately reported, and correctly analysed (Goldhor, 1972, Hafner, 1998).

3.2 ICT in education in the developed countries

The significant impact of Information and Communication Technology (ICT) on education has led many countries to integrate it into their education systems (Birch,

2006). Regarding the provision of ICT in the education system, Clark (2006) stated that: "In some instances and under certain conditions, it has been shown that technology helps students learn more, learn faster, become more motivated, and become more connected to the community and the outside world" (2006, p.483). Furthermore, developed countries keenly put the emphasis on ensuring all school communities could effectively and efficiently manipulate the new technology (Baskin and Williams, 2006; Lai and Pratt, 2004; Hew and Brush, 2007). Various initiatives and schemes showed the disparity between the integration and use of ICT in the education system across Europe, Australia, the USA and a few Asian countries (Johnson and Maddux, 2007; Baron and Bruillard, 2007; Baskin and Williams, 2006; Lim, 2007). Most of these initiatives were precisely studied and examined qualitatively and quantitatively by researches from different approaches. These studies aimed, for instance, to demonstrate SWOT analysis for the new environment. In other words, they were investigating the level of ICT equipment and school community skills, awareness and use of the technology in the school (Frieden and Elliott, 2007; Vannatta and Fordham, 2004; Baker, 2005).

3.3. ICT in schools in the developing countries

Developing countries have striven to pursue the technological revolution and adoption of integration of ICT into the education system (Al-Mekhlafy and Al-Basha, 2000). Al-birini (2006) described the situation in developing countries regarding the deployment of ICT into the education system as:

> Governments in most developing countries have responded to the challenge by initiating national programmes to introduce computers into education. Doing so, these governments have added to their burden of debt…even though the costs are large and the payoffs modest (2006, p.374).

Very few pertinent pieces of literature have had such a powerful impact on ICT in schools. There is, the researcher found, a lack of other research conducted in this field, which cannot be expected to represent the real picture of ICT in education in these countries (Summerline, 2000). Moreover, most of the recent studies which have been undertaken in developing countries have attempted to discover different attitudes through qualitative and quantitative approaches (Bovée et al., 2007; Albirini, 2006, Aduwa-Ogiegbaen and Iyamu, 2005). These approaches include teachers' and pupils' opinions towards information skills, rather than determining how they are used ICT in the classroom, as well as the quantity and quality of the ICT applications in the school (Zeidan, 2007).

3.4 The school library media centre (SLMC) and ICT

The impressive change on the SLMC in recent years has varied its role. The antiquated school library was solely a store of books located in a small room within a school, supporting teachers and students with physical information. However, the school library, and indeed SLMC, is now a learning laboratory situated prominently within schools, providing non-traditional materials such as computers, internet and audio-visual means, in addition to traditional resources such as books, referencing and periodicals. (Morris, 2004; Alyan, 2001; Tilke, 1998; Roys, 2004).

Clabo (2002) expanded upon the meaning of the typical SLMC as a "centralised information and technology centre designed to support the school's curriculum and provide resources that meet the educational and recreational needs of both the faculty and the students" (2002, p.24). Interestingly, the SLMC has played an important role in the school community, especially when ICT was integrated in its services (McDonald, 2006).

3.5 The SLMC in developed and developing countries

The integration of ICT into secondary school library media centres has had a vast influence and is implemented worldwide, particularly in developed countries. This recent technological innovation has created a significant evolution in library services and utilisation over the last few decades (Ingersoll and Culshaw, 2004). However, in spite of the widespread nature of ICT-based applications, there are few documents and studies conducted in this field.

Developed countries' literature indicates that secondary SLMCs provide disparate traditional and non-traditional services. Moreover, many libraries have advanced ICT services that provide sophisticated access to electronic formats that support the curriculum. Surprisingly, other studies have showed that many SLMCs in developed countries lack a decent library collection and basic ICT services (Office for Standards in Education, 2006; Liguète, 2007; Turner, 2006; Tilbian, 2005). In addition, Barstad et al. (2007) found in his study that the majority of teachers and students use the library infrequently. He also added that students claimed that teachers never encouraged them to visit the SLMC.

Turning to the developing countries, the ICT services in libraries have been widely circulated due to their importance. The extensive nature of the new digital environment has dominated the developing countries' considerations in integrating the ICT applications into their SLMCs (Moahi, 2002). However, very few countries have taken real initiatives to supply their schools, or indeed embrace the fusion of ICT tools and services with traditional materials into the school library media centres. In addition, insignificant research has been conducted in the study of SLMCs, their services and school community skills and use of the library.

In brief, most developing countries struggle to enlarge their library services and concentrate on furnishing schools with adequate library equipment, as well as providing sufficient ICT services for the school library community (Magara and Nyumba, 2004). However, the status of the SLMC and the integration of ICT in secondary school libraries in some developing countries is still ambiguous, and negligible in other countries due to its failures in different sectors. There are other factors that influence the development of the SLMC, which include budget, bureaucracy issues and mismanagement (Swee and Abdullah, 2005).

3.6 SLMC Situation in Kuwait

Many developing countries are struggling to supply new technology in their SLMCs. Therefore, a review of the few related literatures provided a critical insight into the efforts of a number of developing countries, which can provide a comparable picture to that in Kuwait. There is no single study that explores the current situation in Kuwaiti SLMCs. Therefore, this paper is a unique study in that it investigates the situation of secondary school library media centres in Kuwait.

4 Research Methodology and Design

Research has adopted various forms of theoretical positions in studying the information and communication technology (ICT) field (Orlikowski and Robey, 1991). It is a fairly constant argument that the purpose of the research determines the method, the approach, and the technique of any study. In that regard, constructing an appropriate and fitting method would achieve significant outcomes (Cohen et al., 2000).

The nature of the ICT and library science fields allow different research approaches and methods to be used. Moreover, the diverse research methods applied in social science studies have improved the standard of the library and information and communication technology researches (Abdulhadi, 2003). In addition, there is potential to study the information technology phenomenon from three philosophical viewpoints: positivist, interpretive and critical (Orlikowski and Baroudi, 1991). However, positivist and interpretive paradigms have been more influential in researching information systems (IS) than the critical research approach (Myers, 1997; Lee, 1991; Paré, 2001; Light, 2003). In addition, ICT is one of the primary drivers of IS phenomenon researches (Orlikowski and Baroudi, 1991; Palvia et al., 2003). Several methodologies are available and can be implemented for IS and ICT researches. The method used in this study is interpretive; it is a case study research and combines qualitative and quantitative data gathering instruments. Bryman (1988) declared that qualitative research is more compatible with interpretive than quantitative research, which is regularly influenced by positivism.

4.1 Case study research

Evidently, case study is the preferred methodology for most researches conducted in IS and ICT topic areas, such as organizational design, system developers, IS and ICT functional applications, and resource management/IS management (Palvia et al., 2003; Paré, 2001; Orlikowski and Baroudi, 1991; Oates, 2006; Fitchman, 2004). Moreover, evidence suggests that qualitative and quantitative methods comprising survey studies, experimental studies, and case study research are the most popular research methods utilised in the field of information technology (Orlikowski and Baroudi`, 1991`; Paré, 2001). Furthermore, the case study method is strongly advocated in studying the library and information science terrain (Abdulhadi, 2003, Goldhor, 1972).

The case studies selected in this research were done so in a fashion that promoted an equal gender selection of boys' and girls' schools from the six counties in Kuwait. A total of twelve cases were targeted: two secondary schools from each county, one boys' and one girls'. In addition, the researcher endeavoured to avoid the bias that might influence the results by adopting multiple sources of inquiry (qualitative and quantitative). Orlikowski and Baroudi (1991) argued that using a single approach for studying IS phenomena is insufficient, therefore the incorporation of other similar cases was critical in order to explore the relationship between ICT, people and organisations. Goldhor (1972) argued that librarianship research was subject to bias because its study was usually reliant on people in interviews and observations.

4.2 Data collection methods

The case study integrates and makes use of multiple qualitative and quantitative data collection methods to capture the features in both types (Kimchi et al., 1991;

Zayton, 2004). Indeed, this variety of data sources is named 'multiple data triangulation', which helps minimize the risks of the validity and the reliability of the data (Richardson, 2003; Yin, 1994; Kimchi et al, 1991; Ingram, 2002). The researcher adopted different approaches to tackle this by: a) using a number of multiple quantitative and qualitative sources of evidence, including questionnaires, interviews, observation and documents; b) being present during the distribution of the questionnaires, emphasizing and describing every single question to the pupils, and understanding the way they understand the questions; and c) making sure the size of the sample was big enough in order to reduce any potential noise.

Four usable qualitative and quantitative sources were designed to gather information from the fieldwork. The following defined the different instruments utilised in the study:

- Questionnaire: is a quantitative technique method aimed at expressing its findings in figures (Rothwell, 1993). The questionnaires were sent to 12 schools, and the response rate was 95.4% (912 completed questionnaires from 955 pupils participated). Within each school, three classes were targeted from each stage.
- One to one interviews: is the first qualitative tool used in the study provides words as data findings. Two interviews were conducted with school staff (teachers) within each school. 12 interviews were also carried out with each school's headmaster.
- Direct observation: aimed also to collect qualitative data about particular behaviour through the observer being actively involved. This technique was utilised in order to gather information through observing the twelve SLMCs in the schools selected.
- Written documents: are suitable qualitative data gathering methods in collecting data from library and information researches. Oates (2006) stressed that ICT research can foster meaningful and tangible information from this kind of data.

5 Discussion and Conclusion

The combination of the four data gathering instruments yielded various qualitative and quantitative results. In addition, the analysis of the data resulted in substantial findings that answered the research questions.

The questionnaire included closed questions and the data gathered was predominantly quantitative. One question sought to identify how often pupils used the SLMC during one semester. Surprisingly, the results indicated 48.1% of respondents stated they used the library only once during the whole semester, whereas 13.7% used the library once a week. Other results showed that 64.4% of the total respondents agreed that they needed ICT in the library and the school for their learning, whilst 14.8% did not. However, only 17.3% of the students often used the ICT services in the SLMC.

45.2% of the pupils were very confident in searching the internet to find information, whilst 32% of the total respondents were only confident in computer basics. 62.3% of the total girls claimed that the teachers often encouraged them to use the ICT facilities in the SLMC, whereas only 37.7% of boys were often encouraged. Equal amounts of girls and boys agreed that ICT within the school would motivate and add value to their learning. Furthermore, 52.2% of the total responses strongly agreed that ICT should be effectively integrated into school activities and the curriculum. Finally, a high ratio of the respondents identified that not only were the ICT levels poor, but also the quantity of ICT equipment within the library was insufficient.

Interviews were used in the research as a qualitative data gathering instrument. At first glance, the interviews' findings involved almost identical answers, especially teachers' responses. This was due to comparable conditions in the public schools: for instance, in budget, training opportunities and learning/teaching processes and environment. All teachers declared that there was a need to enhance ICT within schools, and increasing pupils' skills more towards ICT use. The teachers and the headmasters strongly advocated integrating the use of ICT into the curriculum. Moreover, the majority of the teachers' responses agreed with pupils' answers that the level of the ICT equipment in their SLMCs was unsatisfactory, and confirmed that there was a need to enhance the libraries' services.

By using a direct observation approach, first-hand knowledge from the real environment was obtained. In brief, the researcher observed that many SLMCs were almost empty of visitors most of the school day, and this was because of the SLMC conditions. Moreover, he found that teachers' and pupils' responses were comparable to those regarding ICT-based equipment. The ICT in many schools and libraries was inadequate, especially the lack of computers and internet services. Very few girls' schools provided a reasonable ICT service, and had only one or two PCs and poor internet access.

Evidently, there is a severe lack of research within the ICT and SLMC fields, especially from developing countries. It is clear that there is a discrepancy between developed countries' initiatives, and existing schemes in the developing countries regarding ICT in education. The literature reviewed revealed that there was no single research that had investigated the application and use of ICT in SLMCs in Kuwait. This made the subject under study a unique proposition. From a pupil's viewpoint, it is disappointing that most of the responses expressed dissatisfaction regarding ICT services and its use in their SLMCs. Although the majority of the pupils strongly advocated the exploitation of the new environment, the Ministry of Education was unresponsive.

Adopting multiple qualitative and quantitative sources of data evidence was essential in gathering diverse views on the subject, especially in organisations such as libraries. This study reaped fundamental benefits from a data triangulation method, which critically reinforced the validity of the data gathered (Kimchi et al., 1991). The results proved significant in illustrating the inadequacy within Kuwaiti SLMCs. These outcomes then raised an important question: what factors could have contributed to such changes? (Jakobsdottir et al., 2004).

References

ABDULHADI, M. (2003) *Research Methods in Information Science.* Cairo, Aldar Almasrih Alobnaneniah.

ADUWA-OGIEGBAEN, S. & IYAMU, E. (2005) Using information and communication technology in secondary schools in Nigeria: problems and prospects. *Educational Technology & Society,* 8 (1), pp.104-112.

AL-MEKHLAFY, M. & AL-BASHA, N. (2000) Integration computer in secondary instructional. Sana'a, Research Center.

AL-MUSALAM, M. (1988) A study of the libraries in girls' credit-hour secondary schools in Kuwait. Denver, University of Denver.

AL-SAYER, N. (2001) The provision of school computer lab scheme. *Altawasil Journal,* 8, 2.

AL-TAMMAR, A. & BADAWI, M. (1994) *Public and school libraries in Kuwait.* Kuwait, Dar Alaoroba Publishing.

AL-TERKAIT, A. & REZG, A. (1987) School libraries in Kuwait. *The Kuwaiti teacher union.* Kuwait.

ALBIRINI, A. (2006) Teachers' attitudes toward information and communication technologies: the case of Syrian EFL teachers *Computers & Education,* 47 (4), pp.373-398.

BARRETT, L. & DOUGLAS, J. (Eds.) (2004) *The CILIP guidelines for secondary school libraries,* London, Fact Publishing.

BARSTAD, J., AUDUNSON, R., HJORTSÆTER, E. & OSTLIE, B. (2007) School-libraries in Norway: a study of the situation in Norwegian School-Libraries. *School Libraries and Resource Centers,* June (44), pp.6-11.

BASKIN, C. & WILLIAMS, M. (2006) ICT integration in schools: where are we now and what comes next? *Australasian Journal of Educational Technology,* 22 (4), pp.455-473.

BIRCH, A. (2006) Pedagogic development work: an investigation using activity theory into ICT in primary schools 1999-2003. *Centre for ICT Pedagogy and Learning.* Manchester, Manchester Metropolitan University.

BIRCH, T., DYSON, K., GOLDSTEIN, G. & SHARPLES, B. (2003) School portrait cramlington community high school Northumberland, England. Northumberland.

BOVÉE, C., VOOCT, J. & MEELISSEN, M. (2007) Computer attitudes of primary and secondary students in South Africa. *Computers in Human Behaviour,* 23 (4), pp.1762-1776.

BRYMAN, A. (1988) *Quantity and quality in social research.* London, Routledge.

CILIP (2001) School libraries making a difference. London, CILIP.

CLABO, C. (2002) A study of the library use practices of high school students in three East Tennessee counties. *Department of Educational Leadership and Policy Analysis.* East Tennessee, East Tennessee State.

CLARK, K. (2006) Practices for the use of technology in high schools: a Delphi study. *Journal of Technology and Teacher Education,* 14 (3), pp.481-499.

COHEN, L., MANION, L. & MORISON, K. (2000) *Research methods in education.* 5th ed., 5th ed. London, Routledge.

DENZIN, N. & LINCOLN, Y. (Eds.) (1998) *Strategies of qualitative inquiry,* London, SEGA Publications.

FITCHMAN, R. (2004) Real options and IT platform adoption: implications for theory and practice. *Information Systems Research,* 15 (2), pp.132-154.

FRIEDEN, J. & ELLIOTT, D. (2007) Teach with movies: using the storytelling power of movies to motivate students. *Teacher Librarian,* 34 (3), pp.61-62.

GARNER, S. (2006) High-Level colloquium on information literacy and lifelong learning bibliotheca Alexandrina. Alexandria, Egypt, UNESCO.

GAY, L., MILLS, G. & AIRASIAN, P. (2006) *Educational research competencies for analysis and applications. 8th ed.* New Jersey, Pearson.

GOLDHOR, H. (1972) *An introduction to scientific research in librarianship.* Illinois, University of Illinois Graduate School of Library Science.

HAFNER, A. (1998) *Descriptive statistical techniques for librarians.* 2nd ed, Chicago,

American Library Association.

HAIDAR, A. (1974) A mastre plan for development of school libraries in the State of Kuwait. Pittsburgh, University of Pittsburgh.

INGERSOLL, P. & CULSHAW, J. (2004) *Managing information technology.* Connecticut, Libraries Unlimited.

JAKOBSDOTTIR, S., JONSDOTTIR, B. & HJARTARSON, T. (2004) Gender, ICT related student skills, and the role of a school library in an Icelandic school. *School libraries worldwide,* 10 (1/2), pp.52-72.

JANESICK, V. (1998) The dance of qualitative research design metaphor, methodolatry, and meaning. IN DENZIN, N. & LINCOLN, Y. (Eds.) *Strategies of qualitative inquiry* London, SEGA Publications.

JOHNSON, L. & MADDUX, C. (2007) Introduction: effectiveness of Information technology in education. *Computers in the Schools,* 24 (3/4), pp.1-6.

KIMCHI, J., POLIVKA, B. & STEVENSON, J. (1991) Triangulation: operational definitions. *Nursing Research,* 40 (6), pp.364-366.

LIGHT, B. (2003) An interpretive field study of packaged software selection processes. *Information Systems Research Institute.* Salford, University of Salford.

MAGARA, E. & NYUMBA, B. (2004) Towards a school library development policy for Uganda. *Library Review,* 53 (6), pp.313-322. Available from: http://www.emeraldinsight.com/10.1108/00242530410544402

MCCLURE, C. (1991) Communicating applied library/information science research to decision makers: some methodological considerations. IN MCCLURE, C. & HERNON, P. (Eds.) *Library and information science research perspectives and strategies for improvement.* New Jersey, Ablex Publishing Corporation.

MCDONALD, S. (2006) The role of technology in the interactions between secondary school library media specialists and teachers. *The Department of Educational Leadership, Research, and Counselling.* Louisiana, Louisiana State University.

MOAHI, K. (2002) Issues of just-in-time (access) v. just-in-case (ownership) for libraries in developing countries: lessons to be learnt from developed countries. *Library Review,* 51 (7), pp.341-349. Available from: http://www.emeraldinsight.com/10.1108/00242530210438637

MORRIS, B. (2004) *Administering the school library media centre.* 4th ed, London, Libraries Unlimited.

OATES, B. (2006) *Researching information systems and computing.* London, Sage Publications.

OFFICE FOR STANDARDS IN EDUCATION (2006) Good school libraries: making a difference to learning. London, Ofsted.

ORLIKOWSKI, W. & BAROUDI, J. (1991) Studying information technology in organizations: research approaches and assumptions. *Information Systems Research,* 2 (1), pp.1-28.

ORLIKOWSKI, W. & ROBEY, D. (1991) Information technology and the structuring of organizations. *Information Systems Research,* 2 (2), pp.143-196.

PALVIA, P., MAO, E., SALAM, A. & SOLIMAN, K. (2003) Management information systems research: what's there in a methodology. *Communications of the Association for Information Systems,* 11, 289-309.

PAPAZOGLOU, A. (2001) School libraries and resource centers section. *Newsletter.*

PARÉ, G. (2001) *Using a Positivist Case Study Methodology to Build and Test Theories in Information Systems: Illustrations from Four Exemplary Studies.* Available from: http://gresi.hec.ca/SHAPS/cp/gescah/formajout/ajout/test/uploaded/cahier0109.pdf.

POWELL, R. (1991a) *Basic research methods for librarians.* 2nd ed, New Jersey, Ablex Publishing Corporation.

POWELL, R. (1991b) Guides to conducting research in library and information science. IN MCCLURE, C. & HERNON, P. (Eds.) *Library and information science research perspectives and strategies for improvement.* New Jersey, Ablex Publishing Corporation.

RICHARDSON, L. (2003) Writing a method of inquiry. IN DENZIN, N. & LINCOLN, Y. (Eds.) *Collecting and interpreting qualitative materials. 2nd ed.* London, SAGE Publications.

ROTHWELL, A. (1993) *Questionnaire design.* Leicester, De Montfort University.

SUMMERLINE, M. (2000) Home with ET: Elsik technology. *Campus-Wide Information Systems,* 17 (4), pp.129-133.

SWEE, T. & ABDULLAH, A. (2005) The status of school library automation in Malaysian Chinese secondary schools: a national survey. *Malaysian Journal of Library & Information Science,* 10 (1), pp.29-48.

TILKE, A. (Ed.) (1998) *Library association guidelines for secondary school libraries,* London, Library Association Publishing.

YIN, R. (1994) *Case study research: design and methods.* 2nd ed. London, Sage Publications.

ZAYTON, K. (2004) *Quantitative and qualitative perspective: educational and psychological research method.* Cairo, Alam Alkotob.

ZEHERY, M. (1994) School libraries in Kuwait: before and after the gulf war. *Library Association Publishing,* pp. 131-139.

ZEIDAN, A. (2007) NETGEAR wins AED 1.8 million contract to install wireless network solution in 350 schools in UAE. *Al Bawaba*

Infopragmatics: An Efficient Method for Information Retrieval

Ibarra Rafael and Ballesteros Silvia

National Autonomous University of Mexico

Abstract: Based on a linguistic algorithm, supported by an uncertainty theorem, the *infopragmatics* is a new method that offers an efficient solution, but not limited, to those Spanish speaking users who try to get the most useful information from academic databases which contents is in English. Presents a search analysis, an application of the language of levels understanding table, brief considerations on the ambiguity of the term "relevance" and statistical reasons to put *infopragmatics* into action at our National University Library System.
Keywords: Infopragmatics; Information retrieval (IR); Algorithm; Uncertainty theorem; Pragmatics; Linguistics; Spanish speakers.

1. Introduction

Information Retrieval is an unfinished challenge faced by today's librarians in order to give satisfaction to their users with pertinent information. There are several reasons that make this problem unsolvable, among others: information systems chaotic interfaces; users multiple categories and the unavoidable mismatch between controlled and natural vocabulary. These three critical aspects and their underlying grounds lead users in general to experience an uncertainty phase that overwhelms and inhibits them to get the information they need from information systems (ISs) also known as data bases (DB).

Furthermore, though there have been several alternatives given by ISs providers and uncountable researchers' theoretical contributions, users' demands for a suitable method to their information satisfaction have not been decreased sufficiently: they are still looking for an appropriate method. *Infopragmatics* is offered to relieve those crucial aspects by means of linguistic tools: a *linguistic algorithm*, an *uncertainty theorem* and a *linguistic storm* (*lingstorm*) – that result in an effective approach to get an efficient non-robotic alternative to satisfy users' information demands, specially for, but not limited to, those Non Native English Speakers (NNES).

Before going into deep, it should be mentioned that though there is a variety of DB that provide data in several formats: text, image, sound, video, and their possible combinations, the present paper will only consider commercial ISs companies with academic information, such as the ones offered by ProQuest, EBSCO and Elsevier because they are the ones used by the involved community. Google, Yahoo and the like are not considered in this study due to their nature as search engines, commercial sponsored interests and aims, though they are information alternatives many user take.

Information systems

The commercial ISs above mentioned present chaotic interfaces search pages and a quick access cumbersome help key (F1) that clearly show how unsuitable they might be for the numerous users' kinds, but especially for a novice user whose language is not English. For example, DB interfaces present more than 25 elements that are non essential for a novice user. Some of such elements are: *Pay Per View, Alerts, Favourite Journals, Quick Links, External Links, My settings, Number of pages, Cover story, SmartText searching, Also search within the full text of the articles, New features,* and several other elements which are definitively out of the novice user's interest. The rest of elements – ten - are more appropriate for mid or expert users.

According to the last reported inform, the top three consulted databases at the UNAM in 2006 were *Academic Search Premier* (25,723 consultations), *Elsevier Science* (7753 consultations), *PsychINFO* (5472 consultations). After reviewing the interfaces of each of these providers, it was found that they fit adequately for a certified librarian or user by the companies, as well as for a robot to read and select the check lists presented in an instant, but they are definitively not easy to deal with for a standard librarian or user whose language is Spanish or some other language different than English.

The lack of uniformity and troublesome interfaces of the ISs prevent several users to use them and prefer the search engines as Google Scholar that offers a suitable interface of no more than nine elements in English and five in Spanish language, which is a key component that is dealt in the following section.

2. Spanish Speakers Experience with ISs in English Language

The National Autonomous University of Mexico Library System (UNAM LS) offers access to more than 198 databases to its users concerning their fields of study and 91% of them are in English language. Its services are given in more than 140 libraries, but the analysis presented and referred in this work took place at the

Central Library (CB) where the interaction between a librarian and a user is both: spoken and in Spanish. Nevertheless, the interaction between humans and the ISs must be written and in English, which already sets a series of probable problems: bad spelling, wrong affixation, use of natural language in opposition to the controlled vocabulary and a big and chaotic number of the DB tools that come within as those alluded previously.

Every year more than 9,000 graduate students and more than 37,000 undergraduate enrol as students. Despite the fact that many librarians hold their posts during several years and offer annual courses related to databases use, thousands of users are mostly new to ISs.

2.1 Kinds of users and their language

Users are unique in their ideas, thoughts, and needs, so the way in which they express their information queries is as different as can be. On the other side, Spanish speaker users, either students or librarians, are not one of a kind and internationally share characteristics that can be summed up in the following, but partial categories referred by Stubinz and Whighly (2003): Pip, the impatient; Odysseus, the dogged; Ishmael, the exploratory; Hamlet, the confused; Ophelia, the deranged and Don Quixote, the idealist. Though this is a limited variety of users, it can be appreciated that, besides the human features, users speak different languages and adapted to modern times, their languages would be: English, Greek, Hebrew, Danish and Spanish.

With this scope, it is not difficult to imagine the effects that the merge between these kinds of users, different languages and commercial ISs' chaotic interfaces may cause. In current times it is evident that researchers, teachers at all levels have at hand a great number of strategies with numerous modifications and concerns to know, manage and improve the manners and channels of user services; Katsirikou and Skiadas, (2001) list 23 processing actions that comprise the opening and the closing dialog in an information request and that go from finding the appropriate electronic resource to indirectly and unwittingly provide personal information on one's activities, no matter the language.

2.2 Controlled vocabulary and natural language

One of the oldest antecedents of controlled vocabulary and natural language is the dispute between two groups: the *anomalists* and the *analogists*. The first group stated that human language should be spoken and lived in the way in which it is articulated; and the second one held that humans should express their ideas in an appropriate manner. As the years passed, the groups turned to be prescriptive and descriptive.

This dispute has not finished yet, as it can clearly be appreciated in modern classrooms when users are using their natural language in order to find controlled vocabulary information for their formal research. They are not aware that the semantic cracks that exist between ISs and them (Ibarra, 2007) is, in most cases, the reason why after a fruitless information search they end feeling uncertain and frustrated. They would certainly prefer feeling "found" than feeling "lost" if they knew how. An option would be to handle the theorem of uncertainty presented in here.

3. Infopragmatics

Infopragmatics is an efficient method to get pertinent information form ISs. It is based on a linguistic perspective aimed to those users, whose language is not English, paying particular focus but not limited to – Spanish speakers. Infopragmatics may be of highly considerable help for those academicians who can not get pertinent information from commercial ISs such as the ones provided by Elsevier, Ebsco, ProQuest and the like and it consists of an uncertainty theorem, a linguistic algorithm and a linguistic storm (lingstorm).

3.1 The uncertainty theorem

When users can not get the information they need from a DB, either guided by librarians or by using the quick guides given by ISs providers, they wonder why, and there is not a chance to give them a clue to reveal what the problems were, since they had the chance to read *relevant* displayed records from a scientific ISs. For example, Jaffe (1988: 759) points out that after a test applied to ISs users without more help than the one within DB, students were thwarted by Boolean, however. They sought the quick "hits" possible in an index-controlled database, and they were frequently confused when non-relevant citations appeared in a Boolean search, even though all the search terms were represented in the citation. After long reading sessions users got tired and fall into a state of uncertainty. Ibarra (1999) presented an approach considering diverse linguistic theories from an ethnolinguistic perspective and several analyses based on 120 real information searches with similar results.

So far, ISs do not offer any aid to keep the users away from the resulted perplexity; a gap which is expected to be covered by the following uncertainty theorem as an efficient contrivance to steer users to step more confidently in their information goals:

I.- If there is no information is due to...

User lacks lexical abilities
Syntax is wrong
Used terms are not equivalent in meaning
Context is no the appropriate
There is nothing in the used data base

II.- If the information doles not fit is due to...

Inappropriate technical language
Incorrect spelling
Key words or descriptors are not such

To reinforce the previous considerations, it is convenient to illustrate the diverse and synthesised linguistic possibilities that make Spanish native speakers fall apart from their information goals at the following understanding levels Liddy (2007): *Morphological*, bad spelling; *Lexical*, stating their needs; *Syntactic*, grammar rules; *Semantic*, opposition between the natural language and controlled vocabulary; *Discourse*, the way in which librarian and user interact to offer and receive ISs information respectively and, *Pragmatic*, the set of strategies that allow the users/librarians contrive their information needs. The next figure represents an information request on *Bolsa Mexicana de Valores*.

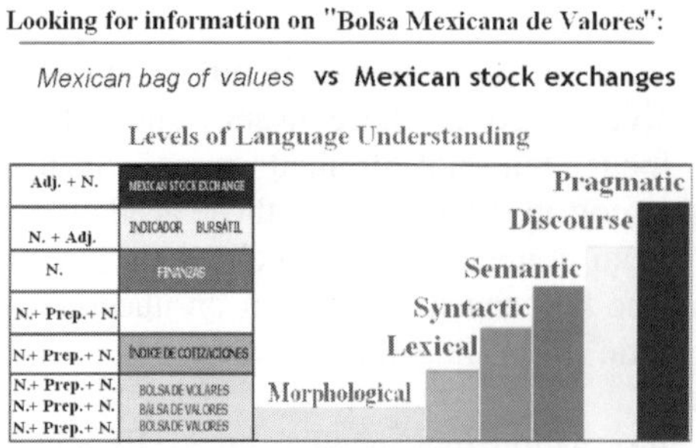

Fig. 1. Levels of language understanding.

It is evident the bad use of English language, but it is not possible to deny that "bag" means "bolsa", "Mexican" mexicana and "values" "valores"; or *sac de valeurs* vs. *Bourse* . Though this information query was taken several years ago, it was made the same trial on April 19, 2009, it was found that Academic Search Premier (Ebsco): and Science Direct (Elsevier), presented *relevant* results: 365540 and 1475 records respectively.

Users may not know much about levels of language and it is common that they follow a critical route: The first step is the lexical confusion, lack of technical dictionaries, indices, subject headings or thesaurus and misspelling. The second step is facing the ISs chaotic interface and dim help. The third step is reading the displayed results and after, selecting and printing or e-mailing undesired records, to justify, in most cases, the usage of ISs. Each of the previously identified errors may cause a variety of problems not just for Spanish Native speakers, but for all those native speakers whose language is not English.

Opportunely, there is another tool that identifies the critical route and suggests and ideal one, besides indicating the steps to be taken to warrant a practical solution to that users' urgent demand to get pertinent records from ISs.

3.2 Relevance

One striking and screened fact that in some way contributes to users' uncertainty is the term *relevance*. On the one hand, the results presented by the DB are offered based on the *relevance* they represent from the ISs, which means, from the engineering point of view, in several cases, the number of times that a term appears on a document.

On the other hand, entering to the definitions of a sense brings within a series of tasks that has come full circle, returning most recently to empirical methods and corpus-based analyses that characterize some of the earliest attempts to solve the problem. Among the numerous efforts that have been done Ide and Véronis (1998) remark AI-base methods, Symbolic methods, connectionist methods, knowledge based-methods, machine readable dictionaries, computational lexicons, corpus based methods (automatic sense-tagging and overcoming data sparseness.. However, the term *relevance* used by the ISs providers to present the results of their Information Retrieval Systems unwillingly masks the meaning *repetition* and *anaphora,* so users tend to follow a critical route shown in the next section.

3.3 Linguistic algorithm

The linguistic algorithm is the illustration of the series of linguistic operations to resolve the problems intrinsic to IR. It can be used as a guiding map to make users aware of the pair of routes within and, alternatively, considering the use of quick actions to satisfy their information needs in opposition to the critical route which issues were discussed previously.

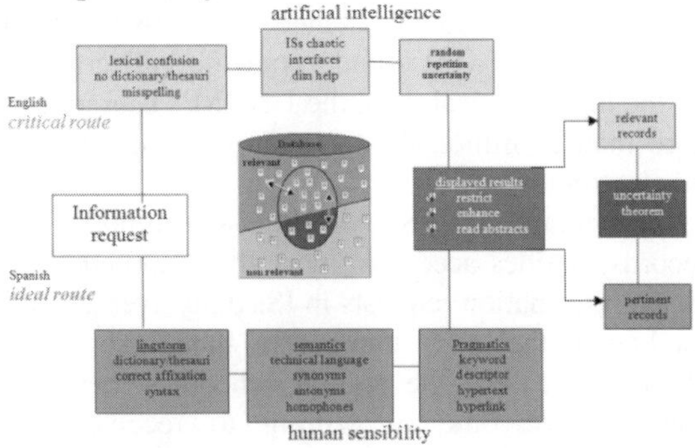

Fig. 2. Linguistic algorithm.

The first element of the ideal route comprises a quick action that requires using linguistic sources, either in print or electronic versions, to ensure the following steps. Specialised dictionary and thesaurus will allow the user to approach the *lingstorm*, "linguistic storm" (Fig. 3), to be used in a similar way as a brainstorm works in a group or individual creativity exercise, a constant along the IR, needed to leap from natural language to controlled vocabulary; the correct affixation deciphers the differences among verbs, nouns and adverbs that commonly cause semantic breaks when users shift from Spanish to English; Syntax determines the results in noun phrases; technical language clinches users´ familiarity with controlled vocabulary; Synonyms enhance semantic horizons and include spelling varieties when dealing with non Latin characters; though antonyms and homophones take place during verbal interaction, they fathom a temporary aphasia; key words and descriptors are easily found along the records´ reading and can be retrieved to set alternative search strategy; hypertext and hyperlinks are options that are attractive to follow as soon as they appear on the information records in order to avoid semantic unsettlement.

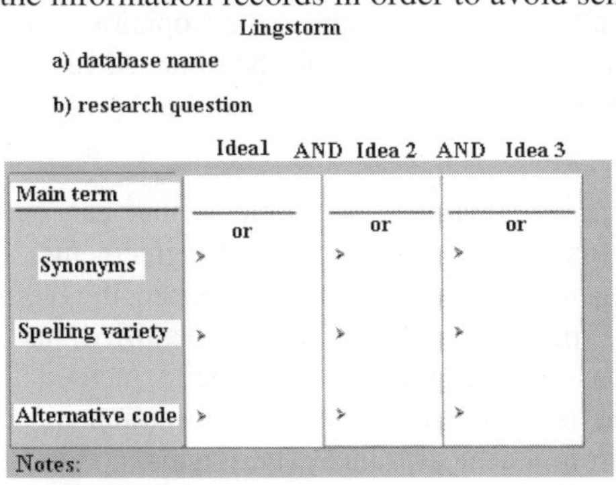

Fig. 3 Linguistic storm.

3.4 Statistical reasons and technical implementation of the *infopragmatics* in the National University Library System

The technical implementation will demand observing the number of users, the collections and two users' scenarios: distance and On-site. As it was mentioned before, the UNAM received 46,000 - undergraduate and graduate – potential ISs users; according to the last statistical data, the UNAM's Library System, up to April, 2009, there is more than 2 million of documents, comprising books, thesis, ISs, serials, printed and electronic.

More specifically, the available 150 ISs – in English - comprise access to more than 400,000,000 of records, besides access to more than 1,000,000 of journals' issues. On the other hand, the information requests in ISs daily average is 20,000.

Though it is not known the exact number of those users who do not receive librarian personal assistance, and the regular schedules they utilise the ISs, it is known not all users have time or willing to receive instructions on the infopragmatics method.

Considering the previous points, besides the level and kind of users, it is being designed a pair of brief workshops: On-site and distance. The first one consists of three parts: 15 minutes to explain the infopragmatics; 15 minutes of practice and; 15 for evaluation and feedback. The second workshop – distance- would be available on line and it is the users themselves who must set their times to profit from it, though there will be suggested steps and a feedback section via e-mail. Currently, there is a quick guide to "Retrieve pertinent information in English" in the Digital Library main web page <bidi.unam.mx>.

From a qualitative point of view, infopragmatics workshops would be more effective in the On-site mode, nevertheless, due to the large quantity of users, and considering the three single steps of the algorithm, a quick guide was designed and entitled "Recupera información pertinente en inglés" (retrieve pertinent information in English) which is available at http://132.248.9.9:8084/infopragmatica/.

It is necessary to mention that this quick guide includes hyperlinks to electronic translators, specialised dictionaries and thesauri, which quality was evaluated and later, catalogued in the UNAM´s Digital Library.

There is a hyperlink that allows users to express their opinions on the utilisation of the quick guide at the bottom of the page. With the obtained results, that are stored in a database, the design would be improved.

4. Conclusions

Information retrieval has a wide variety of problems that can only be solved by appropriate solutions, that is, if there are language disagreements, the clarifications must be given in language agreements. In this paper the common linguistic difficulties that affect Spanish speakers were identified as well as their corresponding explanations. Infopragmatics is an agile method that gives acute dynamism that allows ISs users to get pertinent information in opposition to the *relevant* ones that result from a critical route. The linguistic algorithm presented in here represents an accomplished tool that can be easily adapted to any language, included English, to serve as an information productive device.

References

Ibarra, R., (1999). *Aprovechamiento y optimización de los recursos tecnológicos en la búsqueda y recuperación de información en CD-ROM basados en estrategias lingüísticas.* Masters' dissertation on Applied Linguistics. UNAM.

Ibarra, R., (2009): Algunas grietas semánticas en la recuperación de información: una perspectiva deconstructiva para una solución pragmática. Proceedings of the *I Simposio Internacional sobre Organización del Conocimiento: Bibliotecología y Terminología*, 305-320.

Ide, N. and Véronis, J., (1998). Introduction to the special issue on word sense disambiguation: the state of the art. *Computational Linguistics*, 24, 1, 1-40.

Jaffe, J. G., (1988), For Undergraduates: InfoTrac MAGAZINE INDEX Plus or WILSONDISC with Reader's Guide and Humanities Index? *American Libraries*, Vol. 19, No. 9, 759-61.

Katsirikou, A. and Skiadas C. H., (2001). Chaos in the library environment, *Library Management*, Vol.22, No. 6/7, 278 – 287.

Liddy, Elizabeth D., (2007). Whither Come the Words? Presented at the *CENDI Subject Analysis and Retrieval Working Group Conference:* Controlled Vocabulary and the Internet. [On line].

Stubinz. J. and Whighly, S., (c. 1994) Information Retrieval System Design for Very High Effectiveness. [On line].

Note

[1]http://www.estadistica.unam.mx/agenda/agendas/2008/disco/xls/124.xls

Potential Uses of Web 2.0 Tools for Library Client Communication and Relationship Development

Jadranka Lasic-Lazic[1], Mihaela Banek Zorica[2] and Goran Bubas[3]

[1]University of Zagreb, Faculty of Humanities and Social Sciences, Zagreb, Croatia
[2] University of Zagreb, Faculty of Humanities and Social Sciences, Zagreb, Croatia
[3] University of Zagreb, Faculty of Organization and Informatics, Varazdin, Croatia

Abstract: In this paper, the potential uses of Web 2.0 technologies for the improvement of communication with library clients are examined. Wikis, blogs, RSS, mash-ups and other Web 2.0 tools and services can assist librarians in their efforts to present information online and better connect with their clients, especially the younger generations of Internet users. In three different studies we investigated (1) the familiarity of informatics students with Web 2.0 tools, (2) the computer literacy and Internet use by librarians in higher-education institutions, as well as their assessment of the potential uses of various Web 2.0 tools for interaction with the clients of their library, and (3) the use of Web 2.0 tools on the websites of public libraries in Croatia.

Keywords: Library 2.0; Web 2.0; Library service; Communication; User satisfaction.

1. Introduction

According to the Library 2.0 concept, library service is oriented "towards the needs and expectations of library users" and "makes information available wherever and whenever the user requires it" (Lepik, 2007). Libraries should exploit the new possibilities for interaction with clients that the Internet/web offers and use novel methods and channels to design and deliver their services, keeping in mind the concepts of customer relationship management and relationship marketing (see Wang, 2007). Library 2.0 is a reaction to the web-based developments in ICT and the widespread use of social software (see Curran et al., 2007). To improve communication with their users, libraries can use Web 2.0 tools and services like wikis, blogs, RSS, mash-ups, or even Facebook (Alsbjer, 2008). The use of Web 2.0 tools can enhance the library's communication with the public, the involvement of the community in the planning and evaluation of library services, the sharing of users' knowledge, as well as the overall experience of users (Stephens and Collins, 2007). The use of Web 2.0 tools may also better fulfil the expectations of the growing population of digital natives who "want to create, remix and share content" (Foo & Ng, 2008).

The theoretical explanations of the Library 2.0 concept should take into account that it (1) reflects user-centeredness; (2) is related to multi-media environments and communication channels; (3) provides the customer with the experience of social presence and enables interaction with librarians and other users; (4) is communally innovative, i.e. works as a community service adaptable to change and allows users to initiate and guide this change of services related to seeking and utilizing information (see Manes, 2006). Reflecting on the development of libraries' web services at the University of Houston, Coombs (2007) outlined the fundamentals of Web 2.0 that were used as guidelines for this effort: (1) decentralization of content creation; (2) orientation toward the use of "small pieces" of different technologies for the library web pages like wikis, blogs, and content management systems; (3) "perpetual beta", i.e. graduate introduction of various innovative technologies and services, their testing by small groups of library staff before implementation, evaluation and redesign based on feedback from users; (4) "remixable content" that can be integrated into the websites of other libraries or university departments; (5) encouragement given to users to contribute as content creators; (6) ensuring rich user experience with multimedia, potential for interaction, customization, and personalization.

However, in a study of ICT competencies of students enrolled in school library media programs in the USA, it was found that 50% or more were not familiar with or seldom used Web 2.0 related tools like podcasts, wikis, blogs, RSS feeds, and social bookmarking (Hanson-Baldauf & Hughes Hassel, 2009). Another study of Web 2.0 use by librarians in Israel revealed that 26% rated themselves as having a low level of computer expertise, and that library managers use Web 2.0 more often than ordinary librarians, recognize better the potential of such technologies, and understand that by using them the libraries may attract different types of users (Aharony, 2009).

Even though both large and small libraries tend to use Web 2.0 tools, in the United States they are more frequently used by successful libraries (see Lietzau, 2008). Decision-makers may find it important to include the use of Web 2.0 technologies in library services and develop training programs for librarians (Al-Fadhli, 2008), especially because such training programs have already been successfully implemented (Titangos and Mason, 2009).

This paper presents an overview of the potential uses of various Web 2.0 tools for the improvement of library services and for the online interaction of libraries with their clients. Data on the use of Web 2.0 tools by students of Informatics are also provided to support the argument that library services based on Web 2.0 tools can find potential users. In addition, a survey was also performed among librarians who work in higher education institutions to investigate their use of Web 2.0 tools and their assessment of the potential usefulness and applicability of Web 2.0 tools in their libraries. Finally, the websites of public libraries in cities and towns in Croatia were analyzed regarding the use of Web 2.0 tools.

2. Problem and Hypotheses

The main problem of this study was to investigate the potential of introducing Web 2.0 tools into Croatian libraries. Three different small-scale studies were conducted to at least partly respond to this problem. The goal of the first study was to determine how familiar students of Informatics are with Web 2.0 technologies and how often they use them. The intention of the second study was to investigate computer literacy, the use of the Internet and of Web 2.0 tools, and also to assess the potential usefulness and applicability of Web 2.0 tools by librarians who work in higher education institutions. The goal of the third study was to investigate the implementation of Web 2.0 tools on the websites of public libraries in Croatia.

According to the previously stated problem and research goals, the following hypotheses were formulated.

- H1: *Students of informatics are familiar with Web 2.0 tools.*
- H2a: *Librarians at higher education institutions have sufficient computer/information literacy to use Web 2.0 tools.*
- H2b: *Librarians at higher education institutions find Web 2.0 tools to be potentially useful in their libraries.*
- H3: *Public libraries in Croatia use Web 2.0 tools on their websites for interaction with clients/users.*

3. Method

A survey method was used in the *first study* of the use of Web 2.0 tools by students of Informatics. The subjects of this research were 285 students of the University of Zagreb, Croatia (20-25 years of age; 75% male and 25% female). The students were asked to rate their knowledge of various Web 2.0 tools using a 1-5 point Likert-type scale (5 – excellent knowledge; 4 – good knowledge; 3 – average knowledge; 2 – limited knowledge; 1 – not familiar).

The 51 subjects in the *second study* were librarians who worked in higher education institutions in Croatia. They had 1 to 35 years of work experience in a library (14 years on average) and 92% of them were female. All of them had Internet access at work and 92% of them stated that their clients could also access the Internet from their library. As many as 96% of the librarians accessed the Internet at work for one or more hours per day (it must be noted that 78% of the librarians stated that they used the Internet from work for as many as three or more hours per day). A survey was performed on this set of subjects to determine their level of computer/Internet literacy, their familiarity with popular Internet and Web 2.0 tools, and also their assessment of the potential of Web 2.0 tools to interact with the clients of their library.

In the *third study* an examination was performed on the websites of public libraries of 124 cities and towns in Croatia. Library websites were found in 41 cities and towns and they were searched for the use of Web 2.0 tools. In addition, the libraries with websites were contacted by telephone to check if Web 2.0 tools were used by librarians to interact with clients/users.

4. Results

In our *first study*, the survey of students of Informatics regarding their use of Web 2.0 tools revealed that most of them were familiar with popular tools/services like wikis, blogs, YouTube and MySpace/Facebook (see Table 1). However, less than 50% had more than scarce knowledge of a popular website for the exchange of photographs named Flickr, or a known social bookmarking site named Delicious, and of an even more popular online virtual world Second Life. Only a rather small percentage of students of Informatics stated that they were familiar with other Web 2.0 tools and services like those for creating web forms (JotForm), the placing of audio comments on presentation slides (Slidestory), adding text balloons as comments for video files (Bubbleply), the tagging of video and audio-recordings (Veotag), drawing mind maps (Bubbl.us), creating cartoon strips from Flickr photographs (Bubblr), and drawing block diagrams (Gliffy). Since students of Informatics have a high level of computer/Internet literacy and knowledge of Internet-based tools and services, it can be concluded that for the general public and less ICT literate students at college only the most popular Web 2.0 tools can be recommended for use by libraries. The use of less-known Web 2.0 tools for interaction with clients/users should perhaps be combined with online/offline tutorials, training sessions, or workshops.

Table 1. Percentage of students of Informatics who stated that they had average, good or excellent knowledge of a specific Web 2.0 tool (N=285)

WEB 2.0 TOOL	FUNCTION	%
YouTube	web publishing and exchange of video files	95.4
Wiki	web publishing	90.2
Blog	online diary	88.8
MySpace/Facebook	social networking	78.2
Flickr	exchange and search of photographs	47.7
Second Life	3D online virtual world	32.6
Delicious	social bookmarking	28.4
JotForm	web forms	22.6
Slidestory	placing of audio comments on presentation slides	16.1
Bubbleply	adding text balloons as comments for video files	10.9
Veotag	tagging of video and audio-recordings	10.9
NoteMesh	exchange of notes by students on the same courses	9.5
Bubbl.us	mind maps	8.1

Bubblr	creation of cartoon strips from Flickr photographs	4.9
Gliffy	block diagrams	4.2

In our *second study*, the level of computer literacy of librarians from higher education institutions was investigated (a convenience sample of 51 librarians was used). It was found that all of them stated that they had an average or higher level of knowledge of the use of the MS Windows operating system and the text processor MS Word. As many as 80% stated that they had average or better knowledge of MS Excel. However, only 49% stated that they had average or better knowledge of creating web pages, and 30% or less had knowledge of how to write a text in a wiki or a blog. Even though 84% of librarians stated that they read an online forum at least once a week, only 28% wrote a text in an online forum once a week or more often. Up to 69% of librarians stated that they read a blog at least once a week, but only 14% reported that they actually wrote a text in a blog once a week or more often. Similar percentages were reported for reading a wiki and writing in one. Finally, only 20-25% of librarians reported using instant messaging (ICQ), Skype, or MySpace/Facebook at least 1 to 2 times a week.

In this *second study*, the librarians from higher education institutions were also asked to assess how useful specific Web 2.0 technologies could be and how applicable they would be to improve their work with the users/clients of their library. The rating of usefulness/applicability was performed on a 1-5 Likert-type scale *(1 – totally useless / non-applicable; 2 – mostly useless / difficult to apply; 3 – both useful and useless / possibly applicable; 4 – useful / mostly applicable; 5 – very useful / applicable)*. The respondents could also indicate that they could not perform the rating of a specific Web 2.0 tool. The results of the rating of Web 2.0 tools are presented in Figure 1 (the average ratings were calculated from 30-48 responses of librarians, depending on their ability to perform the rating).

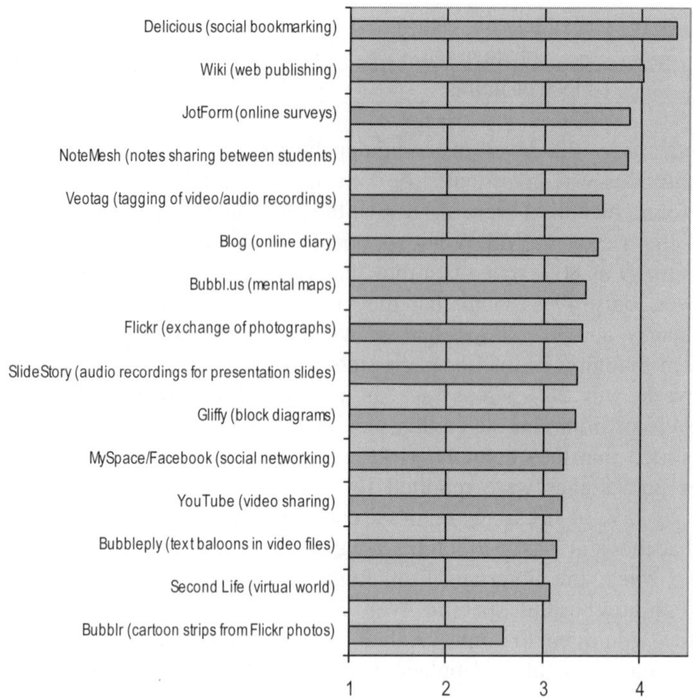

Figure 1. Average ratings by librarians of the potential usefulness and applicability of Web 2.0 technologies in higher education institutions (1 – totally useless / non-applicable; 5 – very useful / applicable)

According to the results of our survey, the social bookmarking tool (Delicious) received the highest average rating for potential usefulness/applicability. The average rating of the use of a wiki tool was also rather high, as was the use of tools for online surveys (JotForm) and exchange of notes taken by students attending the same courses (NoteMesh). It must be noted that the librarians gave on average a rating of 3 or above to most of the other Web 2.0 tools. Therefore, at least some potential use/applicability of the Web 2.0 tools that are listed in Figure 1 was recognized by the librarians from higher education institutions.

Finally, the results of the *third study* were rather discouraging regarding the use of Web 2.0 tools on the websites of public libraries in Croatia. As can be concluded from the data presented in Table 2, most of the public libraries of cities and towns in Croatia had only one web page or almost no web presence at all (except perhaps some general information on the website of their city/town). There was a total of 44 libraries that had a website of more than one webpage and on those websites no use of Web 2.0 tools was noticed during the examination of the respective web pages. However, a subsequent telephone inquiry revealed that two public libraries used a blog and one used a wiki, although not on their websites.

Table 2. Public libraries of cities and towns in Croatia with websites, and their use of Web 2.0 tools

Web presence and use of Web 2.0 tools by public libraries	Number
Libraries without a web page / website	19
Libraries with only one web page	61
Libraries with a website	44
Libraries with a website that used a Web 2.0 tool (wiki, blog)	2

5. Discussion

The survey performed in our *first study* revealed that the majority of the students of Informatics were familiar only with the most popular Web 2.0 tools such as wikis, blogs, and social networking sites. Many tools which are potentially useful to students and educators (NoteMesh, Bubbl.us, Bubblr, Gliffy) were known by less than 10% of students (the related findings are presented in more detail in a paper by Orehovacki et al., 2008). Therefore, the first hypothesis could only partly be confirmed. However, in one university course which used Web 2.0 tools for the design of e-learning activities it was found that the students of Informatics could learn in 15 to 30 minutes to use most of these tools (e.g. wiki, blog, JotForm, Slidestory, Bubbleply, Veotag, NoteMesh, Bubbl.us, Bubblr, Gliffy). This indicates that perhaps it would not be difficult to train librarians in the use of selected Web 2.0 tools to present information and improve their communication over the website of the library, or to use an alternative to an official website (i.e. use something else than a content management system). For instance, those libraries that could not afford to have a website could present their information over a Croatian version of Wikipedia, interact with the public through a blog, perform online surveys with JotForm, present their collections with SlideStory or Veotag, interact with children using Bubbleply of Bubblr, help students learn for specific courses using NoteMesh, or explain specific concepts/ideas or procedures/processes with Bubbl.us or Gliffy.

Our *second survey* of 51 librarians at higher education institutions indicated that most have basic computer skills and use the Internet at least several hours per day. In addition, most of them read content on a wiki or blog at least once a week. On average, those librarians believed that certain Web 2.0 tools could be useful and applicable in their libraries (for instance, Delicious, wiki, JotForm, Notemesh). It must be noted that, when average ratings are considered, none of the Web 2.0 tools listed in Figure 1 was excluded from this possibility. Because of their rather high level of basic computer literacy, it can be taken that librarians at higher education institutions have sufficient computer/information literacy to use Web 2.0 tools and that they find Web 2.0 tools to be of potential usefulness in their libraries. Thus, hypotheses H2a and H2b can be accepted.

However, the third hypothesis of our study could not be confirmed due to the fact that the majority of public libraries in Croatia do not use Web 2.0 tools for interaction with their clients/users. Only a few libraries reported using such tools, but separately of their official web pages. It must be noted that Web 2.0 tools were also not found on the websites of the libraries of 26 research institutes in Croatia, on the websites of 6 university libraries, or on the web pages of 15 museum libraries.

6. Educating the Librarians

The conducted studies and the related results confirm the need to modify the current library curriculum at the Department of Information Sciences, Faculty of Humanities and Social Sciences, University of Zagreb. Improvements have been applied in our part-time curricula intended for students who are already working in public or school/university libraries. This was done mainly since these professionals could benefit from this knowledge and instantly implement the methods and examples learned. Two new courses were introduced: *Information literacy* and *E-learning*, both focusing on the role of librarians in this new informational and educational environment. The objective of these courses is to give students insight into both the theory (information literacy course) and the practical (e-learning course) application of Web 2.0 tools and services in the transformed learning environment. The information literacy course was more oriented towards the theory of information literacy, the transformation of the web environment and its implementation in various library types and workplace environments. On the other hand, the e-learning course was more practically oriented towards new learning modes and different educational environments, focusing on the position and role of the librarians. Courses are offered in two modes: as distance learning and as an on-site course mainly based on using our e-learning system OMEGA (based on Moodle LMS) and the virtual faculty space in the virtual world – Second Life.

The main motivator for these courses is to offer on-hand experience, both from the student's point of view and from the teacher's position, thereby providing the librarians with basic knowledge of tools and services as well as experience in working with the technology that the majority of their users are familiar with. In order to create a successful Library 2.0 environment, we need to give both current and future librarians the theoretical background and practical exercises which can be carried out in attending such classes and workshops. Users who have actively participated in using new technology in learning and training are able to assess all the benefits and shortcomings of introducing new tools and teaching methods in their work environment. As librarians have a mission to provide their users with information and to respond to their users' information needs, this seems one of the best ways to do so.

7. Conclusion

Web 2.0 tools and services have huge potential. This potential is partially recognized and used by students and library users but it is still not utilized by librarians themselves. The majority of public libraries are present in the Web 1.0 world but still need to include and adapt their services in the Web 2.0 environment. Although one cannot say that librarians lack basic computer literacy and skills for the Web 2.0 context, they perhaps lack agility in implementing new technologies and services. Introducing librarians to the potential of various Web 2.0 tools could be one of the solutions to help them adopt these new services. This could be accomplished by offering training programs for librarians in order to help them meet their users' needs. Only educated librarians who are knowledgeable in the usage of social networking tools and services can promote these services to their users who are, in higher education libraries, both students and teachers. The full potential of

Web 2.0 could then be brought out in the whole educational environment, i.e. in the learning and research process.

References

Aharony, N. (2009). Web 2.0 use by librarians, *Library & Information Science Research*, Vol. 31, No. 1, 29-37.

Al-Fadhli, M. S. (2008) *Web 2.0 + Library = Library 2.0 / What is Library 2.0?* [Unpublished Report], Retrieved on 10 January 2009 from http://eprints.rclis.org/12679/1/Web_2.0_%26_Library_2.0.pdf

Alsbjer, P. (2008). Interaction: Anything goes 2.0. *Scandinavian Public Library Quarterly*, Vol. 41, No. 2, 6-9.

Casey, M.E., Savastinuk, L.C. (2006). Library 2.0: service for the next-generation library, *Library Journal* [Online], Vol. 131 No. 14, 40-42, Retrieved on 10 January 2009 from http://www.libraryjournal.com/article/CA6365200.html

Coombs, K.A. (2007). Building a Library Web Site on the Pillars of Web 2.0, *Computers in Libraries* [Online], Vol. 27, No. 1, Retrieved on 10 January 2009 from http://www.infotoday.com/cilmag/jan07/Coombs.shtml

Curran, K., Murray, M. and Christian, M. (2007). Taking the information to the public through Library 2.0, Library Hi Tech, Vol. 25, No. 2, 288-297.

Foo, S., Wee K.W. and Ng,Y. (2008). *Library 2.0, Libraries and Library School* [Unpublished Report], Retrieved on 10 January 2009 from http://www.las.org.sg/pa_sfjn.pdf

Hanson-Baldauf, D. and Hughes Hassell, S. (2009). The information and communication technology competencies of students enrolled in school library media certification programs. Library & Information Science Research, Vol. 31, No. 1, 3–11.

Lepik, A. (2007). Relationship marketing and Library 2.0: successful prospective partnership? *Signum*, Vol. 40, No. 5, 13-16.

Lietzau, Z. (2008). U.S. Public Libraries and Web 2.0 [Presentation], Library Research Service, Denver, Colorado, Retrieved on 10 January 2009 from http://www.lrs.org/documents/web20/pub_libs_web_20_ppt.pdf

Maness, J.M. (2006). Library 2.0 Theory: Web 2.0 and Its Implications for Libraries, *Webology* [Online], Vol. 3, No. 2, Retrieved on 10 January 2009 from http://www.webology.ir/2006/v3n2/a25.html

Orehovacki, T., Konecki, M. and Radosevic, D. (2008). Web 2.0 technologies in university education. *Proceedings of the 31st MIPRO International Convention on Computers in Education*,
Rijeka, Croatia: Croatian Society for Information and Communication Technology, Electronics and Microelectronics, 2008. 269-273

Stephens, M. and Collins, M. (2007). Web 2.0, Library 2.0, and the Hyperlinked Library, *Serials Review*, Vol. 33, No. 4, 253-256.

Titangos, H.-L. H. and Mason, G.L. (2009). Learning Library 2.0: 23 Things @SCPL, *Library Management*, Vol. 30, No. 1/2, 44-56.

Wang, M.Y. (2007). Introducing CRM into an academic library, Library Management, Vol. 28, No. 6/7, 281-291.

Service Quality of Web Information Systems

Yaşar Tonta[1] and İrem Soydal[2]

[1]Department of Information Management, Hacettepe University, 06800 Beytepe, Ankara Turkey
E-mail: tonta@hacettepe.edu.tr
[2]Hacettepe University Medical Library, Hacettepe University, 06100 Sıhhiye, Ankara, Turkey
E-mail: soydal@hacettepe.edu.tr

Abstract: It is essential that web designers understand what users expect of web services, how they perceive service quality dimensions such as security, usability and information quality, and which ones they value the most. In this study, the users' service quality perceptions of two different web sites were investigated. Data were obtained from 1,900 users of web sites of a for-profit online bookstore and a not-for-profit national information center through the E-Qual Index that was administered online. Findings of the study indicate that users of both for-profit and not-for-profit web sites attach more importance to the "trust" and "quality of information" dimensions as web service quality indicators. Users' expectations should therefore be regularly measured to review the design and information structures of both for-profit and non-profit web sites.

Keywords: Web service quality; Usability; Information quality; Trust; E-Qual Index.

1. Introduction

The web sites presenting information about a specific subject that appeals to a specific user group are called as web information systems. These systems may have commercial, information sharing or information presenting purposes, and they need to be designed by taking into consideration the user satisfaction. The level of user satisfaction is determined by the extent to which users' expectations are met. Users often think that the quality of web information systems is closely related with the quality of information provided and the quality of the system design (Shih, 2004a; 2004b; Negash, Ryanb and Igbaria, 2003). Users' expectations increase as the web functionality does. They become more demanding as they experience new web services and technologies (Piccoli, Brohman, Watson and Parasuraman, 2004). This shows that users' expectations can change as fast as the Web itself does. Measuring the service quality in the Web environment is important in terms of increasing the usage rate of the systems. If the web service quality is perceived positively by the users, it significantly affects the users' overall satisfaction, their eagerness to suggest the system to others and their tendencies to purchase/repurchase (Zeithaml, 2000).

This study aims to measure the service quality of web information systems by means of the E-Qual Index. Comprised of 22 Likert-type questions, the E-Qual Index tests the concepts of web site usability, information quality and interaction quality, in general. We applied it to one for-profit web site (Idefix, an online shopping site, www.idefix.com.tr) and one not-for-profit web site (the National Academic Network and Information Center, ULAKBIM, www.ulakbim.gov.tr). Findings were compared to see if users' perceptions of web service dimensions differed in terms of types of web sites.

2. Literature Review

The concept of "traditional" service quality started to attract attention in 1980s (Parasuraman, Zeithaml and Berry, 1985). The SERVQUAL Index with 22 questions and five different dimensions (Tangibles, Reliability, Responsiveness, Assurance, and Empathy) has emerged as a tool to measure the traditional service quality. The dimensions measured by the SERVQUAL Index have since changed as more services and products have increasingly been offered via the Web. Nevertheless, most studies measured the web service quality by using the dimensions of SERVQUAL Index (Van Iwaarden, Van der Wiele, Ball and Millen, 2004; Caruana, Ewing and Ramaseshan, 2000; Cook and Thompson, 2000; Negash, Ryan and Igbaria, 2003).

Several studies were carried out on the web service quality (Lindgaard and Dudek, 2003; Muylle, Moenaert and Despontin, 2004; Shih, 2004b; Yang, Cai, Zhou and Zhou, 2005; Garrity, Glassberg, Kim, Sanders and Shin, 2005). Factor analysis was used to identify the new web service quality dimensions. Among them are: usability, usefulness of content, the adequacy of information, accessibility, and interaction (Yang, Cai, Zhou and Zhou, 2005); responsiveness, competence, quality of information, empathy, web assistance, and callback systems (Li, Tan and Xie, 2002); and, effectiveness, system availability, fulfillment, compensation, and contact (Parasuraman Zeithaml and Malhotra, 2005). Also, the quality of information, the features of perceived usability and the ease of use are significant measures from the users' point of view to evaluate the success of information systems (Shih, 2004a; 2004b).

The E-Qual Index was developed in the beginning of 2000s in order to measure the web service quality. It was based on the literature of information systems, marketing and human-computer interaction (Barnes and Vidgen, 2002). The first versions of E-Qual Index (named "WebQual Index" before 2003) were used to evaluate the web sites of various universities (Barnes and Vidgen, 2000), online auction web sites (Barnes and Vidgen 2001), the web sites of online bookstores (Barnes and Vidgen, 2002) and government institutions providing electronic services (Barnes and Vidgen 2003b; 2005). Using the factor analysis on the data, the dimensions of perceived service quality were identified as Usability, Design, Information Quality, Trust and Empathy. In a different study, an information presenting website of OECD's Forum on Strategic Management Knowledge Exchange (FSMK) was explored by removing the questions on Trust (Barnes and Vidgen 2003a). The results of the study were similar except the Trust dimension. Users' views on the Usability and Design dimensions were positively changed after the web site was redesigned. A similar study was carried out using the official website of the UK Inland Revenue Service in which users' perceptions of service quality were compared. Users who utilized the website to carry out "interactive online transactions" attached more importance to the Usability dimension than those who used it to "gather information" (Barnes and Vidgen 2003b, 2005).

3. Methodology

Research questions addressed in this study are as follows:

- How do users perceive the service quality of web sites in terms of information quality, usability and service interaction?
- Which service dimensions do users value most?

The web sites of Idefix, a for-profit online bookstore, and ULAKBIM, a not-for-profit national information center, were used to collect data using the E-Qual Index (www.webqual.co.uk/instrument.htm). An online questionnaire with 22 questions was filled out by the users of both web sites. Questions addressed the aspects of usability (e.g., "I find the website easy to learn to operate"), information quality (e.g., "The web site provides accurate/timely/believable information") and service interaction (e.g., "My personal information feels secure") of each web site. Users were asked to mark their scores of perception and importance for each question on a 5-point Likert scale (1: "I'm not pleased at all" / "It is not important for me at all" - 5: "I'm very pleased" / "It is very important for me"). The perception scores reveal the users' evaluation of the website while the importance scores reveal their level of expectation for the concepts tested in terms of perceived web service quality.

Analyses were based on 1,782 questionnaires filled out for Idefix and 118 for ULAKBIM. The suitability of the data sets for the factor analysis was examined with the Kaiser-Meyer-Olkin (KMO) and Bartlett test. Factor analysis identifies different dimensions of web sites on the basis of users' perception scores. The importance scores indicate the web site dimensions to which users attach more importance in general. The Principal Component Analysis method was used with varimax rotation. Findings were summarized in tables and radar graphs.

4. Findings and Discussion

Data sets for Idefix and ULAKBIM web sites were suitable for factor analysis (Idefix KMO=0.946, $p<0.05$; ULAKBIM KMO=0.930, $p<0.05$). The reliability of the E-Qual Index was high (Idefix α= 0.934; ULAKBIM α= 0.968).

The Eigen value was selected as 1 for the factor analysis for Idefix data. Five factors obtained after the rotation explained 71% of the total variance. They are as follows:

1. Quality of Information (question numbers 9 through 15);
2. Trust (question numbers 16, 17, 18 and 22);
3. Usability (question numbers 1 through 4);
4. Design (question numbers 5 through 8); and
5. Empathy (question numbers 19 through 21).

The highest factor loadings belonged to the first factor, the Quality of Information. Cronbach's alpha (α) values revealed that perception and importance scores were highly reliable (Table 1). The mean perception score (3.9) was lower than the mean importance score (4.3). The mean scores for the factors Trust, Usability and Quality of Information were the highest (4 and above) while that for Design and Empathy were the lowest (3.6 and 3.3, respectively). As for the importance scores, the Trust factor's mean score was very close to 5 while the mean scores for the Design and Empathy were, once again, the lowest (3.9 and 3.7, respectively).

Table 1. Reliability levels and the mean scores of factors (Idefix)

	Perception		Importance	
Dimensions	α	$\bar{X}$	α	$\bar{X}$
Quality of Information	0.916	4.0	0.881	4.6
Trust	0.837	4.3	0.703	4.8
Usability	0.887	4.2	0.819	4.5
Design	0.850	3.6	0.758	3.9
Empathy	0.759	3.3	0.668	3.7
	$\bar{X}$:	*3.9*	$\bar{X}$:	*4.3*

As for ULAKBIM, four factors explained 77% of the total variance. Identified as separate factors for Idefix, the Quality of Information and Trust, factors merged and became a single factor while the remaining three factors (i.e., Usability, Design and Empathy) did not change (including the question numbers). It appears that users deemed the Trust (and the security of their personal information) and the Quality of Information in the same category, thereby creating a joint factor with the highest loadings that explained a third of the overall variance in the ULAKBIM data. As in Idefix, the perception and importance scores were highly reliable (Table 2). The highest mean perception score belonged to the (combined) Quality of Information and Trust factor (4.0) while the Design factor had the lowest (3.3). The highest mean importance scores belonged to the factors of Quality of Information and Trust (combined) (4.7) and Usability (4.5). It should be noted that the difference between the means of perception and importance scores for the Usability factor was high, indicating that users seemed to be less pleased with ULAKBIM's interface than they had expected.

Table 2. Reliability levels and the mean scores of the dimensions (ULAKBIM)

	Perception		Importance	
Dimensions	α	$\bar{X}$	α	$\bar{X}$
Quality of Information & Trust	0.961	4.0	0.915	4.7
Usability	0.929	3.6	0.848	4.5
Design	0.894	3.3	0.772	3.9
Empathy	0.811	3.5	0.761	4.0
	$\bar{X}$:	*3.6*	$\bar{X}$:	*4.3*

In order to better evaluate the perceived service quality of each web site, both the perception and the importance scores should be taken into account. While the perception scores indicate how much users like the web service quality dimensions of the web site they used at a certain time, the importance scores underline how important users find each dimension on the basis of their prior experience with the web in general.

The mean perception and importance scores of factors for Idefix are shown on a radar graph in Figure 1. The Quality of Information, Trust and Usability factors (with the highest mean scores) appear to be prominent, indicating that users graded them more heavily than the other factors. Factors' mean perception and importance scores were close to each other. The expectations of users seemed to be met more satisfactorily for the Design and Usability factors.

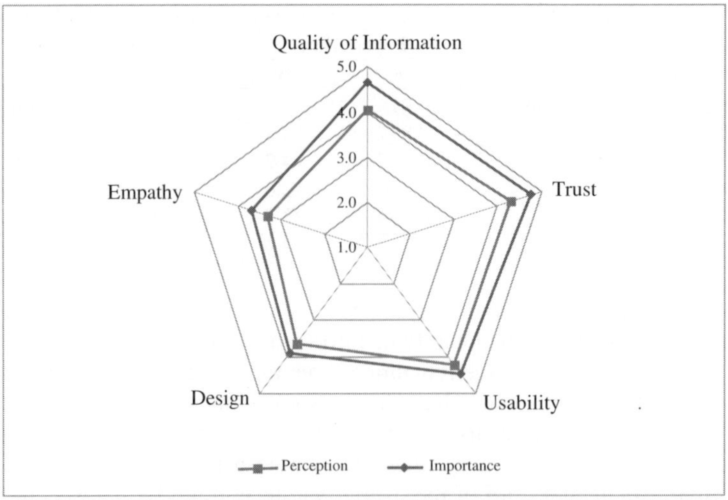

Figure 1. Comparison of factors for Idefix web site according to mean perception and importance scores

The radar graph in Figure 2 shows that ULAKBIM users thought of the Quality of Information and Trust (combined) and Usability factors as the most important. Differences between the mean perception and importance scores for Usability, Design, and the (combined) Quality of Information and Trust factors are noticeable, indicating that there appears to be a gap between the levels of how users perceived these service quality dimensions in ULAKBIM web site and how they expected them to be. In other words, the higher the gap, the less successful the web site in terms of delivering what users expected.

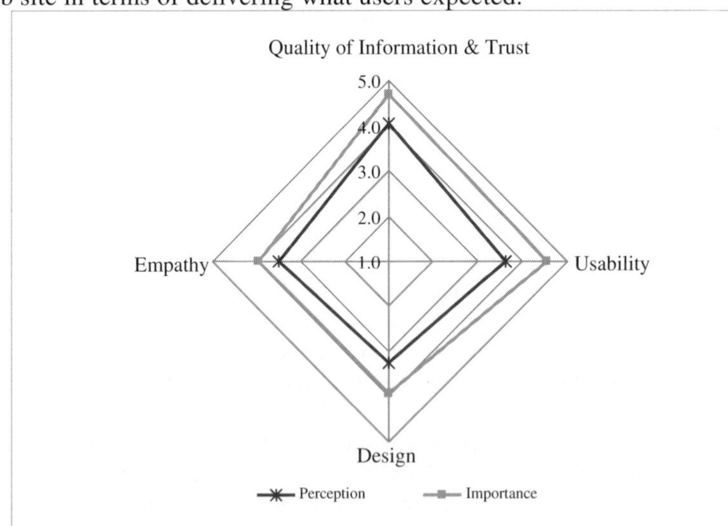

Figure 2. Comparison of factors for ULAKBIM website according to mean perception and importance scores

The results showed that the Usability, Design and Empathy factors (and the questions measuring these dimensions) were the same for both web sites. However, the Quality of Information and Trust factors differed, as ULAKBIM users perceived these two factors as one while the Idefix users differentiated them. The Quality of Information, Usability, Design, Trust and Empathy concepts were also deemed as different dimensions by the users of previous studies that used the E-Qual Index, which confirms our Idefix findings (Barnes and Vidgen, 2002; 2003b). The dimensions revealed in those studies (and question groups comprising these dimensions) were the same as ours except that ULAKBIM users evaluated the Quality of Information and Trust concepts jointly. This may be due to the fact that Idefix is a commercial company. Idefix users can carry out financial transactions by registering with the system and by supplying personal information. Therefore, Idefix users may have special concerns regarding the Trust issue. ULAKBIM, on the other hand, is an official web site of a government institution providing information to its users (both registered and unregistered). Unlike Idefix users, ULAKBIM users cannot perform online financial transactions through the ULAKBIM web site. ULAKBIM users generally use the web site to get access to information and they may perceive the questions measuring the Trust and the Quality of Information in the context of the presentation of information only. It may also be the case that the 22-question EQual Index was used for the first time in an information presenting web site used solely for academic purposes. In that sense, previous studies evaluating the information presenting web sites of OECD's FSMKE and UK Inland Revenue Service might be similar to ULAKBIM (Barnes and Vidgen, 2003a; 2003b). However, the five factors emerged were the same as that of Idefix in one study while the questions measuring the Trust were removed from the E-Qual Index in the other.

The importance scores of factors for both web sites show the expectations of users: they value Trust (combined with the Quality of Information in the case of ULAKBIM) as the most important. Non-profit web site users attach more importance to the concepts concerning the Quality of Information, which was also observed in earlier studies (Barnes and Vidgen 2003b; 2005). As indicated earlier, the concepts of Quality of Information and Trust are interwoven for ULAKBIM users. As for Idefix users, they differentiated the Trust factor from the Quality of Information factor, possibly due to their concerns about the security of their dealings with a commercial website. Interestingly, the users of both web sites rated the Usability as one of the least important factors. This may be either due to the fact that user interfaces of both Idefix and ULAKBIM are well designed or that the users do not seem to be terribly interested in the usability of web sites.

5. Conclusion

This study was carried out in order to compare two different web sites, one for-profit (Idefix) and the other not-for-profit (ULAKBIM) in terms of perceived service quality dimensions, and to determine the most important ones from the users' point of view. The Quality of Information and Trust appear to be the two most important service quality dimensions of the for-profit web site. As for the users of the not-for-profit website, they considered the Quality of Information and Trust factors as a single dimension. The other three factors, namely Usability,

Design and Empathy were similar for both web sites.

When the perception and importance scores were compared, it was observed that the user expectations were not fully met for both web sites, although users did not complain much, in general. The factors to which users attach the most importance were Trust for Idefix and the Quality of Information and Trust (combined) for ULAKBIM, indicating that for-profit web site users are more concerned with the security of web information systems while non-profit web site users value the quality and the reliability of information more highly.

Users' expectations were met less satisfactorily for the factors of Quality of Information, Trust and Usability, suggesting that the perceived usability and design principles were not taken into consideration in designing the non-profit web site. As users attached importance to information and content, the design of the for-profit website seemed to ignore the fact that such web sites are used not only for online interactive transactions but also for finding information.

The importance scores of both web site users differ from each other in terms of service quality dimensions. Yet, our findings show that web users require "good quality information" both from a shopping web site and from an information presenting web site. Although the basic purpose of the existence of a for-profit web site such as that of Idefix may not be presenting information per se, they are an active source of information for books and other information-bearing objects, nevertheless. A non-commercial web site, on the other hand, may collect personal information from the users and require credit card information of users to compensate the costs of some services. This might explain why not-for-profit web site (ULAKBIM) users attached the highest importance to Trust (i.e., safety and security). It is likely that the difference in the perceived service quality dimensions for commercial and non-commercial web sites will disappear in the near future, as more web sites, including commercial ones, offer a wide variety of services.

The results of the study show that users consider the web sites as a valuable source of information no matter what their motivations are in using them. Therefore, designers of web sites should pay attention to the presentation and content of information regardless of their type (e.g., for-profit vs. not-for-profit web sites). Users' expectations also vary, suggesting that studies similar to ours should be carried out regularly to detect the changing user expectations and redesign the web sites accordingly.

References

Barnes, S., & Vidgen, R. (2000). WebQual: An exploration of web-site quality. Proceedings of the Eighth European Conference on Information Systems. Retrieved March 25, 2009, from http://is.lse.ac.uk/asp/aspecis/20000052.pdf.

Barnes, S., & Vidgen, R. (2001). Assessing the quality of auction web sites. Proceedings of the Hawaii International Conference on Systems Sciences. Retrieved March 25, 2009, from http://www.webqual.co.uk/papers/auction.pdf.

Barnes, S., & Vidgen, R. (2002). An integrative approach to the assessment of ecommerce quality. The Journal of Electronic Commerce Research, 3(3), 114-127. Retrieved March 25, 2009, from http://www.webqual.co.uk/papers/bookstore.pdf.

Barnes, S., & Vidgen, R. (2003a). Measuring web site quality improvements: a case study of the forum on strategic management knowledge exchange. Industrial Management and

Data Systems, 103(5), 297-309. Retrieved March 25, 2009, from http://www.webqual.co.uk/papers/webqualfsmke.pdf.

Barnes, S., & Vidgen, R. (2003b). Interactive e-government: evaluating the web site of the UK Inland Revenue. Journal of Electronic Commerce in Organizations, 2(1), 42-63. Retrieved March 25, 2009, from http://www.webqual.co.uk/papers/inlandrevenue.pdf.

Barnes, S., & Vidgen, R. (2005). Data triangulation in action: using comment analysis to refine web quality metrics. Proceedings of the 13 th European Conference on Information Systems. Retrieved March 25, 2009, from http://www.webqual.co.uk/papers/comment.pdf.

Caruana, A., Ewing, M.T., & Ramaseshan, B. (2000). Assessment of the three-column format SERVQUAL: An experimental approach. Journal of Business Research, 49(1), 57-65.

Cook, C., & Thompson, B. (2000). Reliability and validity of SERVQUAL scores used to evaluate perceptions of library service quality. The Journal of Academic Librarianship, 26(4), 248-258.

Garrity, E.J., Glassberg, B., Kim, Y.J., Sanders, G.L., & Shin, S.K. (2005). An experimental investigation of web-based information systems success in the context of electronic commerce. Decision Support Systems, 39, 485-503.

Li, Y.N., Tan, K.C., & Xie, M. (2002). Measuring web-based service quality. Total Quality Management, 13(5), 685-700.

Lindgaard, G., & Dudek C. (2003). What is this evasive beast we call user satisfaction? Interacting with Computers, 15, 429-452.

Muylle, S., Moenaert, R., & Despontin, M. (2004). The conceptualization and empirical validation of web site user satisfaction. Information & Management, 41, 543-560.

Negash, S., Ryan, T., & Igbaria, M. (2003). Quality and effectiveness in web-based customer support systems. Information & Management, 40, 757-768.

Parasuraman, A., Zeithaml, V.A., & Malhotra, A. (2005). ESQUAL: A multiple item scale for assessing electronic service quality. Journal of Service Research, 7(3), 213-234.

Parasuraman, A., Zeithaml, V.A., & Berry, L.L. (1985). A conceptual model of service quality and its implications for future research. Journal of Marketing, 49(4), 41-50.

Piccoli, G., Brohman, M.K., Watson, R.T., & Parasuraman, A. (2004). Net-based customer service systems: Evolution and revolution in website functionalities. Decision Sciences Journal, 35(3), 423-455.

Shih, H.-P. (2004a). An empirical study on predicting user acceptance of e-shopping on the Web. Information & Management, 41, 351-368.

Shih, H.-P. (2004b). Extended technology acceptance model of Internet utilization behavior. Information & Management, 41, 719-729.

Van Iwaarden, J., Van der Wiele, T., Ball, L., & Millen, R. (2004). Perceptions about the quality of web sites: a survey amongst students at Northeastern University and Erasmus University. Information & Management, 41, 947-959.

Yang, Z., Cai, S., Zhou, Z., & Zhou N. (2005). Development and validation of an instrument to measure user perceived service quality of information presenting web portals. Information & Management, 42, 575-589.

Zeithaml, V.A. (2000). Service quality, profitability, and the economic worth of customers: What we know and what we need to learn. Journal of Academy of Marketing Science, 28, 67-85.

Internet Access and Use in Brazil: Concepts, Measures, and Public Libraries as Social Facilitators

Gilda Olinto

Instituto Brasileiro de Informacao em Ciencia e Tecnologia, Ministério de Ciência e Tecnologia, Graduate Program in Information Science, Brazil

Abstract: Evidence about internet access and use in Brazil is presented using 2005 Brazilian Bureau of Census data. The importance of internet access outside home, especially by disadvantaged groups is pointed out as well as the impact of socio-technical factors on types of internet access and use is analysed. The relevance and the complexity involved in identifying and classifying internet use and social factors involved are stressed. The role played by specific "social facilitators" of internet use, with emphasis on the role of the public libraries, is also considered.
Keywords: Internet use; Digital divide; Public libraries; Brazil, Developing countries; ICT literacy.

1. Introduction

This paper starts with evidences about socio-technical dimensions of internet access and use in Brazil, using Brazilian Bureau of Census data, a questionnaire applied in 2005 to a sample of more than 408 individuals (IBGE, 2006). The intention is to initially detach aspects of the country's situation, similar to that of other developing countries, that can have implications on how one focus the subject, and how one chooses concepts (or variables) and analytical models for empirical treatment. I try to point out that certain topics that seem to become uninteresting in developed countries, as it is the case of mere access to the net and its socio-demographic underpinnings, are still very relevant in the Brazilian context and might be fundamental for large comparative studies that take into account the great diversities of internet access and use.

The evidence shown about Brazil also gives support to studies that focus on different dimensions of internet use and on how these uses relate to contextual factors. The study of the ways in which contexts influence internet use and how internet use is effective in promoting changes is an increasing challenge for analysts, involving several theoretical and methodological problems.

Another point that made in this paper is the role that could be played by public libraries, in contributing to the increase of internet in access and use, especially in certain contexts, as Latin American countries, due to the specific characteristics and problems they face in dealing with ICT use and ICT literacy, as initially considered. Libraries are seen by analysts as bridges, "the only bridge" (Schement, 2003), that could be used by those that are technologically and socially disconnected to become a part of the Knowledge society.

2. The low levels of internet access and internet use outside home in Brazil

Analyses based on the above mentioned survey show that a hard reality characterizes internet use by Brazilian adult population[1]: only less than 20%[2] had any kind of access to the internet in 2005.

Contrasts with developed nations are outstanding: in the same year already almost 70% of the US adults were connected to the internet and similar figures were obtained from many OECD nations (Fox, 2005, World Bank, 2006). It is a fact that Brazilian reality is changing rapidly and accompanies patterns shown by Latin American countries. But the point to stress is that any analysis of internet use shown here or elsewhere refers to a very small minority of a very large population: more than 100 million did not access internet.

When the focus of analyses change to the younger ones – to the student population- the figures are equally distressing: the same survey indicated that only 10.7% of elementary school children, from first to fourth grade, had internet access, regardless of place of access. The size of the student population is almost 22 million youngsters (Olinto, 2007).

The socio-economic profile of those that still do not have internet in the country, shown in the next table, highlights the strong contextual forces shaping ICT divide in Brazil. The dimensions selected for analyses follow those used by the PEW Internet and American Life reports and also other international surveys (Horrigan, 2008, Chen & Wellman, 2003, Olinto, 2008b):

TABLE 1. Socio-demographic profile of Brazilians without access to the internet. Brazilian adult population, 2005.

Socio-demographic characteristic	Without access (%)	Population in stratum (in Million)
Age		
18-29	70.1	**39.9**
30-49	80.5	**50.4**
50- 64	89.6	**22.0**
65+	98.0	**12.6**
Gender		
Male	79.3	**59.7**
Female	81.7	**65.3**
Race		
White	73.9	**64.5**
Afro-Brazilian	88.0	**59.4**
Other	64.3	**0.9**
Years of Education		
10 or less	95.5	**83.2**
11 to 14	57.4	**32.8**
15 or more	23.8	**8.6**
Income (minimum wages)		
2 or less	95.5	**41.0**
More than 2 to 5	87.2	**45.4**
More than 5 to 10	67.0	**22.1**
More than 10	39.2	**14.1**

Source: IBGE (PNAD). Olinto, 2008b. Population aged 18 years old or higher.

If one compares Brazil and the US in the same year, similar values indicate the opposite situation: while in the US about 80% of Brazilians in the 30-40 age group had access to the internet, around 80% of Americans already had access (Fox, 2005). Although gender differences in net access are not remarcable in table 1, ethnic differences are clear, highlighting disadvantages of African-Brazilians. The above data also show that it is necessary to belong to higher educational and income level groups to escape the general pattern of very little access to the net. It is also noteworthy the absolute numbers involved in above mentioned percentages as shown in the last column of table 1: the total amount of Afro-Brazilian adults (almost 60 million), of people with less than 10 years of education (83 million) and of two or less minimum wages (41 million) in the country.
Another interesting figure to show, and central to the arguments developed in this paper, refers to places of access to the internet, as shown in table 2:

TABLE 2. Place of Internet access.
Brazilian adult population, 2005.

Place of Access	(N in million)	(%)
Outside home	11.4	9.2
At home	13.0	10.3
Total	24.4	19.5

Source: IBGE (PNAD)

It is noticeable from table 2 that almost half of the lucky ones that had some kind of internet access in 2005 had it outside their homes; and the latter represent only 9.2% of the Brazilian adult population, involving nonetheless 11.4 million of adults. Use outside home is also the reality faced by Brazilian youngsters who make frequent and intensive use of the internet in LAN houses (Cysne, 2007, CGI, 2006, Olinto, 2008a).

The next table shows the types of home access:

TABLE 3. Type of home access.
Brazilian adult population, 2005.

Type of home access	(N in Million)	(%)
Dial up	7.5	6.0
Broadband	6.2	4.9

Source: IBGE (PNAD)

The above data indicate that in Brazil, in the year of 2005, the adult population that possessed internet at home was divided in two groups of about the same size: those with dial up connection and those that mentioned having broadband in their homes. These two groups encompass very small percentages of the Brazilian adult population. Considering the characteristics and frequencies of Internet access in Brazil, this concept – type of access- could in fact be treated as an ordinal measure with the lowest level of access indicating those that only have access outside home, followed by access at home with dial up and the highest level of access being at home with broadband. Each of these levels represents a fair amount of people, with the lowest level – access outside home - with the highest frequencies. The analysis of the social profile of these different types of access revealed that access outside home is characteristic of the majority of the younger age group, of large part of Afro-Brazilians, of people with lower levels of income and education. As one moves to dial up access ant to broadband, the demographics change to socially privileged groups (Olinto, 2008b).

How privileges, expressed by technological accessibility (type of internet access) and by socio-economic characteristics (income level), are related to types of internet use in Brazil is expressed in the graphs that follow. In accordance to evidences already obtained form other contexts, on the whole the graphs suggest that technology has a strong social base, with which it interplays, continuing to reproduce inequalities (Wellman et al, 2002, Horrigan, 2008). Favorable socio-technical conditions contribute to the multiple uses of the internet considered: use for education, use of the media, for maintaining social relations, for accessing government, for having access to good and services and for leisure. As previous evidence suggest, these uses contribute both to quality of life and to active citizenship.

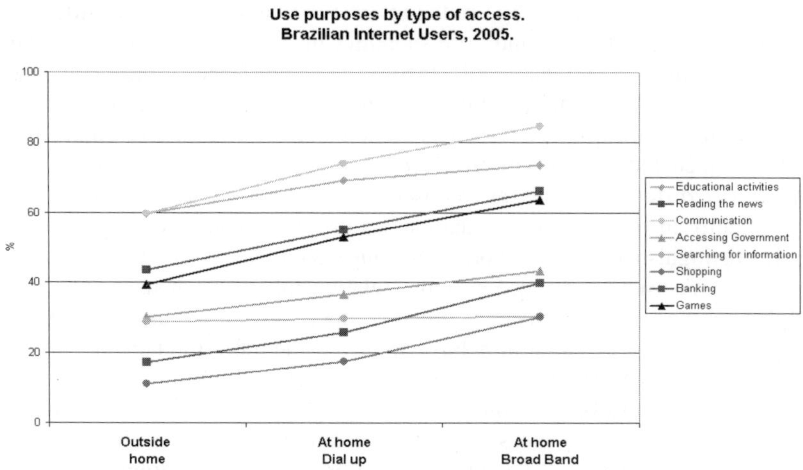

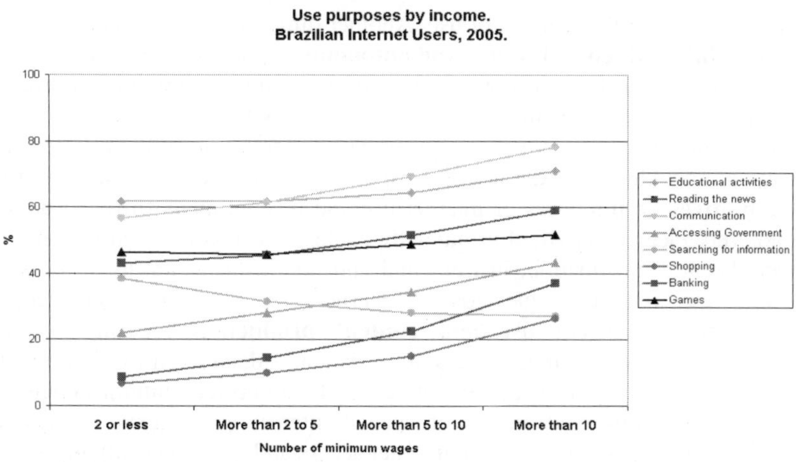

3. Uses of the internet: multiple dimensions and social facilitators

In spite of low levels of access and uses to the internet in Brazil, and mainly for those in lower socioeconomic strata, the focus on the multi-dimensions of internet use imposes itself. It permits to accompany the constant changes that characterize the internet phenomenon, help to identify what kind of uses have an impact on individual lives and it also refines the understanding of the ways social and cultural factors are related to the diverse ways internet is used.

Analyses of multiple dimensions of internet use are being done through the eyes of different disciplinary traditions. Nonetheless most approaches converge to the interest in finding out if internet use is enabling individuals for TICs use guaranteeing information uses that contribute to increasing their life chances; answering questions about conditions and perspectives of community development and democracy, which can be depicted, among other things, from characteristics of individual behavior is another interest of research about internet use.

Studies of internet use also converge in the interest in classifying it. Classifications of dimensions of internet use - and corresponding measures - abound and change constantly reflecting differences of theoretical approaches and contextual characteristics, as well as in the specificities of the object studied – the internet - that undergoes constant and rapid changes. The complexity of the task also comes from the fact that dimensions of use are also related to each other in a complex way. Sometimes also different names are chosen to refer to similar aspects of use. Another difficulty in focusing use is that classes or types of internet uses are often not clearly distinguished from factors that cause them, as it is the case of the technological infrastructure of access or the relationship between uses and socio-demographic characteristics and the social support given to users. However, classification efforts are essential in helping to unveil the more fundamental aspects of net usage and in orienting analyses, especially comparative ones.

Several different dimensions of internet use are taken account, with different conceptual arrangements and measurement propositions, in studies that focus on internet use by general public or the adult population. **Frequency/intensity** of use is a basic dimension often included, mainly in surveys; it can be considered as the first and basic dimension of the concept of use. Another dimension involves notions like **competence, ability, fluency, literacy and autonomy** applied to internet use. These are complementary aspects to the complex idea of mastering the information process necessary the effective use of the internet. This involves the capacity to deal with information channels and resources, requiring close attention to new literacies that accompany internet changes. Another dimension of internet use is the one that tries to capture **motives or purposes** of internet use and receive many different names that are not very clearly classified in mutually exclusive categories: work and non-work, everyday life information, instrumental and non-instrumental uses, problem solving uses, etc. Another dimension of internet use, recently emphasized in analyses, refers to **content use and content production** focusing on the characteristics of content that it is actually being added and retrieved from the internet by users. This latter aspect of use is closely connected cultural milieus in which use is being observed and is of special interest to contexts, as that of developing countries, that lag behind in internet access and use, especially those that do not use the internet lingua franca – the English language. (Barzilai-Nahon, 2006, Chen &Wellman, 2004, DiMaggio, 2004, Gurstein, 2005, Haythornthwaite, 2007, Savolainen, R. 1999, Eastabrook, 2007).

The relationships existent between types of use - as abilities and content production - is a topic that suggests more systematic approaches aiming at the construction of analytical models of internet use that could be useful for comparative studies. Contextual influence on different types of internet use, showing how dimensions of use are related to socio-demographic characteristics of users, have, nonetheless, been the focus of several large of population surveys, including the Brazilian survey here analyzed. Some small surveys and other types of studies reflect efforts in the direction of modeling internet use, especially those that try to capture how internet use affects peoples' lives.

These types of analyses, although relevant in detecting social conditionings of internet use, do not consider other "social facilitators", which seem to play an important role in activating internet access and use (Gurstein, 2005, Haythornthwaite, 2007). Social networks can contribute to internet use and are considered as an example of social facilitator, deriving from theoretical and practical principles of network theory. Among these social facilitators some institutional arrangements seem to be of especial relevance in contexts that face the problem of limited home access. In Brazil, government created telecenters and LAN houses play an important role for internet access and use, being the place of internet access for the majority of youngsters and of low income people. Their contribution for the promotion of internet use and literacy is, however, controversial (Madon et al, 2007).

4. Public libraries as social facilitators of internet use

Public libraries is another "social facilitator" institution. Recent major surveys in the US show that the majority of American adults, despite their high level of home internet access, go to local public libraries. They are the most frequently mentioned location of public access in the United States and also a most cited public place for finding content and resources in the internet, as well as agents of e-government. They use internet resources to provide information for individual problem solving and to get information about the community, contributing to activate and multiply networks of support and to enhance community organizations (Estabrook et al. 2007, Berlot et al, 2007, Durrance et al, 2009). These characteristics enforce Schement's argument that libraries are places for the development of information capability as well for helping individuals in reaching meaningful contents for problem solving. Therefore, libraries are seen as a basic institution for overcoming digital divide: "for most of those Americans of the disconnected side of the 'gap' libraries offer the only bridge" (Schement, 2003, p.121).

In many developing countries reality is very different, as pointed out in a comparative study of 25 countries, focusing on public access to ICT (Coward et al 2009). Public libraries in these countries are mainly used in support for school education; their use by the general public, trying to give support for the solution of information needs of individuals and to help in their access to governmental information, as well as in support to citizenship building, which is a characteristic of the Anglo-Saxon tradition, is very limited and is not a part of their cultures.

There are, however, several reasons to try to diversify social facilitators of ICT use, like NGOs, and also enhance our attention to public libraries in Brazil, Latin American and other developing countries. The first reason is of course the low levels of home access and use in these countries, with access in public places characteristic of the less privileged segments of society. The second one is related to evidences about problems and limited effects of other public places of access like telecenters. Their creation and development in the city of São Paulo, for example, where there are 700 telecenters serving a metropolitan area of 17 million people, can be considered an example. They were intended for the development of digital literacy for the population in general, as well as for community content development. However, those goals changed overtime and telecenters are seen nowadays as places for youngsters, helping to keep them off the streets and in reducing local violence (Madon et al, 2007). Another characteristic of telecenters, and a third reason to value libraries as venues for internet use, is that in the same way as LAN Houses they are more frequently used for boys than for girls, so contributing to maintain of even to generate gender ICT divide (Olinto, 2008a).

There are several other reasons in favor of a new focus on public libraries for the development of ICT literacy in Latin American countries (Suaiden, 2003). The fact that they are already institutionalized, belonging to a national network of libraries, is an important reason. One could also mention non-English cultural environments as yet another reason to place high value for ICT in libraries, for they are better tailored for content production than telecenters. But the most important reason for focusing attention in public libraries is found in successful experiences that try to consider ICT use in a broader context of community development. Seeking to collect and organize information about the community, trying to give voice to local cultural production through the organization of data bases and other initiatives, aiming at the development of citizen empowerment through information services and involving the community in planning of its activities public libraries in Colombia are good examples (Betancur, 2002). The reasons are many but public actions and subsidies in that direction, including the provision of basic ICT infrastructure and human resources, are still very restricted.

5. Concluding remarks

This article showed evidence about the low level of internet access in Brazil. Among those who are lucky enough to have some kind of access, public places are used substantially, especially for people of low socio-economic strata. The analyses of types of uses also pointed out to the vicious circle of social privileges involved: as better technological infrastructure is guaranteed (speed of access) and better income levels are reached so do the uses of the internet for several purposes that seem to contribute to individuals' life chances and his participation as citizens in the knowledge society.

In spite of low access, the relevance of considering multiple dimensions of internet use was pointed out. Content production was highlighted as a particularly important dimension for analyses of internet use in developing countries. The role played by "social facilitators" of internet access was also considered. Among those, public libraries seem to be of special relevance in developing countries. Several factors contribute to this vision, including the great numbers of outside home use, especially by low social standing users. Successful experiences in the use of public libraries for ICT literacy, as those of Colombia, contribute to the argument.

References

Barzilai-Nahon, K. (2006) Gaps and Bits: conceptualizing measurements for digital divide/s. *The Information Society*. http://projects.ischool.washington.edu/karineb/html/pub/DDI-htmlver.html

Berlot, J. C. (2007) Public libraries and the internet 2007: Report to the American Library Association. Florida: Florida State University. Information Institute. Tallahassee. http://www.ii.fsu.edu

CGI - Comitê Gestor da Internet no Brasil (2006). Pesquisa sobre uso das tecnologias de informação e comunicacao no Brasil. http://www.cetic.br/tic/2006/indicadores-2006.pdf

Chen, W. & Wellman, B. (2003) Charting digital divides: comparing socioeconomic, gender, life stage, and rural-urban internet access and use in eight countries. Toronto: Information Institute. University of Toronto.

Cysne, R. (2007). Exclusao digital: desafios para a consolidacao democratica. Unpublished Thesis, IBGE - ENCE (Instituto Brasileiro de Geografia e Estatística – Escola Nacional de Ciencias Estatisticas).

DiMaggio, Hargittai, E., Celeste, C.& Shafer, S. (2004). From unequal access to differentiated use: a literature review and agenda for search on digital inequality. In: Neckerman, K. Social Inequality. New York, Russell Sage.

Durrance, J.C., Pettigrew, K.E. (2009). Toward context-centered methods for evaluating public library networked community information initiatives. *First Monday*, 6(4). http://firstmonday.org

Eastabrook, L. (2007. Information searches that solve problems. Washington: Pew Internet American Life Project. http://www.pewinternet.org/

Fox, S. (2005) Digital Divisions. Washington: Pew Internet American Life Project. 12p. http://www.pewinternet.org/

Gurstein, M. (2003). Effective use: a community informatics strategy beyond the Digital Divide. *FirstMonday, 8 (12).* Retrieved in December, 2004 from http://www.firstmonday.org/issues/issue8_12/gurstein/

Haythornthwaite, C. A. (2007). Social facilitators and inhibitors to online fluency. In: Hawaii International Conference on System Sciences, 2007. Hawaii. Proceedings.

Horrigan, J.B. (2008). Home broadband adoption-2008. Washington: Pew Internet American Life Project. 12p. http://www.pewinternet.org/

IBGE/PNAD (Instituto Brasileiro de Geografia e Estatistica – Pesquisa Nacional por Amostra de Domicílios 2005) (2006). Síntese dos indicadores. Rio de Janeiro: IBGE. http://www.ibge.gov.br/

Schement, J.R. (2003). Measuring what Jefferson knew and De Tocqueville saw: libraries as a bridge across the digital divide. *IT & Society*, 1 (4), 118-125.

Horrigan, J.B. (2008) Home broadband adoption-2008. Washington: Pew Internet American Life Project. 12p. http://www.pewinternet.org/

Madon, S. et al. (2007) Digital inclusion projects in developing countries: processes of institutionalization. In: 9th International Conference on Social Implications of Computers in Developing Countries, São Paulo, Proceedings.

Olinto, Gilda (2007). Desigualdades de acesso a Internet no Brasil. In: XIII Congresso Brasileiro de Sociologia, GT 11, 2007, Recife. http://www.sbsociologia.com.br/congresso_v02/index.asp?idcongresso=9

Olinto, Gilda. (2008). Gender differences in Internet use by Brazilian students: Judicious girls and playful boys. In: Sudweeks, F. & Hrachovec, H. (eds). Cultural Attitudes towards technology and communication 2008, Nîmes, France. Proceedings of the Sixth International Conference on Cultural Attitudes towards Technology and Communication, Proceedings, Murdoch, Australia: Murdoch University. www.catacconterence.org

Olinto, G. (2008b) Everyday life Internet use in Brazil: technological and social conditionings. In: Internet research 9.0, 2008, Copenhagen, Denmark. Proceedings.

Savolainen, R. (1999). The role of the Internet in information seeking. Putting the networked services in context. *Information Processing and Management, 35*, 765-782.

Suaiden, E. J. . The social impact of public libraries. *Library Review*, London, v. 52, n. 8, p. 379-387, 2003.

Wellman, B., Quan-Haase, A., Boase, J. & Chen,W. (2002). Examining the Internet in Everyday life. Keynote address to the Euricom Conference on e-Democracy. Nijmegen, Netherlands, October.

World Bank (2006). Information and communication for development: global trends and policies. Washington: World Bank. Available: http://rru.worldbank.org/documents/other/Chapter4_ICT_in_DoingBusiness.pdf

Acknowledgement

I am grateful to CNPq (Conselho Nacional de Desenvolvimento Científico e Tecnológico) for the financial support provided for the Project: "Social conditions of internet use in Brazil".

---

[1] Individuals 18 years old or older.

[2] The question indicating internet access in the survey was: "In the last three months have you utilized the internet in any place (at home, school, in telecenters, in other people's home or any other place?"

12. Support to Research

The Creation and Development of a Multi-Disciplinary Research Center in an Academic Library

Teresa S. Welsh

Associate Professor, University of Southern Mississippi School of Library and Information Science, USA; Assistant Director, Katrina Research Center, USA

Abstract: Hurricane Katrina was the costliest natural disaster in U.S. history and one of the deadliest. In 2006, the University of Southern Mississippi established the Katrina Research Center (KRC) as an multi-disciplinary center for research and education to facilitate the gathering of information on the effects of and recovery from catastrophic natural disasters such as Katrina. The purpose of this case study is to document the creation and development of the Katrina Research Center, including its mission, vision, organizational structure, funding, collection development, community outreach, research and educational activities.

Keywords: Hurricanes; Disasters; Academic library; Repository; Research center.

1. Introduction

Hurricane Katrina, which struck on August 29, 2005, was the costliest natural disaster in U.S. history and one of the deadliest. At least 1,836 people lost their lives and the cost of damaged and destroyed property is estimated to be over $80 billion. In addition to the flooding in New Orleans, there was extensive destruction across some 12 Mississippi Gulf Coast communities (Scurfield 2008, 2009a). A 34 feet high storm-surge from Katrina in western Mississippi was propelled inland *as far as 10 miles* from the coast through myriad rivers and bayous. An estimated 350 buildings listed in the National Register of Historic Places were washed or blown away, along with most of the evidence of 300 years of Gulf Coast history. According to Huffman (2006), Katrina was *the worst historic preservation disaster* in U.S. history.

The Katrina Research Center (KRC) was originally part of the University Libraries at the Hattiesburg campus but was reorganized in July 2006 as a multi-disciplinary center located on the Southern Miss Gulf Coast campus in Long Beach. The Center, which opened in November 2007, was established to facilitate research and education by gathering information on the natural, physical, social, political and economic effects of and recovery from catastrophic natural disasters such as Hurricane Katrina (McCormack 2007).

The KRC is both a research center and a subject repository, a collection that is focused on a single theme or area of study. Subject repositories may be virtual or may be a combination of both physical and digital formats as in the KRC. Subject repositories are usually a part of a larger organization such as an academic institution.

2. Purpose of the Study

The purpose of this case study is to document and examine the creation and development of the Katrina Research Center, including its mission, vision, organizational structure, funding, collection development, community outreach, research and educational activities.

Research Questions

R1. What is the mission and vision of the KRC?
R2. What is its organizational structure?
R3. How is the KRC funded?
R4. What types of items are in the KRC repository and how are they collected?
R5. What activities are related to community outreach?
R6. What activities are related to scholarship and research?
R7. What activities are related to education?

Limitations

This study is limited to the creation and development of the Southern Miss Katrina Research Center. The results may not be generalizeable to other academic research centers.

3. Methodology

Participant-observation and case study methodology were used in this study. This type of research involves first acknowledging the perspectives of the researcher (Yin 1994). It is relevant to note that the participant–observer is an assistant director of the KRC and had access to primary-source documents related to the creation and development of the KRC.

Theory

Examination of formal and informal documents related to this study is based on Narrative Theory. Humans are narrative beings and human rationality is determined by an "inherent awareness of *narrative probability*, what constitutes a coherent story … and testing *narrative fidelity*, whether the stories they experience ring true with stories they know in their lives" (Fisher 1987, 64)

Validity

Triangulation, "where researchers search for convergence among multiple and different sources of information to form themes or categories in a study" (Creswell and Miller 2000, 126), was used to test the validity of the study. Formal documents such as monthly and yearly reports were compared with informal documents such as email correspondence. The KRC director, historian, and librarian were asked to review the study for accuracy.

4. Results

R1. What is the mission and vision of the KRC?

Mission

The Katrina Research Center (KRC) serves as an inter-disciplinary center and a public clearinghouse to facilitate the gathering of historical and current information and knowledge including the natural, physical, social, political, economic and spiritual aspects of recovery from Hurricane Katrina and other disasters. The KRC includes these major components related to Hurricanes Katrina and Camille as well as other disasters:

- a repository/historical collection
- exhibit center
- digital information clearinghouse
- research and education concerning post-disaster recovery and enhancement of quality of life.

The library of the University of Southern Mississippi - Gulf Coast provides critical support and leadership to the KRC depository and collaborates with the KRC to promote community awareness and provide access to scholars and the general public.

Vision

- To be a world-class inter-disciplinary center that promotes and supports scholarship and education concerning the 2005 Hurricane Katrina and other disasters and contributes to the expansion and preservation of knowledge about Katrina, disasters and their aftermath.
- To facilitate the development of disaster-related research and/or program evaluation studies and knowledge through collaboration with the offices of Research and Economic Development, Research Foundation, the various colleges and departments, and/or for the KRC to develop and submit proposals to various funding sources.
- To develop, promote, implement and consult concerning cross-disciplinary educational, training and other learning opportunities to disseminate knowledge, assessment and actions about the human, social and economic impact of and recovery from disasters.
- To oversee the KRC Repository of historical and scholarly information and materials and to interface with the University's Gulf Coast Library concerning (a) the development and usage of repository and special collection of artifacts, photographs, documents and other items relevant to the impact and aftermath of Hurricane Katrina and other disasters, (b) library resources regarding disaster-related mental health, economic recovery and disaster relief services and (c) developing a comprehensive database of Katrina, post-Katrina and other disaster materials that are accessible locally and nationally.

R2. What is its organizational structure?

The KRC is a research center that is led by a director, several assistant directors, an historian, a librarian/clearinghouse coordinator, and other associated faculty and staff. Initially, the KRC reported to the Gulf Coast Provost but in year two, the Southern Miss organizational structure changed. Now all research centers and institutes report to the Director of University Research Centers and Institutes, who reports to the Vice President for Research and Economic Development, who reports to the President of the University.

Physical structure:

The director, historian, and librarian have offices in the Katrina Research Center, which is located in an area of 3,000+ square feet on the third floor of the Southern Miss Gulf Coast Library. The KRC has a public area with reading tables, reference desk, a section of book shelves, display cases, and an art exhibit space. The private area consists of two offices and a conference room with cabinets for archival materials.

Faculty and staff

The librarian/clearinghouse coordinator, who is an archivist and digitization specialist, is the only full-time person who works at the KRC. Other faculty and staff include:

- KRC Director Dr. Ray Scurfield is a Professor of Social Work who also teaches and has written several books on post-traumatic stress disorder (PTSD).
- Three KRC assistant directors are teaching faculty whose fields are in psychology/mental health, coastal ecosystems/environmental impacts, and library/information science. Another assistant director for economic development served for two years.
- The KRC historian/exhibit coordinator is also teaching faculty in the history department.
- The program development specialist works on a part-time basis with faculty and staff on grant applications.
- The KRC Web developer is the Director for Web-based marketing for the Southern Miss Gulf Coast campus.
- Four graduate assistants, one for each of the assistant directors, were funded in year one, three were funded in year two, and none in year three.

Other

- The KRC is closely affiliated with and works in association with University Libraries, particularly the Gulf Coast Library where the Center is physically located.
- The KRC is affiliated with the Southern Miss Center for Oral History & Cultural Heritage and archives Katrina-related oral histories from the OHCH collection (OHCH 2009).
- Photographer Keith Fishman serves as the Fine Arts Advisor.

R3. How is the KRC funded?

The University originally committed funding for the KRC for two years, but this was later extended to three years. The start-up budget for year one was about $400,000 for personnel costs, furnishings, equipment, and travel. The Gulf Coast Library donated space for the Center and shared in furnishing costs. The budget for year two was about $250,000 and year three about $200,000. The director and assistant directors were allowed one course buy-out in spring and fall semesters and two course buy-outs in summer for the three years. Four graduate assistants were funded in the first year, three in the second year, and none in the third year. The director and assistant directors are expected to obtain research grant money to fund course buy-outs and other research-related expenses after the initial three year funding ends in August 2009.

Donated funds are deposited in a Southern Miss Foundation fund and used for special events and acquisitions. Additional funds have been obtained through silent auctions of donated items.

Due to the recession, all Southern Miss budgets were required to be cut by 5 percent in year three (2009). To meet this requirement, one of the assistant directors who had resigned in 2008 and the graduate assistants were not replaced.

R4. What types of items are in the KRC repository and how are they collected?

Physical repository

In spring 2009, the KRC collection consisted of a set of IMLS reference books, several hundred additional books, several dozen DVDs, archival materials such as newspapers, diaries, letters, meeting notes, and maps. Three sets of limited-edition prints have been donated to the KRC permanent collection by photographer Keith Fishman.

Digital repository

Many hundreds of digital images on CD-ROM have been collected for the KRC digital repository. Selected images have been uploaded to the Mississippi Digital Library available at: http://cdm.lib.usm.edu/cdm4/katrina.php

A memorandum of understanding (MOU) has been signed by the KRC and the *Sun-Herald Newspaper* to archive Katrina-related images and stories on a server at Southern Miss. A similar agreement is being worked on for WLOX-TV, which has a cache of raw news footage from Hurricane Katrina in 2005 and Hurricane Camille in 1969. University Libraries is developing an institutional repository that will house the digitized archival materials.

The KRC collection has been built with limited funding. The Center librarian has successfully solicited Katrina-related and coastal disaster-related books, DVDs, posters, and archival materials from authors and publishers. Some of the authors generously donated signed copies of their books including President Bill Clinton, Dr. Douglas Brinkley, and Anderson Cooper.

The KRC was successful in obtaining two awards for materials: Alibris Award for $1,500 in books and DVDs and an IMLS set of archival reference books, *Connecting to Collections*, worth $800.

R5. What activities are related to community outreach?

Since the Center opened in November 2007, it has hosted two exhibits of Keith Fishman images that are now part of the permanent collection and two traveling mixed-media art exhibits. Each of the traveling exhibits began with an opening reception honoring the artist and their work.

Another exhibit was of donated plates painted by elementary, middle, and high school students from local schools affected by Katrina. The exhibit opening reception was attended by the students, families, teachers, and other interested parties and the plates became part of the Center's permanent collection.

KRC historian supervised local eighth-grade student in an historical survey of a Biloxi neighborhood. A booklet, *As Time Keeps Turning: Biloxi Houses*, was produced and a reception was held in the local school to honor students who contributed. Students and other reception attendees received a copy of the booklet and additional copies were archived in the KRC.

Community service activity includes service work with the Interfaith Disaster Task Force and with African-American church communities on the Gulf Coast by the assistant director in psychology/mental health, the director's work as a traumatic stress counselor after Katrina with the Southern Miss Gulf Coast campus, and the historian's work with local historical societies and school organizations.

Students, teachers, and the general public are invited to view the exhibits on display at the KRC. Numerous tours have been conducted for various organizations and groups such as the Society for Mississippi Archivists, student groups, and the general public.

Books in the collection are catalogued and entered into the University Libraries OPAC. Circulating books may be checked out by faculty, students, staff, and the general public who have membership in the Alumni Association (any interested party can join the Alumni Association for $35 a year). Non-circulating and archival materials may be viewed on-site after patrons fill out a form for researchers.

The KRC Web site includes information about the Center, the faculty and staff, and collections: http://www.usm.edu/katrina

The KRC and Center for Oral History & Cultural Heritage have contributed images and oral histories to the *Hurricane Digital Memory Bank* (http://www.hurricanearchive.org/).

R6. What activities are related to scholarship and research?

KRC faculty presented Katrina-related research in numerous scholarly conferences and their research has been published in scholarly journals and conference proceedings. The director and two of the assistant directors are each under contract for and are working on books related to Katrina (Scurfield 2009b, Aten 2009, Welsh 2009).

The KRC librarian has produced finding aids such as "Hurricane Katrina and other Natural Disasters" and "Hurricane Preparedness Resource Guide" to help educators, researchers, and the general public locate materials.

The KRC librarian has worked with the director, assistant directors, and others associated with the Center to identify Katrina-related research, particularly research conducted by Southern Miss faculty, to update finding aids and for sending requests to archive the researchers' work at the Center.

LIS students, as part of a government publications course, compiled a list of online resources: "Katrina-Related Online Publications: Non-Government Publications, State Government Publications, U.S. Government Publications" (http://www.usm.edu/slis/KatrinaDocs.htm) and "Katrina-Related Oral History Projects" (http://www.usm.edu/slis/KatrinaOralHist.htm).

Grant-writing is an ongoing process that is accomplished with the help of a program development specialist and CREATeS (Southern Miss Center for Research, Evaluation, Assessment and Training Services). The KRC has been successful in obtaining some small grants and awards; several larger federal grant applications have been submitted and are pending.

R7. What activities are related to education?

The KRC Librarian supervised and instructed several part-time graduate assistants whose duties included: organizing news articles; indexing; copy cataloging; desk duties; scanning; metadata entry; and administrative support. An LIS student is scheduled to complete an archival practicum in the Center this summer.

KRC has hosted and provided guided tours to various educational and service groups: elementary, middle, and secondary school students; college and university students; and other interested groups such as archivists, friends of local library group, AmeriCorps, Habitat for Humanity, and a boys/girls club.

For an historical research project funded by a History Channel Save our History

Grant of $10,000, the KRC historian supervised local eighth-grade students in an architectural survey of an historic Biloxi neighborhood. A booklet, *As Time Keeps Turning: Biloxi Houses*, was produced and distributed to students with some copies archived in the KRC collection (Nuwer 2008).

5. Conclusions

Several themes have emerged from formal and informal communication and documentation related to the creation and development of the KRC:

- The professional experiences of the director, who had previously established a research center, and the librarian, who previously worked in a research center and an academic library, have been valuable in guiding the Center through its creation and development.
- The development of the KRC collection can be attributed to having a dedicated archivist/digitization librarian. The librarian's professional affiliation with groups such as the Society of Mississippi Archivists enhanced professional networking, which led to resource-sharing and increased visibility.
- Cooperation/affiliation with related university entities, such as University Libraries, the Center for Oral History & Cultural Heritage, and the Center for Research, Evaluation, Assessment and Training Services, has been essential in effective and efficient use of resources.
- Networking with other community groups, such as local historical societies, public libraries, schools, and media has led to increased visibility in the community and donations of documents, images, and artefacts to the KRC collection.
- Dissemination of Katrina-related research has led to increased visibility and additional professional and academic contacts, such as with the director of the *Hurricane Digital Memory Bank* and faculty associated with the University of Pennsylvania Center for Public Health Preparedness.
- Obtaining funding by large federal grants is a competitive undertaking and each large grant application takes about one year from time of initial conception and planning to receiving word of funding or rejection. Typically, feedback from the first attempt is used to revise and reapply so it may take several years to get a large federal grant.

Research is ongoing but results include:

- Identification of the six stages of disaster recovery (Scurfield 2008)
- Identification of post-catastrophic disaster needs by LIS graduate students affected by Katrina (Welsh and Higgins 2008).

Future of the Katrina Research Center

The KRC, just as any other academic entity, must adapt to a changing academic environment. Possible changes for the future include:

- Collaboration and affiliation with similar university centers such as the Center for Biosecurity and Pubic Health Preparedness at the University of Houston (2009) and the Center for Public Health Preparedness at the University of Pennsylvania (2009)
- Collaboration and affiliation with federal agencies such as the Emergency Management Center (EMC) at Oak Ridge National Laboratory (2009)

- Organizational change from KRC assistant directors to KRC associated or affiliated faculty to include more faculty who are involved in Katrina-related research.

References

Aten, Jamie D. "Jamie D. Aten, Ph.D." (2009) http://www.jamieaten.com/index.html (accessed 2 May 2009).

Creswell, John W. and Miller, Dana L. "Determining Validity in Qualitative Inquiry. *Theory into Practice* 39, no. 3 (2000): 124-131.

Fisher, Walter R. *Human Communication as Narration: Toward a Philosophy of Reason, Value, and Action*. Columbia, SC: University of South Carolina Press, 1987.

Huffman, Alan. "Does it Matter if the World Knows Mississippi's Story? Yes. Here's Why." *Sun Herald,* (February 11, 2006): C-2.

McCormack, Edward. "The Learning Center: A Reconfigured Space at the Gulf Park Library." *Library Focus* (Fall 2007): 1-2.

Nuwer, Deanne, ed. *As Time Keeps Turning: Biloxi House*, an historical research booklet produced by 8th graders of Biloxi Junior High (May 2008).

Oak Ridge National Laboratory. *Emergency Management Center* (2009) http://emc.ornl.gov/EMCWeb/EMC/EMCINFO1.html (accessed 9 May 2009).

OHCH. *Center for Oral History & Cultural Heritage* (2009) http://www.usm.edu/oralhistory/ (accessed 5 May 2009)

Scurfield, Raymond M. "The Nexus between the Iraq War and Katrina Recovery: Clinical and Policy Issues." *Trauma, Violence and Abuse*10, no. 3 (2009a).

Scurfield, Raymond M. "Post-Katrina Aftermath and Helpful Interventions on the Mississippi Gulf Coast." *Traumatology* 12, no. 2 (June, 2006): 104-120.

Scurfield, Raymond M. "Post-Katrina Storm Disorder and Recovery in Mississippi More Than 2 Years Later." *Traumatology* 14, no. 2 (2008): 88-106.

Scurfield, Raymond M. "Ray Scurfield, DSW" (2009b) http://www.usm.edu/gc/health/scurfield/ (accessed May 2, 2009).

University of Pennsylvania Public Health Practice. *Center for Public Health Preparedness* (2009) http://www.prepare.pitt.edu/ (accessed 9 May 2009)

University of Texas Health Science Center. *Center for Biosecurity and Public Health Preparedness* (2009) http://www.sph.uth.tmc.edu/biosecurity/ (accessed 9 May 2009).

Welsh, Teresa S. "Teresa S. Welsh, Ph.D." http://ocean.otr.usm.edu/~w146169/vita.htm (accessed 2 May 2009).

Welsh, Teresa S. and Susan E. Higgins. "Reflections on the Katrina Experience: LIS Students' Stories," In *2008 Hawaii International Conference on Education Conference Proceedings held in Honolulu, HI 5-8January 2008,* 1245-1258.

Yin, Robert K. *Case Study Research: Design and Methods*, 2d ed. Thousand Oaks, CA: Sage, 1994.

What 37000 Citations Can Tell

Adriaan Swanepoel

Library and Information Services Tshwane University of Technology, Pretoria, South Africa
E-mail: Swanepoelaj@tut.ac.za

Abstract: A longitudinal study at the Tshwane University of Technology (TUT) used citation analysis to analyze the reference lists of 480 master's and doctoral (M and D) theses and dissertations submitted at TUT between 2004 and 2007. The purpose was to determine

what types of information sources M and D students at TUT use most, how the patterns of use differ across the seven faculties of the university, and to what extent the Library and Information Services (LIS) keeps or provides access to the journals that are mostly used by M and D students. More than 37 000 citations were analyzed over the four-year period. The study found several similarities but also some distinct differences in the use of information sources across the seven faculties of TUT. It also identified more than 60 different information sources used by M and D students. With regard to journal use, the study found that out of 3 641 different journals cited, most journals were only cited once over a period of four years. However, a small percentage of journals were highly and/or frequently cited.
Keywords: Citation analysis; Theses and dissertations.

1. Introduction

1.1 Aims

The Tshwane University of Technology (TUT) started in 2004 with a longitudinal study to obtain information that would assist its Library and Information Services (LIS) in making sound collection development decisions. The aims of the study were to identify:

- Which types of information sources do master's and doctoral (M and D) students of different faculties in TUT use most and least, and to what extent does this change from year to year?
- Which journals do M and D students of different faculties in TUT use most and least, and to what extent does this change from year to year?
- To what extent does the TUT LIS keep or provide access to journals that are mostly used by M and D students?

1.2 Method

Library science has developed a number of methods for evaluating the use of information sources. Some of the more popular methods include a) studying circulation statistics and in-house use of information sources, b) surveying user opinions, c) analysing interlibrary loan patterns, d) doing shelf-availability studies, and e) analysing bibliographic citations. Although it is generally recognised that no one method alone provides a complete picture in assisting with collection development decisions, this study used citation analysis as the preferred research method to achieve its aims. This method, with its advantages and disadvantages, and how it was applied in this study, was described elsewhere by this author (Swanepoel 2008). It is nevertheless necessary, for the sake of comprehensiveness, to repeat some of that information in this paper.

Citation analysis is known to be a low-cost method whereby researchers can gather and study citation data in an unobtrusive and non-invasive way. Citation analysis is also a flexible method: it can be applied in the assessment of data sources of a group of libraries, or a single collection or a library collection supplemented with external information sources. It is also flexible in terms of the size of samples, types of citation sources (whether a standard list or a specific collection in a library) as well as the manner of citation selection (Ching 2002). Furthermore, it can be used to focus on the type and number of information sources that researchers or library users use in a specific discipline or over a period of time. In this regard, the research of Peritz and Sor (1990) and Allen, Jacobs and Levy (2006) serve as examples.

Citation analysis is also a well-studied method in university library environments. Not only do citations play an important part in the scholarly communications process, but "citations and the composition of bibliographies reflect changes in the information-seeking behaviour of academics", as well (Naudé, Rensleigh & Du Toit 2005). In this regard, theses and dissertations have proved to be particularly appealing to use for assessing library collections because they serve as a convenient source of in-house research. Furthermore, Zipp (1996) found that "the most heavily cited journal titles in theses and dissertations can be used as a surrogate for the titles most heavily used by faculty in their publications". This is because the research interests of graduate students often reflect the research interests of their faculty advisers.

While many studies have reported on the uses and usefulness of citation analysis, some writers, including Loree (2007), Griscom (1983) and Ching (2002) have acknowledged the limitations of the method. Concerning citation analysis of students bibliographies, Sylvia (1998) highlighted several limitations, including the following: a) researchers are more likely to use information sources to which they have local access, b) researchers may add citations to increase a manuscript's length and scholarship, c) manuscripts may include citations of marginal importance, d) researchers may not cite all works used to prepare a manuscript, e) handbooks and textbooks often do not receive citations because those sources are taken for granted by students.

Being aware of the limitations of citation analysis and acknowledging that the method is sensitive to the skill with which it is applied, it was nevertheless decided to use citation analysis as method for this research because it has been proved by many as a valid, reliable and practical tool for comparing a library's holdings to an authoritative list for the purpose of evaluating the quality of a library collection.

1.3 Data collection

Data were collected from the reference lists of all (480) theses and dissertations submitted by M and D students and accepted by TUT from 2004 to 2007. No sample was taken. However, one thesis from the Faculty of Science was not included because its extreme number of citations (3 750) would have skewed results.

A library assistant photocopied the title pages and reference lists of all theses and dissertations and provided each data source with a sequential number. The assistant then captured the following data from the title pages on an Excel worksheet: a) author, b) title, c) date, d) faculty, e) department at the faculty, f) language of the thesis, and g) whether it was a master's thesis or a doctoral dissertation. Subsequently, the researcher collected the following data: h) number of citations per information type, i) number of citations per thesis, j) number of theses per department, k) frequency of journal titles cited, and l) cited periodicals owned or provided access to by the library. All the data collected (a – l) was captured on Excel worksheets.

1.4 Data analysis

With regard to Aim 1: The different types of information sources used by M and D students in each of the seven faculties were counted and the numbers obtained per type were summarized per annum. The data were also sorted and ranked to identify which types of information sources M and D students in different faculties use most and least, and to what extent the pattern changes from year to year.

With regard to Aim 2: A list was made of all the different journal titles that were cited by M and D students in each faculty. The researcher then counted the number of times each title was cited per annum. This enabled him to determine which journals M and D students in different faculties use most and least, and to what extent this changes from year to year.

With regard to Aim 3: Each journal title cited by M and D students was compared against a list of journal titles that the LIS makes available either (a) by keeping those journals in stock or (b) by providing online access to full text versions of the journals. This process resulted in identifying to what extent the LIS keeps or provides access to the journals that are mostly used by M and D students.

2. Findings and discussion

2.1 Types and number of information sources cited

To put the findings of this study into context, it is necessary to present an overview of the types and numbers of information sources cited by the students under discussion. Although M & D students of TUT used 64 different types of information sources from 2004 to 2007, it is clear from Table 1 that they largely relied on books and journals for research purposes. Together, citations to books and journals add up to almost 70 percent of all citations. Furthermore, the top nine sources are typically those that are readily accessible in or through libraries. One should, however, not ignore the fact that several other information types play an important role in the research activities of M & D students, especially in-house documents, course material, technical publications, user manuals and newsletters /bulletins.

Citation analysis studies usually refer to less cited information sources as “other” information sources. Although this study also used the term “other” to group information resources that individually received less than one percent of all citations, it went a step further to actually identify those information sources and rank them according to the number of times they were cited (see footnote to Table 1). In doing so this study found that M and D students used more than 50 types of information sources that are generally regarded as “grey literature”. This indicated that, although M and D students predominantly use books and journals, reference librarians and collection developers should take cognisance of the wide variety of so-called grey-literature that M and D students use.

Table 1: Types and number of information sources cited

Information sources	**Total citations 2004 - 2007**	**Percentage**
Books and chapters in books	14 617	39.11
Journals and magazines	11 503	30.77
Websites and electronic databases	3 740	10.00
Government publications	1 387	3.71
Conference proceedings and papers	1 158	3.10
Reports	956	2.56
Newspapers	676	1.81
Theses and dissertations	601	1.61
Personal communication	571	1.53
Other **	2 169	5.80
TOTAL	37 378	100.00

** Consisting of unidentified types (234), in-house documents (205), course material (200), technical publications (176), operating manuals and user manuals (169), newsletters and bulletins (158), videos (116), standards and test methods (102), policy documents (70), planning documents (65), manuscripts and drafts (61), working papers (48), event programmes (47), statistical data (46), discussion and position papers (45), software and computer files (38), comic books (33), fact sheets (33), speeches (29), surveys and questionnaires (29), patents (27), pamphlets and brochures (25), codes of conduct (19), radio and television programmes (16), briefing documents and position papers (16), case studies (16), specifications (14), media releases (13), trade literature (12), maps (11), photos (11), rules and regulations (11), prospectuses (9), circulars (8), staff lists (8), logbooks (7), company profiles (6), abstracts (5), catalogues (4), kits (4), proposals (4), exhibit captions (3), event invitations (2), microfilm (2), posters (2), graphics (1), sound recordings(1), calendars (1), drawings and diagrams (1), instrumental reviews (1), mathematical models (1), memorabilia (1), notices (1), simulation tools (1) and testimonials (1).

It should be noted that the number of citations to Websites was slightly higher than that reported in Table 1. In the process of classifying citations into different types of information sources, citations were first classified by content and then by form. For instance, a citation to a government publication on the Web was classified as a government publication and not as a Website. Only citations to Websites that were not clearly identified as either a journal on the Web or a government publication on the Web, etc., were classified as 'Websites'. However, Figure 1 presents a more complete picture of the number of citations to electronic sources; it shows the number of citations to all Websites regardless of content, as well as citations to electronic databases and CD-ROMs. Regardless of the way citations to Websites were classified, this study showed that M and D students of TUT still make far less use of electronic formats for research purposes than librarians and faculty members generally suspect. However, seeing that there was a slow but gradual increase of electronic formats over four years, the ratio between citations to paper formats versus electronic formats may seem significantly different over the next four years.

Figure 1: Citations to paper formats versus electronic formats

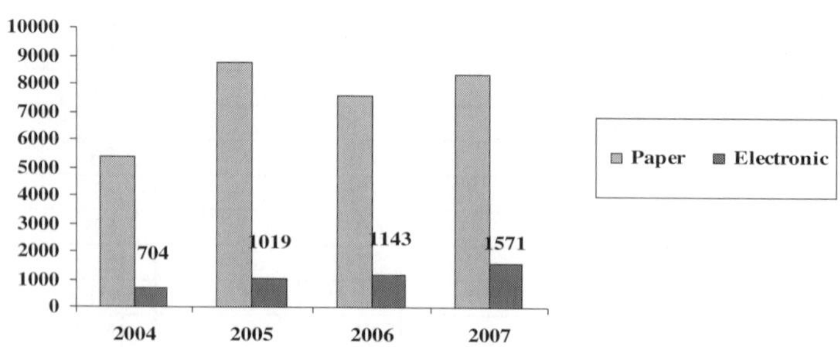

Figure 2 shows some similarities but also distinct differences in the use of information sources by M and D students in the so-called science, engineering and technology (SET) faculties, specifically regarding to books, journals and electronic formats. The Science Faculty clearly uses journals most, followed by books and electronic formats, conference papers and reports. Compared to all other faculties, this faculty uses journals most by far. The Faculty of Engineering also used journals primarily, followed by books, electronic formats, conference papers and reports, but its students use journals far less than students from the Faculty of Science. Engineering students also used electronic formats and conference papers more than science students. Students in the Faculty of Information Communication and Technology (ICT), on the other hand, first and foremost used Web sources; with books and journals respectively the second and third most used sources. It is also worth noting that ICT students were the only students that used Websites and electronic databases more than any other faculty's M & D students. Contrary to this is the relative low use that students of the Faculty of Science made of Websites and electronic databases. Not only was their use of electronic formats the lowest in the SET faculties but is was also the lowest in all faculties. The patterns showed in Figure 2 did not change much over the four years of investigation.

Figure 2: Types of information sources cited most by M and D students of science, engineering and technology (SET) faculties, 2004 - 2007

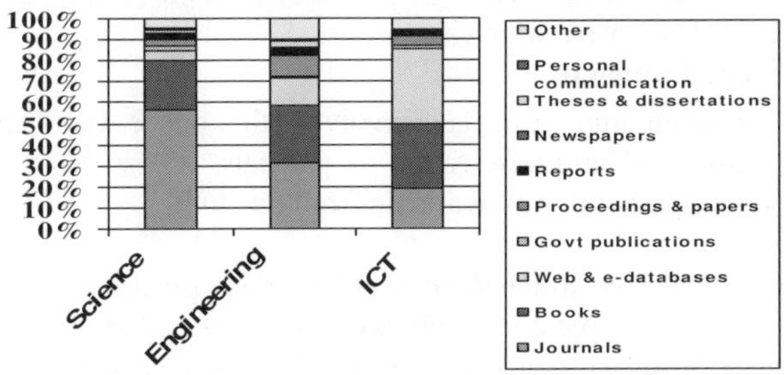

Figure 3 shows a different pattern from the one in Figure 2. M & D students in the social sciences and humanities (SSH) faculties clearly use books most. They also use noticeably fewer journals than students in the science, engineering and technology (SET) faculties. This is especially noticeable in the Faculty of the Arts. The use of journals in the Faculty of Arts ranked only fourth, next to books, electronic formats and newspapers. It is also clear from Figure 3 that the Faculties of Economic Sciences, Humanities, and Management Sciences cited government publications rather highly.

Figure 3: Types of information sources used by M and D students of social sciences and humanities (SSH) faculties, 2004 - 2007

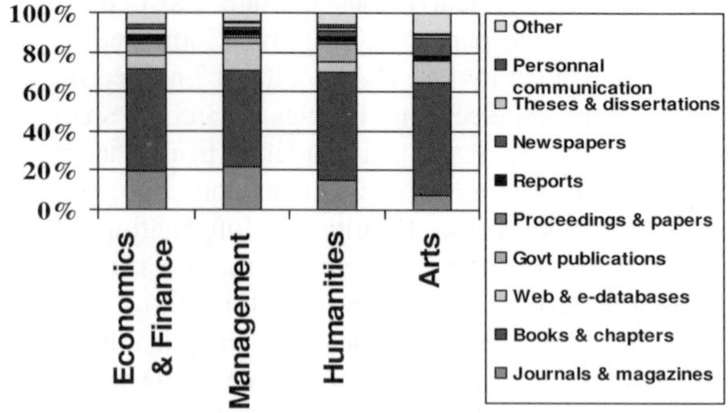

2.2 Journals used by M and D students

One of the aims of this study was to determine which journals M and D students in different faculties use most and least, and to what extent this changes from year to year. The results produced a surprisingly large amount of data. Authors of the 480 theses and dissertations cited altogether 3 610 different journal titles in 2004 to 2007. The 3 610 journals received 11 533 citations. The average number of citations to individual journal titles was 7.49 and the average (mean) citations to journal articles were 23.93 over the four-year period.

2.2.1 Highly cited journals

Because of the large amount of data involved, this paper will display only a list of the top 10 most cited journals. A list of journals, across all seven faculties, that received 20 citations or more is available from the author.

Table 2: Ten most cited journals over a four-year period

The journals listed in Table 2 were not only highly cited but most of them were cited in all four years of investigation. However, when the researcher listed and ranked all journals cited in each faculty it was observed that the vast majority of journals had

Journal	2004	2005	2006	2007	Total
Harvard Business Review	9	73	3	24	109
International Journal of Pharmaceutics	20	52	25	5	102
Medicine and Science in Sports and Exercise	5	51	25	0	81
Journal of Analytical Atomic Spectrometry	25	38	7	8	78
Journal of Controlled Release	11	45	19	3	78
Journal of Applied Physiology	2	67	4	0	73
Spectrochimica Acta Part B	11	39	10	7	67
South African Journal of Higher Education	4	12	11	37	64
Human Reproduction	0	14	47	0	61
Pharmaceutical Research	14	27	19	0	60

only been cited in one or two of the years concerned. For instance, of the 50 topmost cited journals across all seven faculties only 24 journals had been cited in the four years of investigation. This is probably an indication that the majority of journals that M and D students cited were used by a particular student only for a particular research topic. This tendency is more noticeable among some of the SSH faculties. For instance, of the 138 different journals that M and D students of the Faculty of Arts used during the four years of investigation, 133 (96.4%) journals were used only once. Five journals were used in two of the four years but no journals were used more than that. Contrary to this pattern, the M and D students in the SET faculties have shown a more consistent use of journals. Such consistent use will enable the LIS to identify a core list of journals that M and D students in those faculties frequently consult.

2.2.2 Journals that received few citations

Table 3 presents the number of journals that received four or less citations. Note that the numbers in the columns do not overlap. In other words, if a journal was only cited once in 2004, it was not cited again in 2005 or in 2006 or in 2007

Table 3: Number of journals that received fewer than five citations per year

	2004	2005	2006	2007	Total
Journals cited only once	488	999	665	819	2 971
Journals cited twice	110	271	143	172	696
Journals cited three times	49	105	64	57	275
Journals cited four times	26	67	36	39	168

The majority of journals (2 971 or 82.3% of the total) were only cited once over a period of four years. Due to the fact that many journals were cited only once the median and the modus for each of the four years was only one (1) citation per journal title, notwithstanding that the mean was 8.28 in that period. The results in Tables 2 and 3 confirm results from other citation studies that a small number of journals generate the majority of journals cited, and *vice versa*.

2.2.3 The availability of highly cited journals in TUT libraries

A third aim of this study was to determine to what extent the LIS keeps or provides access to the journals that are mostly used by M and D students. The research found that of the 87 journal titles that received 20 citations or more, the LIS either subscribed to or provided online full-text access to a total of 58 titles. In addition it had back copies available in some of its libraries of a further eight (8) titles of which it recently cancelled the subscriptions.

3. Conclusion

From the findings of this study one can conclude that M and D students of TUT are far greater users of paper-based information sources than of electronic information sources. Over time there was a gradual increase in citations to electronic formats but not as much as one would have expected. Citations to electronic formats therefore had no real impact on the composition of reference lists.

With regard to paper-based sources, M and D students of TUT rely to a large extent on books and journals for research purposes. This, however, should not detract attention from the fact that several other information types play an important role in the research activities of M and D students, especially that of government publications, conference proceedings and papers, reports, newspapers, theses and dissertations and personal communication. Since many of the lesser used information sources were not part of the LIS collection one can therefore also conclude that rather than confining their research to what was available in TUT libraries, several M and D students made use of sources elsewhere. Even if lesser used information sources do not qualify to be included in the LIS collection, reference librarians of TUT should recognise the need for such sources and become proficient in searching and retrieving them

This study revealed clearly distinguishable patterns between the information sources that M and D students in different faculties of TUT use most and least. This indicates that the LIS should consider separate collection development strategies for its seven faculties.

Across all faculties the majority of journals were only cited once over a period of four years. However, a small percentage of journals were highly cited and/or frequently cited. This confirms the outcome of other citation studies: A small number of journals generate the majority of journals cited. This confirmation can be used as a rationale for cancelling subscriptions of less-used journals or allocation of funds to faculties who consistently make high use of specific journals.

It is reassuring that TUT libraries are to a large extent able to provide most of the journals that are highly cited by M and D students. Although TUT libraries own only a few of the most cited journals they provide Web access to most of the others.

This study provided information that was previously unavailable to librarians and academic staff of TUT. It revealed what types of information sources M and D students used more frequently than others, how the patterns of use differ across subject disciplines and faculties, and it showed to what extent the LIS keeps or provides access to the journals that are mostly used by M and D students. The continued replication of this study will enable the LIS to determine even more reliable usage trends that will assist it to make informed decisions regarding which information resources to make available to M and D students, especially as Internet and electronic technologies evolve. A continuation of this research will also assist librarians and academics to better understand the research interest of M and D students at TUT.

References

Allan, M., Jacobs, S. and Levy, J.R., (2006). Mapping the literature of nursing: 1996 – 2000. *Journal of the Medical Library Association,* Vol. 94, No.2, 206 – 220.

Ching, J.T.Y., (2002). Collection evaluation through citation analysis techniques: a case study of the Ministry of Education, Singapore. *Library Review*, Vol. 51, No. 8, 398 – 405.

Loree, S., (2007). Is citation analysis worth it: a comparison of local citation analysis, interlibrary loan records and usage statistics for collection development purposes in a special library. Master's Thesis, Chapel Hill, University of North Carolina. [Online]. Available WWW: http://etd.ils.unc.edu/dspace/bitstream/1901/369/1/saraloree.pdf (Accessed 8 January 2008).

Griscom, R., (1983). Periodical use in a university music library: a citation analysis of thesis and dissertations submitted to the Indiana University School of Music from 1975 – 1980. *The Serials Librarian,* Vol. 7, No. 3, 35 – 52.

Naudé, F., Rensleigh, C. & Du Toit, A.S.A., (2005). Analysis of the citation of Web-based information resources by UNISA academic researchers. *South African Journal of Information Management*, Vol. 7, No. 3, 1 - 14. http://www.sajim.co.za/peer99.7nr3.asp?print=1 (Accessed 22 March 2007).

Peritz, B.C. and Sor, D., (1990). The use of libraries by graduate students in psychology as indicated by citations. *Collection Management* 12(3/4), 11 – 23.

Swanepoel, A.J., (2008). Citation analysis of theses and dissertations submitted at the Tshwane University of Technology: 2004 – 2006. *South African Journal of Higher Education*, Vol. 22, No. 5, 1097 – 1113.

Sylvia, M.J., (1998). Citation analysis as an unobtrusive method for journal collection evaluation using psychology student bibliographies. *Collection Building,* Vol. 17, No. 1, 20 – 28.

Zipp, L.S., (1996). Theses and dissertation citations as indicators of faculty research use of university library journal collections. *Library Resources and Technical Services,* Vol. 40, No. 4, 335 – 342.

Knowledge Creation and Flow in Agriculture: The Experience and Role of the Japanese Extension Advisors

Sohaimi Zakaria[1] and Haruki Nagata[2]

[1]Associate Professor, Faculty of Information Management, Universiti Teknologi MARA, Malaysia; Foreign Visiting Research Fellow, Research Center for Knowledge Communities, Graduate School of Library, Information & Media Studies, University of Tsukuba, Japan.
E-mail: sohaimiz@salam.uitm.edu.my
[2]Professor, Research Center for Knowledge Communities, Graduate School of Library, Information & Media Studies, University of Tsukuba, Japan
E-mail: harungt@slis.tsukuba.ac.jp

Abstract: This paper presents findings of a recent study on the experience and roles of agricultural extension advisors in the context of knowledge creation and flow in organizations. Data were collected through interviews with eleven principal and senior extension advisors and a consultant from different Prefectures and organizations as well as questionnaires from 135 extension advisors in the Ibaraki Prefecture, Japan. The purpose of the study was to explore the preferences and roles played by extension advisors in relation to knowledge sharing among advisors, farmers and other stakeholders. Results show that the Japanese agricultural agencies are actively involved in facilitating knowledge creation within their organizations. The extension advisors, as intermediaries and catalysts, are the key links between farmers and the relevant agencies in terms of providing personalized and need-based information for decision-making.

Keywords: Knowledge creation; Knowledge sharing; Information use; Knowledge flow; Agricultural information; Agricultural extension; Information management; Agriculture; Information intermediary.

1. Introduction

The Japanese agriculture has experienced several phases of reforms and modernization for more than a century ago. Since the end of the Second World War Japan started to embark on a concerted effort to revitalize its agriculture sector in order to boost production to meet the escalating demand for food. The Central and Prefectural Governments worked closely to enhance the training of farmers to uplift their technical and managerial skills and to ensure sustainability, and this was remarkably carried out through the activities and programs by the agricultural extension services.

The Japanese extension system for agriculture which started in 1948 was meant for helping farmers to acquire useful, appropriate and practical knowledge in the domain of agriculture (Fujita, n. d.). This system was adapted from the Western extension system into the Japanese culture to suit their local needs and requirements. Traditionally, extension focuses on disseminating R&D information from research laboratories to farmers (Roling, 1990), providing farmers with technical advice as a guide to improved farming methods (Williams, 1968), training of new, youth and women farmers as well as community reorganization.

The Japanese agriculture has thus far been successful and sustainable. This "suggest that farm decision-makers have either been using more and better information or becoming more knowledgeable" (Jones et al., 1987). The food shortage in the recent past has seen how important it is for nations to ensure sustainability of their agriculture sector. In fact, agricultural sustainability has been the focus of many developed nations as well as emerging economies. There have been a few interpretations of sustainable agriculture which could describe a state whereby: a) farm productivity is enhanced over the long-term, b) adverse impacts on the natural resource base and associated ecosystems are ameliorated, minimised or avoided, c) residues resulting from the use of chemicals in agriculture are minimised, d) net social benefit (in both monetary and non-monetary terms) from agriculture is maximised, and e) farming systems are sufficiently flexible to manage risks associated with the vagaries of climate and markets (Australian Standing Committee on Agriculture, 1997).

It would be interesting to understand how a developed country such as Japan manages its agriculture sector through the extension services, hence the study reported in this paper explored the roles and experience of the extension advisors in the context of knowledge creation and flow.

2. Methods and procedures

This study used questionnaire-based survey and interviews for data gathering. Eleven principal and senior extension and agricultural officers from different Prefectures and organizations and a consultant on the Japanese extension system were interviewed and 232 questionnaires were sent out to the extension advisors at the Headquarters and all of the 12 branches of the Ibaraki Prefecture Agricultural Center, Japan. Ibaraki is one of the 47 prefectures in Japan, with an area of 6,093 km^2 situated in the northern part of the Kanto region in Honshu Island. It has close to 3 million population and in terms of productivity, in 2006, Ibaraki was ranked 4th most productive agricultural region with its production of vegetables, crops, flowers, fruits and livestocks (Ibaraki Prefectural Government, 2009).

One hundred and thirty-five completed questionnaires were returned, providing an overall response rate of 58.2%. The breakdown of respondents according to branch is given in Table 1.

TABLE 1: Questionnaire Response Rate

Branches of the Ibaraki Agricultural Center	N (135)	%
Bandou	12	8.9
Chikusei	12	8.9
Hitachiomiya	13	9.6

Hitachiota	10	7.4
Hokota	12	8.9
Inashiki	12	8.9
Kasama	12	8.9
Mito	11	8.1
Namegata	9	6.7
Tsuchiura	12	8.9
Tsukuba	12	8.9
Yuuki	8	5.9

The development of the questionnaire was based on the review of literature where a few open and close-ended questions were derived from themes from previous studies related to information management and agricultural extension services such as those conducted by Jones et al. (1987), Kaniki (1989), Rolling (1990), Majid et al. (2000), Middendorf (2007), and Fukuda (2008). Subsequently, interviews were conducted with several experts in the field of agricultural extension to ensure that the questionnaire items are relevant with the nature and characteristics of the extension advisory services. The survey instrument was reviewed by a number of senior extension advisors before it was distributed to the extension advisors.

Meanwhile, additional information was gathered through interview sessions with principal and senior agriculture officers from a national organization for agricultural extension, a national agricultural research institute, three Prefectural Agricultural Centers, and a retired expert and consultant on agricultural extension system. The purpose of these interviews was to seek further clarifications on their experiences on the overall development of the Japanese agricultural extension system in relation to inter-organizational linkages and co-operations, common practices and leadership of the extension services.

3. Findings and discussion

3.1 Survey demographics

Twenty-three (17.3%) respondents were between 20 and 29 years old while the largest were in the age group of 30-39 years old (30.8%), 32 (24.1%) were between 40 and 49 years old, 34 (25.6%) were between 50 and 59 years old, and only 3 (2.3%) were 60 years old or more. Of the 134 respondents who provided feedback on their gender, 89 (66.4%) were male and 45 (33.6%) were female.

On their highest educational attainment, four (3.1%) respondents held a PhD degree, 29 (22.5%) had a Master's degree. The majority (79 or 61.2%) of them had a Bachelor's degree. Only 1 (0.8%) had only a college or high school education.

More than a third of the extension advisors who participated in this study had five years of working experience or less with the extension service, while 11 (8.9%) had 36 or more years of experience. Table 2 provides detail breakdown about their experience.

TABLE 2: Experience of Respondents

Experience (years)	N (124)	%
Up to 5	46	37.1
6-10	19	15.3
11-15	15	12.1
16-20	10	8.1

21-25	9	7.3
26-30	5	4.0
31-35	9	7.3
36 & above	11	8.9

As extension advisors, respondents were assigned to 1 or more areas of specialty where 55 (40.7%) respondents associated to vegetable farming, followed by rice cropping, 44 (32.6%), upland cropping, 31 (23%). Apart from farming and cropping, respondents also specialized in technology applications, 23 (17%), human resource management, 22 (16.3%) as shown in Table 3.

TABLE 3: Area of Specialty of Respondents

Area	N	%
Vegetable farming	55	40.7
Rice cropping	44	32.6
Upland cropping	31	23.0
Technology applications	23	17.0
Human resource management	22	16.3
Business management	20	14.8
Fruit farming	17	12.6
Community development	16	11.9
Feed cropping	13	9.6
Flower farming	11	8.1
Dairy cow farming	8	5.9
Beef cattle farming	7	5.2
Pig farming	6	4.4
Chicken farming	5	3.7

3.2 Personalized learning activities

Respondents were asked to indicate on a scale of 1-5 (as noted below in Table 4) their preference of the channels of communication when interacting with farmers, the industry as well as with other organizations and related parties. It was discovered that extension advisors used several means to communicate with their clients in performing their advisory tasks and responsibilities. Table 4 provides the list of communication channels preferred and used by extension advisors and their mean score.

From the table, the channels which ware highly rated by the respondents were personal face-to-face meetings with farmers and other clients and visits to their farms and work places. The mean score for this preference was closest to 1 (most preferred). It is observed that the top 3 rated channels of communication (i.e. personal face-to-face meetings, visits; fixed line telephones and cell phones) would relate to the extension advisors' preferences for personal, on-the-spot and interactive communications with their clients.

TABLE 4: Preference of Different Types of Communication Channels

Rating	Types of Communication Channels	N	Mean Score	Standard Deviation
1	Personal face-to-face meetings, visits	135	1.34	0.625
2	Office, residential fixed line telephones	135	1.77	0.712
3	Cellphones, SMSes	132	2.54	1.162

4	Handouts, flyers	132	2.67	1.061
5	Workshops, seminars, classes	131	3.18	1.094
6	Postal correspondences	126	3.33	0.980
7	Emails	128	4.13	0.908
8	Weblogs	127	4.87	0.591

Note: Scale: 1) Most preferred 2) Preferred 3) Neutral 4) Less preferred 5) Least preferred

From the interviews it was possible to highlight that active learning happened during the interactions between extension advisors and farmers and between farmers where the more advanced farmers often provide assistance and guidance to other farmers. It was reported that farmers developed close collaborations between then through the formation of various local societies and groups. The extension services, on the other hand, constantly exchange ideas, experience and tacit knowledge with the farmers. The 'bottom-up' approach which is widely practiced in the Japanese agriculture permeates well with the extension's focus on personalized and repeated interactions. This approach apparently allows farmers to provide direct input to the development of the agriculture field. In addition, through this the extensions are able to gather firsthand information from farmers which are subsequently shared within the community and authorities for further actions.

This phenomenon (of personalization) is further evident by the preference of the extension advisors to meet with farmers at the latter's residence (mean score of 1.38, where 1 = most commonly at/on, 2 = commonly at/on, 3 = neutral, 4 = less commonly at/on, and 5 = least commonly at/on), followed by farmers' farmyard (mean = 1.94). Table 5 provides the list of meeting places rated by extension advisors.

TABLE 5: Preference of Places of Meeting With Farmers

Rating	Places of Meeting	N	Mean Score	Standard Deviation
1	Farmers' residence	134	1.38	0.691
2	Farmers' farmyard	132	1.94	0.955
3	Respondents' office	132	2.64	0.967
4	Workshops/classes/meetings	131	2.69	0.894
5	Local agricultural cooperatives	130	2.92	1.061
6	Experimental plots/sites	129	3.19	1.146

It would be interesting to highlight that the interactions between the players in agriculture provide a platform for formal and informal exchanges of ideas and experience, which gradually formed into what is called communities of practice (Wenger, 1998) where individuals through active social participation contribute to the practices of and learning in their communities and/or organizations. Wenger believes that 'learning is an issue of sustaining the interconnected communities of practice through which an organization knows what it knows and thus becomes effective and valuable as an organization' (p. 8). Sharing of one's experience is an integral part of a community where the alignment of individuals towards common goals may facilitate change within the community (Kahan, 2004).

Therefore, we can conclude that in the context of the agricultural extension, social interactions and participations between advisors and farmers lead to the creation and sharing of new knowledge which would contribute to the enhancement and sustainability of the agriculture sector. In this case, the extension advisors act as intermediaries and key players in the community.

3.3 Need-based and personal sources of information

Respondents were asked to indicate from 17 items on where they acquire and seek the information required to perform their advisory and administrative tasks. Table 6 shows the list of advisory information and the sources used by the extension advisors in performing their advisory tasks. Of the 19 types of advisory information, 12 were acquired from their Prefectural Agricultural Center, 2 each from the Ministry of Agriculture, Forestry and Fisheries (MAFF); mass media; and customers and farmers; and 1 from their superiors, colleagues and subordinates.

It is obvious from Table 6 that the Prefectural Agricultural Center caters for most of the advisors' needs for information which spans from R&D findings, new technology, technical aspects of agriculture to managerial issues. The MAFF meanwhile was referred to for governmental incentives and policies as well as legal and regulatory information. Information pertaining to the needs of specific farmer groups and community development were acquired from their clients themselves. The mass media were relied upon for news on global and local affairs and finally, for information on credit system, they referred to their superiors, colleagues and subordinates.

We can conclude that the Prefectural Agricultural Center possesses a repository of tacit and explicit knowledge which could be easily accessed and used by the extension advisors in performing their advisory tasks. The availability of such facilities is an integral part which would enhance knowledge sharing within the organization.

TABLE 6: Sources of Information for Advisory Purposes

Advisory Information	Source	N	%
New research & experiment findings	Prefectural Agricultural Center	74	55.6
New technology development	Prefectural Agricultural Center	70	52.6
Government incentives & policies	Min of Agriculture, Forestry & Fisheries	61	46.2
Legal and regulatory information	Min of Agriculture, Forestry & Fisheries	67	51.1
Farm management methods	Prefectural Agricultural Center	38	29.0
Technical specifications	Prefectural Agricultural Center	42	33.6
Soil improvement	Prefectural Agricultural Center	57	44.2
Plant/animal breeds	Prefectural Agricultural Center	36	27.9
Pest & disease control	Prefectural Agricultural Center	63	49.2
Natural disaster protection	Prefectural Agricultural Center	57	45.6

Water & irrigation systems	Prefectural Agricultural Center	37	30.8
Farmer groups' needs & requirements (new, young & women farmers)	Customers, farmers	59	46.5
Community reorganization	Customers, farmers	29	22.8
Food safety	Prefectural Agricultural Center	28	21.9
Environmental issues	Prefectural Agricultural Center	34	26.6
Local market information (including prices & consumer demands)	Prefectural Agricultural Center	28	22.0
Credit system	Superiors, colleagues, subordinates	37	28.9
Current global affairs	Mass media	61	47.3
Current local affairs	Mass media	53	41.1

Similarly, the respondents were given a list of 10 types of administrative information to indicate the sources of information in performing them as listed in Table 7. It shows that 6 types of administrative information were acquired from their superiors, colleagues and subordinates. This is followed by 2 each from the Prefectural Agricultural Center and their customers and farmers.

In relation to the high preference for sources of information from the Prefectural Agricultural Center, it could be argued that the concepts of communities of practice and organizational learning with individual active participation and sharing of experience are indeed well observed and activated at this Prefectural Agricultural Center. It is evident that human expertise and experience are the main source of information and shared within the organization as the main ingredients for decision-makings, aligned toward the achievement of organizational goals.

TABLE 7: Sources of Information for Administration Purposes

Administrative Information	Source	N	%
Making predictions and forecasting	Superiors, colleagues, subordinates	32	26.0
Doing research and experiments	Prefectural Agricultural Center	68	55.7
Providing feedback on community issues to research institutions	Customers, farmers	42	33.6
Preparing presentations	Superiors, colleagues, subordinates	33	27.0
Preparing reports for farmers	Superiors, colleagues, subordinates	36	28.8
For personal and private use	Customers, farmers	22	17.5
On-the-job training	Superiors, colleagues, subordinates	43	36.4
Preparing departmental reports	Prefectural Agricultural Center	37	31.1
Preparing institutional strategic plans	Superiors, colleagues, subordinates	42	35.0
Responding to emergency cases	Superiors, colleagues, subordinates	45	37.2

4. Conclusions

This study highlights an integral factor that contributes to the success of an organization that is the ability to generate and share knowledge among members of the organization. Results showed that the agricultural extension system actively promotes and facilitates the sharing of ideas and experiences between extension advisors and farmers as well as other stakeholders.

Farmers have learned that agriculture is a risky business, hence they need to make accurate decisions based on real life experience and specific knowledge to ensure that they could get the appropriate return on investment and to minimise losses. They need constant, accurate and timely advice from the extension services and other advanced farmers. The agricultural extension organizations naturally provide the place or the Japanese concept of 'ba' (Nonaka & Konno, 1998), which means 'a shared space that serves as a foundation for knowledge creation' (p. 40) for the promotion of active interactions, consultations and exchanges between extension and farmers.

An example of the initiative that creates the ba is the on-the-job training (OJT) for farmers through on-site and hands-on sessions, and for extension advisors which is widely practised in most Japanese organizations. It is worth noting that Japanese organizations adapted the OJT concept into their work culture which allows the sharing and flow of implicit knowledge among members. The open office concept where workers are placed closely together in an open office space helps to further enhance the OJT practices, thus allowing for ideas and experience to naturally flow, underpinned by a situation referred to by Nonaka and Konno as 'entrainment' (synchronizing behaviour), and eventually got aligned towards the common culture and goals of the organization.

The findings of this study have provided some insights as to the ways in which knowledge is created and shared within an organization and are expected to serve as an initial framework for organizational leaders to create opportunities and space for such activities to be carried out. Future research may be conducted to find out the state of knowledge creation and sharing in the other Prefectures and in other organizations in general.

5. Acknowledgements

The authors acknowledge with gratitude support from Universiti Teknologi MARA, Malaysia; Research Center for Knowledge Communities, the University of Tsukuba, Japan; and collaboration of the Japan Agricultural Development and Extension Association (JADEA); Japan National Agricultural Research Center (NARC); Agricultural Center of Ibaraki and Toyama Prefectures and Hokkaido; Tochigi; Dr. Yasuki Fujita; Mr. Asahi Kiyokawa; the respondents and consultants.

References

Australia. Standing Committee on Agriculture (1997). *Sustainability indicators for agriculture: introductory guide for regional/national indicators and on-farm indicators.*

Fujita, Y. (n.d.) *Japan's extension system for improvement of agriculture and rural life.* Unpublished paper.

Fukuda, K. (2008). *Study of problems and improvement measures of information activities used with information technology in agricultural extension.* Tokyo: Japan Agricultural Development and Extension Association.

Ibaraki Prefectural Government (2009). *Data on Ibaraki.* Mito: Ibaraki Prefectural Government. Available at http://www.pref.ibaraki.jp/bukyoku/seikan/kokuko/en/data/index.htm

Japan Agricultural Development and Extension Association (2005). Nougyo fukyu jiten = Agricultural extension services overview & perspectives. Tokyo : Maruikoubunsha.

Jones, G. E.; Rolls, M. J. and Tranter, R. B. (1987). *Information management in agriculture : British Library R&D report 5931.* Reading, England : Agricultural Extension and Rural Development Centre.

Kahan, S. (2004). Etienne Wenger on communities of practice: engagement, identity and innovation. *The Journal of Association Leadership,* March 2004.

Kaniki, A. M. (1989). *Agricultural information needs in Zambia: a study of a two-way information flow.* Unpublished doctoral thesis. University of Pittsburgh.

Majid, S.; Anwar, M. A. and Eisenschitz, T. S. (2000). Information needs and information seeking behavior of agricultural scientists in Malaysia. *Library & Information Science Research,* 22(2), 145-163.

Middendorf, G. (2007). Challenges and information needs of organic growers and retailers. *Journal of Extension,* 45(4). Available at: http://www.joe.org/joe/2007august/a7.shtml

Nonaka, I. and Konno, N. (1998). The concept of 'ba': building a foundation for knowledge creation. *California Management Review,* 40: 40-54.

Roling, N. (1990). The agricultural research-technology transfer interface: a knowledge systems perspective. In David Kaimowitz (Ed.). *Making the link: agricultural research and technology transfer in developing countries.* London: Westview.

Wenger, E. (1998). *Communities of practice: meaning, and identity.* London: Cambridge University Press.

Williams, D. (1968). *Agricultural extension: farm extension services in Australia, Britain and the United States of America.* London: Cambridge University Press.

Supporting Knowledge Discovery in a Research Organisation

Steve Thornton

(Formerly) Departmental Programmes Coordinator, Knowledge Services Department, Defence Science and Technology Laboratory, Ministry of Defence, United Kingdom

Abstract: This paper describes the creation, and philosophy of, a Department whose structure and functions were all aimed at supporting knowledge creation by both individuals and project teams for the UK's Ministry of Defence. Underlying these services was a deep understanding gathered over 30 years of how research scientists learn, and how we need to aid that learning process. This process is demonstrated graphically by a development of Max Boisot's "Social Learning Cycle".

1. Introduction

The Defence Science and Technology Organisation (Dstl) is the UK Ministry of Defence's research and development organisation. Created in 2001 following the partial-privatisation of the Defence Evaluation and Research Agency (DERA), its primary functions are to carry out research considered best done within Government and to provide the UK's Ministry of Defence with impartial expert advice.

The division of DERA meant that Dstl lacked virtually all the library and information services needed to support a research organisation some 3,000 strong. Our challenge was to create a new Department – Knowledge Services – to meet the research scientists' requirements and develop tools, facilities and services that would encourage knowledge creation and sharing. Fundamental to the problem we faced was discovering their needs, understanding how they learn, and thus how they create knowledge.

2. Knowledge Transfer

Firstly, what is knowledge? We used a standard dictionary definition that "knowledge is the sum of what is known". New knowledge is created in a person's brain, and its creation is a function of a variety of factors; what that person has read, his education, his societal upbringing, his working environment, in short everything that has gone into creating him as a person.

My contention is that that knowledge itself can never be transferred from one person to another (and as a consequence can never be managed, except by its creator). The knowledge that is created in someone's head is limited to, and unique to, that individual. When they attempt to transfer that knowledge to another person, all they can actually transfer is an imperfect image or subset of what is in their head – an information product. These information products may take the form of a conference paper, article, report, presentation, teaching lesson, conversation, letter, television programme, videoed lecture, web site or whatever. What you can be certain of is that what is transferred via that information product will not be "the sum of what is known" by the person imparting it, but an imperfect and incomplete subset of their knowledge.

We can take cooking recipes as an example. Chefs develop new recipes through practice, experience and trial-and-error. The first way that recipes were transferred from the chef "researcher/inventor" to another person would have been as hands-on one-to-one tuition. This was, and probably still is, the most effective way of learning, and recipes were passed down by word of mouth from one generation to the next. Even so, transfer may not succeed, as often the chef is not a very competent teacher, or may require of the student a level of pre-knowledge and ability which may be lacking - some pupils are unteachable! So, while effective, one-to-one or one-to-small group tuition is not a very efficient means of transferring new knowledge widely or quickly.

The next stage was recording the recipe in writing, and while this allowed transfer to larger numbers than ever before, some writers were more effective than others in describing the process. While Mrs Beaton famously began her recipe for Rabbit Stew with the instruction, ' First catch your rabbit.', not all are as clear. Clarity and details vary – how "hot" is a "hot pan"? I have one recipe at home that says to make dumplings "shilling sized", not very helpful since shillings went out of use in the UK some 35 years ago.

From hand-copied recipe books we progressed to print, to recipes with black-and-white illustrations, to ones with colour plates, and thence to television programmes with chefs again demonstrating how to cook, with some being far better at getting the message across than others. Increasingly useful, but until recordings became available, such demonstrations were always very quick one-offs and separate from the kitchen. Now we can have a Nintendo DS Lite in the kitchen, showing video recipes for each stage – the ultimate so far, but still no guarantee that an amateur can cook as well as a Michelin-starred chef. In short, although the information product has improved greatly over the years, knowledge transfer is still less than perfect.

Given that knowledge transfer is imperfect, how can we support and encourage knowledge creation and aid in its transfer?

3. The Social Learning Cycle

A non-commercial research organisation operates in fundamentally different ways to either academic or commercial research. In academia, research or project teams tend to be small or based on individuals and whose primary task is educational rather than research oriented. Certainly, commercial interests come into play, but the main task is the development of the individual graduate or post-graduate student. For commercial organisations the primary interest is generating profit through viable commercial invention. Teams can be very large, and (perhaps surprisingly) internal self-interest may prevent information being shared freely within the organisation, or indeed within the team itself. In Dstl providing our security forces with the best research and technology support as quickly as possible to counter threats to the UK and our allies is more important that personal self interest or profit generation – although we have been quite successful in the latter, if only as an accidental by-product.

Creating our service from scratch was not a task to be taken lightly. In order to discover the needs of our customer base, we placed particular emphasis on the fact that we were looking at their needs and not their wants. What they wanted was for us to replicate the high quality university-style library service they had had access to in the past, but our investigations showed that what they wanted was very different to their actual needs. There has been a growing tendency within the profession to ask the user community what they want, partly because - I suspect - this is very much easier than actually divining what they need. But the users do not necessarily know what could or should be provided. Often they will ask for what they think you can supply, or what they think is fashionable. Our task should not follow slavishly the demands of the user, but by identifying their real needs and knowing what is both possible and practical, devise and revise our services accordingly to meet as much of those needs as we can with the resources we have at our disposal.

To add to our already extensive knowledge of the research requirements of MoD scientists, we carried out workshops, one-to-one interviews, on-line chat groups and semi-social events to find out how much Dstl's requirements would differ from those of the much larger DERA predecessor. Using the hybrid scheme devised by Peter Brophy (1998) as the framework for our proposed service to meet those needs, we were able to overlay this on our own version of Max Boisot's social learning cycle (1998) to define where each of our services and other facilities and structures provided the framework Dstl had to have.

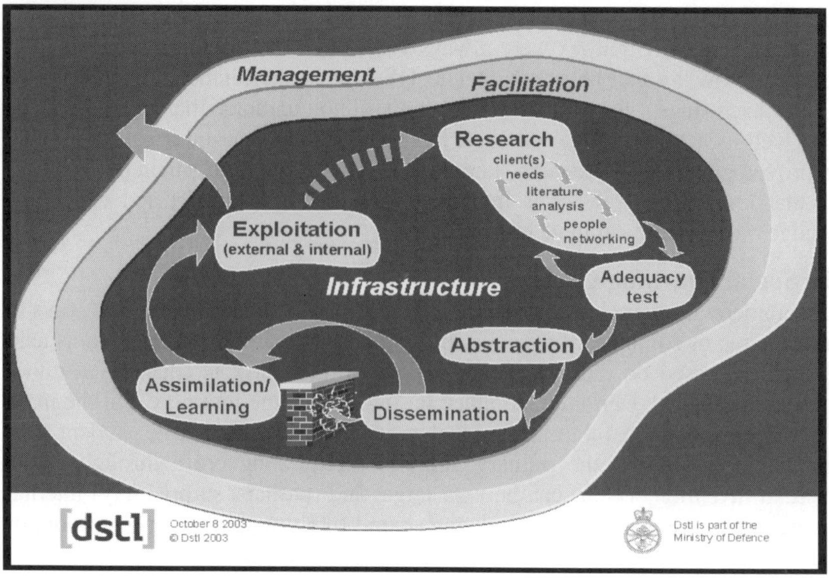

The social learning theory shown here is a graphical representation of how individuals learn, and subsequently create knowledge in themselves and their teams. They are supported by the library and information management professionals within Knowledge Services Department through many of the steps in the cycle. If we were to do our job properly we had to support the learning process through out its cycle.

4 Dstl's Learning Infrastructure

The central element on which the learning cycle sits is an infrastructure which consists of physical and intangible elements without which the process would be extremely hard, if not impossible, for our scientists to carry out. These elements include corporate, cultural, the electronic environment and information provision.

Corporate Culture:

We were fortunate from the start to be supported by a genuine belief among Dstl's senior management that the organisation's role is to provide the best research and advice to our employers. With this came an appreciation among management of the value and cost of learning, training and sharing – as well as the ultimate penalties of not doing so.

They also not only accepted that information provision costs, but also understood research we had undertaken that showed that a former culture of "internal charging" for photocopies, books, quick searches etc. was not only an inefficient way of recovering such costs, but was also found to be detrimental to the scientific/learning process. Finally, there was a genuine acceptance that these were not short-term targets – there is no quick-fix for excellence.

Cultural Philosophy

We moved away from the usual idea of the Library as a collection-building repository of printed information – we had no funds or physical resources for such a monolithic structure, and it wasn't what was needed. Given the vast range of subjects our users worked in, there was no way that we could even scratch the surface of gathering all of the significant material of interest. More importantly our scientists would never have time to digest it all. What we provided was a welcoming reading room with a very small but carefully selected collection of key books, current newspapers, journals and reference works. Most importantly we provide a convivial atmosphere (and coffee!) with specially selected intelligent library staff who know their stock, the customers and their interests, and how to meet their needs as quickly as possible.

We also looked closely at how Dstl's staff communicate. Although we largely have open-plan offices, with an extensive electronic intranet, much useful discussion takes place either when travelling to or from the coffee point, or at the coffee point itself. To mesh with, and encourage, this internal culture of discussion and knowledge sharing, what we put in place in terms of "physical" infrastructure are:

- One, fairly large (for a special library) conventional library;
- Three small focussed collections. - small site libraries - each with a dynamic stock and 2 dynamic staff, as part of an information sharing resource designed to encourage and stimulate thought;
- Tea Boat collections – unmanned tea room sites with small collections of books, internet terminals, white boards, relevant journals etc, scattered around our various sites which were maintained and regularly supported by Knowledge Services staff;

Some of the collections also have Anti-Bistros – the alternative to the busy open-plan office. Small, individual work areas where scientists can get down to serious thinking and study, away from the telephone and the insidious all-pervasive e-mail.

Electronic Infrastructure

Network and related infrastructures need continuous investment and development, and need to be aligned to the needs of the clients. Although Knowledge Services had no direct involvement in service provision, we were often closely involved in development requirement discussions.

Information Infrastructure

Development of the core information infrastructure - much of which either we provide directly or lead on provision - was strongly directed at providing material directly to the desktop, not an easy task in a security environment. Much of what we provided was bought in from commercial suppliers, although we set up an in-house scanning team to create e-versions of our scientific and technical reports holdings. These offerings included:

- Our reports catalogue, including over 200,000 full text documents;
- Web of Knowledge;
- Jane's;
- Electronic journals access;
- E-Learning courses;
- A portal site to many other major sources.

But the infrastructure is just that. It is developing and growing in light of our clients needs, but to limit ourselves to just to those short-term needs and not think ahead would be not carrying out our job properly. Sadly, in our experience, many libraries (and librarians) see the provision of these infrastructure service as their sole role, and go no further. For us this was merely the foundation for a far more active role in supporting the learning cycle.

5 Roles Within The Learning Cycle

Research Phase

Beyond being a key provider of the infrastructure, Knowledge Services plays a greater role in the learning cycle, an information facilitation role. The Research phase is that it which the individual or team defines what it is that is to be researched, carries out some form of literature search, gathers together (and shares) relevant material, and utilising people networks to ensure as broad a coverage as possible.

Conventional library and information services usually support some of the *Research* phase, perhaps defining the client's needs and assisting in the gathering of literature to meet those needs. Knowledge Services however goes further than these limited aims, offering a wide range of consultancy services which can improve the efficiency and sustainability of the research process.

I was, and am still, continually surprised that many organisations provide their experts with a wide range of expensive bibliographic sources, and then leave them to do any and all information gathering, sifting, sorting and analysing themselves. Certainly, our client base contained several individuals not only capable but even expert at carrying out these tasks, but it is generally accepted that this tends to be a very expensive use of their valuable and limited time, and one for which *unless you carry out the task frequently*, the non-expert rapidly becomes inefficient. Our approach is to provide a variety of trained information specialists to handle such tasks, and to facilitate knowledge creation and sharing.

I am sure that we have all experienced a shift in the 1990's from information provision through library services to information provision at the desktop sometimes leading either to the widescale reduction of conventional library services or even to their obliteration. Yet in our case we have not only increased our information staff, but also created three small libraries – a complete reversal of the trend – for three major reasons. Firstly, and possibly most importantly, we received the support of senior management from the outset. Knowledge Services was not seen as just "the Library", but a pool of information expertise on a par with the scientific research departments. Secondly, we were in the (possibly) enviable position of having to start almost from scratch with very few existing facilities and none of the baggage that came along with them. Thirdly, we discovered what our customers what they needed. We didn't provided them with exactly what they wanted – usually a University quality library with massive book stock and journal back-runs - but we identified from information needs gathering exercises what they really <u>needed</u> to do their jobs properly. Among the evidence we gathered was an awareness that while they were capable of meeting a fair proportion of their needs from a variety of sources including desktop, communities of practice, professional or newsy journals etc., they not only wanted but needed high quality information professionals on tap for those occasions where comprehensiveness, certainty and speed were essential, and where they needed to apply analytical techniques beyond their existing skills set.

To meet these needs we have four groups of information experts: Information Specialists, Information Scientists, Knowledge Agents and of Knowledge Research Team.

The Information Specialists are another term for our Librarians and Assistants. Although 'conventionally' trained, we expect far more from them. They must be very active among their community, and be very aware of their clients' needs and expertise. They have very little physical room to play with, so collection building has to be highly selective and effective to make to best use of the space available. They also serve various training roles, teaching clients locally on the resources available at the desktop, either in one-to-one sessions or in more formal courses organised by Knowledge Services. By making these small focussed collections (or libraries as everyone from the Chief Executive down calls them) a social and friendly environment, they make a valuable contribution to helping create a knowledge sharing culture.

Fortunately there is an acceptance amongst the majority of Dstl that if you don't know, you buy the expertise in. Our Information Scientists are either information scientists or scientists trained in many techniques of information work. They are our true specialists, our experts in bibliometric analysis, patent analysis, data visualisation, technology roadmapping, etc., and their expertise is bought in when and where needed in support of specific pieces of work, either directly or in support of our generalists. The Information Scientists, and to a lesser extent the Knowledge Agents, analyse the information at their disposal, identifying research trends and developing technologies. The can also identify key players and groups in the areas of interest, pointing out those people that our clients should be interested in, following, talking to and co-operating with, thus supporting the *people networking* element of learning cycle.

Our generalists, the Knowledge Agents, are spread across four of our sites, but with a remit to go to the clients wherever they may be – a mobile information task force as it were. With either scientific or information qualifications – most have doctorates or MScs – they are trained up to a reasonably high level, and can be bolted into projects to handle anything from basic literature searches to handling the total information requirements of a whole research package. Although their tasks are not usually related to their individual specialism, their scientific expertise and overarching knowledge has lead to widespread acceptance of the concept throughout the organisation. One, bolted into a project as a Knowledge Agent, also fills the role of inorganic chemistry expert within it. Most have received training in facilitation, and act in dual roles in team workshops as facilitators and information experts. In fact, the skills that they have demonstrated have led to them being included in a range of projects for which standard "librarians" would never have been considered, culminating recently in a organisation wide capability analysis, with the unforeseen benefit that they know more about what is going on across Dstl than some senior managers! They tend to be the most widespread public face of the Department, and key to their success is a wide knowledge of all of the skills, strengths and weaknesses of the rest of the Department. They operate singly, or as part of ad hoc teams, drawing in skills and talents wherever needed from the rest of Knowledge Services.

By using these generalists and specialists as support in the research phase our experts, either as teams or individuals, can usually gain access to far more material than they would normally know about.

Adequacy Phase

Going on from the *Research* phase in the cycle, our staff have been trained to identify whether the information supplied and sources used meet *Boisot's "Adequacy Test*". We have all come across clients who have carried out a "comprehensive literature search", which has turned out to a quick delve into Google that has barely scratched the surface. Our staff are trained in, and have access to a far greater range of potential sources than many clients have any idea exist, and can select from this range of material to provide the appropriate depth of research needed for the task in hand. One of our experts thought he had all of the relevant papers – just three - on his subject. An hour later he was given a stand-alone database with details of over 60 more, and 200 more related ones that he ought to know about. Others, about to embark on expensive research, have been put in touch with other experts in the organisation and saved lots of time and money in the process.

Abstraction/Summarisation Phase

They can also supply the *abstraction/summarisation* phase, producing technology reviews to a very high standard. Many of these skills were found among librarians in the past, but sadly do not seem to be taught these days in the UK, either in schools or colleges.

Dissemination Phase

They also can assist in *dissemination*, with expertise in shared network drives, stand-alone bibliographic databases, and a range of other skills aimed at sharing information. For many of our scientists and knowledge integrators, the ability to take sub-sets of bibliographic databases or analysed data to meetings both in this country and abroad or to mount on separate networks, is seen as a real advantage.

Assimilation/Learning Phase

This is the one phase where we can offer no support, except where one of our staff forms a specific part of a research team.

Exploitation Phase

In the final phase of the cycle, we assist in the *exploitation* of the new knowledge created by the *assimilation* phase. Scientific and technical reports form the concrete product of Dstl's research, and these are recorded and indexed not only on our corporate catalogue, but also on databases and hard copy abstract journals which are made available to the rest of MOD and defence community and throughout our allies. By making this information available we are encouraging the exploitation of our research by the wider community.

6. Conclusion

Knowledge creation is a human activity, and as such is subject to all of the vices (and virtues) of including humans in any loop. Technological "solutions" only exaggerate the differences between the individuals involved. Knowledge Services' approach was to create an environment, both physical and cultural, whereby knowledge sharing is encouraged and facilitated, in line with both the client's expressed needs and the organisation's philosophy and strategies. In addition, the ready availability of information/subject experts in the form of the Information Scientists and the Knowledge Agents encourage effective information gathering and use, together with the informal creation of knowledge networks running in parallel to the formal ones within the organisation.

References

1. Peter Brophy. Performance measures for Twenty-First Century libraries. Proceedings of the 4th Northumbria International Conference on Performance Measurement in Library and Information Services, Pittsburgh, PA, August 2001, pp 1-7.

2. Max H. Boisot. Knowledge assets: securing competitive advantage in the information economy; Oxford University Press, May 1998, ISBN: 0198290861

Tools to Develop Effective Research Support in an Academic Library: A Case Study

Helen Young, Peter Lund and Graham Walton

Loughborough University Library, UK

Abstract: As Research Support is becoming an increasingly topical issue within academic libraries in the UK, this paper examines two different surveys that Loughborough University Library undertook to assess the effectiveness of its research support. The first was a benchmarking survey amongst 1994 Group universities, which produced quantitative data to enable the Library to identify its relative strengths and weaknesses and plan for the future. The second was a more inward looking survey which examined the information needs of a sample of research centres. This produced a mixture of qualitative and quantitative data. The paper discusses the strengths and weaknesses of both methods and how the results were carried forward into operational plans.

Keywords: Academic libraries; Research support; Qualitative data; Quantitative data; Case study; Library services; Benchmarking; User surveys.

1. Introduction

In April 2007, the Research Information Network (RIN) and Consortium of University Research Libraries (CURL) published their joint report into *Researchers' use of academic libraries and their services* (2007). This national study raised the profile of research support currently offered within University libraries, whilst identifying the challenges for librarians and researchers in ensuring that this support is effective. Whilst a national survey is a very useful tool to provide a map of the landscape of research support in UK academia, it cannot provide an individual institution with all that it needs to know about the relevance of its own current services or how it should develop them in the future. Institutions range in size, resources and ethos. It is for this reason that Loughborough University Library undertook two projects to aid the development of its own research support services. The first was a benchmarking survey within the 1994 Group of universities conducted by the Research Support Team, whilst the second was a survey into the use of library services by research centres within the University itself and was one of the Library's annual research oriented studies. This paper details the methods used in these surveys, their strengths and weaknesses and provides examples of how the results have been used to enhance research support at Loughborough.

2. Benchmarking Survey

Before the Library decided exactly how it wanted to develop its research support services, it decided to discover what institutions of a similar size and outlook were offering their researchers. This would enable the identification of any services that needed be developed to be on a par with these institutions or to surpass them. The quantitative data that such a benchmarking survey would produce would have strengths, as it would be quick to obtain and to analyse, whilst the main weakness would be that it would not be possible to assess how valued or used the services might be. However, it could identify the institutions to be contacted to discover more about particular services.

The key to the survey's success was to ensure that the institutions that were benchmarked were like-minded institutions. This decision was helped by the fact that Loughborough is part of the 1994 Group of universities which was "established to promote excellence in research and teaching." (2009 1994 Group). In the summer of 2008, when the study was undertaken, there were nineteen institutions in this group, which was felt to be a practical number of potential respondents, as well as providing a reasonable range of comparators.

Having decided who would be surveyed, the data collection method was determined. Given the potential range of research support services and number of respondents, it was felt that a questionnaire was the only practical tool. We knew from our own experience that respondents would not want to spend a long time filling in a questionnaire. We also did not want to ask questions to elicit data that was already available easily elsewhere. It was decided that data that could be drawn from the annual Society of College, National and University Library statistics (2007 SCONUL) should be analysed separately. It was not easy to find data about services offered to researchers, however, and so this was the area on which the questionnaire concentrated.

To ensure that the questions would have some resonance with the potential respondents, the web pages of both 1994 Group libraries and some Russell Group libraries (2009 Russell Group) were scanned to inform us of the services that could be offered. These included those that might be considered core services, such as inter-library loans, as well as 'niche' services, such as delivery of items to departments. One of the aims of the survey was to ascertain exactly how far spread such services were. The areas surveyed were: obtaining materials; mediated searching of databases; special collections; electronic reference; reference management; training; dedicated research space; support for the Research Assessment Exercise; management of research outputs; support for e-research; and a final open question on any areas not covered by the questionnaire.

With the content determined, the data collection tool had to be user-friendly. The Library had used UCCASS open source software (2009 UCCASS) for the construction of online surveys previously and it seemed ideal for our purpose, as it provided a web-based form for both the construction and the completion of the questionnaire, as well producing data for export to Excel for analysis. The majority of the questions were 'tick box' answers, so that it would be quick to complete and straightforward to analyse. The questionnaire was piloted by colleagues at University of Stirling and Loughborough to check the clarity of the wording and for any technical hitches. Once it had been amended, the link to the questionnaire was distributed by the University Librarian via a closed mailing list. It was felt that the endorsement of the Librarian would increase the response rate. The questionnaire was distributed during August for completion by the first week in September. It was hoped that this traditionally 'quiet' time in universities would ensure a good response.

By the end of a slightly extended deadline, we received fourteen responses, a response rate of approximately 79%. It was felt that the timing of distribution and physical method of delivery had been successful. Unfortunately the start of Loughborough University's first semester began at the end of September, which meant there was only a very short time to analyse the data, because of preparations for the busiest period of the academic year. As there were just two people working on the survey, the data analysis was more constrained than was originally planned and stretched well into the autumn term, with the report and recommendations completed at the beginning of December. In retrospect it would have been wiser to have distributed the questionnaire in the equally quiet May/June period, with the report and recommendations published in September, as this would have allowed the analysis and report writing to take place during the less pressured summer months.

The results of the survey (2008 Lund and Young) enabled the Library to discover the services that were being currently offered by other institutions within the 1994 Group. The Library was reassured that Loughborough was offering a similar range of support compared with others in the Group across all of the areas surveyed. The survey enabled us to identify that we were not allocating as much funding as the majority of respondents to electronic reference products, which moved their importance up our purchasing agenda. It also identified areas for further investigation, such as the deposit of data within institutional repositories and the possibility of the electronic submission of interlibrary loan forms. However, even though the majority of other respondents were offering the latter, advice from our copyright expert suggested that it would not be sensible for Loughborough to adopt the system of electronic signatures.

It was also possible to use the analysis of SCONUL electronic journal statistics to demonstrate that Loughborough was not spending as much as some of its most noteworthy competitors on electronic journal subscriptions. A presentation of the survey results to the Library Committee exercised the Committee enough to request increased funding for the Library budget to enable increased purchasing in this area. It is a moot point as to whether the funds that were subsequently forthcoming can be attributed solely to the survey results, but it did provide more evidence to support the argument.

The exercise has proved useful enough to consider repeating it to see how service provision changes over time and to keep ensuring that Loughborough is, at least, providing comparable services with others in the 1994 Group. However, the questions would be refined to look more towards the future. The original survey could not provide a sense of how research support services were likely to develop in the different organisations and so it did not really provide any fresh ideas. One way to develop this might be to include some libraries that are not in the 1994 Group but which are renowned for their research support. It would also be very helpful to discover the usage of the services offered. For example, to know how many PhD students or academic or research staff are being trained within other institutions, not just which courses are being run. Whilst some institutions might struggle to answer such questions, any responses would provide some insight into the success of the services.

A list of recommendations for Loughborough to take forward into future operational plans was drawn up as a result of the survey and so it has influenced the direction of the Library. For example, it is currently organising focus groups, to discover the importance of research space for PhD students, to help assess whether the Library or the University as whole should be providing more segregated areas for researchers. The recommendations are also being translated into measurable targets for research support. However, whilst the benchmarking survey informed us that we are currently offering similar services to other institutions, it was not a tool to provide any insight into what was needed by our own researchers, and for this reason that we turned our spotlight onto the research centres at Loughborough for the next survey.

3. Research Centres Survey

The aim of the survey into the use of the University Library by research centres and research institutes at Loughborough University (2009 Lund, Walton and Young) was to discover more about how the University's research community used information and the Library. Whilst the Library has Academic Librarians whose role is to liaise with departments to ensure that staff and students know about and can use information resources effectively, there was concern that the Research Centres and Institutes of the University were not being as well served, as they could be physically separate from academic departments and therefore are not necessarily so closely networked with the Library. However, their work is essential to a research intensive university, like Loughborough, and it was important to analyse their use of Library services and discover if they simply knew about them.

A team of three worked on the project which started in March 2008 with the publication of the report planned for the end of September 2008. As there were eight research institutes and thirty-nine research centres across the different faculties of the University, a stratified sample was selected for the survey, as there was not the time or resources to survey every one. Two research centres from each of the three faculties were selected to ensure that there was a spread of disciplines and size. It was also decided at an early stage to survey administrative staff, as well as academic staff and research associates. We wanted to find how information needs varied amongst the different roles and whether administrative staff might be being used as information brokers.

Rather than just have one method to survey the sample, a variety was chosen to provide both quantitative and qualitative data. The first phase was to discover how many people in the selected centres were borrowing the Library stock or using the inter-library loan service. This quantitative data was obtained from the library management system, ALEPH, and immediately indicated that usage of both services was not high by the vast majority of research centre staff in the sample.

The second phase was to discover which resources the staff were using; whether they were provided by the Library or not; and whether they were using any of the other research support services or knew about them. All of the staff in the six research centres, we had chosen, were surveyed. There were eighty-nine individuals within the sample and so the only practical method for data collection was a questionnaire. As UCCASS survey software had proved effective in the benchmarking survey, it was used again. Mainly tick box questions were used, to make the questionnaire quick to complete and provide data that could be analysed easily. However, as it was also important to obtain qualitative data to try to provide greater understanding of the reasons behind the statistics, there were free-text areas provided. The survey was piloted by a separate research centre, the Library and Information Statistics Unit, to check that the questionnaire was understandable and easy to complete. The areas covered by the questionnaire included: how often different types of information were used; where information was located; training needs; and use of library research support services at Loughborough and elsewhere.

The construction and revision of the questionnaire took longer than the benchmarking survey as there were more questions and a broader mix of types. This unfortunately meant that it was distributed in June rather than April/May, as had been originally planned. It was distributed via individual, personal emails, which was time-consuming but it was hoped that a personal touch would increase the response rate. There were 47 responses (52%) which included all of the sample centres and types of staff. Individuals were asked to include their name, centre and the type of role they had, so that potential interview candidates for the final stage of the survey could be identified, as well as enabling us to check that there was a mixture of respondents.

The final phase of the survey was to look even deeper into the types of information sources used by individuals in their work and to tease out how they currently used Library services or might want services to develop. The potential interviewees were selected from those who had completed the questionnaire. Their individual staff web pages were checked to see how experienced as researchers or members of staff they were, so that there was a mixture of experience, as well as a variety of roles. There were ten interviews altogether, which included individuals from all of the six research centres. A template for the interviews was constructed so that they all followed a similar structure and covered similar points. This also enabled the data to be collated effectively within key themes. The main sections of the interview included: the individual's use of books and journals (of whatever format); their perceptions and use of Library systems and services; and what the Library could do to help their research or work in the research centre. The interviewer took notes rather than taping the interview, which made the data collection less reliable than transcription but there was not time for this to take place. The interviews were held over the summer vacation, although research trips and holidays meant that this part of the data collection took longer than anticipated with some of the interviews not taking place until late September. This meant that once again data analysis and report writing took place during the busiest time of the year. The report was not published until early 2009, three months later than anticipated.

The research centres survey allowed the Library to deepen its knowledge about how research centres currently use information and library services, as well as providing ideas for the future. It demonstrated where the Library and its resources sat within their research world and, as had been suspected, for many people in the sample, it often had an invisible role, if it had a role at all. It was quite sobering but important to know. However, a weakness with the survey was the size of its sample. Eighty-nine individuals out of the total number of 1042 research and research and teaching staff (2008 Loughborough University) is only 0.09%. Whilst 1042 is not the total number research centre staff, it is the total number of staff that the Library's research support services should be reaching. The sample had to be small to be manageable but it means that care had to be taken not to rely solely on the conclusions for service development. However, despite this, it has provided some evidence to support ideas for new services and developments that could be investigated. For example, there is evidence that some staff do not know about Library services that could be very helpful to them, such as Academic Librarians. Some of the interviewees appreciated learning of their existence during the interview process and have used them since, which suggests that marketing these services more effectively could be productive both for the Library and the individuals concerned. The Library has recently instigated a campaign to include Academic Librarian contact details on all departmental web pages to increase their visibility beyond the Library. The interviews suggested that researchers do not need information at all times in a project and so publicity and services should be targeted at key points in a project, such as at the beginning when researchers could finding their way into a new subject area, or when they are preparing a bid.

All three phases of data collection were successful in providing the information sought and they complemented each other well. In retrospect, the depth of certain questions in the questionnaire could have been improved to have obtained more insight into which 'websites' and which 'electronic Library services' were being used. However, such questions had been consciously sacrificed to ensure that the questionnaire was not too long, in case it became too off-putting to complete. The questions were followed up in the interviews but as interviewees equated to less than a quarter of our respondents, we are uneasy about drawing firm conclusions without further investigations. The research centres survey was a very valuable experience but was ambitious in the time scale. A study using the three different phases could, however, be repeated for just one specific research centre or academic department to learn more about its individual information needs and use of the Library.

4. Conclusion

Both the benchmarking survey and the research centres survey were very valuable tools to discover more about what academic libraries currently offer researchers and how researchers use their services and other information resources. Both surveys provided Loughborough University Library with information that it had not known and is now using to improve its services to current and future researchers. Different methods were tested and proved to have both strengths and weaknesses. The benchmarking survey provided sound results as it was based on a large enough sample to provide trustworthy quantitative results. The qualitative data that was obtained from the small sample in the research centres survey provided the Library with very valuable insight into what it is like to be a researcher. The empathy that this latter type of data produced will be extremely helpful in the construction of future services for this group of Library user (or potential user), admittedly with a little more research to check that it is not unique. The key point for both surveys is that they have both been used to improve Library services to researchers. Whilst no completely new services have been developed as yet, services are being enhanced, such as the improved publicity for academic librarians and extra researcher only training sessions. It is doubtful that either of these initiatives would have taken place without the results of the surveys to prompt them. More changes will come and so the time and effort involved in both projects has been worthwhile and will continue to benefit both researchers and Loughborough University Library itself.

References

1994 Group (2009). *About us*, <http://www.1994group.ac.uk/aboutus.php> [Accessed 1st April 2009].

Loughborough University (2009). *Facts and figures*, <http://www.lboro.ac.uk/admin/ar/planning/stats/factsfigures/2008/35646%20facts%20and%20figures-2008.pdf> [Accessed 30th March 2009].

Lund, P. and Young, H. (2008). *Benchmarking survey of research support provided by 1994 Group libraries, Loughborough University Library*, Loughborough. < http://www.lboro.ac.uk/library/about/PDFs/1994.pdf> [Accessed 24th April 2009].

Lund, P., Walton, G. and Young H. (2009) *Use of the University Library by research centres and research institutes at Loughborough University*, Loughborough University Library, Loughborough.< http://www.lboro.ac.uk/library/about/PDFs/research.pdf> [Accessed 24th April 2009].

RIN and CURL (2007) *Researchers' use of academic libraries and their services,* RIN, London.

Russell Group (2009), *The Russell Group*, <http://www.russellgroup.ac.uk> [Accessed 21st April 2009].

SCONUL (2007). *SCONUL annual library statistics*, SCONUL, London.

UCCASS (2009). *Unit Command Climate Assessment and Survey System (UCCASS)*, <http://www.bigredspark.com/survey.html> [Accessed 21st April 2009].

Access and Use of Information by Primary Health Care Providers in Rural Uganda: A Qualitative Approach[1]

Maria G. N. Musoke

Makerere University, P. O. Box 7062, Kampala, Uganda, Africa
Phone: 256-414-533735; Cell: 256-772-654960; Fax: 256-414-540374
E-mail: mmusoke@med.mak.ac.ug; maria.gnmusoke@yahoo.com

Abstract: The article summarises findings from a qualitative study that was conducted in rural Uganda, East Africa. The main aim of the study was to investigate the accessibility and use of health information in the lower echelons of Primary Health Care (PHC). Women, as PHC providers in an African family, were focussed on, as well as health workers. An interview schedule that consisted of open questions and one relating to health information critical incidents was used. A holistic inductive paradigm was adopted with a grounded theory analysis. The findings highlight a model of information behaviour that was driven by the value and impact of information unlike previous information models, which have been driven by information needs. The value and effect of information on PHC was as experienced and reported by the interviewees. Implications of the study and areas for further research are highlighted.

Keywords: Information models; Value of information; Information use; Information behaviour; Primary health care; Women; Information activities in rural Africa.

1. Introduction

Over the years, information related problems in the health sector have raised the concern of information professionals, health workers and social scientists. Some have suggested that in order to implement the planned health strategies, there is a need to improve not only the health information services but also the understanding of why and how to use the information. To many African health professionals and librarians, information is available but not accessible; while to some, information is neither available nor accessible (Lowan & Bukachi, 1998; Musoke, 2007). Therefore, although there is a need to produce more relevant information in Africa, the greatest challenge is to ensure that what is available so far, can be accessed.

The development of effective information services for rural people, and the policies governing their implementation and use, depends on ample knowledge of rural people's information environment and behaviour. Hardly any empirical data exists on this topic in Uganda. Focusing research on rural health workers, who are professionally isolated, is an important step in improving their information infrastructure. This would indirectly enhance information provision to the communities they serve. At a local level, the study is important because the majority of Ugandans[Ψ2] do not see high level health workers when they seek health care; it is provided within the family, community or health units run by nurses and clinical officers.

Many information studies in the developed world have focused on information systems and retrieval (Spink, 1999; Vakkari, 1999). However, the interest of an information researcher in a rural African setting can hardly be on such topics. Rather, the attention is on information in every day life. In a post civil war situation of an African rural area, can the use of available information make a difference to the lives of rural people?!

The main aim of the study was, therefore, to investigate the accessibility and use of health information by women and health workers, who are at the lowest level of Primary Health Care (PHC) service delivery in rural Uganda. This would advance the understanding of the role of information in the health sector and the information processes involved. Therefore, the main concern of the study was not to quantify data, but rather to understand issues surrounding access and use of information in rural Uganda, and how women and health workers perceived and interpreted these issues.

In this study, the term information was used in a broad sense to include the subjective and objective aspects of information, as well as the behaviours associated with information acquisition or use.

2. Methodology

Given the nature of the study, a holistic inductive paradigm was used with a grounded theory analysis. Although the study took a grounded theory approach, it differed from the grounded theory as originally defined by Glaser & Strauss[5] in that it did not adopt a theoretical sampling strategy. The sample was determined by the PHC set up[6], and followed a purposeful sampling strategy as described by Patton (1990). The study, therefore, focussed on two categories of people who form the base of PHC service delivery, namely the women and health workers. The total sample was eighty-two (48 women leaders and 34 health workers).

Face-to-face interviews were conducted using an interview schedule that consisted of open questions and one relating to health information critical incidents. Two sets were used: one for the women and the other for health workers. As a semi-structured (open-ended) interview method was used to collect data, it was preferred to do a cross-case analysis for each question in the interview schedule. This involved grouping together and comparing answers from different interviewees to common questions. The analyst then abstracted from the data and generated concepts and categories inductively. This was proceeded by open and selective coding, based on the original Glaser & Strauss (1967) approach.

Some interviewee responses are given in the findings. These are based on verbatim records (translated from vernacular to English in the case of women), and are quoted in italics. For confidentiality reasons, each quotation indicates the interviewee number rather than the name.

3. Findings

The interviewees reported the difference information had made in their personal and professional lives, and the frustrations and consequences of failure to find or use the needed information. The article is going to focus on this finding. It should be noted that the fully analysed findings of the study (Musoke, 2001) resulted into an interaction-value model where the value of information was the core category, while the moderation of constraints and the interaction with sources for latent or apparent needs are the two main categories which make up the model (Musoke, 2007). However, given the size limitation of this article, it is not possible to discuss all the findings here.

Role of information

The meaning information made to people after being accessed, used and interpreted, and its significance and role as perceived, experienced and reported by the interviewees were conceptualised as the value people attributed to information. The interviewees, as users of information, judged the information they accessed and attributed, or did not attribute, value to it.

Interviewees reported, for example, that when they accessed information and used it, some of that information changed their states of knowledge, values, beliefs, attitudes and behaviour. This led to the various actions that put the knowledge acquired into practice or applied the information gained in various ways, which improved and promoted health. For example, when women received relevant health information, used it and found it valuable, they carried out various information dissemination sessions both formal and informal about, say, the causes and prevention of illnesses/diseases; so, they interacted with their networks to promote health. The value and impact of information also made health workers disseminate information to others in various ways (print, oral, visual). These information dissemination activities were driven by the value of information, and involved interaction with individuals, groups and communities in the case of women leaders interviewed; or fellow health workers and patients in the case of health workers. Therefore, those individuals who had been constrained to access information in one way, accessed it in another way (and a series of processes of information access and use went on, as value-reported information led to further interactions). Hence, the 'interaction-value' model of health information access and use that emerged from the overall findings (Musoke, 2001; 2007).

The value of information, as reported in the findings, was quite subjective, although it was shared with others as indicated above. Hence, this study's approach to the value of information is what Saracevic & Kantor (1997) referred to as 'perceived value approach', which is "Subjective valuation by users of information, of the value or benefits of given information. This assumes that users can recognise the value of information or the benefits gained/lost. If scales are used, it assumes that they can place the value in some ranking" (p.532).

Health workers reported the value of information mainly from a professional rather than a personal point of view. Information was valuable in clinical work, administration, decision-making, education and training, detection, prevention and control of diseases/health problems. Some examples of the role of information in critical incidents are given below:

"A 12 year old child was brought to the health centre bleeding from the nose profusely. After positioning him properly, I needed to find information about the reaction of one of the medicines I wanted to prescribe because I remembered from my training that this particular medicine, if not administered properly, could cause serious clotting which may result into death. So, I rushed and referred to a manual (Standard treatment guide) which fortunately provided the information about the correct dose of the medicine; I then gave it to the child and he got well" (Clinical officer -Bh8).

"Recently I examined a patient and thought he had an intestinal obstruction; on opening, I found a ruptured gall bladder yet I had never done cholecystectomy before. I called in a colleague; before he came, I decided to read the CME materials, which provided the details of what to do. When my colleague came, he brought a copy of Primary Surgery textbook by King which also gives step by step account of what to do in order to carry out that operation. These assisted us to successfully do the operation (Doctor-Lh1)".

Women reported that most of the information they had accessed was very valuable and they used it in the prevention and treatment of diseases, to know the causes of illness, to promote health, take decisions, make choices, overcome constraints and misconceptions, cope with illnesses, support the community/self help, change behaviour, change attitude, participate in information dissemination/awareness raising, and for general health knowledge. Some examples of the value of information are:

Information was valuable in the prevention of illnesses through knowing their causes. Knowledge of how diseases are caused and transmitted was reported to have led to the control of disease vectors, water borne diseases and health promotion in general.

> *"I learned how to control the breeding of mosquitoes which transmit malaria, so I do everything possible to keep this home free from bushes and stagnant water where mosquitoes breed and to close windows and doors before dark, sleep under a net... Since I started putting these measures in place, my household members take long to suffer from malaria; actually, we may spend almost a year without an attack, yet in the past, it was a frequent problem in this home" (Woman-Bw2).*

Information that was used to prevent diseases was also reported to have had some economic benefits.

> *"I learned about the importance of immunisation and my children got immunised. Since then, they have been a lot healthier... This reduces our medical expenses because they no longer get diseases like measles which used to disturb them" (Woman-Iw5).*

Some women interviewees also reported that the information they received assisted them in disproving concepts and/or overcoming beliefs and attitudes about family planning and other medical practices. Once these were overcome, women made decisions to use contraceptives, use medical instead of traditional practices/services, etc. Hence, 'overcome misconceptions' triggered off various **decisions**. Some decisions were taken as a direct result of overcoming misconceptions, while others were taken as a result of the value of information in general. Some women reported that among the various decisions they took was to change behaviour in order to prevent diseases such as AIDS. This can be illustrated as follows:

Value of information decision making behavioural change prevention

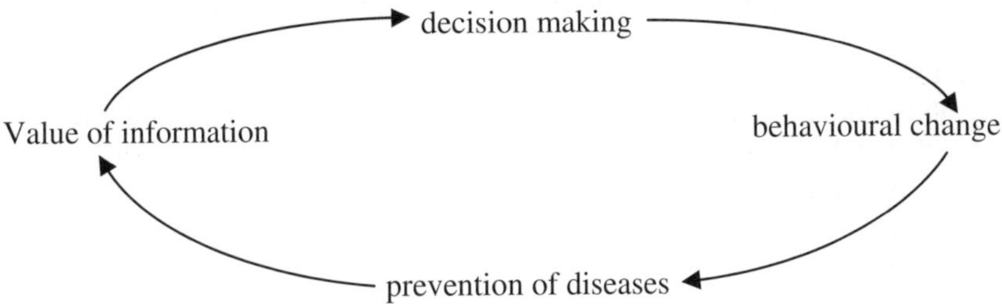

Figure 1: Role of information in promoting health

The study found out that awareness about AIDS was quite high, in fact the highest of all the health topics reported. That high awareness seems to have been translated into behavioural change, which has greatly checked the spread of AIDS in Uganda. This development has been supported by national and international statistics[Ψ3], which indicate that the HIV/AIDS rate had reduced from 30% in 1980 to 6.4% in 2008 mainly due to effective information provision and behavioural interventions[Ψ 3]. While celebrating the World AIDS day (1st December, 2008), it was reported that the reduction in the national prevalence rate is "an achievement attributed largely to the country's rapid acknowledgement of the crisis it faced, the roll out of national prevention and treatment messages and its embrace of open discourse around causes and solutions to the virus" $^{\Psi}$2.

Some examples were cited when health workers reported that the information they had accessed enabled them to make decisions concerning personal health e.g. diet. The data from women, on the other hand, showed that the value of health information was mainly to the family, then personal, and community in that order. What made the findings so distinctly African, was the extended family aspect. Women reported the value of information in relation to its effect or benefit to the nuclear and extended family members.

Therefore, the value of information in this study was mainly at two levels, namely, the social level because it served communities, and an individual level. The two levels were, however, interdependent. Health workers shared their individual valuable experiences with patients on such issues as diet or other professional matters with colleagues. Women leaders did the same.

The value of information in the prevention of diseases and promotion of health as demonstrated in the findings agrees with the WHO report, which points out that: "Both the public health and the personal care interventions have contributed to reversing the urban - rural differences in health status; better health among urban populations is due more to the application of improved knowledge than higher incomes in cities"[11].

It therefore follows that although rural areas had low incomes, they could enjoy better health if they accessed information to enhance their knowledge. Hence, factors which negate information access and use in rural areas need to be addressed in order that rural communities may reap the benefits of improved health knowledge.

Finally, the findings highlighted the various needs for information, as well as the demands people made. Citing an example, health workers reported that when they go for, say, immunisation programmes in rural areas, women insist that the sessions should start with health education. Furthermore, health workers reported throughout the study about the need for continuing education to keep up to date, and how out-dated knowledge had constrained their activities. The study findings, therefore, differ from Nordberg's view[12] who claimed that there was low demand for information from health workers and that they do not use information resources even where they are accessible.

4. Consequences of failure to access or use the needed information

The findings confirmed further the importance of providing timely information. For example, during the interviews, some women and health workers reported that they needed information about Ebola, but they had not been able to get it. If the available information on prevention was disseminated when these needs were identified, and after the Ebola problem was reported in neighbouring countries, Ebola may not have claimed so many lives in 2000 and 2001. In many situations therefore, information is available but not accessible; this leaves many health information needs unmet, which is a challenge to health information providers.

Furthermore, some of the incidents narrated revealed the consequences of delayed access or lack of appropriate advice or information, which led to the death of family members in the critical situations reported by five of the forty-eight women interviewed (Bw1, 4, 9; Lw4 & 9). In some cases, there was conflicting information or advice and it was difficult to judge which one to use. Hence, the need for timely and appropriate information. Provision "of the right information at the right time by the year 2000" was one of WHO's declarations, which seems to have remained on paper. In rural Uganda, it was not easy to access the right information or information source at the right time.

It was also noted that women's perceptions of illness or health problem and their preliminary interpretation of the illness play a role in their choice of source of information and the source tends to vary according to women's own beliefs and knowledge about illness, and the availability of relatives, friends or neighbours who become a primary source of information when they confirm the women's interpretation or assist in identifying and labelling the symptoms.

The study also revealed that factors such as gender or religious practices and values interfered in both women's and health workers' activities especially on topics e.g. contraceptives and AIDS control. Hence, even though women interacted with health workers, accessed information about contraceptives, and derived meaning out of the information they accessed in the interactions, some of them reported that they were not able to use and apply that information due to the social forces around them.

In some situations, unmet information needs led to constraints to information use. The women's data highlight various interdependencies and relationships between unmet information needs, sources of information and constraints to information use, e.g. regarding the immunisation programme. Although all the women interviewed in the study reported that they accessed information about immunisation, the information they had accessed left some unanswered questions. For example, some women needed information about the safety of the vaccine; when this information need remained unsatisfied, those women decided not to have their children immunised, hence they were constrained to use the information they accessed about immunisation dates, venue and age of children to be immunised. If women obtained information/clarification about, for example, the safety of the vaccine and what caused children's deaths after the previous immunisation session (to satisfy their information needs), the constraints could be overcome and the information used by taking children for immunisation. Hence, the more information needs are met or satisfied, other considerations being held constant, the less the constraints to information use, and therefore, the more successful the preventive measures such as polio immunisation or family planning would become.

It was also observed in the study that although there had been massive campaigns for polio immunisation, and only 'rumours' or word of mouth messages about the possible relationship between polio immunisation and the origins of HIV/AIDS, some people seem to have responded to the latter by resisting to participate in the immunisation exercise. Hence, some informal but negative messages from friends or relatives tended to have almost as much impact as the massive positive messages from formal and authoritative sources.

The unmet information needs, therefore, remained a strong constraint to information

use, as well as a challenge to the health of Ugandans.
Information provided by health workers to patients was generally considered insufficient. The findings of this study have shown, for example, that while the majority of women interviewees preferred to get more information (monitors) about their long-term and life-threatening illnesses or the illnesses of those they nursed, two women reported that information would make them more worried and hence, worsen their situation (blunters). It is, therefore, important that health workers assess patients' general orientation to information so that the monitors are provided with as much appropriate information as possible to assist them to cope with the illnesses. Health workers have been reported to provide too little information to people, something that needs to be addressed. On the other hand, the blunters, who may not need information at all or who may need some information but not all, should have their choice respected.

Finally, it was noted that the problems of limited access to information caused by having few or hardly any health workers reaching some rural areas, lack of time for the women to attend meetings, listen to the radio, etc., led the local authority council (LC) executive committee members to take on an information dissemination role (for the benefit of their communities) either by inviting health workers to give talks in LC meetings or by the LC executive members moving door to door to ensure that emergency health information reaches every member of their community. At a slightly higher level of abstraction, this relationship seemed to be one in which the value of information, the need for information access and use, and the prevailing constraints in rural Uganda had led, among other things, to the institution and flourishing of an informal mechanism of health information provision.

Nuijten (1992) observed that such local practices or initiatives are often denied their due importance and labelled as 'disorganised', 'traditional' or 'indigenous' in development studies literature. These debates, however, remain far removed from the everyday practice of the people as this study has demonstrated.

5. Conclusions

The article has illustrated that where appropriate information was available, accessible, used and applied, it solved emergency or critical health needs and saved lives, as well as promoting health; the reverse was true when health workers or women as care givers failed to access and use the required information.

In addition to supporting their professional work, well informed health workers are a key element in informing the women's social network which was reported to be an important source of information, and hence a positive element in the promotion of health and the health care of rural families. Amongst the implications identified are:

- The need to adopt a participatory and multi-sectoral approach involving front-line health workers, the Local Authority (LCs), the Faith-based organisations, women's groups and other development organisations for the effective provision of information to women.
- The use of social networks that have proved valuable and effective as sources of information need to be recognised and supported.
- In this part of the world, there was still a need to pay attention to printed materials which were still inadequately provided in some rural health units,

and yet the infrastructure for accessing electronic sources was not fully developed.

- Improving access to information on radio and other simple technologies was a popular demand by the interviewees. Repackaging information to increase its accessibility was recommended.

Besides advancing our knowledge, qualitative research provides the necessary details needed to design systems and improve service delivery. Furthermore, access to health information has become topical making the study findings relevant to local and international agencies. It is, therefore, not surprising that the topic of "access to health information and knowledge sharing" was, for example, part of the Rockefeller Foundation's eHealth sponsored series of conferences from 12th July to 8th August 2008 entitled "Making the eHealth Connection: Global Partnerships, Local Solutions." International institutions such as the World Health Organisation (WHO), Commonwealth Secretariat, the G8, European Union, the Commission for Africa and the Health Metrics Network have established eHealth action plans and programmes. Despite advancements, substantial questions remain regarding the best strategies for eHealth system design, funding, implementation, and capacity building, particularly in developing or "Global South" countries. The issue of how to leverage eHealth to advance health services, particularly in low-resource settings remains a challenge (Rokefeller Foundation, 2008).

Areas for further research

Several areas for further research were identified in the study (Musoke, 2001); for this paper, only three are presented:

1. The 'interactivity' in the 'Interaction-Value' model was added to the Slawson and Shaugnessy formula by Smith[14].

   The formula is $U = \frac{R \times V}{W}$

   Where U = usefulness of the information to health workers, R= relevance of the information, V= validity of the information, and W= work to access the information. In words, the most useful information for health workers is information that is relevant to their practice, is valid, and does not take too much work to access. "After listening to a presentation by Maria Musoke, a researcher from Uganda, on the usefulness of information to rural health workers in Uganda, I added 'interactivity' to the top line of the equation. The information is still more useful if you can interact with the source and interrogate it. The formula provides a test of the ways in which doctors look for information they need."(Smith, 2002). Studies to test this formula are recommended.

2. Coping and information behaviour: The findings of this study have shed some light on the information needs and information behaviour of people with long-term illnesses, e.g. sickle cell anaemia, asthma, HIV/ AIDS and paralysis. These findings just emerged from the interviews. There is therefore a need for further and more specific research on coping and information behaviour. Baker[15] also observed that because very few studies have focussed on people with chronic diseases, information about monitoring and blunting behaviour in the face of long-term stress remains

relatively scarce.

More extensive research on larger samples should be undertaken to test the findings, which emerged from the qualitative data in this study.

References

Baker, L.M. (1995), “A new method for studying patients' information needs and information seeking patterns”, in Lloyd-Williams, M. (Ed.), Health Information Management Research, Proceedings of the 1st International Symposium, University of Sheffield, Department of Information Studies, Centre for Health Information Management Research, Sheffield, 5-7 April, pp. 67-75.

Glaser, B.G., Strauss, A. (1967), *The Discovery of Grounded Theory: Strategies for Qualitative Research*, Aldine de Gruyter, New York, NY.

Jing Bai et al. (2005). Query expansion using term relationships in language models for information retrieval. Proceedings of the 14th Association for Computing Machinery international conference on Information and knowledge management

Kigongo, C. (1997), "Primary health care: role and functions", *The Uganda Health Information Digest*, Vol. 1 No.1, pp.65-68.

Lowan, B., Bukachi, F. & Xavier, R. (1998). "Health information in the developing world", *Lancet*, **352**, October suppl 34 - 37.

Musoke, M. G. (2001). Health information access and use in rural Uganda: an interaction-value model. PhD. Thesis, University of Sheffield.

Musoke, Maria G. N. (2007). “Access to health information: The African users’ perspective.” In: Mlambo, A. (ed): *African Scholarly Publishing Essays*. African Books Collective Ltd., Oxford. ISBN:1-904855-83-0

Musoke, Maria G. N. (2007). “Information behaviour of primary health care providers in rural Uganda: an interaction-value model”. *Journal of Documentation,* vol. **63** no3, pp. 299-322.

Nordberg E. (1998). The gap between need and demand. In: *Proceedings of Health Information Forum Workshop 3, November 1998.* [www.inasp.org.uk] page 2 -3. Site visited at: 3/4/00.

Nuijten, M. (1992), "Local organisation as organising practices: rethinking rural institutions", in Long, N., Long, A. (Eds),*Battlefields of Knowledge: The Interlocking of Theory and Practice in Social Research and Development*, Routledge, London, .

Rockefeller Foundation (2008). From Silos to Systems: Bellagio eHealth Call to Action on “Better Health for All Through Integrated, Person-Centered eHealth Systems”. http://www.ehealth-connection.org/.

Saracevic, T., Kantor, P. (1997), "Studying the value of library and information services", *Journal of the American Society for Information Science*, Vol. 48 No.6, pp.527-42.

Smith, R. (2002), “Patient-oriented evidence that matters – POEM – a week”, Editorial, BMJ, Vol. 325 No. 983.

Spink, A. (1999), “Towards a theoretical framework for information retrieval in an information seeking context”, in Wilson, T.D. and Allen, D.K. (Eds), Exploring the Contexts of Information Behaviour, Proceedings of the 2nd International Conference on Research in Information Needs, Seeking and Use in Different Contexts, Taylor Graham, London, 13-15 August, .

Patton, M.Q. (1990), *Qualitative Evaluation and Research Methods*, Sage Publications, London

Vakkari, P. (1999), "Task complexity, problem structure and information actions: integrating studies on information seeking and retrieval", *Information Processing & Management*, Vol. 35 pp.819-37.

WHO (2000), Health Systems: Improving Performance, The World Health Organisation (WHO), Geneva (The World Health Report 2000).

Notes

[1] This paper is based on an earlier paper presented at ICML, Brazil, 2005. It has been revised and updated.

Ψ2 Uganda had a population of 31.4 million people in 2008, with slightly more males than females. About 70% of the population live in rural areas. (Source: Uganda Demographics profile, 2008).

Ψ 3 In November 2003, the African-American Institute gave an Award to Uganda in recognition of its fight against HIV/AIDS ...The Institute hailed Uganda's dramatic reduction in HIV/AIDS rate in the last ten years owing to vigorous public education campaigns ...www.monitor.co.ug/news November, 7th 2003.

Ψ2 HIV/AIDS in Uganda by Kelly, A ...www.guardian.co.uk/katine/2008/dec/01/world-aids-day-uganda.

The Impact of the Electronic Resources in Portuguese Academic Libraries: Results of a Qualitative Survey

Luiza Baptista Melo[1] and Cesaltina Pires[2]

[1]CIDEHUS, University of Évora, Portugal
[2]CEFAGE-UE and Management Department, University of Évora, Portugal

Abstract: In the last 10 years there have been big changes in the Portuguese academic libraries services as in other academic libraries over the world. These changes include the adoption of automatic catalogues and the electronic access to bibliographic data bases and scientific journals in full text. Nowadays physical and digital sources are together. Professors, students and researchers are able to access simultaneous to a great amount of quality information pay and open access. The Portuguese Government has been investing to improve the access to the production of knowledge so as to develop the country. It is important to know the return on the investments in university libraries. The purpose of this paper is to identify the impact of the electronic sources in the Portuguese academic libraries. This paper describes an ongoing project to assess:

- The use of electronic scientific information and the correlation to the scientific production of the Portuguese academic community according to standard performance measures indicators and bibliometrics data.
- The economic value of these library services. In order to estimate in monetary terms the value of these services for end-users we use the contingent valuation method (CVM). This study reports the results of a qualitative e-survey of academic community.

Keywords: Academic libraries; Electronic sources; Impact evaluation; Bibliometrics; Contingent valuation.

1. Introduction

During the last two decades, the idea of academic library quality services has been changing. Nowadays, efficiency, effectiveness and users satisfaction are not synonymous of large collections of publications. At present, the university libraries offer several services to disseminate and make available the information and knowledge to users.

Librarians have to manage human and information resources with the following main goals: to provide fast access to information; to satisfy the expectations of the users and to reduce the costs of the services. As a consequence, it is not surprising that one can find a vast and increasing body of literature on these subjects providing multiple methodologies to improve the quality and performance of the library services.

In an age of constant change, due to the information technologies development, to the digitalization of the society and to an increasing pressure to reduce the costs of academic library services, librarians and information managers all over the word have used assessment models and performance indicators in an effort to improve the quality of the services. It is important to evaluate the services because we must know if "we are providing the best possible service at right time, to the right people and at the right price" Davies (2008).

Academic Portuguese users seek for and use information in very different ways. This paper explores some aspects of the outputs, outcomes assessment and the impact of electronic resources services in the Portuguese academic libraries.

Our study has three main steps:

1. Selection of the performance indicators and the scenario of the contingent valuation method (CVM) to be used.
2. Data collection and analysis.
3. Identification of the economic value of these library services in monetary terms, evaluation of the use of the *e*-resources (what type of scientific information, where and how often)

The selection of the performance indicators to be evaluated is based on the International Standards ISO 11620:1998, Amendment 1:2003 additional performance indicators for libraries and ISO 2789:2006.

In order to estimate in monetary terms the value of these services for end-users we use the contingent valuation method (CVM) and we evaluated the electronic scientific information consortium, B-on, available in the Portuguese academic libraries. This study reports the results of a qualitative e-survey of Portuguese academic community.

The remainder of this paper is organized as follows: in Section 2 we present the methodology used. Section 3 describes our sample and Section 4 presents and discusses the results. The final section concludes the paper.

2. Methodology

In order to evaluate the electronic services in the Portuguese universities libraries we have assumed the following International Standards ISO 11620:1998, 1:2003 Amendment, ISO 2789:2006 performance indicators: percentage of the target population using traditional library, percentage of the target population using digital library, percentage of the target population using both libraries, preferred location of use of the electronic services, service used (data bases, electronic collections, pay e-journals or Open Access journals), distribution of the user time saved.

According to Noonan (2003) "contingent valuation methodology (CVM) has been increasingly applied to cultural resources. This valuation employs survey to elicit a willingness to pay (WTP) from individuals for hypothetical changes in some good or services". Mazzanti (2002) refers that "the surveys ask respondents to rate, rank, or choose among several alternatives described in terms of various levels of attributes". In the last decade, some authors have used the contingent valuation method for monetary valuations of public, academic and special libraries services. For special and academic libraries we highlight the following studies: Harless and Frank (1999) estimate the economic value that patrons attach to reference desk service in an academic library; Chung (2007) presents a new approach to measure the economic value of the KDI School Library and Luther (2008) describes a project "that creates a quantifiable measure and a compelling position for the University of Illinois at Urbana-Champaign Library that demonstrated economic value to the university administration."

In our paper we consider the contingent valuation methodology (CVM) to valuate in monetary terms the electronic scientific information consortium, B-on, available in the Portuguese academic libraries. The model developed in our study is based on the time and costs saved by users and the benefits generated by using electronic library resources. Benefit-cost analysis intends to estimate and compare Portuguese electronic scientific information consortium, B-on, costs and the benefits to the academic community.

Data Collection

The data collection process included one questionnaire that we have sent by e-mail to thirty three Public Portuguese Universities, since 15th January 2009 to 15th March 2009. In this study we present the data that we got during these two months. This e-survey is yet ongoing.

The questionnaire was based on the International Standard performance indicators and the contingent valuation method (CVM) to assess academic library electronic services. The scenario designed in this research to valuate electronic services of the Portuguese academic libraries is based on a hypothetical idea. The WTP scenario describes an economic situation which forces the Portuguese electronic scientific information consortium, B-on, to stop. It is suggested that the consortium B-on will continue if the users maintain the cost of these services paying a monthly tax with values between 5 to 50 Euros. The range proposed in this study was based in data from the FCCN (2008).

Since there exists a very large number of potential users among the participating universities, the questionnaire was applied to a sample of the population. In order to make inference about the population, we used stratified sampling in each institution participating in the study.

Data Analysis

The first step of the analysis was to summarize the data collected. The next step involved the comparison between different types of users and between various scientific disciplines. We considered four groups of users: Professor/Researcher, PhD Student, Undergraduate/Master Students and Others. The scientific disciplines were aggregated in the following six groups:

- Physiques and Chemistry Sciences (Physics, Astronomy, Chemistry and Materials Science);
- Humanities and Social Sciences (Social Science, Economics, Accounting, Business, Management, Finance, Humanities Science, Library and Information Science and Decision Science);
- Earth and Planetary Sciences (Environmental Science, Earth and Planetary Sciences);

- Life and Health Sciences (Veterinary, Pharmacology, Nursing, Neuroscience, Medicine, Immunology and Microbiology, Health Professions, Dentistry and Agricultural, Biological Sciences, Biochemistry, Genetics and Molecular Biology);
- Engineering (Engineering, Energy and Chemical Engineering);
- Mathematics and Computer Sciences (Mathematics and Computer Science).

We analyzed the data with descriptive statistics (frequency tables and graphs). Next, for several pairs of variables we computed contingency tables and performed the chi-square test ($\chi 2$). The chi-square test is used to assess two types of comparison: tests of goodness of fit and tests of independence (Maroco, 2007). A test of goodness of fit establishes whether or not an observed frequency distribution differs from a theoretical distribution. A test of independence assesses whether paired observations on two variables, expressed in a contingency table, are independent of each other – for example, whether people from different groups differ in the frequency of the use of electronic scientific journals. In our case we used the chi-square test to analyze whether two variables are independent or not.

Our statistical analysis was performed with the Statistical Package for the Social Sciences (SPSS) and with Excel (using the Data Analysis Tool).

Description of the Sample

The assessment was based on an electronic questionnaire for all the Public Portuguese academic community (professors, researchers, students, administrative staff and everyone who usually uses academic services). During two months we received 1786 answers. We divided the population into four groups: Professor/Researcher 32.4%, PhD Student 7.8%, Master and Undergraduate Students 27.8% and Other 32.0% (administrative and library staff). We also considered six groups of scientific subjects: Physiques and Chemistry Sciences, Humanities and Social Sciences, Earth and Planetary Sciences, Life and Health Sciences, Engineering and Mathematics and Computer Sciences.

3. Analysis of the Results

In this section we present the preliminary results of our study. We start by analyzing the results of user e-surveys. These results are important for knowing the user's behaviour and what users think about the scientific electronic information access in the Portuguese academic institutions. Next we analyse the results obtained for various performance indicators and estimate benefit-cost based on user time saved and the contingent valuation method (CVM).

Results for the performance indicators

The user e-surveys involved 1786 answers. Table 1 and 2 summarize the results of these surveys based on the International Standard performance indicators. Table 1 shows the percentage use of the various types of libraries and the place where users access electronic library services. Table 2 presents the percentage of users who know the Portuguese electronic scientific information consortium, B-on, and the percentage use of the various information e-resources.

The first item in Table 1 indicates the percentages of respondents who said they had used the library services in the previous 12 months. The figure show that this percentage varied from 4.3 to 63.3, depending on the various library services and the type of user. The data reveal the extent to which the services have been used. The higher scores (63.3, 50.4, 40.4 and 58.2) shows that the majority of users have used both digital and traditional academic library services. The only group of users for whom this is not true are the Undergraduate/Master students, who use more traditional libraries. It is also interesting to note that among Professors/Researchers and PhD Students there is a relatively large proportion of users who only use digital library services.

Table 1: Results of user e-surveys (percentages of the target population using traditional library, traditional and digital library, both libraries, preferred location of use of the electronic services)

User	Tradicional library (%)	Digital and tradicional library (%)	Digital library (%)	Do not use libraries (%)	Where do you access library e-resources? (%)			
					In the library	In a computer of the university	University campus with your laptop	At home
Professor/Researcher	6.7	63.3	27.2	2.8	6.7	55.4	54.0	51.4
PhD Student	4.3	50.4	38.1	2.2	10.8	46.0	72.0	51.8
Undergraduate/Master Student	45.7	40.4	4.4	9.5	42.5	27.6	58.9	47.7
Other	23.1	58.2	10.5	8.3	43.5	34.3	50.7	45.8

The next item shows the places where e-resources were used (the percentage varied from 6.7 to 72.0). These data reveal that a lot of users have their own laptop and access these libraries services in the university campus (for instance, 72% of the PhD students use this mode of access). In addition a large percentage of Professors/Researchers access scientific information in a computer in the institution but not in the library (55.4%). Around 50% of the users access the library e-resources at home. This suggests that many users access the electronic scientific information well into the night and over the weekend.

Table 2: Service used (Portuguese consortium B-on, bibliographic data bases, paid e-journals in full text and Open Access journals)

User	Kwnoledge of B-on (%)	What type information resources do you use? (%)		
	Yes	Bibliographic data bases	Paid full text journals	Open Access Information
Professor/Researcher	89.4	40.0	84.0	44.6
PhD Student	87.1	41.0	79.9	52.5
Undergraduate/Master Student	39.4	19.7	28.8	17.3
Other	62.8	30.9	50.2	35.3

The first item in Table shows the percentage of users who know the Portuguese electronic scientific information consortium, B-on. Around 90% of the Professors/Researchers and of the PhD Students know this resource. On the contrary, among the Undergraduate/Master Students only 39.4% know this consortium (we have computed this percentage separately for undergraduates and master students, the results are similar for the two groups). This suggests that it is urgent to promote the knowledge of this e-resource among these students. This is particularly true for master students since master programs require more research work than undergraduate ones.

The last item in Table 2 shows information about the percentage use of bibliographic data bases, paid electronic journals and Open Access information. The paid full text journals have the highest percentage use with values ranging from 84.0 for Professors/Researchers to 28.8 for Undergraduate/Master students.

The aim of this project is to provide a detailed analysis of how academic community in Portugal have responded to the provision of scholarly electronic information and how this has shaped their information-seeking behaviour and their use of such e-resources. The next chart, Figure 1, compares the percentage use according to the type of information (bibliographic data bases, paid full text journals and Open Access information) and by subject. The chart reveals several interesting facts. First the highest percentage use values are for paid full text journal independently of the subject. Second academic users have researched Open Access information but the percentage use varies quite a lot among scientific areas. Third the less research-intensive use is in the bibliographic data bases.

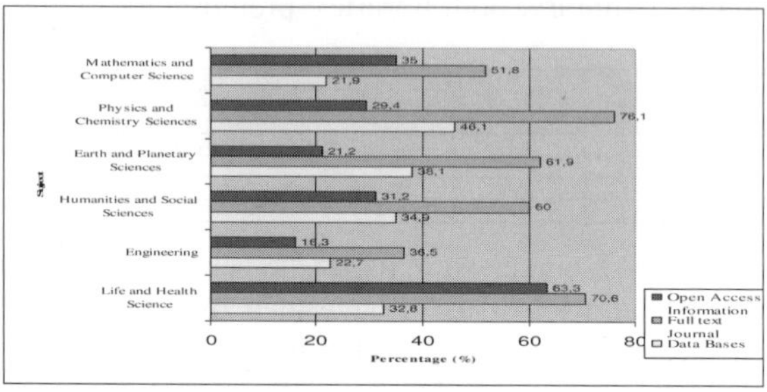

Figure 1: Percentage of use for data bases, paid full text journals and Open Access information by scientific area.

Results for benefit-cost analysis

Table 3 presents the distribution of the user time saved when accessing the Portuguese electronic scientific information consortium B-on. For each group of users we estimated the average time saved per month. The average time saved for Professors/Researcher and PhD Student is quite high (8.79 and 9.85 hours per month, respectively) whereas for Undergraduate/Master Students the average time saved is 4.44 hours per month. The next step involved the calculation of the average time saved in a year as well the estimation of the average time saved for all Professors/Researchers, PhD Students and Undergraduate/Master Students from Portugal, about 402914 users, according to data from GPEARI (2008). The time saved can be converted in monetary terms by multiplying the number of hours saved by the value of time for each type of users. To estimate the value of time we used the salary or scholarships for each group of users, considering data from the Portuguese legislation (professors and researchers salaries, PhD Students financial support and university monitor salary for Undergraduate/Master Students). The idea is that each hour saved in accessing journals can be used in some other activity (for instance, writing papers, working on the PhD or Master theses or preparing classes), thus we can value each hour by the value that it would have in these alternative uses. Adding up the value of the time saved for all the groups we obtained an estimate of the benefits of the Portuguese electronic scientific information consortium, B-on. Using this estimate we calculated the benefit-cost ratio for this resource, obtaining a ratio 1:5.35 based on the estimated benefits of time saved by using the resource.

Table 3: Distribution of the users time saved

User	How much time do you save using B-on (number of hours for month)?							Average time saved
	0 (%)	1 - 3 (%)	4 - 6 (%)	7 - 9 (%)	10 - 12 (%)	13 - 15 (%)	16 or more (%)	(hours/month)
Professor/Researcher	6.7	14.0	20.4	11.6	10.0	5.9	20.8	8.79
PhD Student	7.2	9.4	14.4	11.5	15.1	5.0	24.5	9.85
Undergraduate/Master Student	5.2	14.5	11.1	5.2	2.2	0.6	1.0	4.44
Other	7.5	15.0	15.0	7.9	5.2	2.3	9.6	6.86

Table 4 shows the frequency distribution of the maximum willingness to pay (WTP) to continue access Portuguese electronic scientific information consortium, B-on. The hypothetical scenario considers values ranging from 5 to 50 Euros per each month.

The results on the left side of table show that there is a large percentage of the users declaring that they are not willing to pay anything in order to continue to have access to the B-on services. Harless and Allen (1999) refers that "in contingent valuation studies, it is common to have some participants who, at least initially, refuse to answer or respond that their maximum WTP is zero as a protest response." We believe that this problem also occurred in our study. To solve this problem we decided to analyse the data in two different manners. In the first approach we considered all the users including those who do not want pay anything for this service. This approach will underestimate the true total willingness to pay as some zeros are just protest answer and thus do not really mean that the user does not give any value to the service. In the second approach we excluded all the users who declared to have a zero WTP and consider the frequency distribution among the positive WTP values. This approach overestimates the total WTP since some zeros might be truthful, i.e., some users might not give any value to the service. By using these two approaches we are able to obtain an interval estimate for the users WTP.

Table 4: Frequency of maximum willingness to pay (WTP) to continue to access Portuguese electronic scientific information consortium B-on. The hypothetical scenario considers that the user needs to pay a monthly tax with values ranging from 5 to 50 Euros.

User	How maximun willingness to pay (WTP) to continue access scientific e-resources (Euros for month)?														
	Including the value zero (%)								**Excluding the value zero (%)**						
	0	5	10	15	20	30	40	50	5	10	15	20	30	40	50
Professor/Researcher	27.5	24.0	20.0	6.9	10.1	4.6	0.8	6.1	33.1	27.6	9.5	13.9	6.4	1.1	8.4
PhD Student	37.1	24.1	15.5	6.0	10.3	3.4	0.9	2.6	38.4	24.7	9.6	16.4	5.5	1,4	4.1
Undergraduate/Master Student	34.9	32.3	19.3	5.2	7.3	0.5	0.0	0.5	49.6	29.6	8.0	11.2	0.8	0.0	0.8
Other	36.2	28.9	17.2	4.7	7.0	3.2	0.4	2.9	45.2	26.9	7.3	11.0	5.0	0.0	4.6

We estimated the value for benefit-cost, based on the contingent valuation method accepting null values, 1:2.38, as well as for the case do not accepting null values, 1:3.62.

Bibliometric data from Portugal

The electronic scientific information access in the academic libraries services started in 2000. This has led to a revolution in the scholarly communications landscape. Figure 2 shows the number of scientific Portuguese documents published for the subjects Life and Health Science, Engineering, Humanities and Social Sciences, Earth and Planetary Sciences, Physics and Chemistry Sciences and Mathematics and Computer Science from 1996 to 2007.

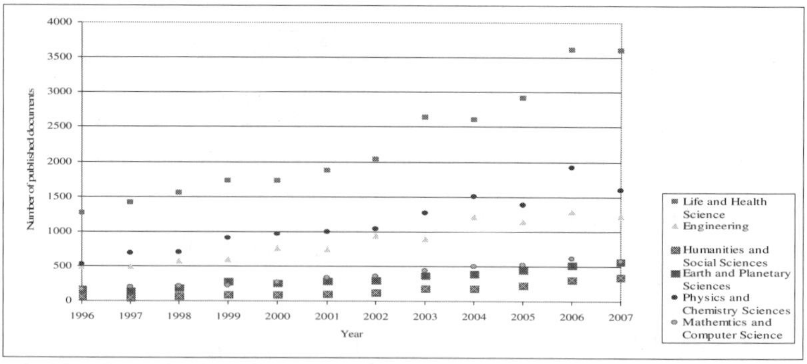

Figure 2: Number of scientific documents published for the following subjects Life and Health Science, Engineering, Humanities and Social Sciences, Earth and Planetary Sciences, Physics and Chemistry Sciences and Mathematics and Computer Science from 1996 to 2007 (SCImago, 2007).

Figure 2 shows a clear increase in the number of articles published since 2001. If we compare the number of articles published in the period 2005-2007 (the last three years) with the number of articles published in the period 1998-2000 (last three years before the introduction of the B-on) we conclude that the number of articles more than duplicates (growth rate is 105.6%). The increase is visible in all scientific domains with growth rates varying from 92.6% in Engineering to 255.9% in Humanities and Social Sciences.

This data supports the statement of the Research Information Network (2009) "Publishers began to provide full-text articles in scholarly journals about ten year ago. This has led to a revolution in the scholarly landscape."

4. Conclusions

F. W. Lancaster (1993) has underlined that is "exceptionally difficult, if not completely impossible, to express the benefits of library service in monetary terms". Nevertheless Hider (2008) refers that in the last decade:

> Has identified some recent "waves" of libraries evaluation where the aim has been to quantify the benefit derived by the end user (…) Moreover, these studies tended to overlook other ways in which organizations benefited from information services, such as by increasing work effectiveness.

Regarding this idea in our article we present some preliminary conclusions of an ongoing project about the valuation of the electronic resources services in Portuguese academic libraries. The results of the study reveal that information-seeking behaviour and the use of the electronic scientific information of the Portuguese academic community have changed. Nowadays a large percentage of professors, researchers and PhD students use traditional and digital library services simultaneous. On the other hand, Undergraduate/Master students do not use both types of services so much, about 40.4%. In this group of users about 60.6% do not know the Portuguese scientific information consortium B-on. This is partially expected since in the first years of graduation the scientific information's needs are less. However this result also suggests that it is necessary to promote and inform potential users about the existence of this resource.

Readers use electronic scientific information from the academic libraries well into the night and over the weekend.

We find evidence that the primary means of gaining access to the knowledge in academic community is now through paid full text e-journal. We agree with the conclusion of the Research Information Network (2009) "electronic journals are a huge success (…) across all subjects". Open Access information evidences to be an excellent e-resource for academic users.

Aabø (2009) refers that:

> As recipients of high proportion of the public funds for cultural activities, public libraries meet demands for more accountability. Academic libraries, too, meet similar types of demands, being asked for performance measurement, cost justifications, and return on investment from administration of their university or college.

This paper tried to answer these demands. We estimated benefit-cost, for the Portuguese electronic scientific information consortium B-on, using the estimated value of the time saved to measure the benefits, obtaining a ratio of 1:5.35. We also calculated benefit-cost, based on the contingent valuation method including nil values, 1:2.38, as well as not including nil values, 1:3.62. Considering these results, we conclude that the Portuguese scientific electronic information services from universities are overall well worth their price as viewed from the academic population's perspective.

References

Aabø S. (2009). Library valuation studies and return of investment. Paper presented at the *17th BOBCATSSS Symposium*: Challenges for the New Information Professional: University of Porto – Faculty of Engineering, Porto, Portugal.

Chung, H.-K. (2007). Measuring the economic value of special libraries, *The Bottom Line: Managing Library Finances*, Vol. 20, No. 1, 30-44.

Davies, E. (2008). What does success look like? Evidence-based assessment of the academic library. Proceedings of *17th Conference of Greek Academic Libraries*: Academic library evaluation as a measure of Institutional Quality Assessment. University of Ioannina, Ioannina, Greece. Retrieved December 10, 2008. Available at: http://17conf.lib.uoi.gr/files/a3.Davies.pdf.

FCCN - Fundação para a Computação Científica Nacional (2008). *B-on: Boletim Estatístico 2007*, Retrieved October 5, 2008. Available at: http://www.b-on.pt/dmdocuments/Boletim_estatistico_2007.pdf.

GPEARI- Gabinete de Planeamento, Estratégia, Avaliação e Relações Internacionais (2008). *Estatísticas Nacionais: Ensino Superior*, Retrieved 6, 2008. Available at: http://www.estatisticas.gpeari.mctes.pt/?action=5&idt=58

Harless, D. W. and Allen, F. R. (1999). Using the Contingent Valuation Method to Measure Patron Benefits of Reference Desk Service in an Academic Library, *College & Research Libraries*, Vol.60, No. 1, 56-69.

Hider, P. (2008) Using the contingent valuation method for dollar valuations of library services, *Library Quarterly*, Vol.78, No.4, 137-158.

ISO 11620 (1998). *Information and documentation – library performance indicators*. International Organisation for Standardisation (ISO), Geneva.

ISO 11620 (2003). *Information and documentation – library performance indicators: amendment1: additional performance des bibliothéques*. International Organisation for

Standardisation (ISO), Geneva.

ISO 2789 (2006). *Information and documentation – international library statistics.* International Organisation for Standardisation (ISO), Geneva.

Lancaster, F. W. (1993) *If You Want to Evaluate Your Library.* 2nd ed. University of Illinois Press, Champaign.

Luther, J. (2008). University investment in library: What's the return? : A case study at University of Illinois at Urbana-Champaign, *Library Connect*, Elsevier, San Diego. Retrieved January 6, 2008. Available at: http://libraryconnect.elsevier.com/whitepapers/lcwp0101.pdf.

Maroco, J. (2007). *Análise estatística: com utilização do SPSS.* Sílabo, Lisboa.

Mazzanti, M. (2002). Valuing Cultural Heritage Services by Choice Modeling Experiments: Visitor Study at the Galleria Borghese in Rome. Paper presented at the *12th Biennial ACEI Conference*, Rotterdam, The Netherlands.

Noonan, D. S. (2003). Contingent Valuation and Cultural Resources: A Meta-analytic Review of Literature, *Journal of Cultural Economics*, 27, 159-176.

SCImago. (2007). *SJR — SCImago Journal & Country Rank.* Retrieved April 03, 2009. Available at: http://www.scimagojr.com

Research Information Network (2009). *E-journals: their use, value and impact: a research information network report.* Retrieved April 01, 2009.
Available at: http://www.rin.ac.uk/files/E-journals_use_value_impact_April2009.pdf

Awareness and Use of Electronic Information Resources by Education Graduate Students: Preliminary Results from the Aristotle University of Thessaloniki

Aspasia Togia[1] and Nikolaos Tsigilis[2]

[1] Department of Library Science and Information Systems, Technological Educational Institute of Thessaloniki, Greece
[2] Department of Physical Education and Sport Sciences, University of Thessaly, Greece

Abstract: The purpose of the present study was to examine the use of electronic information resources by graduate students at the Aristotle University of Thessaloniki. Fifty-nine graduate students affiliated with four Departments of Education voluntarily participated in the study. A specifically designed questionnaire was administered to gather information about the awareness of resources, the frequency of use, the kind of information sources preferred by students, the main reasons for using the resources, the perceived effectiveness of the searches, the factors encouraging their use and the major obstacles in terms of using them effectively. In addition, the authors sought information on the ways students identify the sources they use, the level of training they have received in using the services and their training needs. Results showed that the vast majority of the participants used Internet search engines rather than specialized databases and full-text resources. It is quite interesting, that nearly half of the respondents (49.1%) had never used ERIC, the fundamental resource of education literature. Only 6.8% became familiar with electronic resources by attending the library training programs. The main problem associated with the non-use of resources was lack of adequate searching skills. The above findings suggest limited use of electronic resources by graduate students, mainly due to absence of basic skills. In order to exploit the full potential of electronic information, university library should undertake a more active role in informing, promoting, and educating the members of the academic community.

Keywords: Information services; Electronic media; Postgraduates; Academic libraries; Greece.

1. Introduction

Electronic resources are valuable tools for study, learning and research. Electronic resources can provide many advantages over traditional print-based resources: they contain current information because they updated frequently, they offer advanced search capabilities, they offer flexibility in the storage of the results, and they enable access to information without the restrictions of time and location.

The access to electronic resources in Higher Education Institutions is rapidly increasing. The growth of information in electronic format forces students to learn how to find, select and use a wide variety of resources. Higher education must develop these skills, in order to produce qualified individuals, engaged in the lifelong pursuit of knowledge for personal and professional growth. For education students in particular, the ability to effectively utilize electronic information resources is a key issue, since it may help them to enhance the quality of their teaching when they become professionals. In addition, it is expected that an educator comfortable in using electronic resources may encourage his/her students to do the same, and thus contribute to their computer and information literacy.

2. Literature review

Several studies have been conducted to assess the acceptance and use of electronic resources by library users. These studies employ various methods for data collection, such as observation, experiments, surveys, interviews and transaction log analysis. Questionnaire surveys are the most widely used research method and members of higher education are the most investigated population (Tenopir, 2003).

The project JISC User Surveys: Trends in Electronic Information Services (JUSTEIS) was a three-year research project funded by the Joint Information Systems Committee (JISC) "on the provision and use of electronic information systems (EIS) within higher education in the UK" (Armstrong et al., 2001). The aim of the project was to gather information on information seeking behavior and use of electronic information systems of students and faculty in a number of UK universities. The findings suggested increased use of search-engines, e-mail and OPACs by both under- and postgraduates, and lower use of databases and e-journals (Armstrong, et al., 2001).

Tenopir (2003) identified eight other major research studies carried out between 1995 and 2003 at the UK and the United States on the use of electronic resources. Among other things, these projects indicated that subject area and status of the individuals are significant factors affecting the use of digital resources.

Aside from the large projects engaged to the investigation of large populations in different disciplines and institutions, a number of small-scale studies have been conducted to assess the level of use in specific settings. Back in the 1990's, Adams and Bonk (1995) conducted a survey of faculty use of electronic information technologies and resources at the four University Centers of the State University of New York. The campus library online catalog and the abstract/index databases loaded on it found to be the most widely used resources. All other resources, including electronic journals were used rather infrequently. Respondents perceived lack of information about available resources and lack of training as the main barriers to the use of electronic technologies.

A study at Cornell University (Payette & Rieger, 1998) found that 65% of the faculty and 88% of the students surveyed were ignorant of the wide array of electronic resources available to them. Faculty relied only to one or two databases they were familiar with and overlooked the variety of tools offered by the library through the Web-based gateway. Undergraduate students, on the other hand, "cited Internet search engines as effective tools in identifying information resources for their papers and speeches" (Payette & Rieger, 1998, p. 125). This is in accordance with findings of other studies that indicated student over-reliance on the Web. Crawford and Daye (2000) found that most of the students were using search engines and relatively fewer of them were making use of online databases such as Medline or Psyclit. Majid and Tan (2002) reported that most of the computer engineering undergraduate students they investigated were considering print sources more useful for their study-related needs than electronic ones. Internet was ranked as the most important and bibliographic databases as the least important source. When asked to indicate how often they had used different electronic resources during the previous six months, nearly half of the respondents responded that they were using the library catalog quite frequently. On the contrary, "the use of databases, electronic journals and other electronic information sources was surprisingly low." (Majid & Tan, 2002, p. 324).

Dadzie (2005) found that that the vast majority of students and faculty she surveyed preferred for their searches search engines like Google and Yahoo, while very few of them were making use of the OPAC and of the scholarly databases the library subscribed to. The under-utilization of electronic resources has been highlighted by Rehman and Ramzy (2004), who studied the health care professionals at Health Science Center of Kuwait University. They found that Medline was the most heavily used source, followed by electronic journals. The expensive, specialized databases offered by the library received minimal use. The most frequently mentioned reasons for non use were lack of time and lack of the skills necessary to perform successful searches. In addition, some of the respondents felt that print resources met their needs better than electronic ones. Mawindo and Hoskins (2008) also noted that "only a few electronic resources were actually used by the students", who "preferred websites over the scholarly academic databases and e-journals" (p. 100). Of the electronic resources consulted, online journals seemed to be the most common.

According to Shuling (2006), postgraduate students, who were the most enthusiast users of electronic resources, were frequently using the full-text databases purchased by the library, but they also preferred resources offered online free of charge. Electronic journals reported as the most widely used resource by Kanniyappan, Nithyanandam and Ravichandran (2008), who concluded that most of the respondents faced problems in fully exploiting digital resources mainly because they did not get enough training to use them.

Despite the steady growth in electronic resources offered to the academic community in Greece, Greek libraries have not been engaged to survey research to the same extent as other countries. The aim of this study is to provide preliminary evidence regarding the trends in the use of electronic information resources and services offered by the Aristotle University of Thessaloniki. Postgraduates' use patterns discussed in this study present issues that librarians need to consider in their effort to serve users effectively.

3. Electronic resources at the Aristotle University of Thessaloniki

Aristotle University of Thessaloniki is the largest university in Greece, with a population of 35,000 active students, approximately 3,000 faculty members and 9,000 postgraduate students. At the time of the study, the university library offered access to a wide range of electronic resources, including over 19,000 electronic journals of nearly all major publishers, approximately 400 electronic books and over 80 bibliographic databases. The vast majority of e-journals and a significant number of databases and e-books are available through the Hellenic Academic Libraries Consortium (Heal-Link), while the rest are university's subscriptions.

Usage statistics via the information providers are the library's main source regarding the extent of use of digital resources. Usage statistics however, are unable to provide insights into the levels of use among different groups and to issues like perceived effectiveness of electronic resources or problems associated with their use.

4. Method

Fifty-nine graduate students from four education departments of the Aristotle University of Thessaloniki participated voluntarily in the study. The respondents were affiliated with the Department of Physical Education, Department of Early Childhood Education, Department of Philosophy and Pedagogy, and Department of Primary Education.

A specifically designed questionnaire consisted of 27 items was developed to gather information about the awareness of resources, the frequency of use, the kind of information sources preferred by students, the main reasons for using the resources, the perceived effectiveness of the searches, the factors encouraging their use and the major obstacles in terms of using them effectively. In addition, the authors sought information on the ways students identify the sources they use, the level of training they have received in using the services and their training needs.

5. Results

The vast majority of the respondents were women (89.7%) and their age ranged from 23-46 years old. With regard to their use of computers, nearly half of them (48.3%) claimed to use a computer 2 or 3 times per week. In response to a question about their computer skills, 67.2% of the respondents perceived themselves as novice or intermediate users. Respondents were also asked about their ability to use different electronic resources. The answers demonstrated that most of graduate students were rather incompetent users of library OPAC, electronic journals and abstract/index databases, but very skilled at using the web search engines.

Multiple response analysis was implemented to examine the frequency tables for multiple response sets. Results showed that the vast majority of participants (86%) had used search engines (e.g. Google) more than 6 times during the last three months, followed by full-text electronic journals (33.9%) and the Library OPAC (29.3%) (Table 1). Half of the respondents were making use of the electronic resources from their home, whereas only one out of four (24.5%) were accessing them from the University Library. Most of the respondents (43.6%) who used any one of the listed resources reported that they became aware of its existence through friends and colleagues who had already used it, and only 18.8% through the library.

Kendall's tau-b was used to examine the association between frequency of computer use and levels of the use of selected electronic resources. Results showed that access to and use of computers correlates positively with the use of OPAC (Kendall's tau-b = .33), electronic journals (Kendall's tau-b = .36), Web of Science (Kendall's tau-b = .44), ERIC (Kendall's tau-b = .43) and internet search engines (Kendall's tau-b = .27).

Table 1. Usage of selected electronic information sources during the last three months

	> 6 times	2-5 times	Once	Never	Not aware of the resource
OPAC	29.3	13.8	8.6	25.9	22.4
E-Journals	33.9	23.2	19.6	10.7	12.5
E-Books	-	18.5	22.2	42.6	16.7
Web of Science	5.8	15.4	7.7	34.6	36.5
ERIC	5.7	5.7	1.9	43.4	43.4
PsycInfo	3.8	1.9	13.5	38.5	42.3
SportDiscus	7.8	9.8	13.7	25.5	43.1
Search Engines	86.0	5.3	3.5	5.3	-

Academic assignments were mentioned by all respondents as the main reason for using electronic resources. Background reading and checking or updating a bibliography were next in the list, whereas 45.8% of the students were using digital services in order to find information for their thesis or dissertation. When the respondents were asked to indicate factors that discouraged them from using the electronic resources, most of them mentioned lack of awareness as the main obstacle, and nearly half of them replied they did not know how to use them (Figure 1).

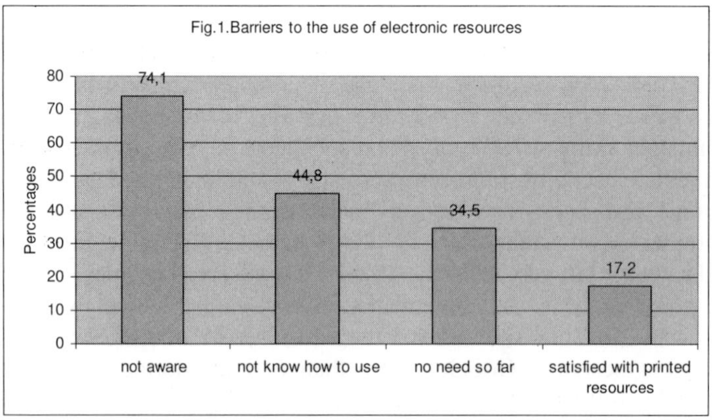

Respondents were also asked to indicate the advantages of electronic resources and the problems associated with their use. Access to current material, the ability to download and print search results and access to wide variety of information were listed as the top three significant features of electronic resources (Figure 2)

Fig.2.Perceived advantages of electronic resources

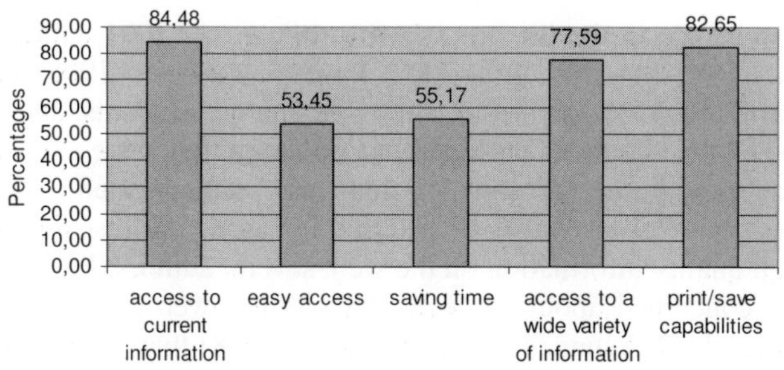

On the other hand, time required to conduct effective searches, and retrieval of too much information – both related to lack of searching skills – were perceived as the main drawbacks (Figure 3).

Fig.3.Perceived drawbacks of electronic resources

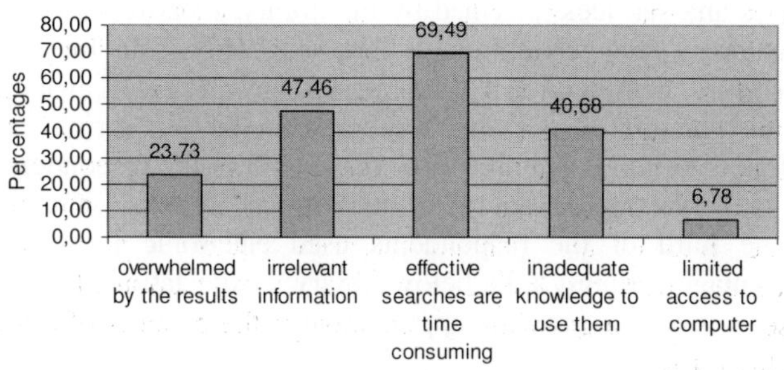

The last section of the questionnaire contained questions about the kind of training participants have had and their training needs. Seminars offered by the Library Instruction Service appeared the most popular method of training. Guidelines given to students by their instructors and course-integrated instruction were the second most common methods. Respondents felt that hands-on sessions would be by far the most useful form of training. Also high on their list was the option of seminars focused on their specific interests and area of study. A high majority of the participants expressed a training need in the selection of the appropriate resource as most urgent, followed by those respondents for whom training was required in the selection of key-words and the development of search strategies.

Mann-Whitney non-parametric test was applied to examine the influence of training on the frequency of use of selected resources. Results demonstrated that participants who had received some kind of training (n = 30) were more regular users of the library OPAC (Mann-Witney U = 188, $p < .001$), full-text journals (Mann-Witney U = 175.5, $p = .034$), ERIC database (Mann-Witney U = 99, $p = .034$ and e-book collections (Mann-Witney U = 204, $p = .009$). in comparison to those who were completely untrained (n = 29).

6. Discussion

There is strong evidence in the literature (Armstrong et al., 2001; Crawford & Daye, 2000; Dadzie, 2005; Majid & Tan, 2002; Payette & Rieger, 1998) that the Internet has an enormous effect on information seeking by students. Our study confirms this finding. The individuals we surveyed, although they were expected, as graduates, to make use of more sophisticated and authenticated resources, overwhelmingly used the Web as the first resource for academic research. While there is plenty of high quality information on the web, several authors (Farber, 1995; Thomson, 2003) are concerned about the way students use web resources. It has been argued (McBridge & Dickstein, 1998; Rothenberg, 1998) that students tend to accept web-based information uncritically, without considering the currency, authority and quality of its content.

Currency of material, possibility of downloading or printing the results or desired parts of them, and access to a wider range of information were the most important issues considered by the users in using electronic resources. However, the results of the study indicate that despite the perceived advantages and the big variety of electronic resources and services provided by the library, most resources, and in particular online databases received extremely low use. This is in line with the results of the most studies mentioned in the literature review. Lack of awareness of the availability and the potential of certain resources seems to be a serious problem associated with underutilization. It is interesting that 43.4% of the respondents were not aware of ERIC, the largest digital source of literature in Education. On the other hand, more than one third of the respondents used electronic journals rather frequently. This percentage certainly falls below library's expectations, but it's also encouraging, because it reveals a growing appreciation of the benefits of e-journals and a move towards their use.

Training and promotion emerged as key factors in the use of electronic resources and services. Lack of training and lack of adequate information of what is available have been highlighted by many studies (Adams & Bonk, 1995; Dadzie, 2005; Kanniyappan, Nithyanandam & Ravichandran, 2008; Mawindo & Hoskins, 2008; Romanov & Aarnio, 2006) as the top impediments to the utilization of information tools. Renwick (2005) proposed that, although the faculty members she investigated were regular users of electronic resources, there was still a need for marketing and user instruction.

Our data suggest that possession of advanced searching skills contributes to better exploitation of electronic tools. Respondents felt insecure about their ability to build a successful search strategy and to select relevant resources, a finding that supports the assumption that limited use may be attributed, among other things, to the ignorance of the scopus and the potential of each electronic source. Library staff can play an important role by educating not only students, but academics as well, who will in turn pass the information to their students and encourage them to consult digital resources for study and course-related assignments. Tenopir (2003) maintains that "the most effective way for students to learn about important resources in academic libraries seems to be for librarians to work directly with faculty to bring relevant electronic resources into the classroom." Of equal importance is the promotion of services. There is a need for aggressive marketing of the available information sources, in order to enhance users' awareness and maximize use.

7. Conclusion

When interpreting the results presenting above, one needs to have in mind that the present study portrays only a glimpse rather than a total picture of the use of electronic resources in the Aristotle University. The small sample and the association of respondents with a specific subject area are the main limitations of the study. Additional research, focused on other groups of the academic community is needed, in order to get a thorough insight into the use of electronic resources at the Aristotle University. Besides, comparative studies of postgraduate students at other institutions will help determine whether the results presented here can be generalized across many universities.

References

Adams, J.A. and Bonk, S.C. (1995). Electronic information technologies and resources: use by university faculty and faculty preferences for related library services, *College and Research Libraries*, Vol.56, No. 2, 119-131.

Armstrong, C., Fenton, R., Lonsdale, R., Stoker, D., Thomas, R. and Urquhart, C. (2001). A study of the use of electronic information systems by higher education students in the UK, *Program,* Vol.35, No. 3, 241-262.

Crawford, J. (2004). The use of electronic information services by students at Glasgow Caledonian University, *Vine,* Vol.34, No. 3, 113-118.

Dadzie, P. S. (2005). Electronic resources: access and usage at Ashesi University College, *Campus-Wide Information Systems,* Vol.22, No.5, 290-297.

Farber, E.I. (1995). Plus Ca Change, *Library Trends*, Vol.44, 430-438.

Kanniyappan, E., Nithyanandam, K. and Ravichandran, P. (2008). Use and impact of e-resources in an academic and research environment: a case study, *Information Studies,* Vol.14, No. 3, 151-162.

Majid, S. and T., A.T. (2002). Usage of information resources by computer engineering students: a case study of Nanyang Technological University, Singapore, *Online Information Review,* Vol.26, No. 5, 318-325.

Mawindo, D. and Hoskins, R. (2008). Use of print and electronic resources by students at the University of Malawi College of Medicine, *Mousaion,* Vol.25, No. 1, 86-110.

McBridge, K.B. and Ruth Dickstein (1998). The Web demands critical thinking by students, *Chronicle of Higher Education*, March 20, B6.

Payette, S. D. and Rieger, O.Y. (1998). Supporting scholarly inquiry: incorporating users in the design of the digital library, *Journal of Academic Librarianship,* March, 121-129.

Rehman, S. U. and Ramzy, V. (2004). Awareness and use of electronic information resources at the health sciences center of Kuwait University, *Library Review,* Vol.53, No. 3, 150-156.

Renwick, S. (2005). Knowledge and use of electronic information resources by medical sciences faculty at The University of the West Indies, *Journal of the Medical Library Association,* Vol.93, No. 1, 21-31.

Romanov, K. and Aarnio, M. (2006). A survey of the use of electronic scientific information

resources among medical and dental students, *BMC Medical Education*, Vol. 6, 28-35.
Rothenberg, D. (1998). How the Web destroys student research papers, *Education Disgest*, Vol.63, February, 59-61.
Shuling, W. (2006). Investigation and analysis of current use of electronic resources in university libraries, *Library Management,* Vol.28, No. 1/2, 72-88.
Tenopir, C. (2003). *Use and users of electronic library resources: an overview and analysis of recent studies*. Council on Library and Information Resources, Washington, DC. Available at: http://www.clir.org/pubs/reports/pub120/contents.html
Thomson, C. (2003). Information illiterate or lazy: how college students use the Web for research, *portal: Libraries and the Academy*, Vol.3, No. 2, 259-268

The Cultural Events Service at the BPI (Public Information Library) or Other Tools for the Acquisition of Knowledge

Marion Loire and V. Bouissou

Centre Pompidou, France
E-mail: loire@bpi.fr, bouissou@bpi.fr

The icing on the cake

Today, most libraries have a cultural department. Whether public or university libraries, big or small, all of them try to propose exhibitions, conferences, lectures, mainly focused on valorizing their collections. Recent big library buildings, like the Alexandrina or the British Library, have large exhibitions and conference rooms.
However, in daily activities, for example dealing with financial capacity, priority is seldom given to cultural events, considering that they're what we would call in French "une danseuse": a cherished mistress, who costs a lot but is a sort of fantasy, not a "serious object" of interest, that comes, anyway, after the supposed "legitimate" object of interest. We would like to show that cultural events are a real and serious proposal to access knowledge, offering a wide range of tools based on re-mediation, popularisation and broadening access in the widest sense.

Over the last several years, the Cultural Events Service of the Public Information Library in the Pompidou Centre has been organising exhibitions, lectures, round table discussions and performances. Through these programmes, we have complemented and enriched the library's written and electronic resources, while facilitating a range of ways to access knowledge. How do these different modes operate, according to the range of events provided and the diversity of the envisaged audience? How does the public perceive this cultural provision? What kind of tools can be used to evaluate this kind of activity?

This study will attempt to answer these questions with reference to our own experience.

I – Bpi : Cultural Events are Part of the Library

1. What is the BPI?

The BPI Public Reference Library -*Bibliothèque publique d'information*- is a public institution under the control of the French Ministry of Culture. Located in the Pompidou Center in Paris since its opening in 1977, the BPI is a general reference library which also provides material on current news topics. Access to the library is free of charge and open to all without any registration formalities. Its reference collections are available to adults in a wide variety of formats for on-site use only and a number of online services are provided via the Internet.

✓ **Some facts and figures**

3 floors, 10,000m2, surface area, seating for 2,100, 14 km of shelves, 400,000 books, documents and printed materials, 400 work stations, open 62 hours per week, 10 information desks, 5,400 visitors per day, 300,000 visitors to the website each month, etc.

The BPI offers...

...on site resources:

- 350,000 books,
- 2,500 different magazines, newspapers and periodicals,
- 7,000 maps and plans
- digitized news articles,
- 1,900 music scores,
- 13,000 compact discs,
- 2,000 spoken word recordings,
- 2,250 documentary films,
- 250 animated films,
- 550 films from ARTE channel (Arte video on demand),
- 400 courseware and software programs and learning websites,
- 1,500 language learning resources (220 languages),
- 11 television channels,
- 2,000 pre-selected websites, reference and multimedia CD-ROMS,
- 9,000 photographs from the Windenberger collection,
- Recorded sound archives (debates, symposiums, seminars… organized by the BPI),

...remote resources: www.bpi.fr

Since the BPI's opening in 1977, cultural democratization has been a main issue for the Library, whether in its functioning, collection and policy of cultural events, or in its international and national cooperation. The main principles that rule the working of the Library are

- free access : free entrance, all is done to encourage reader autonomy
- current news topics : collections are up to date and there's constant attention to renewing collections
- research on new technologies to offer wider access to collections, including online services

2. The Cutural Activities Direction

a. Special Events Department

The library's **Special events** department regularly schedules conferences, debates and workshops at the Pompidou Center, in conference rooms or on the library premises or online on its website http://www.bpi.fr and organizes exhibitions .

b. The Audiovisual Department

Documentaries, animated and performing arts films can be viewed in the Library, including films from ARTE channel (Arte video on demand).

The **Audiovisual** department also regularly screens theme-based series of documentary and animated films in the Pompidou Center's projection theatres as well as fiction films for children.

Since 1978, The BPI has organized the festival *Cinéma du Réel* (http://www.cinereel.org). This international documentary film festival has been an outstanding international meeting point, where the public and professionals discover the films of experienced authors as well as new talents, the history of documentary cinema as well as contemporary works. The festival programs some hundred films for its various sections.

c. The Publishing Department

The BPI **publishes** a magazine entitled the *Bulletin Bpi* (available free of charge at the library): library news and the program of the events.

The BPI/ Pompidou Centre publications *–Editions de la Bibliothèque publique d'information/Centre Pompidou-* have published five collections: *Bonjour/Salut* (language learning methods), *En Actes* (symposium proceedings), *Pratique* (library science), *Etudes et Recherche* (studies on library users and the sociology of reading) and the online collection (*Paroles en réseau*) from symposium proceedings.

Some of the texts are also available on the BPI website (http://www.editionsdelabibliotheque.fr).

d. The Communication Department

This department is in charge of press relations, and communication about the events of the Library

3. Running Cultural Events : a Mission of the BPI which has been Assumed and Reasserted

The organization of cultural events holds a central position at the BPI : these peculiar missions have been assigned to the library from the origin.

The **decree** that created the Library in 1976 placed the running of cultural events as one of the three essential missions of the BPI and as one of the main services the library was to offer.

This mission has been reinforced by **the institution project** that reorganised the library in 2000 and by the publication of the first "**Cultural Policy Charter**" of the library (Charte de l'action culturelle) in 2008.

This charter reasserts the BPI's role of running cultural events and redefines its principles and aims. It insists on the fact that the cultural events have to be conceived in order to facilitate a range of ways of accessing knowledge and information for the widest audience and to open a democratic space for debate, through all kind of special events.

The BPI has to create tools for the public **to understand contemporary world issues** by multiplying points of view and analyses. Its schedule has to offer public (free access) cultural training in the field of thought and contemporary ideas. Creating teaching material by the means of workshops, exhibitions, digital debate archives, etc., has to be one of its most important aims.

The charter also gives the main directions for the subjects covered by our activities: **current news topics and subjects of collective memory, literary and artistic creation, books and publishing, contemporary thought**. These actions must be focused on the quest for all-round knowledge, interdisciplinarity and diversity of tools in order to touch different publics.

The BPI is a public reference library where collections are renewed constantly, which means "*a non patrim*onial" library. Its cultural events policy is therefore more devoted to creation and production of content than to giving value to the library's collections.
Special events are conceived with respect to the fields covered by the collections, serve as another complementary way to provide access to knowledge, thus enriching library's collection, and creating a trace of current news.

The location of the BPI in the Centre Pompidou also contributes to a peculiar position towards the cultural policy. The Centre is focused on modern and contemporary creations, with an interdisciplinary vocation and a core mission to spread knowledge about all creative works from the 20th century and those heralding the new millennium. The BPI takes part, wholly, in this project and completes, in its own specific areas, the offer of the Museum, the cultural departments, and the Ircam (Institut de recherché et de coordination accoustique/musique)

II – Cultural Events as Tools for the Acquisition of Knowledge

The Bpi is running exhibitions, lectures, round table discussions and performances, as well as projections of films and a film festival . We won't be able to deal with the audiovisual program because of lack of time.
Concerning oral events and exhibitions, we will try to find out, according to the range of events, how differents skills for acquisition of knowledge can be used and developped.

Oral Events

The BPI schedules a **large range of oral events**, from one-shot colloquia to long duration cycles, from classical lectures and round table discussions to happenings.
These events follow the principles enacted in the cultural policy charter: the **quest for all-round knowledge, interdisciplinarity and diversity of tools**. Like all BPI services access is **totally free and open to all** without any registration formalities. Events aim at **all kinds of publics**, especially amateurs, the self-taught, or those coming from mere curiosity, but also professionals, or even researchers. The events deal with a large number of subjects, literature, sciences, subjects of society, etc. ; the purpose being to broaden as much as possible the access to culture.

These oral events are consciously conceived to facilitate the approach and understanding of contemporary issues and thought, and/or to offer major public occasions to discover and enjoy contemporary creation. Organizing these events, the BPI has placed itself as a **mediation space different from the university as much as from the media**.
We believe, in fact, that oral events are efficient tools to pass on culture. They act in a different way from written documents. We try to reflect on, and to exploit, in various manners, **speech effects on the subjective construction of knowledge:**

Our purpose is **to allow the circulation of knowledge out of its usual circles and community codes, to enhance popularization** in a positive sense, making collective appropriation possible.
The designers of the BPI's oral events have tried to broaden the access to culture, diversifying the points of view on a same topic and the kinds of presentations and

modes used to address the public.

For each subject, we pay particular attention to **comparing different approaches**, confronting for instance scientific research with professional experience or with associative expertise or even with artistic interpretation. This is a way to prompt the public to consider a problem from all angles.

In a series of colloquia about the evolution of relationships between women and men, which aimed at popularizing gender studies, for instance, we invited historians, sociologists, philosophers, legal experts, doctors, midwives, biologists, and also associations, and writers. We also used **different modes to address the audience**, from classical lectures, round table discussions and interviews, to film projections, and literary readings.

Operating in this way, we have tried to **exploit both emotion and rationality** to awaken public interest. To surprise the audience is in fact a good way to arouse curiosity and to create the desire to learn.

For example, a conference about the origin of space exploration, began with a reading of a literary text on concentration camps, raising emotions and surprise, and making the audience question itself about the link between that fiction and the scientific subject of the evening.

The oral events are organized around three elements: the contributor(s), the discussant and the audience :

We pay peculiar attention to the **choice of the contributors**, to the quality of the information they can pass on, but also to their **desire to communicate**, to express original opinions and to debate with a wide public.

Surveys conducted by our research service have shown indeed that the physical presence of the speaker is very important for the audience, giving them a feeling of authenticity, or even of fascination, and fulfiling in part a desire to get the information at its source, but also to see a show. A successful debate has to present a synthesis, "it avoids having to read big books", but the information also has to be communicated by a really engaged speaker (Agnès CAMUS, "Le public des manifestations orales de la Bpi, synthèse de la phase préparatoire", on line : http://www.bpi.fr).[1]

The **chairperson** is essential too. He must be familiar with the subject or the person he has to interview, know how to organize time allotted to speech of the speakers and the audience, and have empathy for the contributor (s).

We are also attentive to leaving a **real place for public debate**, and always plan time for the exchange of opinions as well as public questions and comments.

We believe indeed that speech and orality are essential vectors of the construction of a cultural background. The conversation between the speaker, the one who knows, and the audience, works as a spiritual game which enables the **construction of authentic knowledge**. During the exchange, the people in the audience can ask for precision, express their opinions and compare their points of view, leading not only to the transfer of information from the contributor to the public, but to the possibility of creating knowledge. Oral events allow the listeners to discuss and share their feelings, and therefore make possible **a collective appropriation of knowledge**.

The first results of the survey, conducted by our research department, on oral events audiences have encouraged us to continue in this direction, increasing

interdisciplinarity, variety of modes of address, and interactivity, appropriate for our will to reach various publics and to answer the two main reasons for people to attend one of our special events: the desire to learn and the desire to take pleasure.
The survey showed, in fact, that we do reach different kinds of audiences in accordance with the subject of the debate and with the mode of address. Example Nothomb/Darwin

Workshops

In order to provide another way for people to discover contemporary literature, the Bpi also planned reading workshops, on short experimental fiction texts, in co-operation with the Inventaire/invention journal and publishing, or about the first novel with the Festival du premier roman de Chambery. In these workshops, the audience was invited to read the most contemporary literature, but also to express opinion about it, to debate about what's literature, and was encouraged to go further, reading essays. These experiences, we'd like to renew shortly, were conceived as an another active and pleasant way to build up culture.

Exhibitions

On this subject, I propose to take the example of the exhibition we're preparing for this autumn. The exhibition will try to explain how the French legal system works through drawings and sketches executed in the courts during trials. We will present around 120 drawings, short films of interviews, archives of tv news, texts and interactive terminals materials.
The aim is to offer as many **different ways as possible to access information** and knowledge. This way of proceeding allows us to identify some of the skills necessary for « **intelligent learning** », as definied by Novak or Ausubel (Ausubel, Hanesian, Novak et al. *Educationnal Psychology : a Cognitive View,* 1978*)*.
As for oral events, we try to use the **surprise effect** to awaken the learning appetite. In our case, visitors of the Pompidou Center will probably come first to see drawings, watercolours and sketches and not specifically to learn about the functioning of the legal system, but through the means of visual media, they can decide to see further. Even in the choice of the items exhibited, we can (photo de la brouette...) arouse intellectual curiosity.
In another way, using art objects to enhance understanding allows **an intuitive, semi-theorical approach** that seems to be much more effective in learning than the classical and academic ones. The pleasure of discovering, through these sketches and drawings, pictures of what is never shown (cameras are prohibited in French courts) can reinforce the feeling of having special access to the world of justice and this positive feeling is also one more stimuli for learning.
The visitor to the exhibition will choose his way through the items and the texts and by this decision, he will engage in a **discovery learning process** and not just be in a reception mode. He will be the one who decides what sort of information he wants to develop, and how he's going to get it : texts, audiovisual or visual elements. This diversity of approaches is a principal element in **autonomy** and can allow each visitor to construct his own learning, based on what he already knows. For this reason, we'll try also to find some elements that can help the public to feel close to the subject. The proximity of the subject (which can apply in many different ways like where, or when it takes place...) is one more possibility to provoke the interest

of the visitors.
Using all these skills, we think that a pedagogical exhibition can offer a real alternative for access to knowledge, allowing for intelligent learning based on discovery, autonomy and self-constructed knowledge. That means that this kind of event has a proper place in a library, like books, films, or databases, and not only as a way to « valorize » the collections of the Library.
After the on-line exhibition on our site, the BPI will offer a travelling exhibition, based on the same content, which can be rented to other libraries (http://www.bpi.fr/fr/professionnels/expositions_itinerantes.html.

Development prospects

The survey conducted in 2007 on oral events audiences showed that the cultural events of the library reach a more diversified audience than the library reading room, and this lets us think that our offer of other tools to access knowledge, without written materials, is convenient and has to be developed.
The survey also showed a significant change of the public's expectation with regard to the first survey conducted in 1993: in 1993 many oral event users referred to the school model to estimate the quality of an event. Nowadays, they're still looking for training and cultural background, but don't approve of the school model anymore, and ask for more interactivity and emotion.
We have noticed a progressive abolition of the borders between the different modes of access to knowledge and a claim for interdisciplinarity and interactivity, linked with web 2.0 and other forms of reappropriation of knowledge by non-specialist audiences.
This has encouraged us to try out new types of cultural events to address different publics and confirm the legitimate of this kind of actions in librairies.

III – Cultural events as a tool to enlarge the Library's collection

Publishing (http://www.editionsdelabibliotheque.fr/)

The BPI/Pompidou publications *–Editions de la Bibliothèque publique d'information/Centre Pompidou-* proceedings of some of the oral events planned by the library, on paper (« En actes » collection) or on-line (« paroles en réseau » collection). The annals of all sessions of the literary festival « d'encre et d'exil » (ink and exile) has for example been published and the three colloquia on genders studies are to be published, on paper for one part and on-line for the other.

Digital Library, Sound Archives (http://archives-sonores.bpi.fr/)

The Public Reference Library has decided to digitalize its sound archive to create a digital library and make it available on the spot or online to the general public through a specific databank and web interface. The notes for the events are integrated to the PRL's general catalogue, thus giving readers direct access to them as they would to any book or periodical.
The interface for the sound archive bank was conceived to make searches as easy as possible. When readers visit the databank homepage for the first time, they can have access to the last six digitalized events. It only takes them a click on the title or picture of the programme to have access to all details (detailed programmes, biographical notes, thesaurus, related documents, links to personal or institutional sites…). They can also make title-, author-, date- or subject-based types of search.
In accordance with the PRL's broadcasting rights, the recordings can be listened to

online or on the spot only. When "unavailable" is mentioned, it means that we have no recording for the event. On the contrary, when "not yet digitalized" is mentioned, it means that we do have a recording which can be digitalized on online request. In case the recording is said to be "not allowed", it cannot be broadcast as the speakers have not allowed it to be publicized yet.

Some of the sessions have been split to make the search easier according to people's centers of interest. The duration of the files is thus shortened for a more agreeable listening. Most recordings are available on a streaming format only, i.e. on an unstorable and continuous mode. Only events taking place after 2007 are on a Creative Commons license, which makes them available for downloading and copying on other computers to be listened to anytime.

We also offer thematic browsing through characteristic « collections » such as "Great figures of the 20th century" or "Cities and territories".

Online exhibitions

For two years, we have begun to produce online exhibitions (http://expositionseuil.bpi.fr/bpiSeuil.html, http://gourmelin.bpi.fr/gourmelin.html). Here again, our desire is to propose information and knowledge in a different way. For example, for the next exhibition we're designing three online games to help visitors understand who the actors in a court are, what their roll is and what the differences are between the Anglo-American judicial system and the continental one.

Interactivity, playful aspects, curiosity, autonomy in the process of learning are our main preoccupations in creating these objects.

IV – The Public of Cultural Events : Proposals for an Evaluation

1. Which Public?

The public of cultural events is still not well known, the last study was done in September 1992, that means nearly 20 years ago ... It's true that free access, with no registration, makes it a bit difficult to run studies. Our service has tried for two years to hand out questionnaires that the public can fill out and leave at the entrance of the conference rooms, if they want to do so. It gave us a first answer, but not enough. What do we know right now ? Apparently our public is a bit different from that of the Library: the working population represents 40% of our public, and students 28 % as they represent 77% of the public of the Library. Half of the public also use the Library and other services in Pompidou Center. They're mainly young, between 25 and 34 years old. They seem to be satisfied with the conferences (between 60 and 80% according to the conferences). We decided to ask the Research and Studies Department of the Library to run another study on our public. The evaluation will take place in 2 phases, the first one, initiated last year, was done by Agnès Camus-Vigué, the second part, the quantitative aspect is being done now with Plein Sens, a survey company, and will end this autumn.

2. The Exploratory Study, the Focus Group

(http://www.bpi.fr/fr/professionnels/etudes_et_recherche/publics_et_usages_a_la_bpi.html

Three groups of users (Focus group) were organised to collect these elements and data. They were collected in order to update the study made by the CREDOC nearly twenty years ago. This qualitative aspect attempts to give information about the motivations of the public to come listen to a conference. Why attend a conference ? What for ?, what is the benefit of doing this pleasure or knowledge ? All theses questions have been worked on with the participants and Agnès Camus report was certainly the beginning of our reflexion. It's very clear to us that what this public wants to find at the Pompidou Center is another way to access knowledge: apart from the university, from TV news, from newspapers, an open-minded way to try to understand our world with scientific but accessible items.

3. The Ongoing Study

The second part of this research has been taking place since September 2008 and will finish in June. With the help of Plein Sens, the Research and Studies Department is running the quantitative study. The first results are quite interesting and seem to show that we have different kinds of publics, depending on our range of conferences. This means we have to work more and more on the variety of our cultural offer.

Conclusion

By running Cultural events, the Library gets an occasion to offer differents ways of accessing knowledge in order to reach all kind of public, specially the one who could be excluded by an access mainly focused on the written sources. It 's a way of reasserting the social role of Libraries.On another hand, with the digitalization of resources and the electronic documents, the role and function of Libraries must be developped in new paths where remediation and human presence will be more and more important. In these pespective, we could think that running cultural events could be one of the solution to keep Libraries alive.

13. Cataloguing and Manuscripts

The Open Catalogue of Manuscripts and Other Information Systems for a New Role of Libraries in Education

Antonio Cartelli and Marco Palma

University of Cassino, Italy

Abstract: The online information systems the authors planned and constructed for research and teaching on the ancient manuscripts are described as first. The corresponding web sites, used to store the bibliography and more general data on ancient manuscripts, are soon after analyzed; it is also shown how they contributed in the creation of communities of learning and practice with the people involved in their use. The special case of the Malatestiana Library is then described; the staff in that library is in fact responsible for the implementation of the Open Catalogue of manuscripts and its continuous updating. At last, some considerations on the influence of new technologies and the role that ancient libraries can play in education are discussed.

Keywords: Ancient library; Community of practice; Community of learners; ICT; Information systems; Learning organizations; Manuscripts; Writing types; Web technologies.

1. Introduction

During the last century multi-media and digital equipments underwent progressive growth and evolution and they are nowadays predominant with respect to printed matter in many communication fields; broadcasting news, propagating more structured and organized information and creating new knowledge, are in fact deeply influenced by these instruments.

The revolution in communication and information transmission induced by digital equipments is usually attributed to the structural features of new media, and especially to electronic media with respect to printed texts, because of their directness, effectiveness and immediateness. Otherwise stated, one can say that *these media talk to the body more than to the mind* (D. de Kerckhove, 1995). Furthermore new media and digital media extend individual capabilities and skills in space and time (i.e., they cancel the response time to external stimuli); they let human beings have at least two new senses: *distance seeing*, letting people see distant events just when they happen, and *distance acting*, letting them modify events without being really present in the context where these events happen.

Digital media do not affect only the perception of reality, they also influence the creation of communities and the way people build knowledge. These results are usually attributed to new dimensions for human communication and knowledge construction induced by the ICT; many authors, based on Ong's (2002) and Olson's (1991) ideas, suggest that these effects are the result of a connection between technology, literacy and new orality (sometimes called *second orality*).

Recently the social effects of new media have been widely analyzed and different levels for the influence of the ICT on knowledge construction have been hypothesized. They are reported in the statements below:

- firstly, the subject's point of view is considered; otherwise stated, subjects build their knowledge autonomously, mostly constructively, by interacting with real or virtual phenomena;
- secondly, a community level is suggested; individuals interact in fact with other subjects in a community, where mediation, interpersonal contacts, informal knowledge sharing and support from peers have a more relevant role (and ICT are important in helping subjects create communities or induce new communities);
- at last a wider social level must to be considered; individuals participate to activities in the society they are immersed in (with respect to community, emulation of behaviours as well as codified and socially accepted rules may modify pre-existing learning strategies or determine new ones).

Main conclusion of the above statements is that subjective knowledge can be thought as made of three components: the individual, the community and the social ones, with their own contents, learning strategies and possible communication channels (Cartelli, 2006). Figure 1 gives a snapshot of the suggested tri-partition.

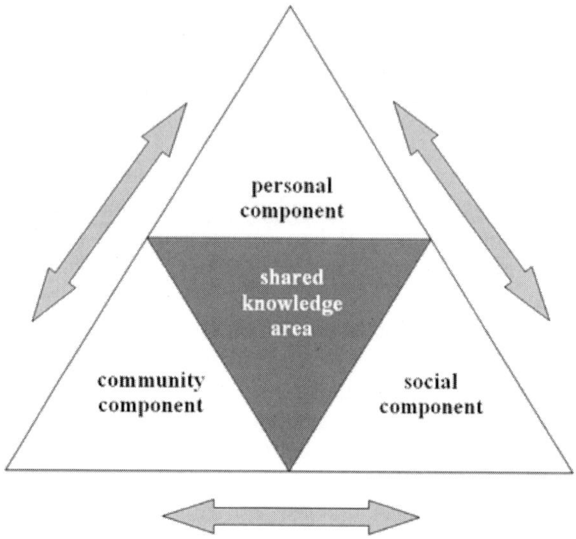

Fig. 1 – Knowledge components and their interactions

Main conclusions are:

- Knowledge construction is the result of the influence of all three components.
- Planning and construction of information systems for the management of information must consider all the reported knowledge components (i.e., a new socio-technical approach to MIS - Management Information Systems, must be considered).
- The use of information systems for the implementation of practices shared by a group of specialists or by subjects working together has the features of a new pedagogical paradigm; it forces people (students, general users etc.) working on

the online system to create a community (or to enter the already existing community), makes easier the socialization and transformation of individuals' tacit knowledge in explicit knowledge and displaces the problem of "information research" to that of "information creation".

In the following sections the instruments and the experiences the authors made while working on the data from ancient manuscripts will be reported; the effects they had on ancient libraries and the changes they induced in historical and humanistic disciplines will be kept separate from each other.

2. The Influence of the ICT and Information Systems on Ancient Libraries and Palaeography Students

In this section the online information systems the authors planned and built for the management of data on ancient manuscripts and the people who wrote them are reported. A separation between the instruments they used in the autonomous context of ancient libraries and the ones concerning palaeography students is made. The first is referred to the Open Catalogue as general proposal and to the case of the Malatestiana Library at Cesena (Italy) for its implementation. The second describes three information systems used for teaching and research in palaeography.

2.1 The Open Catalogue of the Malatestiana Library

It is well known that writing a catalogue of manuscripts is a very difficult task, because it requires a deep competence in a lot of fields, from philology to history, from the art history to palaeography, from literature to library science; furthermore, many different problems affect its realization (i.e., manuscripts can be very difficult to access and analyze by the authors and the final book can have a very limited audience and can be very expensive).

It is probably for the above reasons that radical changes in catalogue publishing intervened in last years. First of all the Internet helped in making available the manuscript heritage all over the world and became the main place where people could publish catalogues (as an example DFG, the German National Research Institute, decided to publish catalogues of manuscripts on the Internet); scholars had from the ICT new and more powerful tools to improve their work and to create *Open Catalogues* (i.e., catalogues in progress, constantly changing with the continuous contribution of new information).

A dynamic web site underpinning an information system looked suitable enough for the creation of an Open Catalogue (Cartelli & Palma, 2002); the following environments were kept separate in it: a closed place, where researchers and scholars had the responsibility of the scientific materials to be published (in the form of images and texts), and an open space, to be used by people occasionally or systematically accessing the information in the site (i.e., not producing it).

In the Open Catalogue five sections, to be intended in a flexible manner, were hypothesized (i.e., the presence of each section depends on the resources the library has at its disposal and on the different solutions it adopts) (Cartelli & Palma, 2003):

a) the first section is devoted to documents explaining the history of the library and its manuscripts;

b) the bibliography ordered by shelfmark and, eventually, alphabetically and chronologically, can be housed in the second section;

c) in the third section the descriptions of the manuscripts, i.e. previous printed catalogues or ancient handwritten catalogues (suitably digitized) and new descriptions (according to nationally/internationally defined standards) can be stored;
d) the fourth section is devoted to the images from the highest number of manuscripts in the library (possibly all);
e) the fifth and last section is based on a communication subsystem including electronic blackboards, chats, forums and special Web solutions granting the easier acquisition, writing and editing of texts among the members of a selected community of scholars/students interested in the study of the materials in the library.
The staff of the Malatestiana Library supported the idea of the Open Catalogue since its beginning and decided to find the resources for building it. The advantages of this choice were:

- the system could be developed in a programmed and gradual manner;
- all the information already acquired could be retrieved even in a partial and non-final form;
- ancient sources, difficult to be accessed by everyone, could be made available and used to extend the research sources;
- the information available by qualified specialists and scholars could be increased interactively and continuously updated.

The Open Catalogue of the Malatestiana Library as made by its staff has four parts:

- The first part credits people working to the project and its carrying out.
- The second section contains general texts on the Library and the manuscript collections (i.e., the history of the library, Cesena humanistic culture, the scriptorium, the illumination, the collections etc.); classical texts suitably digitized have been put on line, special works and graduation theses are continuously added to the former ones, together with the descriptions of the Library coming from foreign visitors.
- A list of all the manuscripts according to shelfmark, author and title can be accessed in the third part. For each codex there is the description and the bibliography (made on the basis of the traditional catalogues and more recent studies). The reproductions of many codices are available and the Library is working to offer the complete reproduction of all the manuscripts.
- The fourth section plays a fundamental role in this project; it hosts users' requests, opinions and articles. Here, scholars and/or persons interested in the Library's manuscript collection can contribute with their observations, as well as with the publishing of online contributions.
  Recently this section enriched of two special functionalities:
  a) collaborative bibliography, where everyone entrusted with the access to the section can insert his/her personal bibliographical records,
  b) works in progress on some manuscripts, by which a community of study and research is granted permission of accessing all the texts in the area and produce new information.

The open catalogue neither excludes nor acts as supplementary to a printed work, which is always possible and even desirable. Instead, the open catalogue is updated constantly by the Library staff, particularly by those who are involved in manuscript preservation. It is their duty to actively administrate the site and to promote research even encouraging interested specialists to provide critical contributions.

2.2 Information Systems for the Teaching of Palaeography

Since 2001 the authors worked at the construction of special web sites (mostly information systems), used both for research and teaching in palaeography. The spreading of the Internet and the easy use of the web for getting information and putting new data in a given database were the main reasons for the construction of the online information systems. The sites described below were used to manage bibliographical data on medieval manuscripts; they also implemented the processes usually adopted by researchers for the collection of bibliographical data.

Women and Written Culture in the Middle Ages (Cartelli, Miglio & Palma, 2001), reports the names of women who wrote manuscripts in the Middle Ages and the manuscripts they wrote; when suitable images are available, people accessing the site can also see the women's handwriting types. The database can be accessed by the authors and allowed people for the management of bibliographical data, images, bibliographies etc. and be only queried by everyone for reading. The site URL is http://edu.let.unicas.it/womediev/

BMB (Bibliography of Beneventan Manuscripts) on line (Cartelli & Palma, 2004) is a pure bibliographical information system; it manages the quotations of Beneventan manuscripts (i.e., an important part of the manuscripts produced in Southern Italy during the Middle Ages). People engaged with the collection of the quotations of those manuscripts are grouped into three categories: contributors, who can access web forms by writing, modifying and deleting bibliographical data; scientific administrators, who can manage all the data contributors are charged with and write, modify, and authorize bibliographical materials (i.e., this last operation can be done only once, because authorized records cannot be reviewed by contributors and scientific administrators; they can only be accessed by general users); the system administrator, who is allowed to do all operations, including the modification or deletion of authorized bibliographical records.

General users can access authorized materials in the site according to different query pages: by author's name, by manuscript, by contributor, and by one or more words or part of them in the title, the location, or the bibliographical abstract of a given publication.

Within the system are also implemented:

- a closed communication subsystem (it can be accessed only by people working on the information system: contributors, scientific administrators and system administrator), letting people quickly exchange messages and texts among themselves,
- special functions, available only to the system administrator, for the production of printed versions of the collected data (to be used to create a printed publication concerning the bibliography yearly collected).

The site URL is: http://edu.let.unicas.it/bmb/

Recently the *DigiSytlus* information system (Cartelli, 2009) has been planned for helping students find in an easier way plates and documents in the site of "Teaching Materials for Latin Palaeography". It does not modify the former site, which is a static web site, so that people who like to access those materials in a more traditional way can use the links in former web pages. The construction of this new web site became a necessity when students' difficulties in finding the materials to be studied became evident.

The *Digistylus* structure is based on a relational database; it is made of tables containing the following data: a) personal identification data of contributors (students) and scientific administrators, b) shelfmarks of the manuscripts containing the plates reproduced in the site, c) the bibliography of the manuscripts and of the medieval documents in the site, d) the writing type of the plates and all the data (as far as they are available) which can be used for a better description of those plates, e) the links to the web pages with the reproduction of any plate and its transcription, f) the keywords letting people access the transcription of a given plate, g) the parameters for the calculation of the difficulty in making the transcription of a given plate, h) the bibliographic records of the documents in the site, with links to the corresponding documents, i) a subsystem letting people working on the system easily communicate, manage bibliographical records and input new data in the DigiStylus database.

People accessing the database have different roles and permissions: general users can only see the plates, the transcriptions, the list of the bibliographies and any other information about materials in the site. The contributors (students) can access a special Web area (by means of their ID and password) with a menu of the allowed operations, i.e. they can manage the records on the plates and their transcriptions, the bibliographic cards and the electronic blackboard. The scientific administrator/s can manage all the data in the database and write, modify and authorize the bibliography. This last operation can be done only once because when the bibliography has been verified it can no longer be accessed by the administrator. The system administrator can do all the operations allowed to the scientific administrator/s and access the verified bibliography in order to modify or delete it.

As soon as the systems were available they have been used for research and teaching. Students attending the courses of Latin palaeography have in fact been involved in the data management of the above information systems.

The observation of students behaviours during the lectures and at the final examinations led to the detection of complex and articulated effects. A selected list of phenomena obtained by comparing the results of North American researchers on communities of learning and the experiences described in former sections is reported below (Cartelli, 2007):

1. information systems contributed in the creation of constructivist learning environments and helped students develop cognitive apprenticeship strategies, as they were defined by D. H. Jonassen (1994); they were also very useful for the improvement of students' learning and performances,
2. the features of communities of learners (CoLs) and fostered communities of learners (FCL), as defined by A. L. Brown and J. Campione (1996) were detected in the classes involved in the use of the described systems; otherwise stated, the online information systems not only supported and extended traditional learning strategies, they also induced the creation of special communities never detected in traditional courses,
3. new skills emerged in the students while working on the information systems

described above (Scardamalia & Bereiter, 1996): a) talent in group work, b) easier facing of complex tasks and c) raising of the individual skills,

4. new transversal competences were detected (Cartelli, 2008): a) better computing skills than those students who attended traditional computing literacy courses, b) development of meta-cognitive strategies.

3. Conclusion

Two different remarks follow the considerations reported in former sections:

- ancient libraries can play a relevant role on university students education; they have in fact the documents for any philological, historical and bibliographical analysis of reality and can make them available to students by means of the ICT and online information systems,
- ancient libraries can have a new role in adult education by adopting the strategies the authors used with palaeography students or adapt them to a wider audience.

It is not an aim of this paper the analysis and discussion of the analogies between the education induced by ancient libraries and museum education, but new technologies have undoubtedly a great role in opening libraries to people and in overcoming the difficulty that people have in accessing the materials stored within ancient libraries.

The hypotheses mentioned in the introduction on the effects of online information systems on students draw new scenarios for libraries because:

- students are now the creators of the information on the web site (they organize and input into the system a part or all the data concerned with the documents in the site),
- the information in the database is available not only to the students but to everyone who may be interested in it, by means of the web,
- any information the students put in the system has to be verified by one or more scientific coordinators before being publicly available on the web,
- a closed forum within the information system letting students communicate and discuss among themselves and with the library staff and scholars, is needed,
- the evaluation of the students' work includes different elements: the evaluation of the work they made, the support they gave to colleagues, the accessibility and usability of the information retrieved by external readers (i.e., general users), the suggestions they gave to the system and its functions.

It can be easily recognized that students involved in the use of systems with the above features will participate in the activities at different levels:

- individually, by critically studying and meaningfully understanding the materials in the library (or they reproductions on the web) and writing the records in the databases (this job is made easier by the presence of supporting materials and the use of communication subsystems letting them easily ask for suggestions from colleagues and library staff),
- at a community level, by adopting different strategies: a) the legitimate peripheral participation (LPP) suggested by Lave and Wenger (1991), helping the management of the community by including the weakest subjects, b) the implementation of practices with the ICT (Information Communication Technology), proposed by Cartelli (2008), letting the online information system

implement processes the community had to conform to, and governing the management of the information acquisition, storing and validation, c) team competency learning, suggested by Jewels and Albon (2006), inducing the library staff to act as coach and assign to every student the best role with respect to his basic knowledge and skills,

- socially, by considering the effects of the information they produce on the people who can access systematically or not the materials in the site.

The same strategies, with little or no change, could be adopted for people who are willing to participate in works and researches on materials in the library. It might be a good occasion for ancient libraries to get out from the routine paperwork of the administration of their materials, to recover the central function of culture promoters they progressively lost and enter a new phase of knowledge construction and development by creating communities of learning and practices actively cooperating on the study of their materials.

References

Brown, A. L., and Campione, J. (1996). Psychological Theory and the Design of Innovative Learning Environments: On Procedure, Principles and Systems. In L. Schaube & R. Glaser (Eds.), *Innovation in learning*. Mahwah (NJ): Erlbaum, 289-375.

Cartelli, A. (2006). Semantics, Ontologies and Information Systems in Education: Concerns and Proposals. *Journal of Issues in Informing Science and Information Technology: The Information Universe*, vol. 3, 113-125.

Cartelli, A. (2007). From Socio-Technical Approach To Open Education: MIS and ICT for the Definition of New Teaching Paradigms. In D. Remenyi (Ed.), *Proceedings of ECEL 2007 International Conference*. Reading (UK): Academic Conferences Limited, 97-106.

Cartelli, A. (2008). The Implementation of Practices with ICT as a New Teaching-Learning Paradigm. In A. Cartelli & M. Palma (Ed.s), *Encyclopedia of Information Communication Technology*. Hershey (PA): Information Science Reference, 413-418.

Cartelli, A. (2009). Digistylus: a Socio-Technical Approach to Teaching and Research in Education. Accepted for publication in the *Journal of Issues in Informing Science and Information Technology*, vol. 6.

Cartelli, A., Miglio, L. and Palma, M. (2001). New Technologies and New Paradigms in Historical Research. *Informing Science, Special Issue "Widening the Focus"* 4 2, 61-66.

Cartelli, A. and Palma, M. (2002). Towards the Project of an Open Catalogue of Manuscripts. In E. Cohen & E. Boyd (Ed.s), *Proceedings of IS 2002 Informing Science + IT Education Conference*. Santa Rosa (CA): ISI, 217-224.

Cartelli, A. and Palma, M. (2003). The Open Catalogue of Manuscripts between Palaeographic Research and Didactic Application. In M. Khosrow-Pour. (Ed.), *Proceedings of the IRMA 2003 Conference "Information Technology & Organization: Trends, Issues, Challenges and Solutions"*. Hershey (PA): Idea Group Publishing, 51-54.

Cartelli, A. and Palma, M. (2004). BMB on line: An Information System for Palaeographic and Didactic Research. In M. Khosrow-Pour (Ed.), *Proceedings of the IRMA 2004 Conference "Innovation through Information Technology"*. Hershey (PA): Idea Group Publishing, 45-47.

Cartelli, A. and Palma, M. (2005). Computer and Information Systems in Latin Palaeography between Research and Didactic Application. In D. Carbonara (Ed.), *Technology Literacy Applications in Learning Environments*. Hershey (PA): IGI Global, 288-298.

de Kerckhove, D. (1995). *The Skin of Culture*, Toronto: Somerville House Books Ltd.

Jewels, T., & Albon, R. (2006). Teaching Team Competences. In A. Cartelli (ed.), *Teaching in the Knowledge Society: New Skills and Instruments for Teachers*. Hershey (PA):

Information Science Publishing, 174-186.
Jonassen, D. H. (1994). Thinking Technology. Towards a Constructivist Design Model. *Educational Technology*, *34*(4), 34-37.
Lave, J., and Wenger, E. (1991). *Situated Learning. Legitimate Peripheral Participation.* Cambridge (MA): Cambridge University Press.
Olson, D. R., & Torrence N. (1991). *Literacy and Orality.* Cambridge (MA): Cambridge University Press.
Ong, W. J. (2002). *Orality and Literacy: the Technologizing of the Word.* New York (NJ): Routledge.
Scardamalia, M., & Bereiter, C. (1996). Engaging Students in a Knowledge Society. *Educational Leadership*, *54*(3), 6-10.

Novel Comparative Study of the Dating of Bulgarian Parchment Manuscripts

Jordan Tabov[1], Svilena Hristova[1] and Milena Dobreva[1,2]

[1] Institute of Mathematics and Informatics, bl. 8, Acad. G. Bonchev St., 1113 Sofia, Bulgaria, E-mail: tabov@math.bas.bg, svilenajh@yahoo.com
[2] Centre for Digital Library Research, Information Resources Directorate, University of Strathclyde, Livingstone Tower, 26 Richmond Street Glasgow, G1 1XH UK
E-mail: milena.dobreva@strath.ac.uk

Abstract: There is an ongoing scholarly debate on the exact time and speed of replacement of parchment with paper. There are three different hypotheses about the time of change: the first one based on Sobolevskij research suggests that paper completely replaced parchment as early as in 14th century; the second one put forward by Hunter is that parchment was still widely used during the 15th century; and the third ones dates the change as late as 16th century. Nowadays it is relatively easier to gather mass evidence on the writing materials using digital catalogues of European manuscripts; this allows to apply quantitative methods on a larger scale studying the process of replacement of parchment by paper on the wider European context. In this paper we present a statistical study based on the data within an electronic catalogue of manuscripts including 823 Bulgarian manuscripts currently stored in Bulgaria. We then extend our study with more than thousand parchment manuscripts from the Delorez's Codicology, 45 volumes of documents in Dubrovnik archives and over 1000 parchment manuscripts from the Bodleian and British libraries. This study is based on the manuscript dating provided in the catalogues. Our basic conclusion is that while there is rare evidence of any Bulgarian parchment manuscripts dated after 1350, and this is in controversy with manuscript collections from libraries in Central and Western Europe.

Keywords: Parchment; Paper; Mediaeval manuscripts.

1. The Scholarly Debate on the Spread of Paper

According to the Pliny the Elder's Natural History xiii.21, the parchment has been invented in the 2nd century BC in the town of Pergam in Asia Minor. Another point of view (see Bogdanov (1978), p. 53) claims that the Latin word "pergamen" – parchment comes indeed from the name of Pergam, but because of the fine quality of the parchment produced in this town.
The parchment has been widely used at least until the end of the 14th century.

Scholars agree that paper had replaced parchment at a great extent, almost totally, before the end of the 16th century. However, among the specialists there are different opinions about the time when the paper became the basic writing material.
The Slavic palaeography suggests this happened in the period 1350-1400. E.g. the famous Russian Slavic palaeographer Sobolevskij (1908) wrote: "14th century was time of battle between parchment and paper. The paper, which is more convenient in many respects, and, which is most important, cheaper, took over." Approximately the same vision was expressed by Shchepkin (1999): "parchment is indicative of 11th -14th centuries, latest to the beginning of the 15th century". Sobolevskij (1908) pointed out the important detail that all paper used in South Slavic and Russian manuscripts in the 14th and 15th centuries is of Western origin.
A large group of scientists date ***the decline of parchment in the 15th century***. A typical example is the opinion of Hunter (1970, p. 153): according to him, in the earlier times the paper was more expensive and less durable than the parchment. Stutermeister (1954, p. 11) states: "In the course of the 15th century vellum (the finest/highest quality parchment) was gradually superseded by paper. Some later manuscripts would use a mixture of vellum and paper. Usually a vellum sheet would form the outer, or the outer and inner, leaves of a quire while the rest were paper".
A third group of specialists shifts ***the decline of the parchment to a century later***, *namely to 16th century*. "Parchment was itself largely replaced by paper ***in the sixteenth*** century (with the rise of printing), but remained in use for certain high-grade books", states the British Library Catalogue of illuminated manuscripts (see http://www.bl.uk/catalogues/illuminatedmanuscripts/welcome.htm).
The analysis of these opinions shows an anomaly: in Eastern Europe, where all paper was imported from the West, according to Sobolevskij (1908), prevails the opinions for an early (in the fourteenth century) "triumph" of the paper over the parchment, while in the West, where papermaking was concentrated, and therefore this gradual change should have been finished at least several decades earlier, the specialists provide a later dating.
Below we describe the main details and the results of our quantitative study, which aimed to compare the time of decreased parchment use in Bulgaria and in the Central and Western European countries.

2. Chronological Distribution of the Bulgarian Mediaeval Manuscripts

There are hundreds of Bulgarian manuscripts, which have survived and are being kept currently in different collections (basically in libraries, museums and monasteries). They were created during different periods in the past.
How does their quantity vary from one time interval to another? Which is the period in our past from which the greatest number of manuscripts survived?
It is not easy to give a precise answer to such questions. The paper of Tabov, Velchev, Dobreva and Sotirova (2004), presents an approach for obtaining approximate results in this direction for the Bulgarian manuscripts. Using quantitative data on the Bulgarian manuscripts, being stored in our national repositories, we constructed an *appropriate function of the chronological distribution* of the extant Bulgarian manuscripts. Its graph, obtained by standard computer software tools (Microsoft Excel), provides a good visual presentation of

the function. This method follows the ideas of the *volume function* introduced by Fomenko (1981) and Fomenko and Rachev (1980). It is also similar to the function *chronological distribution of information in historical texts*, introduced by Tabov (2003).

We collected data on 823 Bulgarian manuscripts based on the catalogue of Ikonomova, Karadjova and Hristova (1982). They are spread over the period between 900 and 1900. We should stress here that we rely on the dating made by specialists and given in the catalogue of Ikonomova, Karadjova and Hristova (1982).

The graph of the chronological distribution of these manuscripts is presented in **Figure 1**. Since the number 823 of the manuscripts included in our study is large enough – perhaps about 10-20 % of the number of all extant old Bulgarian manuscripts, the same graph could be used as the chronological distribution of all extant old Bulgarian manuscripts since it gives a good approximation of the whole.

After extracting from the above 823 manuscripts only those of parchment, we constructed similarly a respective chronological distribution: of the extant old Bulgarian parchment manuscripts within our experimental sample (**Figure 2**).

It is not surprising that smaller amount of objects survived from earlier time periods. In cases where we find a decline of the volume in later time periods compared to earlier ones, we should seek for a significant historical or cultural reason.

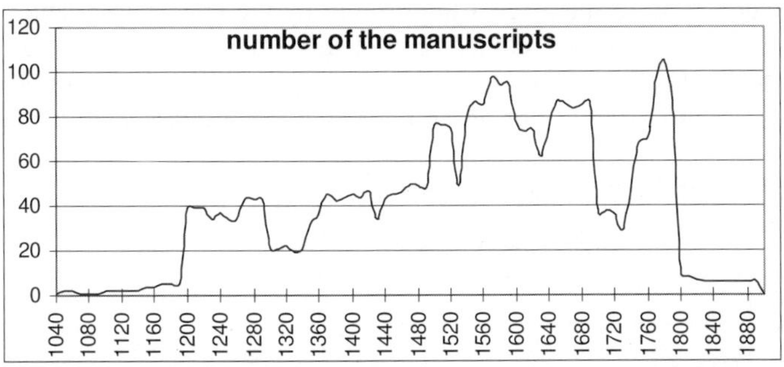

Figure 1. Chronological distribution of the extant old Bulgarian manuscripts.

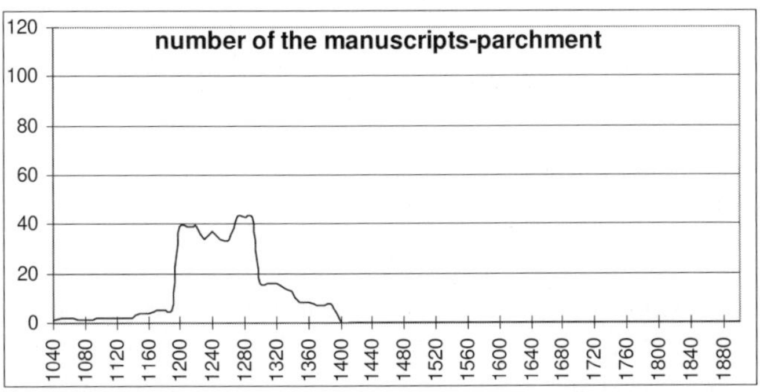

Figure 2. Chronological distribution of the extant old Bulgarian parchment manuscripts.

The careful study of the two graphs highlights a number of anomalies, we discuss below two of them.

The first one is related with the decline of the graph in Figure 1 about 1280-1290 and its relatively low level in the period 1290-1360, compared to the earlier period 1200-1280. This behaviour of the graph seems to be in contradiction with the natural expectation, that the Tartar invasion and pillaging in the Bulgarian lands in the period 1260-1290 influenced negatively the production of manuscripts, while the economical and cultural growth in the next several decades stimulated it.

The second anomaly is closely related with our investigations on the parchment manuscripts.

The graph in **Figure 2** shows that the peak of use of parchment as a writing material for the Bulgarian manuscripts was in the interval 1200-1280, and that among the extant Bulgarian manuscripts written after 1400 any parchment manuscripts are relatively rare exception. This picture leads to ***the conclusion that in Bulgaria by the year 1400 parchment was superseded by paper***.

3. Chronological Distribution of the Mediaeval Parchment Manuscripts in Central and Western Europe

Data from Delorez' Codicology

In the second volume of his Codicology A. Delorez provides a list of 15th century manuscripts on parchment, dated from 1406 to 1491; altogether it contains data on more than thousand such manuscripts. According to him by the end of 15th century handwriting of manuscripts stopped almost completely following the already widely-spread printing. However, the list of parchment manuscripts in his monograph illustrates the ***intensive use of parchment as a writing material during the 15th century***.

Parchment manuscripts in the Bodleian Library

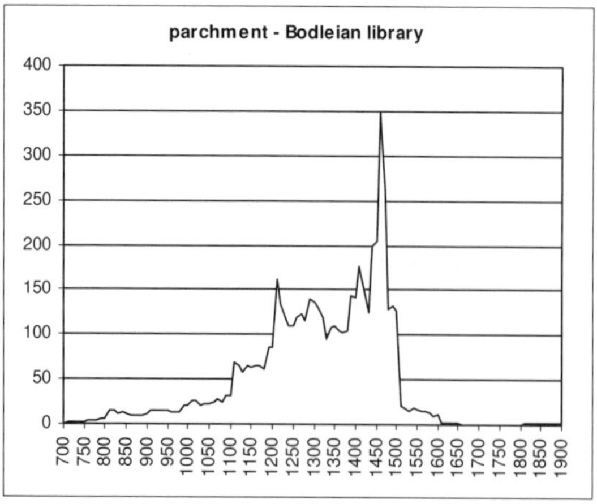

Figure 3. Chronological distribution of the old Parchment manuscripts in Bodleian Library

The chronological distribution of the old parchment manuscripts in the Bodleian Library of Oxford University (see **Figure 3**) supports the hypothesis that ***the use of***

***parchment as a writing material attains its maximum in the 15th century*.**

Parchment manuscripts in The British Library

The command "search" in the Catalogue of illuminated manuscripts of The British Library (in August 2008) returned the following results for the number of the manuscripts from the respective intervals of time:

22 manuscripts for the period 1000-1100
118 manuscripts for the period 1100-1200
189 manuscripts for the period 1200-1300
240 manuscripts for the period 1300-1400
437 manuscripts for the period 1400-1500
60 manuscripts for the period 1500-1600
4 manuscripts for the period 1600-1700

From these results it is clear, that the majority of the illuminated parchment manuscripts in The British Library originates from the 15th century; in fact, about 1/3 of all illuminated parchment manuscripts in the Catalogue comes from this century. This is yet another argument which supports the statement that in Western Europe the production of parchment manuscripts had its peak in the 15th century.

Parchment manuscripts in Dubrovnik archives

Spisarevska (2000) presents information about Bulgarian history from the archival findings in Dubrovnik archives. In connection with this she describes the documents in these archives used in her study: they consist of volumes 62-106 of the series Diversa Cancellariae, for the period 1450-1515. According to Spisarevska, each of these volumes contains 300-400 sheets, ***written usually on parchment and rarely on paper*** (Spisarvska (2000), pp. 9 and 17).

This example shows that in the beginning of 16th century parchment has been preferred by the merchants and lowers as writing material for documents.

4. Contradictions and Conclusions

The above brief analysis of randomly chosen quantitative information from the Central and Western parts of Europe about the survived old parchment manuscripts provide evidence in support of the following:

(1) Parchment has been used intensively as writing material at least till the end of 15th century.

In the same time the graph in **Figure 2** shows that in the Bulgarian lands the use of parchment after 1400 tends to zero, because, according to the opinion of the palaeographers, parchment has been replaced by paper.

However, it is well known that during the Middle Ages skin formed a great part of the Bulgarian export to Italy and other countries in Central Europe, since it was cheaper (see e.g. Spisarevska (2000)). From sheep skins the monks in the Bulgarian monasteries made parchment for their religious books. If paper was cheap enough to replace parchment for the Christian books in Bulgaria, it should be relatively much cheaper compared to parchment in the West, say in Italy, and

(2) Paper should supersede parchment there as well – at least by the year 1400.

The contradiction between (1) and (2) is evident; what could be the explanation for it?

It seems most probable that the roots of the controversy lie in the dating of the old Bulgarian parchment manuscripts. Therefore we suggest the **hypothesis** that ***many of these manuscripts are dated incorrectly, and are made "older" by 2-3 centuries in average***.

Since this hypothesis is based on a relatively small piece of information about the Western parchment manuscripts, to confirm or to reject it further investigations are necessary and will require thorough analysis of the individual manuscripts' datings.

References

British Library. *Catalogue of illuminated manuscripts.* Available: http://www.bl.uk/catalogues/illuminatedmanuscripts/welcome.htm

Bogdanov I. (1978) *The Bulgarian Book across the Centuries.* Narodna prosveta, Sofia (in Bulgarian)

Derolez, A., (1984). *Codicologie des manuscrits en ecriture humanistique sur parchement.* T. I. Texte. T. II. Catalogue. Brepols – Turnhout.

Electronic Catalogue of Medieval & Renaissance Manuscripts. Bodleian Library. http://www.bodley.ox.ac.uk/dept/scwmss/wmss/online/medieval/

Fomenko, A., (1981). *New Experimental and Statistical Methods of Dating Ancient Events and Application to The Global Chronology of Ancient World.* Preprint Gos. Kom. Telev. Radiovesht. Vol. 3672 (1981), B07201 (9/XI-81), Moscow. (in Russian)

Fomenko, A. and Rachev, S., (1990). Volume Functions of Historical Texts and The Amplitude Correlation Principle. *Computers and the Humanities,* Vol. 24, 187-206.

Hunter, D., (1970). *Papermaking. The History and Technique of and Ancient Craft.* Dover publications, New York.

Ikonomova, A., Karadjova, D., and Hristova, B., (1982). *Bulgarian manuscripts from XI to XVIII centiry, preserved in Bulgaria.* Catalogue, Vol. I, Nationa Library St. St. Cyril and Methodius, Sofia. (in Bulgarian)

Pliny the Elder. *Natural History.* Loeb Classical Library.

Shchepkin, P.N., (1999). *Russian Paleography.* Aspect Press, Moscow. (In Russian)

Sobolevskij, A.I., (1908). *Slavic-Russian Paleography.* Sanct-Petersburg. (In Russian) http://www.textology.ru/drevnost/sobolevsky.html

Spisarevska, I., (2000). Sources about Bulgarian history from Dubrovnik. (In Bulgarian)

Stutermeister, E., (1954). *The Story of Papermaking.* R.R. Bowker Company, New York.

Tabov, J., (2003). Chronological Distribution of Information in Historical Texts. *Computers and the Humanities*, Vol. 37, 235-240.

Tabov, J., Velchev, A., Dobreva, M. and Sotirova, K., (2004). Chronological distribution of the Bulgarian mediaeval manuscripts preserved in Bulgaria. In: *Mathematics and Education in Mathematics.* Proc. Of the Thirty Third Spring Conference of the Union of Bulgarian Mathematicions, Borovets, April 1-4, 257-261.

Bringing FRBR Model into Current Cataloguing Process via Liberty3, a Library Oriented Software

Gabriela Costea

Library of "Transilvania" University of Brasov, Romania

Abstract: Analyzing the type of material or media for the benefit of all users and taking into account the developing electronic and networked environment, the new cataloguing rules must closely interconnect with ISBDs and FRBR standards and at the same time with the library oriented softwares. ISBDs and cataloguing rules must keep their own specific terminology and must provide accurate definitions showing how each term in this specific terminology is conceptually related to the FRBR terminology. On the other hand, library oriented software must be understood and used accordingly.
That is why one of the most challenging issues of today knowledge and library management is bringing FRBR model into current cataloguing process. This also stands for the theme of the proposed paper.

Keywords: Cataloguing; FRBR; ISBD; Software; Case study.

1. Introduction

Few years ago I had to prepare a paper on „Frankfurt 2003 Cataloguing Principles" subject. It was then when I've got into „their" new FRBR world. At that time I understood but one thing: that FRBR model wasn't mine. Mine were the Paris Principles, and ISBDs, and the word „book" with its simple, classical, friendly meaning.
After a while, another paper, the same subject yet more detailed: „FRBR attributes". This second approach revealed to me new dimensions inside the space of cataloguing. And I was glad of having the opportunity to explore them. I was intreagued but also curious. The more FRBR I read the better understanding for that new world I got. And the more lost I felt. New FRBR world. Brave New FRBR World. And Its soldiers.
So there I found myself between my old(fashioned) but still-in-function world and that Brave new one, cyber-equipped in Liberty style, trying to do my best in bibliographic describing not only books but all kinds of new forms of publishing, harassed by lots of confusing questions: (where) do I find ISBD elements among FRBR concepts; (where) may I place FRBR elements throughout Liberty fields; could the specialized ISBDs be merged into one consolidated ISBD; (are there any) reasons for consolidation of ISBDs; should ISBD become a new or revised standard?!
The only way of clearing my cataloguing problems up was to put each of these cataloguing patterns on the same topic and then tile the outcame „models" onto the same table like pieces gathered together in order to get the whole image of a

puzzle. An enlightened image where the new cataloguing rules interconnect with ISBDs and FRBR standards and at the same time with a library oriented software.

Background

Today's bibliographic foundation for cataloguing codes are the ISBDs and FRBR Principles. This requires a better understanding of FRBR concepts and clarifying the relationship between the ISBDs and the FRBR model. An important impact on cataloguing had the automation of libraries which made the international exchange of bibliographic records possible between national bibliographic agencies and troughout the international library and information community.

The paper studies the relationship between ISBDs and FRBR model with appliance to Liberty3 (the 2005 version), a web based Library Management System developed by Softlink International, which is the available software for cataloguers at the Library of „Transilvania" University in Brasov.

2. Case study

ISBD cataloguing

An electronic audiobook was chosen to be analysed.

The ISBD(ER) bibliographic description for this resource is as it follows:

Fratii Karamazov [Resursa electronica] : discursul Marelui Inchizitor / Fiodor Mihailovici Dostoievski ; traducere Izabela Dumbrava si Ovidiu Constantinescu ; lectura Gabriel Liiceanu. – Bucuresti : Humanitas Multimedia, cop. 2008. – 1 disc optic electronic (CD-ROM, 1 h., 7 min.) : sd. ; 12 cm. – (Audio Fiction) Cerinte de sistem: PC 486; 8 MB RAM; Windows 3.1 or higher; placa de sunet MPC pe 16-biti; boxe; mouse ISBN 9789731709307

Fig.1

Comments I

Electronic resources and audiovisual materials require special attention with cataloguing treatment.

Each audiovisual medium (and often each format as applied within that medium) is part of an audiovisual culture unique to itself. In turn, that audiovisual culture is related to its historical era, and to the type of content (including duration of the record piece and its genre or style) in the format. The ability to recognize and respond appropriately to each particular era and culture relating to the various audiovisual media and forms is also necessary for cataloguing purposes.

With today's new technology and media, some moving image and electronic resource products could be considered as contemporary means of communicating content which may otherwise have been exclusive to the recorded sound and radio media of the past (e.g. video histories vs oral histories; music videos vs long play recordings or singles, film or television productions of opera and ballet vs sound recordings and radio productions, and sound excerpts in interactive multimedia and other electronic resources). For this reason electronic resources are addresed in this case study.

These aspects are related to the „gmd", „area 3", „area 5" and „area 7" problems. GMD is unsatisfactory because the notion of "type of document" (text, map, music, etc.) and the notion of „type of material presentation (=appearance) or type of format" (print, manuscript, microform, etc.) are mixed. For example, the notion of „electronic resource" may be applied both to a type of document (e.g. a data base) or to a type of material presentation (e.g. a digital map).

Another cataloguing problem raised here is about „the statement of responsibility". Because the responsibility is most often complex and highly diverse for these types of materials (electronic resources and audiovisual materials) the cataloguers determine the types of functions they wish to include in this area, and also if they want to present the functions in a given order, and also if part of those functions are to be given in a note.

Some of the recommendations made along the process of updating and consolidating ISBD[1] are: gmd should be mandatory; gmd should be moved to another location; alternatives to gmd that would clarify the element as being a mode of expression[2] versus a form of manifestation[3]; more precise terminology for „content/carrier" or „content/medium" designation is needed; use a separate, unique, mandatory component for recording „content/carrier" or „content/medium" designation; „types of electronic resources" in area 3 is omitted and could be put into notes; further stipulations in area 5 (physical description area) for remote-access electronic resources; the term „nonbook" was deleted; use the term „resource" rather than „item" or „publication"; name of area 4 : Publication, production, distribution etc. area.

FRBRising attempt

As we already know, to FRBRise is to „produce a framework that would provide a clear, precisely stated, and commonly shared understanding of what it is that the bibliographic record aims to provide information about, and what it is that we expect the record to achieve in terms of answering user needs."[4]

The process requires a good knowledge of both ISBD and FRBR terminologies, and also the understanding of the relationship between the ISBDs and FRBR model.

The correlation of both systems is revealed by mapping each of the elements specified in the ISBDs to its corresponding entity, attribute or relationship as defined in the FRBR model.

FRBR Group 1 entities (W=work, E=expression, M=manifestation, I=item)

W: Fratii Karamazov monographic work (whose form is a novel) created by Fiodor Mihailovici Dostoievski

E: Fratii Karamazov : discursul Marelui Inchizitor fragments translated in romanian by Izabela Dumbrava and Ovidiu Constantinescu, read by Gabriel Liiceanu

M: Fratii Karamazov : discursul Marelui Inchizitor sound recording on electronic optical disc in 2008 at Humanitas Mltimedia

I: Fratii Karamazov : discursul Marelui Inchizitor Item (at the „Transilvania" Library)

Fig. 2

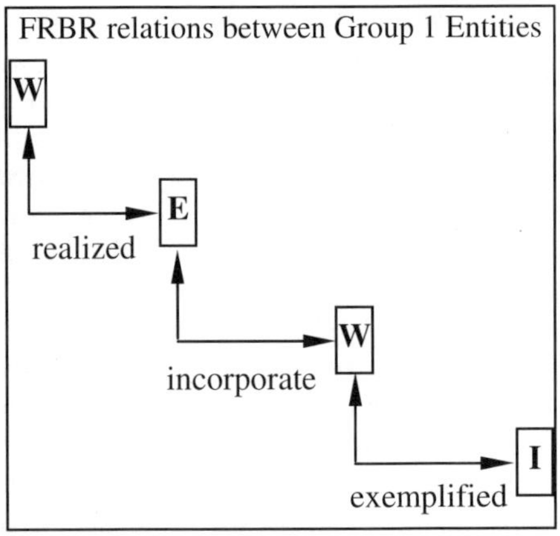

Fig. 3

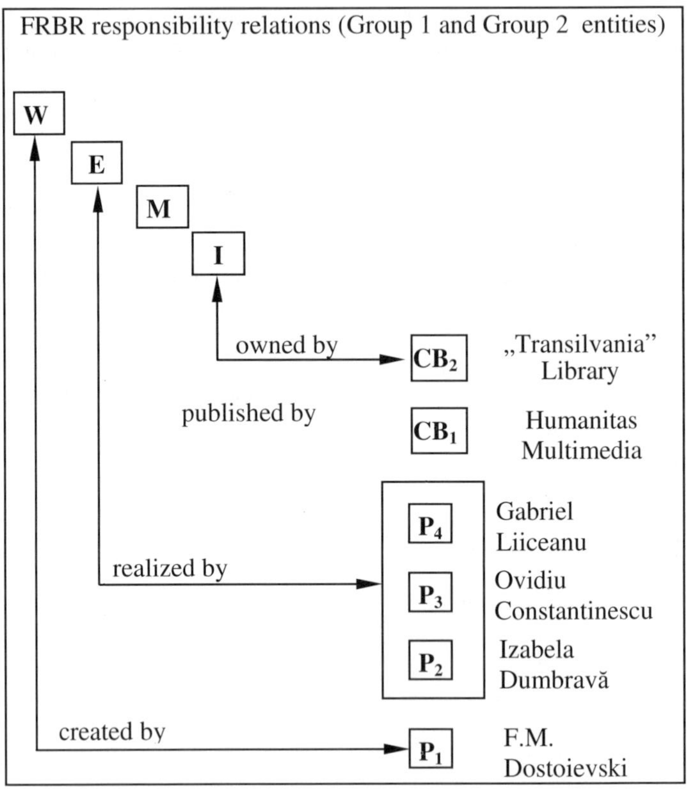

Fig. 4

ISBD Area[5]	ISBD Element	FRBR Entity	FRBR Attribute/Relationship
1.Title and statement of responsibility	1.1Title proper	3.2.3Manifestation	4.4.1Title of Manifestation[6]
	1.2 General material designation	3.2.1Work	Category of work[7]
		3.2.2 Expression	4.3.2 Form of expression[8]
		3.2.3 Manifestation	Category of carrier or medium[9]
		See Note 10	
	1.4 Other title information	See Note 11	
	1.5 Statement of responsibility	3.2.3 Manifestation	4.4.2 Statement of responsibility[12]
4. Publication	4.1 Place of publication	3.2.3 Manifestation	4.4.4 Place of publication
	4.2 Name of publication	3.2.3 Manifestation	4.4.5 Publisher[13]
	4.4 Date of publication	3.2.3 Manifestation	4.4.6 Date of publication
5.Physical description area	5.1 Specific material designation and extent of resource	3.2.3 Manifestation	4.4.9 Form of carrier
			4.4.10 Extent of carrier
		3.2.2 Expression	4.3.8 Extent of the expression
	5.2 Other physical details	3.2.3 Manifestation	Integral sound[14]
	5.3 Dimensions	3.2.3 Manifestation	4.4.13 Dimensions of the carrier
6. Series area	6.1Title proper of series	3.2.3 Manifestation	4.4.8 Series statement
7. Notes area	7.5 Notes on system requirements(ER)	3.2.3 Manifestation	4.4.35 System requirements
	Notes relating to mode of access(ER)	3.2.3 Manifestation	4.4.37 Mode of access

Comments II

The table follows the numberings of ISBDs and FRBR with respect to the studied case of the audiobook. The elements shown in the table are the elements within the bibliographic description of the audiobook.[15]

Notes

1. IFLA´s ISBD Review Group
2. FRBR terminology
3. FRBR terminology
4. Le Boeuf, Patrick. Brave New FRBR World (2007)
5. See Fig.1
6. See Fig.3

7. GMD in ISBD(CM) is „cartographic material" term which reflects a broad category of work. Among GMDs in ISBD(NBM) are „graphic", „multimedia" and „object" that reflect broad categories of work. GMDs in ISBD(PM) are „printed music" and „Braille music"; „music" reflects a broad category of work, „printed" reflects the method of production of the manifestation (printing or embossing). There is no attribute currently defined in FRBR that corresponds to category of work.
8. GMD in ISBD(M), ISBD(A) is „printed text" and „Braille text"; „text" reflects a form of expression; „printed" reflects the method of production of the manifestation (printing or embossing) („Braille" likewise).
9. Among GMDs in ISBD(NBM) are „microform", „motion picture", „sound recording" and „videorecording", terms that reflect broad categories of carrier. GMD in ISBD(ER) is „electronic resource" that reflects a broad category of medium. The term „hologram" specified for use with ISBD(NBM) also reflects a subcategory of medium. There is no attribute currently defined in FRBR that corresponds to category of carrier or medium.
10. A monographic Work (Fratii Karamazov) whose Form has the value of „novel" is artistically realized as an audio content recorded on an electronic medium.
11. Other title information cannot be mapped to specific entities or attributes in FRBR. Because other title information is defined in ISBD not in terms of its content but in terms of its proximity and relationship to the title of the manifestation, it may encompass a broad range of different kinds of information, and can be associated with a variety of attributes (e.g. form of work, intended audience, medium of performance, language of expression, etc.).
12. A statement of responsability as defined in ISBD corresponds to statement of responsability in FRBR, an attribute of manifestation. However, a statement of responsability will also reflect an „is created by" relationship between work and a person or corporate body responsible for the creation of the intellectual or artistic content of the work (author, composer, etc.) or an „is realized by" relationship between the work and a person or corporate body responsible for the realization of the work (translator, lecturer, etc.). See Fig.2 and Fig.4
13. The name of publisher as defined in ISBD corresponds to publisher in FRBR (an attribute of manifestation). However, the name of publisher will also normally reflect an „is produced by" relationship between the manifestation and a person responsible for its production
14. In ISBD(ER) and ISBD(NBM) the specifications for other physical details provide for indicating the presence or absence of integral sound for materials for which the presence of sound is not implicit in the specific material designation. There is currently no attribute corresponding to integral sound defined in FRBR.
15. See Fig.1

FRBR accents in Liberty3 cataloguing practice

How do we apply the ISBD and FRBR cataloguing rules while working with Liberty3?

Setting – that is either choosing or defining - a relationship between the Bibtype and GMD for a resource is a way the cataloguer creates a FRBRised bibliographic description. At the same time, the access points in the OPAC are to be considered among the FRBR elements (attributes).
Details on this section will be included in Conference presentation.

3. Conclusions

With „physical" and „abstract„ features, the new cataloguing era targets to accomodate different levels of cataloguing to different needs of the different users via a more and more challenging issue : the library oriented software.

References

ISBD(G) : General International Standard Bibliographic Description, 2004 Revision

ISBD(M) : International Standard Bibliographic Description for Monographic Publications, 2002 Revision

ISBD(A) : International Standard Bibliographic Description for Older Monographic Publications (Antiquarian). Second revised edition, 1991

ISBD(CM) : International Standard Bibliographic Description for Cartographic Materials, Revised Edition 1987

ISBD(CR) : International Standard Bibliographic Description for Serials and Other Continuing Resources, 2002 Revision

ISBD(PM) : International Standard Bibliographic Description for Printed Music, Second revised edition, 1991

ISBD(NBM) : International Standard Bibliographic Description for Non-Book Materials, Revised edition 1987

ISBD(ER) : International Standard Bibliographic Description for Electronic Resources, 1997

FRBR Review Group-IFLA Cataloguing Section. Available at: archive.ifla.org/VII/s13/wgfrbr/index.htm

Le Boeuf, Patrick (2007) . *Brave New FRBR World* (Version 5): Prepared for IMEICC5. Available at: www.imeicc5.com/download/BraveNewFRBR

Mapping ISBD elements to FRBR Entity Attributes and Relationships (2004). Available at: archive.ifla.org/VII/s13/pubs/ISBD-FRBR- mappingFinal.pdf

Rodriguez, Elena Escolano (2007). *Consolidated ISBD* : a step forward : for IME ICC5. Pretoria- SouthAfrica. Available at www.imeicc5.com/download/ISBD/%20-Presentation%20-Pretoria.pdf

IASA : International Association of Sound and Audiovisual Archives : sound recordings. Available at : www.iasa-web.org/special_publications/cataloguing_rules/ icat001.htm

*Liberty*3 : 3.1E reference manual (2005). Softlink International Limited

Author Index